Technology in the Law Office

Third Edition

Thomas F. Goldman, JD
Attorney at Law
Professor Emeritus
Bucks County Community College

PEARSON

Boston   Columbus   Indianapolis   New York   San Francisco   Upper Saddle River
Amsterdam   Cape Town   Dubai   London   Madrid   Milan   Munich   Paris   Montréal   Toron
Delhi   Mexico City   São Paulo   Sydney   Hong Kong   Seoul   Singapore   Taipei   Tokyo

Editorial Director: Vernon Anthony
Executive Acquisitions Editor: Gary Bauer
Editorial Assistant: Tanika Henderson
Director of Marketing: David Gesell
Marketing Manager: Stacey Martinez
Marketing Assistant: Les Roberts
Senior Managing Editor: JoEllen Gohr
Project Manager: Christina Taylor
Senior Operations Supervisor: Pat Tonneman

Senior Art Director: Diane Ernsberger
Full-Service Project Management: Integra-Chicago
Composition: Integra
Printer/Binder: Edwards Brothers
Cover Printer: Lehigh Phoenix Color/Hagerstown
Text Font: 11/13 Goudy
Chapter Opener photographs: David Graham

Credits and acknowledgments borrowed from other sources and reproduced, with permission, in this textbook appear on appropriate pages within the text.

Microsoft® and Windows® are registered trademarks of the Microsoft Corporation in the U.S.A. and other countries. Screen shots and icons reprinted with permission from the Microsoft Corporation. This book is not sponsored or endorsed by or affiliated with the Microsoft Corporation.

Many of the designations by manufacturers and sellers to distinguish their products are claimed as trademarks. Where those designations appear in this book, and the publisher was aware of a trademark claim, the designations have been printed in initial caps or all caps.

Library of Congress Cataloging-in-Publication Data

Goldman, Thomas F.
  Technology in the law office/Thomas F. Goldman.—3rd ed.
    p. cm.
  Includes index.
  ISBN-13: 978-0-13-272299-5
  ISBN-10: 0-13-272299-2
  1. Law offices—United States—Automation—Popular works. I. Title.
KF320.A9G645 2011
340.068—dc23

2011045849

10 9 8 7 6 5 4 3 2 1

ISBN 10:   0-13-272299-2
ISBN 13: 978-0-13-272299-5

CONTENTS

iv CONTENTS

CHAPTER 4
The Internet, the Cloud, and Communications 81
  Learning Objectives 81
Introduction to the Internet and Electronic Mail 82
Internet Fundamentals 82
  Modem 82
  Hubs 84

CHAPTER 5
The Electronic Courthouse and Virtual Law Office 113

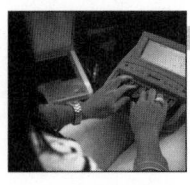

CHAPTER 12
Evolving Issues in
E-Discovery   323

CHAPTER 13
E-Discovery—
The Process   345

LEARNING OBJECTIVES

The following list describes the outcomes you should expect from completing the course or reading this book.

1. Describe the impact and use of technology in the legal workplace.
2. Explain the ethical issues in using technology in the practice of law.
3. Describe the different types of software and hardware used by the legal team.
4. Explain the use of the Internet and cloud computing in the law office and the courthouse.
5. Describe how courts and legal professionals are using computers and the Internet in the administration of justice.
6. Describe how to use word processing tools and specialty features.
7. Describe how to use spreadsheet programs and create specialty spreadsheets for use in the law office.
8. Explain the functions and uses of databases in the law office.
9. Explain the value of office management programs for the efficient operation of the law office.
10. Describe the value and use of case management programs.
11. Explain how technology has changed discovery practice.
12. Describe the obligations and issues in the preservation of electronically stored information and the potential sanctions for its spoliation.
13. Explain the electronic discovery process and the issues in discovering relevant electronically stored evidence.
14. Describe the ethical issues in the review of electronically stored information.
15. Describe the elements of the electronic courtroom and their uses by the legal team.
16. Explain the value of the use of graphics in litigation and create a PowerPoint presentation.
17. Describe the use of trial presentation programs and create an electronic trial presentation.

PREFACE

■ FROM THE AUTHOR

In prior editions I have said that change was a certainty. In the few short years since the second edition of *Technology in the Law Office*, the uses of technology in the law office, courthouse, and courtroom have accelerated. The most notable are the changes in the adoption and use of computer hardware, including smartphones and the iPad. The use of the Internet has also evolved from very basic functionality to a sophisticated method for legal research, remote storage of data, and a source of software-solutions-on-demand in the form of cloud computing. Where few law offices had an Internet presence just a few years ago, almost every attorney, from solo practitioners to the largest firms, now has a website, and many use social media like Facebook and Twitter to communicate with current and potential clients.

We have also seen a major shift in the past few years from paper-based systems to a paperless working environment. Individuals as well as corporate clients are using computers and the Internet for everything from written communication and audio-video chats to the creation and storage of personal and business information. Increasingly, the courts are also shifting to a paperless process utilizing the Internet, with many now mandating the use of electronic filing.

For those in the legal profession, the change from paper files and court dockets to electronic files and computerized document storage requires learning new skills, as well as learning to use the enhanced features of older, more familiar computer programs. Today, obtaining and keeping a position as a legal professional requires understanding the role of technology and its use by the courts, law offices, and clients.

As courts require electronic filing in both the federal and state jurisdictions, the legal team must be prepared to learn the specific systems dictated by their local courts. Without a national standard, this may require the legal team to learn the different systems used in the various courts in which they practice. These changes spur the introduction of new or enhanced software and hardware. The successful member of the legal team—whether paralegal, litigation support, or lawyer—must understand the basic functions of the software, the ethical issues related to the use of technology (particularly in the area of Internet usage), the process of electronic discovery, and be prepared to learn the new and enhanced features of these tools. The ability to adapt and learn new features and programs, including those required by the courts and by clients, is a critical soft skill that every legal professional must develop.

In a competitive work environment, it is important that students have experience using the actual software found in the workplace in order to develop an understanding of how these programs are used. Through the courtesy of many legal software providers, we are fortunate to be able to provide actual versions of the software used in law offices. In addition to the traditional extended demonstration versions provided on the Technology Resources Website, we are also able to provide multiyear versions of several programs, with tutorials allowing the use of these programs across the entire curriculum.

To provide real-world work experience, we have created a virtual law office internship experience in a new online course called MyLegalStudiesLab Virtual Law Office Experience. This multimedia environment simulates the actual working experience of a paralegal shadowing a supervising attorney or senior paralegal. Videos pertaining to many areas of practice allow the student to observe what goes on behind closed doors in client interviews, meetings with judges in chambers, the deposition room, arbitration, and trial. Cases are followed from initial client meeting, with students preparing a complete portfolio of documents and work product that may be used in applying for positions in law firms and for reference in the workplace.

As in prior editions, the third edition focuses on teaching students how to use the training tutorials and Help functions in the software, rather than on how to execute rote keystroke instructions. Many instructors and students have told me that learning how to find and use Help programs is the most important skill that they developed while using this text. Working paralegals have emphasized to me that an understanding of the basic programs enables new employees to get up to speed in the workplace quickly.

The practice of law is evolving more quickly than ever before as electronic tools provide new methods of creation, storage, production, and access to information by clients, lawyers, and the courts. The courts are imposing greater responsibilities on the legal team to understand technology applications and to monitor their use not only internally, but by clients as well. Even the smallest law firms must be aware of the new rules of procedure and evidence to avoid court sanctions and ethical violations. In this edition, I have greatly expanded material on the ethical implications of using technology in legal practice in response to the increased number of ethical violations reported in cases and in the press. I hope that references throughout the text to the potential ethical impact of each application will help students avoid major problems in practice.

Change in the law is also inevitable. We were first introduced to the "new" federal rules in December 2006: a restatement of the "new" rules and the passage of the new rule of evidence, section 502. Consequently, I have expanded the coverage of electronic discovery from one chapter in the first edition to four chapters in this edition. Case law also continues to evolve in this area, so while there is no absolute set of rules to follow, there are some well-reasoned opinions that can be used as a starting point for further research and guidance. In addition, I have also addressed the growing field of litigation support, which is becoming a major area of practice support.

This edition continues to provide a basic foundation in legal technology applications. Sources of help and references for learning about new programs, features, and changes in the law relating to electronic applications are provided in every chapter. You will also find a wealth of new video and print tutorials online at the Technology Resources Website at www.pearsonhighered.com/goldman.

Thomas F. Goldman

ORGANIZATION OF THE BOOK

UNIT ONE—THE FUNDAMENTALS presents an introduction to the use of computers and technology in the practice of law, including an overview of the ethical issues facing the legal team. For the new paralegal, the information technologist, or the lawyer quickly trying to come up to speed with the use of technology and computers, this unit covers:

Chapter 1 Technology in the Law Office
Chapter 2 Legal Ethics in a Technology Age
Chapter 3 Computers in the Law Office
Chapter 4 The Internet, the Cloud, and Communications

UNIT TWO—THE BUILDING BLOCKS shows the uses of law-related applications software that are the building blocks on which all other specialty applications software is built: the database, the word processor, and the spreadsheet. With these conceptual building blocks in mind, students, paralegals, and lawyers have a better understanding about how to use the more complex software applications built around these building blocks.

Chapter 5 The Electronic Courthouse and Virtual Law Office
Chapter 6 Word Processing
Chapter 7 Spreadsheets
Chapter 8 Electronic Databases

UNIT THREE—SPECIALTY APPLICATIONS SOFTWARE offers an introduction to some of the classes of specialty applications software in use in the law office and the court system.

Chapter 9 Office Management Software
Chapter 10 Case Organization and Management Software

UNIT FOUR—E-DISCOVERY provides an overview of the underlying court rules and judicial interpretations in the rapidly evolving electronic discovery process. Without a national standard, it is important to understand the underlying court rules and the judicial interpretation of those rules as they apply to the duties and obligations of the legal team.

Chapter 11 The Changing Face of Discovery and the Basics of E-Discovery
Chapter 12 Evolving Issues in E-Discovery
Chapter 13 E-Discovery—The Process
Chapter 14 Analysis and Review of E-Discovery

UNIT FOUR—COMPUTER APPLICATIONS IN LITIGATION presents the ways in which technology is being used by the courts and by litigators and suggests how it may be used in the future.

Chapter 15 The Electronic Courtroom
Chapter 16 Presentation and Trial Graphics
Chapter 17 Electronic Trial Presentation

NEW TO THE THIRD EDITION

The applications of technology in the law office continue to evolve at a rapid pace. Changes found in the third edition are numerous, reflecting changes in technology, software applications, and legal software applications, and changes in law relating to technology's usage. In addition, many users of previous editions of the book provided feedback that led to refinement in coverage, presentation, hands-on tutorials, and exercises. Here is a list of some of the most important changes:

VIDEO INTRODUCTIONS TO EACH CHAPTER

- In videos located on this book's MyLegalStudiesLab or Technology Resources Website, the author introduces the chapter topics and reinforces the importance of the topics for paralegal students.

MORE EXERCISES AND EXAMPLES

- More tutorials, exercises, and examples were added throughout the textbook to provide students more hands-on experiences with technology concepts and applications.

ETHICS AND TECHNOLOGY CHAPTER

- A full chapter on ethics in the age of technology reflects the importance of being aware of ethical issues related to technology applications in practice.
- Ethical perspectives and guideline notes are also integrated throughout the text.

EXPANDED COVERAGE OF MICROSOFT OFFICE APPLICATIONS

- Coverage of law-related Office Suite functions has been expanded.
- Additional law office case studies have been added, along with data to be used in application exercises.

FOUR CHAPTERS ON E-DISCOVERY

- Chapter 11: The Changing Face of Discovery and the Basics of E-Discovery
- Chapter 12: Evolving Issues in E-Discovery
- Chapter 13: E-Discovery—The Process
- Chapter 14: Analysis and Review of E-Discovery

NEW VIDEO CASE STUDIES

- Case study videos dealing with technology topics have been added to the textbook as end-of-chapter MyLegalStudiesLab assignments.

TEXTBOOK FEATURES

■ OPENING SCENARIOS

Each chapter contains a scenario designed to focus the reader on the relationship of the chapter content to law office practice. The scenarios follow the activities of a fictional law office starting from scratch.

■ LEGAL SOFTWARE COVERAGE

Material covered in the book has been divided into chapters representing functional aspects of the use of technology. The core programs found in legal specialty applications software, including word processing, electronic spreadsheets, and databases, are covered from the view of the law office application and the specific features and applications commonly used in the legal environment. Specialty applications software is divided into classifications and covered by class, including law office applications, case management, litigation support, and presentation graphics. Emerging topics covered are use of the Internet, the paperless office, the electronic courtroom, and electronic research. Contemporary legal software programs are presented, where applicable, with an overview of the software and end-of-chapter exercises utilizing real-world software. Tutorial learning modules can be downloaded from the Technology Resources Website to ensure that the latest versions are covered and taught. A primary learning objective of the end-of-chapter software exercises is teaching the student how to use the built-in Help features of software programs, how to locate and use the training materials available from the software vendor, how to learn new or rarely used features of the program, and when to call for outside assistance.

OPENING SCENARIO

At first, the litigation team had what seemed to be a simple vehicle collision case between a school bus and a truck. However, the evidence obtained in discovery revealed the possibility of a defect in the truck, either because of faulty maintenance or defective parts. This new evidence in turn raised new issues and options, and it was becoming clear that new areas of discovery would have to be explored. At the very least, the truck had to be inspected by the plaintiffs' own experts, and the trucking company's records had to be reviewed for anything related to the truck, including its use, maintenance, and repairs.

Meanwhile, the team working on the new airplane crash case was concerned about a flood of new information. They worried that the mass of information and data from federal investigators and individual corporate defendants might potentially overwhelm them. In addition, they were representing only one of the plaintiffs in the case, with a number of other attorneys representing the families of the other victims. Thus all of the attorneys needed access to the same data, and all needed to be able to sift through it to find usable evidence to support their legal theory. This was the first case the firm had handled where the defendants were large national firms with massive amounts of electronically stored data. The team members would also be dealing with federal agencies, which had similarly large amounts of electronic information.

■ END-OF-CHAPTER EXERCISES AND MATERIALS

End-of-chapter practice materials, continuing case studies, and two comprehensive case studies reflect the actual information and documents frequently found in legal practice and use the appropriate application software.

■ GETTING READY TO USE SOFTWARE

To prepare your computer for some of the software learning modules, you will need to select "plug-ins" and "viewers." Okay, so I started with the geek talk already. These and the other technical terms are explained in the text itself, in the Frequently Asked Questions appendix located on the Technology Resources Website, and in the technical Glossary.

For some of the advanced software learning topics, you will need Microsoft Internet Explorer. To view the webinars in certain software learning modules, you will need the WebEx Player. To hear the sound files, you will need one of the sound programs available, such as SoundRec, iTunes, MS Media Player, or a similar program. Again, all of these will be explained in the Technology Resources Website. You may want to take a moment to check your computer for these plug-ins and viewers and download them before you start the first chapter.

Lessons in the chapters on word processing, spreadsheets, databases, and presentation graphics require the student to have a copy of Microsoft Office in order to access the Microsoft Internet site. Microsoft makes available a "test drive" version of Office 2010 at http://www.microsoft.com/office/trial/default.mspx. However, Microsoft recommends that only broadband users try this version. When you log onto the Microsoft site, it will check your computer for the needed plug-in. You may need to install the test drive browser plug-in if your computer doesn't already have it.

Student Warning

Do not download software until told to do so by your instructor. Some of the programs are time-limited, meaning that you can download them only once or twice, or that they will be active for a period of only 30, 90, or 120 days. Download too early, and you may not have access to the software when it is time to use the software in the course.

Technology Resources Website

Students can download the latest (time-limited) versions of the most popular legal software from the open access Technology Resources Website at www.pearsonhighered.com/goldman. There you will find links to software tutorials, video overviews, teaching notes, and a variety of other useful resources, including forms for requesting lab copies of software from vendors.

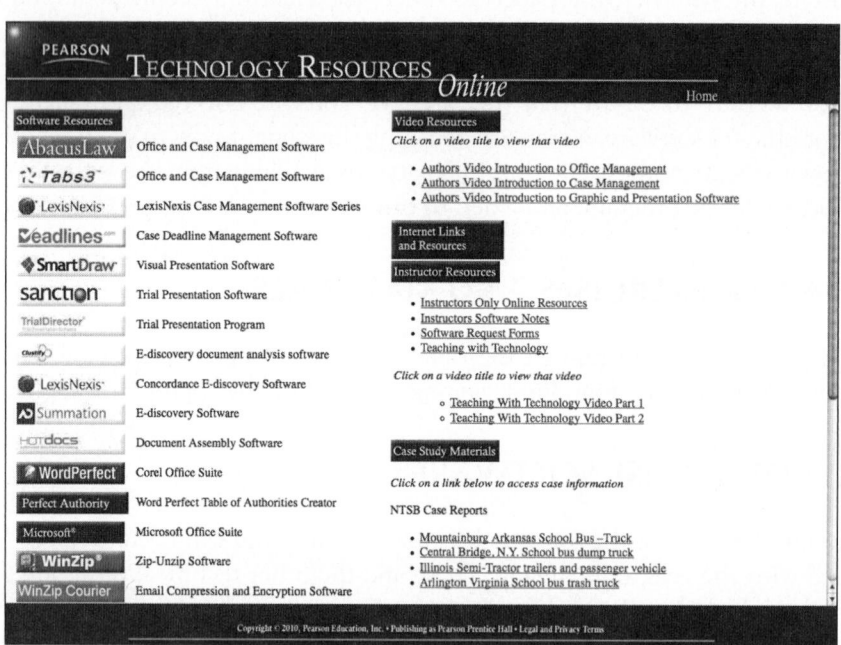

TECHNOLOGY RESOURCES WEBSITE DOWNLOADS

■ OFFICE MANAGEMENT AND ACCOUNTING SOFTWARE

Office management and accounting software is used extensively in most law firms, from the sole practitioner to large, multi-office practices. Such software is used to keep accurate calendars of appointments, schedules, and deadlines; to track time and billing information, client funds, and costs; and to prepare accurate billing records. **AbacusLaw** is one of the most popular and best supported programs.

■ CASE ORGANIZATION AND MANAGEMENT SOFTWARE

Case management software can be used to organize the cast of characters in a case, the documents, the relevant timetables, the issues, the legal authorities, and other desired information. Top programs include **LexisNexis CaseMap** and **LexisNexis TimeMap.**

■ PRESENTATION AND TRIAL GRAPHICS SOFTWARE

Graphic-creation programs such as **SmartDraw** are used to create graphics for either stand-alone presentations or as part of a graphics presentation, such as a PowerPoint presentation. The obvious advantage to this class of software is the ability of the legal team to create its own graphics without the need of graphic artists and outside consultants.

■ THE ELECTRONIC COURTHOUSE

Litigation support software such as **Sanction** and **TrialDirector** are used in trial to display documentary evidence, graphic presentations, and simulations of accident cases in court. Relevant portions of illustrations and documents can be displayed as a witness testifies without the need to pass around paper copies to everyone.

■ DOWNLOADABLE AND PRINTABLE SOFTWARE TUTORIALS

The author has created tutorials for several of the most commonly used software packages, including **Word, PowerPoint, Excel, AbacusLaw, SmartDraw, Sanction,** and **CaseMap.** These tutorials make it easy for students to get started using the programs.

■ EXTENDED USAGE SOFTWARE AND PACKAGES:

AbacusLaw Tutorial and Guide with 3-year Access Code ISBN: 0-13-249071-4

AbacusLaw 3-year Access Code ISBN: 0-13-139169-0

SmartDraw VP Tutorial and Guide with Access Code ISBN: 0-13-276284-6

SmartDraw VP Access Code ISBN: 0-13-702616-1

Sanction 2-year Access Code ISBN: 0-13-249950-9

Check with your local Pearson representative to find out about other new tutorial guides with extended software.

MYLEGALSTUDIESLAB VIRTUAL LAW OFFICE EXPERIENCE FOR TECHNOLOGY IN THE LAW OFFICE

The MyLegalStudiesLab Virtual Law Office Experience for *Technology in the Law Office* is a multimedia course program that includes an integrated e-book and is designed to provide students with the tools they need to confirm their mastery of legal concepts and applications, and then apply their knowledge and skills in a workplace context. Students watch realistic video scenarios, work with case files and documents, and use the technology tools found in the law office to do the work a paralegal will be asked to do in practice. Throughout the course, students build a portfolio of work that demonstrates that they have the training and experience employers are looking for.

- Students engage in a workplace experience as a law office intern.

- Students can see technology being used in the law office and develop an understanding of how best to deploy technology in practice.

- Students build a comprehensive portfolio of workplace products to show potential employers.

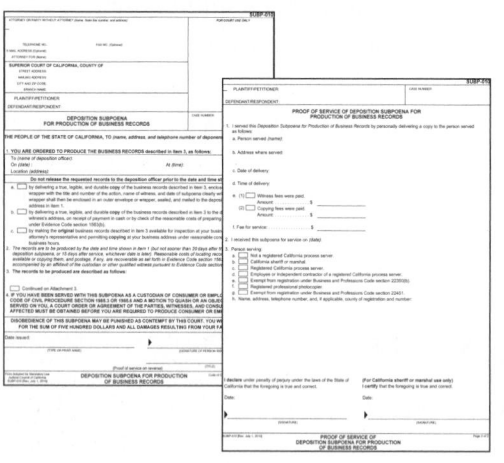 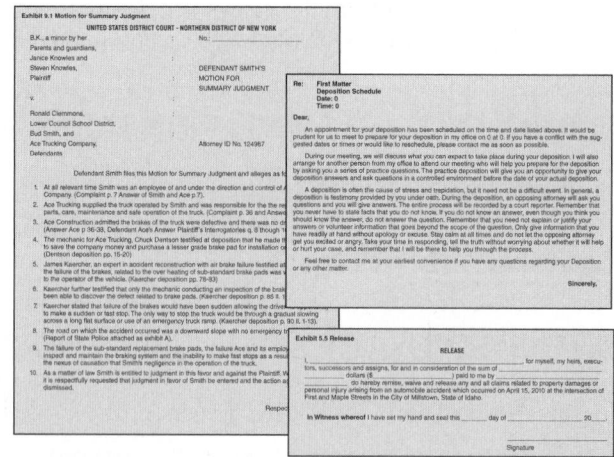

- Students can test their mastery of concepts and concept application by taking quizzes and receiving feedback and a link to e-book content.

Within MyLegalStudiesLab, students can access a wealth of resources to complete assignments, including:

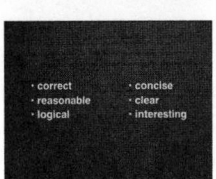

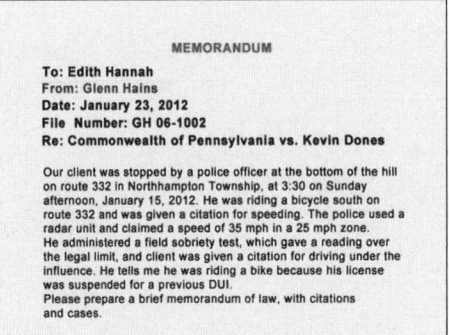

- ■ *Ask the Law Librarian Instructional Videos* answer students' research and writing questions.

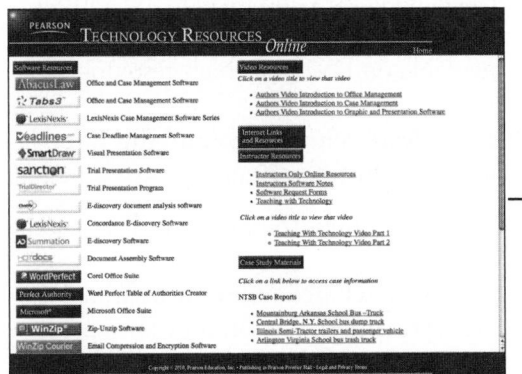

- ■ *Ask Technical Support* links to the Technology Resources Website for technology and legal software support.

  AbacusLaw Tutorials
  LexisNexis CaseMap Tutorials
  SmartDraw Tutorials
  Sanction Tutorials
  Microsoft Office Tutorials

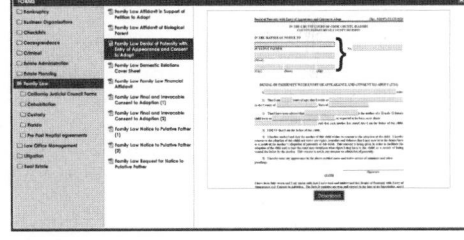

- ■ *Forms File* contains hundreds of examples of commonly used legal documents for the major legal specialties.

- ■ *Case Materials* contain all of the case information and documents needed to complete assignments.

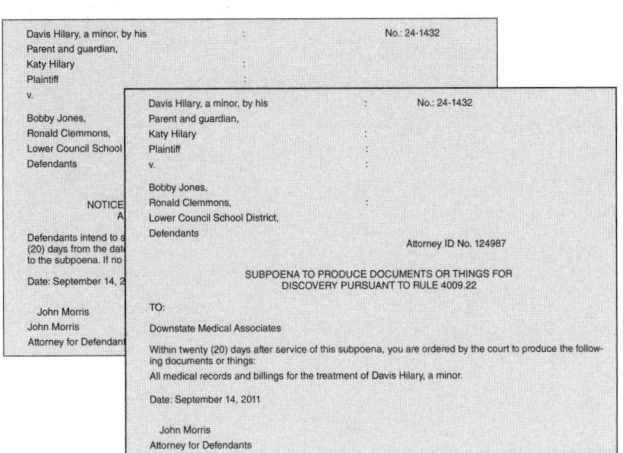

ACCIDENT SCENE

PROGRAM BENEFITS AND INSTRUCTOR RESOURCES FOR MYLEGALSTUDIESLAB VIRTUAL LAW OFFICE EXPERIENCE FOR TECHNOLOGY IN THE LAW OFFICE

- MyLegalStudiesLab makes it easy for you to confirm that students are achieving measurable outcomes for knowledge of the law, procedural knowledge, and administrative work place skills.
- MyLegalStudiesLab content is book-specific, with an integrated e-book built into the program.
- All course outcomes are assessed and include all AAFPE-recommended learning objectives.
- Legal concept and legal application quiz questions feed an instructor gradebook.
- Assessments for all Virtual Law Office Experience assignments include grading rubrics.
- Instructor supplements, including the Instructor's Manual, PowerPoint Lecture Screens, and MyTest, have been upgraded and include the Virtual Law Office Experience assignment teaching notes and rubrics.
- All videos within the lab are also available on DVD in a high-resolution format for use in the classroom.
- For selected assignments, use of legal software is integrated into the Virtual Law Office Experience to be assigned at the instructor's option.

A MyLegalStudiesLab access code with or without the Pearson eText can be packaged with the print textbook at a value price.

Access to MyLegalStudiesLab can also be purchased online at www.mylegalstudieslab.com. Please contact your local representative to arrange for a preview or for packaging and pricing options.

The Instructor's Manual, MyTest, and PowerPoint package are available for download from Pearson Instructor's Resource Center. To access supplementary materials online, instructors need to request an instructor access code. Go to www.pearsonhighered.com/irc, where you can register for an instructor access code. Within forty-eight hours of registering, you will receive a confirming email that includes an instructor access code. Once you have received your code, locate your text in the online catalog, and click on the Instructor Resources button on the left side of the catalog product page. Select a supplement, and a log-in page will appear. Once you have logged in, you can access instructor material for all Prentice Hall textbooks.

■ INSTRUCTOR'S MANUAL

The Instructor's Manual, written by Thomas Goldman and Marissa Moran and updated by Evan Voboril contains sample syllabi, chapter outlines and summaries, Web Resources results, answers to questions and exercises, and software teaching notes.

■ MYTEST

MyTest allows you to generate quizzes and tests composed of questions from the Test Item File, modify them, and add your own.

■ POWERPOINT LECTURE PRESENTATION

The PowerPoint Lecture Presentation includes key concept screens and exhibits from the textbook.

■ *TECHNOLOGY IN THE LAW OFFICE*, 3E, VIDEO CASE STUDY SERIES ON DVD

The end-of-chapter video case studies in the textbook are available for classroom use on DVD, free to adopters. Students can view the video cases within MyLegalStudiesLab or the Technology Resources Website.

ACKNOWLEDGMENTS

◼ REVIEWERS

The following individuals were very helpful in their review of this text. I am grateful for their insights and contributions.

John Bradley,
Bucks County Community College

Matthew Cornick,
Clayton State University

Katherine Currier,
Elms College

Stephanie Delaney,
Edmonds Community College

Veronica Dufresne,
Finger Lakes Community College

Dora Dye,
City College of San Francisco

David Freeman,
Community College of Philadelphia

Cathy Kennedy,
Minnesota School of Business

Bryce Letterman,
Coastline Community College

Marissa Moran,
New York City College of Technology

William Mulkeen,
Thomas Edison State College

Kathryn L. Myers,
Saint Mary-of-the-Woods College

Deborah K. Periman,
University of Alaska

Jennifer Severson,
University of California San Diego

Kathleen Smith,
Community College of Philadelphia

Robert Van Der Velde,
Eastern Michigan University

William Weston,
Kaplan University

◼ SOFTWARE COMPANIES

Thanks also go out to the software companies who contributed and reviewed material for this text.

Abacus

Judd Kessler
Bob Elliott

CaseSoft

Robert Wiss
Greg Kehel
Ivan Browning

LexisNexis

Dianne Callahan

Sanction

Mike Hahn

SmartDraw

Paul Stannard
Todd Savitt

Summation

Kate Paslin

Tabs3

Kent Merkl

WordPerfect

Gillian Darby
Cynthia Howard

ABOUT THE AUTHOR

THOMAS F. GOLDMAN, JD, is Professor Emeritus of Bucks County Community College, where he was a Professor of Law and Management and Director of the Center for Legal Studies and the Paralegal Studies Program. He is currently a member of the Paralegal Studies Advisory Board and a mentor at Thomas Edison State College, where he has developed the Advanced Litigation Support and Technology Certificate Program in the School of Professional Studies.

He is an author of textbooks in paralegal studies and technology, including *The Paralegal Professional*, Third Edition; *Accounting and Taxation for Paralegals*; *Civil Litigation: Process and Procedures*, Second Edition; *SmartDraw: A Hands-On Tutorial and Guide*; *Litigation Practice: E-Discovery and Technology*; *and AbacusLaw: A Hands-On Tutorial and Guide*.

An accounting and economics graduate of Boston University and of Temple University School of Law, Professor Goldman has an active international law, technology law, and litigation practice. He has worked extensively with paralegals and received the award of the Legal Support Staff Guild. He was elected the Legal Secretaries Association Boss of the Year for his contribution to cooperative education by encouraging the use of paralegals and legal assistants in law offices. He also received the Bucks County Community College Alumni Association Professional Achievement Award. He has been an educational consultant on technology to educational institutions and major corporations and a frequent speaker and lecturer on educational, legal, and technology issues.

"I do not fear computers. I fear the lack of them."

—*Isaac Asimov*

Technology in the Law Office

CHAPTER 1

OPENING SCENARIO

Mrs. Hannah had worked in large, center-city law firms for twenty years, rising to the level of senior paralegal. In the course of working on a case for which she was responsible for technical support, she met Owen Mason, an attorney fresh out of law school. Owen had just passed the bar, and was clerking for a federal judge. He confided in Mrs. Hannah that after many months of sitting in on the judge's cases and watching the trial attorneys in action, he wanted to open his own firm and try cases. However, he admitted that he was reluctant to go out on his own because he was unfamiliar with managing a law practice. He realized how much he didn't know about setting up a law office when he started looking around at actual law offices in the area. He said, "I can do the law part, but the internal operations of a law office are something I never thought about or had to worry about when I was clerking for the judge. It certainly wasn't something they taught in law school."

He asked Mrs. Hannah if she would help him, and offered her employment with his new firm. She agreed to leave her current law firm—not only for the challenge of establishing a new office, but also for a chance to work closer to home.

Owen's first question to her was, "What do I need at the minimum, and what tools will help me manage a practice if I am frequently out of the office trying cases?"

LEARNING OBJECTIVES

After studying this chapter, you should be able to:

1. Explain the use of technology in the law office.

2. Discuss the impact of the Federal Rules of Civil Procedure on electronic documents and the use of technology in the law.

3. Explain the role of the technology support staff.

4. Describe the need to understand the language of technology.

5. Identify technologies that can help the legal team.

VIDEO INTRODUCTION

Professor Thomas F. Goldman, Esq.

TECHNOLOGY IN THE LAW OFFICE
After watching the video in MyLegalStudiesLab, answer the following questions.

1. How has technology changed the way traditional procedures are performed in the law office?
2. What role does the internet play in the contemporary law office?

■ INTRODUCTION TO TECHNOLOGY IN THE LAW OFFICE

LEARNING OBJECTIVE 1
Explain the use of technology in the law office.

Technology in the law office, the court system, and the courtroom has changed the way many traditional procedures are performed. Paper-laden files are giving way to electronic documents that reside on computer servers instead of in boxes and file cabinets. The computer and the Internet are increasingly used not just for traditional document preparation, but also for maintaining client databases, keeping office and client accounting records, engaging in electronic communications, researching, filing documents with the court, presenting cases at trial, and attracting new clients through firm websites.

Computer technology is used in the following ways in the law office:

word processing—preparing documents
electronic spreadsheets—performing financial calculations and financial presentations
time and billing programs—recording billable time accurately, and invoicing clients
accounting programs—managing firm financial records, payroll, and client escrow accounts
calendaring—tracking deadlines, appointments, and hearing dates
graphic presentation software—preparing persuasive presentations
trial presentation software—organizing trial presentations
Internet search engines—searching for accurate and current legal information and factual information to support a case
databases—maintaining records and documents
document scanning—converting documents to electronic format
document search features—locating relevant material in documents and exhibits
email and document delivery—communicating electronically
e-discovery—finding and reviewing discoverable electronic data
online collaboration—using the Internet to work collaboratively
online electronic document repositories—storing and accessing documents remotely

digital format
A computerized format that allows information to be transmitted electronically.

attachments
A popular method of transmitting text files and graphic images by attaching the file to an email.

Computers are also being used with greater frequency to communicate and share information in **digital format** between remote offices, courthouses, government agencies, and clients. In the past, paper had to be physically copied and sent, frequently by a costly messenger service or express mail service. Now, electronic files are increasingly shared as **attachments** to emails. Large files can be exchanged almost instantaneously anywhere in the world, without any

hard copy. Electronic files do not have the same issues with physical safety as paper documents. However, electronic files do have their own issues with security and **confidentiality.**

The legal team is increasingly using the Internet for more than just pure legal research. Most government information can be obtained through the Internet. Finding businesses and individuals through private service providers, such as the yellow pages and white pages, is now handled most efficiently through web search engines such as Google and Yahoo!. More legal firms are developing and using websites for their own businesses, as shown in Exhibit 1.1. However, only the best of these sites are designed in a way that is effective in helping to attract and retain clients.

hard copy
The paper copy of a document.

confidentiality
In the law field, any information with regard to a client, learned from whatever sources, that is to be kept in confidence by the legal team.

Exhibit 1.1 A typical law firm website, the new yellow pages

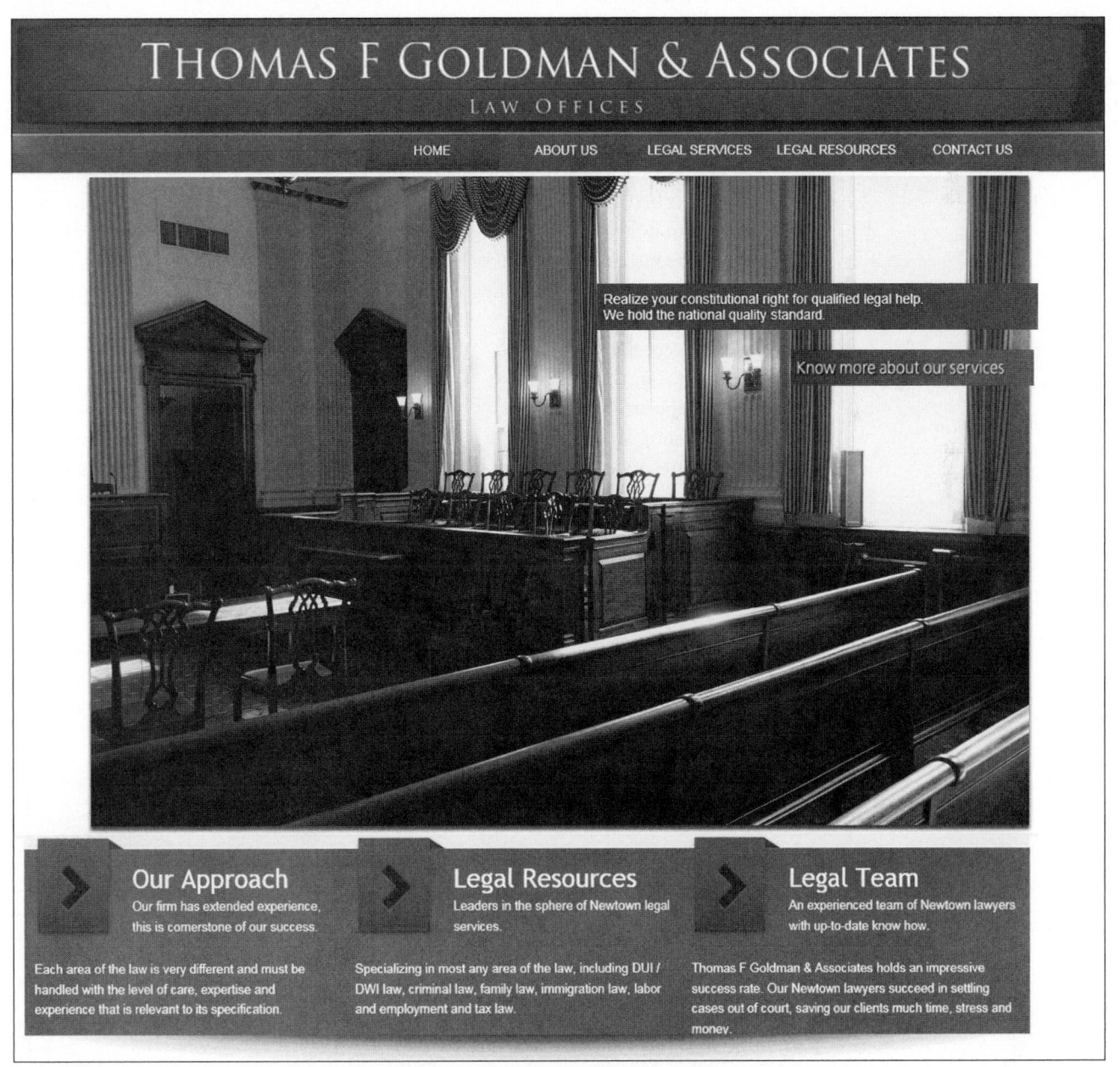

The increase in the use of electronic documents in litigation, and new federal and state rules and case law on electronic discovery, are increasing the demand for skills and knowledge in the use of technology in civil litigation. Increasingly, the legal team must work with technology professionals in order to use computers and electronic data effectively. Thus everyone on the legal team must now have a working familiarity with computers and the types of computer programs used in the law office.

At one time, the equipment in the average law office consisted of a typewriter, an adding machine, and a basic duplicating machine. Paper was king, with every document being typed, edited, retyped—and frequently retyped again. In each instance, a paper copy was produced and delivered to the supervising attorney for review and additional changes. It was then returned for retyping and eventually sent to the client, to the opposing counsel, or filed with the court. File cabinets abounded in the law office, and numerous boxes of paper files were stored in back rooms, warehouses, and other storage locations. But now, the trend is toward eliminating paper in the law office through the use of computer technology and software. In most law offices today, there are no typewriters; instead, computers are used to prepare documents using word processing software. The typical duplicating machine is now a multifunction device that can scan, print, copy, and fax documents.

Members of the legal team frequently work from locations other than the firm's main office, such as a home office, satellite office, or another firm. In some cases, they may be working in a different part of the country or world. But no matter where each team member works, he or she may need access to the case data or electronic files. One solution is to have all of the files stored electronically in an **electronic repository** on a secure, protected file server that authorized users may access over the Internet.

Members of the team may also use the Internet to work together using **online collaboration** software. This software allows several persons to see the same document simultaneously and, in some cases, to make on-screen notes and comments. A number of companies provide services and software that converts case documents to electronic format and stores the documents on a secure server. Exhibit 1.2 shows a typical secure remote litigation network.

electronic repository
An off-site computer used to store records that may be accessed over secure Internet connections.

online collaboration
Using the Internet to conduct meetings and share documents.

Exhibit 1.2 Secure remote access for the legal profession

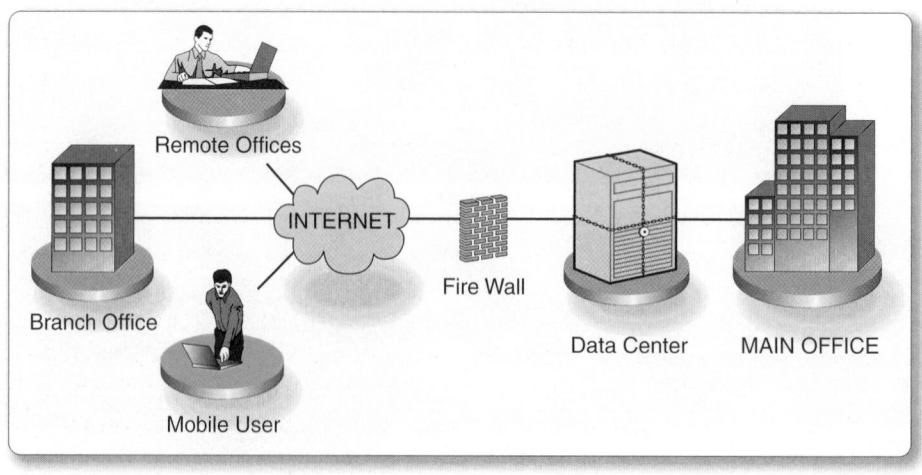

■ THE IMPACT OF THE FEDERAL RULES OF CIVIL PROCEDURE

The December 2006 revision to the Federal Rules of Civil Procedure has had a major impact on our thinking about technology in the practice of law. Members of the legal team who had given only passing notice to the inroads of computers and electronic documents can no longer ignore the impact of this technology. The new federal rules organize and formalize what had once been a patchwork of court rules and case law on electronic discovery. There are also many new rules on electronic discovery in both the state and federal courts.

The new rules specifically address the issue of the increased use of electronic documentation in all aspects of business and personal life. Whereas people once used a pen or a typewriter to write a letter, today the communication method of choice is more likely an email or text message. The federal courts have, through the new rules of civil procedure, acknowledged the role of electronically stored information and the impact it has on litigation. The state courts are also looking at the issue, and many have implemented their own rules, which are often fashioned after the federal rules.

The legal team must always consider the impact of technology on documents connected with current litigation. But they must also address the impact of technology on documents that could be connected with potential litigation. One important consideration is document retention. The ability to retain documents is limited mainly by available storage space. The more space available, the greater the number of documents that can be stored, and the longer they can be retained. With electronic files, the ability to retain documents is virtually limitless. It is therefore necessary for the legal team to carefully consider the rules and procedures for retaining and storing potentially sensitive documents.

Technology has had a significant impact not only on the ability to retain documents, but also on the ability to find and access those documents. For a litigator, stored documents can be a source of a potential **"smoking gun"**—a document on which the case hinges, and that may be introduced into evidence. For example, a document may admit a course of conduct, such as removing a safety feature for the sake of saving money. In some classic product liability or antitrust cases, tractor-trailer loads of documents have been produced, and a document may be "hiding" in a maze of possibly thousands of pieces of paper, waiting for other parties to find it. For example, in a well-known product liability case, Ford was alleged to have sold a dangerous product despite knowing that it was defective. The smoking gun was an internal company report stating that the potential monetary damages from lawsuits would be less costly than changing the design. But the plaintiff team's serendipitous discovery of this document was like finding a needle in a haystack.

With technology and a big enough budget, all of the paper documents in a case can be scanned electronically, a form that allows an electronic search for the smoking gun. The search can be made easier if the documents are delivered by the opponent in a searchable electronic format pursuant to a proper discovery request.

The potentially massive delivery of documents in electronic form also raises concerns that these electronic documents may contain privileged or confidential information. These documents may need to be delivered to the opposing side in compliance with an electronic discovery request without the opportunity to check each document for privileged or confidential material.

LEARNING OBJECTIVE 2
Discuss the impact of the Federal Rules of Civil Procedure on electronic documents and the use of technology in the law.

smoking gun
A document hidden among old files that would conclusively impeach or destroy the credibility of a witness or be evidence that conclusively determines an issue.

No longer can the legal team ignore the role of technology in law practice, whether the legal team is a sole practitioner with a legal secretary, or a mega-member international law firm with in-house technical support. Thus everyone on the legal team must understand the role of various technologies in counseling and representing clients.

■ TECHNOLOGY SUPPORT IN THE LAW OFFICE

LEARNING OBJECTIVE 3
Explain the role of the technology support staff.

IT
Information technology, or the technology support staff within organizations.

Larger law offices, corporate legal departments, and government offices usually have a technical support staff, frequently called the **IT,** or information technology, department. The IT staff handles questions and issues concerning the use and implementation of technology in general, and computers and software in particular. Smaller offices may have a person who is unofficially responsible for the same type of support. This person is usually the most tech-savvy member of the staff—a lawyer, a paralegal, a secretary, a "friend" of the office, or a relative of a staff member—and is sometimes referred to affectionately as the office "geek."

ADVICE FROM THE FIELD

TAKING YOUR CAREER IN A NEW DIRECTION—AN INSIDE GLIMPSE AT LIT SUPPORT CAREERS
by Sally Kane, J.D.

Advances in technology, the growth of electronically stored information and amendments to federal and state e-discovery rules have transformed litigation support into one of the hottest careers in today's legal market. The e-discovery/litigation support industry [was] predicted to...[reach] $21.8 billion by the year 2011.

As the market heats up, new positions are opening within law firms, litigation support vendors, the government and corporate legal departments across the globe. The unprecedented number of opportunities in the litigation support marketplace has created a new market dynamic as supply/demand economics fuel salary growth and lateral hiring. As a result, "litigation support professionals are moving with increasing frequency between what I call the three silos of the litigation support market: law firms, litigation support vendors and corporate legal departments," says David Cowen of The Cowen Group, a global provider of e-discovery and litigation support staffing services.

These three market silos differ significantly in terms of benefits, challenges, professional development opportunities, career paths, work/life balance, compensation and career growth.... So, how does employment in a law firm compare with employment with litigation support vendor[s] or corporate legal department[s]? Who is paying top dollar? What is the best career move for you right now?

Below, attorneys, recruiting experts and litigation support professionals share their insight into the pros and cons of working in the three silos of litigation support.

Law Firm Life

Employment within a law firm offers litigation support professionals many distinct advantages including a well-defined career path, extensive firm resources, access to the latest technology, a large support staff, well-developed training programs, challenging work and a diverse client base.

As the profession evolves, law firms are creating more well-defined career paths in order to attract and retain talented litigation support professionals. The typical path at a major firm with a large litigation support department progresses from analyst level one, analyst level two and specialist to coordinator, project manager, senior project manager, supervisor, manager and director, according to Cowen. Many of these positions did not exist five years ago and, as the industry evolves, law firms continue to offer significant advancement opportunities.

Brian Stempel, firm wide litigation services manager for Kirkland & Ellis, LLP, notes that one of the primary advantages of working for a law firm over other practice environments is the big-picture perspective and insight into the entire litigation life cycle. "It's where the rubber meets the road," Stempel says. "You see the actual legal

(*continued*)

representation in terms of what the issues are and what the client's needs are."

Scott Cohen, Director of Practice Support at Proskauer Rose, agrees. "The breadth and diversity of the work is substantially greater than what I experienced in a corporation," notes Cohen[,] who has spent his twenty-year litigation support career in law firms, corporations and vendors. "In a corporation, you are only working for one client. In a law firm, you could be working on a white collar crime matter today, a complex commercial litigation tomorrow and everything in between."

Salaries paid to litigation support professionals in law firms are among the highest in the industry. Project managers in top markets such as New York earn between $95,000 and $125,000 in a law firm; managers and directors are making between $150,000 and $200,000, Cowen says.

Since law firms pay top dollar, they can afford to recruit the most skilled and experienced professionals. Litigation support professionals in law firms are surrounded by and benefit from knowledgeable, well-credentialed colleagues. The large pool of qualified candidates within a firm may also fuel competition as a number of high-caliber candidates compete for the best assignments and advancement opportunities.

Law firms also offer ample opportunities for professional development ranging from in-house training sessions to certification in specific software programs. Stempel's firm sends employees to industry training programs and certification classes on litigation support technology.

Law firm life as a litigation professional also presents challenges. The hours can be long and evening and weekend work is often required. The "support" aspect of litigation support requires that services be available when the client—firm partners, associates and outside clients—need[s] them. Law firm litigation support departments may need 24/7 capabilities as the firm gears up for trial or another large matter. "It is a delicate balancing act," says Gyorgy Pados, director of litigation support at Hughes Hubbard & Reed, LLP. "You may have multiple cases going on at the same time, each with competing demands.... You must measure the triangle of scope, time and money [and staff the matter accordingly]."

Moreover, litigation support professionals are required to track and bill time, both billable and administrative. This requirement seems to be fairly universal, whether the law firm treats its litigation support department as a capital expense with the goal of cost-recovery or as a profit center with the goal of raising revenue. Stempel reports that his level one through level three employees are required to be 70% billable (about 35 to 40 hours a week) while managers are expected to bill 50% of their work week.

Litigation support professionals looking to transition to a law firm generally need several years of experience.

"Law firms, for the most part, are not willing to train," says Cowen. "Firms want experience—any combination of hands-on technical skills, project management experience and high level communication skills. Litigation support professionals must have the ability to interact with IT, litigation support, attorneys and, in some cases, clients," Cowen says.

Corporate Legal Departments

Compared to the frenzied environment of law firms and vendor[s], professionals employed in the corporate legal environment often enjoy a more relaxed work pace. Large corporations (i.e., those that typically employ litigation support and e-discovery professionals) are notoriously slower to embrace change, purchase new technological tools, implement new processes and make hiring decisions....

Litigation Support Vendors

Employment with a litigation support vendor offers a different landscape and perspective than the law firm and corporate environment. Spending on e-discovery software technologies and services [was] forecasted to grow more than 35% annually through 2011, fueling growth in the vendor space.

While law firms and corporations are often characterized as linear, traditional and conventional, the vendor environment is entrepreneurial, flexible, informal, innovative and fast-paced. These qualities may stem from the recent arrival of many vendors to the litigation support arena. Most litigation support vendors have been established within the last five to ten years and are in the nascent stages of development, boasting smaller workforces, dynamic growth and a more informal business environment....

The Perfect Fit

Every law firm, corporation and vendor boasts its own unique structure, business practices and culture. Determining the perfect fit for you is "a combination of timing, luck and personal career goals," Cowen says. When preparing to transition from one practice environment to another, it is important to understand the differences within each organization. By conducting a thorough due diligence and considering how the move will impact your future career, you will more surely find personal fulfillment in today's competitive job market....

About the Author: Sally A. Kane is an attorney and writer specializing in legal and career topics. Visit Sally's legal careers website at www.legalcareers.about.com/ or post questions and comments about this article on her forum at www.legalcareers.about.com/mpboards.htm.

Source: Originally published in *Litigation Support Today* May/July 2008. Reprinted with permission from *Litigation Support Today* magazine.

Technology Usage in the Law

The role of technology in the law has evolved in a few years from a minor role, such as the stand-alone word processor, to a ubiquitous element in the management of law offices of all sizes. Computers are now being used for everything from word processing to accounting functions, such as computerized timekeeping, payroll, or tax return preparation. In some offices, telephone systems even use a computerized attendant to answer the phone without human intervention. The use of technology in litigation was once limited to large law firms working on big cases for wealthy clients, who could afford to pay for the technology. Today, however, even the smallest law firm and litigator must use technology. Some courts and government agencies, such as the Internal Revenue Service, are encouraging computerized filing. Records previously available in paper form, such as medical records in litigation cases, are now provided electronically. The result is that offices of all sizes now need to have computer or technology support.

Working with In-House Technology Support Staff

In the past, technology support was limited to supporting on-site computer systems and software. The advances in portable computers and wireless technologies, however, have expanded the demand placed on IT departments to include supporting the legal team outside the office. Members of the legal team who are working from remote locations on their wireless laptops or devices may need to be able to access to files on office file servers or in remote electronic repositories. In addition, services must be provided for technology beyond computers and software. Litigation teams may require support for videotaping depositions at out-of-office or out-of-town locations, and trials may require the use of sophisticated presentation equipment.

The IT department may not have the resources in people, hardware, or software to support every demand. If the IT staff is frequently called in at the last moment, they may not have the time to gear up to support the immediate needs of the legal team. But when the support staff has time to prepare, they can usually find a way to support many potential applications, whether they are **remote access** issues or graphic-intense litigation needs. Of course, IT staff can offer the best support to the legal team when they are involved early in the process, and when it is clear what the legal team needs to accomplish. For instance, if the use of a computer simulation is considered for presenting a case at trial, calling in the IT staff in the early stage of the litigation may save time and money. In that situation, for example, the IT staff may need time to consider such issues as whether the courthouse has the necessary equipment to show the simulation, whether specialty equipment must be obtained or used, or whether the graphics will be delivered in a format compatible with the law firm's trial presentation software.

remote access
Accessing a file server or computer from a remote location using the Internet.

Issues in Working with Outside Technology Consultants

There are many types of independent technology consultants who can provide services with computer, software, and multimedia technology. Selecting the correct consultant is a matter of understanding what is needed. Consultants may be needed to fix a computer or peripherals such as a printer or monitor. Many outside companies are retained on a maintenance contract to provide coverage as needed for a period of time at a fixed rate. Others are hired for support or maintenance as needed at an hourly rate.

Media consultants are also frequently called to assist in a variety of situations. Some are called upon to prepare graphic presentations ranging from individual exhibits to multimedia simulations. Others are called upon simply to operate equipment or assist in trial presentations.

To obtain the best service from the consultant, the legal team must speak the same language as the consultant when defining the scope of service and the desired results. Hiring a consultant who uses a system that is incompatible with the legal team's system can be a costly mistake, or even a disaster—one sometimes not discovered until the actual day of trial. For example, if the legal team is using PC-based hardware and software and the consultant is using Mac OS (the operating system used by Apple computers), the consultant might produce the final product in a version that works only on an Apple computer. Although such a gross oversight might seem unlikely, it has been known to happen.

The ownership of the consultant's work product must also be addressed. Is it "work for hire" that will be owned by the law firm or client, or is it a creative work that is owned by the consultant and may be used in any way he or she wishes?

Outsourcing

Outsourcing has become a buzzword for shipping work out of the office or overseas to save money. Some of the services that can be performed in-house are better outsourced. For years, many law firms have outsourced the payroll function instead of preparing payroll checks and tax returns in-house. The confidentiality of information about salaries may dictate that an outside firm handle the payroll process so that only a few people in the office have access to the critical payroll information. In a similar vein, the accounting functions may be outsourced to an outside bookkeeping or accounting firm.

IT support may also be outsourced. For example, using an outside computer consultant to provide support for hardware and software is a form of outsourcing. Such support may simply involve a help desk in a foreign location answering questions.

outsourcing
The use of persons or services outside of the office staff.

Information Technologists as Members of the Legal Team

Electronic data is created and stored in many formats using many different software applications. While there are some commonly used protocols, formats, and methods for data creation and storage, the lawyers and paralegals on the legal team cannot be expected to have the same specialized technical knowledge that an **information technologist** has. The handling of electronic records requires the input of these information technology specialists. Even the IT specialist may need to engage the assistance of additional specialists in rarely used methods, software, or hardware. In some cases, such as those involving erased data or damaged storage media, a forensic expert may need to be called in.

IT specialists understand current information systems; the methods of producing, reproducing, and accessing electronic documents; and the problems that may be encountered in handling documents. IT specialists must therefore be part of the legal team.

information technologist
A member of the legal team who has legal and technology skills and primarily supports electronic discovery activities.

■ TRAINING FOR HARDWARE AND SOFTWARE SUPPORT

To be efficient, each user of the office computer system must be trained in the features and procedures of that system. Each office tends to have its own method of filing documents, either on individual personal computer workstations or on the office network file server. In the ideal world, a reference guide—where everything is documented, easy to read, and completely understandable—would be available to each employee. But in the real world, people may need instruction on everything from the basics, such as where the on-off switch is located, to the more sophisticated tasks, such as how to connect with a remote office file server and download a file.

Someone must do the training. Again, in the ideal world, an IT person would do the training in-house. In the real world, however, few offices have this resource. Often, some of the basics are taught by the more-experienced people in the office. But in most law practices, one or more outside sources are used. The person or company who sold or installed the hardware or software may also offer training. Manufacturers may offer online help or telephone support. In some cases, classes may be offered at local educational institutions for credit or as noncredit offerings. Many specialty software vendors also offer training from a basic to an advanced level.

How Much Do I Really Need to Know?

No one can be an expert in everything. What is important is knowing enough to know what you do not know and to be able to find someone who does know. It is thus necessary for members of the law team to understand basic computer concepts and be able to communicate with those who are the experts. Having a basic understanding of what different programs are used for in the legal environment is a good starting point. For instance, find out what word processing, spreadsheet, or database programs are used in the daily support of the legal team. Understand the differences in the software and computer tools used by the litigation specialist and those used by the in-house legal support team. Most importantly, communicate

---

International Legal Technology Association (ILTA) IT Staffing Survey

Outsourcing

"There are simply too many IT functions to be performed in today's law firm and too many different skill sets required to go it alone; outsourcing some IT function, either in whole or in part, is the norm for firms of all sizes.

The most commonly outsourced function, regardless of firm size, is printer maintenance. Across the board, eight out of ten firms report outsourcing all or part of this function.

Outsourcing the help desk function is more commonly seen at very large firms than at their smaller counterparts, not so much for providing the basic services during office hours, but for providing extended coverage after-hours, on weekends and on holidays."

Source: ILTA Staffing Survey, December 2006 www.iltanet.org.

ETHICAL Perspectives

WEST VIRGINIA RULES OF PROFESSIONAL CONDUCT

Rule 1.1. Competence

A lawyer shall provide competent representation to a client. Competent representation requires the legal knowledge, skill, thoroughness and preparation reasonably necessary for the representation.

 WEB RESOURCES

Contrast and compare West Virginia Rules of Professional Conduct Rule 1.1 at http://www.wvbar.org/BARINFO/rulesprofconduct/rules1.htm with the analogous rule in the American Bar Association Model Rules of Professional Responsibility at http://www.abanet.org/cpr/mrpc/mrpc_toc.html. Then compare these to the ethical rule in your jurisdiction.

with both the legal side and the technology side of a firm. Learn the language of the IT specialists—what some refer to as "geek talk." Keep current by reading the professional journals and legal papers for new tools and services being offered to make the job of legal and litigation teams more efficient. Attend the local, regional, and national technology shows for the legal industry to see the products and services available. Ask questions, and learn enough to make suggestions for updating and changing the tools of your profession.

■ UNDERSTANDING THE LANGUAGE OF TECHNOLOGY

The field of law has developed its own lexicon of terms that enables those in the legal community to communicate effectively and with precision. The technology world also has developed its own lexicon. An understanding of the language of technology is thus a prerequisite to understanding the technology found in the law office, the courthouse, and the client's business. The legal team and the technology support team must learn each other's language in order for one team to communicate its needs and solutions to the other.

In some cases, each group thinks it is communicating to the other, but in reality, the words used by one group may have a different meaning to the other group. For example, the word *protocol* has multiple definitions. To the legal team, *protocol* is defined as "a summary of a document or treaty; or, a treaty amending another treaty, or the rules of diplomatic etiquette" (*Black's Law Dictionary*—West Group). To the technology specialist, *protocol* is defined as "a set of formal rules describing how to transmit data, especially across a network" (Free On-Line Dictionary of Computing [http://foldoc.org]). Another example is the word *cell*. To the criminal lawyer, a cell is a place where clients are held in jail. To the computer support staff, it is a space on a spreadsheet where a piece of data is displayed. Lawyers, paralegals, other members of the legal team, and the members of the technology support team must learn each other's language because understanding such differences in terminology is essential to working together effectively and meeting the needs of clients.

LEARNING OBJECTIVE 4
Describe the need to understand the language of technology.

■ FUTURE TRENDS IN LAW OFFICE TECHNOLOGY

Law offices are constantly under pressure to be more productive. Increased costs have led law office managers to look for new ways to use technology to increase productivity. Further, clients and the courts are not willing to approve fees and costs when more cost-effective methods are available. In addition, the demand

LEARNING OBJECTIVE 5
Identify technologies that can help the legal team.

for speedy justice in the courts has resulted in less time to prepare and present cases. Thus the legal team must work faster and become more productive. Advances in computer technology are providing solutions to help deal with these constraints.

Looking ahead to what's on the technological horizon is imperative to the smooth and profitable functioning of the law office. Anticipating and incorporating new technology in turn requires IT knowledge and savvy, whether it is provided by in-house staff or external technology consultants. A chief information officer or chief technology officer at a corporate firm must anticipate change and plan for it in concrete and innovative ways. Those responsible for IT at smaller firms must also be well-informed of technology trends. They must assess when a new tool should be added to their technology repertoire—and when it should be avoided.

The legal team is an increasingly mobile workforce. Working outside of the office is a fact of life for trial attorneys and their support staff. The litigation team may spend much of their time in courthouses, or by taking depositions at other offices. These activities may take place across the street, across the country, or around the globe. Increasingly, the support staff must also work outside the traditional law office. In some cases, this work is outsourced to other firms or companies in remote locations. In addition, some lawyers, paralegals, and litigation support staff work from home. With advances in technology, it is possible for these team members to connect with the main office and access all the needed files and electronic resources through a computer at home. These workers are sometimes referred to as **teleworkers.**

teleworkers
People who work from remote locations, typically from home.

Technology is developing much faster than we could have expected even a few years ago. As Raymond Kurzweil writes in his essay "The Law of Accelerating Returns" (2001),

> An analysis of the history of technology shows that technological change is exponential, contrary to the common-sense "intuitive linear" view. So we won't experience 100 years of progress in the 21st century—it will be more like 20,000 years of progress (at today's rate). The "returns," such as chip speed and cost-effectiveness, also increase exponentially. There's even exponential growth in the rate of exponential growth.

The following section describes some of the emerging technology, some of which is currently available now and in use at some law firms, while some of which is still under development. The list is not exhaustive but gives an idea of what businesses might expect to see in the near and distant future.

Videoconferencing

videoconferencing
Conferencing from multiple locations using high-speed Internet connections to transmit sound and images.

Videoconferencing is the use of the Internet, telephone lines, or special satellite systems to transmit and receive video and audio signals in real time. This technology allows parties in several locations to see and hear each other during a conference. Many law firms and their clients currently use videoconferencing on a regular basis as a method of "face-to-face" communication when parties are at remote sites, such as depositions, hearings, or conferences.

Videoconferencing is also used in many courts at various stages of court proceedings, most often at the early stages of a criminal case. This technology is now being recognized by some court rules. For example, Section 885.52(3) of the Wisconsin Supreme Court Rules defines videoconferencing as "interactive technology that sends video, voice, and data signals over a transmission circuit so that two or more individuals or groups can communicate with each other simultaneously using video monitors." The Wisconsin rules further establish the requirements under which videoconferencing can be used in court proceedings. They are some of the most advanced rules on videoconferencing in the country, permitting the use of this technology in all aspects of criminal and civil litigation. Rules such as these are designed to make emerging web-based technologies available to litigants, as long as certain requirements are met. With Wisconsin leading the way, videoconferencing and other technologies can be expected to become important tools in litigation practice.

VoIP

Voice over Internet Protocol **(VoIP)** is a method for transmitting voice communication over the Internet rather than through traditional telephone company services. A computer with a microphone and headset or speaker is used to complete a call to another computer or telephone over the Internet. The communication operates through software installed on a computer, and may include both voice and images. At first, VoIP was limited by the inability to connect calls to or from a conventional telephone. But services like Yahoo Messenger now provide options that permit calling conventional phones at a very nominal rate, sometimes as low as one cent per minute.

At one time, conducting a videoconference required going to a special location and paying a substantial fee. Now, the relatively low cost and ease of use of VoIP make teleconferencing, including videoconferencing, a reality for those who previously could not afford such services. Anyone with a laptop, a built-in microphone and speakers, and an inexpensive video camera can set up a videoconference from almost anywhere an Internet connection is available.

Voice Recognition

Voice recognition software has been around for a number of years as an alternative to typing. This software converts spoken words into text on the screen. Many will remember trying out earlier versions of speech recognition programs, and finding them to be lacking in accuracy. But improved technology has brought this software to a level of accuracy approaching, and in some cases exceeding, the accuracy of typing. Speech-enabled devices include smartphones, pad devices, and GPS devices. With programs like Dragon Naturally Speaking (Legal Version), it is now possible to dictate working drafts of legal documents directly into almost any other program, including word processors, spreadsheets, and databases, without touching a computer keyboard. The document may then be sent to another member of the legal team electronically, as shown in Exhibit 1.3. This software has become so advanced that portable dictation devices can be used outside of the office and later connected to the office computer to transcribe documents without the intervention of a typist. And the benefits to the legal team in productivity and efficiency are significant. Transcribing speech at up to 160 words a minute, voice recognition software far outpaces the average typist's speed.

The underlying technology found in voice recognition software is now being used in automated response systems that replace live operators and receptionists at some firms. It is also used in products that help those who cannot use a keyboard because of physical disabilities, such as carpal tunnel syndrome.

WEB RESOURCES

Read the article on the use of videoconferencing in Wisconsin in the *Wisconsin Lawyer* Vol. 81, No. 7, July 2008, at http://www.wisbar.org/AM/Template.cfm?Section=Wisconsin_Lawyer&template=/CM/ContentDisplay.cfm&contentid=73013. What potential issues with videoconferencing does the Wisconsin rule attempt to address?

VoIP
An Internet replacement for traditional telephone connections.

voice recognition
Computer programs for converting speech into text or commands without the use of other input devices such as keyboards.

Exhibit 1.3 A paralegal using The Boom from UmeVoice, a high-quality noise-reduction microphone with Dragon Naturally Speaking that achieves high-accuracy speech recognition

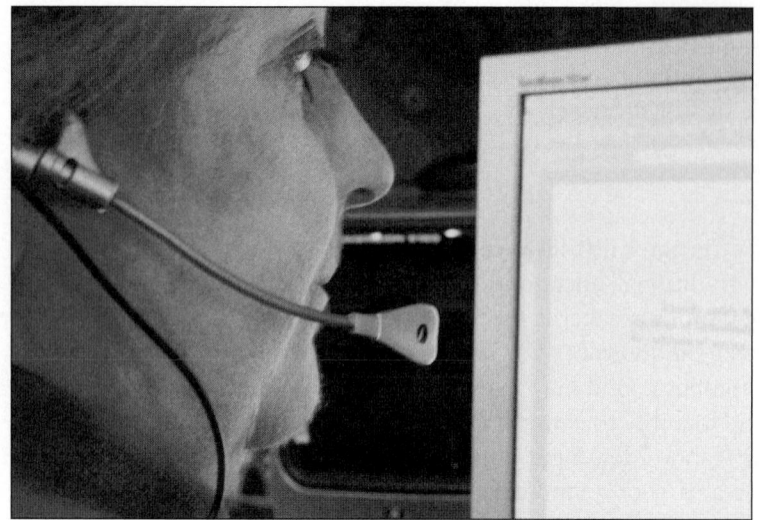

Miniaturization and Portability

The trend in computers and related computer devices has been toward light weight, portability, and extended battery life. Some laptops now weigh less than three pounds, and are more powerful than some older desktop systems. They may include all of the capabilities of desktop systems, including built-in web cameras for videoconferencing. Similarly, cell phones such as the Apple iPhone and the Google Android are now capable of taking and displaying photos and video, preparing documents, sending emails, and accessing the Internet—functions that formerly required large, hard-wired computer devices.

Wireless Technology

Only a few years ago, wires or cables were necessary to access networks or to set up network connections. Today, networks may be set up among workstations, servers, and peripherals using wireless technology. Remote access is also possible with the use of a wireless Internet connection using laptops and cell phones with built-in Internet access.

Many offices today are equipped with wireless telephones and wireless Internet networks. In addition, the worldwide availability of inexpensive high-speed Internet connections, or "hotspots," has expanded the use of wireless technologies. Wireless devices allow constant communication and enable work to be performed virtually anywhere, such as at home, the courthouse, an airport lounge, or a coffee shop. Staff members may connect to their office's wireless network through the Internet or cellular network using wireless hardware built into the computer, or through an external adapter card.

Remote Access

Remote access allows members of the legal team working on cases out of the office to connect with the office file server to retrieve documents, work on them, and send them to other members of the team anywhere in the world. If a hard copy is needed, documents may be printed on any printer accessible over the Internet, including printers in remote office locations, public access points in airports, clients' offices, and courthouses. Exhibit 1.2, shown on page 6, is an example of a typical remote access configuration that provides security for the data and limits access to authorized users.

Remote Collaboration

remote collaboration
Two or more parties working on a common document through remote access.

Remote collaboration involves members of the team at multiple locations working together as if they were in the same physical location. Software conferencing programs allow team members to share files while communicating and seeing each other on the same screen with the use of small cameras on the desktop or built into their laptop computers. The same remote access technology also allows the taking of witness statements from remote locations while the parties see each other or view exhibits on the computer screen.

With high-speed Internet connections, true real-time videoconferencing has become a reality. In the past, slower connections restricted how much information could be transmitted, and increased the time needed to send a document. Slower speeds also prevented the availability of full-motion, full-screen video. High-speed Internet connections now allow users to transmit both sound and images simultaneously. With the introduction of fiber-optic and cable Internet services, videoconferencing from multiple locations is now available at many offices.

Wireless Computer Networks

Wireless computer networks are like cell phone networks in that both use radio waves to transmit signals to a receiver. Cell phone systems use cell towers located at strategic points all over the world that receive the signals from cellular devices. Similarly, wireless networks use wireless access points, which are essentially receivers of radio signals that convert the signals so that they can be transmitted to a computer or to the Internet.

wireless computer networks
Networks using wireless technology instead of wires and cables for connecting people and equipment.

Unlike cell phone towers, these access points have the more limited range of only a few hundred feet. Many of these access points, or "hotspots," are provided in coffee shops, airport lounges, hotels, libraries, bookstores, and other locations. Businesses often offer wireless access without charge, or at a nominal fee, to encourage customers to patronize them.

With the growth of wireless **hotspots,** lawyers and paralegals may be connected anywhere in the world and may send documents electronically back and forth with the same ease as sending them within the same building. And with the cellular connections provided through internal or plug-in accessories, computers can access the Internet over areas where the Internet was not previously accessible.

hotspot
A wireless access point, usually in a public area.

Wireless Laptop Connections

With the use of USB plug-in devices, laptops may be wirelessly connected to the Internet without the need of a hotspot. Subscriptions to data services are provided by most major cellular providers such as AT&T, Verizon, and Sprint. These services can provide Internet access virtually anywhere there is cellular coverage. The popularity of these wireless services has resulted in many newer-generation laptops having the feature built in, thus eliminating the need for external cards.

"Cloud computing" or **"thin client,"** as it has been called, is now emerging in which all programs and files are maintained on a centralized server. Each user has access through a dumb terminal (a terminal without programs or data). The thin client model offers some additional level of control and prevents the loss of information that would occur if someone's computer were lost or damaged. Another example of cloud computing is Software as a Service (SaaS), such as Office 365 from Microsoft. The service charges a monthly fee for use of its software when needed.

thin client
A computer system where programs and files are maintained on a centralized server.

Checklist ☑

Use the following checklist as a tool to assess how your firm uses technology and to discover areas you might want to address in the future.

- Which functions are automated now? Which additional functions do you wish to automate?
- Are existing pieces of equipment mutually compatible?
- Does everyone in the office use the same software?
- Are word processing procedures standardized?
- Is the billing system interfaced with the accounting system?
- Are checks drawn on law firm accounts computer-generated or prepared manually?
- Are you using software to keep track of client expenses, such as copies, faxes, long-distance calls, and postage?
- Are telephone messages delivered accurately and in a timely manner?
- Does the office get flooded with paper interoffice memoranda?
- Is the payroll prepared in-house? Is payroll handled manually, or with software?
- Do the attorneys often carry boxes of documents to the courthouse?
- Do the paralegals spend hours preparing manual document index systems?
- How does the firm check for conflicts of interest?
- What type of calendaring system do you use for docket control and scheduling?

Source: Gisela Bradley, Law Practice Management Program, State Bar of Texas.

CONCEPT REVIEW AND REINFORCEMENT

KEY TERMS

attachments 5
confidentiality 5
digital format 5
electronic repository 6
hard copy 5
hotspot 17
information technologist 11

IT 7
online collaboration 6
outsourcing 11
remote access 10
remote collaboration 16
smoking gun 7
teleworkers 14

thin client 17
videoconferencing 14
voice recognition 15
VoIP 15
wireless computer network 17

CHAPTER SUMMARY

Introduction to Technology in the Law Office	Computer technology is used in many ways in the law office:
	word processing
	electronic spreadsheets
	time and billing programs
	accounting programs
	calendaring
	graphic presentation software
	trial presentation software

	Internet search engines databases document scanning document search features email and document delivery online collaboration online document repositories
Impact of the Federal Rules of Civil Procedure	New Federal Rules that became effective December 2006 specifically address the issue of the increased use of electronically stored documentation. New federal court rules on electronic discovery and electronically stored documents, and emerging case law on electronic discovery, are creating increased demand for skills and knowledge in the use of technology in civil litigation.
Technology Support in the Law Office	In larger law offices, corporate legal departments, and government offices, there is usually a technical support staff.
Technology Usage in the Law	The role of technology in the law has evolved in a very small number of years from a minor function to a ubiquitous element in the management of law offices of all sizes.
Working with In-House Technology Support Staff	Litigation teams may require support for videotaping depositions at out-of-office or out-of-town locations. Trials may require the use of sophisticated presentation equipment. All members of the legal team may need access to the home office files on the office file servers from remote locations on their wireless laptops.
Issues in Working with Outside Technology Consultants	Outside companies may be retained to service hardware or provide support to software used in the office. They may be retained on a maintenance contract basis to provide coverage as needed for a period of time, or for a fixed rate. Others may be hired as needed at an hourly rate.
Outsourcing	Work may be shipped out of the office to an outside contractor to save money. Some service providers are located overseas.
Information Technologists as Members of the Legal Team	Information technologists are members of the legal team who combine legal skills and technology skills.
Training for Hardware and Software Support	To be efficient, each user of the office computer system must be trained in the features and procedures of that system.
How Much Do I Really Need to Know?	What is important is knowing enough to know what you do not know, and to be able to find someone who does know.
Understanding the Language of Technology	An understanding of the language of technology is a prerequisite to understanding the technology found in the law office, the courthouse, and the client's business.

Future Trends in Law Office Technology	The legal team is under pressure to be more productive. Advances in computer technology are providing ways for the team to achieve this greater productivity.
Videoconferencing	Videoconferencing employs technology that transmits sound and video simultaneously, in real time. It allows remote conferences, hearings, and depositions among parties located at separate sites.
VoIP	Voice over Internet Protocol is a computer substitute for the use of traditional telephone connections.
Voice Recognition	Voice recognition software allows spoken words to be converted directly into text. Speech-enabled devices include cell phones, personal digital assistants (PDAs), and other handheld devices.
Miniaturization and Portability	The trend in computers and related devices has been toward miniaturization and portability.
Wireless Technology	Wires and cables are no longer necessary to access networks or to set up network connections. Today, they may be set up using wireless technology in a wireless network.
Remote Access	Team members working on cases outside of the office can connect with the office file server to access documents.
Remote Collaboration	The legal team can work collaboratively from multiple locations as if in the same physical location through software conferencing programs. This technology allows the sharing of files while team members communicate with and see each other on the same screen using small cameras on the desktop or built into laptop computers.
Wireless Computer Networks	Wireless computers use radio signals to transmit information to wireless access points. These wireless networks can be used to connect to the Internet.
Wireless Laptop Connections	Laptops may access the Internet using built-in or plug-in devices and a subscription service that provides access anywhere there is a cellular connection. In cloud computing, programs and files are maintained on a centralized server. Each user has access through a terminal called a thin client.

REVIEW QUESTIONS AND EXERCISES

1. Prepare a detailed list of the ways technology is used in the law office and courts.
2. How can law offices use computers to share information?
3. How can the Internet be used to attract new business for the law office?
4. How has the use of technology changed the skills needed to work in a law office?
5. How can the computer help members of a legal team work together when they are not in the same physical location?
6. Explain, with examples, how the Internet is used today by law offices and the courts.
7. Why does the legal team need to have a working familiarity with computers and the different types of computer software programs? Give examples.

8. How have the new Federal Rules of Civil Procedure impacted the legal profession?
9. What is the role of the information technology department in a law office?
10. How can "hotspots" be used by the legal team?
11. Why is it necessary for the members of the legal team to be able to communicate with those in a support or user position about technology as it relates to the legal community? Give examples.
12. Why is the quantity of documents increasing in litigation?
13. How has technology changed the roles of the members of the legal team?
14. Why would a law firm use an outside technology support firm?
15. What are the underlying reasons for the difficulty some legal team members may have in communicating with the IT staff?
16. Do the members of the legal team need to know everything about the computers and software they use?
17. How can a member of the legal team learn about the technology used in a law office? Give specific examples.
18. How will videoconferencing change the way law is practiced in the future?
19. Is it realistic for members of a legal team to do work from home?

BUILDING YOUR PARALEGAL SKILLS

INTERNET AND TECHNOLOGY EXERCISES

1. Use an Internet search engine to find an article on the use of outsourcing in the legal community.

2. Locate at least three Internet resources on technology used in law practices. Save the Internet addresses for future use.

CHAPTER OPENING SCENARIO CASE STUDY

Use the Opening Scenario for this chapter to answer the following questions. A new attorney is having a discussion with an experienced paralegal who has agreed to help him open an office.

1. What are office and legal functions for which technology can be used in a start-up law office? What technologies would best serve those functions?
2. What technologies would be most helpful in a litigation practice where the attorney is frequently in court? How would those technologies help a trial attorney be more efficient and productive?
3. What issues are involved in using an outside software, hardware, or Internet consultant in setting up a law office?

4. Prepare a checklist of *minimum* software and hardware requirements for a start-up office. Prepare a second checklist of *recommended* technology needs. Be specific. Print out and save a copy for future reference.
5. What, if any, additional minimum or recommended items should be added to the list in question 4 for a trial attorney establishing a new law practice?
6. Use the Internet to find the prices for the equipment and software on the checklists in questions 4 and 5. Prepare a budget for acquiring hardware and software for the new law office.

CONTINUING CASES AND EXERCISES

1. Internet Resources
   Start a list of resources available on the Internet as you progress through the chapters and complete assignments. To get started, the Internet resources from Chapter 1 have been inserted. Remember that web addresses change often, so update your list regularly.

Subject	Source	Topic	URL	Date of entry
Ethics	ABA	Model rules of professional conduct	www.abanet.org/cpr/mrpc/home.html	
State ethics opinions		Your state ethical rule opinions		
Dictionary	FOLDOC	Computing	http://foldoc.org	
Federal Court Rules—Civil	Legal Information Institute	FRCP	www.law.cornell.edu/rules/frcp	
Federal Court Rules—Criminal		FRCRMP	www.law.cornell.edu/Rules/FRCRMP	
State and Local Court Rules—Civil				
State and Local Court Rules—Criminal				

2. Keep a log of the time you spend in this course. Use the following format:

	Time				
Date	Start	Stop	Elapsed	Code	Description
8-19-2012	8:00			AC	Attend Class on ethics

Record the actual time spent (you can round to 1/10 of an hour) using these suggested codes. The descriptions in parentheses are analogous activities that would be billed in a real law practice.
  a. class attendance (conference with supervising attorney)—AC
  b. travel to and from class (travel)—T
  c. time reading and researching material (research)—RRM
  d. time preparing assignments (drafting documents)—PA
  e. time spent preparing for tests (preparation)—TP
  f. time taking tests (trial)—T
  g. other miscellaneous items (miscellaneous)—M

3. Prepare a list of calendar items for the course, including times and locations for class, library sessions, tests, assignment deadlines, and other class-related calendar items. Using an electronic calendar program, create a schedule as if it were a docket control system. Set up warnings or alarms in the system to alert you when certain dates are approaching.

4. Owen Mason, Esq., is a young, technology-aware attorney just starting out in a new legal practice. He thought the World Wide Web would be a good source of potential business. However, as a clerk in the federal court, he did not have the opportunity to look at many law office websites. He asks for your help in designing his web page.
  a. Using the Internet search tools available to you, locate the websites of law firms in your area, as well as around the country. Make a list of the best and the worst features of these websites.
  b. Prepare your recommendations for Mr. Mason, including details and, if possible, screen printouts. Make a list of the web addresses of each of the sites that you feel demonstrate the good, the bad, and the ugly.
  c. Outline which features would be most useful in attracting and assisting clients. Sketch a design for each page, including the information that would be presented on each page.

d. What are the ethical issues and potential UPL issues in the use of a website in your jurisdiction? Research the ethical rules that would apply to lawyers advertising on the Internet.

e. ADVANCED STUDENTS. Create a website using available resources and software.

Note: A number of lawyers use the web to promote their specialty practices. Use the generic terminology—civil litigation—to locate other web pages of attorneys specializing in civil litigation.

BUILDING YOUR PROFESSIONAL PORTFOLIO

1. Prepare a job description for each of the different members of a legal team. Include descriptions of the skills that are necessary to manage a law practice in the age of technology.

2. Prepare a memo to the legal team on how the IT department can aid the paralegal support staff.

"During my eighty-seven years I have witnessed a whole succession of technological revolutions. But none of them has done away with the need for character in the individual or the ability to think."

—*Bernard Mannes Baruch*

Legal Ethics in a Technology Age | CHAPTER 2

OPENING SCENARIO

Each lawyer in the firm was required to attend a minimum number of continuing legal education (CLE) programs as part of the licensing requirements for lawyers in their jurisdiction. At least one hour of this time had to be on ethics. To make sure the new knowledge was shared with the entire firm, those attending the CLE programs had to recount any particularly interesting information they had learned at the firm's morning staff meetings. Ethan had just fulfilled his required hour of ethics at a litigation update seminar. At the next staff meeting, he shared advice from the seminar regarding "need to know" policies. In firms who had adopted such policies, only those with a "need to know" had access to client information and files, and guidelines were established to define what constituted a "need to know."

This resulted in a question from his paralegal, Caitlin. She had a twin sister named Emily, who was a paralegal in the firm's other office. She and Caitlin often discussed cases that were interesting but that they were not personally assigned to. Caitlin said that she and her sister often used their personal access codes to access these files over the Internet connection maintained by the firm. Ethan told her that no one in the firm has the right to use his or her personal access code to access files unless he or she was personally directed to do so by the supervising attorney. Caitlin then suggested that everyone in the firm should be instructed in the "need to know" guidelines, and wondered aloud who might be responsible for this instruction. She also wondered if these guidelines really mattered.

LEARNING OBJECTIVES

After studying this chapter, you should be able to:

1. Define *legal ethics* in terms of duties owed to the client and the legal system.

2. Explain the difference between the duty of confidentiality and attorney–client privilege.

3. Explain the function of the work product doctrine.

4. Explain the potential consequences of an inadvertent disclosure of confidential information.

5. Discuss the reasons for conflict of interest rules.

6. Discuss the duty of competency in a technology age.

7. Explain the rationale for the obligations of candor and fairness in litigation.

8. Describe the ethical obligation of appropriate hiring, delegating, and supervising owed by managing and supervising attorneys.

LEGAL ETHICS IN A TECHNOLOGY AGE
After watching the video in MyLegalStudiesLab, answer the following questions.

1. What is the role of the legal profession ethical code?
2. Are paralegals expected to comply with the lawyers rules of professional conduct?

■ INTRODUCTION TO ETHICS IN TECHNOLOGY

ethics
Minimally acceptable standards of conduct in a profession.

Every profession has a set of rules that members of that profession are expected to follow. These rules typically set forth the minimum standards for ethical behavior—the very least each professional should do. In the field of law, these rules are referred to as "the rules of **ethics**" or "the rules of professional responsibility." Each state controls the right to practice law, and therefore each state has adopted its own rules of ethics. The highest court or legislature of each state has created a committee or board that is authorized to enforce state rules of professional responsibility. States also typically use a "bar association" to receive and investigate complaints against lawyers. With only a few exceptions, most states have adopted some form of the American Bar Association's **Model Rules of Professional Conduct** (MRPC). This provides a high degree of consistency in the ethical guidelines for the legal profession across the country. Exhibit 2.1 shows the links and resources provided by the American Bar Association regarding ethics. The ABA also provides a report on the status of individual state review of the ethical rules (Exhibit 2.2).

Model Rules of Professional Conduct
The American Bar Association's set of proposed ethical standards for the legal profession.

Members of national paralegal associations, such the National Association of Legal Assistants (NALA) and the National Federation of Paralegal Associations (NFPA), also have ethics guidelines. These organizations require members to conduct themselves in accordance with these guidelines, observance of which is a condition of continued membership in the organization.

WEB RESOURCES

The links to state ethics resources on the ABA website may be found at http://www.americanbar.org/groups/professional_responsibility/resources/links_of_interest.html

■ ETHICAL DUTIES OF THE LEGAL TEAM

LEARNING OBJECTIVE 1
Define *legal ethics* in terms of duties owed to the client and the legal system.

Ethical behavior is expected and required of every member of the legal team, whether he or she is an attorney, a paralegal, a litigation support specialist, an information technologist, or an outside consultant. Ethical guidelines are enforced by the court in the jurisdiction where the attorney is practicing or where a case is being tried. The supervising attorney of every legal team must follow the ethics rules and ensure that the members of the legal team follow the same rules as the supervising attorney. These rules are as much a part of the administration of justice as the rules of civil or criminal procedure or the rules of evidence.

Many nonlawyer members of the legal team may not be familiar with what ethical obligations they have and how the ethics rules are to be followed and enforced. An important issue in the technology age is determining who has the responsibility to instruct the nonlawyer members of the legal or trial team, and who is responsible for ensuring their compliance. While it is ultimately the responsibility of the lawyer to supervise these nonlawyers, in many cases this obligation falls to the paralegal or litigation manager.

Exhibit 2.1 A portion of the American Bar Association Center
for Professional Responsibility website

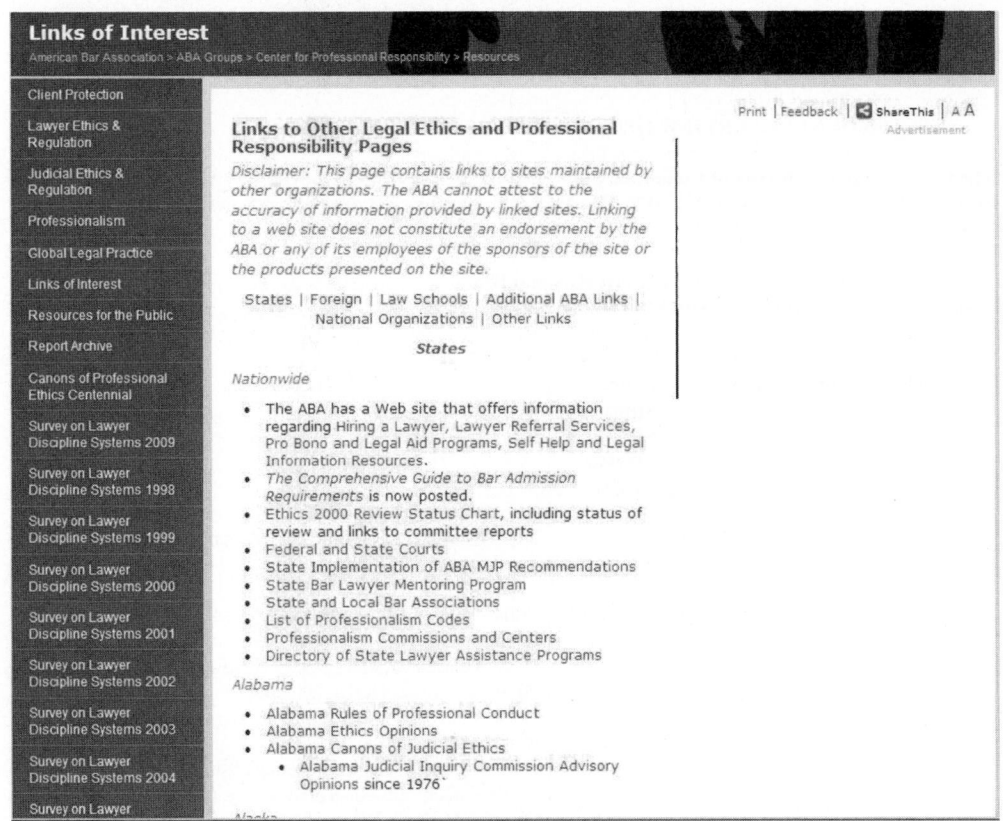

Under Rules 5.1 and 5.3 of the Model Rules of Professional Conduct, the **supervising attorney** has the obligation to supervise all who work on the case for him or her, including their ethical conduct. Each person working for or supervised by the attorney is in fact the **agent** of the attorney. Under the fundamentals of agency law, the **principal** (the attorney) and the agent (the person working under the attorney) have a **fiduciary relationship** to each other. Thus the agent must obey the reasonable instructions of the principal, and the principal is presumed to know everything the agent learns in the ordinary course of working for the attorney on the case. The attorney is ultimately responsible for the ethical conduct of the agent.

Among the ethical obligations of the attorney and the legal team acting as agent of the attorney are:

Rule 1.1, Competency,
Rule 1.6(A), Confidentiality,
Rule 1.7, Conflicts of Interest,
Rule 3.3, Candor,
Rule 3.4, Fairness to Opposing Party and Counsel, and
Rules 5.1 and 5.3, Duty to Supervise.

Related to the issues of ethical conduct are the rules of evidence that bar the legal team from having to testify under the attorney–client privilege and protect

supervising attorney
The attorney managing or supervising the members of the legal team.

agent
A person authorized to act on behalf of another.

principal
One who authorizes another to act on his or her behalf.

fiduciary relationship
A relationship where one is under a duty to act for the benefit of another under the scope of the relationship.

 WEB RESOURCES

The complete State Review of Professional Conduct chart may be viewed at http://www.americanbar.org/content/dam/aba/migrated/cpr/pic/ethics_2000_status_chart.authcheckdam.pdf

Exhibit 2.2 Portion of the ABA Status of State Review of Professional
Conduct Rules as of November 3, 2010

As of September 14, 2011

STATUS OF STATE REVIEW OF PROFESSIONAL CONDUCT RULES

Forty-six (46) jurisdictions, including the District of Columbia, have adopted revised rules (AL, AK, AZ, AR, CO, CT, DE, DC, FL, IL, ID, IN, IA, KS, KY, LA, MA, ME, MD, MI, MN, MS, MO, MT, NE, NV, NH, NJ, NM, NY, NC, ND, OH, OK, OR, PA, RI, SC, SD, TN, UT, VT, VA, WA, WI, WY).
One (1) state has circulated proposed rules (WV).
Two (2) states have committees that have not yet issued a report (GA and HI).
Two (2) state did not adopt Model Rules (CA (has its own rules) and TX).

State	Committee Reviewing Rules	Committee Issued Report	Supreme Court Approved Rule Amend-ments	Notes
Alabama			X	Revised rules effective 6/23/08 http://www.alabar.org/ogc/PDF/Amendments-to-theAlabama_RPC.pdf Proposed advertising rules changes submitted to Supreme Court http://www.alabar.org/ogc/PDF/Petition_A_filed_Supreme_Court%20Oct12_2007.pdf Revised 5.5 effective 9/1/06. http://www.alabar.org/rulechanges/Rule%205.5_Rules%20of%20Professional%20Code_Unauthorized%20Practice%20of%20Law_Supreme%20Court%20order.pdf
Alaska			X	Revised rules effective 4/15/09 http://www.state.ak.us/courts/sco/sco1680.pdf
Arizona			X	Revised rules effective 12/1/03. http://www.supreme.state.az.us/media/pdf/test%20ule%2042%20%2043.pdf

work product
In the law field, material prepared for trial that is protected from disclosure.

Federal Rules of Evidence
The rules governing the admissibility of evidence in federal court.

the **work product** of the legal team prepared for trial from disclosure (**Federal Rules of Evidence** 501).

Confidentiality issues must be carefully considered when adding technical staff to the legal team. The technical consultants and other support staff are nonlegal staff who may have access to files that contain privileged or confidential client information and trial strategy. Technology staff must understand their ethical obligations and the confidential nature of the files on which they are working.

Many persons may be added to the legal team who do not fit the traditional roles of lawyer, paralegal, legal assistant, clerk, or legal secretary. The addition of these staff broadens the concern as to how the rules of confidentiality and privilege will be applied and enforced. The courts have recognized that the lawyer must engage others to help in the representation of clients, and numerous cases have touched upon the use of traditional legal support staff like paralegals and investigators. However, the application of ethical rules to the use of technology or computer consultants may not be as clear. These consultants are often essential where large volumes of electronic discovery are involved. Yet most computer consultants are not adequately educated in the ethical rules of the legal profession.

■ CONFIDENTIALITY AND PRIVILEGE

Technical support personnel and computer consultants must understand the nature and obligations of the legal profession with regard to the duty of confidentiality and the attorney–client privilege. The differences between these concepts, and the obligations imposed by them, can be confusing even to members of the legal team, let alone to IT staff whose training and education were not in the legal profession. At the most basic level, it is important for them to understand that there are two sets of rules: ethical rules, and rules of evidence. **Confidentiality** is an ethical obligation. **Privilege** is a rule of evidence.

LEARNING OBJECTIVE 2
Explain the difference between the duty of confidentiality and attorney–client privilege.

confidentiality
An obligation to not reveal information, which is based on a relationship of trust placed in one person by another.

privilege
A rule of evidence that protects certain forms of communication from disclosure at trial.

ETHICAL Perspectives

PENNSYLVANIA BAR ASSOCIATION PROFESSIONALISM COMMITTEE—WORKING RULES

1. Treat with civility the lawyers, clients, opposing parties, the Court, and all the officials with whom we work. Professional courtesy is compatible with vigorous advocacy and zealous representation.
2. Communications are life lines. Keep the lines open. Telephone calls and correspondence are a two-way channel; respond to them promptly.
3. Respect other lawyers' schedules as your own. Seek agreement on meetings, depositions, hearings and trial dates. A reasonable request for a scheduling accommodation should never be unreasonably refused.
4. Be punctual in appointments, communications and in honoring scheduled appearances. Neglect and tardiness are demeaning to others and to the judicial system.
5. Procedural rules are necessary to judicial order and decorum. Be mindful that pleadings, discovery processes and motions cost time and money. They should not be heedlessly used. If an adversary is entitled to something, provide it without unnecessary formalities.
6. Grant extensions of time when they are reasonable and when they will not have a material, adverse effect on your client's interest.
7. Resolve differences through negotiation, expeditiously and without needless expense.
8. Enjoy what you are doing and the company you keep. You and the world will be better for it.

Beyond all this, the respect of our peers and the society which we serve is the ultimate measure of responsible professional conduct.

I hereby endorse the PBA Working Rules for Professionalism.

Signature _____

Date _____

Attorney ID Number _____

Firm/Office _____

Address _____

Subchapter I Client–Lawyer Relationship

SCR 20:1.1 Competence

A lawyer shall provide competent representation to a client. Competent representation requires the legal knowledge, skill, thoroughness and preparation reasonably necessary for the representation.

History: Sup. Ct. Order No. 04–07, 2007 WI 4, 293 Wis. 2d xv.

ABA Comment: Legal Knowledge and Skill

[1] In determining whether a lawyer employs the requisite knowledge and skill in a particular matter, relevant factors include the relative complexity and specialized nature of the matter, the lawyer's general experience, the lawyer's training and experience in the field in question, the preparation and study the lawyer is able to give the matter and whether it is feasible to refer the matter to, or associate or consult with, a lawyer of established competence in the field in question. In many instances, the required proficiency is that of a general practitioner. Expertise in a particular field of law may be required in some circumstances.

[2] A lawyer need not necessarily have special training or prior experience to handle legal problems of a type with which the lawyer is unfamiliar. A newly admitted lawyer can be as competent as a practitioner with long experience. Some important legal skills, such as the analysis of precedent, the evaluation of evidence and legal drafting, are required in all legal problems. Perhaps the most fundamental legal skill consists of determining what kind of legal problems a situation may involve, a skill that necessarily transcends any particular specialized knowledge. A lawyer can provide adequate representation in a wholly novel field through necessary study. Competent representation can also be provided through the association of a lawyer of established competence in the field in question.

[3] In an emergency a lawyer may give advice or assistance in a matter in which the lawyer does not have the skill ordinarily required where referral to or consultation or association with another lawyer would be impractical. Even in an emergency, however, assistance should be limited to that reasonably necessary in the circumstances, for ill-considered action under emergency conditions can jeopardize the client's interest.

[4] A lawyer may accept representation where the requisite level of competence can be achieved by reasonable preparation. This applies as well to a lawyer who is appointed as counsel for an unrepresented person. See also Rule 6.2.

Thoroughness and Preparation

[5] Competent handling of a particular matter includes inquiry into and analysis of the factual and legal elements of the problem, and use of methods and procedures meeting the standards of competent practitioners. It also includes adequate preparation. The required attention and preparation are determined in part by what is at stake; major litigation and complex transactions ordinarily require more extensive treatment than matters of lesser complexity and consequence. An agreement between the lawyer and the client regarding the scope of the representation may limit the matters for which the lawyer is responsible. See Rule 1.2(c).

(continued)

> ### Maintaining Competence
>
> [6] To maintain the requisite knowledge and skill, a lawyer should keep abreast of changes in the law and its practice, engage in continuing study and education and comply with all continuing legal education requirements to which the lawyer is subject.
>
> http://www.legis.state.wi.us/rsb/scr/5200.pdf2006

Confidentiality

The ethical obligation to keep client information confidential is founded on the belief that clients should be able to tell their attorneys everything about their case so that the attorney can give proper legal advice to the client. Confidentiality is an ethical obligation. Rule 1.6 of the ABA Model Rules of Professional Conduct requires that lawyers "not reveal information relating to representation of a client" until the client gives informed consent to the disclosure after being advised of the consequences of disclosure, except for disclosures that are "impliedly authorized." Everything the lawyer or other members of the legal team learn about the case from every possible source is to be kept confidential. For example, if the client's case is written up in the local newspaper, the story may report details of the case. Even though these details are made public, the members of the legal team are not free to discuss them. The details are still to be kept confidential. They may not be discussed with someone who has read the newspaper and who is not on the team.

> # Implied Attorney–Client Relationship
>
> An implied attorney–client relationship may result when a prospective client divulges confidential information during a consultation with an attorney for the purpose of retaining the attorney, even if actual employment does not result.
>
> *Trust v. Monthei*, 49 P.3d 56, 59 (Mont. 2002).

Privilege

All communication between the client and the lawyer for the purpose of obtaining legal advice is protected by the attorney–client privilege. The **attorney–client privilege** is a rule of evidence that protects the client from the attorney being required to reveal the information. (Note that the information given by the client is also confidential, but the privilege is different from the duty of confidentiality.) The privilege applies only when the lawyer is questioned under oath. At that point, the attorney must invoke the privilege, saying, *"I refuse to answer because that is confidential information covered by the attorney–client privilege."* This could happen any time the attorney is under oath. Some examples include responses to interrogatories or requests for production of documents, or testimony in court, in a deposition, or before a grand jury. The privilege may not be waived by the attorney—only the client can waive the privilege and allow the attorney to reveal protected information. It is the client's right to preserve the privilege,

attorney–client privilege
A rule of evidence permitting an attorney to refuse to testify as to confidential client information, and specifically protecting the communication between the attorney and client for the purpose of obtaining legal advice.

IN THE WORDS OF THE COURT...

Trammell v. United States, 445 U.S. 40 (1980)[i]

Burger C. J.

"The privileges between priest and penitent, attorney and client, and physician and patient limit protection to private communication. These privileges are rooted in the imperative need for confidence and trust. The priest-penitent privilege recognizes the human need to disclose to a spiritual counselor, in total and absolute confidence, what are believed to be flawed acts or thoughts and to receive priestly consolation and guidance in return. The lawyer-client privilege rests on the need for the advocate and counselor to know all that relates to the client's reasons for seeking representation if the professional mission is to be carried out. Similarly, the physician must know all that a patient can articulate in order to identify and to treat disease; barriers to full disclosure would impair diagnosis and treatment."

except in limited circumstances such as when the information is about a crime of violence that the client is about to commit. The concept of privilege also extends to persons while acting within certain roles such as:

1. spouse
2. clergy–penitent
3. doctor–patient
4. psychotherapist–patient
5. participants in settlement negotiations

Claim of Privilege

The attorney–client privilege is not automatically invoked. Rather, the person claiming the privilege—usually the client—has the burden to establish its existence, called a **claim of privilege**.

> "To sustain a claim of privilege, the party invoking it must demonstrate that the information at issue was a communication between client and counsel or his employee, that it was intended to be and was in fact kept confidential, and that it was made in order to assist in obtaining or providing legal advice or services to the client" *SR International Bus. Ins. Co v. World Trade Center* Prop No 01 Civ 9291 (S.D.N.Y. 2002), quoting *Browne of New York City, Inc. v. Ambase Corp.*[ii]

claim of privilege
Prevents the disclosure of confidential communications as evidence based on a recognized privilege.

Extension of Attorney–Client Privilege to Others

It is now accepted that the efficient administration of justice requires lawyers to engage others, such as legal assistants, accountants, and other experts, to assist in the vigorous representation of the client. These "agents" must also be covered by the attorney–client privilege; to do otherwise would obligate the attorney to guard every document, exhibit, and pretrial memorandum from the eyes of everyone on the legal team. Attorneys would have to perform every task personally, such as interviewing clients and witnesses, typing reports and memoranda of law, conducting factual and legal research, and preparing trial exhibits and documents. This would clearly not be desirable or cost effective for the client or the administration of justice. As one court has held,

---

[i] *Trammell v. U.S.,* 445 U.S. 40 (1980).
[ii] *SR International Bus. Ins. Co. v. World Trade Center* Prop No 01 Civ 9291 (S.D.N.Y. 2002), quoting *Browne of New York City, Inc. v. Ambase Corp.*

IN THE WORDS OF THE COURT...

Extension of Attorney–Client Privilege to Others

IN RE Grand Jury subpoenas dated March 24, 2003, directed to (A) Grand Jury Witness Firm and (B) Grand Jury Witness, M11-188 (USDC, S.D.N.Y.) (June 2, 2003).

The U.S. District Court for the Southern District of New York summarized the law, stating:

> "...the privilege in appropriate circumstances extends to otherwise privileged communications that involve persons assisting the lawyer in the rendition of legal services. [fn17] This principle has been applied universally to cover office personnel, such as secretaries and law clerks, who assist lawyers in performing their tasks. [fn16] But it has been applied more broadly as well. For example, in *United States v. Kovel*, [fn19] the Second Circuit held that a client's communication with an accountant employed by his attorney were privileged where made for the purpose of enabling the attorney to understand the client situation in order to provide legal advice. [fn20]"

"The attorney–client privilege is founded on the assumption that encouraging clients to make the fullest disclosure to their attorneys enables the latter to act more effectively. We have recognized that an attorney's effectiveness depends upon his ability to rely on the assistance of various aides, be they secretaries, file clerks, telephone operators, messengers, clerks not yet admitted to the bar, and aids of other sorts. The privilege must include all the persons who act as the attorney's agents." (*Von Bulow v. Von Bulow*, 811 F. 2d 136 (2d Cir. 1987))

If the client reveals the same information to someone outside of the attorney or legal staff, the privilege is lost. Thus, the client must truly keep the information secret for the privilege to apply.

Self-Defense Exception

The rules concerning the duty of confidentiality and the attorney–client privilege are not absolute. Lawyers who are accused of wrongdoing by their clients must be able to defend themselves. This defense may require the use of confidential and/or privileged information. Therefore, lawyers will not be bound by the rules of confidentiality and privilege in this instance because of an inherent right to **due process**. This is frequently referred to as the "**self-defense exception**."

The Pennsylvania Rules of Professional Conduct Rule 1.6(c)(4) Provides

(c) A lawyer may reveal such information to the extent that the lawyer reasonably believes necessary:

...(4) to establish a claim or defense on behalf of the lawyer in a controversy between the lawyer and the client, to establish a defense to a criminal charge or civil claim or disciplinary proceeding against the lawyer based upon conduct in which the client was involved, or to respond to allegations in any proceeding concerning the lawyer's representation of the client; or [...]

WEB RESOURCES
ETHICAL Perspectives

Review the most current version and comments to Rule 1.6 on Confidentiality of Information of the American Bar Association Model Rules of Professional Conduct at the American Bar Association website: http://www.abanet.org/cpr/mrpc/rule_1_6.html. Read Comment 4 to Rule 1.6. What is a "hypothetical," as discussed in the comment? What must an attorney do when using a hypothetical to counsel a client?

due process
An established course of judicial proceedings or other activity designed to ensure the legal rights of an individual.

self-defense exception
The right of an attorney to reveal a client confidence when necessary to defend himself or herself against a claim of wrongful conduct.

WEB RESOURCES

Contrast and compare Rule 1.6(c)(4) of the Pennsylvania Rules of Professional Conduct at http://www.padisciplinaryboard/board.org/documents/PA9.2.Rpc.pdf, with the American Bar Association Model Rules of Professional Conduct at http://www.abanet.org/cpr/mrpc/mrpc_toc.html. How does the Pennsylvania rule differ from the MRPC rule? Which rule do you think best addresses the issue of confidentiality? Then compare to the analogous ethical rule in your jurisdiction.

 # IN THE WORDS OF THE COURT...

UNITED STATES DISTRICT COURT SOUTHERN DISTRICT OF CALIFORNIA

Case No. 05CV1958-RMB (BLM)

Qualcomm, Inc, Plaintiff

Vs

Broadcom Corp, Defendant

**ORDER REMANDING PART OF ORDER OF MAGISTRATE COURT
RE MOTIONS FOR SANCTIONS DATED 1/07/08**

...Qualcomm filed four declarations of employees, in spite of the fact it had maintained its position of invoking attorney-client privilege. All four declarations were exonerative of Qualcomm and critical of the services and advice of their retained counsel. None were filed under seal.

This introduction of accusatory adversity between Qualcomm and its retained counsel regarding the issue of assessing responsibility for the failure of discovery changes the factual basis which supported the court's earlier order denying the self-defense exception to Qualcomm's attorney-client privilege. *Meyerhofer v. Empire Fire & Marine Ins. Co.,* 497 F.2d 1190, 1194-95 (2d Cir. 1974); *Hearn v. Rhay,* 68 F.R.D. 574, 581 (E.D. Wash. 1975); *First Fed. Sav. & Loan Ass'n v. Oppenheim, Appel, Dixon & Co.,* 110 F.R.D. 557, 560-68 (S.D.N.Y. 1986); A.B.A. Model Rules of Prof. Conduct 1.6(b)(5) & comment 10.

Accordingly, the court's order denying the self-defense exception to the attorney-client privilege is vacated. The attorneys have a due process right to defend themselves under the totality of circumstances presented in this sanctions hearing where their alleged conduct regarding discovery is in conflict with that alleged by Qualcomm concerning performance of discovery responsibilities. See, e.g., *Miranda v. So. Pac. Transp. Co.,* 710 F.2d 516, 522-23 (9th Cir. 1983)....

The full opinion of the court may be viewed at www.ediscoverylaw.com/Brewster.pdf

---

WEB RESOURCES

Review the current language of the Federal Rules of Civil Procedure Rule 26. One source of the rule may be found on the website of the Cornell Law School Legal Information Institute at http://www.law.cornell.edu/rules/frcp/Rule26.htm and the related Federal Rules of Criminal Procedure Rule 16 at http://www.law.cornell.edu/rules/frcrmp/Rule16.htm. How does the rule balance the need for full disclosure in discovery with the ethical obligation of confidentiality?

work product doctrine
The rule of evidence that allows the attorney to treat work product as confidential, and protects it from disclosure to the opposing side.

LEARNING OBJECTIVE 3
Explain the function of the work product doctrine.

One of the most significant technology cases involving the self-defense exception is *Qualcomm, Inc. v. Broadcom Corp.* In this case, substantial sanctions were assessed against the client. In response, the client made accusations of wrongdoing by outside counsel as part of its attempt to exonerate itself.

◼ WORK PRODUCT DOCTRINE

The **work product doctrine** provides a limited protection for material prepared by the attorney, or those working for the attorney, in anticipation of litigation or for trial. The work product doctrine is different from both the attorney–client privilege and the duty of confidentiality. The attorney–client privilege and the duty of confidentiality relate to information provided by the client, and apply regardless of whether it involves potential litigation.

Exceptions and Limitations to the Work Product Doctrine

The work product doctrine has some exceptions. For example, it does not cover documents prepared in the normal operation of the client's business, such as sales reports, data analysis, or summaries of business operations.

"The work product doctrine does not extend to documents in an attorney's possession that were prepared by a third party in the ordinary course of business and that would have been created in essentially similar form irrespective of any litigation anticipated by counsel." In Re Grand Jury Subpoenas, 318 F.3d 379 (2nd Cir. 2002) at 3851.

In other words, simply giving internal business documents to the attorney does not make them work product, and they are not protected from discovery by the other side simply because they are in the possession of the attorney.

Internal Investigations and Evidentiary Privileges

Businesses, and particularly corporations with publicly traded securities, are required under state and federal laws and regulations to take a proactive approach to determine wrongdoing and identify violations of statutes and regulations. These investigations and "audits" create a body of documents of which some,

IN THE WORDS OF THE COURT...

Work Product Doctrine

Electronic Data Systems Corporation v. Steingraber
Case 4:02 CV 225 USDC, E.D. Texas, 2003.

The work product doctrine is narrower than the attorney–client privilege in that it only protects materials prepared "in anticipation of litigation [Fed. R. Civ. P. 26(b)(3)], whereas the attorney–client privilege protects confidential legal communications between an attorney and client regardless of whether they involve possible litigation."

IN THE WORDS OF THE COURT...

Work Product Doctrine

Hickman v. Taylor 329 U.S. 496 (1947), page 511.

The U.S. Supreme Court recognized the work product doctrine and its importance, saying:

> "Proper preparation of a client's case demands that he assemble information, sift what he considers to be the relevant from the irrelevant facts, prepare his legal theories and plan his strategy without undue and needless interference. That is the historical and the necessary way in which lawyers act within the framework of our system of jurisprudence to promote justice and to protect their clients' interests. This work is reflected, of course, in interviews, statements, memoranda, correspondence, briefs, mental impressions, personal beliefs, and countless other tangible and intangible ways—aptly though roughly termed by the Circuit Court of Appeals in this case as the 'work product of the lawyer.' Were such materials open to opposing counsel on mere demand, much of what is now put down in writing would remain unwritten. An attorney's thoughts, heretofore inviolate, would not be his own. Inefficiency, unfairness and sharp practices would inevitably develop in the giving of legal advice and in the preparation of cases for trial. The effect on the legal profession would be demoralizing. And the interests of the clients and the cause of justice would be poorly served... '...where relevant and non-privileged facts remain hidden in an attorney's file and where production of those facts is essential to the preparation of one's case, discovery may be properly had.'"

none, or all may be subject to evidentiary privilege. Without the protection of the privilege, businesses would be hesitant to conduct audits for fear of prosecution. Therefore, the courts have extended the privilege to these documents. However, the privilege applies differently in each jurisdiction.

■ INADVERTENT DISCLOSURE OF CONFIDENTIAL INFORMATION

LEARNING OBJECTIVE 4
Explain the potential consequences of an inadvertent disclosure of confidential information.

Inadvertent disclosure of confidential or privileged information does happen. It may result from a slip of the finger in sending an email, an accidental pushing of the wrong number on the speed dial of a fax machine, or the sending of a misaddressed envelope.

The admissibility of inadvertently disclosed documents may hinge on the steps the firm takes before and after the disclosure. Having an effective process in place to review documents for privileged information may prevent a claim of negligence.[iii] The treatment of inadvertently disclosed documents will depend on the individual jurisdiction, and the courts follow no single policy.

Judicial Views

There are three judicial views on handling the inadvertent disclosure of confidential and privileged information: (1) Automatic waiver; (2) no waiver; and (3) balancing test.[iv]

> *Automatic waiver*—This view holds that once the confidentiality is breached, the privilege is automatically waived. There is nothing that will redeem the privilege, and therefore the documents may be used by the party that received them by accident.
> *No waiver*—Under this view, the privilege is destroyed only when a client makes a knowing and voluntary waiver of the privilege. Therefore, the attorney's inadvertent disclosure does not constitute a waiver.
> *Balancing test*—The courts using the balancing test look at several factors: (1) the nature of the methods taken to protect the information, (2) the efforts made to correct the error, (3) the extent of the disclosure, and (4) fairness. Remedies under this test range from unlimited use of the disclosed materials, to court-ordered return of documents, to disqualification of attorneys who have reviewed inadvertently disclosed privileged documents.

ABA Ethics Opinion

The ABA has issued an opinion that imposes a burden upon attorneys who receive what appear to be privileged materials to not review the materials and to return them following instructions given to them by the disclosing attorney. The ABA's Formal Opinion 05-437 states:

> A lawyer who receives a document from opposing parties or their lawyers and knows or reasonably should know that the document was inadvertently sent should promptly notify the sender in order to permit the sender to take protective measures.

[iii] *VLT Inc. Lucent Technologies*, No 00–11049-PBS (D. Mass. 01/21/03).
[iv] Inadvertent Disclosure: Approaches and Remedies, *The Practical Lawyer*, Philadelphia, April 2001, by Kevin M. McCarthy.

However, the ABA's opinion does not answer the question of what should happen to the attorney who reads the inadvertently disclosed document. It also does not answer the question of whether the information can be used by the other side. Each jurisdiction may have a different rule. The California courts have addressed these questions in *Rico v. Mitsubishi Motors Corp.*

IN THE WORDS OF THE COURT...

Rico v. Mitsubishi Motors Corp., 42 Cal.4th 807 (2007)
171 P.3d 1092, 68 Cal.Rptr.3d 758

...Here we consider what action is required of an attorney who receives privileged documents through inadvertence and whether the remedy of disqualification is appropriate. We conclude that, under the authority of *State Comp. Ins. Fund v. WPS, Inc.* (1999) 70 Cal. App. 4th 644 (State Fund), an attorney in these circumstances may not read a document any more closely than is necessary to ascertain that it is privileged. Once it becomes apparent that the content is privileged, counsel must immediately notify opposing counsel and try to resolve the situation....

Moreover, we agree with the Court of Appeal that, "when a writing is protected under the absolute attorney work product privilege, courts do not invade upon the attorney's thought processes by evaluating the content of the writing. Once [it is apparent] that the writing contains an attorney's impressions, conclusions, opinions, legal research or theories, the reading stops and the contents of the document for all practical purposes are off limits. In the same way, once the court determines that the writing is absolutely privileged, the inquiry ends. Courts do not make exceptions based on the content of the writing." Thus, "regardless of its potential impeachment value, Yukevich's personal notes should never have been subject to opposing counsel's scrutiny and use."

ETHICAL Perspectives

ARIZONA ETHICS RULES

ER 1.6. Confidentiality of Information.

(a) A lawyer shall not reveal information relating to the representation of a client unless the client gives informed consent, the disclosure is impliedly authorized in order to carry out the representation or the disclosure is permitted or required by paragraphs (b), (c) or (d), or ER 3.3(a)(3).

(b) A lawyer shall reveal such information to the extent the lawyer reasonably believes necessary to prevent the client from committing a criminal act that the lawyer believes is likely to result in death or substantial bodily harm.

(c) A lawyer may reveal the intention of the lawyer's client to commit a crime and the information necessary to prevent the crime.

(d) A lawyer may reveal such information relating to the representation of a client to the extent the lawyer reasonably believes necessary:

(1) to prevent the client from committing a crime or fraud that is reasonably certain to result in substantial injury to the financial interests or

WEB RESOURCES

Contrast and compare the **Arizona Ethics Rules** at http://www.myazbar.org/Ethics/ruleview.cfm?id=27, with the American Bar Association's Model Rules of Professional Conduct at http://www.abanet.org/cpr/mrpc/mrpc_toc.html. On which rules do they differ the most? Then compare to the ethical rules in your jurisdiction.

property of another and in furtherance of which the client has used or is using the lawyer's services;

(2) to mitigate or rectify substantial injury to the financial interests or property of another that is reasonably certain to result or has resulted from the client's commission of a crime or fraud in furtherance of which the client has used the lawyer's services;

(3) to secure legal advice about the lawyer's compliance with these Rules;

(4) to establish a claim or defense on behalf of the lawyer in a controversy between the lawyer and the client, to establish a defense to a criminal charge or civil claim against the lawyer based upon conduct in which the client was involved, or to respond to allegations in any proceeding concerning the lawyer's representation of the client; or

(5) to comply with other law or a final order of a court or tribunal of competent jurisdiction directing the lawyer to disclose such information.

■ CONFLICT OF INTEREST

LEARNING OBJECTIVE 5
Discuss the reasons for conflict of interest rules.

conflict of interest
Representation of one client that will be directly adverse to the interest of another client, the attorney, or another third party that is not a client.

WEB RESOURCES

ETHICAL Perspectives

Review the most current version and comments to Rule 1.7 on Conflict of Interest in the American Bar Association Model Rules of Professional Conduct at the American Bar Association website at http://www.abanet.org/cpr/mrpc/rule_1_7.html. Read Comment 5 to the rule. When an "unforeseeable development occurs," what steps must a lawyer take to remove himself or herself from the case?

The basis of the **conflict of interest** rule is the belief that a person cannot be loyal to two clients. Lawyers cannot represent two clients with potentially conflicting interests, such as a husband and wife in a domestic relations case. A lawyer cannot represent a client when the attorney has a financial interest in the subject matter of the case, such as where the lawyer and client are partners in a real estate transaction. Conflict of interest is clearly an issue for every lawyer on the legal team, but what about the nonlawyer members—the paralegals and the computer and technology consultants? The line is not clear. If both sides of a case wish to use the same paralegal, the answer to the conflict of interest question is probably the same: do not employ the same paralegal. For technology consultants, however, the distinction is less clear. Consultants do not offer legal advice. But they are privy to trial strategy and confidential information. To whom is the obligation to keep the confidences owed? If the consultant is an agent of the lawyer-principal, what about the agent's duty to advise the principal of information learned as an agent of another principal? Does the consultant have a duty to tell one attorney what was learned while working for another attorney? The legal team should be certain the client's rights are not jeopardized and obtain the same assurance from the outside consultants that they demand of in-house staff.

Loyalty to the client is the essence of Rule 1.7 of the Model Rules of Professional Conduct, which defines a conflict of interest. A lawyer should not represent another client if "representation of one client will be directly adverse to another client," unless both clients give their informed consent to the dual representation, and the consent is confirmed in writing. The lawyer's personal interests, or those of third parties who are not clients such as family members, may also create a risk of a conflict that must be avoided.

Clearly, a lawyer should not accept the engagement if there is a reasonable probability that the lawyer's personal interests or desires will adversely affect the advice to be given or services to be rendered to the prospective client. The client is entitled to independent advice from members of the legal team. In this instance, "independent" means free from concern for personal gain. However, the information that may create a conflict of interest is not limited solely to that of the attorney representing a client. It also includes the information held by another member of the legal team, including the legal assistant—and yes, the technology consultant.

ETHICAL Perspectives

ARKANSAS RULES OF PROFESSIONAL CONDUCT

Rule 1.7. Conflict of Interest: Current Clients.

(a) Except as provided in paragraph (b), a lawyer shall not represent a client if the representation involves a concurrent conflict of interest. A concurrent conflict of interest exists if:

  (1) the representation of one client will be directly adverse to another client; or

  (2) there is a significant risk that the representation of one or more clients will be materially limited by the lawyer's responsibilities to another client, a former client or a third person or by a personal interest of the lawyer.

(b) Notwithstanding the existence of a concurrent conflict of interest under paragraph (a), a lawyer may represent a client if:

  (1) the lawyer reasonably believes that the lawyer will be able to provide competent and diligent representation to each affected client;

  (2) the representation is not prohibited by law;

  (3) the representation does not involve the assertion of a claim by one client against another client represented by the lawyer in the same litigation or other proceeding before a tribunal; and

  (4) each affected client gives informed consent, confirmed in writing.

■ COMPETENCE

LEARNING OBJECTIVE 6
Discuss the duty of competency in a technology age.

ABA Model Rule of Professional Conduct 1.1 requires that lawyers provide competent representation to a client. **Competent** representation means providing the legal knowledge, skill, thoroughness, and preparation reasonably necessary for the representation. Few ethics opinions have been written on the subject of competent representation required under Rule 1.1 as it relates to the nonspecific requirement of workload and legal knowledge. However, the minimum standards clearly require an understanding of the **rules of court.** These rules continue to grow in number and complexity, including the adoption of rules regarding electronic discovery. New rules require a higher level of knowledge to competently represent clients. Further, lawyers must be able to communicate with clients in the language of technology about the methods used to create electronic documents and the methods for retrieving and processing them for submission to opposing counsel and the court. As explained in the Formal Opinion of the Association of the Bar of the City of New York, excerpted below, attorneys may need to use foreign language interpreters to represent a client competently. Similarly, attorneys may need to use "interpreters of the language of technology" to meet their ethical duty of competence.

competent
Having or providing the requisite knowledge, skill, thoroughness, and preparation necessary for representation of a client.

rules of court
Rules governing the practice or procedure in a specific court.

Wisconsin Rules of Professional Conduct for Attorneys

SCR 20:1.1 Competence

A lawyer shall provide competent representation to a client. Competent representation requires the legal knowledge, skill, thoroughness and preparation reasonably necessary for the representation.

WEB RESOURCES
The complete version of the Formal Opinion can be found at: http://www.abcny.org/Publications/reports/show_html.php?rid=168

ETHICAL Perspectives

**THE ASSOCIATION OF THE BAR OF THE CITY OF NEW YORK
FORMAL OPINION 1995-12
COMMITTEE ON PROFESSIONAL AND JUDICIAL ETHICS
JULY 6, 1995
ACTION: FORMAL OPINION**

...DR 6-101(A)(2) mandates that "[a] lawyer shall not... [h]andle a legal matter without preparation adequate in the circumstances." Adequate preparation requires, not only that a lawyer conduct necessary legal research, but also that he or she gather information material to the claims or defenses of the client. See *Mason v. Balcom*, 531 F.2d 717, 724 (5th Cir. 1976). The lawyer's inability, because of a language barrier, to understand fully what the client is telling him or her may unnecessarily impede the lawyer's ability to gather the information from the client needed to familiarize the lawyer with the circumstances of the case. This makes communication via the interpreter vital since it may be the only practical way that a free-flowing dialogue can be maintained with the client, and the only means by which the lawyer can actually and substantially assist the client.

The duty to represent a client competently, embodied in DR 6-101(A)(1), requires a lawyer confronted with a legal matter calling for legal skills or knowledge outside the lawyer's experience or ability, to associate with lawyers with skills or knowledge necessary to handle the legal matter. When a lawyer is confronted with a legal matter requiring non-legal skills or knowledge outside the lawyer's experience or ability and these skills or knowledge are necessary for the proper preparation of the legal matter, DR 6-101(A) (2) appears to require that the lawyer associate with professionals in other disciplines who possess the requisite skills or knowledge needed by the lawyer to prepare the legal matter. The interpreter appears to be the type of professional envisioned by EC 6-3's observation that "[p]roper preparation and representation may require the association by the lawyer of professionals in other disciplines." When the need for an interpreter is apparent or it is reasonable to conclude that an interpreter is required for effective communication, failure to take steps with the client to secure an interpreter may be a breach of the duty to represent the client competently....

■ CANDOR AND FAIRNESS IN LITGATION

LEARNING OBJECTIVE 7
Explain the rationale for the obligations of candor and fairness in litigation.

candor
The ethical obligation to not mislead the court or opposing counsel with false statements of law or of facts that the lawyer knows to be false.

Litigation is the practice of advocacy. It involves advocating a legal position to the court or trying to persuade a trier of fact to accept the facts as presented. It is also the duty of the advocate to avoid any conduct that undermines the integrity of the process. But the duty to persuasively present the client's case is a qualified duty, limited by the ethical obligation of **candor**—to not mislead the court or opposing counsel with false statements of law or of facts that the lawyer knows to be false. Without mutual respect, honesty, and fairness, the system cannot function properly.

It may appear to be a simple ethical duty to competently research and present the current statutory and case law, even when the most current version is not favorable to the position taken. But this duty requires making a complete search for ALL the law, statutory enactments and case law, and not just the part that is favorable to the client's position. In a technological age of vast numbers of electronic cases, it is easy to miss a few cases if the search is not conducted as thoroughly as possible. Not making the proper inquiry of the client's staff to find all of the applicable law may lead to sanctions, or potentially something worse—disbarment.

ETHICAL Perspectives

WEB RESOURCES

The entire set of Michigan's proposed standards for imposing lawyer sanctions are at: http://courts.michigan.gov/supremecourt/Resources/Administrative/2002-29-ADB-proposal.pdf

PROPOSED MICHIGAN STANDARDS FOR IMPOSING LAWYER SANCTIONS [WITHOUT COMMENTARY] (SUBMITTED IN JUNE 2002 BY THE ATTORNEY DISCIPLINE BOARD)

"**Preface**

These Michigan Standards for Imposing Lawyer Sanctions were adopted by the State of Michigan Attorney Discipline Board (ADB or Board) on [date] under the authority granted by the Michigan Supreme Court in its order dated [date], and are intended for use by the Attorney Discipline Board and its hearing panels in imposing discipline following a finding or acknowledgment of professional misconduct. Pursuant to the Court's order, these standards may be amended by the Board from time to time. The Court may at any time modify these standards or direct the Board to modify them.

...6.0 *Violations of Duties* Owed to the Legal System

   6.1 False Statements, Fraud, and Misrepresentation to a Tribunal. The following sanctions are generally appropriate in cases involving conduct that is prejudicial to the administration of justice or that involves dishonesty, fraud, deceit, or misrepresentation to a tribunal:

      6.11 Disbarment is generally appropriate when a lawyer, with the intent to deceive the tribunal, makes a false statement, submits a false document, or improperly withholds material information, and causes serious or potentially serious injury.

      6.12 Suspension is generally appropriate when a lawyer knows that false statements or documents are being submitted to the tribunal or that material information is improperly being withheld, and takes no remedial action, and causes injury or potential injury.

      6.13 Reprimand is generally appropriate when a lawyer is negligent either in determining whether statements or documents submitted to a tribunal are false or in taking remedial action when material information is being withheld and causes injury or potential injury...."

Rhode Island Rules of Professional Conduct

WEB RESOURCES

Contrast and compare the **Rhode Island Rules of Professional Conduct** at http://www.courts.ri.gov/supreme/pdf-files/Rules_Of_Professional_Conduct.pdf, with the American Bar Association Model Rules of Professional Conduct at http://www.abanet.org/cpr/mrpc/mrpc_toc.html, and the ethical rules in your jurisdiction.

Rule 3.3 Candor Toward The Tribunal

(a) A lawyer shall not knowingly:

   (1) make a false statement of fact or law to a tribunal or fail to correct a false statement of material fact or law previously made to the tribunal by the lawyer;

   (2) fail to disclose to the tribunal legal authority in the controlling jurisdiction known to the lawyer to be directly adverse to the position of the client and not disclosed by opposing counsel; or

   (3) offer evidence that the lawyer knows to be false. If a lawyer, the lawyer's client, or a witness called by the lawyer, has offered material evidence and the lawyer comes to know of its falsity, the lawyer shall take reasonable remedial measures, including, if necessary, disclosure to the tribunal. A lawyer may refuse to offer evidence, other than the testimony of a defendant in a criminal matter, that the lawyer reasonably believes is false.

(b) A lawyer who represents a client in an adjudicative proceeding and who knows that a person intends to engage, is engaging or has engaged in criminal or fraudulent conduct related to the proceeding shall take reasonable remedial measures, including, if necessary, disclosure to the tribunal.

(c) The duties stated in paragraphs (a) and (b) continue to the conclusion of the proceeding, and apply even if compliance requires disclosure of information otherwise protected by Rule 1.6.

(d) In an ex parte proceeding, a lawyer shall inform the tribunal of all material facts known to the lawyer that will enable the tribunal to make an informed decision, whether or not the facts are adverse.

Fairness to Opposing Party and Counsel

Fairness in the practice of law has been an important issue for probably as long as there has been an adversarial justice system. A number of states have established professionalism centers, such as that of the Pennsylvania Bar Association shown in Exhibit 2.3. Attorneys are advocates for their clients and occasionally forget that the ultimate purpose of the legal system is justice for all. The ethical rule of fairness to opposing parties and counsel is an attempt to ensure that justice is done even if one's client loses the case. Each side is expected to use its best skills and knowledge and present its position fairly so that the trier of fact may determine where the truth lies. Destroying, falsifying, or tampering with evidence destroys the fabric of the system. If these unfair tactics are permitted, society will lose confidence in the system, and it will break down. Just consider the criminal cases where the prosecutor does not turn over, as required, exculpatory evidence that might show a defendant is innocent.

WEB RESOURCES

Contrast and compare the **Oregon Rules of Professional Conduct** at http://www.osbar.org/_docs/rulesregs/orpc.pdf, with the American Bar Association Model Rules of Professional Conduct at http://www.abanet.org/cpr/mrpc/mrpc_toc.html, and the ethical rules in your jurisdiction.

Oregon Rules of Professional Conduct (12/01/06)

Rule 3.4 Fairness to Opposing Party and Counsel

A lawyer shall not:

(a) knowingly and unlawfully obstruct another party's access to evidence or unlawfully alter, destroy or conceal a document or other material having potential evidentiary value. A lawyer shall not counsel or assist another person to do any such act;

(b) falsify evidence; counsel or assist a witness to testify falsely; offer an inducement to a witness that is prohibited by law; or pay, offer to pay, or acquiesce in payment of compensation to a witness contingent upon the content of the witness's testimony or the outcome of the case; except that a lawyer may advance, guarantee or acquiesce in the payment of:

   (1) expenses reasonably incurred by a witness in attending or testifying;

   (2) reasonable compensation to a witness for the witness's loss of time in attending or testifying; or

   (3) a reasonable fee for the professional services of an expert witness.

(c) knowingly disobey an obligation under the rules of a tribunal, except for an open refusal based on an assertion that no valid obligation exists;

(d) in pretrial procedure, knowingly make a frivolous discovery request or fail to make reasonably diligent effort to comply with a legally proper discovery request by an opposing party;

(e) in trial, allude to any matter that the lawyer does not reasonably believe is relevant or that will not be supported by admissible evidence, assert personal knowledge of facts in issue except when testifying as a witness, or state a personal opinion as to the justness of a cause, the credibility of a witness, the culpability of a civil litigant or the guilt or innocence of an accused;

(f) advise or cause a person to secrete himself or herself or to leave the jurisdiction of a tribunal for purposes of making the person unavailable as a witness therein; or

(g) threaten to present criminal charges to obtain an advantage in a civil matter unless the lawyer reasonably believes the charge to be true and if the purpose of the lawyer is to compel or induce the person threatened to take reasonable action to make good the wrong which is the subject of the charge.

Adopted 01/01/05

http://www.osbar.org/_docs/rulesregs/orpc.pdf

Exhibit 2.3 Pennsylvania Bar Association Professionalism Committee website

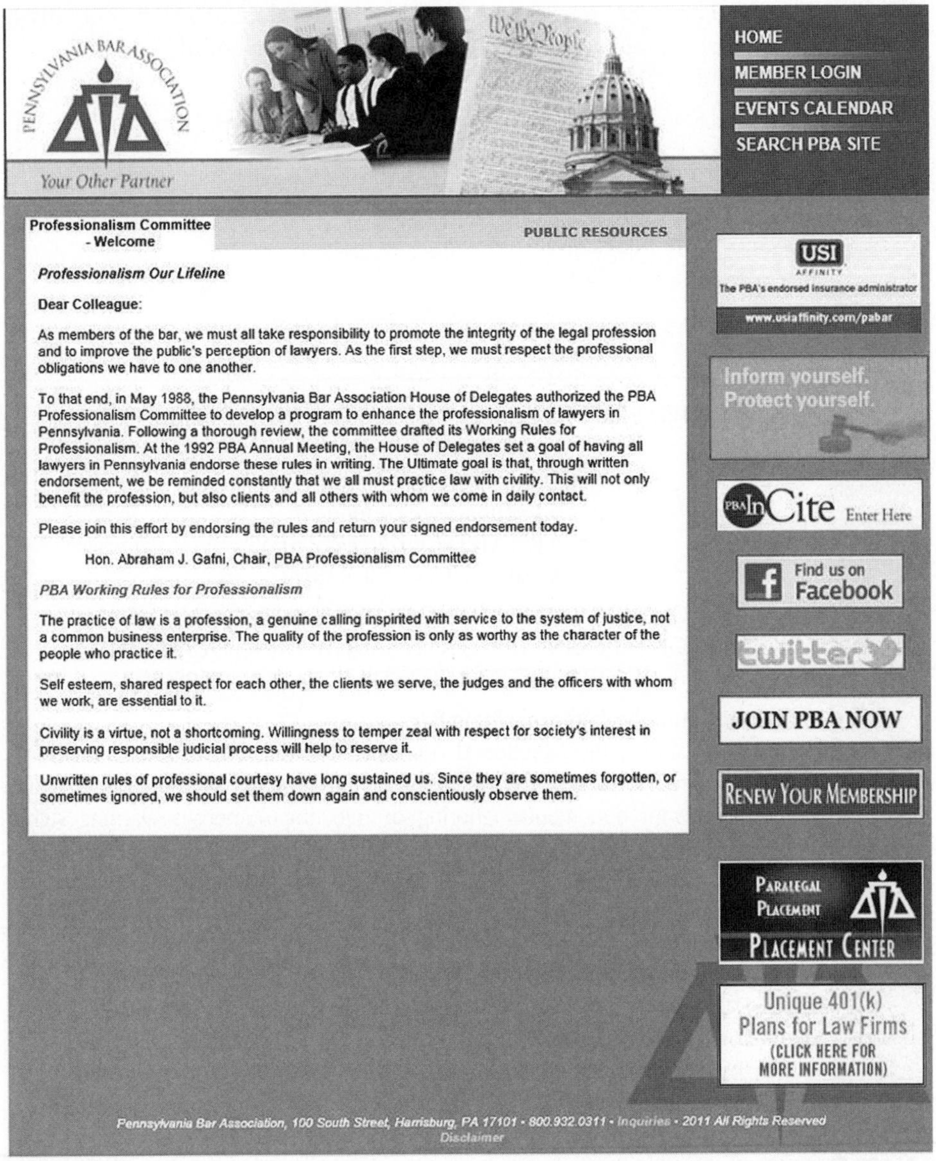

WEB RESOURCES

The Pennsylvania Bar Association Professionlism Committee website may be viewed at: http://www.pabar.org/public/committees/proflism/about/welcome.asp

PENNSYLVANIA BAR ASSOCIATION

Your Other Partner

HOME
MEMBER LOGIN
EVENTS CALENDAR
SEARCH PBA SITE

Professionalism Committee - Welcome

PUBLIC RESOURCES

Professionalism Our Lifeline

Dear Colleague:

As members of the bar, we must all take responsibility to promote the integrity of the legal profession and to improve the public's perception of lawyers. As the first step, we must respect the professional obligations we have to one another.

To that end, in May 1988, the Pennsylvania Bar Association House of Delegates authorized the PBA Professionalism Committee to develop a program to enhance the professionalism of lawyers in Pennsylvania. Following a thorough review, the committee drafted its Working Rules for Professionalism. At the 1992 PBA Annual Meeting, the House of Delegates set a goal of having all lawyers in Pennsylvania endorse these rules in writing. The Ultimate goal is that, through written endorsement, we be reminded constantly that we all must practice law with civility. This will not only benefit the profession, but also clients and all others with whom we come in daily contact.

Please join this effort by endorsing the rules and return your signed endorsement today.

Hon. Abraham J. Gafni, Chair, PBA Professionalism Committee

PBA Working Rules for Professionalism

The practice of law is a profession, a genuine calling inspirited with service to the system of justice, not a common business enterprise. The quality of the profession is only as worthy as the character of the people who practice it.

Self esteem, shared respect for each other, the clients we serve, the judges and the officers with whom we work, are essential to it.

Civility is a virtue, not a shortcoming. Willingness to temper zeal with respect for society's interest in preserving responsible judicial process will help to reserve it.

Unwritten rules of professional courtesy have long sustained us. Since they are sometimes forgotten, or sometimes ignored, we should set them down again and conscientiously observe them.

USI AFFINITY
The PBA's endorsed insurance administrator
www.usiaffinity.com/pabar

Inform yourself. Protect yourself.

PBA**In**Cite Enter Here

Find us on **Facebook**

twitter

JOIN PBA NOW

RENEW YOUR MEMBERSHIP

PARALEGAL PLACEMENT
PLACEMENT CENTER

Unique 401(k) Plans for Law Firms
(CLICK HERE FOR MORE INFORMATION)

Pennsylvania Bar Association, 100 South Street, Harrisburg, PA 17101 · 800.932.0311 · Inquiries · 2011 All Rights Reserved
Disclaimer

Pennsylvania Bar Association.

WEB RESOURCES
Contrast and compare the **Colorado Supreme Court Rules of Professional Conduct** at http://www.coloradosupremecourt.com/Regulation/Rules/appendix20/statdspp88f6.html, with the American Bar Association Model Rules of Professional Conduct at http://www.abanet.org/cpr/mrpc/mrpc_toc.html, and the ethical rules in your jurisdiction.

ETHICAL Perspectives

COLORADO SUPREME COURT

Rule 3.4. Fairness to Opposing Party and Counsel.

Annotations

Comment

[1]The procedure of the adversary system contemplates that the evidence in a case is to be marshalled competitively by the contending parties. Fair competition in the adversary system is secured by prohibitions against destruction or concealment of evidence, improperly influencing witnesses, obstructive tactics in discovery procedure, and the like.

[2]Documents and other items of evidence are often essential to establish a claim or defense. Subject to evidentiary privileges, the right of an opposing party, including the government, to obtain evidence through discovery or subpoena is an important procedural right. The exercise of that right can be frustrated if relevant material is altered, concealed or destroyed. Applicable law in many jurisdictions makes it an offense to destroy material for [the] purpose of impairing its availability in a pending proceeding or one whose commencement can be foreseen. Falsifying evidence is also generally a criminal offense. Paragraph (a) applies to evidentiary material generally, including computerized information.

http://www.coloradosupremecourt.com/Regulation/Rules/appendix20/statdspp88f6.html

IN THE WORDS OF THE COURT...

UNITED STATES DISTRICT COURT SOUTHERN DISTRICT OF CALIFORNIA
Qualcomm Incorporated, Plaintiff, v. Broadcom Corporation, Defendant.
and RELATED COUNTERCLAIMS.
Case No. 05cv1958-B (BLM)

ORDER GRANTING IN PART AND DENYING IN PART DEFENDANT'S MOTION FOR SANCTIONS AND SANCTIONING QUALCOMM, INCORPORATED AND INDIVIDUAL LAWYERS

...b. Referral to the California State Bar
As set forth above, the Sanctioned Attorneys assisted Qualcomm in committing this incredible discovery violation by intentionally hiding or recklessly ignoring relevant documents, ignoring or rejecting numerous warning signs that Qualcomm's document search was inadequate, and blindly accepting Qualcomm's unsupported assurances that its document search was adequate. The Sanctioned Attorneys then used the lack of evidence to repeatedly and forcefully make false statements and arguments to the court and jury. As such, the Sanctioned Attorneys violated their discovery obligations and also may have violated their ethical duties. See e.g., The State Bar of California, Rules of Professional Conduct, Rule 5-200 (a lawyer shall not seek to mislead the judge or jury by a false statement of fact or law), Rule 5-220 (a lawyer shall not suppress evidence that the lawyer or the lawyer's client has a legal obligation to reveal or to produce)....

■ DUTY TO SUPERVISE

The duty of supervision, set forth in Rule 5.1 of the Model Rules of Professional Conduct, requires that partners, and lawyers with managerial authority in the firm, ensure that the conduct of lawyers working beneath them conforms to the ethical code. Rule 5.3(b) further requires that supervising attorneys with direct authority over nonlawyers have an ethical obligation to ensure that those persons' conduct is compatible with the ethical obligations of a lawyer. Any ethical breaches or lapses are ultimately the responsibility of the supervising attorney, under the ethical guidelines and under common law principles of agency law (the principal is responsible for the acts of the agent when the agent is acting within the scope of the principal's employment). The attorney is the one to whom the client looks for professional advice and the outcome of the case. As noted in the *Qualcomm v. Broadcom* case, the obligation to ensure full compliance with the rules of court may also extend to the attorney supervising the client and its staff.

The supervising attorney will suffer any sanctions that result from a failure of the members of the legal team to follow and enforce the ethical rules. Sanctions can come from two sources: the court hearing the underlying action (as in the *Qualcomm* case above) and the attorney disciplinary agency. The court typically punishes this sort of misbehavior with monetary sanctions, the purpose of which is to recompense the other side for the time and effort they have expended or will expend because of the discovery abuse. The attorney disciplinary agency's punishment can include, in extreme cases, disbarment or suspension from practice before the court for a period of time, or in less extreme cases, public or private censure. In addition, under some circumstances, "unfair" litigation tactics may result in a suit for malpractice by the client against the attorney and the law firm.

LEARNING OBJECTIVE 8
Describe the ethical obligation of appropriate hiring, delegating, and supervising owed by managing and supervising attorneys.

Rules Governing the Missouri Bar and the Judiciary Rules of Professional Conduct

Rule 4-5.3: Responsibilities Regarding Nonlawyer Assistants

With respect to a nonlawyer employed or retained by or associated with a lawyer:

(a) a partner, and a lawyer who individually or together with other lawyers possesses comparable managerial authority in a law firm, shall make reasonable efforts to ensure that the firm has in effect measures giving reasonable assurance that the person's conduct is compatible with the professional obligations of the lawyer;

(b) a lawyer having direct supervisory authority over the nonlawyer shall make reasonable efforts to ensure that the person's conduct is compatible with the professional obligations of the lawyer; and

(c) a lawyer shall be responsible for conduct of such a person that would be a violation of the Rules of Professional Conduct if engaged in by a lawyer if:

    (1) the lawyer orders or, with the knowledge of the specific conduct, ratifies the conduct involved; or

    (2) the lawyer is a partner, or has comparable managerial authority in the law firm in which the person is employed, or has direct supervisory authority over the person and knows of the conduct at a time when its consequences can be avoided or mitigated but fails to take reasonable remedial action.

Source: http://www.courts.mo.gov/courts/ClerkHandbooksP2RulesOnly.nsf/c0c6ffa99df4993f86256ba50057dcb8/ f264eb01f0599e3186256ca6005211e3?OpenDocument

 WEB RESOURCES
Contrast and compare the **Rules Governing the Missouri Bar and the Judiciary Rules of Professional Conduct** at http://www.courts.mo.gov/courts/ ClerkHandbooksP2RulesOnly.nsf/ c0c6ffa99df4993f86256ba 50057dcb8/f264eb01f0599e 3186256ca6005211e3?Open Document, with the American Bar Association Model Rules of Professional Conduct at http:// www.abanet.org/cpr/mrpc/mrpc_ toc.html, and the ethical rules in your jurisdiction.

Temporary Attorneys

It has become a common practice to hire temporary attorneys to do "privilege reviews" of documents as part of the electronic discovery process. Model Rule 7.5(d) states that clients are entitled to know who or what entity is providing their legal services. However, the Rule requires notice only when a temporary lawyer is providing work for a client without the close supervision of a lawyer associated with the law firm. See ABA Op. 88-356 (1988). If the temporary lawyer is working under the direct supervision of a lawyer associated with the firm, there may be no duty of disclosure.

CONCEPT REVIEW AND REINFORCEMENT

KEY TERMS

CHAPTER SUMMARY

Introduction to Ethics in Technology	Ethics are the minimally acceptable standards of conduct in a profession. Ethical guidelines are enforced by the court in the jurisdiction where the attorney is practicing or where the case is being tried.
Ethical Duties of the Legal Team	The supervising attorney of every legal team must follow the ethics rules and ensure that the members of the legal team follow the same rules.
Confidentiality and Privilege	Every member of the legal team, including technical support personnel and computer consultants, must understand the nature and obligations of the legal profession with regard to confidentiality and the attorney–client privilege.
Confidentiality	Confidentiality is an ethical obligation. Attorneys have a duty to treat client information obtained in the course of representation in confidence under ABA Rule 1.6.

Privilege	Privilege is a rule of evidence. The attorney–client privilege protects the client from the attorney revealing the confidential information. The concept of privilege also applies to: 1. Spouses 2. Clergy–penitent 3. Doctor–patient 4. Psychotherapist–patient 5. Participants in settlement negotiations
Claim of Privilege	Privilege is not automatic. The person claiming the privilege has the burden of establishing the privilege, called a claim of privilege.
Extension of Attorney–Client Privilege to Others	"…the privilege in appropriate circumstances extends to otherwise privileged communications that involve persons assisting the lawyer in the rendition of legal services…." (U.S. District Court for the Southern District of New York)
Self-Defense Exception	Lawyers who are accused of wrongdoing by their clients must be able to defend themselves and not be bound by the rules of confidentiality and privilege.
Work Product Doctrine	The work product doctrine provides limited protection for material prepared by the attorney, or those working for the attorney, in anticipation of litigation or for trial.
Exceptions and Limitations to the Work Product Doctrine	The work product doctrine does not apply to documents created in the normal course of a client's business, nor does it apply to some materials prepared as part of government case preparation or internal investigation required by law.
Internal Investigations and Evidentiary Privileges	Internal business investigations required by statute or regulation that would not be performed properly if the court did not extend privilege to documents created during these audits.
Inadvertent Disclosure of Confidential Information	The admissibility will depend on the judicial view in a particular jurisdiction. There are three judicial views: Automatic waiver: Once divulged, there is no confidentiality. No Waiver: Only a waiver if knowingly made. Balancing Test: Depends on steps taken to prevent disclosure and efforts to retrieve information after disclosure.
Conflict of Interest	A lawyer should not accept an engagement (representation) if the lawyer's personal interests or desires will, or if there is a reasonable probability that they will, adversely affect the advice to be given or the services to be rendered to the prospective client.
Competence	Ethical guidelines require lawyers to provide competent representation. In the technology age, lawyers need to be able to communicate with clients about how electronic documents are created, the sources of electronic documents, and the methods used to retrieve the documents.

Candor and Fairness in Litigation	A lawyer has an ethical duty of candor to not mislead the court, even when the most current version of the law is not favorable to the client's legal position. Candor requires all members of the legal team to make an accurate inquiry and present the most current information.
Fairness to Opposing Party and Counsel	Lawyers are expected to use their best skills in presenting a case but also must avoid destroying or tampering with evidence or ignoring rules of the court.
Duty to Supervise	All lawyers and partners in law firms are required to supervise everyone over whom they have supervisory authority. All ethical breaches by members of the legal team are ultimately those of the supervising attorney.
Temporary Attorneys	Attorneys hired for a specific case on a temporary basis must be supervised by the responsible supervising attorney on the case.

REVIEW QUESTIONS AND EXERCISES

1. What is ethics? How is it defined with respect to the attorney–client relationship?
2. What is the purpose of the confidentiality rule in the legal setting?
3. What are the differences between the duty of confidentiality and attorney–client privilege?
4. Can the duty of confidentiality between attorney and client be lost? Give an example of how this can occur.
5. Can the attorney–client privilege be lost? Give an example of how this can occur.
6. What are the three judicial approaches to the inadvertent disclosure of confidential information? How might each of these approaches result in a different outcome for the client?
7. What ethical guidelines, if any, does your state follow?
8. What is the ethical obligation of a paralegal to the firm's clients?
9. What is the ethical obligation of the paralegal to the court?
10. What is the ethical obligation of a litigation support staff member to the clients? To the court? Of a litigation support person from an outside firm or a consultant? Explain.
11. In addition to the attorney–client relationship, are there others who are protected by a privilege? Why would it apply to these persons?
12. How is a claim of privilege made?
13. Why is the attorney–client privilege extended to others working for the attorney?
14. What is the purpose of the self-defense exception to the confidentiality rule?
15. Why is conflict of interest an issue for the legal team? Give an example in which a conflict of interest may prevent a lawyer from representing a particular client.
16. What are the ethical duties of computer or technology consultants regarding information and documents they handle for a law firm? How should a law firm avoid potential ethical issues associated with using a computer or technology consultant?
17. What is required to invoke the attorney–client privilege? Explain the privilege in terms that a nonlegal team member can understand.
18. What work is protected by the work product doctrine? Give examples of protected and nonprotected documents or materials.
19. How has technology changed the concept of competence for lawyers? What knowledge and skills must attorneys now possess that they didn't need twenty or thirty years ago?
20. Do the ethical rules of "fairness" prevent lawyers from aggressively advocating their client's position? What duties do lawyers have with regard to their opponents?

21. Why would a partner in a law firm be required to supervise the lawyers working underneath him or her in the firm? What duties does a partner have with regard to these other lawyers?

22. What are the potential consequences of a failure to adequately supervise other staff members at a firm? Who will ultimately bear the consequences of any ethical lapses or errors?

BUILDING YOUR PARALEGAL SKILLS

INTERNET AND TECHNOLOGY EXERCISES

1. Find a copy of the most current version of the Model Rules of Professional Conduct (MRPC) as published by the American Bar Association. Compare the current version to a previous version of the MRPC. Choose one rule that was changed from the previous version, and note how the rule was changed. Research the reasons for the change and what ethical problem the change was intended to solve.

2. Use the Internet to locate the most current version of the ethical rules as used in your jurisdiction. Save the Internet address for future reference.

3. Use the Internet to find three or four ethics opinions from the attorney disciplinary authority in your jurisdiction. Choose one opinion that you think is interesting. Explain, in your own words, the ethical issue at stake and how a legal team can avoid the ethical problem.

4. Use the Internet to find the continuing legal education requirements in your jurisdiction, including any ethical education elements. Prepare a memo for members of the legal team on the requirements.

VIDEO CASE STUDIES

CONFIDENTIALITY: PUBLIC INFORMATION

The law firm has a case that has received coverage by the local press. Two paralegals from the same firm are on a coffee break at a public coffee shop. One of the paralegals is working on the case, and the other is not assigned to the case but is curious about it.

Watch this video case in MyLegalStudiesLab and answer the following questions.

1. Does the legal team working on a case have a duty to remain silent when information about the case has been made public?

2. If incorrect information about a case has been made public, can the members of the legal team correct this misinformation? Why or why not?

3. Can confidential information about cases be shared between members of the same law firm? Why or why not?

4. What is the difference between confidentiality and attorney–client privilege? Who is protected by each doctrine? What information does each of these doctrines protect?

DESTROYING EVIDENCE FOUND BY PARALEGALS

A paralegal discovers a document that is detrimental to the clients case. Only the paralegals working on the case are aware of its existance.

Watch this video case in MyLegalStudiesLab and answer the following questions.

1. What are the ethical issues in destroying evidence under the Model Rules of Professional Conduct?

2. Are there any ethics opinions in your jurisdiction addressing destruction of evidence?

CHAPTER OPENING SCENARIO CASE STUDY

Use the Opening Scenario for this chapter to answer the following questions. The setting is the daily meeting of the partners, and the ethical obligations of staff are discussed.

1. What policy should the firm institute with regard to the discussion of cases among the litigation team and among those in the law firm who are not working on a particular case?
2. Should the firm have a firm-wide program of ethics training on a regular basis, independent of any jurisdictional requirement for ethics training?

Who should be included in that program? What would be the benefit of this additional training?
3. What guidelines should the partners institute to ensure that all staff members are properly supervised?
4. What steps should the firm take to ensure that the attorneys and staff are competent in their technology knowledge and skills?
5. What policies or procedures should be instituted to protect confidential information and litigation work product?

CONTINUING CASES AND EXERCISES

1. Internet Resources. Update your list of Internet resources to include the ABA Model Rules of Professional Conduct, the ethics rules of your local jurisdiction, and sources for ethics opinions from attorney disciplinary authorities.

2. Locate and save information on sources of continuing education on ethics, including updates to the ethics rules in your jurisdiction.
3. Continue to maintain a time log of your activity in the course.

BUILDING YOUR PROFESSIONAL PORTFOLIO

1. Choose one of the ethical rules discussed in this chapter that you find especially interesting. Prepare a memo for distribution to members of the legal team on their obligations to obey this ethical rule.
2. Prepare a memo to a supervising attorney regarding the ethical rules governing conflicts of

interest. Outline methods for ensuring compliance with these rules by the members of the attorney's staff.
3. Prepare a brief note to a supervising attorney on why a failure to supervise the proper handling of confidential documents could result in a problem for the client, the attorney, and the firm.

"The advance of technology is based on making it fit in so that you don't really even notice it, so it's part of everyday life."

—*Bill Gates, Microsoft*

Computers in the Law Office | CHAPTER 3

OPENING SCENARIO

It was obvious to Mrs. Hannah that the attorney for whom she had left the large, center-city law firm to work had no experience in setting up a law office. Owen's experience as a law clerk in federal court had done nothing to prepare him for the realities of getting a practice off the ground. While working in the federal court system, he had grown accustomed to having complete computer support. He had access to e-filing and online research, and a complete IT staff to support all of the computer users and to answer every computer question.

But in setting up the new office, he would need to provide his own computer equipment and research tools, and cost was a major concern. His immediate inclination was to buy just one inexpensive desktop computer with a very basic word processing program. With a little input from Mrs. H., however, he realized they needed a computer for both of them and more software than a basic word processing program. He quickly began to depend on her advice as she explained the problems she and other members of her paralegal association encountered in their offices. She advised him that they would need a system that could grow as the practice expanded. She particularly wanted to make sure that when they eventually added a secretary and an associate, they would not have to start over again with new computers and software. She recalled that her old firm had had to make a lot of changes when they added more people.

They finally decided that it would be a good idea to attend a legal technology trade show and see what was available.

LEARNING OBJECTIVES

After studying this chapter, you should be able to:

1. Discuss the different types of computer systems used in a law office.

2. Describe the different computer operating systems.

3. Explain the differences between general applications and specialty applications software.

4. Understand basic issues in installing and using software.

5. Understand how a network functions and the issues involved with network security.

VIDEO INTRODUCTION

Professor Thomas F. Goldman, Esq.

COMPUTERS IN THE LAW OFFICE
After watching the video in MyLegalStudiesLab, answer the following questions.

1. How can members of the legal team improve communication with technical support people?
2. Why does the legal team need technical expertise?

■ INTRODUCTION TO COMPUTER HARDWARE AND SOFTWARE

Computers and computer accessories have become an integral part of the practice of law. The variety and sophistication of computer-controlled devices have exploded in recent years, and this trend shows no sign of slowing down. Members of the legal team thus have to be able to communicate with an online support services help desk, or a courthouse technology support person to get help in setting up a courtroom for trial. In larger firms, the team must be able to communicate with an in-house information technologist. Understanding the terminology of computer hardware and software will help the legal team explain their needs, and will make dealing with computer problems less stressful. The modern legal staff must also be able to solve basic computer issues on the spot when time does not allow for consultation with support services.

Hardware

computer hardware
A tangible or physical part of a computer system.

Computer hardware is the tangible or physical parts of a computer system. A **computer system** includes at least one input device, a central processor, and at least one output device. A system may be as small and portable as a multifunction digital watch or as large as a classic **mainframe** computer requiring a large room to house it.

computer system
A combination of an input device, a processor, and an output device.

Older models of computers, occasionally found in some law offices, are large metal boxes connected to bulky, heavy desktop monitors, sometimes taking up half of the desktop. Newer models are smaller and less obtrusive. In some offices, the heart of the computer system is a portable laptop computer the size of a book and weighing as little as two to three pounds. The laptop may have a docking station at the user's desk to connect it to a flat-screen monitor, an external keyboard, a mouse, an Internet connection, and a network.

mainframe
A large computer system used primarily for bulk processing of data and financial information.

As the size of computers has decreased, speed and functionality have increased. On older models, opening more than one document used most of the system's resources, slowing it down or even stopping ("freezing") the processing of data. Newer models, however, typically run faster while also allowing the display of multiple documents from multiple applications running at the same time. Word files, Excel spreadsheets, calendaring programs, and timekeeping applications can thus be run simultaneously. Exhibit 3.1 shows a monitor display of four programs running at the same time.

central processing unit (CPU)
The computer chip and memory module that perform the basic computer functions.

The ability to perform multiple functions simultaneously is in part the result of the increased processing speed of newer **central processing units (CPUs).** It is also the result of inexpensive dynamic or volatile computer memory, called

Exhibit 3.1 A monitor display of four programs running at the same time

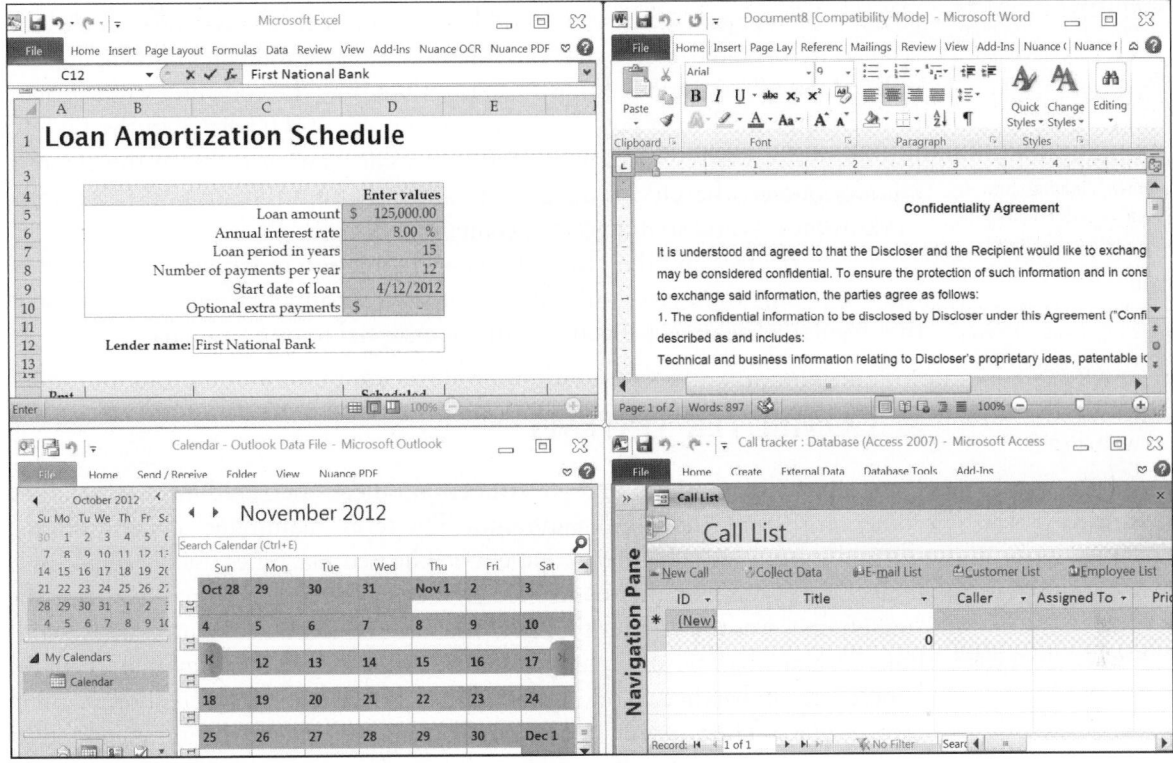

random access memory (RAM). A CPU is the computer "chip" that interprets computer instructions and processes data, and RAM is the temporary computer memory that stores work in progress.

Operating Systems

All hardware requires instructions from software to run and perform desired functions. An **operating system** is software that provides the basic instructions for starting up the computer and processing the basic input and output. The processing of data requires additional software such as word processing and financial data applications.

Power

Just as an automobile depends on fuel to continue to operate, so the computer is dependent on a power source. All computer components, including the CPU, the RAM, and output devices like the computer monitor and printer, must have a power source (such as an electrical outlet or a battery) to operate.

After the power is turned off, computers cannot remember information or work in progress unless it has been saved to a permanent memory device, such as an internal hard drive, a removable memory card, or a USB memory device. Power is also needed to save (or "write") the information to these devices. Once the data is saved, these memory devices do not require power to retain the data. Power is needed only to save or retrieve the data to or from a computer.

Unless data has been saved to a permanent memory device, an unexpected loss of power to a computer can result in all the work done on a document to be lost. One solution is to constantly back up or transfer the work-in-process to the

random access memory (RAM)
Temporary computer memory that stores work-in-process

WEB RESOURCES
Explore the components inside your computer at: http://www.videojug.com/film/what-components-are-inside-my-computer

operating system
The software that the rest of the software depends on to make the computer functional. On most PCs this is Windows or the Macintosh OS. Unix and Linux are other operating systems often found in scientific and technical environments.

uninterruptible power supply (UPS)
A battery system that can supply power to a computer or computer peripheral for a short period of time.

PC
Personal computer.

stand-alone computer
A computer on which all of the software used is installed and on which all of the data or files are electronically stored.

networked computer
Any combination of workstations (stand-alone computers) electronically connected, usually to a central computer that acts as a server on which files and data are stored for access by all other computers and shared software programs.

LEARNING OBJECTIVE 1
Discuss the different types of computer systems used in a law office.

workstation
Consists of a computer, monitor, and input device and is connected to a network that is used for access.

server
Any computer on a network that contains data or applications accessed by users of the network on their client PCs.

more permanent internal hard drive or to a removable memory device. Another solution is an **uninterruptible power supply (UPS),** which alerts users when the power is off and provides a short period of time for users to save the data. A UPS is a battery-operated system that can supply power to a computer or computer peripheral for a short period of time. The length of time the computer will continue to work after the loss of power depends on the size of the battery in the UPS. It may be as short as a few minutes or as long as an hour or more. In the event of a power outage, the UPS is designed to allow the user time to save the current work-in-process and shut down the computer normally.

Power outages and the physical loss or destruction of hardware can result in the loss of important electronic data. Therefore, it cannot be emphasized enough that regularly backing up electronic files is essential to protecting data.

■ COMPUTER SYSTEMS

Large firms, corporations, and governmental offices once used large, centralized computer systems known as mainframes. The term "mainframe" comes from the original computers, which were large, complicated machines usually requiring a temperature- and humidity-controlled environment for operational stability. The "mainframe" was the cabinet that held the massive central computer. Early mainframe systems had no direct user interface and processed information on paper punch cards in batches. Later, "dumb terminals" were used, which allowed direct user interface. These terminals were used on a timesharing basis and supported up to thousands of users simultaneously.

Today, most small and medium-size offices use personal computers **(PCs),** and large firms and organizations are switching to PC-based systems. But the old mainframe systems have provided the model for the networked systems found in offices today, where a number of PCs are connected to a main server on which most of the data is stored. The main difference is that in mainframe systems, dumb terminals could only transmit information to the mainframe for computation, whereas in modern networks, PCs have enough memory and processing capability to perform stand-alone computation functions.

Today, mainframes are typically used by large organizations such as the U.S. government to handle the processing of bulk data such as census information, statistical computations, and financial transactions. Most law firms have moved to PC-based systems, some of which are more powerful than the largest of the original mainframes. The scope of this book is limited to the personal computer system.

The typical systems in use today are either stand-alone computers or networked computers. A **stand-alone computer** is a system in which all the necessary software and all the data or files are stored within one computer. A **networked computer** is part of a system of stand-alone computers, called **workstations,** that are connected to a central computer. The central computer acts as a **server** on which files and data are stored and accessed by other computers in the network. Exhibit 3.2 shows

Exhibit 3.2 A small office or home computer network consisting of a file server and two workstations

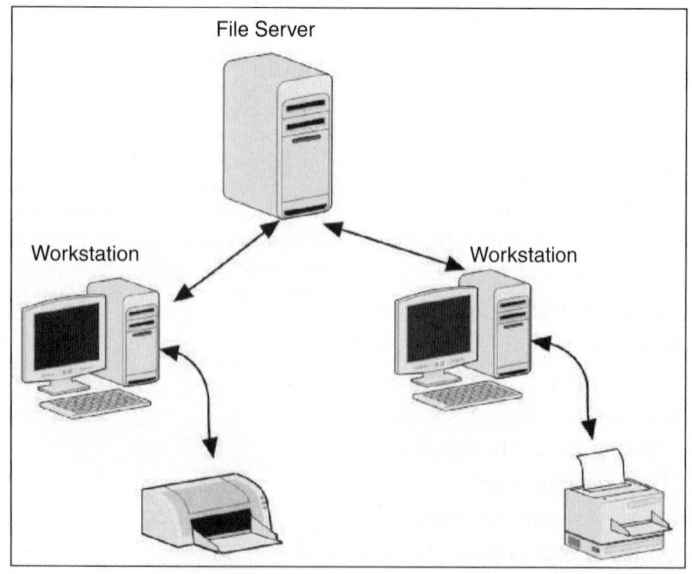

File Server

Workstation

Workstation

an example of a small office or home network. The server acts as a traffic cop for the connected computers, allowing or denying access as needed. Advanced systems may include multiple networks of workstations and servers connected to each other in the same location or in remote locations such as offices in other cities.

All computers, from handheld smartphones to large mainframes, have devices for input, output, and data processing. Examples of input devices are the keyboard, the mouse, and the scanner. Devices that provide output are the monitor and the printer. Other devices may be used for storage of information, such as backup drives, rewritable CDs, and USB memory cards.

Some of the components of a computer system are inside the computer; others are external devices that plug into the computer using a number of standardized connectors or plugs. Part of the confusion for users is that there is no standard location for some of these connections. The interfaces in Exhibit 3.3 are on the front; others may be found on the back of the computer.

Exhibit 3.3 Connectors on a personal computer (PC)

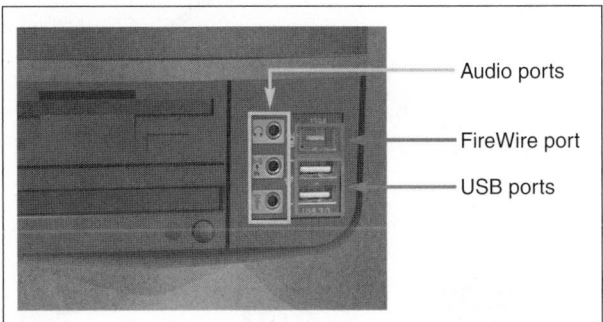

PRACTICE TIP

The universal service bus (USB) is the most commonly used interface for connecting external devices like printers, keyboards, and external memory devices. While the USB connections on the computer may look the same, there are variations. Currently, most are either USB 1.1 or USB 2.0, with some of the newer models using USB 3.0. The higher the number of the USB version, the greater the number of resources that can be connected with it. For example, USB 1.1 can transfer data at 12 Mbps, and USB 2.0 at a rate of 480 Mbps. USB 3 connectors have increased data transfer rates of up to 5 Gbps (1,000 Mbps = 1 Gbps) and increased power capability.

The higher-number versions also allow the computer to supply power to the external device. This ability to transfer both data and power allows some devices such as smartphones to be charged from the USB connection on a computer. Some computers have both powered and non-powered USB connections, and external devices requiring power will not work on an unpowered connector.

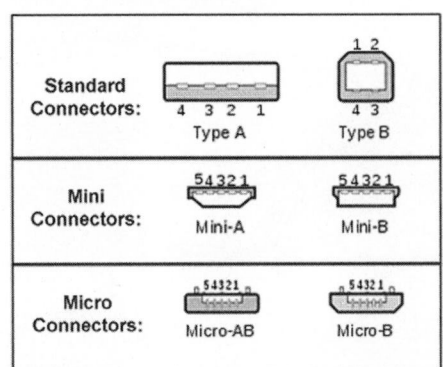

There are six types of USB connectors: Type A, Type B, Mini-B, and Mini-A, Micro AB and Micro B.

Source: Computer Cable Inc.
10,000 W. 100th Avenue Westminister, CO 80021

Telephone	**Email**
(303) 469 0638	info@computercableinc.com
1-888 576 9363 (toll free)	http://www.computercableinc.com/
(303) 469 5970 (fax)	

Exhibit 3.4 Sample computer plugs and connectors

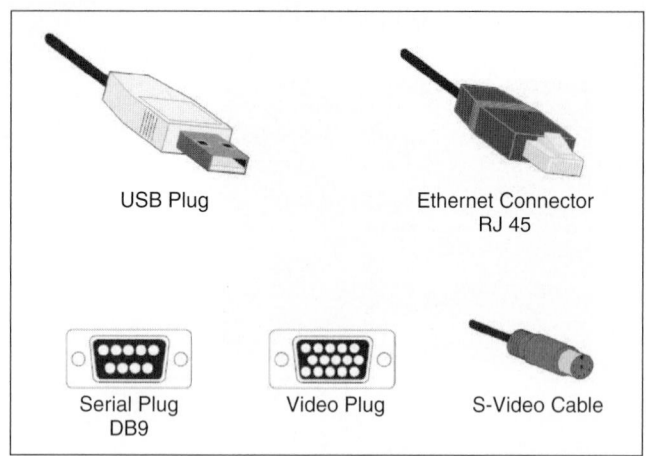

USB Plug

Ethernet Connector
RJ 45

Serial Plug
DB9

Video Plug

S-Video Cable

adapters
Devices for changing the connection on
a connector to a different configuration.

motherboard
A printed circuit board that holds electronic components of the computer.

Some of the standard plugs and connectors
are shown in Exhibit 3.4.

Understanding the differences in the types
of plugs, **adapters,** and connectors should reduce
some of the mystery of how things connect and
allow you to immediately solve many connection issues. But more importantly, being able to
identify the connections will allow you to communicate your needs with support staff with less
confusion and wasted time.

The inside of a computer may be intimidating
to someone who isn't an expert in electronics.
But some of its parts are easily identified. The
largest item in a computer is the **motherboard.**
The motherboard is a printed circuit board that
holds some of the most critical components of
the computer. Some of these components are installed permanently, while others
may be added or replaced, such as the computer's CPU and RAM memory modules. The motherboard has connectors and sockets into which these items are
plugged. Desktop computers are easily opened to access the main components on
the motherboard, as shown in Exhibit 3.5.

Most desktops are designed to allow the user to add additional components or replace existing components. Each add-on device has its own
type of slot and a system of notches to prevent improper installation. The
components most commonly added to desktops are memory modules. New

Exhibit 3.5 Inside of a typical desktop PC, showing the motherboard and components

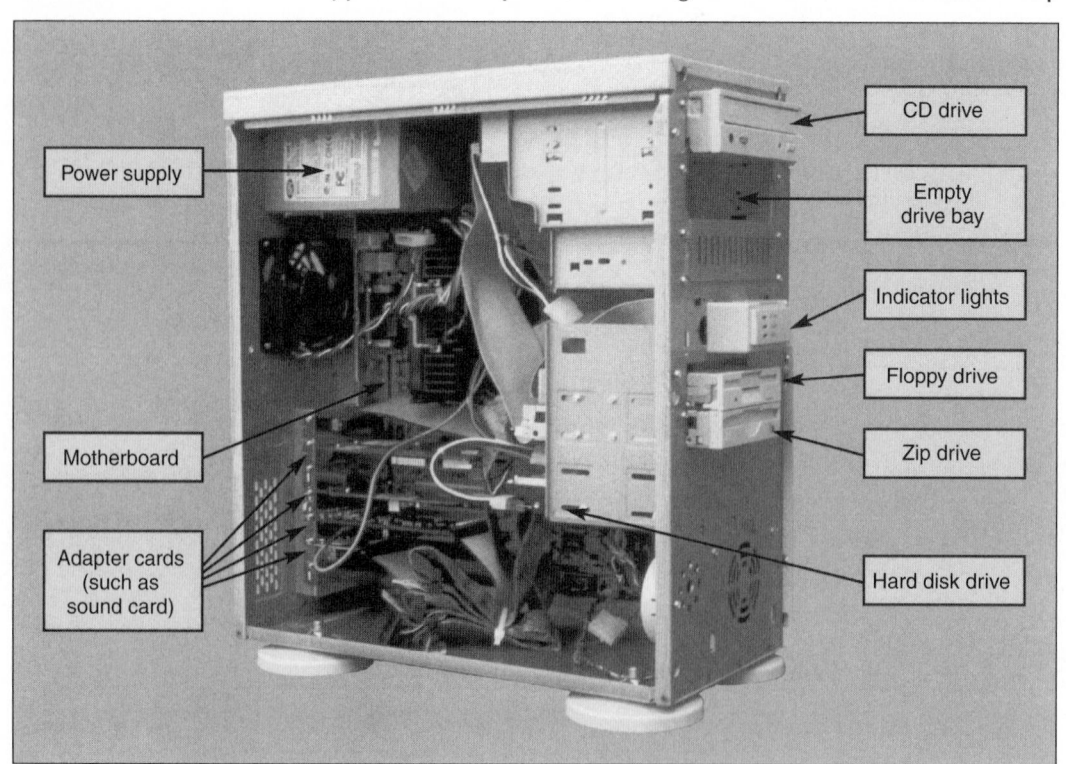

Power supply

Motherboard

Adapter cards
(such as
sound card)

CD drive

Empty
drive bay

Indicator lights

Floppy drive

Zip drive

Hard disk drive

Exhibit 3.6 A PC memory module in a motherboard

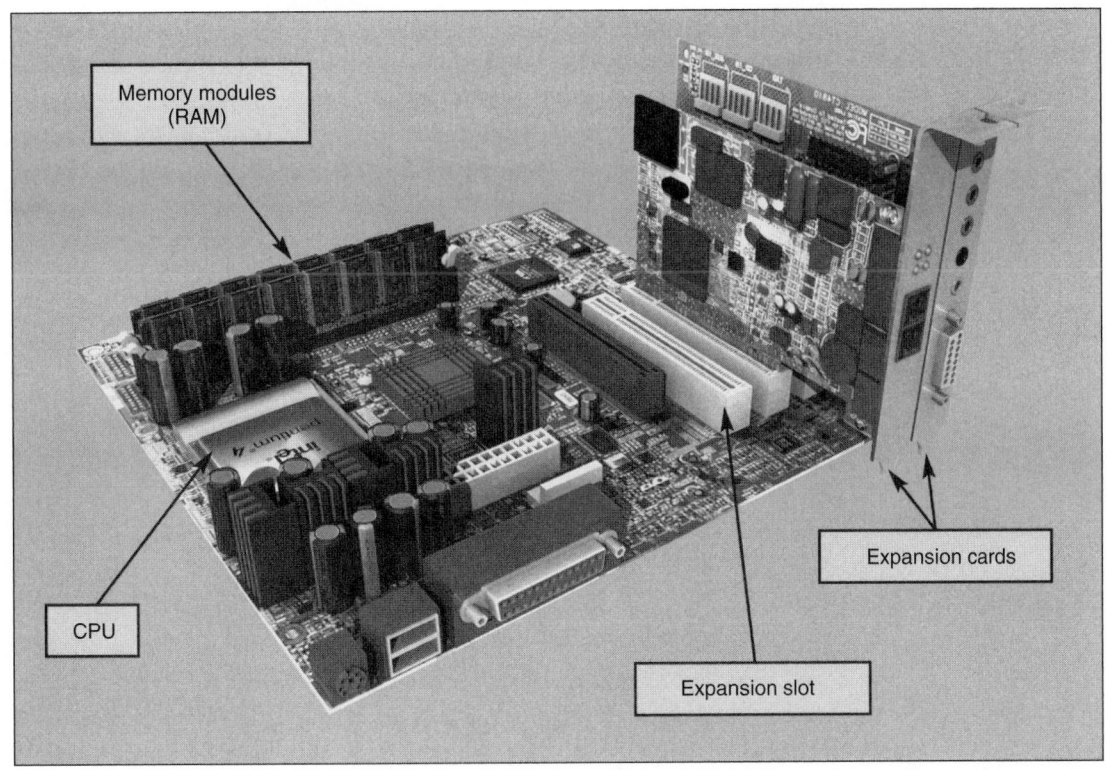

or updated versions of software programs frequently require more memory for efficient processing of the information. Adding additional memory is as simple as plugging in a new memory module that is compatible with that particular computer in an available memory slot. Exhibit 3.6 shows a memory module in a motherboard.

Adding components or memory is usually a function of the support staff, but in smaller offices, members of the legal team may find that they themselves *are* the support staff, and they should at least understand the process. It should be noted that on most laptops, the only services users may perform themselves are adding memory modules or replacing a hard disk drive. On many portable devices such as the iPad, internal batteries and components that are part of the motherboard are not replaceable except by factory-authorized repair facilities.

PRACTICE TIP
Caution should always be taken to prevent static electricity by grounding oneself by touching a metal part of the case before touching the components or the inside of the computer.

■ PORTABLE COMPUTER SYSTEMS

With the increase in wireless communications, the contemporary legal team has become more mobile. The legal team frequently will work outside the traditional office. They may need to work at home, clients' places of business, government offices, courthouses, and other locations across the state, the country, or the world. The personal computer is thus no longer tied to the desk like the practically immovable desktop PC. Computers are now highly portable in the form of laptops, tablet computers, and smartphones.

Laptops

laptop
Small, portable computer.

The modern **laptop** is a powerful, full-function wireless device. Most laptop computers can support multiple peripheral input and output devices, such as document scanners or projection devices used for making courtroom presentations. Most models of the newer generation of laptops also have built-in wireless Internet and network connections.

One issue with laptops is battery life. Older models of laptops had CPUs that required more power than today's CPUs, resulting in shorter battery life before recharging was necessary. But newer CPUs, in addition to being faster and more powerful, use less battery power, which results in longer work sessions before the battery needs recharging. New battery and CPU technology has further reduced power consumption, allowing the newest generation of laptops to run faster and for periods of up to 24 hours, depending on the device. Some laptops weigh less than three pounds, with full keyboards, large screens, and the ability to plug in many of the same peripherals that are plugged into a desktop system.

drivers
A program that allows the computer to communicate with a peripheral and tell it what to do.

Connecting with peripherals outside the office may require adding the software necessary to run these peripherals, called **drivers.** A driver is a program that allows the computer to communicate with a peripheral and tell it what to do. The newest operating systems, such as Windows 7, automatically install most of the drivers for newer peripherals without user action. However, for older computers and devices (often called "legacy systems"), installing a driver may still be necessary. In these cases, the driver may be provided on a CD supplied with the device. A specific driver may also be obtained from the manufacturer's website and downloaded directly to the computer.

Although laptops have the advantage of reduced size, the portability of these computers raises a major security concern. Laptops are frequently stolen from airports, hotel rooms, and unattended automobiles, or are accidentally left behind on restaurant tables, in public bathrooms, and at security checkpoints. A lost, stolen, or "missing" laptop may contain confidential information. For the legal team, if this confidential information belongs to the client, its loss or misuse may be considered a breach of ethical standards.

Tablet PCs

tablet PC
Laptop that allows input from a pen device or fingers instead of a mouse or keyboard.

Tablet computers such as the iPad allow input from touching the screen, instead of using a mouse or keyboard. The screen becomes the writing surface, like a pad of paper. Fingers, or a special pen called a stylus, are used to write on the screen. With appropriate software, handwriting can be converted to text, or saved as graphic images.

Mobile Devices

Mobile devices include small laptops, tablet computers, and smartphones such as Android, BlackBerry, and iPhone products. They are designed with screens in a variety of sizes, from those the size of traditional cell phone screens to the screens of ten or more inches found on some tablet computers. They can perform a variety of functions—making telephone calls, videoconferencing, taking photos, sending email, text messaging, playing music and videos, connecting to the Internet, scheduling, and keeping notes. With the growth of apps for the Apple and Android devices, new features are introduced every day. It is not unusual to see attorneys in court receiving emails and text messages on their mobile devices. For many, mobile devices have become the portable office assistant, replacing the pocket calendar or address book. In many cases, mobile devices eliminate the need to carry a portable or laptop computer just to send and receive email when out of the office.

Smartphones combine both mobile phone and handheld computer functions into a single device. For many people, smartphones have replaced portable computers. With the release of the Apple iPad and the Android tablet devices, the distinction between smartphone and computer has vanished, as the functions performed by each have been combined. The user can receive calls, send and receive email and text messages, and browse the web on one device. In addition, a personal calendar, telephone contact list, and task list can be synchronized with a desktop computer containing a copy of the same information. Most smartphones also have built-in maps and global positioning systems (GPS) that are usable wirelessly almost anywhere in the world.

WEB RESOURCES
For more information on smartphones, go to www.palm.com or http://www.blackberry.com

smartphone
Generally a wireless telephone with features such as a camera and an Internet connection.

WEB RESOURCES
For an overview of mobile devices, go to http://www.webopedia.com/quick_ref/mobile_OS.asp

■ SOFTWARE

Software provides instructions to the computer for performing internal operations and specific tasks, such as preparing documents, sorting information, performing computations, and creating and presenting graphic displays. Software includes programs used in the management of the law office and the management of client cases.

software
Coded instructions (programs) that make a computer do useful work.

■ OPERATING SYSTEMS

The operating system is software that provides instructions to the computer on how to handle basic functions, such as how to process information from input devices, the order in which to process information, and what to show on the computer monitor. The operating system is like the ringmaster of a circus directing the flow of performers and the timing of the performance. The portion of the basic operating system needed to start up the CPU is contained in **read-only memory (ROM).** This is a type of nonvolatile memory that does not require power to retain its contents. When the system is started, the basic set of instructions in the ROM tells the CPU to look for the main operating system on a designated device, usually a hard drive. This setup also allows a user during start-up to install a new operating system from a CD.

LEARNING OBJECTVE 2
Describe the different computer operating systems.

read only memory (ROM)
A type of nonvolatile memory that does not require power to retain its contents.

PC, Apple, and Linux Operating Systems

The two most popular computer systems are referred to as "PC" and "Apple." The original designs of these two systems were built around different central processor system chips manufactured by different companies—Intel in the case of the PC, and Motorola in the case of Apple. Each computer system requires its own unique operating system.

Although both computer systems have advocates, the PC has a dominant position in the legal and business communities, where its main uses are text production and mathematical computations in the form of word processing and spreadsheets. The Apple system has achieved a dominant position in

Exhibit 3.7 A Windows screen showing the command line within a GUI interface

© 2011 Microsoft.

the graphic, education, and artistic communities. New models of both systems have software that permits files created on one system to be used on the competitor's system. In 2006, Apple started to utilize the same CPUs the PC manufacturers use, allowing new Apple computers to use software for both systems.

Microsoft Windows is the most commonly used operating system for the PC. A number of different versions of the Windows operating systems are found in the workplace. The latest versions, such as Windows 7, are designed to take advantage of increased computer operating speeds and can better display graphics. Windows provides a **graphic user interface (GUI),** which allows a user to interface with the computer using graphic commands such as icons, windows, and menus. Exhibit 3.7 shows a command line interface and a graphic user interface.

The analogous operating system for Apple computers is Mac OS, which also uses a GUI. Over time, the Windows and Mac OS operating systems have come to have similar appearances, and software for both systems is generally provided by most software companies, sometimes on the same CD.

Among the newer computer operating systems gaining followers is the Linux operating system, created by Sun Microsystems. This is an operating system offered by its developer as an alternative to the Microsoft operating system, and is provided without a licensing or royalty fee. Any improvements are made available without a fee to anyone using the Linux operating system.

graphic user interface (GUI)
A set of screen presentations and metaphors that utilize graphic elements such as icons in an attempt to make an operating system easier to use.

Mobile Operating Systems (Mobile OS)

A **mobile operating system** is the software platform for programs running on mobile or handheld devices. The operating system determines the functions and features available on the device, including which third-party applications can be used.

iOS is the proprietary system used in Apple iPhones and iPads. Windows Mobile is the mobile operating system from Microsoft and is used on a variety of devices from manufacturers like Dell, HP, Motorola, and Palm.

mobile operating system
The software that controls the functions of mobile operating devices.

Utility Software

Utility software, sometimes referred to simply as "utilities," are programs that perform functions in the background that are related to the operation of the computer. Perhaps the most commonly used utilities are antivirus software, like Norton AntiVirus, which search for, block, and isolate or eliminate computer viruses. Other utilities are used for viewing documents, such as Adobe Reader for PDF files, Quicktime or Realplayer for videos, and Webex for viewing online webinars. Some utilities are used to compress (zip) or extract (unzip) files, back up software and data on hard drives, and limit access to computer systems, such as firewall and parental blocking programs.

utility software
Programs that perform functions in the background that are related to the operation of the computer.

applications software
A collection of one or more related software programs that enables a user to enter, store, view, modify, or extract information from files or databases. The term is commonly used in place of "program" or "software." Applications may include word processors, Internet browsing tools, and spreadsheets.

■ APPLICATIONS

An **application** is a type of software used to perform a specific function, or a set of related functions, such as word processing, presentations, and electronic spreadsheets. These are programs that are often used across many different professions and industries.

Office suites are sets of commonly used office applications that are designed to work together. For example, a suite may contain a word processing application, a database application, a spreadsheet application, and a graphics and presentation application. Each of the programs can be used alone, such as Microsoft Word or Corel WordPerfect, but is packaged together with other stand-alone programs. Some of the programs in the two most common office suites, Microsoft Office and Corel WordPerfect Office, are shown in Exhibit 3.8.

The software suites usually are delivered on one CD or as a set of CDs, enabling all the programs to be loaded at one time, saving installation time. With common features and appearance, it is easier to switch between programs and copy information among the programs. For example, a spreadsheet may be copied into a word processing document.

LEARNING OBJECTIVE 3
Explain the differences between general applications and specialty applications software.

office suites
Software consisting of commonly used office software programs that manage data and database programs; manipulate financial or numeric information and spreadsheet programs; and include displayed images and presentation graphics programs.

Exhibit 3.8 Software suite comparison chart

	Microsoft Office Corel	**WordPerfect Office X5**
Word processor	Word	WordPerfect X5
Spreadsheet	Excel	Quattro Pro X5
Database	Access	Paradox X5
Presentation graphics	PowerPoint	Presentation X5
Graphics	Visio	Presentation Graphics X5

Software Integration

integration
Direct input from one program into another program.

Suites are designed for **integration** among the different applications in the suite. Charts, graphs, and spreadsheets are easily copied and inserted among word processor, spreadsheet, and graphics programs. Some applications can export files directly into other programs. For instance, Lexis Nexis NoteMap can export a file directly into Microsoft Word. Some applications even add a button on a toolbar for exporting files. For example, a button for exporting a Microsoft Word file to Adobe Acrobat® is included on the Word screen.

During the life cycle of a case, the legal team may frequently use different applications to serve specific needs. At the beginning of a case, CaseMap might be used to organize the factual issues and the documents. Near the end, trial presentations may be prepared using Sanction or TrialDirector. With applications designed to allow for the integration of the data, a seamless workflow is possible, saving time and money for the client.

Specialty Applications

specialty applications
Specialty programs combine many of the basic functions found in software suites: word processing, database management, spreadsheets, and graphic presentations.

A **specialty application** is software that is industry-specific. These applications are created to perform functions that are unique to an industry, such as case management in the law office. As computers become more powerful, software likewise becomes more powerful and capable of performing more complex functions involving more data. In the past, many companies needed to have software custom-written to perform functions specific to their industry. Today, off-the-shelf specialty applications can perform these specialized functions, saving the time and cost previously needed to write, install, and test custom software. To some extent, specialty applications allow for some limited customization, such as specialized input screens or reports.

Specialty applications designed for the law office combine many of the basic functions found in software suites, such as word processing, database management, spreadsheets, and graphic presentations. With the use of customized input screens and preset report generators tailored to the law office, these applications make the management of cases and litigation easier and more efficient.

legal specialty software
Programs that combine functions found in software suites for performing law office management functions.

Legal specialty software falls generally into the following categories:

- Office management
- Case management
- Litigation support
- Transcript management
- Trial presentation

Of the office management specialty applications, the most basic are the time and billing programs. These provide an input screen to record and store the time spent on a client's case. The data is then automatically sorted, the billing rates are applied, and an invoice is prepared.

Popular programs in this group are:

- AbacusLaw from Abacus Data Systems, Inc.
- ProLaw from Thomson Reuters Elite
- PCLaw from LexisNexis
- Tabs3 from Software Technology, Inc.
- Timeslips from Sage

Early versions of time reporting software were limited to timekeeping. With today's faster computers and greater memory capacity, however, most of these programs now have other features integrated into them, such as accounting functions to track costs and expenses, and practice management functions such as calendar and contact management.

■ SOFTWARE INSTALLATION

Installing software is usually very easy. Most software is provided in a format that initiates automatic installation. Just insert the CD, and the program launches its own installation or setup program—at least, that is the ideal situation. Many computers and computing devices such as ultra-light PCs and tablet computers do not have CD readers built into them. As will be discussed later, software today may be downloaded using the Internet, eliminating the need for CDs. In some cases, achieving automatic installation requires a little preliminary effort to determine compatibility and capacity.

Compatibility is usually a matter of buying software for the type of computer used. Some programs are offered in both Windows and Mac OS formats, but many are not. Software packaging typically specifies the "platform" as Windows or Mac OS on a side panel.

Another issue in the installation of software is **capacity,** or the ability of a particular computer to run the software. Capacity refers to the technical specifications of the system: the speed of the CPU, the available space on the hard drive, the RAM needed to run the program, and the necessary input and output devices, such as a scanner, a color printer, or a high-resolution graphics system. If the system does not have the required capacity, the software will either perform poorly on that system, or will not perform at all.

Minimum requirements can change as software is revised and upgraded. Exhibit 3.9 shows how the requirements have changed from version 2007 to version 2010 of the Microsoft Office Suite. In addition to the *minimum* and *recommended* computer requirements, there are also requirements for optimal use of software, as shown in the configurations for Sanction trial presentation software in Exhibit 3.10.

The **minimum requirements** will allow the computer to function with one program open at a time, but the program may not run as fast as desired.

LEARNING OBJECTIVE 4
Understand basic issues in installing and using software.

compatibility
In software usage, means software is designed to work on a particular type of computer or operating system.

capacity
Technical specifications such as CPU speed and computer memory.

minimum requirements
The minimum computer requirements in terms of memory, speed, and other characteristics necessary for software to run properly.

Exhibit 3.9 Comparison of system requirements for recent versions of the Microsoft Office Suite

Overview

From the outset, a key design criterion for Office 2010 was to minimize the need for additional system resources. A comparison of the system requirements for recent Office versions is shown in the following table.

Component	Office 2003	Office 2007	Office 2010
Computer and processor	233 MHz	500 MHz	500 MHz
Memory (RAM)	128 MB	256 MB	256 MB
Hard disk	400 MB	2 GB	3 GB
Display	800 × 600	1024 × 768	1024 × 576*

*All display requirements for Office 2010 are designed to allow for good performance on both portable and desktop computers.

Processor and RAM requirements for Office 2010 are the same as for the 2007 Office system. Therefore, if your computer meets the 2007 Office system requirements, you can run Office 2010.

The recommended hard disk space has increased with Office 2010 because of new features, Office-wide ribbon implementation, and in some cases different applications that are included in the Office suites. For example, Microsoft Office Professional 2010 includes OneNote, whereas Microsoft Office Professional 2007 did not. Also, the system requirements are rounded up to the nearest 0.5 GB to be conservative. For example, if we measure an application's required hard disk space to be 1.99 GB, our recommendation will be 2.5 GB. Our hard disk system requirements are intentionally larger than the actual disk space usage of the software.

A graphics processor will help increase the performance of certain features, such as drawing charts in Microsoft Excel 2010 or transitions, animations, and video integration in Microsoft PowerPoint 2010. Use of a graphics processor with Office 2010 requires a Microsoft DirectX 9.0c compliant graphics processor with 64-MB video memory. These processors were widely available in 2007, and most computers available today include a graphics processor that meets or exceeds this standard. However, if you or your users do not have a graphics processor, you can still run Office 2010.

When you choose the product suite or individual program to deploy in the environment, evaluate the computer before deployment to ensure it meets the minimum operating system requirements.

© 2011 Microsoft.

Exhibit 3.10 Sanction Trial Presentation software minimum, recommended, and optimal system requirements

Sanctions System Requirements

Minimum configuration	Recommended configuration	Optimal Configuration
Intel Celeron Processor	Intel Core 2 Duo Processor	Intel Core 2 Duo Processor
1GB RAM	2GB RAM	4GB Ram
120MB for Application Installation space	120MB for Application Installation Space	120MB for Application Installation Sapce.
80GB Internal Hard Drive (For Data Storage*)	100GB Internal Hard Drive (Data Storage*)	160GB Internal hard Drive (For Data Storage*)
128MB Video Card	256MB Video Card	256MB Video Card.

Copyright © AG/Sanction LLC. Used with permission.

recommended requirements
Computer system configurations of memory, speed, and other characteristics for the maximum utilization of the software.

The **recommended requirements** allow for the full utilization of the software. Running multiple programs at the same time may cause a slowdown in overall performance and may result in a computer "crash" if there are conflicts in sharing the memory and CPU.

■ LICENSE ISSUES

Software is rarely sold outright to the end user. Instead, it is usually licensed for use by the end user, subject to certain limitations and restrictions. These are found in the end user license agreement that the user must, as part of the installation process, accept to continue the installation.

End User License Agreement (EULA)

end user license agreement (EULA)
The contract between the software company and the user authorizing the use of the program and setting the limitations of that use.

An **end user license agreement (EULA)** is the agreement with the software vendor that authorizes and specifies the terms for the legal use of the software. For example, an end user license for an educational version of software is violated when the software is used for commercial purposes. Also, a license for one user is violated when the software is used by multiple simultaneous users. There are three major variations among the types of license agreements sold.

single-user license
Authorizes the installation of software on one computer.

A **single-user license** authorizes installation of the software on one computer. Some companies permit installation on one main computer and on one secondary computer (like a portable or home computer) where both are used by the same person, but not at the same time.

multi-user license
Authorizes the installation of software on multiple computers.

A **multi-user license** authorizes installation on multiple computers. Software is authorized for the number of computers for which a license is purchased, which could include many computers.

network license
Authorizes the use of software on a computer network with a specified number of simultaneous users on the network.

A **network license** authorizes the use of the software on a computer network with a specified number of simultaneous users. In some network environments such as schools, corporate settings, and large law firms, the number of simultaneous users covered under a license may be in the hundreds or thousands.

Demo Version

Demo or trial versions of software are offered to consumers to help them make a determination of suitability for purchase. Most trial or demo versions include in the EULA the restrictions on the use of the software. Continued use beyond the scope of the trial or demonstration period is usually a violation of the EULA unless the software is purchased by the user.

Shareware or Freeware

Shareware or **freeware** is generally software that the author has chosen to make available free to the public on the honor system. Some developers restrict the software's use to noncommercial applications; others set no limitations. Shareware has become the term used to describe the "try it before buying" software that can be downloaded from the Internet. In some cases, a contribution may be required to continue to use the software or to receive software updates or to be able to use all the features of the software. Some freeware is widely used. But other freeware is not reliable and may in fact have a negative impact on one's computer. Thus before using freeware, it is wise to check with a respected reviewer of software like *PC Magazine* or ZDNet.com for reviews and user experiences.

shareware
Software that the author has chosen to make available free to the using public on the honor system.

freeware
Software distributed, generally over the Internet, at no charge to the user.

■ INSTALLATION AND ANTIVIRUS PROGRAMS

It is generally a good idea to turn off or close all other programs when installing new software. This avoids potential conflicts in the use of common program elements. Also, in some cases, the computer's antivirus software must be turned off to allow the computer to install the necessary files and the necessary entries in the operating system, because if left on, the antivirus program may interpret the software installation as a potential attack on the integrity of the computer system and will ask if the installation should proceed, or will block the installation of the program. Antivirus programs like Norton will allow the antivirus protection to be stopped temporarily and will display a screen showing a suggested time period during which the antivirus program will not be protecting the computer. Once the time has elapsed, the antivirus program resumes automatically. The danger in turning off the antivirus program is that the Internet connection may still be active during the installation period, and viruses may get into the computer's system. Thus unless the user is downloading the software from the Internet, the safest installation procedure is to disconnect from the network completely before installing the new software. Reconnection can be resumed if necessary to allow the new program to connect with the software vendor for registration or activation.

Making a Backup of the Program

For software that cannot be downloaded from the publisher, it is a good idea to have archived copies of your programs for that one time when the entire computer crashes or is hit by a power surge on an evening when you are facing a deadline.

If your computer has a CD or DVD drive that allows you to make CDs and DVDs, the process of copying, or "burning," the program onto the new media is simple. It is a good idea to store the license key or activation codes with the backup copies so that the reinstallation copy can be activated. In cases of crashed systems, the software vendor support desk may be able to help you reactivate the software on the new computer.

 WEB RESOURCES
For an excellent source of information on starting and managing a law office, see the South Carolina Bar website at http://www.scbar.org/MemberResources/PracticeManagementPMAP.aspx

Checklist ✓ TECHNOLOGY NEEDED FOR YOUR OFFICE

- Individual workstations for each member of legal team
- Automatic battery backup and power surge system
- Backup system or remote backup service
- Scanner
- Printer
- Copier/scanner/printer/fax
- Digital camera
- Computer camera for videoconferencing
- Portable computer for out of office use and docking station if used in office as primary computer
- Smartphone—phone system
- Software:
    - Computer operating system (Apple, Microsoft, Linux)
    - Office Suite including word processing, spreadsheet, and presentation
    - Data compression software (i.e., WinZip)
    - Time and Billing software
    - Check Register software
    - Calendaring software
    - Internet Browser
    - Practice area specific software (litigation, bankruptcy, real estate)
    - Digital Dictation software
- Server operating system if computers networked
- Cloud storage/sharing program or account

LEARNING OBJECTIVE 5
Understand how a network functions and the issues involved with network security.

network
A group of computers or devices that is connected together for the exchange of data and the sharing of resources.

network file server
A computer that controls the flow of information over the network.

host
Every computerized device, like a computer, printer, or fax machine, that is connected to a network.

file server
A computer in a network that controls the flow of information in the network.

connections
The way in which workstations, file servers, and other peripheral devices are joined to the network.

■ NETWORKS

The first computer systems in law offices generally consisted of a computer, a monitor, and a printer. In the contemporary law office, this system is called a workstation. A **network** is a group of workstations connected together. In a small law firm, the network may be as small as two workstations. In a large law firm, the network may have hundreds of workstations and peripherals connected through a **network file server.**

Every device that is connected to a network is referred to as a **host.** A host that shares its resources is also called a server. Exhibit 3.11 shows a typical computer network system in a small law office.

A network **file server** is a separate computer that acts as the traffic cop of the system, controlling the flow of information among the workstations, the file server, and peripheral devices. It also manages requests to use the system's resources or to access data stored on the system.

Just as a computer requires an operating system in order to function, the server requires network operating software that tells it how to communicate with the connected workstations and peripheral devices. These computers and devices are referred to as **connections.** Networks may also be connected to one another, such as a main office network and a branch office network. In fact, the Internet itself is one large network consisting of many smaller networks linked together.

Checklist ☑️   PURCHASING HARDWARE OR SOFTWARE

- Determine the need to automate a function.
- Is the computer or technology the best way to solve the problem?
- Is this a function best performed in-house or by using a consultant?
- What will it cost to implement the software, including training?
- What software or hardware is available?
- Is there a demo version to try out before buying?
- How many licensed copies will be needed?
- How many hardware items will be needed?
- Who will install and support it?
- Can it be supported by the in-house team?
- How much will an outside maintenance contract cost?
- Will computers currently in place support the new software or hardware?

Exhibit 3.11 A small office network with a file server and workstations connected through a hub

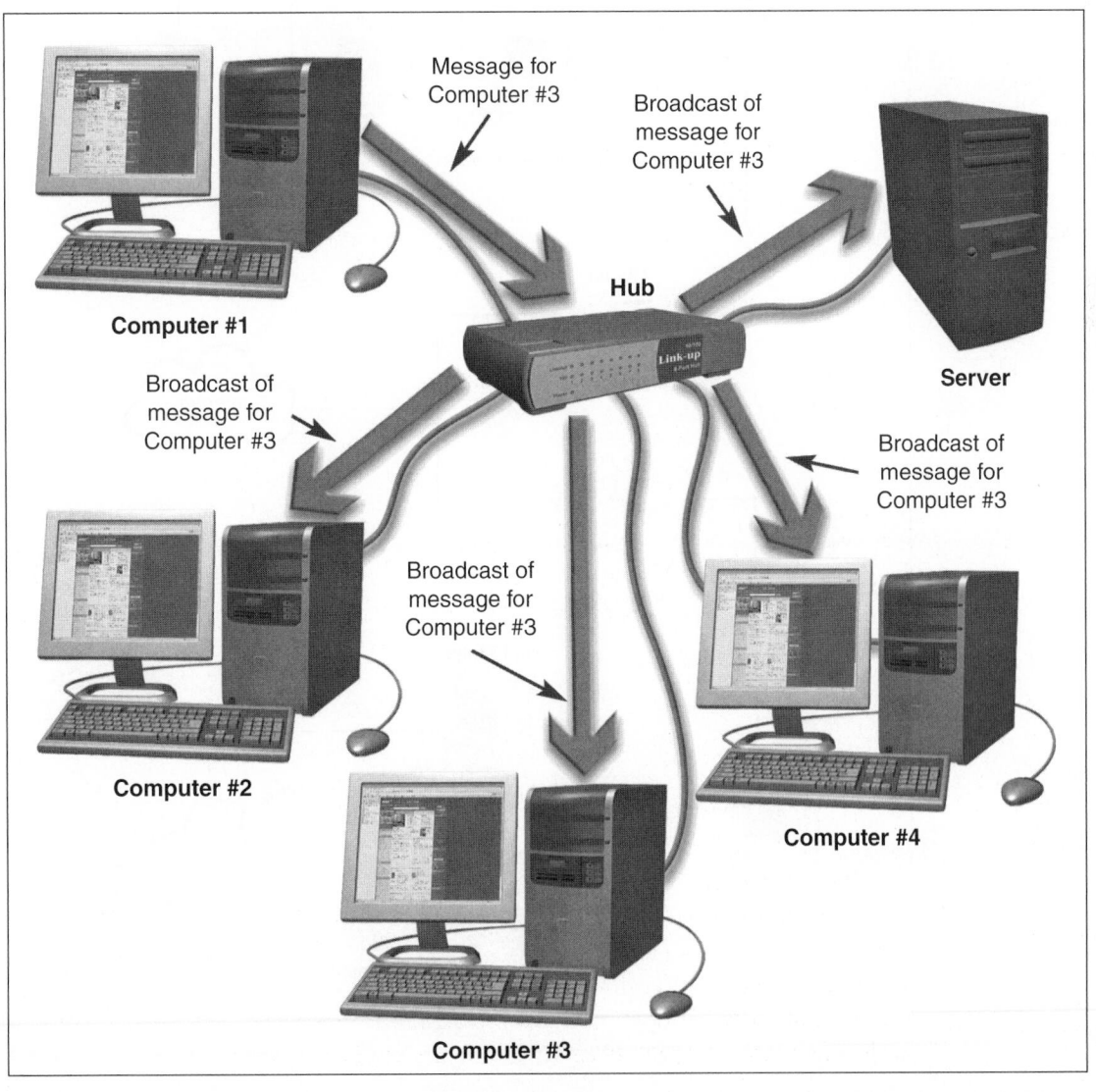

Local Area and Wide Area Networks

local area network (LAN)
Usually refers to a network of computers in a single building or other discrete location.

wide area network (WAN)
A network generally covering a large geographic area and made up of other networks; a network of networks.

A **local area network (LAN)** is a computer network covering a local area like an office, a home, or a building. A **wide area network (WAN)** is a network covering a large geographic area and is made up of other networks—a "network of networks." The largest WAN is the Internet. Time can be saved by sharing information electronically over a WAN instead of meeting someone personally or having a courier deliver hard copies of documents. Many firms—some as small as two people—maintain multiple office sites, such as a center-city and a suburban office location, or a main office and a satellite office across from the courthouse. Each of these offices may have a separate computer network that is connected to the other networks over a WAN.

Exhibit 3.12 shows a WAN of three office networks connected using the Internet. With high-speed communications lines, these separate networks may

Exhibit 3.12 Typical WAN of two office locations using the Internet

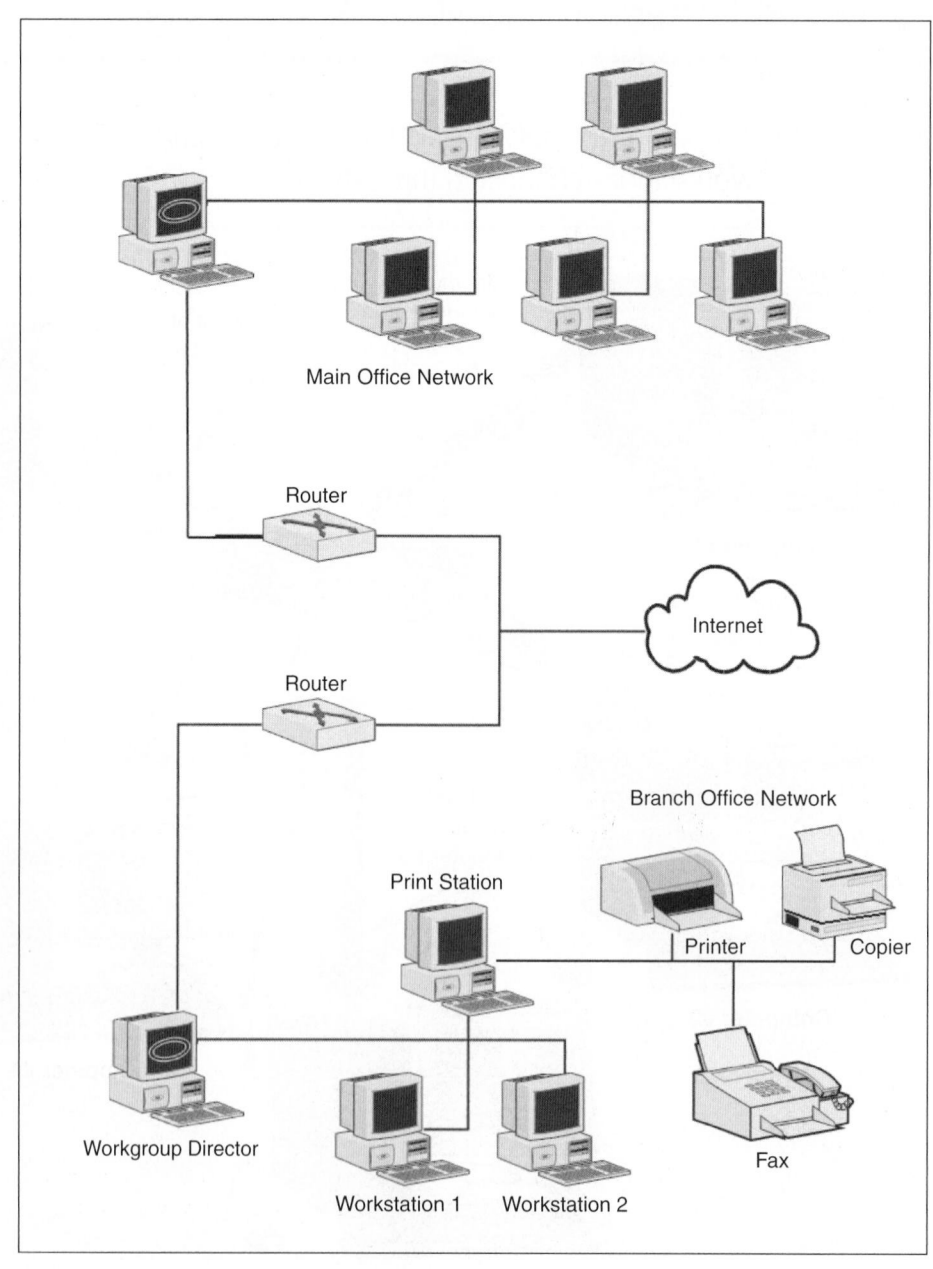

be connected to form a network of networks. Any workstation on one of the networks has access to the other networks in the system and the peripherals attached to the network, including network printers. This allows a person in one office to print documents on a printer in another office. Files may be shared among all the members of the legal team regardless of the office where they are physically located.

Wireless Networks

A **wireless network** is one in which computers communicate over the airwaves instead of through wired connections. The advantages are ease of setup and freedom to work without a cable or wire connection. Laptops are seen everywhere using wireless technology to connect to the Internet. They may also be connected to the company or firm through the Internet and can access company or firm files. Within the large office environment, a laptop or workstation may use a wireless connection without an Internet intermediary. In both cases, however, users must take security precautions. If data is sent using wireless tools, others may be able to intercept the files.

wireless network
A network in which computers communicate over the airwaves wirelessly instead of through wired connections.

Wireless Hotspots

In the early days of the Internet, a few municipalities tried to make the Internet available to residents and visitors using a **municipal area network (MAN)**—a wireless network in a specific geographic municipality. Today, wireless hotspots, or points of wireless access, are provided in many locations such as coffee shops, restaurants, airports, commuter and interstate rail systems, buses, and businesses. These hotspots may be provided free or for a nominal daily or hourly charge. Even airlines are offering wireless access on select flights for a fee.

municipal area network (MAN)
A network in a specific geographic municipality; usually wireless.

■ COMPUTER AND NETWORK SECURITY ISSUES

Security has become a critical issue as law offices, courts, and clients become more dependent upon the use of the computer and the Internet. When there is only a single computer, the security concern is limited to the software and files on that system. With computer networks, however, there is the potential to adversely impact every workstation on the network and the network file server itself. On a network, any workstation is a potential source of problems. Damaged software at one workstation could corrupt other software on the network or the files stored on the file server. While not common, there have been instances of employees introducing annoying or potentially harmful programs as a method of getting even with an employer.

Part of the solution to these kinds of issues is to limit access to the network, including limiting the ability to access the file server, limiting the ability to make changes to operating systems, or preventing any activity other than the saving of documents. Limiting access to files on a file server is one method to ensure confidentiality in a large office, and this can be done by protecting files with passwords. Because each file or set of files (called "folders") can be password-protected, ethical walls can be established by restricting access to only those on the legal team who are working on a particular case.

Network Rights and Privileges

security protocols
Software programs that limit access to the file server and peripherals such as printers or other workstations.

network rights and privileges
Rights to access the different information on the network.

network administrator
The person with the highest level of access to or authority over the network.

Network software programs have **security protocols**—methods used to limit access to workstations, the file server, and peripherals such as printers. These rights to access other devices are sometimes called **network rights and privileges.** The rights or privileges determine who has access to the server, the data stored on the server, and the flow of information among devices.

The person with the highest level of access is called the **network administrator.**

Although an individual workstation can store documents or data, office files are usually stored centrally. Using a central file server makes it easier to limit access to files. It also makes backing up data easier. Law offices that use network servers generally use one server as the central repository for all electronic files.

Passwords

passwords
Combinations of letters, numbers, and symbols used to restrict access to files and computers.

Network connections can be restricted in a number of ways. **Passwords,** in the form of letter and number combinations, offer some degree of protection. But that protection is lost if passwords are used improperly. For instance, although they may be hard to remember, passwords should not be left in open view on the sides of computer monitors or keyboards. They should also not be obvious words, like a person's birthday, a pet's name, or the word *password.*

A more secure option is using a preapproved computerized device on which a code has been stored. Newer methods to limit access include devices that scan the thumbprint of the user. Retinal scanners, once seen only in science fiction, are also becoming a reality in some security systems.

Unauthorized Network Access

Breaking into a computer network by unauthorized parties is sometimes referred to as "hacking." In some instances the unauthorized party is attempting to gain access to information in files stored on the network. In other cases, the purpose of the unauthorized access is to undermine the integrity of the system by modifying files and programs or introducing computer viruses. These intrusions can cause a minor inconvenience—or can destroy entire systems by deleting files, programs, and operating systems.

Network administrators must also monitor the network for authorized users who use the network to access unauthorized material. Businesses and schools do not want their networks and Internet connections used for certain kinds of activity, such as accessing pornography or gambling sites. The display and storage of illegal material can also create liability issues for the owner of the network. Employees may also use the network for personal business, such as monitoring the stock market, which may place a burden on the system by slowing it down, and in some cases causing a complete shutdown.

Firewalls

firewalls
Programs designed to limit access to the authorized users of an application.

A **firewall** is a program designed to limit access to a computer or a computer network system. Depending upon the complexity of the program, it may block all access to those who do not have a password, or block access to only certain kinds of programs or sources not deemed to be acceptable by the network administrator. For example, many parents use a form of firewall designed to limit children's access to certain kinds of programs and sites on the Internet. But a firewall can be a two-edged sword: it can prevent unauthorized access to the network, such as hackers accessing files on the firm's system, but it may also prevent the ability to work at an off-site location like a courthouse or client's office or to connect with an educational institution to take an online course. It is thus important for a legal team to check a connection to be sure it will allow data to be accessed from a remote location before the data is needed for a trial, depositions, or a presentation. Given enough time, almost any issue can be resolved with the local system administrator.

Computer Viruses

Unfortunately, some computer-knowledgeable people take sadistic pleasure in developing and disseminating programs that attack and destroy computer programs, internal computer operating systems, and the hard drives of computers. These programs are known as **computer viruses.** Viruses range from those that create minor inconveniences to those that can destroy data and cause computer shutdowns.

 Some simple precautions can prevent disaster. Virus protection programs, such as those sold by Norton, McAfee, and others, are as important to have on your computer as the computer operating system itself. Indeed, this should be the first program loaded onto a new computer.

computer virus
A program that attacks and destroys computer programs, internal computer operating systems, and occasionally computer hard drives.

Antivirus Software

Antivirus software programs scan the computer for the presence of viruses and eliminate them. The software does this by scanning the computer for code patterns of known viruses. Most of the major antivirus software companies are constantly checking on reports of new viruses and downloading the new patterns to subscribers on a daily basis. Anyone who uses a computer must accept the possibility that if he or she is the first one to receive a new virus or if his or her computer does not have a current version of the antivirus software, the computer may be vulnerable to attack.

 Preventing viruses is not easy, but there are some preliminary precautions that can be taken. For example, files or attachments in emails from unknown sources should not be opened. Every removable memory device should be scanned with an antivirus program before being used. Files that are downloaded from other computers or over the Internet should also be checked. Even the best antivirus software becomes out-of-date as soon as new viruses are created and unleashed. Therefore, all antivirus programs should be updated regularly.

antivirus software
Programs that scour the computer for the presence of viruses; the better programs eliminate the virus.

Backing Up Data

Imagine trying to reconstruct files, court-filed documents, and other essential information after a devastating hurricane and resulting flood destroys all of a law firm's paper records. This type of event has occurred, with severe consequences. Backing up data regularly is thus essential to prevent the loss of critical files and office data in the event of a disaster such as a flood, fire, earthquake, or tornado. With everything on one file server, the **backup** of data can be automated to make copies of everyone's files. A good backup policy includes backing up the file server daily and storing the duplicate copy in a safe location away from the main server, such as a fireproof safe or a bank safe deposit box.

backup
A copy of data created as a precaution against the loss of or damage to the original data.

CONCEPT REVIEW AND REINFORCEMENT

KEY TERMS

CHAPTER SUMMARY

Introduction to Computer Hardware and Software	Computer hardware is the tangible or physical parts of a computer system that must have a power source. Operating system software provides the basic instructions for starting up the computer and processing the basic input and output activities.
Computer Systems	Most small and medium-size offices use personal computers (PCs). A typical system is a workstation connected to a network. A stand-alone computer stores all the software, files, and data. A networked computer is one of any number of stand-alone computers electronically connected. These computers are called workstations, and they are usually connected to a central computer that acts as a server on which files, data, and shared software are stored for access by the workstations.
Portable Computer Systems	A laptop computer is a highly portable form of personal computer.

	The modern laptop is a powerful, full-function device that can support multiple input and output devices and provide wireless access to computer networks. A tablet PC or pad device is a computer that allows input from finger touch or the use of a pen device instead of from a mouse or keyboard. Some devices like smartphones and tablet computers have many of the features of a laptop, including Internet connectivity.
Mobile Devices	The contemporary mobile device is also a multifunction device allowing use as a telephone or camera, permitting email and text messaging, playing music and videos, connecting to the Internet, and maintaining calendars, telephone directories, and reminder notes.
Operating Systems	An operating system is software that provides instructions to the computer hardware for internal operations and to perform specific tasks such as preparing documents, sorting information, performing computations, and creating and presenting graphic displays. The operating system is a basic set of instructions to the computer on how to handle basic functions such as how to process information from input devices such as the keyboard and the mouse, the order in which to process information, and what to show on the computer monitor.
PC, Apple, and Linux Operating Systems	Microsoft Windows is the most commonly used computer operating system for the personal computer. Mac OS is the operating system for current Apple computers. Windows and Mac OS systems have come to have similar appearances, and software is generally provided by most software companies for both systems. Among the newer operating systems is Sun Microsystems' Linux.
Mobile Operating Systems	Mobile devices use operating systems such as Apple's iOS, Android OS, and Windows Mobile OS.
Utility Software	Utility software performs background functions related to the operation of the computer.
Applications	Applications are programs that perform specific functions used in many professions, such as word processing, preparing presentations, or electronic spreadsheets. Office suites are sets of commonly used office software programs that work together.
Software Integration	Programs are often designed to allow the integration of data from one program into another, frequently between software applications of different vendors. Software suites typically provide direct integration between the different software programs in the suite.
Specialty Applications	Specialty applications combine many of the basic functions found in software suites.
Software Installation	Most software is provided in a format that initiates automatic installation.

	Software must be compatible with the type of computer on which it will be used. The software is compatible if it is written for that type of computer. A computer must have adequate capacity to handle the software to be run on it. Capacity refers to the technical specifications of the computer, such as memory size and processor speed. An end user license agreement (EULA) is the agreement with the software vendor that authorizes and specifies the terms for the legal use of the software. Backup copies of programs should be kept.
Installation and Antivirus Programs	It is generally a good idea to turn off or close all other programs when installing software. This avoids potential conflicts in the use of common program elements.
Networks	A network is a group of workstations connected together. A file server is a separate computer that acts as a traffic cop controlling the flow of information on the network. It is also the location where files are frequently stored.
Local Area and Wide Area Networks	A LAN is a small network in a location like a home or an office. Separate networks may be connected to form a "network of networks," otherwise known as a WAN. The computers on the network may communicate over the airwaves wirelessly instead of through wired connections.
Wireless Hotspots	Municipal area networks provide network connections in an entire town or city.
Computer and Network Security Issues	With computer networks, there is the potential to adversely impact every workstation on the network and the network file server itself. On a network, any workstation is a potential source of problems.
Network Rights and Privileges	Security protocols are procedures that limit access to the file server. A network administrator is the person with the highest level of security access.
Unauthorized Network Access	The use of the Internet from workstations has introduced security concerns about unauthorized parties gaining access to the computer network; this is sometimes referred to as "hacking."
Firewalls	A firewall is a program designed to limit access to a computer or a computer network system.
Computer Viruses	Viruses are programs that attack and destroy legitimate programs, internal computer operating systems, and the hard drives of computers.
Antivirus Software	Antivirus software scans the computer for the presence of viruses and eliminate them.
Backing Up Data	Backing up data regularly is essential to prevent the loss of critical files and office data in the event of a natural disaster.

REVIEW QUESTIONS AND EXERCISES

1. Discuss the different types of computer systems used in a law office.
2. Describe the different computer hardware used by the legal team.
3. Explain the differences between applications and specialty applications software.
4. Explain the difference between a suite of programs and integrated software.
5. Why should passwords not be obvious or left in the open?
6. Describe how a computer network may be used by a law firm.
7. Explain the importance of and the steps that maybe taken to maintain computer and network security.
8. Explain the difference in the operation of a computer with the minimum requirements and the operation of a computer with the recommended requirements. How can the user determine if his or her computer meets the minimum or the recommended requirements?
9. What are the ethical issues of using unlicensed software?
10. Prepare a list of the computer hardware components, including names and model numbers, of the system you use at:
    a. home
    b. work
    c. school
    d. other (e.g., public library or Internet café)
11. If you are using a PC, use the Control Panel in the Start Menu to find the System icon. Prepare a detailed description of:
    a. general information about the *system*
    b. the *registered* party
    c. the type of *processor* and its speed and memory
    d. the *name* of the computer as shown in System Properties
    e. the *full computer name* and the *workgroup*
12. Prepare a list of the applications software on your personal computer:
    a. manufacturers
    b. program names
    c. version
    d. registered owner
13. What ethical issues might be raised in a review of a list of applications software programs on computers in the law office?
14. Explain the functions of the components of a computer system in the law office.
15. Describe the different classes of software and the functions they perform in the law office.
16. What law office functions can be performed with the use of legal-specific applications programs?
17. What, if any, policies should be in place in the law office regarding the use of personal computers by the members of the legal team? Explain why or why not policies should be created.
18. What does the end user license for one of the Office Suite programs say about multiple uses of the software?

BUILDING YOUR PARALEGAL SKILLS

INTERNET AND TECHNOLOGY EXERCISES

1. a. Use the list from Chapter 1 or prepare a checklist of *minimum* software and hardware requirements and a second list of *recommended* technology needs for the start-up office. Be specific. What, if any, additional minimum or recommended items should be added to the list for a trial attorney regarding office setup?
   b. Use the Internet to find prices on the items in the checklist you prepare.
2. Use the Internet to find information on backup software and hardware. Then use the Internet to locate a copy of at least one of the EULAs for a software program on your personal computer. Does it permit use on multiple machines at the same time?

VIDEO CASE STUDIES

VIDEO CONFERENCING

 A small multi-office law firm has been retained in a case involving a large number of passengers who were injured on a bus that collided with a large truck. The case has been filed in federal court. The legal team has decided to conduct in-house conferences, using videoconferencing.

Watch this video case study in MyLegalStudiesLab and answer the following questions.

1. What confidentiality issues arise in using videoconferencing?
2. Is the cost of videoconferencing justified by the travel time saved?
3. What are the advantages of using videoconferencing instead of telephone conference calls?
4. What are the ethical duties of the legal team when information about the case has been made public?

CHAPTER OPENING SCENARIO CASE STUDY

Use the Opening Scenario for this chapter to answer the following questions. The scene is a new attorney in solo practice discussing with his newly hired paralegal, who has experience working in a large law firm, how to set up the technology systems for the new firm.

1. What procedure or protocol should be established for adding users to the office network?
2. How can access to confidential files be limited?
3. What are the advantages of attending a technology show for the legal profession?

4. What questions should the paralegal and attorney be prepared to ask at the show?
5. What role does the future office expansion have in the initial technology decisions?
6. What hardware should be initially purchased? Be specific regarding functions and capabilities. Is this different from the list prepared in Chapter 1?
7. What software should be purchased first? Prepare a list in order of priority, with essential software at the top. Explain your reasons for the selections and priority.

CONTINUING CASES AND EXERCISES

1. Update the Internet resources list from Chapter 1.
2. Download the latest version of Adobe Reader from the Adobe website: www.Adobe.com.
3. Download a new Internet browser that is different from the one you usually use. You may use

any search engine available to locate the new browser.
4. Continue to maintain a time record as outlined in Chapter 1.

ADVANCED EXERCISES

Detailed tutorials for AbacusLaw and Tabs3 can be found on the Technology Resources Website: www.pearsonhighered.com/goldman. As assigned by your instructor:

1. Click on the AbacusLaw icon, download and install the AbacusLaw Software, and complete the tutorial for AbacusLaw.

2. Click on the Tabs3 icon, download and install the Tabs3 Software, and complete the tutorial for Tabs3.

BUILDING YOUR PROFESSIONAL PORTFOLIO

1. Based on the Opening Scenario, prepare a plan for setting up the technology systems for the new firm that can be presented to the attorney and that he can share with others who are working in the office or subletting space. Explain the reasons for the plan.

2. Prepare an office policy on the use of passwords in the law office. Explain the reasons for using passwords and the methods to be used to create the most secure passwords.

"A computer terminal is not some clunky old television with a typewriter in front of it. It is an interface where the mind and body can connect with the universe and move bits of it about."

—Douglas Adams, Mostly Harmless

The Internet, the Cloud, and Communications | CHAPTER 4

OPENING SCENARIO

Owen Mason felt very fortunate in many ways. He had landed a federal clerkship after law school and was well-trained in the use of the Internet for legal and factual research. He had hired Mrs. Hannah, the best paralegal downtown, to help him set up his own practice. The judges he had met as a clerk were keeping him busy by appointing him counsel, if at a significantly reduced fee. But the realities of managing a practice soon became evident. In addition to rent, there was the expense of basic computers and other equipment, the fees for using the Internet, as well as other costs he had never had to think about before.

Mrs. Hannah reminded him that there were alternatives to using the Internet that might save costs. There were also issues with sharing their Internet service with Ariel Marshall, a lawyer who was subletting space in the office with her paralegal, Emily. Mrs. Hannah expressed a concern to both attorneys about a potential ethical breach after seeing a list serve posting on Emily's computer screen that had a similar fact pattern to a case that both attorneys were working on.

Mrs. Hannah also expressed concern that Ms. Marshall and Emily were both addicted to the Internet for legal and factual research as well as for social networking and constantly checking the stock market. Their overuse of the Internet had increased to the point that it was slowing down the entire system for both offices. And if they did not stop downloading unnecessary information and freeware and saving everything on the file server, they would be out of storage space on their shared server very soon.

LEARNING OBJECTIVES

After studying this chapter, you should be able to:

1. Explain how the Internet works.

2. Explain the concept of cloud computing.

3. Discuss issues in the use of the Internet.

4. Describe the issues in downloading and installing software from the Internet.

5. Define metadata.

6. Explain the role of list serves and the etiquette in using them.

VIDEO INTRODUCTION _____

THE INTERNET, THE CLOUD, AND COMMUNICATIONS
After watching the video in MyLegalStudiesLab, answer the following questions.

1. How can the Internet be of use to the members of the legal team?
2. What is the role of the Internet in the law office?

■ INTRODUCTION TO THE INTERNET AND ELECTRONIC MAIL

Internet resources have become ubiquitous, and are used by everyone on a daily basis. As the number of websites has increased, the Internet has become a source of information on every conceivable topic. As the services used to access the Internet have improved, it has become an important method of communicating, not just with email and text messaging, but with voice and video as well. The ability to communicate wirelessly with portable devices has also enabled people to work from remote locations and to collaborate with anyone from virtually anywhere. With vendors offering services and software on demand, the need for high-capacity computers is reduced, allowing greater access and efficiency on smaller, cheaper devices.

■ INTERNET FUNDAMENTALS

LEARNING OBJECTIVE 1
Explain how the Internet works.

Internet backbone
The Internet connection between countries that carries information around the world.

Internet service provider (ISP)
A company that provides users with local access to the Internet.

The Internet may be thought of as a network of networks—a huge collection of networks linked together and sharing information.

At the highest level of the Internet are the main data routes between large, high-capacity academic, commercial, and government routers. This high-level network is called the **Internet backbone.** The term is also used to refer to the Internet connection between countries that carries information around the world. The average user is many layers below this backbone. User connections are made through local or national Internet service providers (ISPs), who themselves connect to higher-level national services, as shown in Exhibit 4.1.

Internet service providers (ISPs) are companies that provide users with access to the World Wide Web. In many communities, service is provided by the local cable or telephone company. In the past, only larger offices, schools, and companies had a direct connection. This direct connection was in the form of a cable, a fiber-optic line, or a dedicated telephone line that eliminated the need to dial up the ISP. Increasingly, small offices and homes are able to obtain the same dedicated service from their cable or telephone company, including low-cost, high-speed connections. Special devices, such as modems and routers, enable computers to "talk" over these cable and fiber-optic systems. Exhibit 4.2 shows a modem with a network connection to the Internet.

Modem

modem
A piece of hardware that lets a computer talk to another computer over a phone line.

A **modem** is a device used to translate the electrical signals for transmission over these connections so that computers can "talk" to each other. Higher-speed

Exhibit 4.1 Internet service providers

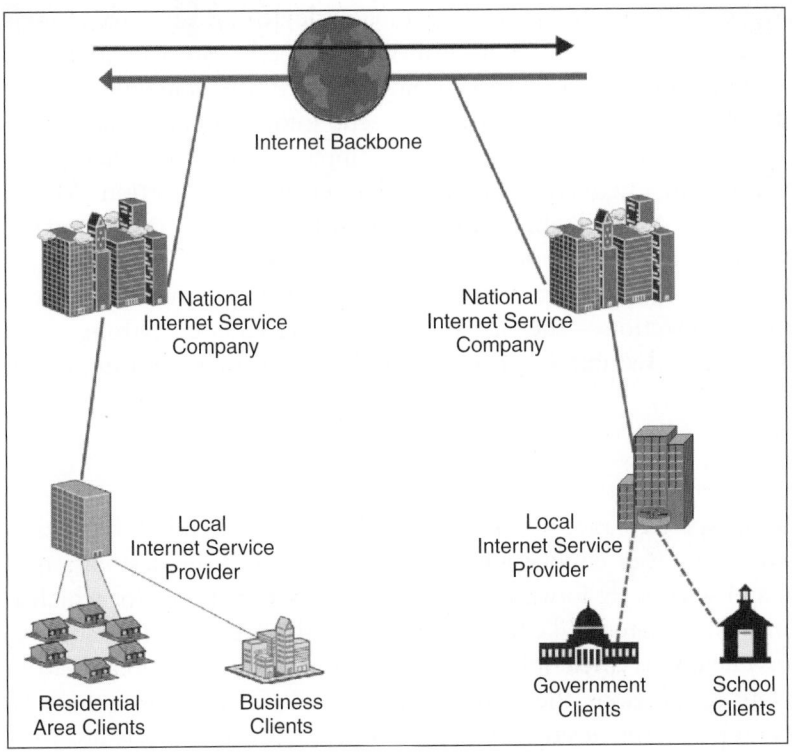

Exhibit 4.2 A modem with a network connection to the Internet

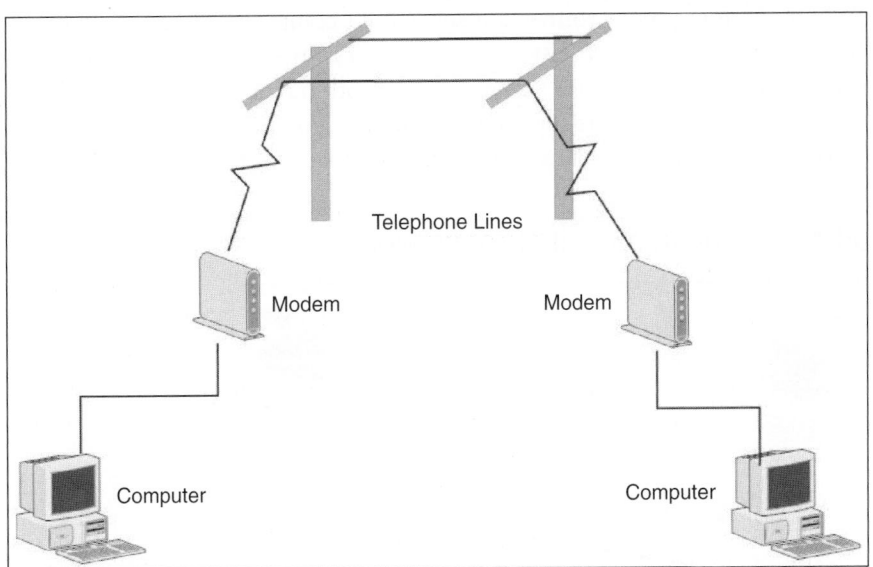

access is rapidly becoming available in most parts of the country and in many parts of the world at relatively affordable prices. In the past, most connections depended on the limited capacity of the copper wires of the telephone company. However, cable and telephone companies are now installing higher-speed infrastructures using fiber optics and satellite technologies to deliver higher speeds and capacity.

hub
A device used for sharing a signal among multiple computer devices.

switch
A high-performance alternative to a hub.

router
A piece of hardware that routes data from a local area network (LAN) to a phone line.

Hubs

A **hub** is a device for connecting multiple computer devices. If you have a single computer, you can plug your Internet connection directly into the computer. With two computers in a small office or home network, the computers can be connected directly with one wire, and they can send information back and forth. When there are more than two computers or computerized devices, like printers or fax machines, on a network, a hub is used as a central connection. All the devices that are plugged into the hub can communicate with each other, and the hub may have an Internet connection that all the devices share through separate wires or connections. Whatever comes through one of the connections is sent to all the other connections—the hub essentially broadcasts everything to all the other connections. Exhibit 4.3 shows a hub broadcasting to and from each connection.

Switches

A **switch** is a high-performance alternative to a hub. Whereas a hub broadcasts every signal to every other connection, a switch determines the destination of each message and selectively forwards it to the computer or device for which it is intended. In smaller systems like home networks with fewer than four connections, a hub may be just as efficient but less costly than a switch. But in a network of more than four connections, the switch is more efficient. By directing the message to the intended recipient and not to the entire network, there is less total traffic, resulting in higher-speed connections.

Routers

In its most basic function, a **router** is a specialized computing device that routes messages to their intended destinations, much like a coin sorter sorts coins into the proper slots or bins. Each message sent over a network has an address where it is to be delivered. Some messages are directed to other computerized devices in the local office network. Others are destined for some computerized device located outside

Exhibit 4.3 A hub in a small office network

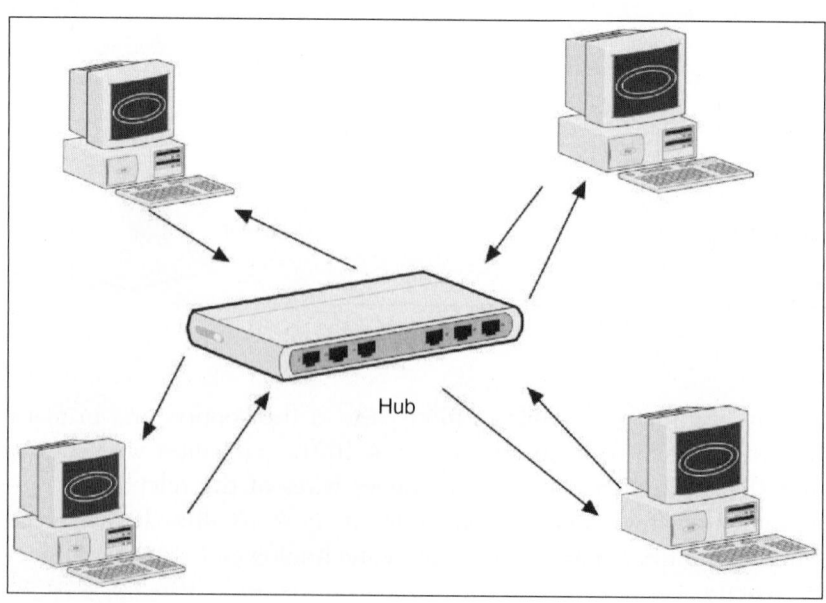

Hub

of the local network somewhere on the Internet. Routers use software to make the decision where to send the message by interpreting the address. The software also "looks" at the devices attached to the router to see if the message is to be sent to a device in the local network or sent to a higher-level router outside the local network and somewhere on the Internet. The routing software may be on a computer or in a separate, stand-alone router. When you send a message, the routing software in your computer looks at the address to see if the destination address is one of the devices attached to your computer or some other device.

The first decision the router makes is whether the message stays inside the local network or goes outside the network. If it decides that the message stays inside the local network, the router sends it to the intended device. If it is not intended for a local device, the message is then passed on to a router further along the Internet, where the decision is made again whether to send the message to another router or to a device that is attached to the current router's network. The process is repeated until the message gets to a network with a router that has the intended recipient device attached to it. The system is like forks in a road, with directions to another fork, which in turn has more directions, and so forth.

You are probably thinking that a router sounds much like a switch. A switch does indeed perform some routing functions, such as sending traffic from one device to the intended device connected to the switch. Modern switches may contain the necessary software to act as modem, router, and high-performance hub, all in one device.

Addresses

Routing software found on computers, routers, and switches uses addresses for delivering messages, much like the post office uses street addresses to locate and deliver the mail. The routing software uses a **logical address**—meaning that it gives information on how to find the place. This should be distinguished from the **physical address,** where the message is to be received.

logical address
Addresses for delivering messages.

physical address
The media access control, or MAC, address.

Every computerized device has a unique physical address that is stored in a special memory location in the device. This physical address is called the **media access control (MAC) address.** Since each device has a different MAC or physical address, the router can direct the incoming message to the particular device intended.

media access control (MAC) address
A physical address that is unique and that is stored in a special memory location in a computerized device.

Internet Addresses

The Internet uses an address to deliver data to a specific computer or computerized device, just as a mail carrier uses an address to deliver a letter to a specific post office box. Each computerized device that connects to the Internet is assigned a numeric address, called the **IP** address. The IP address contains a set of numbers separated by periods. For example, the numeric address for the website for *Technology in the Law Office* is 216.13.106.54.

IP
Internet protocol address. A string of four numbers separated by periods used to represent a computer on the Internet.

Most people do not use the numeric IP address when referring to a location on the Internet. Each location also has a text version of the address to access a website, called the domain name. For example, the domain name for the *Technology in the Law Office* website is www.technologyinthelawoffice.com. An interpretation service on the Internet called a domain name service (DNS) converts the text name to the numeric IP address. The domain is the entryway to the computers and devices in that particular website.

Every device, whether connected to the Internet or not, has a MAC address. When a device is connected to the Internet, it is assigned an IP address. By way of example, a law office may have a server, a router, three workstations, and several

Exhibit 4.4 Network with IP and MAC addresses

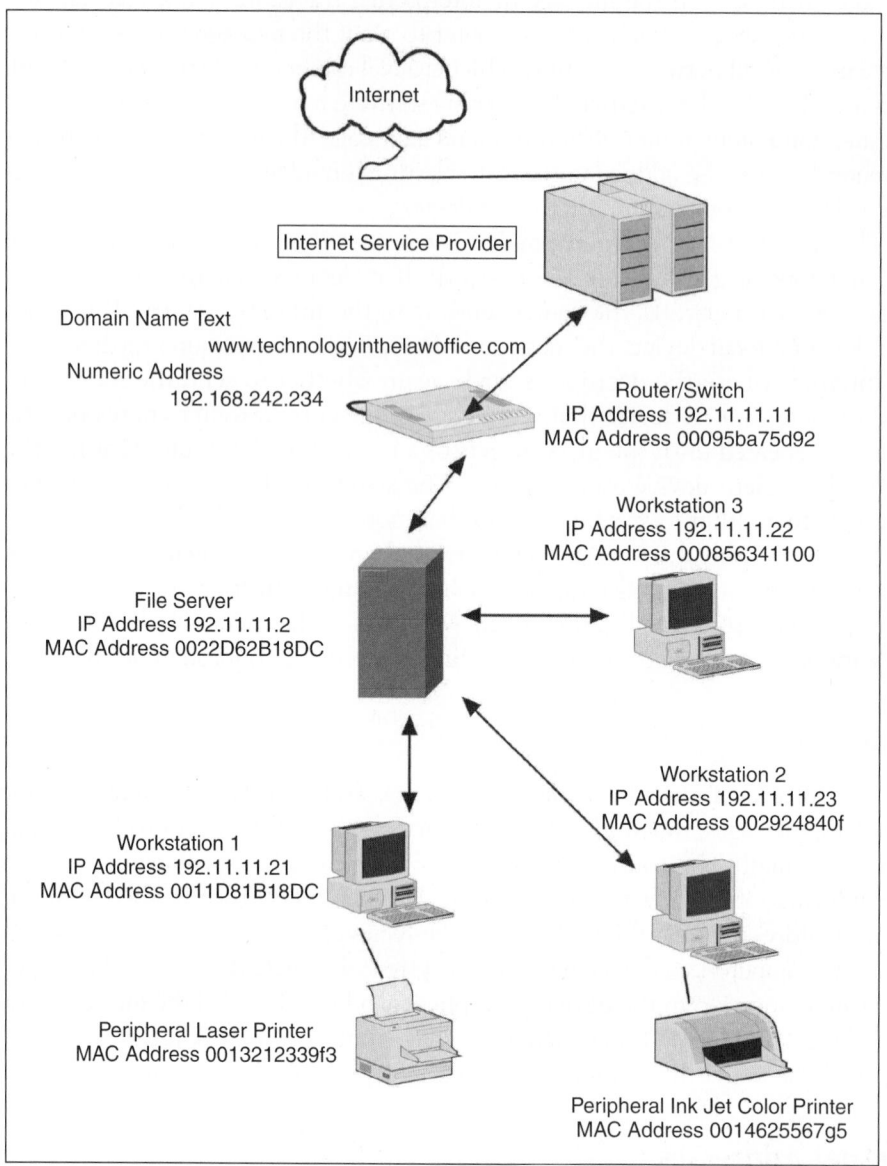

WEB RESOURCES

Find the MAC address of a Windows PC using Windows:

Go to the Start menu

Click on Run

Type cmd

When the window opens, type IPCONFIG/all

computerized devices. Each of these computerized devices is assigned an IP address when it connects to the Internet. Each computerized device also has a physical address, the MAC address. The routing software in the router takes the IP addresses and translates them into the MAC addresses of the devices connected to the router. The router then stores this information in a look-up table and translates the IP address of the Internet to the physical MAC address of the particular device. Each address assigned is as unique as the number on a post office box in the local post office. Exhibit 4.4 shows a network, with IP addresses and MAC addresses, that is connected to the Internet through an Internet service provider.

Internet Browsers

Finding the desired information on the Internet is easy when you know the specific source of that information. In those cases you can enter the computer address of the specific page or document, and have your results almost instantly. More frequently, information must be located without knowing where to find it. Information can

Exhibit 4.5 Microsoft Internet Explorer

be found on the Internet using an **internet browser** such as Firefox or Internet Explorer. A browser is a program that helps a user search the Internet. Microsoft Internet Explorer is shown in Exhibit 4.5. All browsers basically provide two main screens—one to display email (see Exhibit 4.6) and one to display content and Internet search results (see Exhibit 4.7).

Internet Browser
A program that allows the user to access the Internet.

Exhibit 4.6 Email display

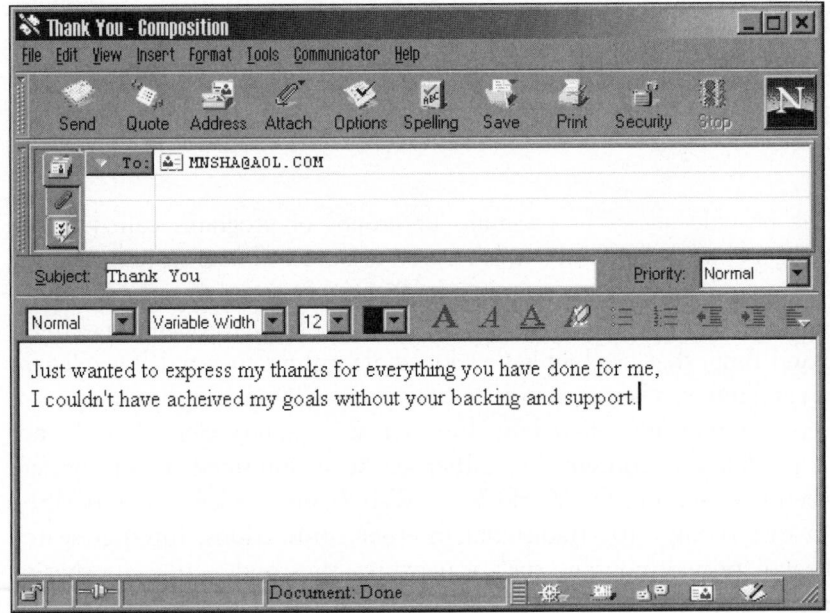

Exhibit 4.7 Internet search results

© 2011 Microsoft.

browser
A software program that allows a person to use a computer to access the Internet.

specialized search engines
Search engines that use highly developed algorithms to search for relevant information and return a listing in order of relevancy with amazing accuracy.

Browsers provide access to programs or groups of programs called search engines that generate a search of available web resources. These searches require only the input of a word or phrase to obtain a listing of potentially relevant information. Also useful are **specialized search engines,** accessible through the websites of Google and Bing, that use highly developed algorithms to search for relevant information and return a listing in order of relevancy with amazing accuracy.

Browsers are typically offered by Internet service providers that do not themselves provide any content, but rather act as an intermediary, or connection, between the user and the World Wide Web. Some services, such as MSN, in addition to providing the traditional Internet connections, Internet search tools, and email, provide content, such as news, weather, and sections for sharing information.

Firefox is another Internet browser that is gaining rapid acceptance. According to its developers, Firefox is more secure than Internet Explorer because it is not attached to an operating system. This way, malicious code in the form of viruses and other threats cannot enter the operating system from the browser and possibly harm the system.

Locating Information

Obviously, finding something requires knowing where it is located. We find people by looking for their home or business address or by their telephone number. The modern equivalent of a telephone number is the email address. A web page also has an address, known as a **uniform resource locator (URL).** The URL is made up of three parts, separated by symbols, in this format: Protocol://Computer/Path. The "protocol" is usually http (hypertext transfer protocol). The "computer" is the Internet computer name, such as www.bucks.edu. And the "path" is the directory or subdirectory on the computer where the information can be found. The URL may be thought of as a file cabinet in which the protocol is the name of the file cabinet, the computer is the drawer in the file cabinet, and the path is the file folder in the drawer. Not all URLs have a path as part of the address.

Part of the naming protocol is the **domain nomenclature,** with extensions that denote a category of websites. Common domain extensions are:

.org	organizations
.edu	educational institutions
.com	commercial operations
.gov	government agencies
.bus	business
.mil	military

In addition, there are extensions referring to countries, such as

.jp	Japan
.fr	France
.uk	United Kingdom

These designations refer to the country where the computer is located.

In determining the authenticity or reliability of information found on the Internet, knowing if the computer is a commercial site (.com or .bus) or a government site (.gov) is sometimes useful. Some websites may appear to be official government websites or may appear to contain official information, but actually are private sites.

For example, the official URL for the Internal Revenue Service is www.irs .gov. This is not to be confused with the unofficial private website, www.irs.com. To obtain the official Internal Revenue Service forms and information, you must use the government site, www.irs.gov.

Potentially, one of the biggest time-savers for the legal team is the ready availability of information, forms, and files on the Internet. Public information that would have required a trip to the courthouse or other government office is now instantly available, twenty-four hours a day, seven days a week, without leaving the office. This information may come from public or private sources.

WEB RESOURCES
Review the information about Firefox and its features at www.firefoxuserguide .com and download a copy if desired. Or, visit the website of the Mozilla Foundation, a nonprofit corporation established to promote innovation on the Internet that also provides a version of Firefox at www.mozilla.org.

URL (uniform resource locator)
The Internet address for a website.

domain nomenclature
Part of the URL naming protocol.

Government information typically is available without cost or at minimum cost. Private information may be free to all, or at a cost per use, per page, or per time period (such as a minute, hour, day, or month).

■ THE CLOUD AND THE INTERNET

LEARNING OBJECTIVE 2
Explain the concept of cloud computing.

Internet
The interconnecting global public network made by connecting smaller shared public networks. The most well-known is the Internet, the world-wide network of networks, which uses the TCP/IP protocol to facilitate information exchange.

World Wide Web
The WWW is made up of all of the computers on the Internet that use HTML-capable software (Netscape, Explorer, etc.) to exchange data. Data exchange on the WWW is characterized by easy-to-use graphical interfaces, hypertext links, images, and sound. Today the WWW has become synonymous with the Internet, although technically it is really just one component of it.

networked
A group of computers or devices that is connected together for the exchange of data and sharing of resources.

The term "cloud computing" or "the Cloud" is a way of describing the utilization of resources and features of the **Internet** or the **World Wide Web.** The term "cloud" comes from early drawings of Internet connections, where cloud images represented the Internet. The Internet may be thought of as nothing more than a group of computers linked together, or a network of networks. If you work in an office in which all of the computers are **networked,** you have a small version of the Internet. Each person's computer is connected to other people's computers, usually with a central or main computer on which the frequently shared data files reside. This main computer also has the network operating system software that controls the connections and how the requests from each computer are handled and directed. In a local area network (LAN), this main control computer is usually referred to as the file server. In a LAN, everything goes through a device, such as a hub or router, that allows each device to access every other device and data. In this system, the device through which all users access the resources available on the Internet may be thought of as the "cloud."

Cloud Computing

The term "cloud computing" is used to describe the advanced uses of the Internet to not only share information, but to also obtain software, access online services, store documents on remote severs or e-repositories, and communicate in real time with voice and video.

Cloud computing has been defined by the National Institute of Standards as follows:

> "…Cloud computing is a model for enabling convenient, on demand network access to a shared pool of configurable computing resources (e.g. networks, servers, storage, applications, and services) that can be rapidly provisioned and released with minimal management effort or service provider interaction…." National Institute of Standards and Technology, Information Technology Laboratory. 10-7-2009

Public Clouds

Access to the resources in the cloud may be restricted to specific users, or may be open to the public. A public cloud uses shared hardware, software, and applications that are available to almost anyone. Examples of public clouds include Google Apps, Office 365, and Amazon EC2. Public cloud resources are most useful to personal and business users when security and access controls are not essential. In many cloud applications, the vendor may use a number of different servers that may be located locally, across the country, or around the world. In most cases there is no way to determine the location of the responding server, but for most users this is not an issue.

Private Clouds

Private clouds limit the use of hardware and software to subscribers. Law firms and their clients will use private clouds for such things as data storage when the access and location of the specific servers can be identified and restrictions on access imposed. Law firms and some businesses must store their proprietary information only in designated locations. The laws of the jurisdiction where the server is located may allow access to government officials or, in the case of lawsuits, to opposing parties. For example, companies working on government contracts should not have their data stored on servers in other countries that may be run by a hostile government. In addition, the laws of some jurisdictions may not protect confidential or proprietary information.

The Use of the Cloud by Law Offices

Many law firms use the cloud for remote storage of data such as client files involved in litigation. In using these remote data storage services or e-repositories, lawyers must contend with issues of security, privacy, and control of the data. Legal professionals are always concerned with maintaining the confidentiality of client data as required under the ethics rules of a jurisdiction. When using an off-site location for storage of data, whether hard copy or electronic, the duty to ensure its confidentiality is an affirmative obligation.

Some major corporate clients, such as insurance companies, may use a number of different law firms around the country for different matters. Such clients may use an e-repository for their data and allow the assigned law firms access as needed without the firm taking charge of the files itself.

Cloud Applications

A growing number of cloud-based programs and services are available.

Microsoft has released a cloud-based solution in Microsoft Office 365, a subscription-based offering that is a combination of online services: MS Exchange (email, calendar, and contacts), MS SharePoint (document sharing and team collaboration), and MS Lync (instant messaging, videoconferencing, and meeting).

Google provides users with applications and storage directly from the popular Google website, as shown in the Google Apps comparison website in Exhibit 4.8.

■ ELECTRONIC COMMUNICATIONS

Email has become a standard method of communication for businesses across the globe, including law practices. But legal teams face issues that other businesses do not face. Most obvious are the issues of confidentiality and privilege. Who will see it and who will read it? Will it be sent only to the correct person, or will it be accidentally sent to a potentially large list of recipients that should never have received it?

According to a survey by the International Legal Technology Association (ILTA), 91 percent of firms have not disabled the automatic **type-ahead feature** in their email programs. This feature completes the address after a few letters of the address are typed. For example, if you type "Jones," the program finishes the address by adding the @ symbol and any email address in your address book that has Jones as part of the address. If you have more than one Jones in your email address book, accidentally hitting the "Enter" or the "Send" key could send the message to the wrong Jones, such as an opposing attorney with the name "Jones," instead of to the client named "Jones." According to the ILTA survey, 92 percent do not give the user a prompt to warn about "Reply to All" being selected for sending an email (in other words, users are not warned, "Are you sure you want to Reply to All?").

Email documents are a large part of the discoverable documentation in cases. How long they should be retained is an important question for the firm

LEARNING OBJECTIVE 3
Discuss issues in the use of the Internet.

type-ahead feature
This feature completes the address after a few letters of the address are typed.

 WEB RESOURCES
ILTA is a peer-networking organization providing information resources to members in order to make technology work for the legal profession. The full ILTA's 2006 E-Mail Survey is available at www.ILTAnet.org, or check for the latest email white paper at www.iltanet.org.

Exhibit 4.8 Google Apps comparison website

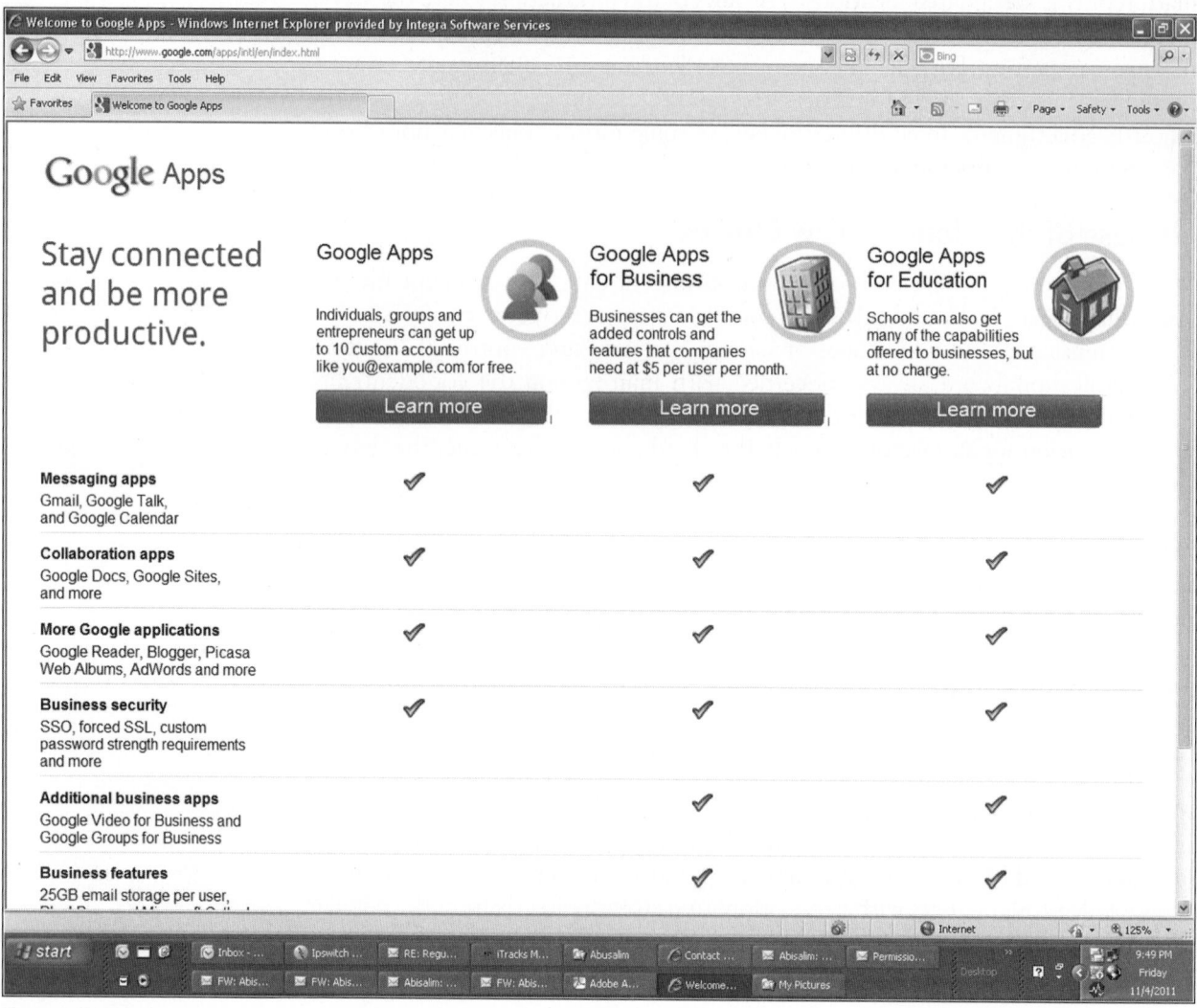

Source: Google.

and for the client, particularly when attachments are part of the email. As email becomes easier to use on all types of devices, the number of emails will increase, with attachments of larger and larger files. And along with the exploding use of emails is the tendency to save every document.

Email is saved on a computer or a file server in a file or folder called a **mailbox.** Limits on mailbox capacity may restrict how much can be saved. However, with email as the standard for correspondence, larger mailboxes are necessary to store the emails, unless some other offline storage is provided.

One of the issues for the legal team is whether emails should be made part of a client's file. In the days of paper letters, copies routinely were printed and placed in the file. With an email management program, they may also be made a part of the electronic file and potentially part of the discoverable record in litigation.

File Attachments

Text files and graphic images may be transmitted by including them as part of an email. An **attachment** is a file that is sent with an email. This is much easier than it sounds. Today, almost everyone has an email address, whether at home, at work, or both. To send or receive emails requires the use of an Internet service provider and a browser such as Internet Explorer, Netscape, or a specialty email program.

mailbox
An electronic storage location for email messages.

attachment
An attachment is a record or file associated with another record for the purpose of storage or transfer.

In traditional email, text is entered via the keyboard and transmitted to the email account of a recipient, who reads it online. Virtually any file can be attached and sent with an email. The receiver need only double-click the mouse on the attachment, which may appear as an icon. In most cases, the file will open using the same program from which it was created, such as Microsoft Word, Corel WordPerfect, or Adobe Acrobat®, provided the receiver has that application on his or her system. Occasionally, a file may be transmitted in a format that the receiver does not have the application for. This is particularly common with regard to graphic images, pictures, and drawings.

Files and Folders

Having a system for saving electronic document files is essential for finding and using them. In the traditional paper office, file cabinets with file folders and subfile folders form the basic structure. For example, a file cabinet may be set up to contain client material, and each client may have an individual folder with subfiles in that folder for specific items like correspondence and billing information. A large client might have its own file drawer, file cabinet, or even its own file room. A filing structure for electronic files uses the same basic format, but with virtual folders and files.

In a networked computer system, most, if not all files from everyone on the network are filed on the central file server. See Exhibit 4.9 for an example of a typical filing hierarchy. Having a system in place and a standardized procedure for setting up and maintaining files avoids the possibility of a staff member setting up his or her own system, which can result in only that person knowing where documents are filed. Establishing a system can also avoid the duplication of files, in which someone re-created a file to replace one he or she couldn't find.

Setting up and organizing documents in folders is simplified by the use of drop-and-drag tools in applications and software such as ScanSoft PaperPort 14, which shows thumbnails of the documents, as shown in Exhibit 4.10.

Exhibit 4.9 Example of a typical filing hierarchy

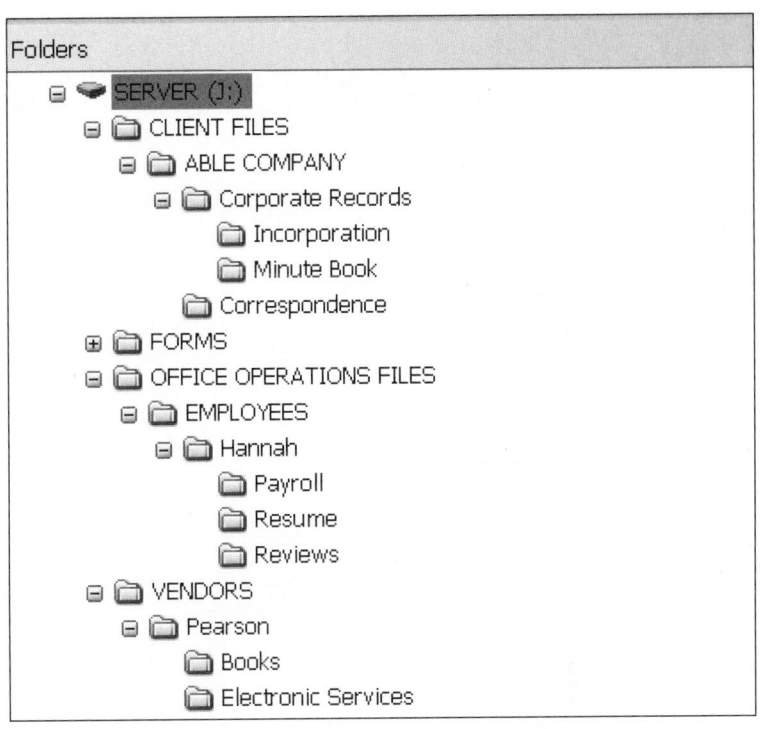

■ SECURITY ISSUES

Access to Files and Folders—Ethical Considerations

Ethical issues must be considered whenever an electronic filing system is designed. Provisions must be made for protecting confidential and privileged documents. Such protection is like locking the file cabinet and restricting the key to only those with a need to have access. Like locking the file cabinet, access to electronic files can be restricted electronically.

It is sometimes necessary in cases of potential conflicts of interest to restrict access to information about a client or a case by building an **ethical wall** around case information. These walls may be needed because of a merger of firms, regulatory requirements, or new hires who have had previous contact with a party or

ethical wall
Restricting access to information or files from those with a potential conflict of interest or who do not have a need to know the client information.

Exhibit 4.10 Thumbnails of documents in Nuance PaperPort 14

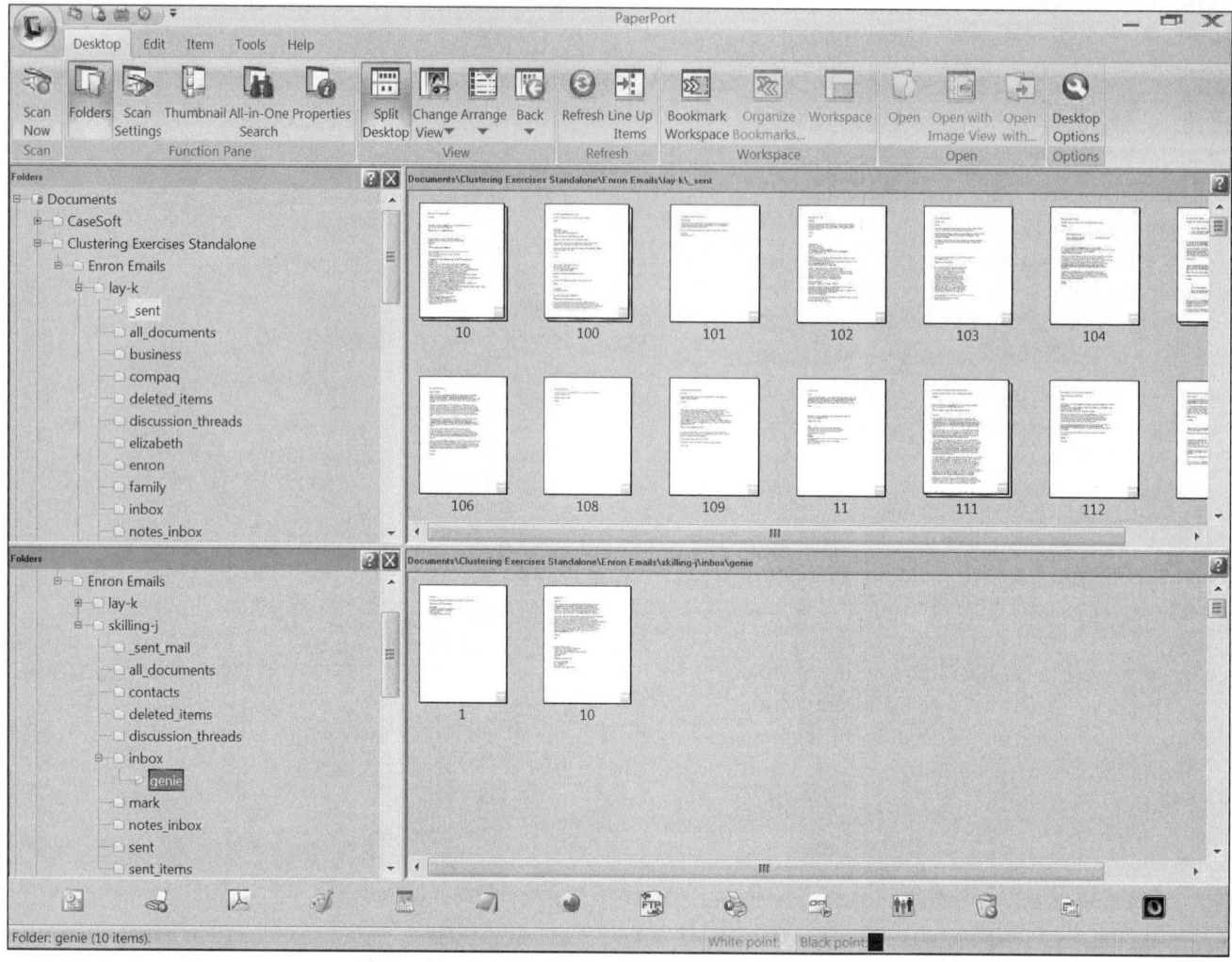

Nuance Communications.

firm with whom the present firm has a potential conflict of interest. An ethical wall on a computer system or network may be created by password protecting access to the restricted files or information.

At the highest level of file protection, only those with the password can open the file. At a lesser security level, others may be able to access the file but not make changes. At the highest level of network protection, access to the entire network may be restricted by password. At a lower level, access may be restricted to only certain features of the network.

The network administrator is the person with the highest level of access to the network and has the ability to add, delete, or change individual users' access rights and permissions to files, folders, and connections on the network. In the law office it must be a person who has the right to see and access everything on the network. In many offices, the network administrator is a member of the IT staff. Similar rights as a network administrator's may also be given to a high-level member of the firm, such as the managing partner.

Another possible security measure is to set up separate file servers for different clients or sensitive cases, with access limited exclusively to those working on the case. In other situations it may be necessary to put an ethical wall around

Exhibit 4.11 Microsoft security features

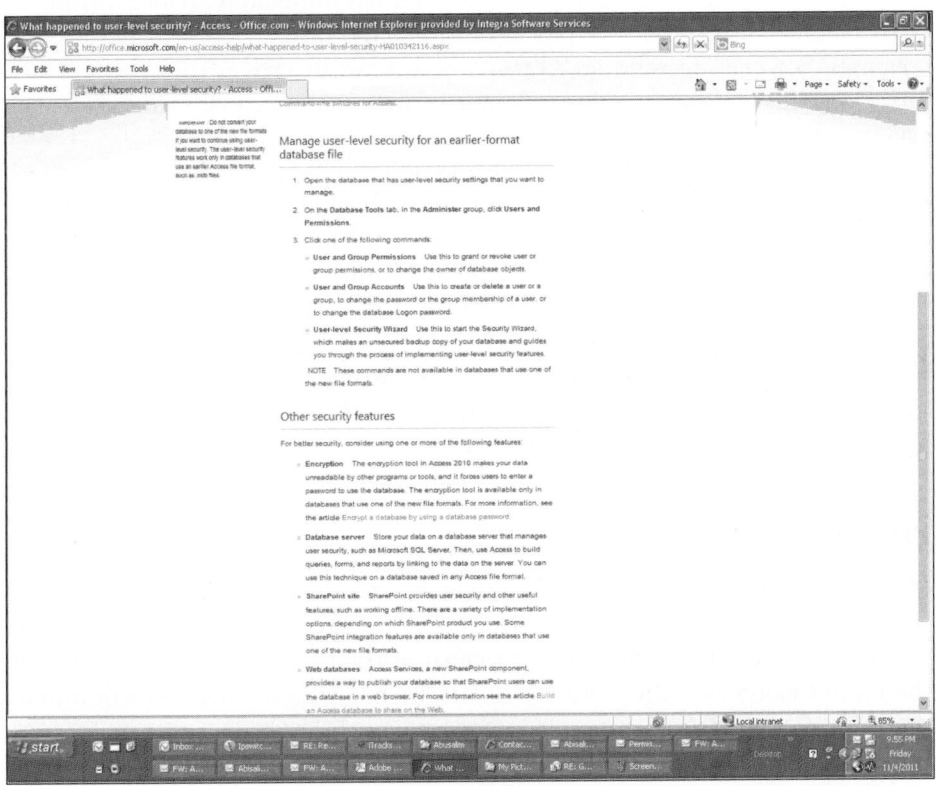

© 2011 Microsoft.

certain folders or files to avoid a conflict of interest, such as a member of the legal team who had previously worked for the opposing party.

Limiting Access to Electronic Files

Security and privacy can be maintained by controlling access, as discussed above. Various programs have different ways of limiting access. Exhibit 4.11 displays the Microsoft Access help menu discussing security features that replace those of earlier versions of Access User-Level Security.

Receiving and Downloading Files and Attachments

When downloading files or attachments to emails, users must first determine the directory, or folder, into which they will be downloading the files. In Windows, this usually is a folder called "My Downloads" or "My Files." If there is no existing folder, a Windows feature called Explorer can be used to create a folder with a name such as "Downloads." Windows Explorer is a program accessed in the Start directory under Programs. Note that Windows Explorer is not the same as Windows Internet Explorer, which is an Internet browser.

Most of the files attached as part of an email will be document files created and saved as either Microsoft Word documents, WordPerfect documents, or PDF documents. The user may want to save these files directly into the client directory. Saving them in the computer download folder is one option, as is immediately opening the file on the screen instead of saving it for later use.

LEARNING OBJECTIVE 4
Describe the issues in downloading and installing software from the Internet.

static files
A file that contains only data.

macros
Small programs that execute software functions when activated.

Normally, text files and graphic images are **static files,** meaning that by themselves, they do not perform any function but are merely usable within another program such as a word processor or graphic image viewer. It has become common, however, to send attachments that have **macros** within them. These mini-programs perform functions when activated, such as those used to calculate sums in spreadsheets.

Some program files have an extension of either ".exe" or ".com." Files with these extensions may run automatically after downloading. Therefore, greater caution must be taken in downloading files with these or other file extensions because they may run automatically upon opening or may contain computer viruses, discussed later in this chapter. Remember that it is not enough to rely on the sender being a reliable source, as even the most reliable source may have had a security breach that allowed a virus to be attached to a file. Or, the source may be forwarding files from other, less reliable sources without checking them first.

Printing

Most items that are displayed on the screen can be sent to a printer attached to a computer. At the top of most web browsers is a printer icon or a Print command in the File selection in the menu or toolbar at the top of the page. Clicking on the printer icon or on the word "Print" in the File pull-down menu will initiate the print process. Patience may be necessary, as the computer may need some time to access the original source of the information. Clicking several times will not speed up the process and actually may result in several copies of the same information being printed.

Sending Files

WEB RESOURCES
Full description and information on types of service available can be found at: http://www.webopedia.com/ quick_ref/internet_connection _types.asp

Some Internet service providers limit the amount of information that may be sent at one time, depending on the speed of the connection or how busy the system is at different times of the day. This may limit the number of pages that may be sent at one time. With increased transmission speed (also referred to as bandwidth) comes the ability to transmit much larger files and more pages at the same time.

Increasingly, large-size graphics files and images such as photographs are sent or attached to emails. The larger files being transmitted require more bandwidth to avoid slowing down the system. Bandwidth may be thought of as a "pipeline" that determines the amount of data that can be sent in a given time period The speed of transmission is usually expressed in "bits per second," with a "bit" being the smallest piece of computer information. "Kbps" means a thousand bits per second, and "Mbps" means a million bits per second.

For example:

dial-up access
Uses a modem connected to a PC to connect to the Internet by dialing a phone number.

ISDN
Integrated services digital network, uses digital telephone lines.

Digital subscriber line (DSL)
A line that is always connected using existing telephone lines.

Dial-up access—uses a modem connected to a PC to connect to the Internet by dialing a phone number provided by the Internet service provider. Typical dial-up connection speeds range from 2400 bps to 56 Kbps.
ISDN (integrated services digital network)—uses digital telephone lines or normal telephone wires to transmit typically at 64 Kbps to 128 Kbps.
DSL (digital subscriber line)—is always connected using existing telephone lines.

ADSL (asymmetric digital subscriber line)—is the most common type of DSL. Typical speeds range from 1.5 to 9 Mbps for downloading (receiving) data, and 16 to 640 Kbps when uploading (sending) data.

Cable—uses a modem that operates over cable TV lines. Typical cable speeds range from 6 Mbps to 50 Mbps download and 1 Mbps to 10 Mbps uploads.

cable
Operates over cable TV lines.

T-1 lines (T for terrestrial, as opposed to satellite)—are leased, dedicated phone connections. A typical speed is 1.544 Mbps.

Satellite or Internet over Satellite (IoS)—allows a user to access the Internet via a satellite. Typical Internet over satellite connection speeds range from 492 to 512 Kbps.

FIOS (fiber-optic service)—uses a dedicated fiber-optic connection, with typical speeds for home use of up to 50 Mbps download speed and 20–25 Mbps upload speed.

As with any pipeline, only a limited amount of product can be transmitted at any one time. To more equitably share the limited pipeline, ISPs and network operators may, during peak usage times, temporarily limit the number of files or the size of files that one user may transmit. In some offices, the same limitations may be imposed to overcome file size limits. Files may be transmitted in a compressed format, frequently referred to as **ZIP files,** in which large files are run through a program that compresses them before they are sent. The recipient of the compressed file then must uncompress the file before being able to read it.

A number of programs are available to compress and decompress files. Some of these require several manual steps, and other programs perform the task automatically. For occasional use, the manual method is acceptable, but with the increasing number of compressed files, it may be more time-efficient to purchase one of the automatic programs. Limited time-trial versions of some of these decompression programs may be downloaded without charge over the Internet from software companies who encourage users to buy the full version. One of the most widely used zip/unzip programs is WinZip. WinZip provides an extensive Help menu for learning and using the program and a wizard to walk the user through the process, as shown in Exhibit 4.12.

ZIP file
An open standard for compression and decompression used widely for PC download archives. ZIP is used on Windows-based programs such as WinZip and Drag and Zip. The file extension given to ZIP files is .zip.

WEB RESOURCES

Download an evaluation copy of WinZip from the Technology Resources Website at http://www.pearsonhighered.com/goldman/.

Exhibit 4.12 WinZip

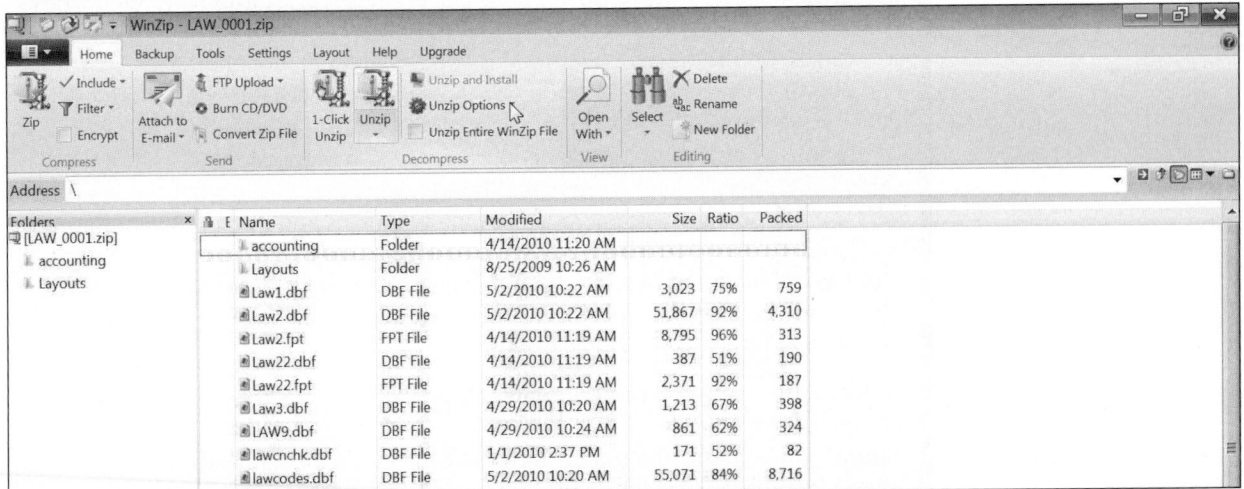

ETHICAL Perspectives

LETTER TO ETHICS BOARD CONCERNING ATTORNEYS' USE OF PRETEXTING

February 21, 2006

Re: Ethical Concerns Regarding Attorneys' Use of Private Investigators and Pretexting

Dear State Bar Ethics Committee:

We are writing on behalf of the Electronic Privacy Information Center (EPIC). EPIC is a not-for-profit research center that focuses on promoting personal privacy.

In July 2005, EPIC began a campaign to end the practice of "pretexting."[1] Pretexting is the use of impersonation or fraud to trick another person into releasing personal information. Through pretexting, online data brokers and investigators offer to obtain private calling records, the identities of individuals who use dating services, and the identities of people who use P.O. Boxes. Many of these services are advertised online for any member of the public to buy data on others.

EPIC identified dozens of websites that offered to obtain personal information through pretexting, and submitted a list of 40 such sites to the Federal Trade Commission for investigation.[2] We also petitioned the Federal Communications Commission to protect individuals' phone records from pretexting.[3]

In the course of investigating pretexting, it has become increasingly clear that attorneys are major consumers of pretexting services. In this letter, we request that appropriate action be taken to ensure that attorneys in your state are not employing investigators or other companies to engage in pretexting or other fraud. We believe that pretexting is incompatible with ABA Model Rules 1.2, 3.4, 4.1, 4.4, and 8.4. We provide documentation below of the mounting evidence showing that attorneys are purchasing the services of pretexters, and urge you to take action to prevent attorneys from using pretexting services.

Attorneys Are Purchasing Private Records Through Pretexting

There is mounting evidence that attorneys are top consumers of pretexting services that acquire private records through impersonation, fraud, or false pretenses. In fact, the operators of these sites offering records claim that attorneys are employing their services:

In an e-mail sent to the Tribune, the manager of one of the Web sites—www .abika.com—defended the business as a legitimate investigative tool for people trying to make sense of their personal lives or track down someone who owes them money. The site recently stopped selling cell phone records, wrote Jay Patel, whose business is registered in Wyoming.

Patel's Web site even contended it could deliver the location from which cell phone calls were being made. Wireless phone companies can produce that data through federally mandated GPS technology that most cell phones have.

"Spouses, girlfriends and boyfriends use it to review and understand their significant others," Patel wrote. "Bail bond agents use it to locate fugitives, lawyers use it for their investigations to locate witnesses and other relevant info."

Noah Wieder, president of www.bestpeoplesearch.com, said he hired former law enforcement officials to collect cell phone records for his customers, mostly private investigators and the occasional doubting spouse referred to him by a lawyer.[4]

A story in the National Law Journal focused directly on attorneys' purchase of phone records:

Attorneys are among the top customers of the controversial Web sites [selling phone records acquired through pretexting], according to private investigators, privacy advocates and Web site operators who sell the phone records.

"Let's put it this way, the legal profession is keeping it alive," said Rob Douglas, a former private eye turned security consultant who has helped the Federal Trade Commission (FTC) investigate and prosecute online operators that sell phone records.

"I've investigated them with the federal government and in private lawsuits…and in every single case, the overwhelming majority of users of these companies are attorneys," Douglas said.

These attorneys include divorce lawyers, who want to know who feuding spouses are talking to; business lawyers, who want to know who their clients' competitors are talking to; and employment lawyers, who want to know if employees are selling any trade secrets.

[…]

Given all the controversy surrounding the sale of cellphone records, attorneys were reluctant to comment on the subject. Of the more than a dozen divorce, business and criminal defense attorneys contacted for this story, none said they used the tactic. Most wouldn't even talk about the subject. One lawyer said, "Good luck finding anyone to admit to it."[5]

These revelations concerning attorneys hiring private investigators to perform illegal services comes at the same time that the government has levied a 110-count indictment against a Los Angeles investigator who worked for many attorneys. Anthony Pellicano and six others were accused earlier this month of conspiracy and blackmail in a case where the investigator obtained private records in the course of litigation:

The 110-count federal indictment outlines a complicated web of payoffs to police, high-tech eavesdropping and other skullduggery. Prosecutors allege that Pellicano scoured confidential communications and law enforcement databases for scandalous details that would scare off lawsuits or provide his clients with the upper hand in courtroom battles.

[…]

Although no lawyers or marquee Hollywood celebrities were named, the indictment alleges that Pellicano and his clients used the information to secure "a tactical advantage in litigation by learning their opponents' plans, strategies, perceived strengths and weaknesses, settlement positions and other confidential information."

[…]

The indictment describes Pellicano as the conspiracy's organizer and leader and charges that the trio used wiretaps, protected computers, bribery, identity theft and obstruction to further the Hollywood private eye's reputation and ongoing relationship with "lucrative clients, including entertainment celebrities and executives, attorneys and law firms."[6]

Last week, a California attorney was indicted for allegedly hiring Pellicano to place wiretaps.[7]

Attorneys' Use of Pretexting Through Agents is Unethical

We believe that attorneys who hire investigators or other companies to engage in pretexting violate ethical norms. Attorneys have a duty to be zealous advocates of their clients, but must operate within the bounds of the law.[8] An attorney cannot hire others to operate outside the bounds of the law, and we believe that this practice of hiring pretexters or counseling clients to hire them implicates ABA Model Rules 1.2, 3.4, 4.1, 4.4, and 8.4. We accordingly urge your ethics committee to review the attorneys' use of pretexting under applicable state versions of these model ethical rules.

(continued)

Model Rule 1.2 prohibits attorneys from advising their clients to engage in fraudulent behavior:

(d) A lawyer shall not counsel a client to engage, or assist a client, in conduct that the lawyer knows is criminal or fraudulent, but a lawyer may discuss the legal consequences of any proposed course of conduct with a client and may counsel or assist a client to make a good faith effort to determine the validity, scope, meaning or application of the law.

Model Rule 3.4 specifies that attorneys shall not perpetuate fraud:

[...]

(b) A lawyer who represents a client in an adjudicative proceeding and who knows that a person intends to engage, is engaging or has engaged in criminal or fraudulent conduct related to the proceeding shall take reasonable remedial measures, including, if necessary, disclosure to the tribunal.

Model Rule 4.1 bars attorneys from lying to others in the course of representation: In the course of representing a client a lawyer shall not knowingly:

(a) make a false statement of material fact or law to a third person;

Model Rule 4.4 prohibits attorneys from gaining evidence in a way that violates the rights of another:

(a) In representing a client, a lawyer shall not use means that have no substantial purpose other than to embarrass, delay, or burden a third person, or use methods of obtaining evidence that violate the legal rights of such a person.

Finally, Model Rule 8.4 prohibits a wide range of behavior related to misrepresentation and fraud, and bars attorneys from hiring agents to engage in unethical practices:

It is professional misconduct for a lawyer to:

(a) violate or attempt to violate the Rules of Professional Conduct, knowingly assist or induce another to do so, or do so through the acts of another;

(b) commit a criminal act that reflects adversely on the lawyer's honesty, trustworthiness or fitness as a lawyer in other respects;

(c) engage in conduct involving dishonesty, fraud, deceit or misrepresentation;

State Ethical Boards Must Take Action to Protect the Integrity of the Profession

We urge you to take action to review these practices under the ethical rules of your state. Pretexting involves using fraud to trick a company into releasing private personal information. We believe that hiring investigators or other services to engage in pretexting implicates ABA Model Rules 1.2, 3.4, 4.1, 4.4, and 8.4. We urge you to analyze the practice of pretexting under the ethical rules in force in your State.

We realize that attorneys may [be] unwitting participants in this practice. They may hire investigators to locate witnesses or perform other functions without being aware that pretexting was being employed. Accordingly, issuing an advisory opinion or highlighting this issue in communications to members of the Bar may be appropriate action to addressing use of pretexting.

Sincerely,

Chris Jay Hoofnagle
Director
Electronic Privacy Information Center West Coast Office
944 Market St. #709
San Francisco, CA 94102
415-981-6400
Hoofnagle@epic.org

[1] EPIC maintains an archive on pretexting online at http://epic.org/privacy/iei/.

[2] In re Intelligent E-Commerce, Inc, Jul. 8, 2005, available at http://epic.org/privacy/iei/ftccomplaint.html.

[3] Petition of EPIC for Enhanced Security and Authentication Standards, In re Implementation of the Telecommunications Act of 1996, CC Docket No. 96-115, available at http://www.epic.org/privacy/iei/cpnipet.html.

[4] Aamer Madhani and Liam Ford, Brokers of phone records targeted Illinois files suit, joins fight to bar practice, Chicago Tribune, Jan. 21, 2006, available at http://www.chicagotribune.com/news/nationworld/chi-0601210074jan21,1,6840972.story?coll=chi-newsnationworld-hed&ctrack=1&cset=true.

[5] Tresa Baldas, Who surfs for cell records? Lawyers, National Law Journal, Feb. 2, 2006, available at http://www.law.com/jsp/nlj/PubArticleNLJ.jsp?id=1138874715046. See also, Matt Richtel & Ken Belson, House Panel to Press Cellphone Industry on Improving Protection of Customer Records, New York Times, Feb. 1, 2006, available at http://www.nytimes.com/2006/02/01/technology/01cell.html; Dave Gussow, Verizon lawsuit says phony callers are committing fraud, St. Petersburg Times, Jan. 30, 2006, available at http://www.sptimes.com/2006/01/30/Technology/Verizon_lawsuit_says_.shtml.

[6] Greg Krikorian and Andrew Blankstein, Pellicano and 6 Others Are Indicted, Los Angeles Times, Feb. 7, 2006, available at http://www.latimes.com/news/local/la-me-pellicano7feb07,0,5599372.story?coll=la-home-headlines.

[7] Greg Risling, Kerkorian attorney indicted in Hollywood wiretapping scandal, San Francisco Chronicle, Feb. 16, 2006, available at http://sfgate.com/cgi-bin/article.cgi?f=/n/a/2006/02/15/state/n133146S99.DTL.

[8] ABA Model Rule, Preamble at ¶9.

EPIC Privacy Page | EPIC Home Page

Last Updated: February 21, 2006
Page URL: http://www.epic.org/privacy/iei/attyltr22106.html

WEB RESOURCES

Read the entire report of the disciplinary action at http://www.state.wv.us/wvsca/docs/Spring08/33256.htm.

IN THE WORDS OF THE COURT...

Supreme Court of Appeals of West Virginia

January 2008 Term

No. 33256

LAWYER DISCIPLINARY BOARD, *Petitioner v. Michael P. Markins*, A MEMBER OF THE WEST VIRGINIA STATE BAR, Respondent

LAWYER DISCIPLINARY PROCEEDING TWO-YEAR SUSPENSION, WITH ADDITIONAL SANCTIONS

Submitted: April 1, 2008

Filed: May 23, 2008

The Opinion of the Court was delivered PER CURIAM. SYLLABUS BY THE COURT

(1) "A *de novo* standard applies to a review of the adjudicatory record made before the [Lawyer Disciplinary Board] as to questions of law, questions of application of the law to the facts, and questions of appropriate

(continued)

WEB RESOURCES

Contrast and compare Rule 8.4 **of the West Virginia State Bar** at http://www.wvbar.org/BARINFO/rulesprofconduct/rules8.htm with the American Bar Association Model Rules of Professional Conduct at http://www.abanet.org/cpr/mrpc/mrpc_toc.html, and the ethical rule in your jurisdiction.

sanctions; this Court gives respectful consideration to the [Board's] recommendations while ultimately exercising its own independent judgment. On the other hand, substantial deference is given to the [Board's] findings of fact, unless such findings are not supported by reliable, probative, and substantial evidence on the whole record." Syl. Pt. 3, *Committee on Legal Ethics v. McCorkle,* 192 W.Va. 286, 452 S.E.2d 377 (1994).

(2) "This Court is the final arbiter of legal ethics problems and must make the ultimate decisions about public reprimands, suspensions or annulments of attorneys' licenses to practice law." Syl. Pt. 3, *Committee on Legal Ethics v. Blair,* 174 W.Va. 494, 327 S.E.2d 671 (1984).

(3) "'"'In deciding on the appropriate disciplinary action for ethical violations, this Court must consider not only what steps would appropriately punish the respondent attorney, but also whether the discipline imposed is adequate to serve as an effective deterrent to other members of the Bar and at the same time restore public confidence in the ethical standards of the legal profession.' Syllabus point 3, *Committee on Legal Ethics v. Walker,* 178 W.Va. 150, 358 S.E.2d 234 (1987)." Syl. Pt. 5, *Committee on Legal Ethics v. Roark,* 181 W.Va. 260, 382 S.E.2d 313 (1989).' Syllabus point 7, *Office of Lawyer Disciplinary Counsel v. Jordan,* 204 W.Va. 495, 513 S.E.2d 722 (1998)." Syl. Pt. 4, *Lawyer Disciplinary Bd. v. Wade,* 217 W.Va. 58, 614 S.E.2d 705 (2005).

(4) "'Rule 3.16. of the West Virginia Rules of Lawyer Disciplinary Procedure enumerates factors to be considered in imposing sanctions and provides as follows: "In imposing a sanction after a finding of lawyer misconduct, unless otherwise provided in these rules, the Court [West Virginia Supreme Court of Appeals] or Board [Lawyer Disciplinary Board] shall consider the following factors: (1) whether the lawyer has violated a duty owed to a client, to the public, to the legal system or to the profession; (2) whether the lawyer acted intentionally, knowingly or negligently; (3) the amount of the actual or potential injury caused by the lawyer's misconduct; and (4) the existence of any aggravating or mitigating factors.'" Syl. pt. 4, *Office of Lawyer Disciplinary Counsel v. Jordan,* 204 W.Va. 495, 513 S.E.2d 722 (1998)." Syl. Pt. 2, *Lawyer Disciplinary Bd. v. Lakin,* 217 W.Va. 134, 617 S.E.2d 484 (2005).

...Finally, we recognize that with the widespread use of computer e-mail as an important method of communication between and among attorneys and their clients come the potentiality that the communication might be improperly infiltrated. This Court does not take lightly the fact that, in this case, it was an attorney who repeatedly accessed the confidential e-mails of other attorneys without their knowledge or permission. Thus, the imposition of a suitable sanction in a case such as this is not exclusively dictated by what sanction would appropriately punish the offending attorney,...but, just as importantly, this Court must ensure that the discipline imposed adequately serve[s] as an effective deterrent to other attorneys,..."to protect the public, to reassure it as to the reliability and integrity of attorneys and to safeguard its interest in the administration of justice." *Battistelli,* 206 W.Va. at 201, 523 S.E.2d at 261, quoting *Lawyer Disciplinary Board v. Taylor,* 192 W.Va. at 144, 451 S.E.2d at 445. Accordingly, based upon the foregoing, we are compelled to adopt the recommendation of discipline tendered by the Board.

IV. Conclusion

For the reasons stated above, we adopt the Board's recommendations and hereby impose the following sanctions upon Respondent:

(1) Respondent is suspended from the practice of law in West Virginia for a period of two years; (2) upon reinstatement, Respondent's private practice shall be supervised for a period of one year; (3) Respondent is ordered to complete twelve hours of CLE in ethics in addition to such ethics hours he is otherwise required to complete to maintain his active license to practice, said additional twelve hours to be completed before he is reinstated; and (4) Respondent is ordered to pay the costs of these proceedings.

License suspended, with additional sanctions.

ETHICAL Perspectives

WEST VIRGINIA STATE BAR
Rule 8.4. Misconduct.

It is professional misconduct for a lawyer to:

(a) violate or attempt to violate the Rules of Professional Conduct, knowingly assist or induce another to do so, or do so through the acts of another;
(b) commit a criminal act that reflects adversely on the lawyer's honesty, trustworthiness or fitness as a lawyer in other respects;
(c) engage in conduct involving dishonesty, fraud, deceit or misrepresentation;
(d) engage in conduct that is prejudicial to the administration of justice;
(e) state or imply an ability to influence improperly a government agency or official;
(f) knowingly assist a judge or judicial officer in conduct that is a violation of applicable rules of judicial conduct or other law; or
(g) have sexual relations with a client whom the lawyer personally represents during the legal representation unless a consensual sexual relationship existed between them at the commencement of the lawyer/client relationship. For purposes of this rule, "sexual relations" means sexual intercourse or any touching of the sexual or other intimate parts of a client or causing such client to touch the sexual or other intimate parts of the lawyer for the purpose of arousing or gratifying the sexual desire of either party or as a means of abuse. (Amended by order entered July 12, 1995, effective September 1, 1995.)

Email Archiving

Email archiving is the continuous saving of emails to a specified file. Traditional computer backups save only what is on the computer at the time of the backup. Archiving ensures that data is not lost between backups. An archiving of emails saves every incoming and outgoing message in a separate folder. In some industries, clients are required by federal or state law to preserve all records, including emails, for a period of time. Initial archiving software was a response to the requirements of such laws as the Sarbanes-Oxley Act, the Securities and Exchange Commission rule on electronic storage, and the Health Insurance Portability and Accountability Act (HIPAA), which in some cases requires archiving of emails for two years following the death of a patient.

email archiving
The continuous saving of email data.

The rules of confidentiality and privilege must be maintained with respect to all client emails. However, in claims of malpractice against a law firm, emails may provide a defense. If a client makes such a claim against the firm, the firm may be released from the ethical duty of confidentiality and attorney–client privilege in order to defend itself. In these cases, an archive of properly kept emails may be a source of evidence for the defense.

ADVICE FROM THE FIELD

E-MAIL ARCHIVING FOR DUMMIES

Foreward

What's in That E-mail and Why Does It Matter?
By Laura Dubois, Research Director, Storage Software IDC

Today's businesses are focused on managing valuable information while at the same time mitigating potential risk from it. Corporate information needs to be protected from compromise, retained according to regulatory requirements, and be available in the event of audits or legal discovery or for general business use. The pervasiveness of e-mail in today's corporate environment to communicate and conduct business continues to fuel e-mail growth. However, today's businesses must be able to manage e-mail growth while satisfying requirements for e-mail availability, retention, and content-oriented retrieval. Content-oriented retrieval is of particular relevance in regulatory audits or electronic discovery, in which e-mails associated with a particular keyword or relevant to a specific topic are frequently sought. E-mail archiving applications and solutions address both of these technical and business requirements.

E-mail archiving applications provide an automated and efficient way of storing, indexing, and retrieving individual e-mail messages and file attachments in real time by individual users, IT staff, and other authorized parties from both inside and outside the firm. E-mail archiving differs from backup and retrieval solutions in that the latter are designed only to provide regularly scheduled copies of an e-mail server or disk. Backup and retrieval solutions enable e-mail to be brought back up and running after an e-mail server or disk fails, but these solutions don't maintain copies of e-mails exchanged between backups, retain copies of e-mails deleted by users after the backup is replaced with a newer one, or move e-mail content off primary e-mail servers to more efficient storage systems. Today's e-mail archiving applications, on the other hand, are designed to handle these tasks, and can be delivered as an on-premises software solution, preinstalled on an appliance, or as a hosted service.

According to IDC, the e-mail archiving applications market was a $477 million market in 2006, realizing 45 percent growth over 2005. The e-mail archiving applications market continues to be fueled by litigation and electronic discovery, regulatory requirements for record retention, as well as overall mailbox management. In comparison, the overall IT industry has been hovering around 5 percent growth year over year. The phenomenal growth of e-mail archiving applications is driven by electronic discovery, in particular by amendments to the Federal Rules of Civil Procedure, regulatory compliance, and the overall need for storage and e-mail application performance optimization.

Because e-mail users tend to express themselves in an informal manner, and because metadata is associated with email, these communications are often sought during the discovery phase of corporate litigation. E-mail archiving solutions can help companies more quickly find relevant e-mail and reduce the cost of electronic discovery. Regulations in different industries may stipulate that related content contained in electronic records be retained for specified time periods or outline rules to secure the privacy, security, and lack of compromise to sensitive information. E-mail archiving supports records retention requirements and also enables content indexing for easy search and retrieval of relevant messages and attachments based on audit requests. In addition, e-mail archiving can be used to manage mailbox size by regularly archiving older or infrequently accessed data. Archiving saves space by moving messages from the email server into an archive repository, thus improving performance while giving users access to their archived e-mail.

E-mail is a core component of business communications today, and firms need to ensure that they have adequate controls in place to protect, retain, and preserve relevant e-mail content. With the volume of e-mail increasing annually, firms also need to find a way to manage growth with relatively flat budgets and limited IT administration. Today's e-mail archiving applications provide a solution to meet these legal, regulatory, and business needs. Through e-mail archiving, companies have an automated and efficient way to store, index, and retrieve individual e-mail messages and file attachments by individual users, IT staff, and other authorized parties.

Obtaining Software on the Internet

WEB RESOURCES
For a more detailed description of metadata, see http://en.wikipedia.org/wiki/Metadata#Types_of_metadata

Software may be purchased locally, by mail order, or from an Internet source in the cloud. Many software vendors sell their software directly from their Internet websites in immediately downloadable form or on a CD mailed to the buyer. One advantage of the downloadable version is immediate delivery.

Downloading software can be a simple operation. The user may select the option to download and, after payment with a credit card, the software is downloaded to a computer over the Internet. The software usually allows the recipient to designate where on the user's computer the software file should be downloaded—in a particular folder or on a specific disk drive. As with e-mail attachments, the software will be downloaded to a default location, or to a location designated by the user. The program files are usually not in usable form, but must still be installed on the computer. One of the options in a download manager is to launch the software. Prudent practice is to make a backup copy of the program before installing it.

Download Issues

Enough Memory for the Program. Does the computer have enough random access memory (RAM) to run the program as well as the other programs normally opened and used at the same time?

Speed of the Internet Connection. If large numbers of documents or graphic-intense files or programs are to be downloaded from another location over the Internet, is the Internet connection fast enough to accomplish the job in a reasonable period of time?

Continual Connection. Downloading long documents may take time. If the connection is interrupted or terminated, the download may have to be started over.

Firewalls. Firewalls are installed to prevent unauthorized access to computer systems and networks. In some cases they are set up to block everything that is not preauthorized or not recognized as coming from an allowed source. This type of firewall restriction is like the parental blocking of undesirable Internet content.

Trusted Sources. Downloading anything from a website has dangers. The document or program may have intended or unintended viruses, Trojan horses, or other spyware attached or embedded within it. Downloading from strangers only increases the potential for problems. Downloading from a trusted site may not eliminate the potential for problems, but it does minimize the risk. For example, viruses may be attached to a document from a trusted site, like that of another law firm. Although they may be trustworthy persons, someone may have sent a virus to them, and they may not have checked their incoming documents for viruses and other problems.

metadata
Information about a particular data set, which may describe, for example, how, when, and by whom it was received, created, accessed, and/or modified, and how it is formatted.

system metadata
The data such as file names, size, and location.

■ METADATA

Metadata is "data about data." Every electronic document has information about that document attached to the electronic file. Metadata is the information about the document, such as who created it; the date it was created, modified, or accessed; and other information related to its existence and location.

Metadata is divided into two types: the **system metadata,** and the **content metadata.** The system metadata is used to track or locate the file containing the data, such as the file name, size, and location. Content metadata is about the

LEARNING OBJECTIVE 5
Define metadata.

content metadata
Information about the contents of a document.

content of the file itself, such as the name of the author of the document, any tracked changes, and the document version.

Each time a file is sent as an email or an attachment to an email, metadata is part of the transmission. The recipient can often see the content metadata by selecting the "properties" function in the application used to view the documents, such as Word or WordPerfect.

ADVICE FROM THE FIELD

PRODUCING METADATA IN E-DISCOVERY—WHAT YOU NEED TO KNOW
By Leonard Deutchman and Brian Wolfinger

As e-discovery requests and productions increase exponentially, many of those requests will, implicitly or explicitly, seek the production of metadata. This article will help you understand metadata production by discussing what "metadata" is, how to preserve and gather metadata, what form of production e-discovery with metadata should take, and issues regarding its production. By understanding the technical and legal issues regarding metadata, you can diminish the occasions upon which you will have to produce metadata and insure that when it is produced it is done so properly.

What is Metadata?

The Committee Note to amended F.R.Civ.P. 26(f) defines "metadata" as "information describing the history, tracking, or management of an electronic document." In the influential opinion, *Williams v. Sprint,* 230 F.R.D. 640, 646-647 (D. Kan. 2005), the court cited with favor the description of metadata in The Sedona Guidelines (The Sedona Conference Working Group Series, Sept. 2005 Version) as "information about a particular data set which describes how, when and by whom it was collected, created, accessed, or modified and how it is formatted (including data demographics such as size, location, storage requirements and media information.)" The Sedona Guidelines noted that metadata included "all of the contextual, processing, and use information needed to identify and certify the scope, authenticity, and integrity of active or archival electronic information or records."

File- and Application-Level Metadata

It is important to distinguish between two types of metadata a file could have associated to it, "File-Level" metadata ("FLM") and "Application-Level" metadata ("ALM"). All files have FLM, while certain files, such as Microsoft Word documents, Excel spreadsheets, etc. will have both. While there are some exceptions, FLM is generally stored separately from where the actual file content is stored on a hard drive, while ALM is commingled with the file content.

"File-Level" Metadata

"File-level" (or "file system") metadata about a computer file may include its size, the date/time of its creation or modification, if it is able to be written to further (as opposed to being read-only) and other information. File-level metadata is created by the computer's file system and changed due to end-user interactions with the file on that computer. Some FLM file attributes include Last Modified, Last Accessed and Creation dates and times ("MAC times"), File Physical and Logical Size, File Name and File Path.

Different user or system actions will "trip" the MAC times, causing them to be updated. Opening a new MS Office document, typing something and then saving the file to a disk or server will stamp the Created attribute with the date/time of this first save, and the Accessed and Modified attributes will show the same, since the user did all of these things to the file. On the other hand, when files are transferred between drive volumes and/or between pieces of computer media (i.e., saved from one location to another without modification) the Created date of the file is normally changed to reflect the time of the creation of the copy, but the Modified date will remain the same. This will often result in the counterintuitive situation of having file-level metadata that shows a file was modified before it was created.

"Application-Level" Metadata

In addition to FLM, certain files contain "Application-Level" metadata, that is, additional metadata within themselves. Microsoft Office documents such as PowerPoint, Excel, and Word have ALM, as do other files such as PDF files. The following is a list of some ALM file attributes that are tracked by Microsoft Office: Track changes, comments and deleted text; Author—assigned during installation of the application software (e.g., Microsoft Office) on the computer; Company—same type of value as Author, assigned during installation of the software; Revision Number—a count of every instance where the file was opened, edited and saved; Creation date and time—the

Date/Time a document was first saved by a user with the stored value in the "Author" field; and, Last Save date and time—the Date/Time a document was last saved by a user with the stored value in the "Last Author" field.

Data Gathering to Preserve Metadata

As the discussion above about copying files to other media makes clear, if data is not gathered properly, metadata such as the dates of file creation, last access and last modification can be changed. If that happens, you simply cannot produce accurate metadata.

Forensic data gathering avoids this problem by gathering all data initially and exactly as it was on the media imaged. Even if only a handful of files are sought from a hard drive, for example, an exact, "bit stream" image of the hard drive should be made and, later, forensically searched. The image would be verified by submitting both it and the original to a complex algorithm to generate identical "hash values." Bit stream imaging with hash value verification is the standard practice of law enforcement and widely accepted by peer groups and courts as scientifically reliable.

Forensic data gathering through a vendor is more expensive than in-house copying of files by the client. However, if metadata must be produced, the data has to be gathered properly, period.

So, what do you do if you are handed some DVDs produced by the client, you have no idea how the data was copied to the DVDs and you have to produce file creation and last accessed and modified dates? You must make clear that you cannot do that—that is, your firm cannot discharge its discovery duties—unless the data is properly collected.

This will not make you the most popular person at the firm, but you will be doing your job properly.

The Form of Production

Form of production will dictate access to metadata. If you produce the data in TIFF or PDF form, the only access to any metadata will be what is found in the fields for each record in the database. If, however, the data is produced with a link to the file in its native form, then the user, i.e. your opponent, can view the metadata as found in the file....

Leonard Deutchman, Esquire is General Counsel and Managing Partner, and Brian Wolfinger, CIFI is Vice President of Electronic Discovery and Forensic Services LegisDiscovery, LLC, a firm based in Fort Washington, PA and McLean, VA that specializes in electronic digital discovery and digital forensics. You may contact them at ldeutchman@legisdiscovery.com and bwolfinger@ legisdiscovery.com.

The full article originally appeared in May/July 2007 • *Litigation Support TODAY.*

Reprinted with permission from Litigation Support Today magazine.

■ LIST SERVES

List serves, or "list servs," are, according to webopedia (www.webopedia.com):

> An automatic mailing list server developed by Eric Thomas for BITNET in 1986. When e-mail is addressed to a LISTSERV mailing list, it is automatically broadcast to everyone on the list. The result is similar to a newsgroup or forum, except that the messages are transmitted as e-mail and are therefore available only to individuals on the list.
>
> LISTSERV is currently a commercial product marketed by L-Soft International. Although LISTSERV refers to a specific mailing list server, the term is sometimes used incorrectly to refer to any mailing list server. Another popular mailing list server is Majordomo, which is freeware.

The Internet has spawned the creation of communities of people with common interests who use the Internet to exchange information. There are list serves for most of the sections of the American Bar Association, the American Trial Lawyers Association, and many other special interest groups. Some list serves have guidelines for the content of the postings Some of these groups are moderated by list managers, who screen the postings to be sure they comply with the guidelines of the list. Some list serves have no limitation on what is posted other than the list members' own sense of propriety.

The ABA hosts over 1,900 email lists for both discussion and broadcast distribution. Subscription to the majority of these is a benefit of ABA/Section Membership.

LEARNING OBJECTIVE 6
Explain the role of list serves and the etiquette in using them.

list serves
An automatic mailing list, usually for specific topics.

CONCEPT REVIEW AND REINFORCEMENT

KEY TERMS

attachment   92

browser   88

cable   97

content metadata   105

dial-up access   96

digital subscriber line
  (DSL)   96

domain nomenclature   89

e-mail archiving   103

ethical wall   93

hub   84

Internet   90

Internet backbone   82

Internet browser   87

Internet service provider
  (ISP)   82

IP   85

ISDN   96

list serves (list servs)   107

logical address   85

macro   96

mailbox   92

media access control (MAC)
  address   85

metadata   105

modem   82

networked   90

physical address   85

router   84

specialized search
  engines   88

static files   96

switch   84

system metadata   105

type-ahead feature   91

URL (uniform resource
  locator)   89

World Wide Web   90

ZIP file   97

CHAPTER SUMMARY

Introduction to the Internet	A group of computers linked together with the added ability to search all the connections for information: a network of networks.
Internet Fundamentals	*Internet backbone:* The highest-level connection. *ISP:* Internet service providers, who provide access to the Internet at a local level for users. *Modem:* A device that translates electrical signals so computers can communicate over public connections like telephone, cable, and satellites. *Hubs:* Devices for sharing signals in a local network. *Switch:* A high-efficiency hub. May also include software that allows it to act as a modem and router. *Router:* Software and computerized devices that translate Internet addresses and route signals by translating IP addresses into MAC addresses using a look-up table of the conversions. *Computer and Internet addresses:* Each computerized device has an address for use in getting messages, referred to as the logical address. *Media access control:* Each computerized device has an imbedded address called a MAC address, referred to as the physical address. *Internet protocol:* Each computerized device is assigned an Internet protocol (IP) address when it accesses the Internet. *Domain name service:* Translates the numbers of an IP address into more familiar word names. *Internet browsers:* Software programs that allow a person to use a computer to access the Internet. *Uniform resource locator (URL):* The Internet equivalent of a phone number that identifies the protocol used, the computer, and the extension called the domain nomenclature.

The Cloud and the Internet	Local networks are searched with Windows Explorer. The Internet is searched with Internet browsers.
Electronic Communication	Electronic communication that raises issues of confidentiality and privilege for the legal team.
Type-Ahead Feature	A feature of email that anticipates the desired remaining letters based on entries in an address book. May result in the wrong party receiving confidential information. Email is received and stored in an electronic mailbox. The number of items is determined by the available memory. A popular method for transmitting text files and graphic images is by attachment of the file to an email.
Receiving and Downloading Files and Attachments	Users must first determine the directory (folder) into which they will be downloading these files. Most of the files attached as part of email will be document files created and saved as either Microsoft Word documents or WordPerfect documents.
Printing	Most of the items that are displayed can be printed by a printer attached to a computer.
Sending Files	Some Internet service providers (ISPs) limit the amount of information that may be sent at one time. A number of programs are available to compress and decompress files.
Email Archiving	A traditional email backup would not capture the emails received and deleted between the backups.
Obtaining Software on the Internet	Software may be obtained and downloaded over the Internet.
Download Issues	1. Having enough memory for the program. 2. Speed of the connection will determine how long it takes to download. Large files may take a long time with a slow connection. 3. Interruption in connection will require a restart of the download. 4. Will the firewall allow the download to come into the network? 5. Is it from a trusted source?
Metadata	Data about data. Information about a document attached to the electronic file. Resource or system metadata is used to track or locate the file containing the data such as file names, size, and location. Content metadata is in the file itself such as who the author of the document is, any tracked changes, and the version.
List Serves	List serves are for communities of people with common interests who use the Internet to exchange information.

REVIEW QUESTIONS AND EXERCISES

1. Why should passwords be changed on a regular basis?
2. Describe how a computer network may be used by a law firm.
3. Explain the importance and the steps that may be taken to maintain computer and network security.
4. What are some of the ways the Internet can be used in the law office?
5. What is an Internet browser? Give several examples.
6. Describe the use of Internet browsers for finding information on the World Wide Web.
7. Explain some of the issues in obtaining and installing software.
8. What is a list serve?
9. How can list serves benefit the legal team?

10. What is the difference between the functions of the network server and the users' workstations?

11. Give examples of how network security can be breached and the possible ways to prevent the breach of network security in the future.

BUILDING YOUR PARALEGAL SKILLS

INTERNET AND TECHNOLOGY EXERCISES

1. Conduct a search on the following topics using four different Internet or search browsers for the same term or item. Are all results shown in the same order? Why or why not?

   Search topics
   a. Legal ethics
   b. Law office technology
   c. Presentation graphics
   d. Internet security
   e. Metadata

2. Use the Internet to locate a definition of the term *metadata*; what is its importance to the legal team?

3. Find list serves available for lawyers through the American Bar Association.

4. Use an Internet search engine to find organizations involved with technology in the law.

5. Use the Internet to find and download a free firewall program.

6. Use the Internet to find Internet service providers in your area and prepare a list of available services and prices.

7. Use the Internet to locate a list of the ABA list serves that might be of value to a litigator.

8. Use a file compression program to "zip" a file and send it as an attachment to an email. You may send it to your own email address and then unzip the file on receipt.

VIDEO CASE STUDIES

ZEALOUS REPRESENTATION ISSUE: WHEN YOU ARE ASKED TO LIE

A paralegal has been instructed by the supervising attorney to do whatever is necessary to obtain information needed in a particular case.

Watch this video case study in MyLegalStudiesLab and answer the following questions.

1. What are the ethical issues when lying to obtain information?

2. May information posted on social media sites be used in the preparation or presentation of a case?

CHAPTER OPENING SCENARIO CASE STUDY

Use the Opening Scenario for this chapter to answer the following questions. The setting is the attorney and paralegal discussing renting space to another attorney who is not a member of the same firm.

1. What additional hardware or software will be required to support a new person in the office? Does it matter if it is a lawyer or a paralegal or secretary?

2. Prepare a memo requesting a faster-than-dial-up Internet connection and explain why the cost is justified.

3. What procedures should be set up to protect data but allow use of the Internet by others in the office?

4. Is there any additional hardware that should be considered or purchased? Is this different from the list prepared in Chapter 3?

5. What are the ethical issues in sharing a common website to attract clients for the plaintiff and defense attorney in this office? See the firm website exhibit (1.2) in Chapter 1 for reference.

6. Are there any ethical issues in unrelated attorneys sharing an Internet connection?

7. Are there any ethical issues in sharing a web page for attracting clients?

CONTINUING CASES AND EXERCISES

1. Update the Internet resources list from Chapter 1.
2. Continue to maintain a time record as outlined in Chapter 1.
3. Review the information presented in Advanced Exercises for the First Client.

a. Set up a file for the client for use in answering the questions and preparing the documents.
b. This exercise will require information found in future chapters and is a continuing exercise.
c. Your instructor may give you additional instructions.

ADVANCED EXERCISES

1. Use Tabs3 to enter and maintain the time records assigned in Chapter 1.
    a. You will need to add yourself as a timekeeper and set a rate. For this continuing exercise, list yourself as timekeeper 30, at a rate of $40 per hour.
    b. Create a list of functions to be billed.

    c. Enter a client for billing purposes; you may use your instructor with the college information as the client.
2. Enter all of the calendar information for the course (see the list of suggested items in the exercise in Chapter 1) in the calendar functions in AbacusLaw.

FIRST CLIENT

The first client for a young attorney is always someone who will be remembered. Suddenly all the textbook theory comes face-to-face with reality. In a modern law office a series of decisions must also be made on law office management issues.

1. The client has requested information on preparing an advance medical directive, also referred to as a living will. What is the applicable law in your jurisdiction?
2. Are forms available from the Internet for your state? Locate any free forms available and download a copy to use as a template.
3. Use the following information to create a new client interview form that can be saved as a template in a word processing program.
4. How should the office files be set up? Some of the options include filing by client's name, by type of documents prepared, or a combination of both. What recommendations would you make to Mr. Mason?

5. How should time records be maintained for billing individual clients?
6. Should the office be a paperless environment, with copies of all client materials maintained electronically, or should paper copies be retained?

Note: As a reference, a sample Advance Medical Directive brochure is available from the University of Arkansas for Medical Sciences at http://www.uams.edu/patienteducation/Handouts/advance_medical_directives.pdf.

Client Information
Adam First
1 Major Road
New Hope, Your State and Zip
Phone 555-123-4567

Mr. Mason spends thirty minutes interviewing the client.

Mr. Mason reviews information with the client and disburses $5.00 to have the document notarized.

BUILDING YOUR PROFESSIONAL PORTFOLIO

1. Prepare an office policy on the use of passwords in the law office. Explain the reasons and methods to be used for the most and the least secure passwords.

2. Prepare an office policy on the use of the Internet for sending and receiving electronic communications and documents.

"It may not always be profitable at first for businesses to
be online, but it is certainly going to be unprofitable not
to be online."

—*Esther Dyson*

The Electronic Courthouse and Virtual Law Office

CHAPTER 5

OPENING SCENARIO

The partners were pleased with the way the firm was growing as cases kept coming in. As their reputation grew, they attracted clients from farther and farther away. But the drawback to representing clients over a large geographic area was the time needed to commute between the main office and the branch office to complete work and collaborate on cases. With financial resources improving, they considered ways to bring in more business while working more efficiently. With the cost of transportation increasing, they were also interested in being able to work from home or while traveling. Electronic filing in the federal courts and their local court was now available, and they looked into the costs of the hardware and technical support needed to adopt these new systems.

LEARNING OBJECTIVES

After studying this chapter, you should be able to:

1. Describe how courts are implementing technology.

2. Explain the use of electronic access to cases and e-filing in the federal court system.

3. Describe the concept of the virtual law office.

4. Discuss the ethical issues in e-lawyering.

VIDEO INTRODUCTION

Professor Thomas F. Goldman, Esq.

THE ELECTRONIC COURT HOUSE AND VIRTUAL LAW OFFICE
After watching the video in MyLegalStudiesLab, answer the following questions.

1. How has technology changed the way lawyers and courts interact?
2. How has technology changed the way people communicate?

■ INTRODUCTION TO THE ELECTRONIC COURTHOUSE

Computer technology is changing the way law offices and court systems perform traditional functions. It has also changed the way lawyers and courts work together. At one time, starting a lawsuit involved preparing a set of paper documents for the signatures of the client and the attorney, and hand-delivering the documents to the court for filing during normal courthouse business hours. Now, some courts permit the filing of documents electronically as well as in conventional paper form. Other courts, including the federal court system, are requiring that pleadings and other documents be filed electronically.

The ease of creating and sending electronic documents in all forms of personal and business communication has resulted in a document explosion. The huge volume of documents involved in litigation requires more time to obtain and review them. At the same time, cases are moving ahead faster because of the demand for "quicker justice," and less time is allowed to prepare and present a case. The result has been a rapid growth in computerized case management and other uses of computers in every aspect of litigation.

Computer-savvy lawyers have embraced the use of technology not only for filing documents, but also for promoting their services and communicating with clients electronically. More law firms are using Internet websites to increase their exposure and, in some cases, to conduct their practice from what is described as a "virtual law office." These lawyers operate their practices from wherever they can connect a laptop to the Internet.

Computerization of the Courthouse

LEARNING OBJECTIVE 1
Describe how courts are implementing technology.

Perhaps the earliest introduction of technology in the courthouse was the use of multimedia devices in the courtroom. Overhead projectors for showing movies and images were the forerunners of the more sophisticated computer-based projection systems that have become common elements in the courtroom.

Courthouse administrators have always been concerned about the increasing volume of documents that are filed, recorded, and maintained for litigation and other public purposes. The first computer systems in the courts were used for indexing documents such as wills and deeds. These systems stored and indexed images of the paper documents, replacing microfilm and microfiches. New systems are now being installed in courthouses for filing, indexing, and storing pleadings as well. It may not be long before all court documents are submitted and stored in electronic form.

Electronic Filing

One of the most significant changes for a large segment of the legal community is the implementation of electronic filing, or "e-filing," by some courts. As of 2009,

Exhibit 5.1 Connecticut e-filing website

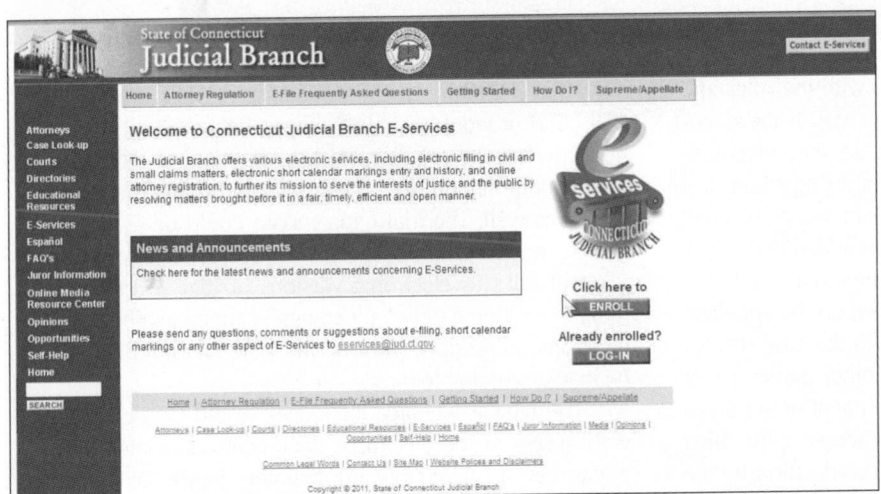

WEB RESOURCES
The Connecticut Judicial Branch E-Service website may be accessed at http://www.jud.state.ct.us/external/super/e-services/efile/

all of the federal district courts have implemented e-filing. The state courts have not embraced this technology as completely, although increasing numbers of jurisdictions are permitting or requiring e-filing.

However, some states, such as Connecticut, not only allow e-filing, but mandate it, and have set up websites for e-filing, as shown in Exhibit 5.1. In the Connecticut system, counsels are advised in the court rules as follows:

> If an attorney or law firm without an exclusion from E-services requirements submits, on paper, any document that is required to be filed electronically, the clerk will not file the document and will write "Not Accepted" across the file stamp on the document. The clerk will then return the document to the sender with a notice explaining why it was not filed.

Source: http://www.jud.ct.gov/external/super/e-services/efile/mandatory_require_except.pdf

It is expected that more courts will also adopt e-filing systems. The legal team must therefore be prepared to use the e-filing systems where required and stay current on the status of e-filing implementation in the courts in which they practice.

WEB RESOURCES
Read the entire article at: http://www.appellatecourtclerks.org/NCACC_E-Filing_White_Paper.pdf

ADVICE FROM THE FIELD

E-FILING IN STATE APPELLATE COURTS: AN APPRAISAL
by David Schanker, Clerk, Wisconsin Supreme Court and Court of Appeals, on behalf of the NCACC

...

E-Filing Systems

In fact, the e-filing systems offered by most e-filing vendors resemble each other far more than they differ. Nearly all are based on the federal model and provide interfaces designed with the differing perspectives of filers, the clerk's office, and the courts in mind.

In a typical (or ideal) e-filing system, filers prepare the document using conventional word processing software, then save it as a PDF file. The filer then (1) logs onto the court's e-filing interface with a court-issued username and password, (2) enters basic information relating to the case and the document, (3) uploads the document, (4) submits it to the system, and (5) pays any applicable filing fees online. The filer receives a notice verifying the submission of the document.

The appellate court clerk's office receives notification that the document has been submitted to the system, usually by the appearance of the newly submitted document in an e-filing review queue. A clerk's office employee

(continued)

(continued)

reviews the document for compliance with the rules and deadlines and either accepts it or rejects it. If the document is rejected, it is returned to the attorney electronically with a note describing the reason for rejection. If it is accepted, (1) the document is file-stamped or receive-stamped with an electronic stamp that is added to the PDF version of the document, (2) the document is added to the electronic case file, (3) the filing is noted on the appellate case docket, and (4) the other parties to the case receive notice of the filing. At that time, the other parties either receive a service copy of the PDF document or are given access to the document on the court's server. If the filing is a motion that requires immediate consideration by the court (e.g., a motion for extension of time), it is transmitted electronically to the appropriate court. The court then issues an order (through the clerk's office) electronically to the parties.

Once the document has been added to the electronic case file, it can also be made available to the public, depending upon the court's policy. In a number of states, documents filed through the e-filing system are available on the court's website, either as part of the appellate docket case search or as a briefs database. In states where the court requires the filing of documents in text-searchable PDF, the database can be configured to be searchable by terms and phrases, making it a valuable tool for attorneys and judges who want to read how other attorneys have handled a particular issue.

If, in addition, the system had an interface with the trial court, it would enable the appellate court to receive not only case information (parties, charges, case type, financial information, etc.) electronically but the trial court record as well. The trial court record could be as simple as a scanned version of the paper record, or it could be a set of links to electronic versions of trial court documents—including e-filed pleadings, scanned exhibits, and electronic transcripts. Most of this material could thereby be in text-searchable form.

The typical interface for judges would provide them with access to the electronic documents associated with a case in a straightforward manner; judges and their law clerks are interested, of course, in the content of the documents, not when and how they were filed. A simple web-based interface would permit a judge (wherever in the world he or she may be) to sign on to the system, enter a case number, and retrieve a list of the electronic documents in that case. Double-clicking on a document would open that document in Adobe Reader. Once open, the document can be saved, printed, downloaded, or e-mailed; it can be copied; pieces of text can be copied from within it; and, if hyperlinks have been included, cases or statutes can be accessed via the Internet from within the document.

Source: http://www.appellatecourtclerks.org/NCACC_E-Filing_White_Paper.pdf

Secretariat: National Center for State Courts, 300 Newport Ave., Williamsburg, VA 23185

■ FEDERAL COURT ELECTRONIC ACCESS

The federal courts, including Appellate, District, and Bankruptcy courts, have established a common electronic system for filing documents and locating case information. This system is accessed through the Public Access to Court Electronic Records (PACER) website, as shown in Exhibit 5.2.

Anyone may use the PACER system by registering and setting up an account. The public may register or access the PACER site from the PACER login page, shown in Exhibit 5.3.

PACER Case Locator

The PACER case locator is a national index for Appellate, District, and Bankruptcy courts. The PACER index is updated each night with new information for each case. PACER may also be used to conduct a nationwide search for parties involved in federal litigation.

Electronic Filing Standards

While there is no national standard for courthouse software on a state level, the federal courts have adopted a single system, called **Case Management/Electronic**

Exhibit 5.2 Public Access to Court Electronic
Records website

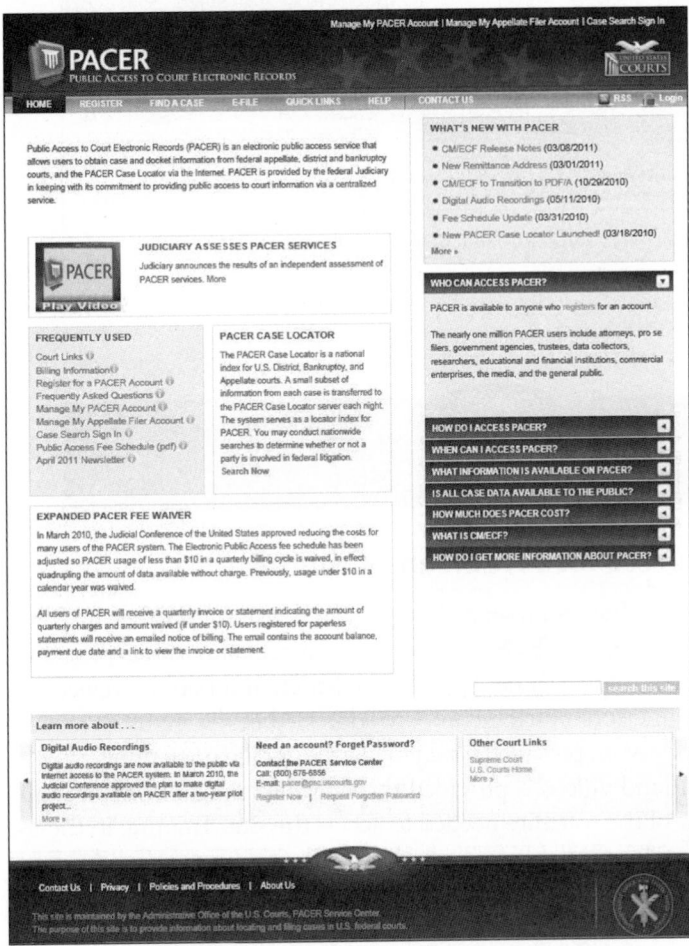

Case Files (CM/ECF). This system is the companion to the PACER website for electronic filing in the federal courts (see Exhibit 5.4). CM/ECF provides courts with enhanced and updated docket management and allows courts to maintain case documents in electronic form. CM/ECF also gives each court the option of permitting case documents—pleadings, motions, or petitions—to be filed with the court over the Internet.

**Case Management/Electronic
Case Files (CM/ECF)**
The federal court's electronic access
and filing system.

Exhibit 5.3 PACER login website

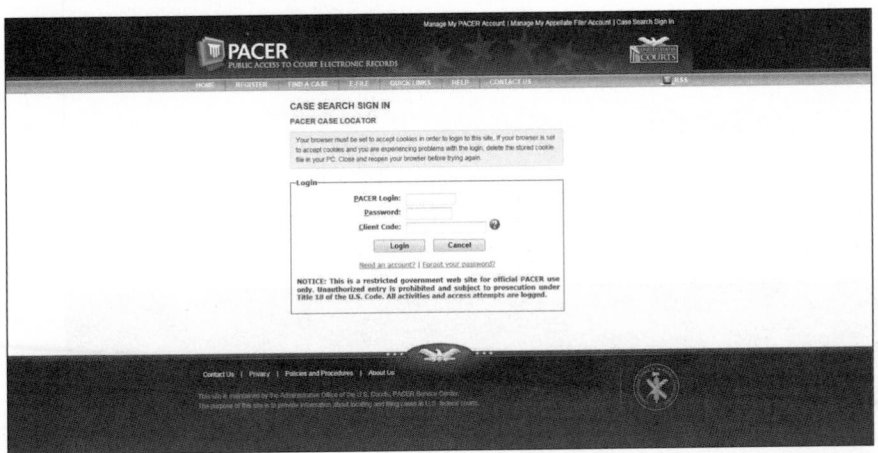

Exhibit 5.4 Case Management/Electronic Case Files website

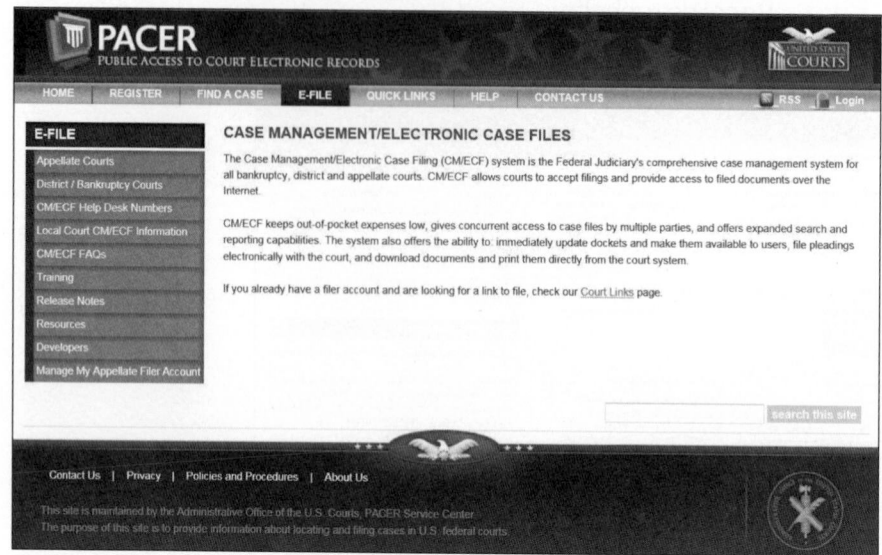

Educational Resources for PACER and CM/ECF

As we have seen, every software program has its own features and user-interface screens. The federal PACER-CM/ECF system is similar to many other programs, and uses similar interfaces for the three Appellate, District, and Bankruptcy courts. The differences in the functions of each court are addressed in the input screens for each, and separate tutorials are provided for each court's unique procedures.

A series of tutorials and videos is provided through the main PACER website, which describes the use of the software needed to access the site. Training in the use of the PACER system is also available from the HELP page, shown in Exhibit 5.5.

Exhibit 5.5 PACER training options website

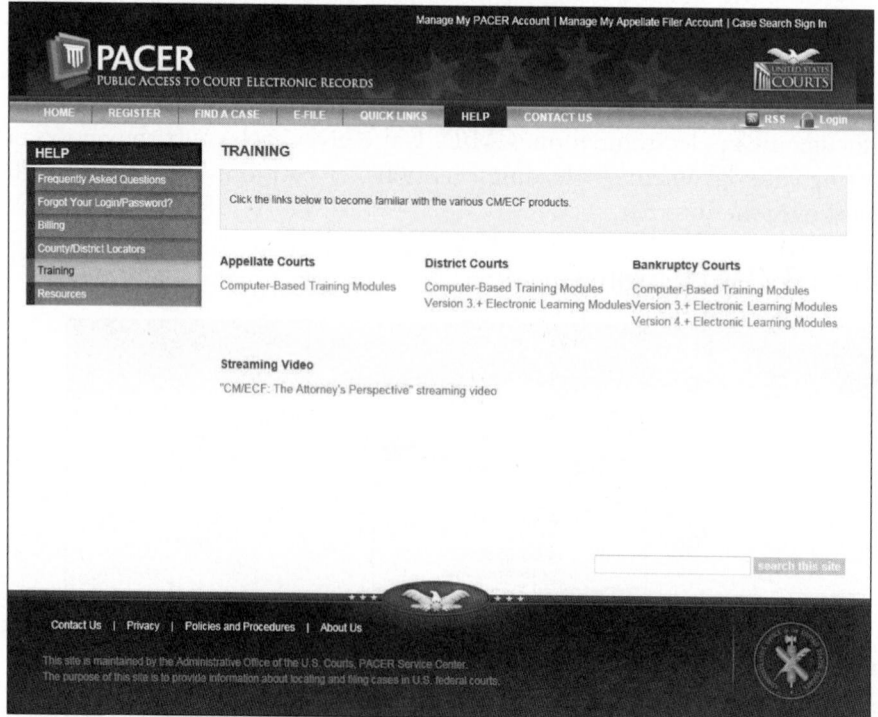

E-Filing in Federal Court

Separate accounts are required for each of the PACER and CM/ECF systems. As discussed below, the legal team prepares the documents on its own computer system, and then uploads the files to the court using the CM/ECF system. An example of the online screen in CM/ECF when the filing is completed is shown in Exhibit 5.6, which is a screen from the online District Court CM/ECF training program.

An example of the pages in the District Court Computer-Based Training Module for accessing and filing a pleading online is shown in Exhibits 5.7– 5.9.

The training modules are interactive, requiring keyboard and mouse input to simulate the same steps that are used in actual practice.

Separate training is provided for each of the Appellate, District, and Bankruptcy court systems. For example, separate training is provided to introduce the Appellate Court docketing system, as shown in Exhibit 5.10.

PRACTICE TIP
EXPANDED PACER FEE WAIVER

In March 2010, the Judicial Conference of the United States reduced the costs for many users of the PACER system. The Electronic Public Access fee schedule was adjusted so that if PACER usage is less than $10 in a quarterly billing cycle, the fee is waived. This change, in effect, quadruples the amount of data available without charge (previously, only usage under $10 in a calendar year was waived).

All users of PACER receive a quarterly invoice or statement indicating the amount of quarterly charges and the amount waived. Users registered for paperless statements receive an emailed notice of billing that contains the account balance, the payment due date, and a link to view the invoice or statement.

Exhibit 5.6 Example of completed filing of complaint on the CM/ECF website

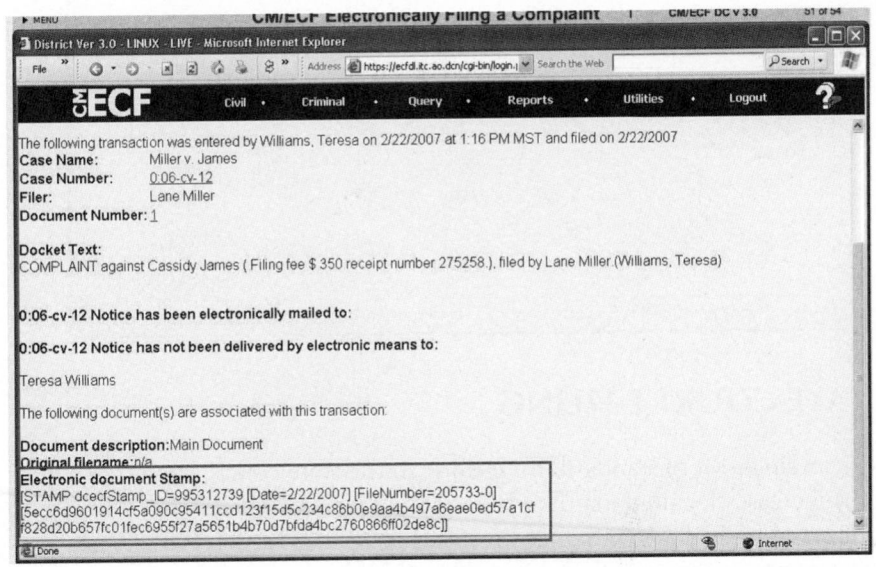

Exhibit 5.7 PACER District Court CM/ECF e-filing training options website

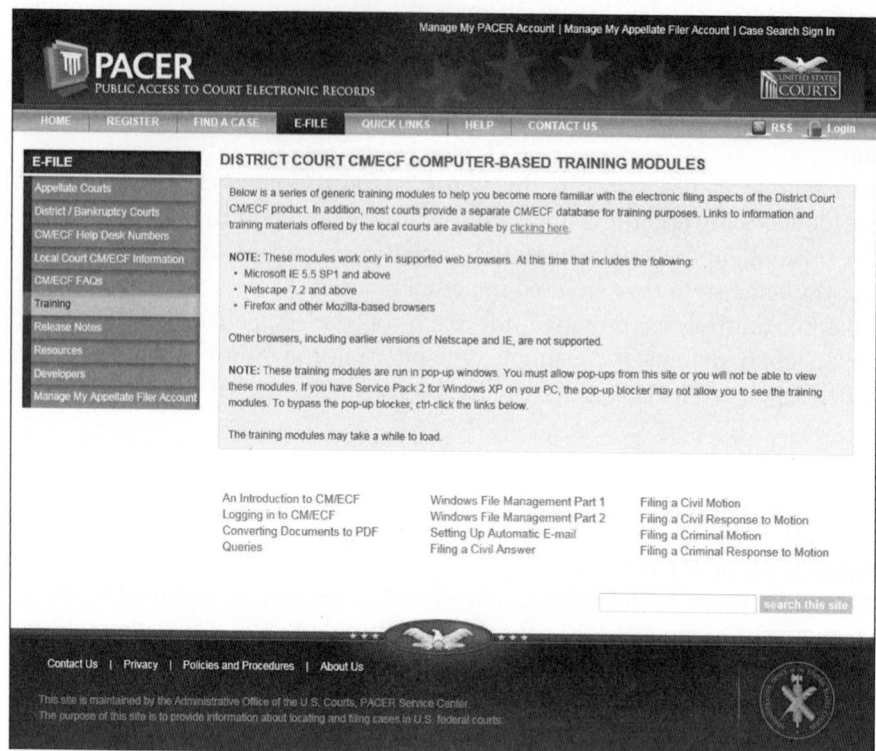

Exhibit 5.8 PACER District Court CM/ECF e-filing party selection training website

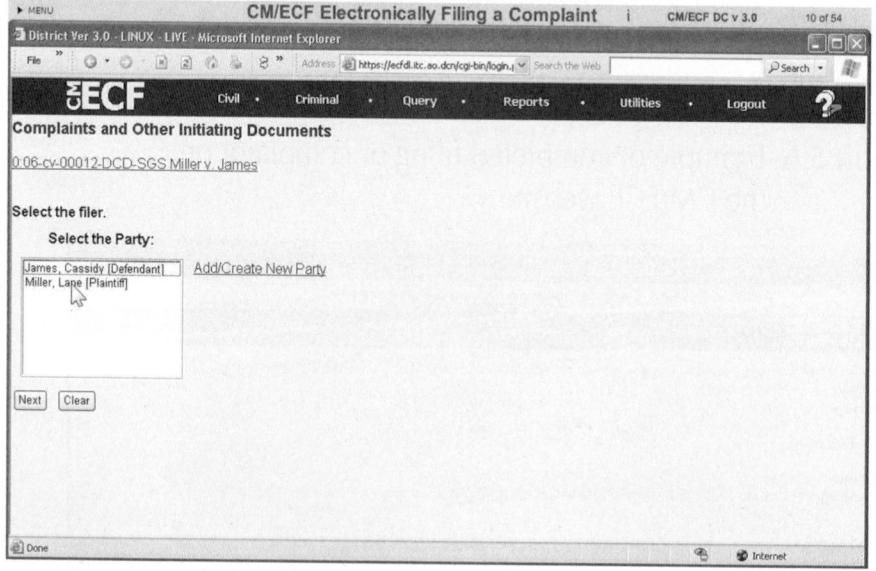

■ STATE COURT E-FILING

There is no single set of standards for e-filing in the state courts. Each state court, and in some cases local courts, like that of the City of Philadelphia, have their own rules and procedures. Among the states providing Internet access are New York and Texas, as shown in Exhibits 5.11 and 5.12.

Exhibit 5.9 PACER District Court CM/ECF e-uploading files training options website

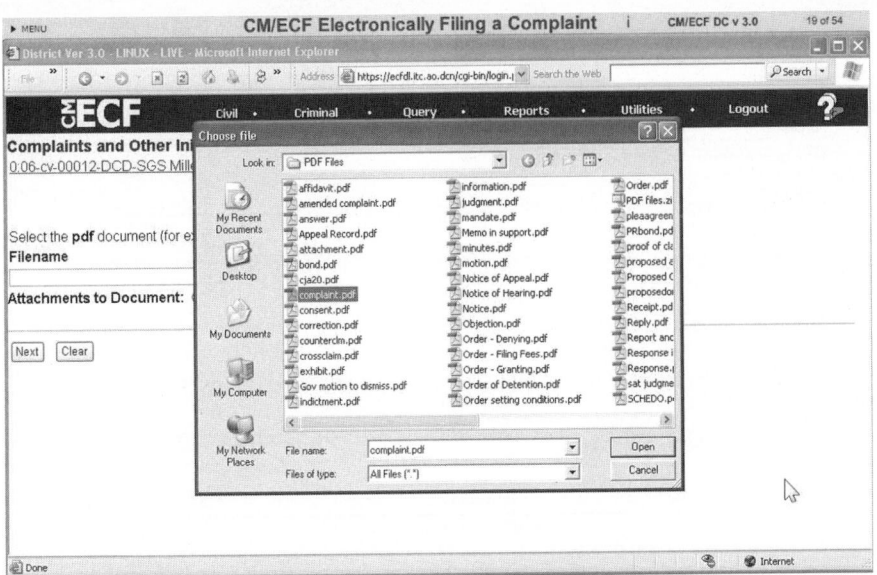

Exhibit 5.10 PACER Appellate Court CM/ECF docketing training options website

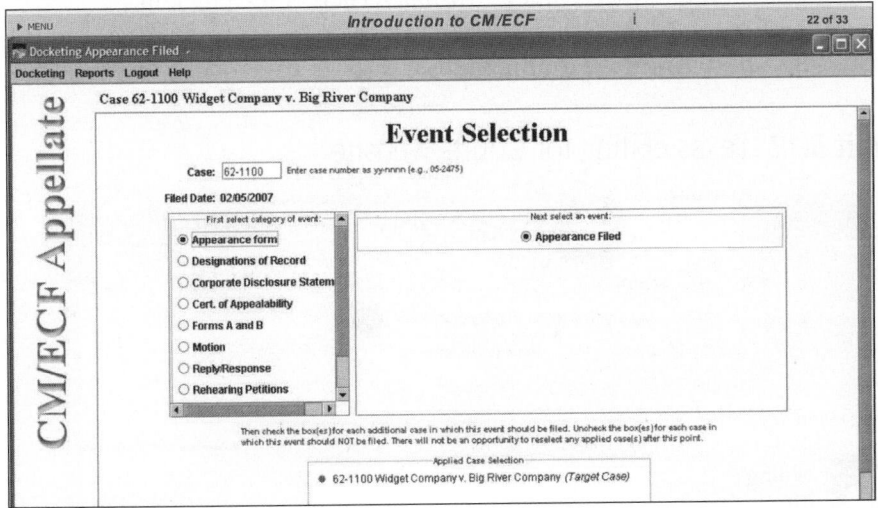

■ ELECTRONIC DOCUMENT FORMATS

PDF Format

The Portable Document Format (PDF) has become standard for sharing documents because PDF documents can be viewed on different computer platforms regardless of their operating system. Unlike documents in **native format,** which is the format used by the creating software such as Word, PDF documents may be viewed without the original program. PDF documents may also be viewed using PDF viewers. Free downloads of software for reading PDFs, such as Adobe Reader or Nuance PDF Reader, have accelerated the acceptance of the PDF format. These applications are limited versions of the Acrobat and PDF Creator programs and allow the opening and reading of files that were created using their proprietary

native format
A file structure defined by the original creating application.

Exhibit 5.11 New York State eCourts website

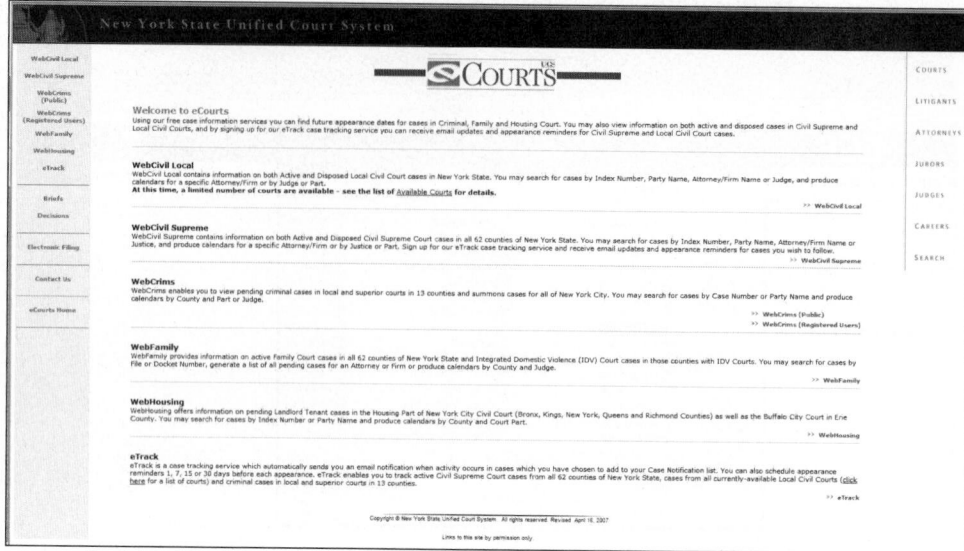

software formats. The websites of many organizations such as the Internal Revenue Service provide forms and documentation in PDF format, and often give links to websites that offer downloads of PDF reader software. These programs are limited in that they allow the user to open and read files but do not allow the user to create new document files, which requires the full version of the program.

Products such as Adobe Acrobat and Nuance PDF Converter have become standard software tools for creating PDF files in both paper-based and paperless

Exhibit 5.12 Texas eFiling for Courts website

offices. With each new version or update to the PDF software, additional features have been added to allow more collaboration and sharing of documents as well as a higher level of security.

In new versions of these programs, the creator of a PDF document, by adding a password, can limit the ability of the receiver of the PDF file to print the document. This feature allows the legal team to send documents that can be viewed by others on the legal team without permitting changes to the original document. Although the document may not be altered, comments can be submitted to the original author.

Typically, the attorney or paralegal creates a document in a word processor such as Word or WordPerfect and then converts the document to a PDF. The PDF format reduces the risk of sending sensitive metadata found in the original word processor document.

Nuance PDF Converter 7 is a lower-cost alternative to the more widely used Adobe Acrobat. In addition to creating PDF documents, Nuance PDF Converter 7 also provides a number of other useful options. For example, its converter feature can be used to convert PDF files into fully formatted Word, WordPerfect, and Excel documents. Another interesting feature in the professional version of this software is its ability to convert documents into audio files that can be played back on a computer or an MP3 player. Anyone who has tried to proofread technical language such as the legal description in a real estate agreement or deed will appreciate the ability to have the language "read to" him or her while following along in the text document. As with Acrobat, Nuance PDF Converter 7 allows security settings for documents created with the program, including password limitations for changes and printing.

WEB RESOURCES

A detailed description of the archiving requirements is available from the Library of Congress Digital Preservation website at http://www.digitalpreservation.gov/index.html

Court and Government Requirements for Digital Documents

Digital formats for documents have evolved over time. A major concern of the courts and government institutions is the integrity of documents filed electronically. These documents must be in a digital archive that will be readable in the future even if the software in use at that time does not support the native file format. The requirements for an acceptable digital document format include:

Device independence
Self-containment
All fonts embedded for unlimited universal rendering
Use of standards-based metadata

PDF/A is a newer version of the original PDF format. It is an open-source, international standard that meets the needs of courts and government agencies internationally, and in some cases has been mandated as the only acceptable format.

The federal judiciary has announced through the PACER system that it is transitioning from PDF format to PDF/A format, as shown in the PACER website in Exhibit 5.13.

PDF/A, or archival PDF format, is a variation of the PDF standard and includes enhanced features for archival purposes and the characteristics required by the Library of Congress.

Exhibit 5.13 PACER PDF/A transition announcement

ADVICE FROM THE FIELD

HOW DO PDF FILES WORK?

PDF files display texts correctly wherever they are viewed because they carry their typographic information with them. Fonts in the document are embedded in the PDF file and are used after distribution to reconstruct the document. The display does not depend on the needed font files being available on the viewing machine, nor on the language of its operating system. PDF documents present their pages as images. They can be marked-up and commented, but the ability to change the basic text is limited. Most PDF files can be searched, because the file has two layers. There is an image layer that is presented on-screen. Behind that there is usually a text layer that can be matched to the characters displayed on the screen.

When the starting point for a PDF file is a set of images, or a scanning process, this text layer is not present and the result is an image-only PDF. When the starting point is an editable document, the text layer can be created and the PDF is called 'Normal' or 'Searchable.' The creator of a PDF can require provision of a password to allow access to the text layer.

Source: Nuance Communications.

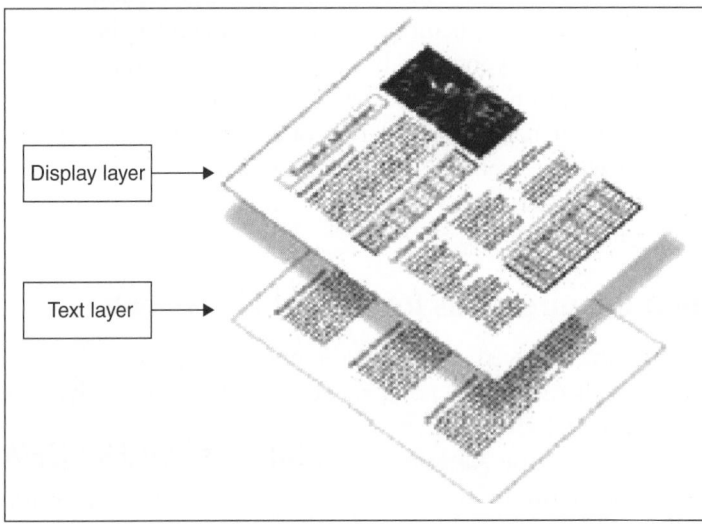

With increasing frequency, the Internet is being used to obtain current forms and documentation. These may be government agency forms, tax forms, or court forms. Even the best-equipped law office will sometimes require one form or another that is not in the office supply room or on the firm file server. For example, an attorney may need an unusual federal tax form or some other form that is rarely used.

The PDF format is the most frequently used format for web-based government forms. With the use of newer PDF programs, these forms can have blank fields that may have information entered directly into them, thus eliminating the need to print out, fill in, and then scan or photocopy the form.

■ THE VIRTUAL LAW OFFICE

LEARNING OBJECTIVE 3
Describe the concept of the virtual law office.

"Virtual law office" or "e-lawyering" are terms used to describe a law practice that exists online, as opposed to the traditional "storefront" law office. In a completely virtual law practice, the lawyer and client may never actually meet face-to-face; all communication is through the Internet. Even telephone conversations may be conducted using the Internet equivalent of the telephone—Voice over Internet Protocol (VoIP). The most well-known version of VoIP is Skype.

With a computer and access to the Internet, a lawyer may practice from any-where in the world. The practitioner may work with clients solely online, and electronically prepare and file documents with courts and government agencies. Local bar admission and ethics rules may allow or even encourage the complete use of a cloud-based law practice, as explained below. In theory, a lawyer may never need to enter a traditional law office, courthouse, or administrative agency.

■ ETHICAL ISSUES IN VIRTUAL LAW PRACTICE

It is common for lawyers to use the Internet to promote their legal services through websites and social networking sites like Facebook and Twitter. Almost every law firm maintains a website promoting its achievements and services. But to the casual observer, it may not always be clear where the law firm or lawyer is located or in which jurisdictions the lawyer is admitted to practice (the disclaim-ers frequently appear in very small print).

LEARNING OBJECTIVE 4
Discuss the ethical issues in e-lawyering.

Some states, like New Jersey, require a physical office as a condition of prac-tice within the state, as described below:

2 1. Bona Fide Office

Rule 1:21-1(a) requires that a New Jersey attorney maintain a *bona fide* office for the practice of law.

For the purpose of this section, a *bona fide* office is a place where clients are met, files are kept, the telephone is answered, mail is received and the attorney or a responsible person acting on the attorney's behalf can be reached in person and by telephone during normal business hours to answer questions posed by the courts, clients or adversaries and to ensure that competent advice from the attorney can be obtained within a reasonable period of time.

[R. 1:21-1(a).] ADVISORY COMMITTEE ON PROFESSIONAL ETHICS
    COMMITTEE ON ATTORNEY ADVERTISING Appointed by the Supreme Court of New Jersey
    JOINT OPINION 718 ADVISORY COMMITTEE ON PROFESSIONAL ETHICS
    OPINION 41 COMMITTEE ON ATTORNEY ADVERTISING

The purpose of the *bona fide* office rule is to ensure that attorneys are available and can be found by clients, courts, and adversaries.

Other states, such as Pennsylvania, do not require a lawyer to have a physical office, and the lawyer need not provide a street address to clients, adversaries, or the court:

An attorney may maintain a virtual law office in Pennsylvania;

- An attorney may maintain a virtual law office in which the attorney works from home, and associates work from their homes in various locations, in-cluding locations outside of Pennsylvania;
- An attorney practicing in a virtual office is not required to list a physical address in advertisements and on letterheads;
- An attorney with a virtual office is not required to meet with clients at the address listed in any advertisements and/or in the geographic location where the attorney will perform the services advertised, but must disclose to the cli-ent all of the information required under the Rules of Professional Conduct;

PENNSYLVANIA BAR ASSOCIATION COMMITTEE ON LEGAL ETHICS AND PROFESSIONAL RESPONSIBILITY FORMAL OPINION 2010-200

There is no single rule as to what is or is not acceptable across jurisdictions, and care must be exercised before establishing a virtual law office.

Unauthorized Practice of Law

The use of the Internet and other forms of electronic communications do not change the rules regarding the unauthorized practice of law. Lawyers must still be licensed in the jurisdiction where the client is located. A client seeking a lawyer to handle a case may use a web search engine to find a lawyer without indicating in which state the advice is needed. To avoid a claim of the unauthorized practice of law, the burden is on the attorney to verify that he or she is properly admitted to practice law in the state in which the client is located, or the state in which documents, such as wills or pleadings, will be used. Paralegals and other legal support personnel using the virtual office concept must also be sure they are not violating any state laws or regulations regarding professional practices.

■ CONFIDENTIALITY

Confidentiality of client information is one of the most important obligations of the legal team. In a traditional law office, this is accomplished primarily by protecting the physical copies of client records and office records. Lawyers and support staff are often reminded at continuing education seminars of the importance of not discussing client information except with those with a need to know and not allowing others to read or see any documents considered confidential.

However, the virtual law office creates new issues in protecting the confidential information of clients. While some documents may be exchanged only in paper form, most will be shared electronically. The law firm is not the only user of electronic media and related hardware. Clients frequently have the ability to scan documents at home, at the workplace, or at a public vendor, and can send them to the lawyer electronically as attachments to emails or can fax them. Lawyers may then create documents and return them to the client as attachments in word processing format or in PDF format, or fax them to the client using the same email address or fax number from which the documents were received.

The danger in using electronic transmission is the potential access by unauthorized parties of the data.

It may be paper copies sent by fax that are accessible or readable by anyone using or near the fax machine. Sending and receiving faxed documents on a fax machine in a public area is an obvious danger. Anyone walking by or using the machine may read the document. In some cases, this alone may result in a breach of the attorney–client privilege.

Another obvious violation involves the display of confidential documents on laptops and computer monitors viewable by others. It is not uncommon to see people on airplanes or in waiting areas reading confidential documents and not taking precautions to prevent others from also reading the confidential information. Perhaps not as obvious is the use of computers in business centers, where the monitors of necessity face outward for anyone walking by to see.

A less obvious violation is the way electronic files are saved and accessible by unauthorized persons. There are regularly reported stories of lost laptops and memory devices containing confidential information. Most notorious are those involving credit card information or personal medical information. For the lawyer operating in a virtual office, the loss of a laptop or removable memory device may open the door to others reading and potentially misusing confidential information, or even offering to provide it to an adversary.

It is common for families to share computers and for co-workers to have access to common computer devices on which electronic documents may be received or

ETHICAL Perspectives

THE STATE BAR OF CALIFORNIA STANDING COMMITTEE ON PROFESSIONAL RESPONSIBILITY AND CONDUCT FORMAL OPINION NO. 2010-179

ISSUE: Does an attorney violate the duties of confidentiality and competence he or she owes to a client by using technology to transmit or store confidential client information when the technology may be susceptible to unauthorized access by third parties?

DIGEST: Whether an attorney violates his or her duties of confidentiality and competence when using technology to transmit or store confidential client information will depend on the particular technology being used and the circumstances surrounding such use. Before using a particular technology in the course of representing a client, an attorney must take appropriate steps to evaluate: 1) the level of security attendant to the use of that technology, including whether reasonable precautions may be taken when using the technology to increase the level of security; 2) the legal ramifications to a third party who intercepts, accesses or exceeds authorized use of the electronic information; 3) the degree of sensitivity of the information; 4) the possible impact on the client of an inadvertent disclosure of privileged or confidential information or work product; 5) the urgency of the situation; and 6) the client's instructions and circumstances, such as access by others to the client's devices and communications.

Conclusion

An attorney's duties of confidentiality and competence require the attorney to take appropriate steps to ensure that his or her use of technology in conjunction with a client's representation does not subject confidential client information to an undue risk of unauthorized disclosure. Because of the evolving nature of technology and differences in security features that are available, the attorney must ensure the steps are sufficient for each form of technology being used and must continue to monitor the efficacy of such steps.

This opinion is issued by the standing committee on professional responsibility and conduct of the state bar of California. It is advisory only. It is not binding upon the courts, the state bar of California, its board of governors, any persons, or tribunals charged with regulatory responsibilities, or any member of the state bar.

stored. Without a procedure to protect the electronic document against access, anyone with computer access may be able to open and read what is intended to be a confidential document. Consider the case of an employee using a work computer to discuss a discrimination claim against an employer or a spouse seeking advice about a potential marital dissolution. A less likely, but still potential, hazard is the outsider who gains unauthorized access to the computer, whether a student as a mental challenge or a malicious individual out to destroy electronic files or obtain them for their contents such as credit card information, trade secrets, or insider information.

◼ ENCRYPTION

Access to files may be minimized by using passwords embedded in the file that limit access only to those to whom the password has been provided. For example, Microsoft Word and Corel WordPerfect allow each file to be password-protected when created. As long as the password is not sent with the email containing the document, access will be limited. A password may then be provided separately by telephone or by using a previously agreed-upon word or phrase.

Encryption Technology

encryption
Scrambling documents using algorithms (mathematical formulas).

Electronic documents may also be sent using encryption technology. **Encryption** technology essentially permits a user to put a lock around his or her information to protect it from being discovered by others. This technology is like a lock on a house. Without the lock in place, unwanted persons can easily enter the house and steal its contents. With the lock in place, it is more difficult to enter. Encryption software serves a similar function in that it lets computer users scramble information so that only those who have the encryption code can enter the database and access the information.

Encryption Software

When confidential or privileged information is sent over the Internet, there is a risk that it will be intercepted. Such transmissions may be encrypted by the sender, and then unencrypted by the receiver. Encryption programs use mathematical formulas called algorithms to scramble documents. Without the proper password or encryption key, unauthorized persons are not able to read the files or determine their content.

The levels of protection offered by the different encryption programs may be compared to different types of combination locks. The lowest level of security is provided by two-number combination locks like the ones frequently found on inexpensive luggage. A heavy-duty lock with four numbers in the combination offers greater protection. As the number of digits in the combination increases, the level of security increases. A simple encryption-breaking program, might be thought of as the equivalent of a two- or three-number combination lock. A higher-level program, with tougher algorithms designed to thwart a professional code-breaker, is like a lock with four or more numbers in the combination. As computers become faster, more sophisticated encryption programs will be required.

Email Encryption

The use of email for communication in the legal environment presents one of the biggest risks of breach of confidentiality. Clients provide details in an email that the attorney uses to give legal advice and answer legal questions. Attorneys reply in an email with legal advice intended solely for the client. A misdirected or intercepted email containing confidential content may be a breach of attorney–client confidentiality and may void the attorney–client privilege.

One way to protect confidential email is to use a program that can encrypt the email and authenticate both the sender and the receiver. WinZip E-Mail Companion is a program that compresses, or "zips," a file, and encrypts documents that are attached to emails. While this does not eliminate all risks, it does offer a level of protection for an attachment that may contain confidential or privileged information. However, the email itself is still readable and potentially accessible to those who have access but don't have the password. But only the intended recipient, who was provided with the agreed-on password in another communication in person, by telephone, or via another method, can open the attachment.

The security provided by the encryption process depends on the quality or strength of the password. As stated in the WinZip manual:

You should keep the following considerations in mind when choosing passwords for your files:

In general, longer passwords are more secure than shorter passwords. In fact, taking maximum advantage of the full strength of AES encryption requires a password of approximately 32 characters for 128-bit encryption and 64 characters for 256-bit encryption.

Passwords that contain a mixture of letters (upper and lower case), digits, and punctuation are more secure than passwords containing only letters.

Because you can use spaces and punctuation, you can create "pass phrases" that are long enough but still easy to remember and type.

Avoid using easily guessed passwords such as names, birthdays, Social Security numbers, addresses, telephone numbers, etc.

Be sure to keep a record of the passwords you use and to keep this record in a secure place. WinZip has no way to access the contents of an encrypted file unless you supply the correct password. Before storing your only copies of critical information in encrypted form, you should carefully consider the risks associated with losing or forgetting the passwords involved.

ETHICAL Perspectives

NY STATE OPINION 842 (9/10/10)
NEW YORK STATE BAR ASSOCIATION COMMITTEE ON PROFESSIONAL ETHICS

Opinion 842 (9/10/10)

Topic: Using an outside online storage provider to store client confidential information.

Digest: A lawyer may use an online data storage system to store and back up client confidential information provided that the lawyer takes reasonable care to ensure that confidentiality will be maintained in a manner consistent with the lawyer's obligations under Rule 1.6. In addition, the lawyer should stay abreast of technological advances to ensure that the storage system remains sufficiently advanced to protect the client's information, and should monitor the changing law of privilege to ensure that storing the information online will not cause loss or waiver of any privilege.

Source: NYSBA One Elk Street, Albany, New York 12207 • 518.463.3200 • www.nysba.org

■ SCANNING

Any discussion of the paperless work environment or the virtual office must include a discussion of scanning. Even with the rise of electronic documents, the world still uses paper documents in many ways. Clients may need to use older paper documents to support their cases, or paper documents may be used in estate administration and contract reviews. In the virtual work space, these documents need to be converted to electronic format.

Scanners and scanning software have become highly compact and extremely accurate. Typically, documents are scanned in an image format, usually PDF. They may also be scanned using OCR software like Nuance OmniPage 18, which converts scanned documents to word processor files, or to a format that allows them to be searched electronically, as shown in Exhibit 5.14.

Exhibit 5.14 Nuance OmniPage 18

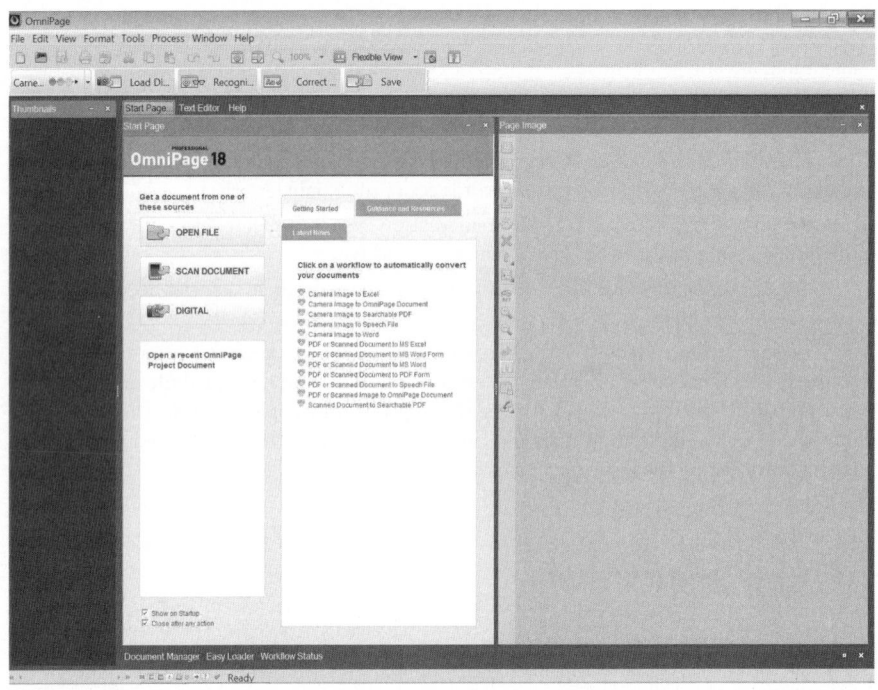

Nuance Communications

Checklist ✓

VIRTUAL LAW OFFICE

What is required for a virtual law office?

- Website
- Portable PC
- Portable scanner
- Portable printer

- Internet connection
- Smartphone
- Briefcase to carry it all, as shown in Exhibit 5.15

Exhibit 5.15 Virtual office

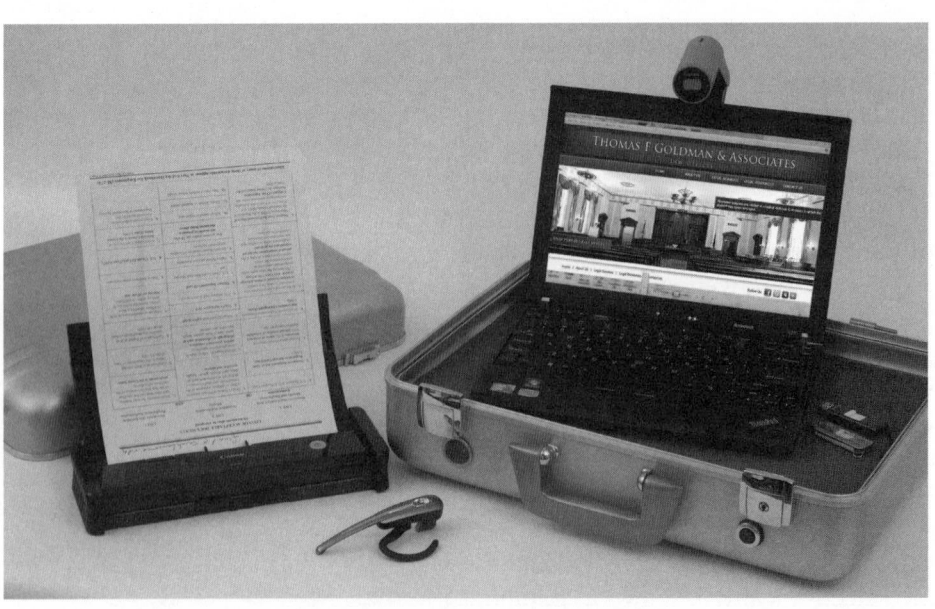

CONCEPT REVIEW AND REINFORCEMENT

KEY TERMS

Case Management/Electronic
Case Files (CM/ECF)   117

encryption   128

native format   121

CHAPTER SUMMARY

Introduction to the Electronic Courthouse	Technology is changing the way that courts perform their traditional function of recognizing the demand for swift justice.
Electronic Filing	The federal courts have implemented e-filing. State courts are making the use of e-filing either optionally available or mandatory.
Federal Court Electronic Access	The federal courts, including Appellate, District and Bankruptcy have established a common electronic system for filing documents and locating case information, PACER.
PACER	PACER or Public Access to Court Electronic Records provides a national index for federal appellate, district and bankruptcy cases that is updated each night to allow a nation-wide search for parties involved in federal litigation.
CM/ECF	CM/ECF- Case Management/Electronic Case Files is a companion website to the PACER system adopted by the federal courts for electronic filing in the federal courts.
Educational resources for PACER and CM/ECF	On-line interactive training is provided for each of the main features of the PACER system and the CM/ECF system
Filing in Federal Court	Separate accounts are required to use the PACER and CM/ECF systems.
State court filing	There is no uniform system for state court filing.
Electronic Document Formats	PDF or Portable Document Format has become the standard for sharing documents. PDF documents may be viewed without the original program used to create the document with the use of free PDF viewers such as Adobe reader or Nuance PDF reader.
Vitual Law Office	Virtual Law Office or e-lawyering is a term used to describe a law practice that exists online. It also refers to lawyers using the internet to communicate, electronically create and file documents using the internet.
Ethical issues in virtual law practice	Some states require a lawyer admitted to practice to have physical presence in the state.
UPL	The use of the Internet does not change the requirement that a person be properly licensed to practice law in a jurisdiction before rendering legal advice to persons within the state.

Confidentiality	Virtual law offices present new issues in protecting the confidentiality of client information transmitted or available over the Internet. Use of electronic transmission opens the potential of access by unauthorized parties, and lawyers must be constantly vigilant to ensure that they are using the latest technology to protect the client's information.
Encryption	In some cases files may be protected by encryption (use of mathematical algorithms) to scramble the data. Only those provided with the unlock encryption code can then open the files.
Scanning	Paper documents may be converted to electronic format by use of scanners and scanning software that can save the document as an image, such as a PDF, or convert the content using optical character recognition into word processor format files.

REVIEW QUESTIONS AND EXERCISES

1. List and explain some of the advantages of the use of technology in litigation.
2. Explain how technology has caused an increase in the amount of documentation.
3. Explain how a lawyer can practice without a physical location.
4. What are the advantages and disadvantages of electronic filing of documents with the court?
5. What is the difference between the PACER system and the CM/ECF system?
6. What are the advantages of the PDF format?
7. How can docments be converted to the PDF system?
8. What are three requirements for acceptable digital document formats filed with governemnt agencies?
9. What are some ethical issues in the virtual practice of law?
10. How can client confidentiality be protected when using the Internet?
11. How does encrytion protect the client?

BUILDING YOUR PARALEGAL SKILLS

INTERNET AND TECHNOLOGY EXERCISES

1. Use the Internet to locate resources for e-filing in your federal and state jurisdictions.
2. Use the Internet to find information on the electronic courthouse and courtroom in your federal and state jurisdictions.

VIDEO CASE STUDIES

FILING DOCUMENTS AND COURT DEADLINES

A paralegal tries to file a pleading to avoid the statute of limitation deadline.

Watch this video case study in MyLegalStudiesLab and answer the following questions.

1. Does electronic filing prevent missing deadlines?
2. Are there preliminary steps that must be taken before using electronic filing?
3. Does the attorney need to sign documents filed electronically?
4. May the paralegal sign pleadings for the attorney?

CHAPTER OPENING SCENARIO CASE STUDY

Use the Opening Scenario for this chapter to answer the following questions.

1. What equipment will the trial team need to work away from the office and try cases in electronic courthouses?

2. What are the advantages and disadvantages of electronic display?

CONTINUING CASES AND EXERCISES

1. Prepare a list of the electronic equipment available in the federal and state courts in your jurisdiction where you may be assigned to try a case.

2. Prepare a memo to the trial team explaining the local rules for bringing in and using multimedia equipment in trial.

BUILDING YOUR PROFESSIONAL PORTFOLIO

Procedures

1. Prepare a memo on the requirements for using the federal court electronic filing system.
2. Prepare a checklist of the steps for electronically filing documents in the federal court and in your

state court, or if e-filing is not available in your state, the requirements for filing including the physical locations (street address and room number) and required items and fees.

"There will still be things that machines cannot do.
They will not produce great art or great literature or
great philosophy; they will not be able to discover the
secret springs of happiness in the human heart; they
will know nothing of love and friendship."

—*Bertrand Russell (1872–1970),*
British logician and philosopher

CHAPTER 6

Word Processing

OPENING SCENARIO

Ethan Benjamin had worked for many years at a law firm that relied on older versions of software, including the word processing program used to prepare documents. The senior partners said that this was not because of personal choice, but because they did not want to spend the money to upgrade to a new program that would require buying multiple licenses. But the truth was that many of the older partners, secretaries, and paralegals were comfortable with the current programs. They did not like change, and so they did not want to learn new programs.

Ethan left this firm to work for the Newtown office of a small, progressive law firm. On his first day at this new job, he discovered that the staff had newer versions of software than he was familiar with, and they did not use the programs he used in his old job. For example, when he arrived the first morning, he saw on his computer screen that they were using a word processing program that was different from the one he'd used at his old firm. After many hours of trying to prepare documents, it was obvious to him that there were substantial improvements and differences in the word processing software at his new job. He was frustrated at not being as efficient as he had been with the other word processing program, but at the same time, he was thrilled with many of the new features. With a few mouse clicks, he could quickly perform many tasks that had required a lot of time and effort with the word processing program at the old firm.

In a casual conversation in the coffee room later that day, he learned they were soon going to upgrade to the newest version of the software, news that

LEARNING OBJECTIVES

After studying this chapter, you should be able to:

1. Explain why the ability to adapt to changes in software is an important job skill.

2. Navigate and find desired functions in word processors.

3. Find resources for learning how to use a program and its features.

4. Create and save a document with a word processor.

5. Discuss security issues and solutions in saving word processing documents.

6. Use some of the special features in word processors for creating documents.

7. Recognize changes and updates to major word processing software.

VIDEO INTRODUCTION

WORD PROCESSING

After watching the video in MyLegalStudiesLab, answer the following questions.

1. Why is clear accurate communication vital in the law office?
2. How does word processing improve communications?

Professor Thomas F. Goldman, Esq.

---

increased his anxiety. Part of his frustration and stress was due to his being unable to ask anyone for help because the legal team of Mr. Mason and Mrs. Hannah was constantly in court, leaving him alone in the office. Also, unlike when he worked at his old office in the large city, there was no corner bookstore where he could get a "non-geek" guide to using software.

■ INTRODUCTION TO WORD PROCESSING

Clear and accurately written communication is vital to every law office. Achieving clarity and accuracy requires repeatedly revising and editing the same document, often by more than one member of the legal team. This revising and editing process is necessary for any kind of document, whether it is a letter, contract, or pleading.

Computerized word processing makes it easier to make changes to written communication. Documents can be sent electronically to any member of the legal team for review, and the convenience of word processing gives every team member the ability to suggest or make changes. As files are sent electronically to the appropriate members of the legal team, changes or revisions are frequently made to the electronic file by each reviewer. These changes may be monitored by using built-in features such as MS Word's Track Changes tool. This feature shows the original text, the deleted text, and the new text. Deletions are indicated by a line through the deleted text, and by margin notes on the document. When the final document is completed, it may be sent quickly by email or fax. In some jurisdictions, it may be filed electronically with the court.

Because of the importance of written communication in the legal profession, the word processor is the most frequently used software in almost any law office. Although many different word processing programs are available, the programs most often used in the legal community are Corel WordPerfect and Microsoft Word. Exhibit 6.1 shows a comparison between the menus and toolbars of WordPerfect X5 and MS Word 2010.

Exhibit 6.1 a) Word 2010 b) WordPerfect X5

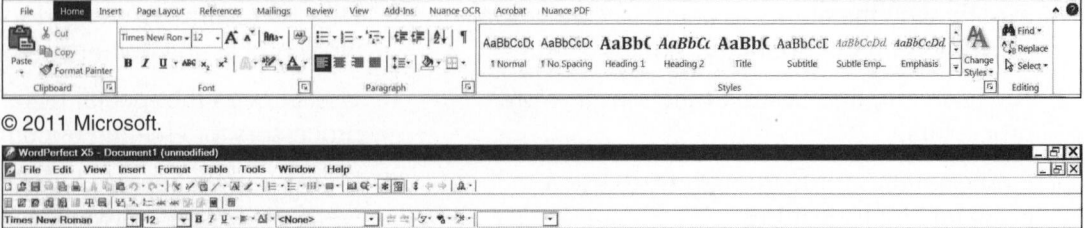

© 2011 Microsoft.

© Copyright 2012 Corel Corporation and Corel Corporation Limited, reprinted by permission.

Exhibit 6.2 Microsoft Office Backstage

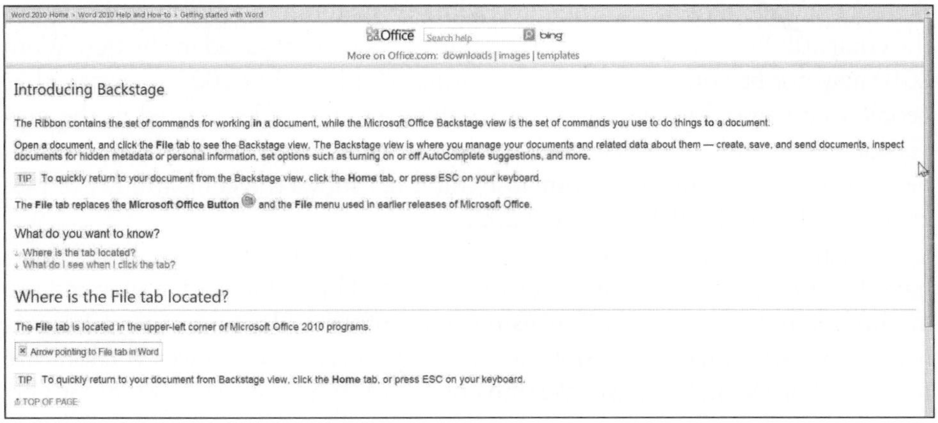

© 2011 Microsoft.

These programs perform a number of tasks that automate and streamline the process of writing and editing. For example, they allow customized formats using a variety of type sizes and font styles within the same document. They also have built-in software tools that check spelling and grammar. Additional features allow you to compare documents, prepare mass mailings, and automatically create tables of authorities. These tasks are performed by running built-in mini-programs called **macros.**

Each new version of WordPerfect and Word has additional functions and improved features. A new user interface, called the **Ribbon,** was first introduced in the 2007 Microsoft Office Suite. Other companies have also added interfaces similar to the Ribbon, such as SmartDraw for creating graphics and Sanction3 for trial presentations. This type of interface makes these programs easier for first-time users. A further change made for the 2010 version of Microsoft Office is a File tab in place of the Office Button. This tab feature opens the Microsoft Office Backstage commands, as explained in Exhibit 6.2.

macro
A set of instructions or keystrokes (a program within a program).

Ribbon
A term used to describe the new user interface in the Microsoft Office suite of products.

■ ADAPTING TO CHANGE

Change is sometimes unsettling, but it is inevitable in almost everything we do. For the paralegal, legal assistant, or lawyer, change is constant. The courts and legislators make changes to the law. Technology changes the way we work. For many, job changes are also an important concern. Many legal professionals are independent contractors who may serve many different firms. Other legal professionals leave firms for better positions, or change jobs as firms merge or become absorbed into other organizations.

Because of this mobility, legal professionals must be prepared to use new software in new positions. They may need to use different programs for the same tasks, such as WordPerfect instead of Word. Or, they may need to use a different version of the same program, such as Word 2010 instead of Word 2007 or 2003. Changes in software are more manageable when users learn to recognize common software features and learn to adapt to the differences in programs. In this chapter, you will learn the common elements found across word processing programs, as well as new features that can improve productivity. As you look at the different programs, and new versions of existing programs, look for the common elements and the ways of navigating to familiar tools and features. Finally, learn how to use the built-in Help features to master the use of the new features and tools.

LEARNING OBJECTIVE 1
Explain why the ability to adapt to changes in software is an important job skill.

Compatibility

A frequent issue that arises when upgrading or switching to different software is the compatibility of file formats. For example, documents saved in the new Word 2010 may not be compatible with the earlier Word 2003 or 2007 versions. Thus people using an old version may not be able to use the files created in the new version, or newer features may be lost when the files are opened. Files must often be converted to a compatible format. Exhibit 6.3 shows the compatibility of files created with Word 2010, 2003, and 2007.

Documents created long ago, such as contracts, wills, or briefs, may have been prepared using an older file format. These documents may require modification or updating when using new software. In some cases, formats from very early software versions are not supported when newer versions are released. For example, newer versions of Word do not support the older versions of Word. Some software updates may also have newer features that are incompatible with older formats. WordPerfect Office does support the older versions of file formats, including some of the oldest versions of Microsoft Word, which Word may not support. WordPerfect addresses this issue by providing the ability to open a file in almost any format and to save it as almost any other word processer format. In addition, Microsoft has made a compatibility pack available for Word, Excel and PowerPoint, as shown in the Office website screen shot in Exhibit 6.4.

> **PRACTICE TIP**
>
> Use WordPerfect as a document conversion tool for formats not supported by other programs, such as old formats of the early versions of Microsoft Word, which Word no longer supports.
>
> *Note:* WordPerfect offers conversions for Word formats, but Word does not offer conversion utilities for WordPerfect.

Exhibit 6.3 Word compatibility chart

WORD 2010 ELEMENT	CHANGE WHEN OPENED IN WORD 2007	CHANGE WHEN OPENED IN WORD 97-2003
New numbering formats	New numbering formats are converted to Arabic numerals (1, 2, 3, 4, …).	New numbering formats are converted to Arabic numerals (1, 2, 3, 4, …).
New shapes and text boxes	Shapes and text boxes are converted to effects available in this format.	Shapes and text boxes are converted to effects available in this format.
Text effects	Effects on text are permanently removed unless the effects are applied by using a custom style. If they are applied by using the style, the text effects will appear again when the document is reopened in Word 2010.	Effects on text are permanently removed unless the effects are applied by using a custom style. If they are applied by using the style, the text effects will appear again when the document is reopened in Word 2010.
Alternative text on tables	Tables lose alternative-text information.	Tables lose alternative-text information.
OpenType features	New type features are removed.	New type features are removed.
Blocking authors	Blocks applied to regions of the document will be removed.	Blocks applied to regions of the document will be removed.
New WordArt effects	Effects on text are permanently removed.	Effects on text are permanently removed.
New content controls	Permanently converted to static content.	Permanently converted to static content.
Word 2007 Content controls	No change.	Permanently converted to static text.
Themes	No change.	Permanently converted to styles. If the file is later opened in Word 2010, you cannot automatically change the style by using themes.
Major/minor fonts	No change.	Permanently converted to static formatting. If the file is later opened in Word 2010, heading and body fonts won't automatically change if you use a different style.
Tracked moves	No change.	Permanently converted to insertions and deletions.
Tabs	No change.	Alignment tabs will be converted to traditional tabs.
SmartArt graphics	No change.	Become a single object that cannot be edited unless no changes are made and it is reopened in Word 2010.
Charts and diagrams	No change.	Some charts and diagrams will be converted to images that cannot be changed. Data beyond supported rows is lost.
Open XML Embedded objects	No change.	Converted to static content.
Building blocks	No change.	Building Blocks and AutoText entries may lose some information.
Bibliography	No change.	Permanently converted to static text.
Citations	No change.	Permanently converted to static text.
Equations	No change.	Become graphics and cannot be changed. Any comments, endnotes, or footnotes in the equations will be permanently lost when the document is saved.
Relative text boxes	No change.	Permanently converted to absolute positioning.

© 2011 Microsoft.

Exhibit 6.4 Compatibility Mode instructions

Word 2010 Home > Word 2010 Help and How-to > File migration

Office   Search help   bing

More on Office.com: downloads | images | templates

Create a document to be used by previous versions of Word

If you create a document to send to people who are working in earlier versions of Word and you know that they have installed the Microsoft Office Compatibility Pack for Word, Excel, and PowerPoint 2007 File Formats, you can work in Microsoft Word 2010 mode.

If you aren't sure whether the people you send your document to have installed the Microsoft Office Compatibility Pack for Word, Excel and PowerPoint Open XML File Formats, you can work in Compatibility Mode. Compatibility Mode makes sure that no new or enhanced features in Word 2010 are available while you work in a document, so that people who are using previous versions of Word will have full editing capabilities.

NOTE   If you already created a document, and you want to find out what content won't be available for editing in earlier versions, see Features that behave differently in earlier versions.

Turn on Compatibility Mode

When you create a new document that will be used in an earlier version, you can turn on Compatibility Mode by saving the file in Word 97-2003 format.

1. Open a new document.
2. Click the **File** tab.
3. Click **Save As**.
4. In the **Save as type** list, click **Word 97-2003 Document**. This changes the file format to .doc.
5. In the **File name** box, type a name for the document.
6. Click **Save**.

© 2011 Microsoft.

Exhibit 6.5 Microsoft Download Center options

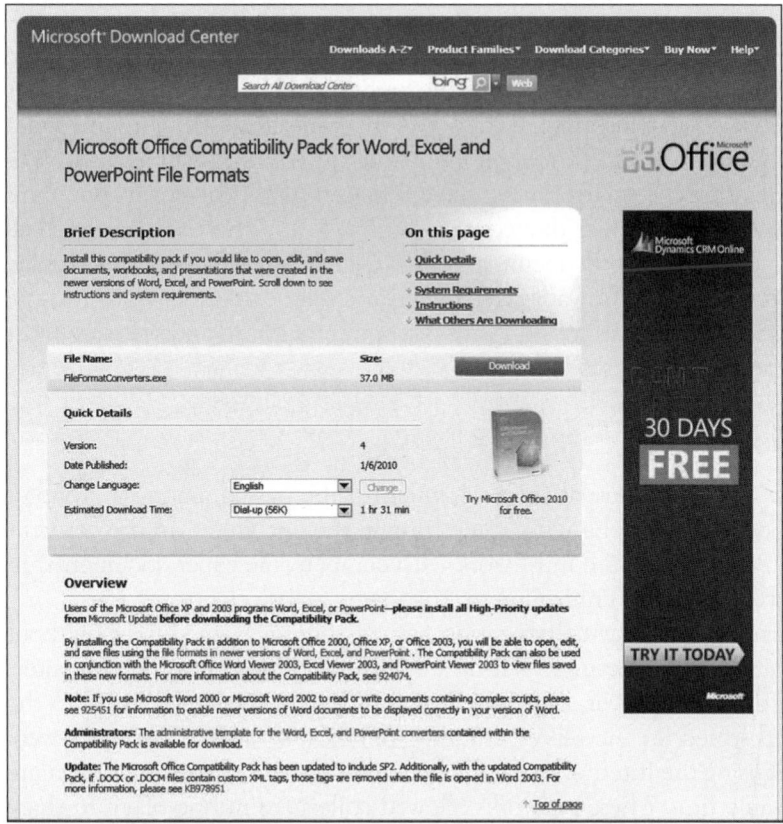

© 2011 Microsoft.

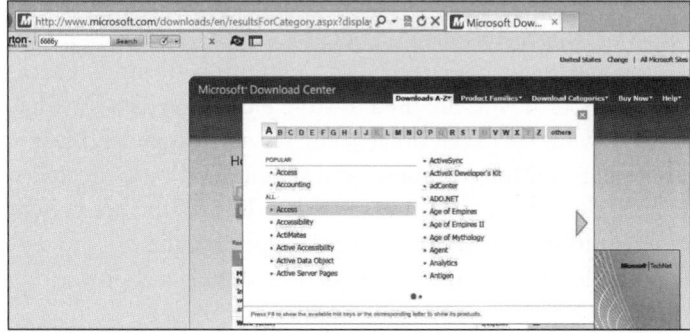

© 2011 Microsoft.

Exhibit 6.6 Microsoft Word compatibility save warning

Microsoft Word	? X

You are about to save your document to one of the new file formats. This action will allow you to use all the new features in Word, but may cause changes in the layout of the document.

Click OK to continue, or click Cancel and select the "Maintain compatibility with previous versions of Word" checkbox to preserve the layout of your document.

☐ Do not ask me again

Tell Me More...   OK   Cancel

© 2011 Microsoft.

The compatibility pack may be downloaded from the Microsoft Download Center, the main source for all Office downloads, as shown in Exhibit 6.5.

Also, before Word 2010 allows documents to be saved, it provides a warning that compatibility may be an issue, as shown in Exhibit 6.6.

Changes in Technology Impacting Word Processing

It is expected that software companies will update and change their programs periodically. Some of these changes are made to keep pace with improvements, such as faster processors and expanded memory, in the hardware used to run the programs.

Changes in hardware also impact how the programs are used. The introductions of tablet computers like the Apple iPad and the Android tablets, as well as the newer generations of smartphones, have required modifications in programs to make them usable on these devices. Many people use these devices instead of office computers to create documents, send email, and create and display PowerPoint presentations. Nowadays, it sometimes seems that everyone is using smartphones or tablet devices for all forms of communication, and software must change to accommodate these uses.

Collaboration

In a law office, it is not unusual for a document to be passed among a group of people, each one adding or changing something in the document. In the conventional office environment, staff must work with cumbersome paper documents. In the computerized, paperless environment, the team can use electronic files.

Computer networks allow collaboration among colleagues and clients without the need for face-to-face meetings. Within a traditional office network, computers are connected through a server, and only those on the network have access to the files shared and stored on the server. Initially, only a few, limited networks were linked together using the Internet to communicate, such as two networks in separate offices of the same firm. These networks allowed colleagues in one office to share documents with colleagues in a remote office. Today, many firms use the Internet as a primary method for sharing files. A popular Internet resource is companies that specialize in allowing off-site storage of electronic data files. These services are increasingly referred to as "cloud applications." Instead of maintaining files and records on servers in the law office, remote servers are used to store electronic data for a fee. Cloud applications have the advantage of offering backup services in safe and secure facilities that are spread among multiple locations and maintained by a specialist. These multiple facilities provide redundancy in case of data loss. A further benefit is the ability of the system administrators to limit access to specific files only to designated individuals. For example, some ethical issues can be avoided by preventing access to certain files by those who have a potential conflict of interest.

Cloud-Based Collaboration Services

Microsoft and Google each offer cloud-based services that provide word processing capability and remote storage of documents. These services allow collaborative sharing of files without the need for in-house servers. In their purest form, they also eliminate the need for word processing software or other programs on individual computers. Word processing software is provided over the Internet, or "cloud," only as needed. Exhibit 6.7 shows Microsoft's Office 365 in its beta view, and Exhibit 6.8 shows Google Apps.

Help Features

No one is expected to know every feature of every program that he or she uses. However, it is important for everyone to be able to find help at those times when a deadline looms or there is no support available in the office. Help for various software is available offline and online from the user's workstation. The online

Exhibit 6.7 Microsoft Office 365 (beta)

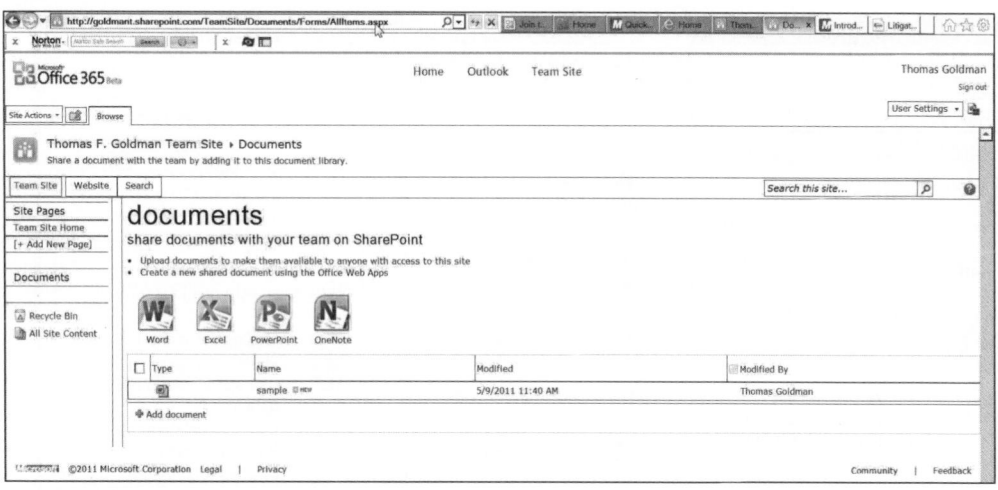

© 2011 Microsoft.

Exhibit 6.8 Google Apps for Business

Google.

content includes an extensive group of self-paced tutorials. These tutorials can also provide a "refresher" of those features that are not used on a regular basis.

Word processing programs are usually included as part of an office suite of integrated programs, such as Microsoft Office or Corel WordPerfect Office. The Help features of the programs within the individual suites are presented in a consistent format. The Help features for Microsoft Word and Excel are shown in Exhibit 6.9.

Help features are available in Microsoft Office both offline as part of the software, and online using a connection to the Microsoft Office website, as shown in Exhibit 6.10.

It cannot be emphasized enough that unless software features such as creating a table of authorities are used on a regular basis, a refresher may be needed. If a new feature or one not previously utilized must be used, such as mail merge, help is available offline and online at the desktop workstation. No one is expected to know every feature of every program that they will use. What is expected is the ability to learn the new feature or find the necessary help when a deadline looms or there is no support line available.

Exhibit 6.9 Microsoft Word and Excel Help

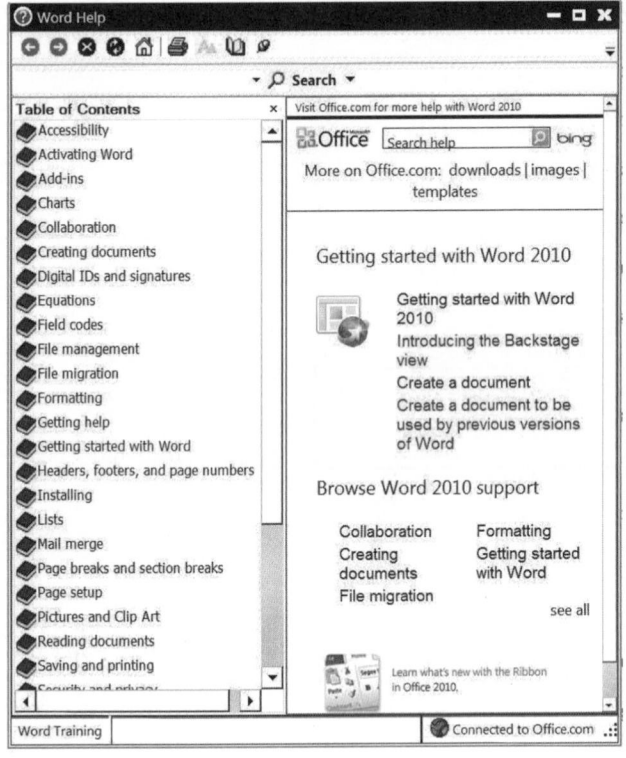

© 2011 Microsoft.

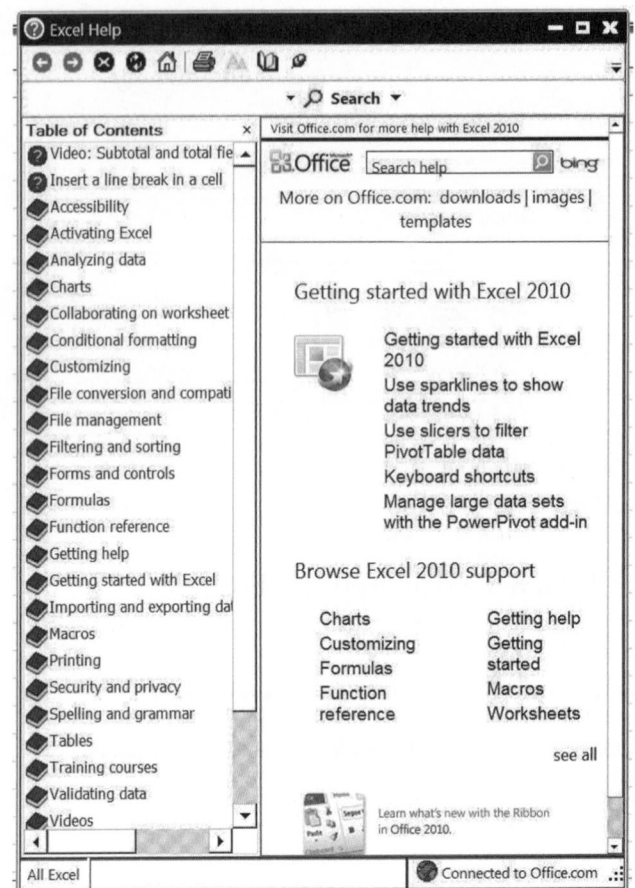

© 2011 Microsoft.

■ NAVIGATING IN WORD PROCESSOR PROGRAMS

LEARNING OBJECTIVE 2
Navigate and find desired functions in word processors.

When using a word processor program, as with using any software, it is important to become familiar with the location of the tools you need to work efficiently. Users will find, with experience, that different programs share many of same structures for organizing tools and features. For example, Microsoft Office 2003 was updated in Office 2007 to have an interface called a "ribbon." In Office 2010, the ribbon remains much the same, with a minor change—the Office Button has been changed to a File tab. A menu of document options, called a "Backstage," is provided, as shown in Exhibit 6.11 on page 144.

Users of previous versions of the Office suite may initially have the feeling that everything about the software must be relearned in order to use Word 2010. In reality, all of the same functions are still available—only the locations and styles of the interface have changed. For example, to open a new file in Word 2003, the File pull-down menu was selected and "New" chosen from within that menu. In the Word 2007 Ribbon, the Office Button is selected and "New" chosen from that listing. In the 2010 version, the File tab is selected, and "New" is chosen, as shown in Exhibit 6.11. The New option in these and most other programs opens a blank document. Existing files are opened with the Open command, and the desired file is selected using the Open File window.

Exhibit 6.10 Microsoft website tutorials

Exhibit 6.11 Microsoft Office 2010 file tab—Backstage

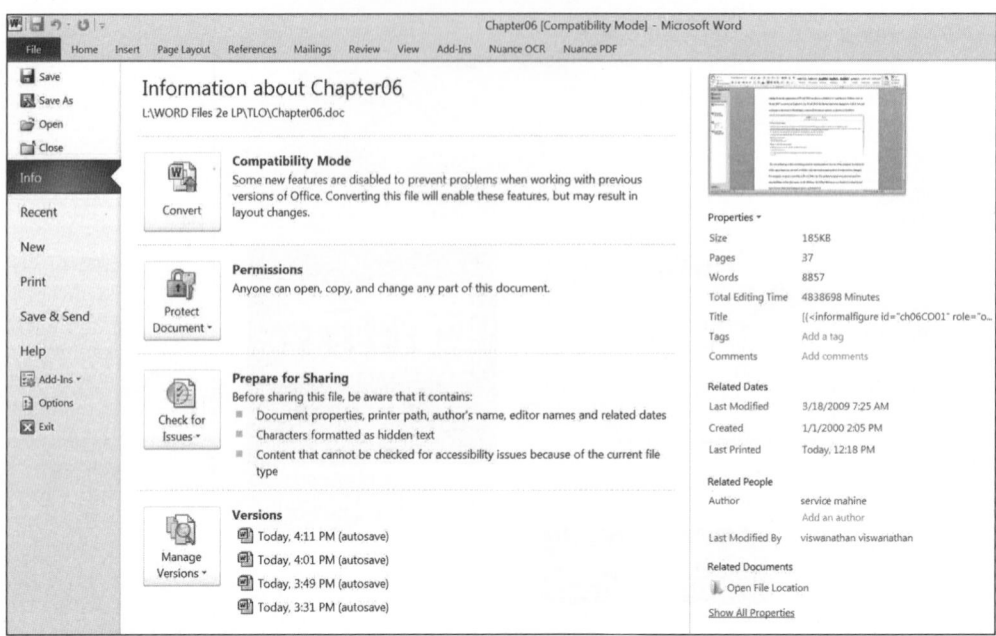

© 2011 Microsoft

Menus and Toolbars

In most software, tools and features are accessed through menus and toolbars. A menu is a list of available commands. A toolbar is located across the top of the window, and may contain menus, buttons, or a combination of both.

The principal difference between the interface in Office 2010 and the interface of older versions is the grouping of commands. In Office 2010's tab format for the Groups commands are grouped by tasks most frequently used, as shown in Exhibit 6.12.

There is consistency in menus and toolbar options in the different programs across the same suite of programs, such as Microsoft Office or WordPerfect Office. As shown in Exhibit 6.1 above, there is also a surprising similarity in locations and menu options in most other software used in the legal community. For example, the first menu item on most traditional program menu toolbars is "File," and one of the last items in the row on the menu toolbar is "Help." The use of similar terminology also makes switching between programs easier. For example, the menu and toolbar items within each of the programs in a suite perform the same functions.

Exhibit 6.12 Microsoft Office 2010 tab format for Groups

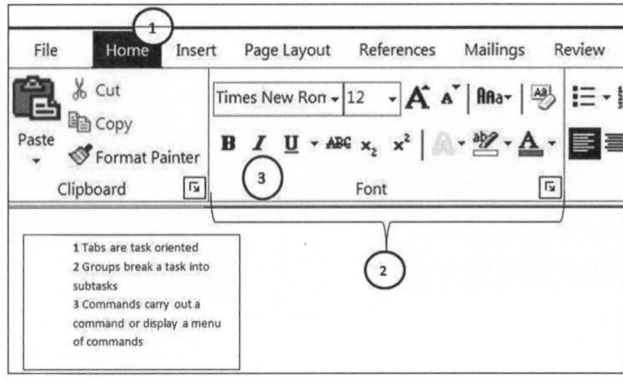

© 2011 Microsoft

■ RESOURCES FOR LEARNING AND USING WORD PROCESSOR SOFTWARE

Every program has some level of instruction or help available. This help may be in the form of online resources including updates, tutorials, and answers to frequently asked questions. Almost all programs have built-in learning resources such as user guides and instructions.

LEARNING OBJECTIVE 3
Find resources for learning how to use a program and its features.

Online Resources

A variety of resources may be provided on the software vendor's website, including tutorials on using different software features. Some of these tutorials, such as the tutorial for Word, require the user to have the same version of the program installed on his or her computer. Many tutorials are interactive and allow the user to take part in the tutorial in some fashion. Some may even have audio narration that can be heard with speakers or headsets, such as the Word tutorial shown in Exhibit 6.10.

Program Resources

All programs have some form of Help function within the program itself. Help functions may provide assistance with standardized features found in all programs, as well as with specialized features. All Help features provide a table of contents showing the topics covered. These tables of contents usually expand to show details or step-by-step instructions. In addition, all offer some connection to the vendor website for information on updates as well as access to online help and tutorials. An example of a Help feature, WordPerfect Tutor, is shown in Exhibit 6.13.

WordPerfect also offers help in moving between Microsoft Word and WordPerfect, as shown in Exhibit 6.14.

Exhibit 6.13 WordPerfect step-by-step tutorial

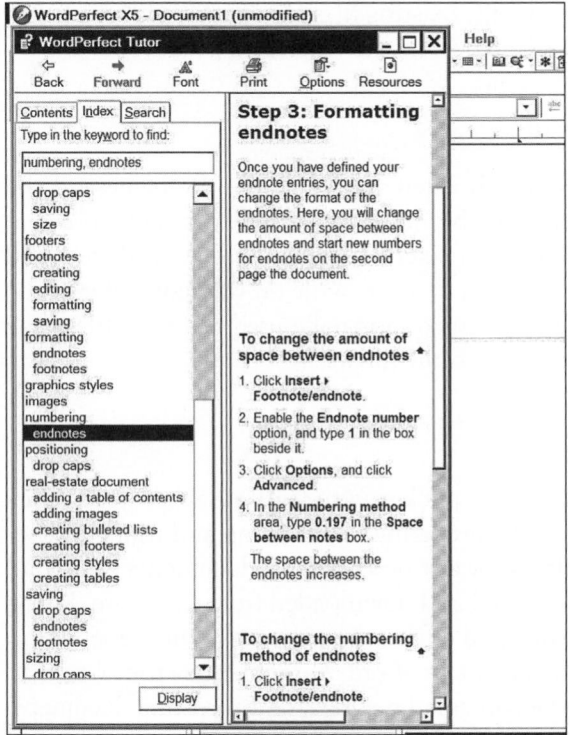

© Copyright 2012 Corel Corporation and Corel Corporation Limited, reprinted by permission.

Exhibit 6.14 WordPerfect help in moving between Word and WordPerfect

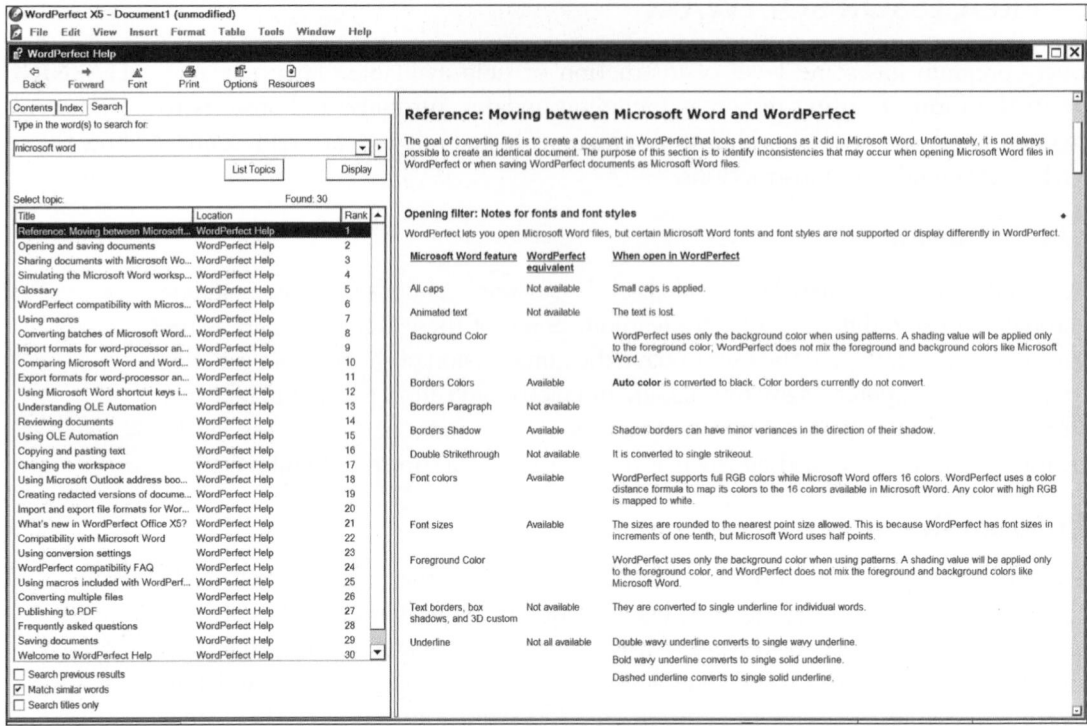

■ STARTING A DOCUMENT

LEARNING OBJECTIVE 4
Create and save a document with a word processor.

The first step in creating a document is to select and start the desired program. Once the program is running, the next step, in most cases, is to open the File menu or, in Office 2007, the Office Button. The "New" option in these and most other programs opens a blank document. Existing files are opened with the Open command, and the desired file is selected using the Open File window.

File Search Function

Opening an existing file is easy enough when you know the file name and the file's location on your computer or on the network file server. However, sometimes you've forgotten or don't know the exact file name. Both WordPerfect and Word have a search tool that can be used to locate a file on your computer or the file server, as shown in Exhibit 6.15. This tool may be used to find a file using only part of the file name, or words within the file itself.

Templates

template
A form or standard document.

Templates are special files that offer a quick way to start a new project. They are essentially blank documents with predefined formatting and fonts for specific types of documents. Templates for a wide variety of documents are found in the program itself or can be accessed and downloaded from a website. Using a template can sometimes save time and effort when creating a new document.

When a user opens a new document in Word, he or she has the option to open a blank document, a web page, an email message, or an existing document.

Exhibit 6.15 Word and WordPerfect search for file

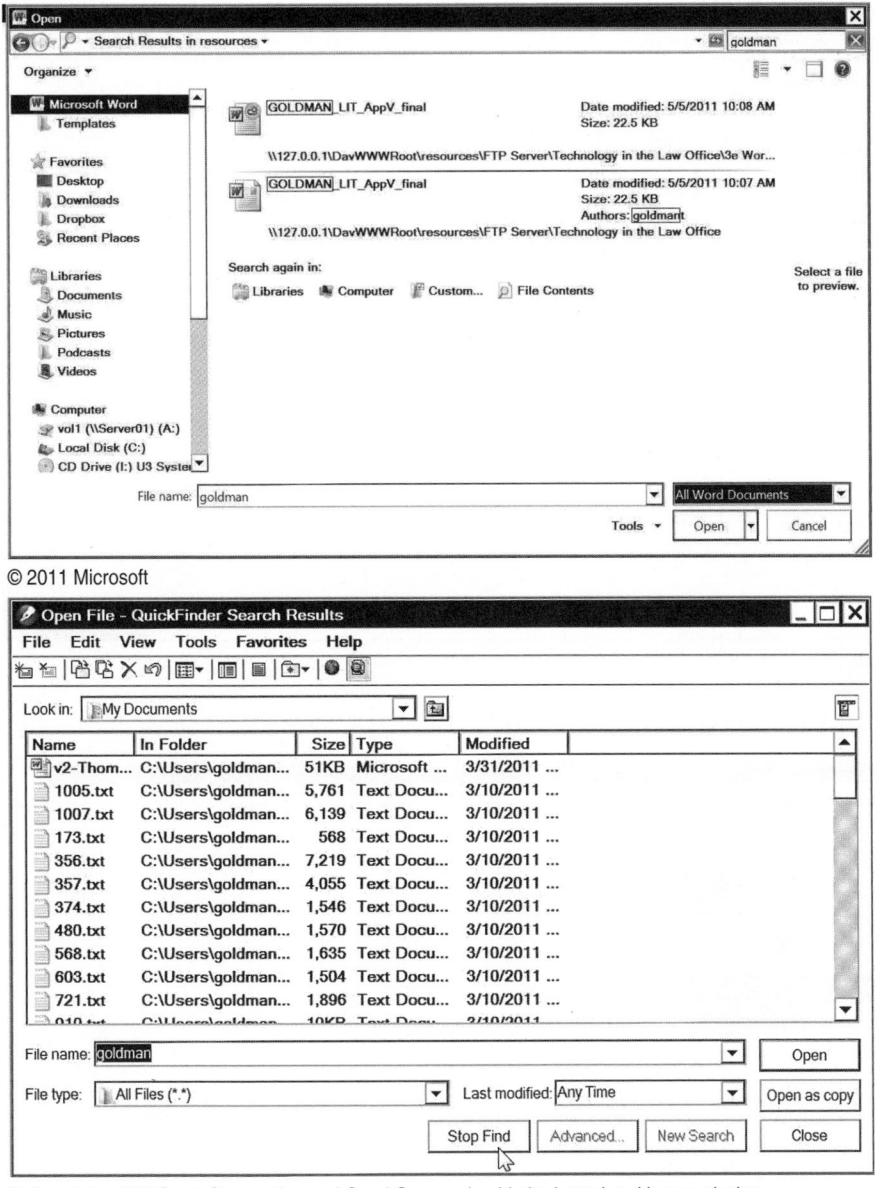

© 2011 Microsoft

© Copyright 2012 Corel Corporation and Corel Corporation Limited, reprinted by permission.

The user is also offered the opportunity to use a template. Exhibit 6.16 shows a sample of the available templates for download.

If a template is not selected, a new document in Word is opened using the default template, Normal.doc. Changes to the Normal template may be made and saved, or the user may create new templates with fonts and formatting for specific purposes. For example, a user may create a template for a specific type of contract that uses predetermined margins, spacing, and headings. The template is then saved with a file name. When the template is opened, a blank document will appear with that formatting, ready for contract language to be entered. Word provides quick access to the saved templates when the New option is selected from the File tab in 2010 (or from the Office Button in 2007), as shown in Exhibit 6.17.

Exhibit 6.16 Word templates

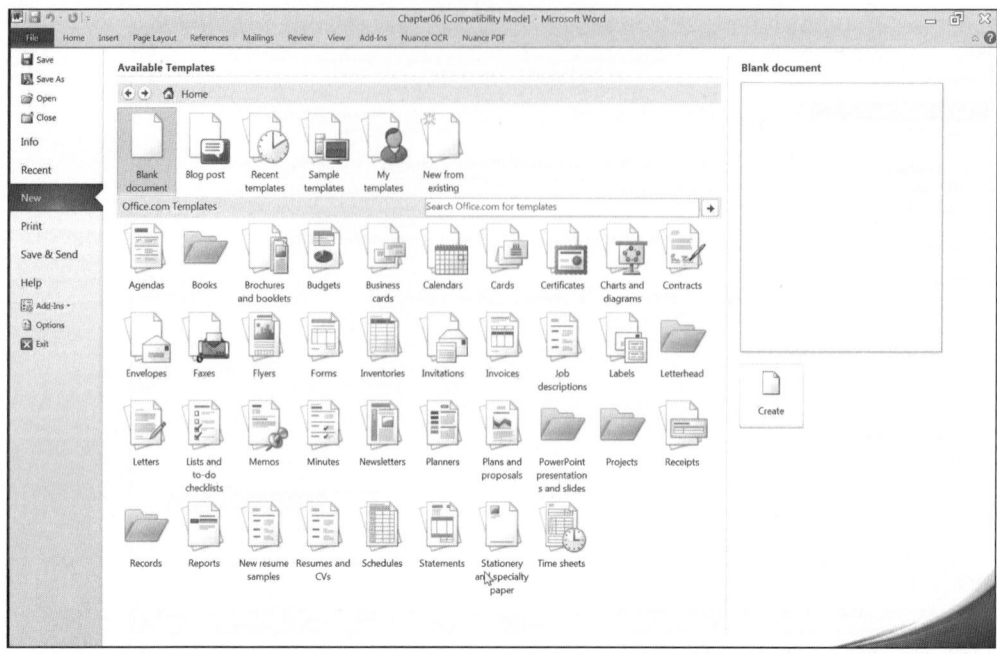

© 2011 Microsoft

Exhibit 6.17 Saved templates in Word

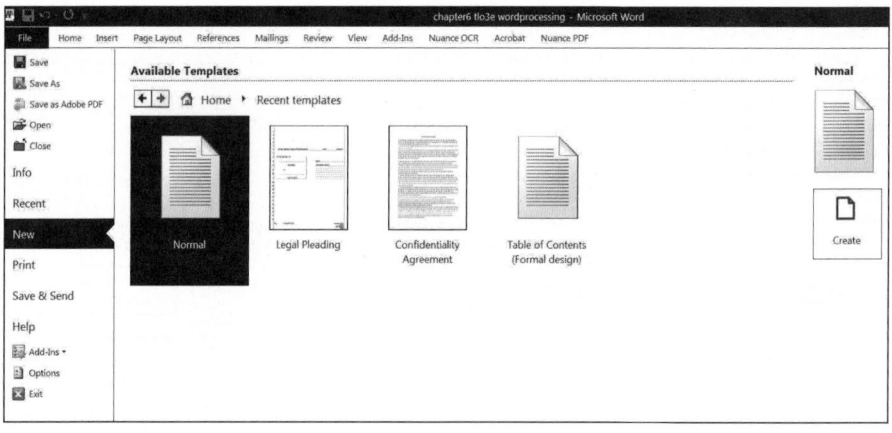

© 2011 Microsoft

■ SAVING THE FILE

When saving a new file, the user is asked to choose a name for the file and a location where the new file should be saved. But if the document was opened from an existing file, the user has two options for saving the file: "Save" or "Save As."

The **Save** command will save the document using the same file name and location from which it was opened. When the file is saved, the previous file of the same name is replaced with a new document having all the changes that were made since the last time it was saved. It is important to note that when the Save command is selected, there is no warning to the user that the previous document is about to be erased.

The **Save As** command allows the user, before saving the file, to change the name and the location in which the file is to be saved. A new file is created and

Save
A command that writes (saves) the document using the original file name and location from which it was opened.

Save As
A command that allows the user to select the location and file name before writing (saving) the file, allowing the user to change the original file name and location from which it was originally opened.

saved to the new location, but the old file is retained as a separate file. The Save As command is useful if a file contains frequently used **"boilerplate"** language that you may want to use in several documents. The old file can then be kept and re-used for future files. When you select Save As, the program will prompt you to change the name of the file so that a new file can be created. Otherwise, the old file will be replaced with the new one.

Converting File Formats

Most word processing programs have the capability to open or save files in different file formats. A **file format** is the way word processor files are saved with document properties such as type font and type size and formatting details. The saved files also include instructions to the computer on how to display the document, on security features, and on hidden information such as Track Changes information.

When a file is saved, a **file extension** is added to the end of the file name that identifies the format in which the file has been saved. Each file extension is a period followed by three letters. For example:

boilerplate
Standard language used in other documents.

file format
The internal structure of a file, which defines the way it is stored and used.

file extension
A tag of three or four letters, preceded by a period, that identifies a data file's format or the application used to create the file.

Program	Name.ext
Microsoft Word 2010 Microsoft Word 2003–2007	filename.docx filename.doc
WordPerfect	filename.wpd
Microsoft Works	filename.wps
Web documents	filename.htm
Generic (rich text file) word processing format	filename.rtf
Generic (text file) word processing format	filename.txt

WordPerfect has an option that allows it to run in Word simulation and open and save files in Word file format. Almost all programs allow files to be saved in selected file formats. However, as previously mentioned, files saved using the newer versions of programs, such as Word 2010, might not be able to be opened in other versions of that program. Some of the new features in Word 2010 are new to that version and are not available in older versions of Word. As a result, files saved in the Word 2010 format may not work in older versions like Word 2003. However, Word does allow files to be saved in generic formats like rich text file (RTF) or plain text format, which may be imported into other programs, but it does not provide for saving in WordPerfect format. Word 2010 permits files to be saved in older formats when the user selects the file format option under the Save As feature, as shown in Exhibit 6.18.

WordPerfect allows files to be saved in a number of formats using the Save As—File Type screen shown in Exhibit 6.19. It will convert most documents from other formats into the WordPerfect format. However, if files are going to be shared among users of different word processing programs, a compatible generic format like RTF format should be agreed upon as the format for all exchanged files. Alternatively, users may agree to save files using an older Word format such as Word 2003, and avoid features that can be used only in Word 2010.

Exhibit 6.18 Microsoft Word Save As options

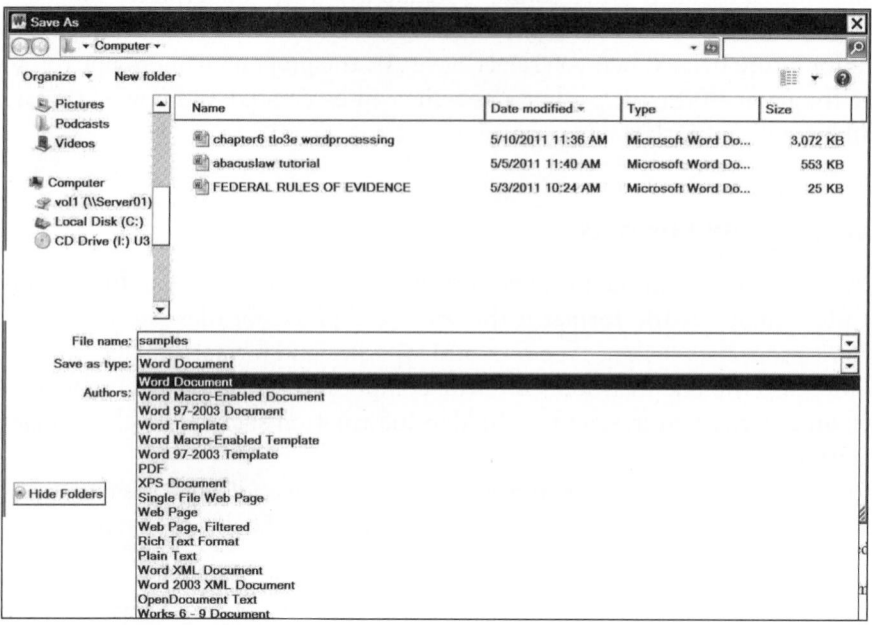

© 2011 Microsoft

Exhibit 6.19 WordPerfect Save As options

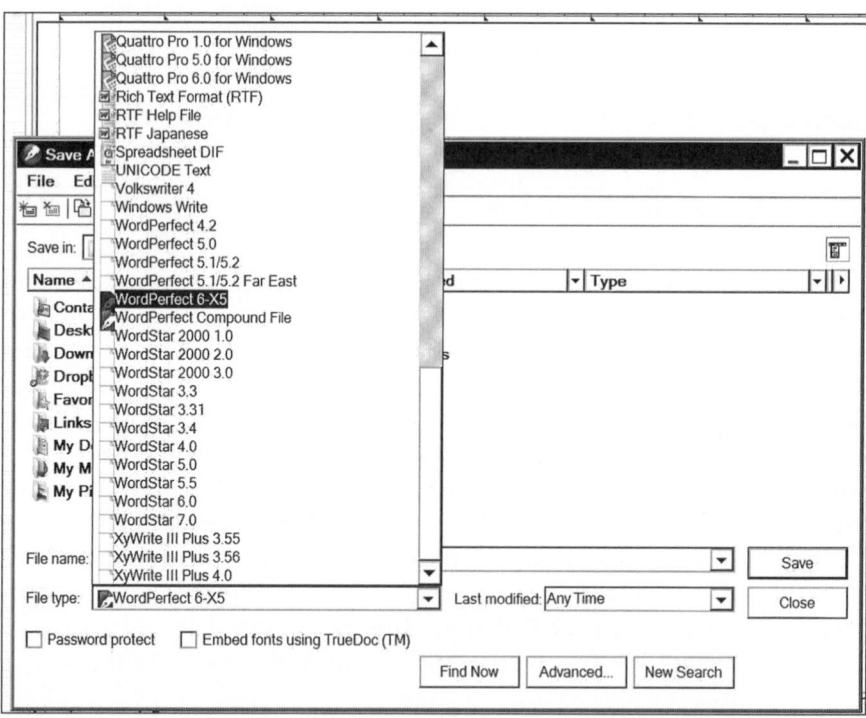

© Copyright 2012 Corel Corporation and Corel Corporation Limited, reprinted by permission.

■ SECURITY FEATURES

LEARNING OBJECTIVE 5
Discuss security issues and solutions in saving word processing documents.

Word processors can do much more than just type and edit documents. They provide tools that can promote collaboration and enhance the productivity of the legal team. But some of these tools, particularly the security features, can raise ethical concerns if not understood and used when appropriate. All word processing programs allow for some degree of security in the process of saving or sharing the file.

Protect Documents

When a file is shared, the author of the file may not want other parties to have the ability to make changes to the document. The Protect Document option restricts how people may access the document, and protects the document from changes to the formatting or text. Exhibit 6.20 shows the File tab Protect Document options in Word 2010. The Protect Document Group is located under the Review tab in Word 2007.

The security options also allow the creator of the document to restrict access to the document or the functions that may be performed with it. A password can be used to totally restrict access or to limit the ability to edit or change the document.

Document Properties

Document properties are data or information about a document, such as the date the document was created or the name of the document's author. This information is often referred to as "metadata."

In certain situations, the user may not want others, such as opposing counsel, to have access to this data. For example, the date a document was created may reveal when the author knew certain information. This date could be critical in a case where the author claimed he or she was unaware of a certain condition or activity at a certain time. The date of the document, found in the metadata, could prove otherwise. If a document is being sent to opposing counsel, it would be prudent to restrict access to this metadata.

For example, a document admitting harassment in the workplace that was created by the defendant on a specific date is a smoking gun document if the date and author's identity are in the metadata. Both Word and WordPerfect offer specific instructions for removing the metadata or other hidden information.

Exhibit 6.20 File tab Protect Document options

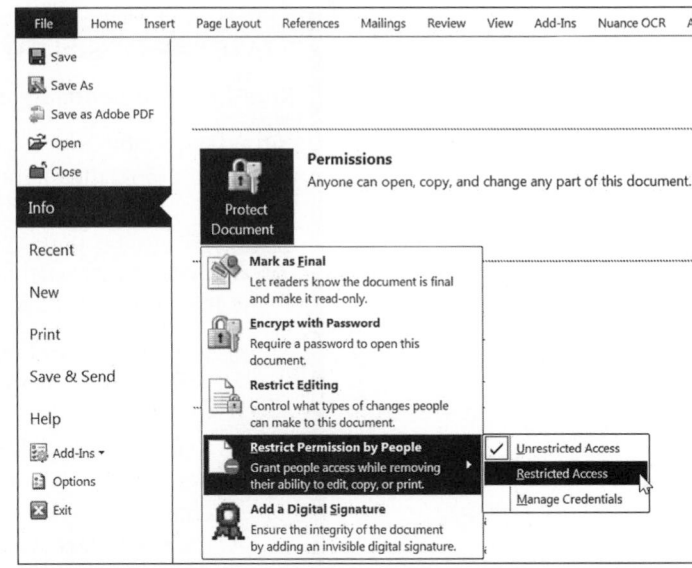

© Copyright 2012 Corel Corporation and Corel Corporation Limited, reprinted by permission.

ETHICAL Perspectives

SENSITIVE INFORMATION IN DOCUMENT DRAFTS

If Track Changes, or a similar tool, has been used while editing a document, it is important to remove the editing history before sending it to opposing counsel, the client, or the court. The history of changes to the document may reveal sensitive or damaging information. For example, during settlement negotiations, the original draft of a letter may show the final settlement offer the client was willing to pay, while the final draft sent to opposing counsel may contain a lower, initial offer. The deleted amount may have been retained in the editing history by the Track Changes tool, and can be discovered among the document's metadata by the other party.

Microsoft Word Help offers instructions on how to remove this information. WordPerfect makes it easy to quickly remove sensitive information by allowing documents to be saved using the *Save without metadata* option. Note that Word uses the term *personal information,* while WordPerfect uses the term *metadata* to refer to this information.

WEB RESOURCES

Contrast and compare Rule 1.6 of the State Bar of South Dakota at: http://www.sdbar.org/Rules/rules.shtm with the American Bar Association Model Rules of Professional Conduct at http://www.abanet.org/cpr/mrpc/mrpc_toc.html, and the ethical rule in your jurisdiction.

ETHICAL Perspectives

STATE BAR OF SOUTH DAKOTA

Rule 1.6. Confidentiality of Information

(a) A lawyer shall not reveal information relating to the representation of a client unless the client gives informed consent except for disclosures that are impliedly authorized in order to carry out the representation or the disclosure it is permitted by, and except as stated in paragraph (b).

(b) A lawyer may reveal information relating to the representation of a client to the extent the lawyer reasonably believes necessary:

(1) to prevent the client from committing a criminal act that the lawyer believes is likely to result in imminent death or substantial bodily harm;

(2) to secure legal advice about the lawyer's compliance with these Rules;

(3) to establish a claim or defense on behalf of the lawyer in a controversy between the lawyer and the client, to establish a defense to a criminal charge or civil claim against the lawyer based upon conduct in which the client was involved, or to respond to allegations in any proceeding concerning the lawyer's representation of the client;

(4) to the extent that revelation appears to be necessary to rectify the consequences of a client's criminal or fraudulent act in which the lawyer's services had been used; or

(5) to comply with other law or a court order.

In Word 2010, the basic details about the document are accessed through the Info section of the File menu. The Document Inspector tool provides options for removing the metadata, as shown in Exhibit 6.21. In Word 2007, this tool is part of the Office Button options, under Prepare.

Exhibit 6.21 Word properties and Document Inspector

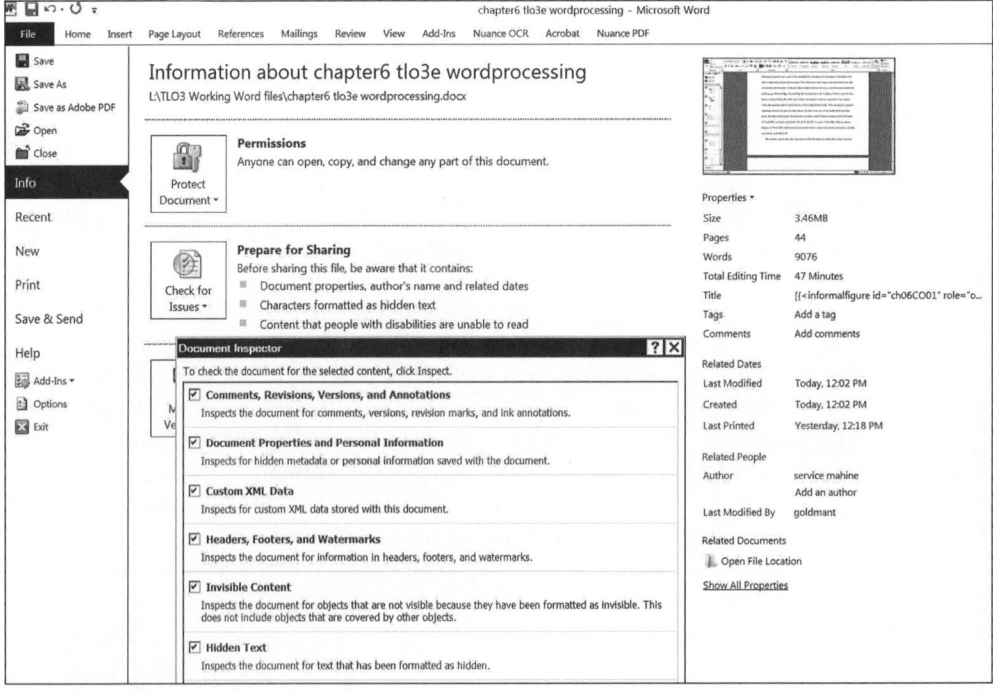

■ SPECIAL FEATURES OF WORD PROCESSOR PROGRAMS

Every software program has some special features that differentiate it from other software. Switching between programs or learning a new program may require learning these special features. Some features can be utilized through "wizards," which are tools that guide the user through a series of steps.

Headers and Footers

Headers and **footers** are the areas at the top and bottom, respectively, of each page in the document that provide information the author wants repeated on every page, such as the page number, a document title, or a copyright notice. To add a header or footer:

In Word 2010:
- use the Insert tab, and
- select Header or Footer (Exhibit 6.22).

In Word 2003:
- use the View tab, and
- select Header and Footer option; a left mouse click opens selection options.

In WordPerfect:
- select the Insert pull-down menu, and
- select Header/Footer (Exhibit 6.23).

header
Items at the top of each page of the document.

footer
Items at the bottom of each page of the document.

Track Changes

In most law offices, several persons may have input in the creation of a document before it is finalized. After each person reviews and edits the document, it is sent to the next reviewer electronically, either over an office network or as an attachment to an email. A document may also be shared for review, additions,

Exhibit 6.22 Word 2010 Insert tab—Header Footer options

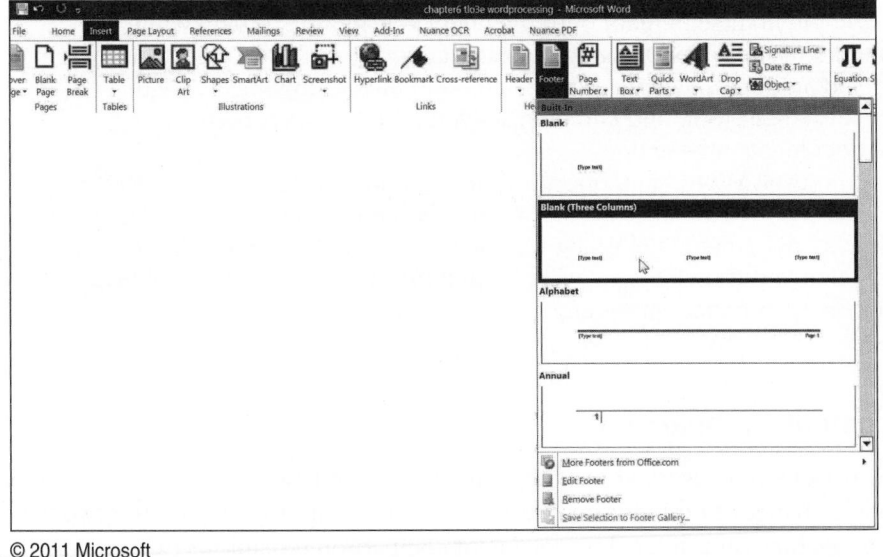

© 2011 Microsoft

Exhibit 6.23 WordPerfect Insert tab Header/ Footer menu

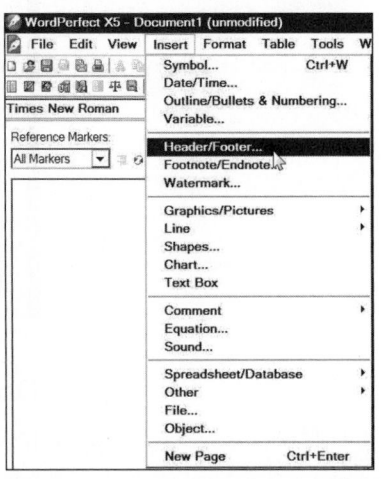

© Copyright 2012 Corel Corporation and Corel Corporation Limited, reprinted by permission.

Exhibit 6.24 Track Change options

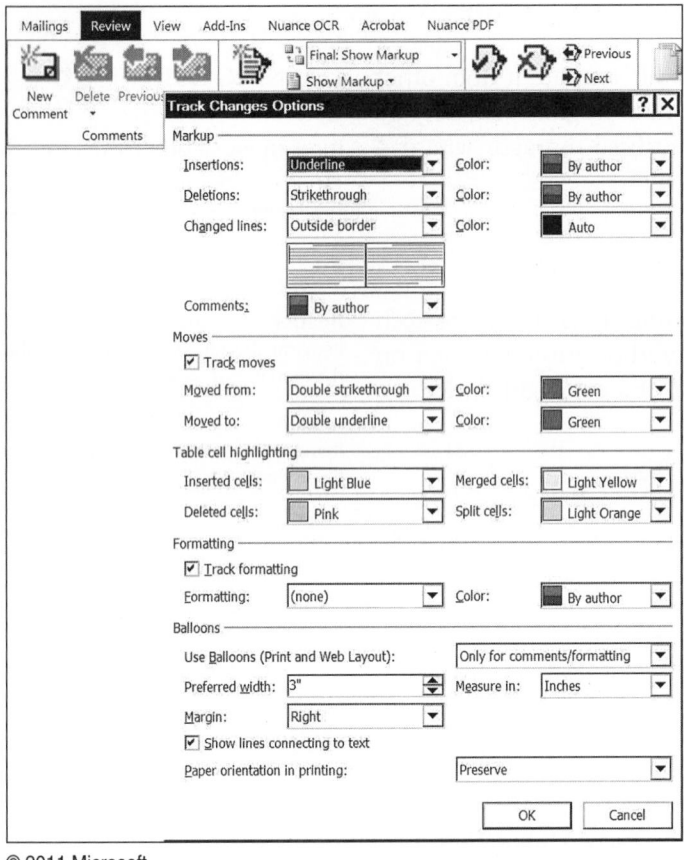

© 2011 Microsoft

and corrections using an Internet or cloud application, like Office 365 or Google Apps. Word's Track Changes feature allows each reviewer to see, in a single document, all the changes that have been made, instead of having to look at multiple drafts. In Word, Track Changes is found under the Review tab. When this feature is selected, the user can see

- the original text,
- the deleted text, and
- the new text.

If the user chooses to view the changes inline, the deleted text is shown with a strikethrough, and the new text is indicated with an underscore. If the user chooses to have edits shown in balloons, the deleted text is set in the margin in a balloon, with a line indicating where it was removed from. Exhibit 6.24 shows the Track Changes options.

Exhibit 6.25 shows the original Word file, with additions indicated by a double underline and deleted text indicated with a strikethrough.

The reviewer may accept or reject each change using the commands Accept or Reject under the Review tab, as shown in Exhibit 6.26.

ETHICAL Perspectives

SENSITIVE INFORMATION IN DOCUMENT DRAFTS

If Track Changes, or a similar tool, has been used while editing a document, it is important to remove the editing history before sending it to opposing counsel, the client, or the court. The history of changes to the document may reveal sensitive or damaging information. For example, during settlement negotiations, the original draft of a letter may have shown the final settlement offer the client was willing to pay, while the final draft sent to opposing counsel contains a lower, initial offer. The deleted amount may have been retained in the editing history by the Track Changes tool, and can be discovered by the other party among the document's metadata.

Microsoft Word Help offers information on how to remove this information. WordPerfect makes is easy to quickly remove sensitive information by allowing documents to be saved using the *Save without metadata* option. Note that Word uses the term *personal information*, while Wordperfect uses the term *metadata* to refer to this information.

Document Comparison

If two persons have worked on a document independently, or opposing counsel has made changes to the document, it may be necessary to compare the two versions to see how they differ. The document comparison tool allows two documents

Exhibit 6.25 Word file with changes

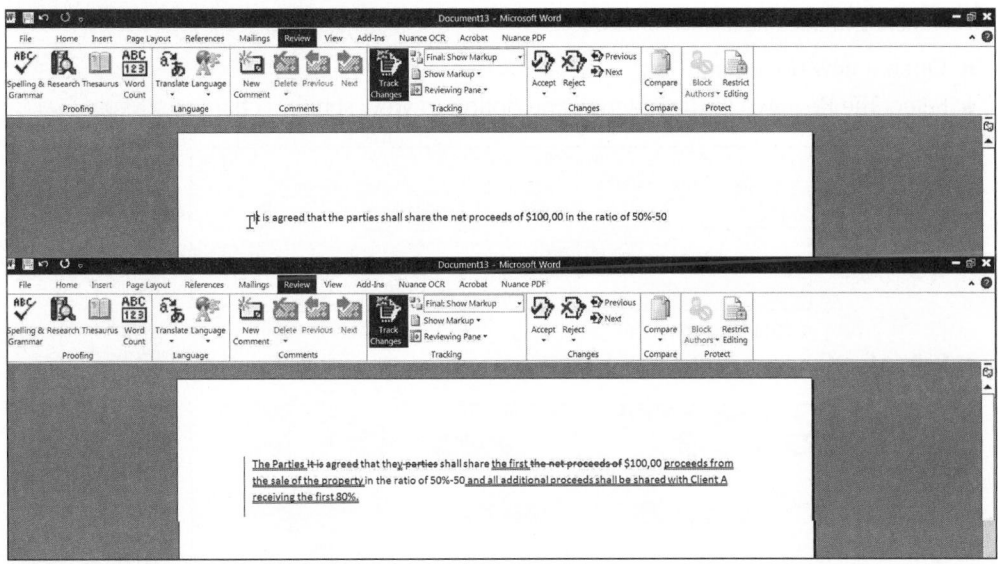

© 2011 Microsoft

Exhibit 6.26 Accept or Reject under the Review tab

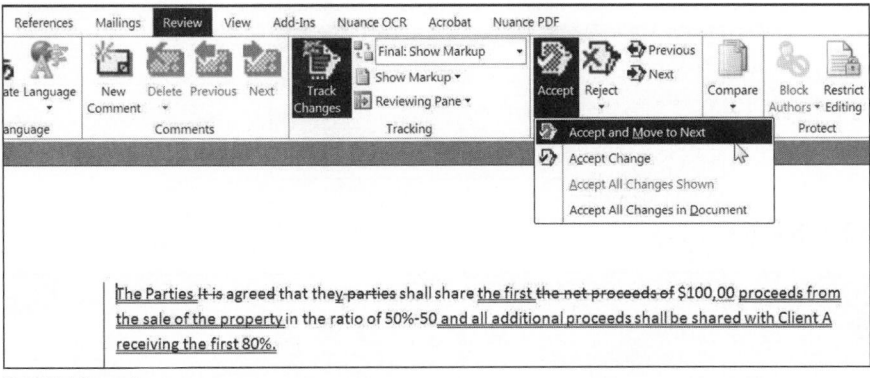

© 2011 Microsoft

to be compared and the differences shown. A final version, a merging of the two documents, can then be created, as shown in Exhibit 6.27.

Mail Merge

The **Mail Merge** feature allows a user to create mass mailings by automatically combining a document, such as a form letter, with a list of recipients. Each person on the list then receives what appears to be a personalized letter. The feature is essentially a program within a program, or a macro, that creates the mailings in a series of steps. In Word, a mail merge may be complete using the Mail Merge Wizard, as shown in Exhibit 6.28. The user may create a new letter or use an existing letter, and then add an address block and greeting line that will be filled for each recipient. The user can then select the list of names and addresses to be used.

Mail Merge
A macro that combines a document with a list of recipients.

Table of Authorities

A **table of authorities** is a listing of the citations or other references in a document and the numbers of the pages where they are located. In Word 2010, a table

table of authorities
A list of the references in a document and the numbers of the pages where they are located.

Exhibit 6.27 Word 2010 Compare Documents

To compare two documents in Word 2010:

- Open a new document.
- Select the Review tab Reviewing Pane option to view specific changes.

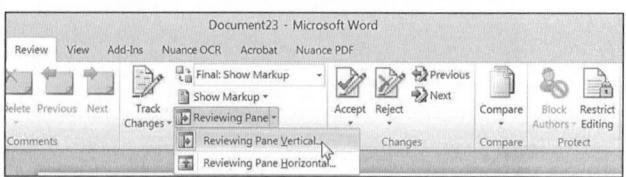

© 2011 Microsoft

- Select the Compare option in the Review tab.

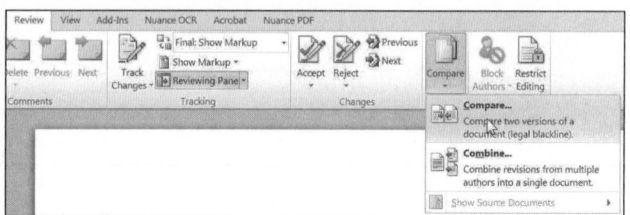

© 2011 Microsoft

- Select the two documents to compare.

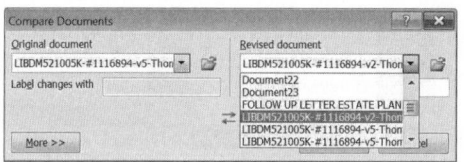

© 2011 Microsoft

- Review the changes.

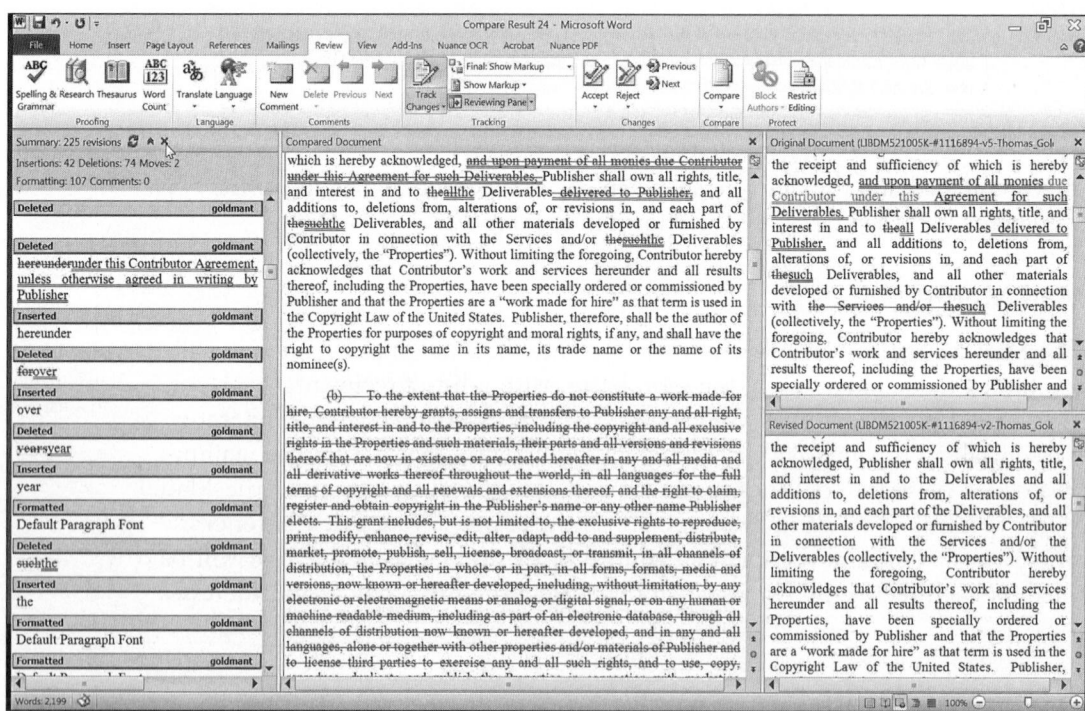

© 2011 Microsoft

Exhibit 6.28 Word Mail Merge Wizard

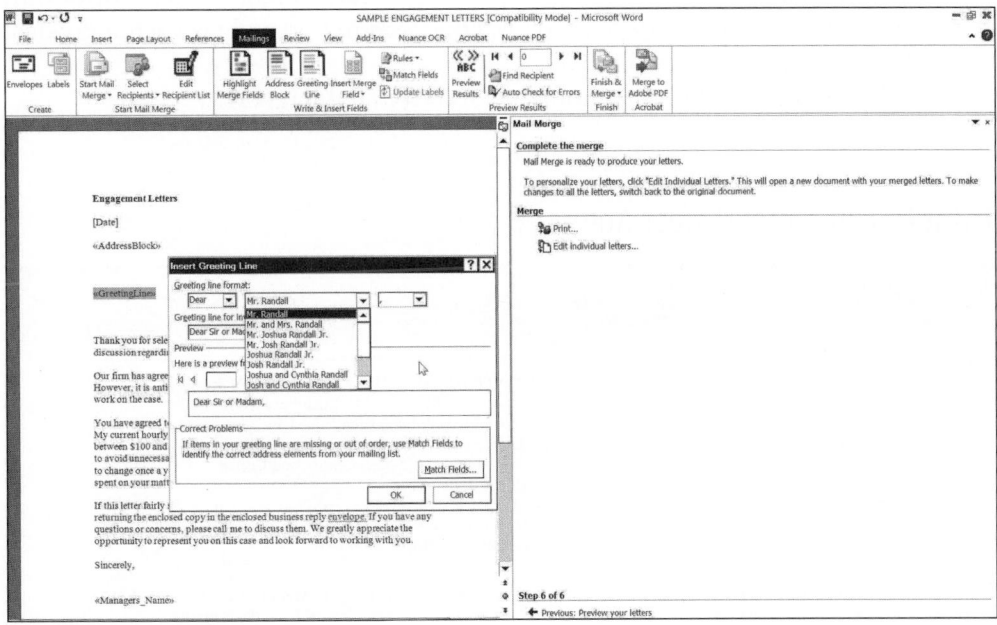

© 2011 Microsoft

can be started by marking each citation by pressing ALT + SHIFT + I. The table of authorities is inserted into the document using the Insert Table of Authorities selection in the References tab. The citations in the table may be organized by category. Each authority is marked and identified by inserting a TA, or Table of Authority, entry. These marks are visible when the Hidden Marks button (¶) is selected, as shown in Exhibit 6.29. The table of authorities may be inserted by choosing Insert Table of Authorities in the References tab.

Exhibit 6.29 Word Table of Authorities tool

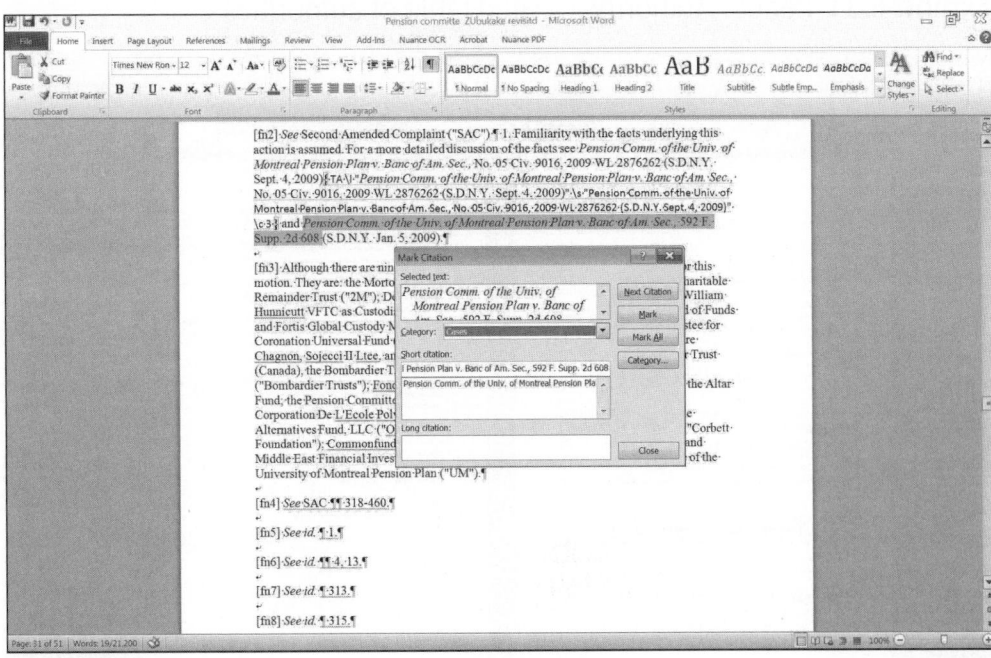

© 2011 Microsoft

WordPerfect offers an add-on tool, called "Perfect Authority," for creating a table of authorities. This tool automatically creates a table of authorities with a single click of the mouse, eliminating the need to find and tag each individual citation, as shown in Exhibit 6.30.

The resulting table of authorities is shown in Exhibit 6.31.

Exhibit 6.30 Corel Perfect Authority

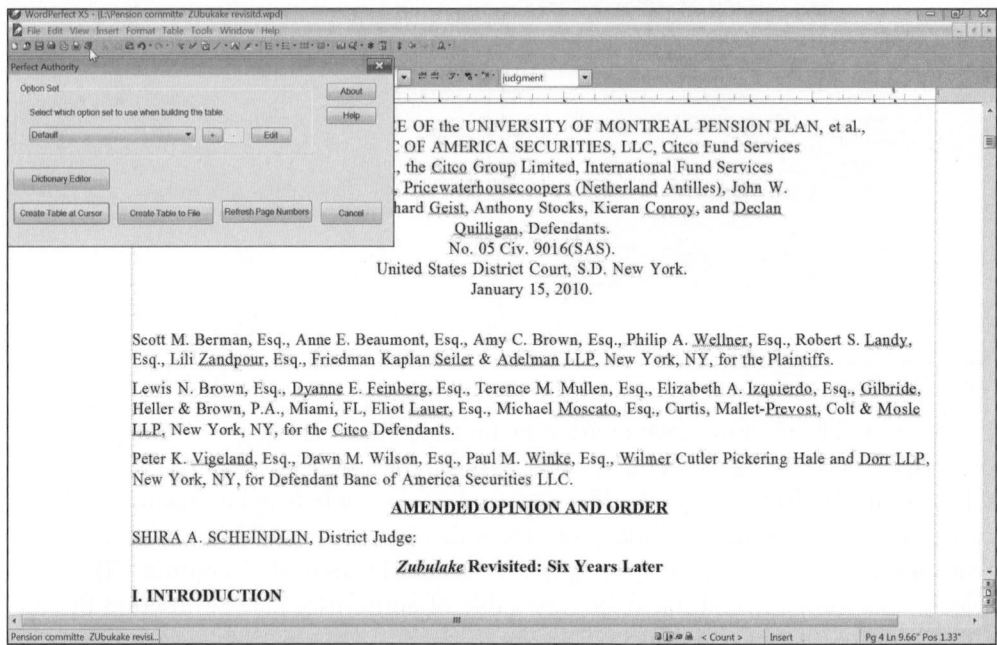

Exhibit 6.31 Perfect Authority–created table of authorities

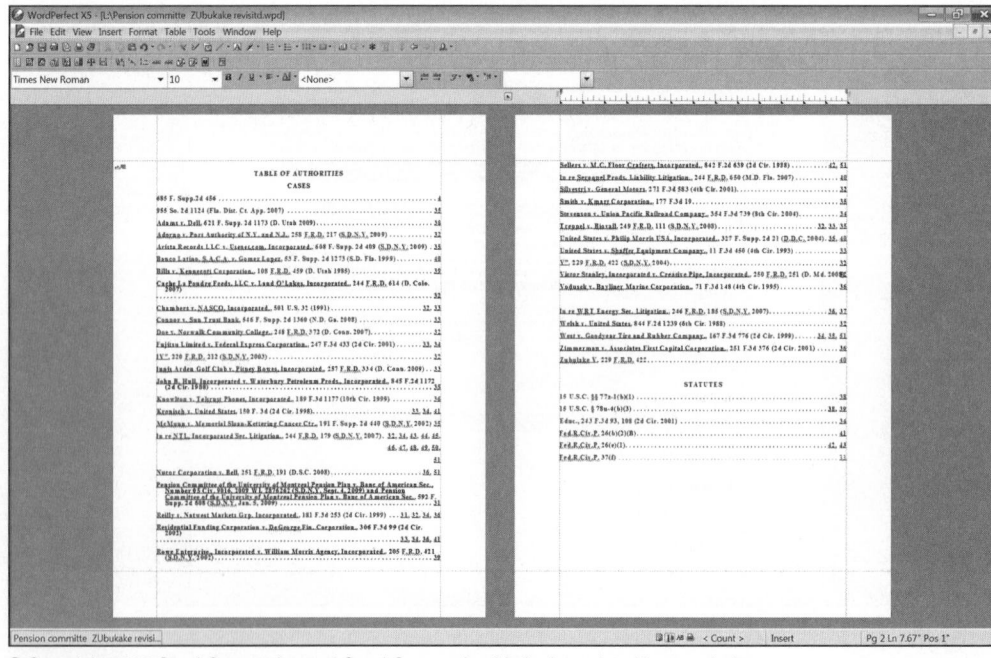

■ UPDATES TO WORD PROCESSING PROGRAMS

Software is continually updated and upgraded, sometimes several times in a year. These changes are designed to fix problems, called bugs; improve existing features; or add new features. Usually, the changes made do not affect the use of files created and saved with previous software versions. However, with some updates, older versions and features may not be supported; in addition, new versions may create files that cannot be opened or used with older versions that are still in use. Most programs feature a "What's New" item as part of the Help feature. New releases of software are usually accompanied by press releases, and special notations on the software package highlight the changes.

Word 2010

Some of the new features of Microsoft Office 2010 make use of the suite's programs more efficient and effective. Other features allow a level of collaboration not possible with older versions. However, not everyone will upgrade to the 2010 version of Office. The decision to upgrade is often based on a combination of considerations. Because of the different issues involved with upgrading, some offices use programs that are two or three versions old, such as Word 97. But if you understand that the basic functions among these versions are the same, you can find the help needed to use them.

For the "power" law office user, a number of tools and features in Word 2010 reduce the number of keystrokes or mouse clicks needed to accomplish the desired result. For example, symbols such as § and ¶ can be inserted with the Insert tab's Symbols group, shown in Exhibit 6.32.

Sometimes legal briefs or documents require footnotes, citations, and tables of figures, and each of these functions can be quickly and easily accessed from the References tab, shown in Exhibit 6.33, using just a few keystrokes.

LEARNING OBJECTIVE 7
Recognize changes in updates to major word processing software.

WEB RESOURCES
Search for changes in software by using your web browser. For example, try entering the search terms "WordPerfect X5 updates." How do these updates change or improve the software? What problems are they designed to correct?

Exhibit 6.32 Insert tab's Symbols group

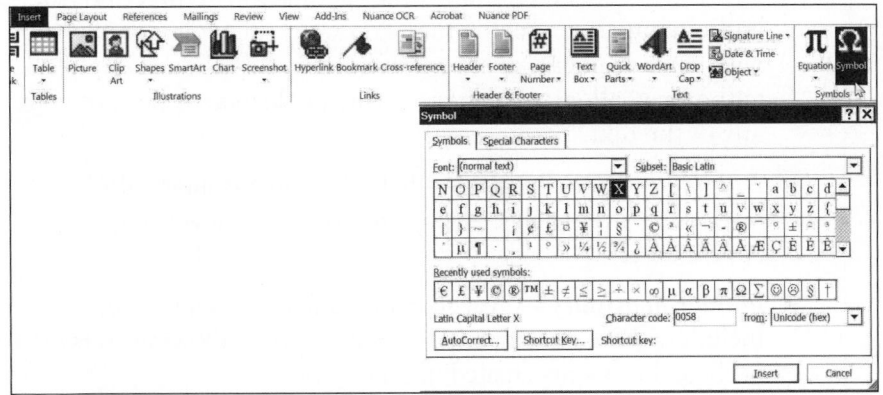

© 2011 Microsoft.

Exhibit 6.33 References tab

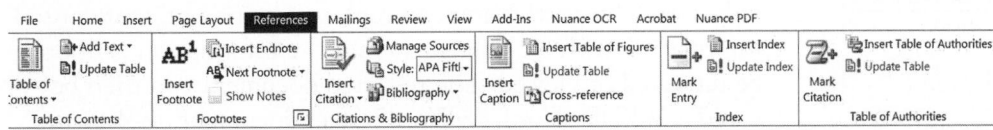

© 2011 Microsoft.

Among other new features are the following:

- Quick styles and document themes can change the appearance throughout a document.
- Live Word Count at the bottom of the word screen can track the length of documents. This feature is useful when there is a word limit, as in some court filings.
- Documents in different formats can be shared.

WordPerfect X5

WordPerfect has added many new enhancements to aid users' productivity, particularly in the use of PDF (portable document format) files. This file format has become as common as some of the proprietary word processor formats from companies such as Microsoft. With the increased use of PDF documents in every aspect of legal practice, flexibility in sharing these files is essential, especially when Adobe Acrobat or Nuance PDF Creator software is not installed on a user's computer.

In its X5 version, WordPerfect supports PDF files through these features:

Exhibit 6.34 WordPerfect Publish to PDF settings

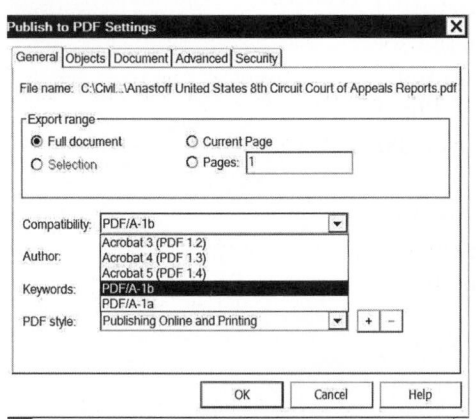

© Copyright 2012 Corel Corporation and Corel Corporation Limited, reprinted by permission.

Exhibit 6.35 WordPerfect tools— Redaction options

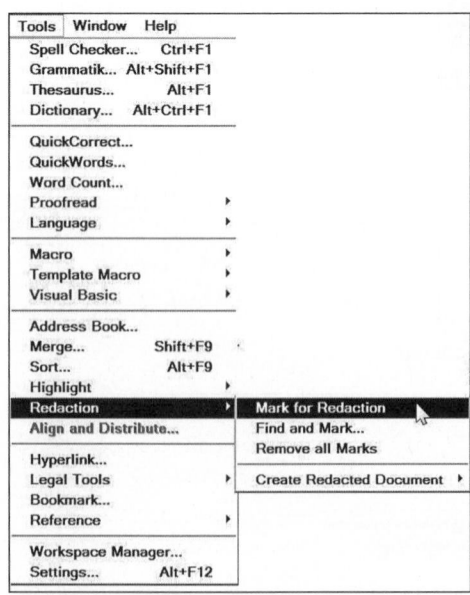

© Copyright 2012 Corel Corporation and Corel Corporation Limited, reprinted by permission.

- ***Import Scanned PDF Files***—Built-in features allow the import, edit, and export of PDF documents without the use of Adobe Acrobat®.

- ***Add Password Protection***—Because PDF files aren't inherently secure, text can be copied and pasted from the files. However, WordPerfect provides built-in password controls that regulate who may view, copy, edit, or print the document. Two levels of password protection are provided: "open" and "permission." With the "open" protection, if the recipient has the password, he or she has full privileges to edit, copy, save, or print the document. With the "permission" protection, the author may place specific limits on what the recipient may do with the document, as shown in Exhibit 6.34. For example, the author may allow someone to print the document but not copy any of the text.

- ***Automatic PDF Preview***—PDF files can automatically be opened after their creation in order to review their appearance.

- *Format-neutrality*—Over sixty file formats are supported, including those of competitors' products, thus allowing users to share documents created in other programs.

- *Redaction*—Confidential personal information, such as names, addresses, social security numbers, and account numbers, must often be redacted, or blacked out, from court filings. With the redaction feature, the user can replace sensitive or confidential information with a black bar so that the information cannot be retrieved or viewed. The redacted document can then be saved as a PDF, Word, or WordPerfect document, as shown in Exhibit 6.35.

CONCEPT REVIEW AND REINFORCEMENT

KEY TERMS

boilerplate 149	header 153	Save 148
file extension 149	macro 137	Save As 148
file format 149	Mail Merge 155	table of authorities 155
footer 153	Ribbon 137	template 146

CHAPTER SUMMARY

Introduction to Word Processing	Written communication and document preparation are at the heart of every law office.
	Changes or revisions are frequently made to electronic file copies by reviewers.
	Changes made by each person on the legal team may be monitored by using built-in features such as Microsoft Word's Track Changes tool.
	All word processing programs have a set of basic word processing functions, such as format, style, and saving options. Some programs offer additional features like document comparison.
	Microsoft Office 2010 offers the same traditional functions as previous versions, plus a File tab in place of the Office Button.
Adapting to Change	For the paralegal, legal assistant, lawyer, or other members of the legal team, change is constant. Adapting to change includes being prepared for updates in the software used in the workplace.
	Change is easier to adapt to if the user recognizes the common features and functions across programs, and can quickly learn the differences or new features in software.
Navigating in Word Processor Programs	Menus and toolbars are the most common ways to access the features of software.
	Office 2007 introduced the Ribbon view. Office 2010 introduced the File tab to replace the Office Button.
	The principal difference between the traditional interface and the new Ribbon interface is the grouping of commands by tasks most frequently used in a tab format.
	Menus display a list of commands and are located on the menu bar, also called a toolbar, at the top of the page in the program.
	Toolbars can contain menus, buttons, or a combination of both. Microsoft Office 2007 changed the traditional appearance from earlier versions while retaining the basic functions of the programs. The 2010 version further enhances usability by grouping features.

Resources for Learning and Using Word Processor Software	Every program has some level of instruction or help available for using the program. Resources include: information available over the Internet from the software vendors; guides, instructions, or formal documentation; built-in Help function.
Starting a Document	The first step in creating a document is to select and start (launch) the desired program. The next step, in most cases, is to open the File menu.
File Search Function	Each program has a search tool that performs a search of the computer and the file server for files with designated names, terms, or words.
Templates	A preset, predesigned page, such as a pleading layout with line numbers. A template may have predefined borders, margins, type font, and type size.
Saving the File	Saving the new document requires selecting an appropriate name for the file, a location in which it is to be filed or stored, and the format in which it is to be saved. The Save command saves the file with the same name and in the same location from which it was opened. The Save command effectively erases the previous file with the same name. The Save As command prompts the user to indicate the name and the location in which the file is to be saved before saving the file.
Converting File Formats	A file format is the way the word processor files are saved, including document properties such as type font and type size and formatting details. A file extension (a period followed by characters) is added to the end of the file name to identify the program or format in which the file has been saved.
Security Features	All programs allow for some degree of security in the process of saving the file or sharing the file.
Protect Documents	The Protect Documents options restrict how people may access the document.
Document Properties	Document properties are a part of the metadata for word processor documents.
Special Features of Word Processor Programs	Metadata is the data or information about the document. Two of the most basic items in the metadata are the date of creation and the author.
Headers and Footers	The items at the top or bottom of each page in the document, like page numbering in a footer or the location where the document is filed (path) in a header.
Track Changes	A feature that shows the original text, the deleted text, and the new text using a series of lines that appear as a strikethroughs and margin notes in the document.

Document Comparison	Allows two documents to be compared and the differences shown, with the final version being a merger of the two documents.
Mail Merge	A macro that combines one document with information from another, such as a letter combined with a list of recipients.
Table of Authorities	A macro that automates the creation of a list of authorities, such as statutes or cases, as a table that can be inserted into a document.
Updates to Word Processing Programs	Some of the new features of Office Suite 2010 make using the programs more efficient and time effective. Other features allow a level of collaboration not easily attained with older versions. WordPerfect X5 addresses the increased use of different file formats by allowing file saving and converting into over sixty formats, including some legacy formats and those of other word processing programs.

REVIEW QUESTIONS AND EXERCISES

1. What are the advantages and the disadvantages in using passwords with word processor documents?
2. What are the security features available in Word and WordPerfect?
3. Explain the functions of the word processing software as used by the legal team.
4. Describe what might be found in a word processor menu and toolbar.
5. How can you identify the document format by referring to the file extension?
6. What are the ethical issues in saving word processing documents?
7. How can you control the degree to which others can access and change specific areas of your documents and specify the types of changes, such as tracked changes, comments, and formatting, that can be made? Why would you want to allow different levels of access?
8. How can you find and remove hidden data, such as tracked changes, comments, and hidden text, from the documents you send to others?
9. Find information on mail merge in your word processor. Create a simple one-paragraph letter and a list of five recipients with addresses. Use the instructions to do the mail merge and print out the results.
10. How can you help protect sensitive information in your documents?
11. How does the ethical duty of confidentiality affect the way word processor documents are saved?
12. Choose a tool or feature in your word processing software that you would like to know more about. Find an online learning resource and locate the information that applies to that tool or feature.
13. Write a step-by-step guide to creating and saving a document in your word processor program. Be sure to explain the distinction between Save and Save As commands, and the implications of using each.
14. Identify five persons with whom you might interact at a law firm. Each person should hold a different working relationship with you, such as an attorney at the firm, a client, opposing counsel, or the court. Using a sample document, create a separate copy for each of the five people, and set appropriate permissions for each copy using password protection, the Protect Document feature of Microsoft Office.
15. Use Word to create a document with at least three case names and citations. The cases should be cited within the text. Neither the text nor the cases need to be authentic; they can be made-up information. Create a table of authorities and place it at the end of the document.
16. Use Word to create a sample form letter. Use Mail Merge to address it to five or more people in your address book.

BUILDING YOUR PARALEGAL SKILLS

INTERNET AND TECHNOLOGY EXERCISES

1. View the demo "Create a legal team notebook" at http://office.microsoft.com/en-us/assistance/HA012190161033.aspx
2. Complete the online Microsoft training course on protecting Word documents.
3. Complete the Microsoft Office lesson on Security for Word.

CHAPTER OPENING SCENARIO CASE STUDY

Use the Opening Scenario for this chapter to answer the following questions:

1. Prepare a list of the three online tutorials you would recommend to someone switching from Word to WordPerfect, from WordPerfect to Word, or from an older version to a newer version of the same program. Explain what features you found most helpful and why.

2. Prepare a section for the employee handbook of a law firm explaining how to find help with using new software. Be sure to explain what steps may be taken to locate and use the resources for learning how to use specific programs.

CONTINUING CASES AND EXERCISES

1. Use the Internet to locate a sample fee agreement letter. Use the letter to create a template in Word or WordPerfect. Be sure to include only the boilerplate language in the template, and provide fields in which to enter the names of the parties, the amounts, and other variables.

2. Use the fee agreement template to prepare a fee agreement letter for a fictional client for services in preparing wills and documents for a family trip. Use the following billing rates:
   a. Attorney, $200 per hour
   b. Paralegal, $75 per hour

   Activate Track Changes before drafting the letter. Then change the date, the billing rates, and the client address, and print a copy showing the tracked changes for attorney review.

3. Prepare a contingent fee agreement for use with the clients involved in the accident described in Appendix II Case A.
   a. Write the first draft of the agreement. In this draft, the contingent fee is 30 percent of the net recovery, plus all out-of-pocket costs. Prepare the document to be sent to the clients electronically.
   b. Write a second draft of the agreement. Use the same contingent fee agreement, but reduce the fee to 20 percent for the driver who brought the case into the office. When saving the second draft of the agreement, use the appropriate features in Word or WordPerfect to remove all sensitive information from the file.

ADVANCED EXERCISES

1. Review the program's Help feature to learn how to insert a table in a document.
2. Use the Table function to set up a table with information on the office staff, including names, address, social security numbers, and the other information required on federal IRS forms W-4 and W-9.
3. Is the Sort function of any value in using the form created using the Table function?
4. Use the Table function to set up a table with the information on the clients in the accident case. Use the information on the sample client interview sheet for the headings.

BUILDING YOUR PROFESSIONAL PORTFOLIO

1. Write a proposed law firm policy for ensuring that metadata and earlier edits to documents have been eliminated from the final version. Include step-by-step procedures for both Word and WordPerfect.
2. Write a memo for a small office on the dangers of using the Track Changes feature. Explain how to eliminate the dangers by properly saving completed files.

"Computers are useless. They can only give you answers."

—*Pablo Picasso (1881–1973), Spanish painter*

CHAPTER 7

Spreadsheets

OPENING SCENARIO

Owen Mason, Esq. and his paralegal Caitlin were preparing for a negotiating session the following day. Their client was working out a new labor contract with a union, and they had been working on different proposals and counterproposals for a number of days. The costs among the demands and offers varied widely.

During the negotiations, Owen wanted to be able to quickly calculate what the cost for each proposal would be, based on the proposed salary increases and changes to individual fringe benefits. As these figures changed, he would need to be able to calculate the total cost per employee, and the total for all employees. These figures would need to be calculated during the negotiating session, as new proposals were presented. He needed to quickly assess whether the total employee salaries and benefits in each proposal were within his client's negotiating authority and budgets.

Caitlin had taken a course in preparing spreadsheets, and had some experience using them in estate planning. Spreadsheets had saved a lot of time in performing calculations in a complex estate in which a number of alternative tax and estate planning strategies were considered. Owen was hoping Caitlin could do something similar in the labor negotiations. Without a spreadsheet to perform the calculations, it would take hours to get through the session, and it seemed that the other side always had the numbers at their fingertips.

LEARNING OBJECTIVES

After studying this chapter, you should be able to:

1. Identify the parts of a spreadsheet.

2. Find resources for learning how to use a spreadsheet and its features.

3. Create, edit, and save a spreadsheet.

4. Use some of the special features of spreadsheets, including graphics.

VIDEO INTRODUCTION

SPREADSHEETS
After watching the video in MyLegalStudiesLab, answer the following questions.

1. How can spreadsheets save the legal team time?
2. What are the dangers in using spreadsheets?

Professor Thomas F. Goldman, Esq.

■ INTRODUCTION TO SPREADSHEETS

Most areas of legal practice involve calculating and presenting financial information. For example, in a family law practice, balance sheets and income and expense reports are routinely prepared for hearings regarding child support, or the distribution of marital assets. In wills, trusts, and estate practices, lawyers must frequently calculate the financial impact of taxes on different estate plans, or submit an account to beneficiaries or to the court showing how the fiduciary handled the financial affairs of an estate or trust. Trial attorneys must provide account statements to clients for the proceeds of settlements, including details of the receipts and disbursements. In some cases, like minors' compromises and class action cases, statements must be given to the court for approval. The spreadsheet, when laid out in the format specified by the court, can be printed without re-entering the data, or copied into word processor documents.

Many applications used in legal practice provide templates with formulas for calculating the information needed. For example, one application provides a spreadsheet version of the Housing and Urban Development (HUD) statement used in real estate settlements or closings. Spreadsheets have reduced the potential for error when manually calculating or retyping amounts. In situations where only a small change is needed, the tedium of manually completing a worksheet is eliminated. The spreadsheet can be instantly reproduced with the number changed, along with the effects on the rest of the calculations. However, caution must be taken to ensure that the formula is accurate and performs the desired calculation. Expert spreadsheet users will test the formulas by inputting a set of sample numbers with a known result.

■ CREATING AND WORKING WITH SPREADSHEETS

LEARNING OBJECTIVE 1
Identify the parts of
a spreadsheet.

As you look at the following spreadsheet and template examples, you will note the variety of presentation styles and degrees of complexity. A spreadsheet, in its most basic form, is any two items with some mathematical relationship, with the result presented in a specific location called a cell. Spreadsheets are frequently used in situations requiring many complex calculations, such as "what-if" tables used in complex estate planning. Some people specialize in developing these complex spreadsheets and then designing a user-friendly appearance or format. Spreadsheets are also valuable for performing basic tasks such as preparing a list of items that can be added up and then saved to later verify that each number was inputted correctly. With an understanding of what the spreadsheet can accomplish, you will be able to express your needs to the person who is preparing the spreadsheet, like the in-house IT specialist or computer consultant.

NAVIGATING IN SPREADSHEETS

Spreadsheets use a set of standard terms to describe the parts of the spreadsheet, such as **rows, columns, cells,** formulas, **workbooks,** the **formula bar,** and the active cell, as shown in Exhibit 7.1.

The 2007 and later versions of Excel introduced a Ribbon design for the user interface. Excel 2010 further refined the Ribbon design as well as other features such as the menus, toolbar, and layout, as shown in Exhibit 7.1. However, the basic parts and functions of a spreadsheet are unchanged, as shown in Exhibit 7.2.

As with other applications in the Microsoft Office Suite, the 2010 version of Excel provides tabs, groups, and command buttons that allow users to access features and functions that were accessed using menus and toolbars in earlier versions. The most visible change in the 2010 version is the substitution of the Microsoft Office Button with the File tab that opens the Microsoft Office Backstage commands.

RESOURCES FOR LEARNING HOW TO USE SPREADSHEETS

As seen in Chapter 6, most software vendors provide help in learning how to use their software. Microsoft offers a number of online tutorials, some of which are listed in the Excel Help and How-to website, as shown in Exhibit 7.3.

row
A horizontal set of cells in a spreadsheet.

column
A vertical set of cells in a spreadsheet.

cell
In a spreadsheet, the box at the intersection of a row and a column for text or numerical data.

workbook
A collection of worksheets.

formula bar
In Excel, the area at the top of the spreadsheet for entering formulas and data into spreadsheet cells.

LEARNING OBJECTIVE 2
Find resources for learning how to use a spreadsheet and its features.

Exhibit 7.1 Parts of a spreadsheet shown in Excel 2003

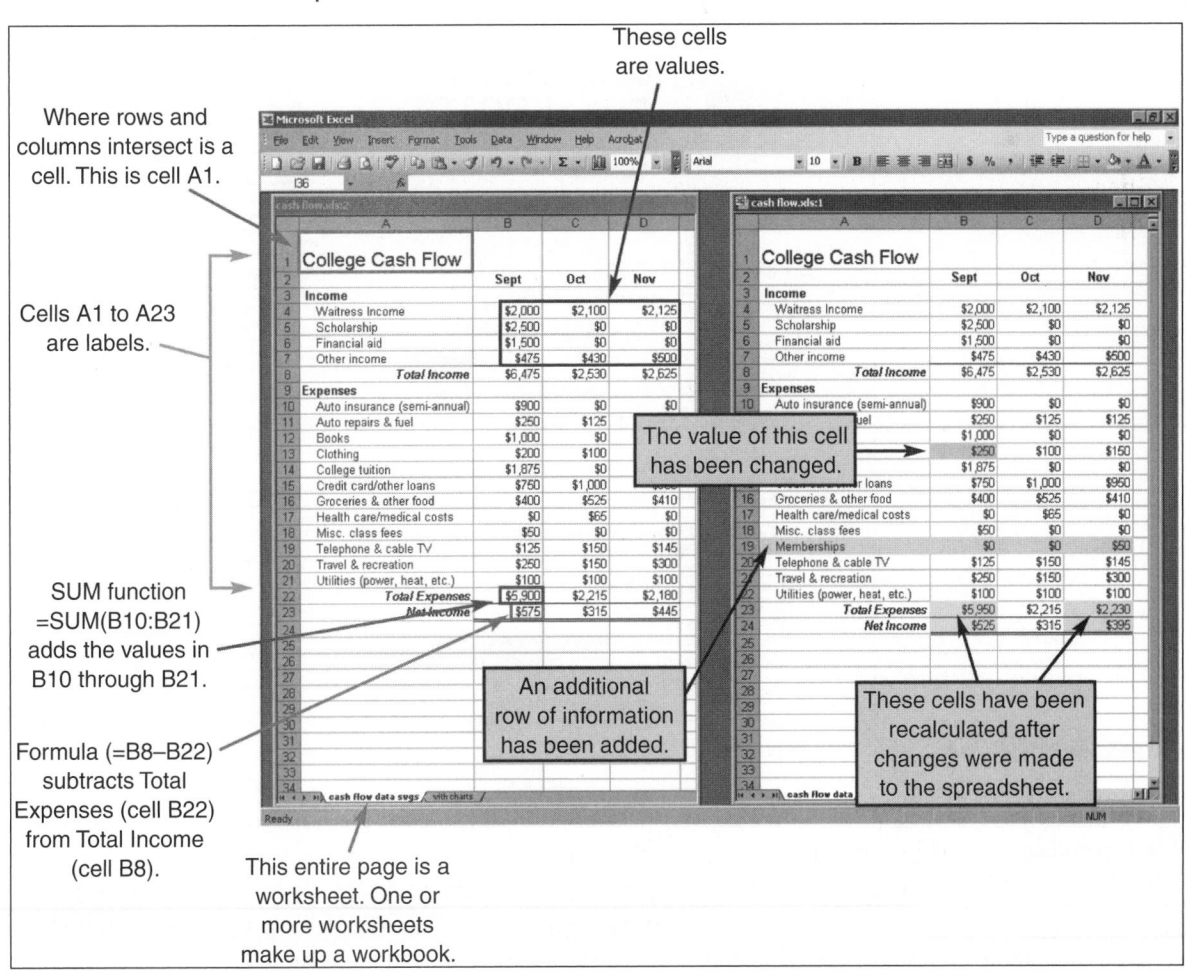

Exhibit 7.2 Excel 2010 Ribbon view

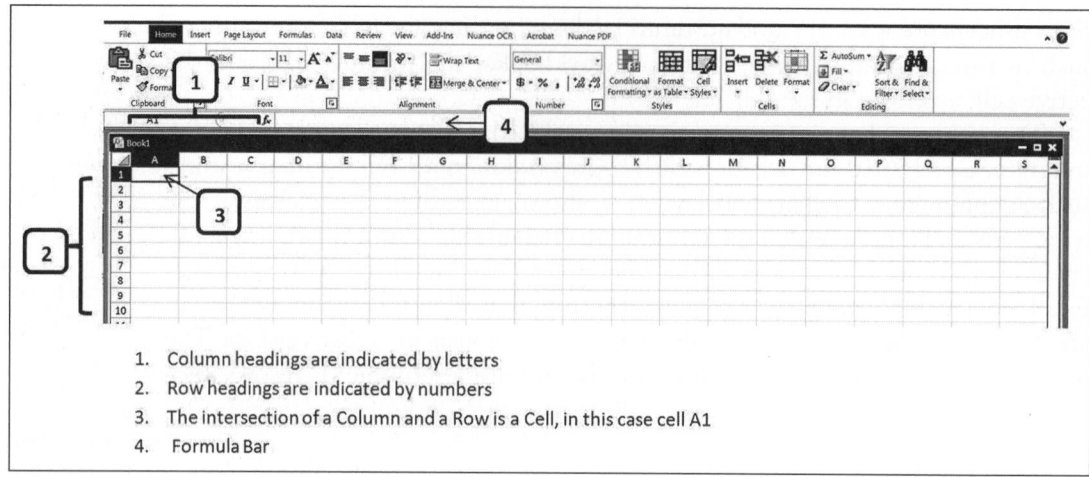

1. Column headings are indicated by letters
2. Row headings are indicated by numbers
3. The intersection of a Column and a Row is a Cell, in this case cell A1
4. Formula Bar

© 2011 Microsoft.

Exhibit 7.3 Excel Help and How-to website

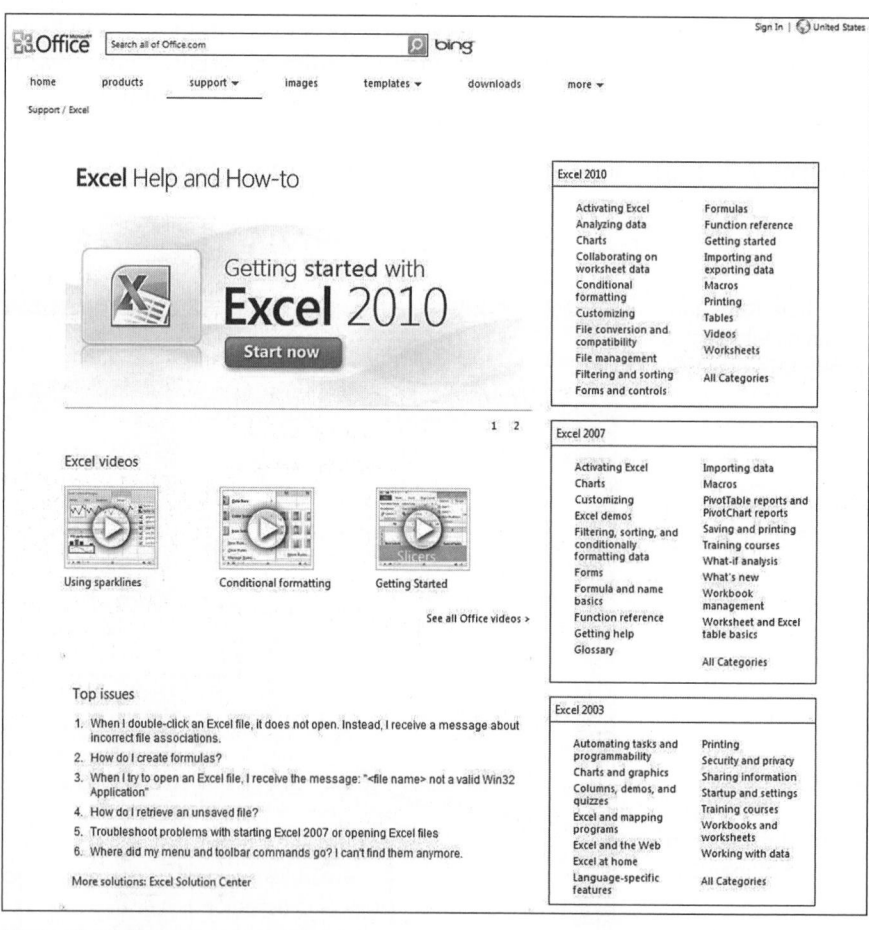

© 2011 Microsoft.

An example of one of the video-audio tutorials for Excel 2010 is shown in Exhibit 7.4.

Excel 2010 Help is opened from within an Excel file by clicking on the question mark (?) symbol. Doing so opens a collection of Help options including direct links to the online video tutorials, as shown in Exhibit 7.5.

Exhibit 7.4 "Getting started with Excel 2010" video tutorial website

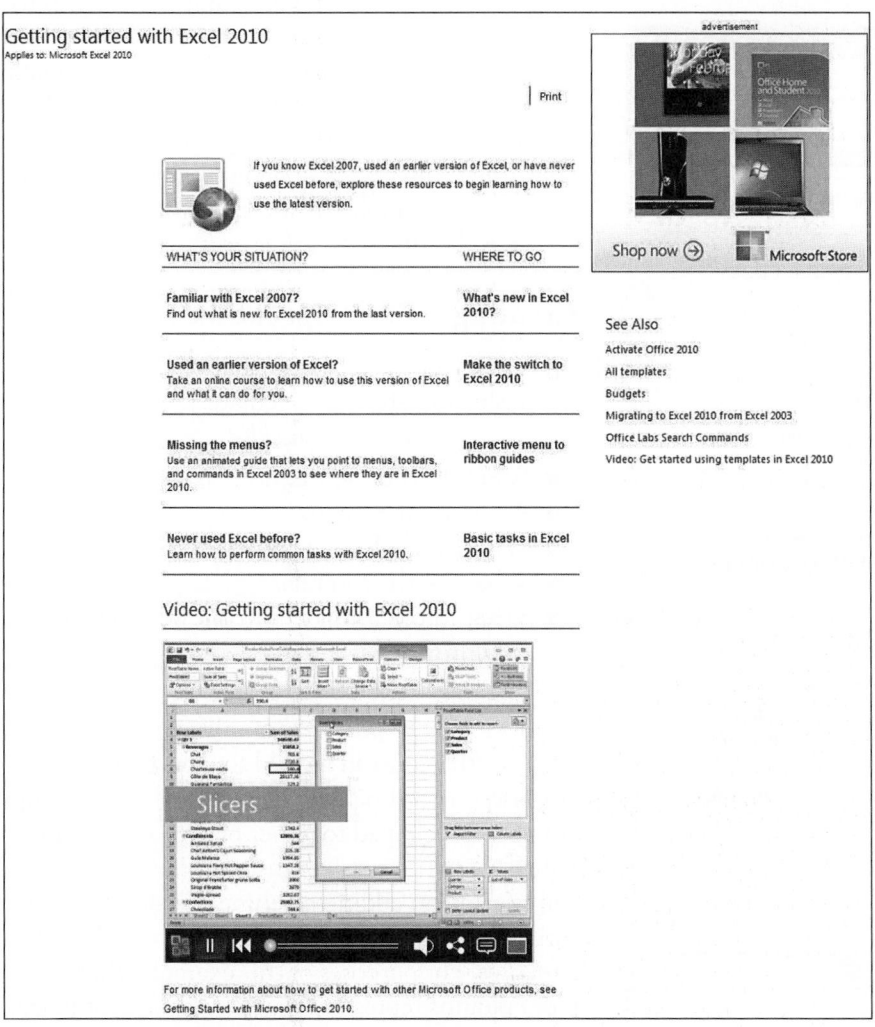

© 2011 Microsoft.

Corel's Quattro ProX5 provides tutorials within the program that can be used without the need for an Internet connection. Exhibit 7.6 shows a partial list of the available tutorials, and Exhibit 7.7 shows the contents of a tutorial. In this case, a tutorial is given on using the **property bar.** In Quattro Pro, the property bar appears above the column letters and is a "context-sensitive" set of commands, meaning that it changes according to what is being worked on.

property bar
In Quattro Pro, the area at the top of the spreadsheet for entering formulas and data into spreadsheet cells.

■ CREATING A SPREADSHEET

A spreadsheet can simplify the task of making computations. For example, in a decedent's estate, the executor may need to calculate the profit or loss realized by a sale of stock owned by the decedent. The profit or loss is calculated by multiplying the number of shares owned by the decedent by the share price on the date of death, and then subtracting this amount from the value of the stock on the date it was sold. This calculation could involve many assets. Without a spreadsheet, all of the calculations would have to be done manually using a multicolumn form known as a ledger, or accountant's working papers. The information would then have to be typed in a report for submission to the court, the beneficiaries, and the taxing authorities.

LEARNING OBJECTIVE 3
Create, edit, and save a spreadsheet.

Exhibit 7.5 Excel 2010 Help

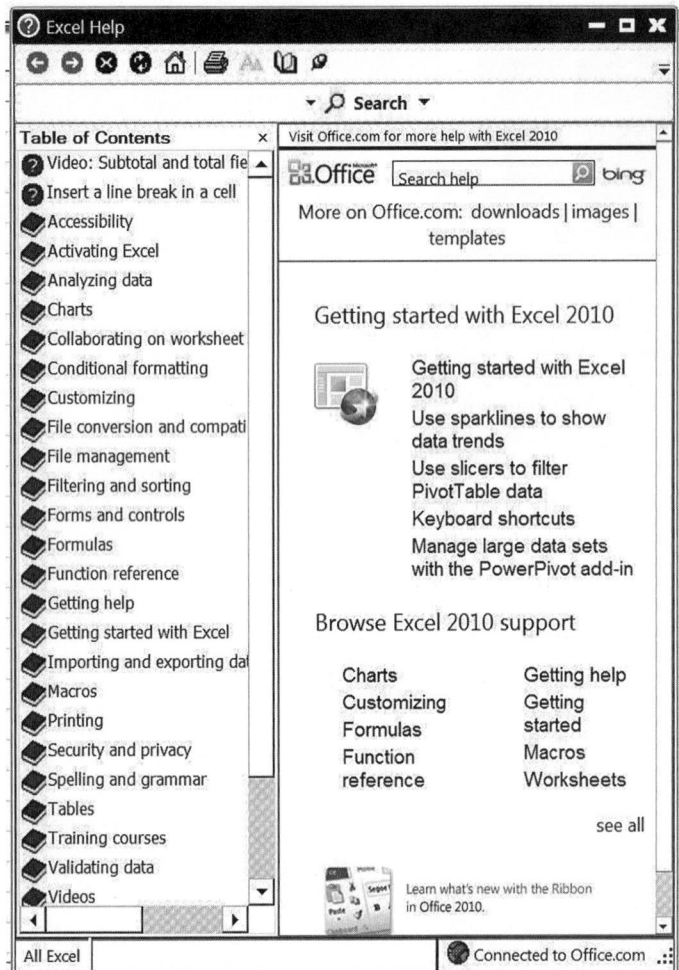

© 2011 Microsoft.

Using a spreadsheet such as Microsoft Excel or Corel Quattro Pro, the numbers are entered into cells, and a formula is assigned to the cell in which the result is to be displayed. In the example described above, a formula might say, *"multiply Column E [Number of Units] by Column F [Cost per Unit]"* and *"display the result in Column G [Original Cost]."* An example of an estate asset ledger is shown in Exhibit 7.8.

Creating a Basic Spreadsheet

First—Start by describing what you want the spreadsheet to show or calculate.
Creating a Spreadsheet Checklist

- What do you want to do?
- What are the inputs?
- What is the desired outcome?
- What are the formulas?
- What information will be shown in each column?

For example:

You need to prepare a family expense summary for the court in a child support case. The client brings in a shoebox full of receipts. These slips of paper are clipped together by type of expense, but they are not totaled. Instead of adding the receipts using an adding machine or calculator, you can use a spreadsheet that creates a record of the expenses. For purposes of this example, there are four columns representing the categories of items, and thirteen rows for the weeks in which the expenses occurred, as shown in Exhibit 7.9.

Exhibit 7.6 Quattro ProX5 Help menu

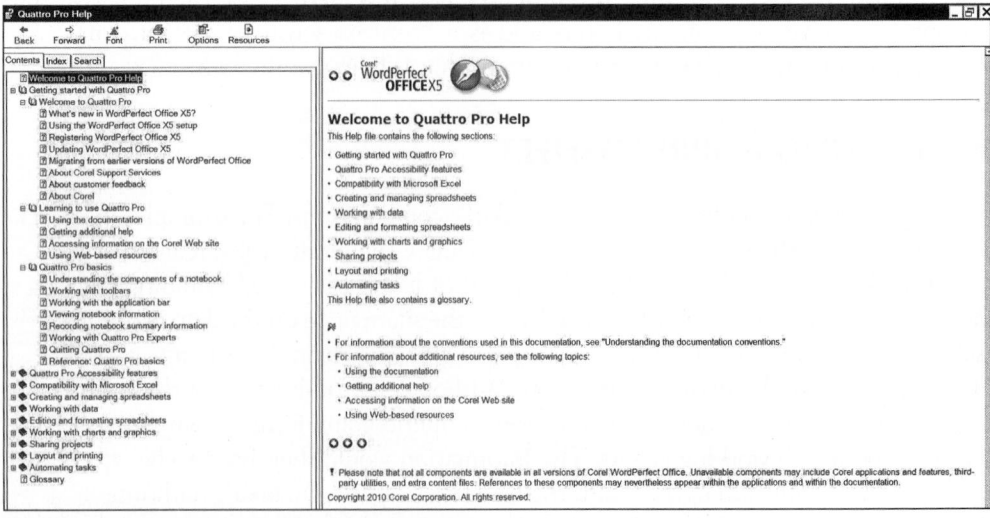

© Copyright 2012 Corel Corporation and Corel Corporation Limited, reprinted by permission.

Exhibit 7.7 Quattro Pro X5 Help menu detail

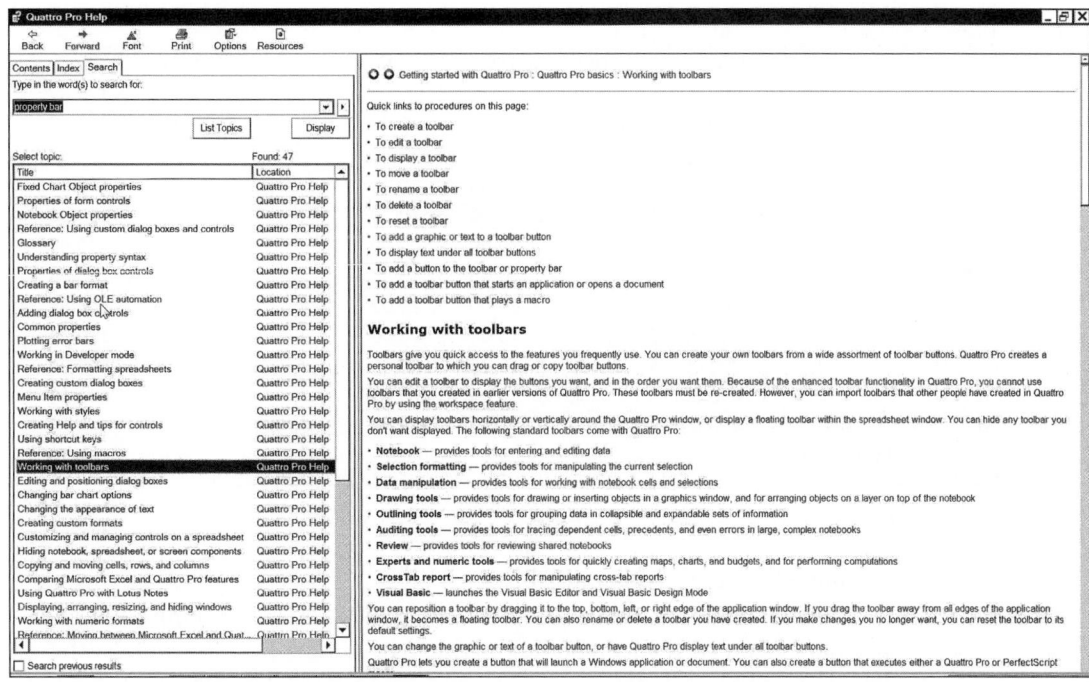

Exhibit 7.8 Estate asset ledger

Estate of Ethel Morris
Asset Ledger

Gray cells are calculated for you. You do not need to enter anything into them.

Investment type	Investment description	Purchase date	Number of units (shares)	Cost per unit (share)	Original cost (basis)	Date of Death Value	Unrecognized Gain (Loss)
Stocks	800 common shares–Fourth Coffee	5/4/03	1,800.00	$67.00	$120,600.00	$197,500.00	$76,900.00
					$0.00		0.00
					$0.00		0.00
					$0.00		0.00
Bonds	10-year treasury (4.76% yield)	5/20/03	1,500.00	$102.26	$153,390.00	$148,500.00	($4,890.00)
					$0.00		0.00
					$0.00		0.00
					$0.00		0.00
					$0.00		0.00
Mutual funds	Woodgroove Bank equity fund	6/30/03	2,000.00	$25.50	$51,000.00	$50,000.00	($1,000.00)
					$0.00		0.00
					$0.00		0.00
					$0.00		0.00
					$0.00		0.00
Minority interests	Litware, Inc. (20% ownership)	1/15/99	$1,000.00	$500.00	$500,000.00	$550,000.00	$50,000.00
					$0.00		0.00
					$0.00		0.00
Other					$0.00	$18,000.00	$18,000.00
					$0.00		0.00
					$0.00		0.00
					$0.00		0.00
					$0.00		0.00
					$0.00		0.00

What do you want to do?	Calculate the total expenses per category
What are the inputs?	Individual receipts, cancelled checks, and credit card statements
What is the desired outcome?	Individual expense item totals, the grand total of all expenses, and the average for each week
What are the formulas?	Sum of each column, and sum of the column totals

Exhibit 7.9 Sample family expense worksheet

	A	B	C	D	E	F	G	H
1		FOOD	UTILITIES	MEDICAL	SCHOOL	YEAR	MONTH	WEEK
2		$ 400.00	$ 125.00	$ -	$ 20.00		$ 545.00	$ 125.87
3		$ 400.00	$ 135.00	$ 25.00	$ 20.00		$ 580.00	$ 133.95
4		$ 400.00	$ 140.00	$ 10.00	$ 20.00		$ 570.00	$ 131.64
5		$ 500.00	$ 110.00	$ 20.00	$ 20.00		$ 650.00	$ 150.12
6		$ 500.00	$ 125.00	$ 20.00	$ 20.00		$ 665.00	$ 153.58
7		$ 550.00	$ 160.00	$ 50.00	$ 500.00		$1,260.00	$ 290.99
8		$ 550.00	$ 170.00	$ 250.00	$ 20.00		$ 990.00	$ 228.64
9		$ 500.00	$ 125.00	$ 30.00	$ 20.00		$ 675.00	$ 155.89
10		$ 500.00	$ 120.00	$ 10.00	$ 20.00		$ 650.00	$ 150.12
11		$ 700.00	$ 110.00	$ 20.00	$ 20.00		$ 850.00	$ 196.30
12		$ 450.00	$ 102.00	$ 80.00	$ 20.00		$ 652.00	$ 150.58
13	TOTAL	$5,450.00	$1,422.00	$ 515.00	$ 700.00	$8,087.00		
14	WEEKLY AVERAGE							$ 169.79

© 2011 Microsoft.

Second—Create the column labels.

Setting up a spreadsheet is a little like setting up the columns in a paper worksheet, with each column having a heading—in this example, the headings are *Food, Utilities, Medical,* and *School Fees.* The labels can be in any row, but in this example they are in Row 1.

Third—Enter a formula.

The cell in which an answer will be calculated must contain the desired formula. In this case, we are assuming that we have monthly receipts. In the example shown in Exhibit 7.10, the formulas are in cells A13, B13, C13, and D13. For each cell name, the letter is the column, and the number is the row.

A step-by-step tutorial for creating this basic spreadsheet is provided at the end of the chapter.

Formulas

The formulas used in spreadsheets can be very simple (add two numbers) or can be complex (calculate the present or future value of a number). In Quattro Pro, the *@sum( )* formula is the most basic. It tells the program you want to calculate the information found between the parentheses ( ). In this example, you want to add the amounts in Columns A, B, C, and D.

Note: In Microsoft Excel the = sign is used instead of the @ used in Quattro Pro.

Exhibit 7.10 Formula for column

© 2011 Microsoft.

Basic Mathematical Function Symbols Used in Spreadsheets

- Multiply   *
- Divide   ÷
- Add   +
- Subtract   –

To add a set of numbers, you enter a formula such as:

@sum(A1+B1+C1)

To multiply a series of numbers:

@sum(A1*B1*C1)

To divide one number by another:

@sum(A1/B1)

Exhibit 7.11 Formula in Excel formula bar

H14		f_x	=AVERAGE(H2:H12)				
A	B	C	D	E	F	G	H

© 2011 Microsoft.

Note that there are no spaces between formula symbols, letters, and numbers. While the example places the numbers in adjacent columns, they don't have to be next to each other. The cells can be from anywhere in the spreadsheet. For example, a formula can add cells A1, C3, and E40, as shown:

@sum(A1+C3+E40).

Editing a Label

A label and a formula can be entered or changed by editing it in the Excel formula bar or the Quattro Pro property bar, as shown in Exhibit 7.11.

A label can be entered by typing it in a cell, or by selecting the cell and typing it in the formula or property bar, as illustrated in Exhibit 7.12.

■ SPREADSHEET TEMPLATES

Many offices save spreadsheet templates in the same way they save sample word processing documents for future use. For example, a real estate settlement spreadsheet with formulas and headings may be saved without amounts filled in. Because the formulas do not change and the form has proven accurate, it may be used as a template for the real estate settlements of other clients. Exhibit 7.13 shows a HUD real estate settlement in an Excel spreadsheet.

Corel's Quattro Pro spreadsheet is similar in function and appearance to Microsoft's Excel spreadsheet. As shown in Exhibit 7.14, Quattro also allows for customization in the way the program calculates and displays items. In most programs, an item on the active screen is selected by pointing to it with the mouse and clicking the left mouse button.

In many applications, the right mouse button usually brings up context-sensitive options, like the Quattro Pro Options menu, as shown in Exhibit 7.14.

In Quattro, right-clicking the bar with the file name brings up the Options menu. A selection is made using the left button.

Project Templates

When creating a new spreadsheet, Quattro provides the option to use project templates (see Exhibit 7.15). These are similar to the templates in Excel.

Microsoft Templates

A number of spreadsheet templates are available for download from the Microsoft website. Most of the templates will work with the more current versions of Excel. However, some will work only with a specific version, such as Excel 2010. Always check the compatibility of a template before downloading it.

The spreadsheet in Exhibit 7.16 is a weekly time sheet template downloaded from Microsoft.

Cell N31 in Exhibit 7.16 has been selected and highlighted to show the formula in the formula bar (Excel) or the property bar (Quattro) used to calculate the total of the entries that will be made in column N. In this example, the

Exhibit 7.12 Formula bar with label

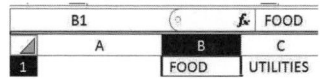

B1		f_x	FOOD
A	B	C
1	FOOD	UTILITIES

© 2011 Microsoft.

Exhibit 7.13 Excel HUD-1 spreadsheet template for real estate

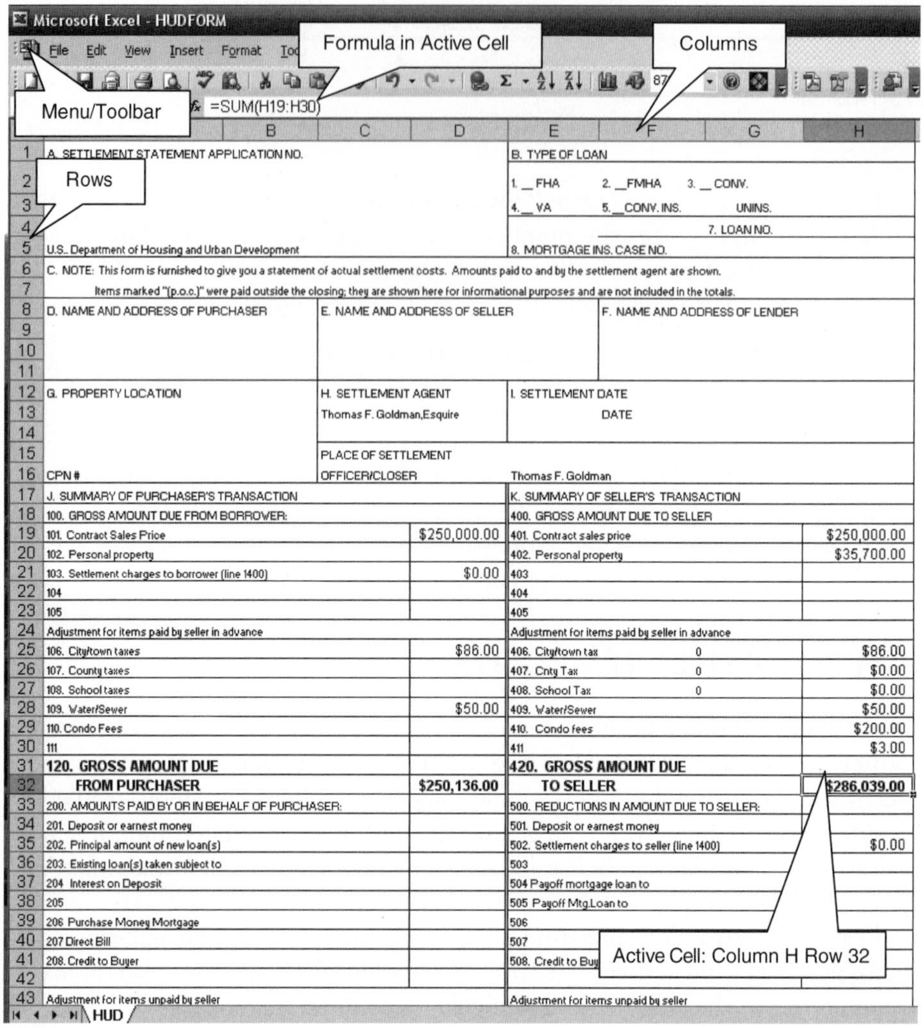

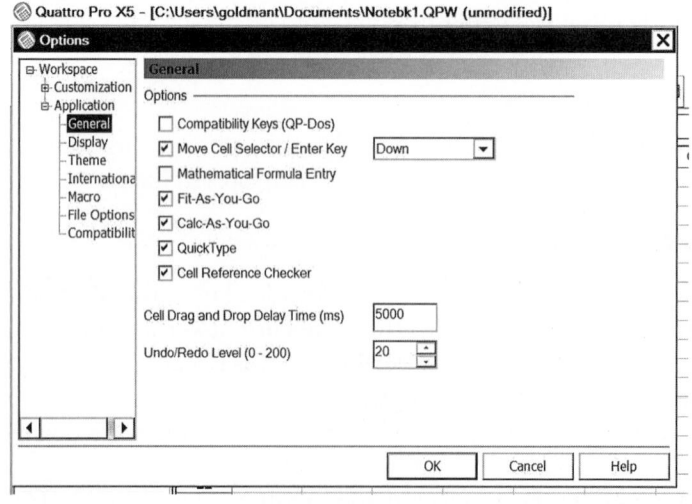

© 2011 Microsoft.

Exhibit 7.14 Corel's Quattro Pro Options menu

© Copyright 2012 Corel Corporation and Corel Corporation Limited, reprinted by permission.

Exhibit 7.15 Quattro Pro project templates

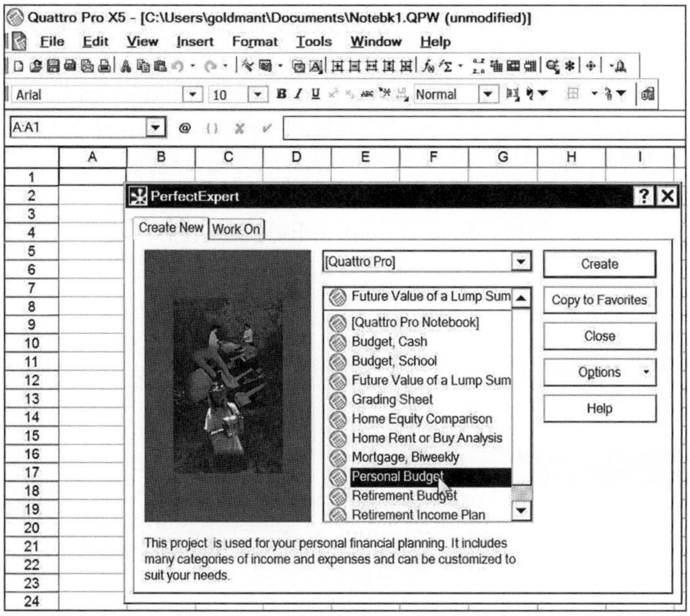

© Copyright 2012 Corel Corporation and Corel Corporation Limited, reprinted by permission.

Exhibit 7.16 Sample template for Excel

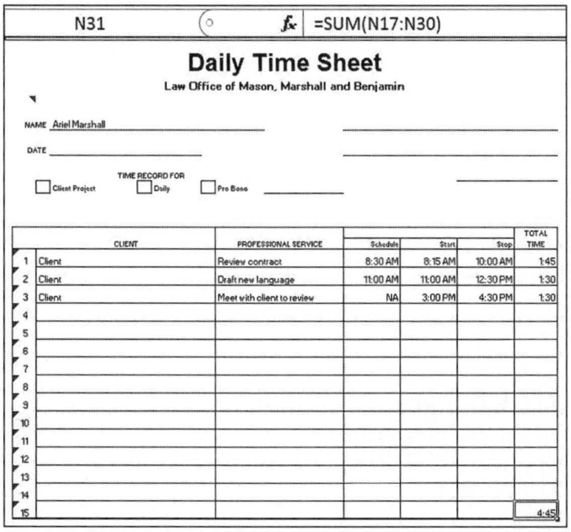

© 2011 Microsoft.

column letters and row numbers have been removed to show only the final document. Note the formula to total cells N17 through N30 using this formula shortcut:

$$=SUM(N17:N30).$$

The same total could be calculated using the formula:

$$= SUM(N17+N18+N19+N20+N21+N22+N23+N24$$
$$+N25+N26+N27+N28+N29+N30)$$

Notice again that there are no spaces between symbols, numbers, and letters.

■ SPREADSHEET SECURITY

Most office suite applications can be password-controlled. Exhibit 7.17 shows the method for limiting access to an Excel spreadsheet using the File tab's Backstage tools.

For comparison purposes, Exhibit 7.18 shows the Review tab, Changes group options, Protect Sheet commands, and the Protect Workbook options in Excel 2010.

As in other Office 2010 programs, the Prepare feature provides a number of security options, including inspecting a document for hidden metadata. This is a "backstage" feature found on the File tab, as shown in Exhibit 7.19.

Exhibit 7.17 Excel Backstage permission option

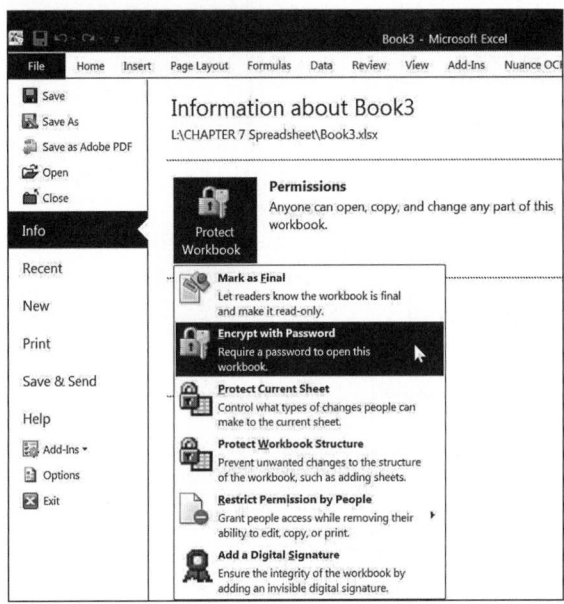

© 2011 Microsoft.

Exhibit 7.18 Excel Review tab, Changes group options, Protect Sheet commands, and Protect Workbook options

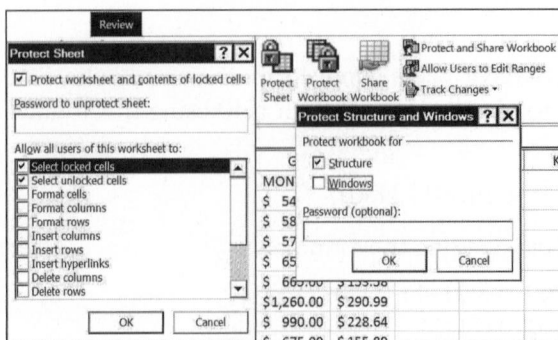

© 2011 Microsoft.

Exhibit 7.19 Excel Backstage Document Inspector

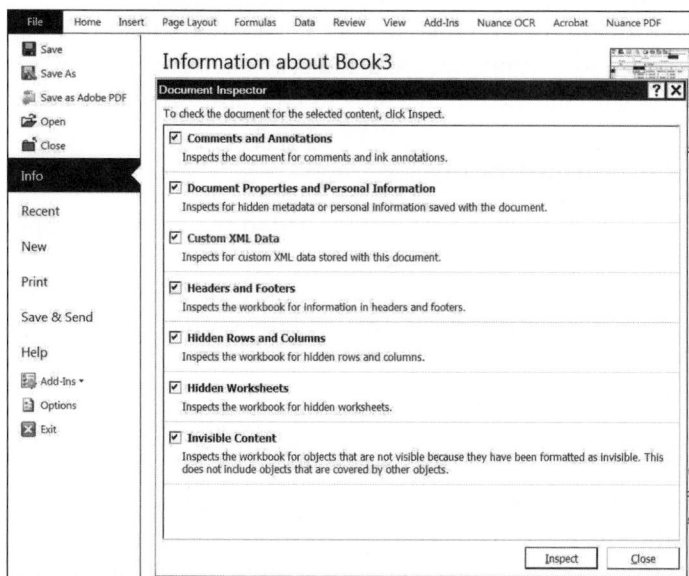

■ SPECIAL FEATURES OF SPREADSHEETS

Each spreadsheet has tools and features that are displayed on toolbars, on the Ribbon in Microsoft programs, and on a Quick Access Toolbar. Exhibit 7.20 shows the options to customize the Ribbon or Quick Access Toolbar in Excel.

LEARNING OBJECTIVE 4
Use some of the special features of spreadsheets, including graphics.

Exhibit 7.20 Options to customize the Ribbon or Quick Access Toolbar in Excel

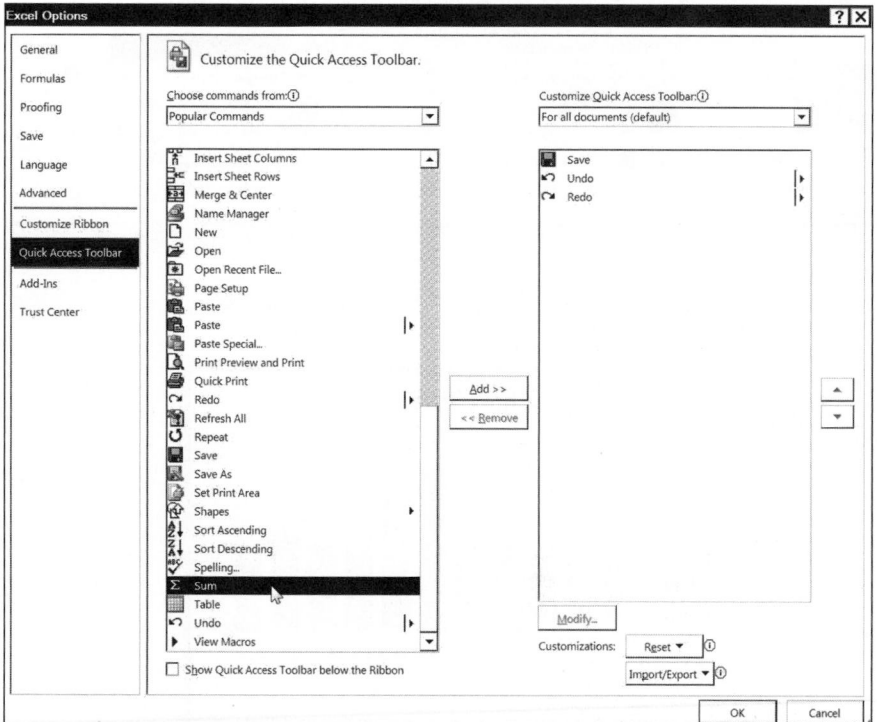

Exhibit 7.21 AutoSum in Excel

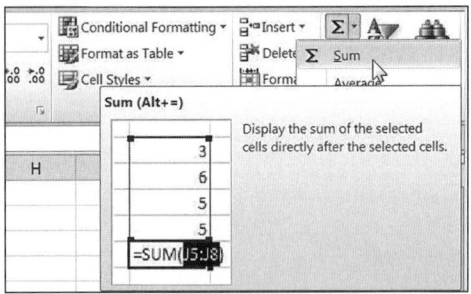

One of the more useful features is the AutoSum button, shown as the Greek letter sigma (Σ). In Excel 2010, this feature is found in the Home tab and in the Formulas tab of the Function Library Group. AutoSum, shown in Exhibit 7.21, will add up the selected cells in any row or column without the user needing to type any formula.

Graphing in Spreadsheets

Data in a spreadsheet is often better expressed in the form of a graph. In Excel, any selection of cells can be converted to a graph using the Insert tab's Charts tools. Selected information is automatically converted into any of a number of graphic representations, as shown in Exhibit 7.22.

Adapting to Change

As mentioned in Chapter 6, change is as inevitable in software as it is in life. There have been significant changes in the functionality of the Quattro Pro and Excel spreadsheets from prior versions. What have not changed are the basic functions for computing rows and columns of numerical data. The changes generally make the job easier by minimizing the number of keystrokes required, as in the use of the AutoSum function shown in Exhibit 7.21. Users of the old versions will find the original functions, but possibly in different locations.

Integrated Software Solutions

A number of specialty software programs provide practice-area-specific software. These programs integrate many functions in a single application, whereas the

Exhibit 7.22 Cell data converted to a graph

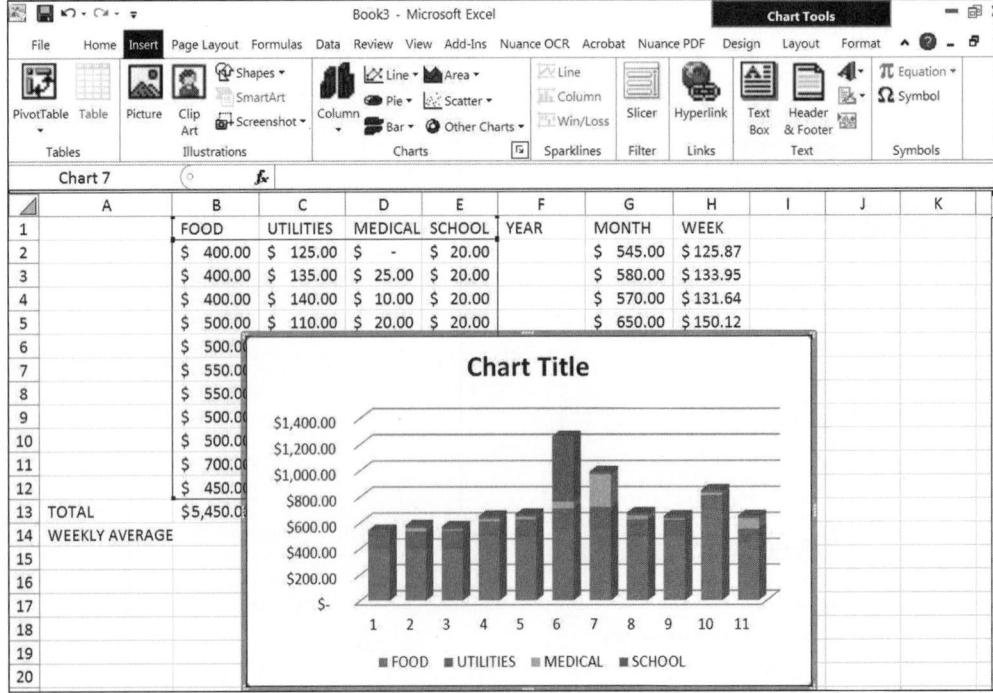

user once needed to use multiple applications. For example, real estate practice software such as that from SoftPro prepares all the necessary forms to complete a real estate transaction.

The Excel spreadsheet template in Exhibit 7.16 is one of a variety of spreadsheet templates used in many offices. The template provides spaces for the entry of information, and embedded formulas are used for automatic computations. Programs such as SoftPro use a series of input screens, as shown in Exhibit 7.23, to capture and calculate the necessary information. The data is then transferred to the appropriate forms, as shown in the HUD-1 form in Exhibit 7.24. The information is saved in a database for use in producing the other documents required for the real estate closing and title documents, such as deed descriptions and tax-reporting forms.

Exhibit 7.23 SoftPro escrow automation solutions

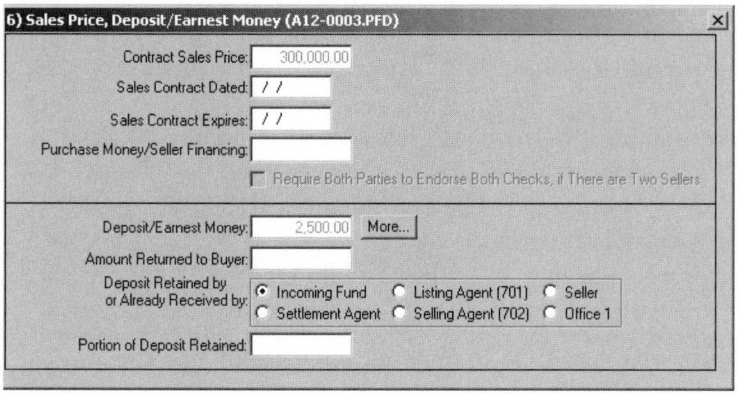

SoftPro.

Exhibit 7.24 HUD-1 produced using SoftPro

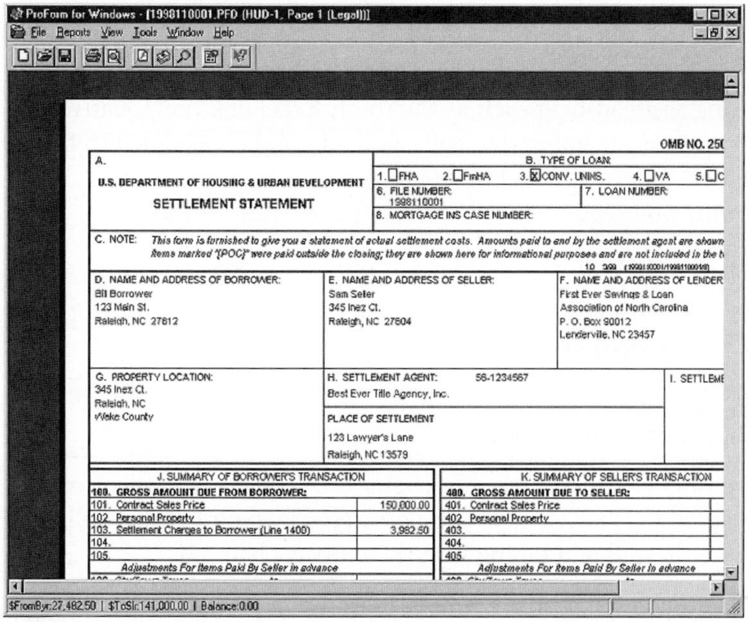

SoftPro.

CONCEPT REVIEW AND REINFORCEMENT

KEY TERMS

cell 169	formula bar 169	row 169
column 169	property bar 171	workbook 169

CHAPTER SUMMARY

Introduction to Spreadsheets	Many areas of legal practice involve calculating and presenting financial information. The spreadsheet, when laid out in the format acceptable to the court, can be printed without re-entering the data, or copied into Word documents. For many applications there are templates with formulas for calculating the information needed, such as an electronic spreadsheet version of the Housing and Urban Development (HUD) sheet used in real estate settlements. The use of spreadsheets reduces the possibility of errors associated with manual mathematical calculations and with retyping the information.
Creating and Working with Spreadsheets	A spreadsheet in its most basic form is any two related items that are acted upon mathematically, with the result presented in a third location.
Navigating in Spreadsheets	Spreadsheets have standard terms to describe their parts, such as rows, columns, cells, formula bar, active cell, formula, and workbooks.
Resources for Learning How to Use Spreadsheets	As seen in the chapter on word processing, most vendors of software provide help in learning and using the software. Microsoft offers a number of online tutorials.
Creating a Spreadsheet	When using a spreadsheet such as Microsoft Excel or Corel Quattro Pro, the numbers are entered in cells, and a formula is assigned to the cell in which the result is to be displayed. Start with what you want the spreadsheet to show or calculate. ■ What do you want to do? ■ What are the inputs? ■ What is the desired outcome? ■ What are the formulas? ■ What columns are needed?
Editing a Label	Just as a formula can be entered or changed by editing it in the property bar, so can a label. A label can be entered by typing it in a cell, or by selecting the cell and typing it in the property bar.
Spreadsheet Templates	Many offices save spreadsheet templates in the same way they save sample word processing documents for future use.

Spreadsheet Security	Most office suite applications can be password-controlled for security.
Special Features of Spreadsheets	Each spreadsheet has a choice of tools and features that may be displayed on the toolbars for quick use. The AutoSum button, shown as the Greek letter sigma (Σ), applies the selected function—for example, Sum (add up) the selected cells in any row or column—without the user needing to type any formula.
Graphing in Spreadsheets	Data in a spreadsheet are frequently better explained in the form of a graph.

REVIEW QUESTIONS AND EXERCISES

1. What are the security features available in Excel? How can these features help the legal team avoid ethical problems with sensitive information?
2. Name three parts of a spreadsheet. In your own words, write definitions of these terms as if you were explaining them to another member of the law firm staff.
3. What steps may be taken to locate and use the resources for learning the Excel or Quattro Pro programs and their features?
4. List the steps in creating and saving a spreadsheet.
5. Create a spreadsheet that shows your grades for a course, or a list of five numbers in the range of 1 to 100, including a formula for computing the average of all the grades listed or the average of the five numbers listed. Use the graphics feature to prepare a graph.
6. What are the steps that can be taken to protect an Excel workbook?

BUILDING YOUR PARALEGAL SKILLS

INTERNET AND TECHNOLOGY EXERCISES

1. Download the Investment Ledger from the Microsoft website. Print out the graph "Investment Chart."
2. Complete the Microsoft Office online tutorial "Audio Course: Get to Know Excel: Create Your First Workbook."
3. Complete the Microsoft Office online tutorial "Get to Know Excel: Enter Formulas."

CHAPTER OPENING SCENARIO CASE STUDY

Use the Opening Scenario for this chapter to answer the following questions. The setting is an attorney and a paralegal preparing for a labor negotiation session.

1. What should the attorney know about using a spreadsheet in a negotiation session? How can a spreadsheet aid in managing the session? Prepare a memo for the attorney to use in preparing for the negotiation session. Explain how the spreadsheet is to be used, and the different pieces of information that are included within it.

2. What information should the attorney convey to the paralegal to enable the paralegal to prepare the spreadsheet?
3. How much of the spreadsheet can be set up ahead of time? What data fields will be left open? Explain fully, with examples.
4. What hardware or software will the attorney need for the meeting? Be specific and explain the reasons for each item.

CONTINUING CASES AND EXERCISES

1. Prepare a spreadsheet for recording the time slips for the office.

    a. What headings are needed? Place these headings in the appropriate columns.

    b. Use the rates provided in previous exercises to create formulas for calculating fees.

    c. Enter all of your time information accumulated since Chapter 1. Be sure to describe each task appropriately in the spreadsheet rows. Provide dates and times to the nearest quarter of an hour.

    d. Sort the information by the billing function performed so that the spreadsheet is organized in a readable format.

2. Prepare a spreadsheet for calculating the payroll for a small law office staff consisting of two partners, an associate, a paralegal, a legal assistant, a clerk, and a receptionist. Create formulas for calculating withholding for federal and state taxes, an office health insurance plan, and 401(k) contributions.

BUILDING YOUR PROFESSIONAL PORTFOLIO

1. Prepare a memo to the legal team outlining the procedure for creating a spreadsheet for the settlement of a basic residential real estate transaction. Use the HUD form discussed in the chapter.

2. Prepare a presentation on the use of a spreadsheet as a productivity tool in a ligation practice. In the presentation, explain how a spreadsheet can make closing a case more efficient by streamlining the settlement of client accounts.

SPREADSHEET TUTORIAL

■ HOW DO I CREATE A FAMILY EXPENSE SPREADSHEET?

NOTE: If you do not have Microsoft Office Suite or Excel, you may download a 60 day trial version to use in completing this tutorial. The Excel website is a good source of additional information and answers. You may want to save the link address for future reference.

Create a New Blank Spreadsheet

Type column labels—for purposes of example we will first enter the labels in Columns A-D—click mouse cursor in desired cell and type, i.e. click in cell A1 and type FOOD. Notice the text is shown in the formula bar as well as in the cell. Editing can be done in the formula bar instead of retyping the entire word or phrase in the cell.

DOWNLOADING AND INSTALLING 60 DAY TRIAL VERSION OF MICROSOFT OFFICE

GOAL	ACTION	RESULT
DOWNLOAD AND SAVE 60 DAY TRIAL VERSION OF MICROSOFT OFFICE	**START** Your Internet web browser **ENTER** http://office.microsoft.com/en-us/excel for 60-day demo **CLICK** *Download a free trial*	

(continued)

GOAL	ACTION	RESULT
SELECT VERSION OF MICROSOFT OFFICE 2010 and REGISTER FOR DOWNLOAD	**CLICK** *Try it free* **COMPLETE** *Registration*	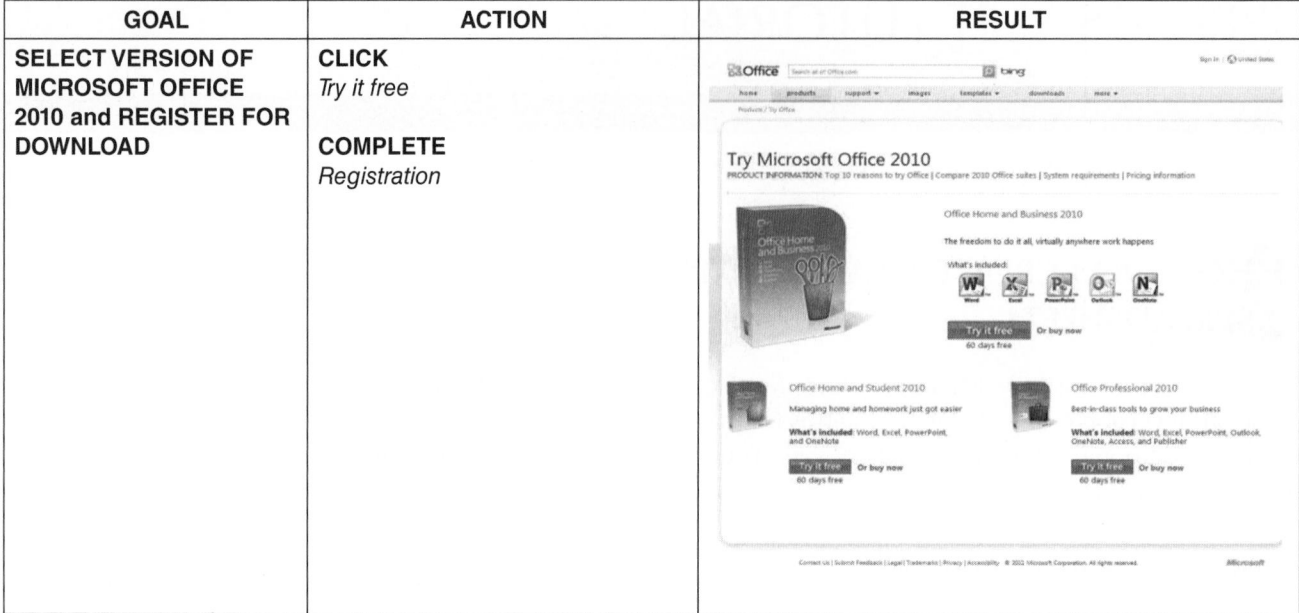

■ HOW DO I CREATE AN EXCEL SPREADSHEET?

GOAL	ACTION	RESULT
START EXCEL	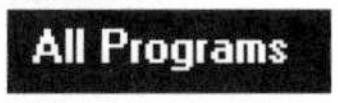 **CLICK** *EXCEL Icon on desktop* *or* **CLICK** 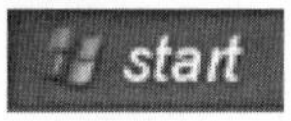 start **SELECT** All Programs **CLICK** EXCEL	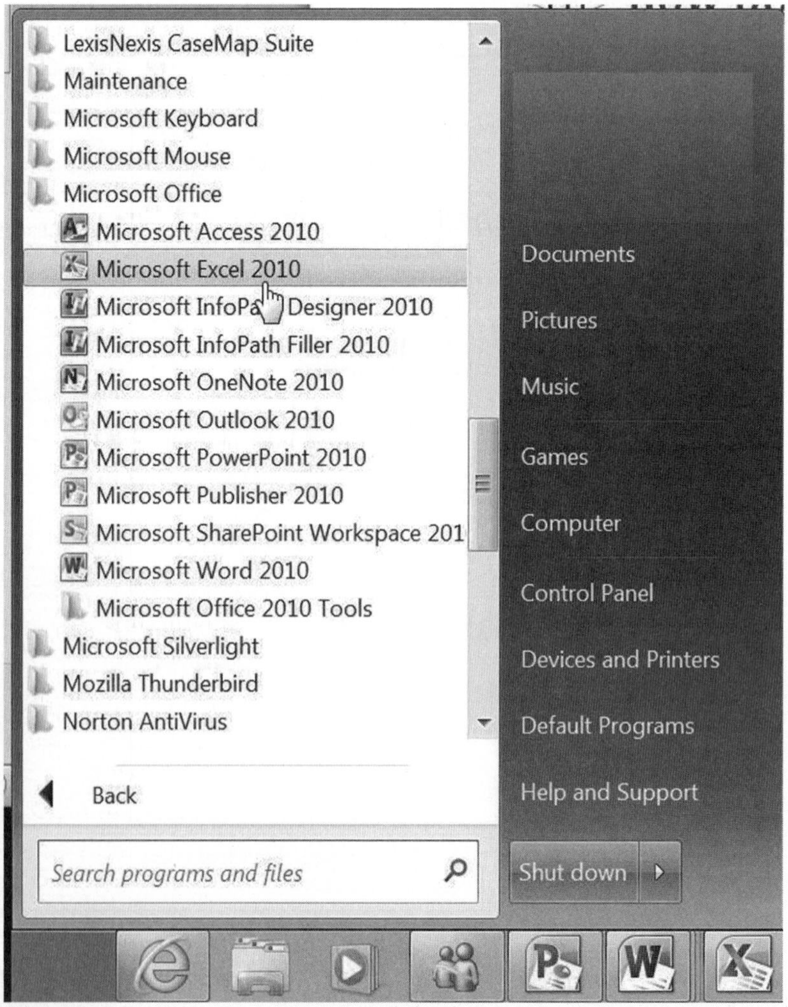 LexisNexis CaseMap Suite Maintenance Microsoft Keyboard Microsoft Mouse Microsoft Office Microsoft Access 2010 Microsoft Excel 2010 Microsoft InfoPath Designer 2010 Microsoft InfoPath Filler 2010 Microsoft OneNote 2010 Microsoft Outlook 2010 Microsoft PowerPoint 2010 Microsoft Publisher 2010 Microsoft SharePoint Workspace 201 Microsoft Word 2010 Microsoft Office 2010 Tools Microsoft Silverlight Mozilla Thunderbird Norton AntiVirus Back Search programs and files Documents Pictures Music Games Computer Control Panel Devices and Printers Default Programs Help and Support Shut down

(continued)

GOAL	ACTION	RESULT
ADD LABELS	**CLICK** *Left mouse in Cell A1* **TYPE** *FOOD* **CLICK** *Left mouse in Cell B1* **TYPE** *UTILITIES* **CLICK** *Left mouse in Cell C1* **TYPE** *MEDICAL* **CLICK** *Left mouse in Cell D1* **TYPE** *SCHOOL*	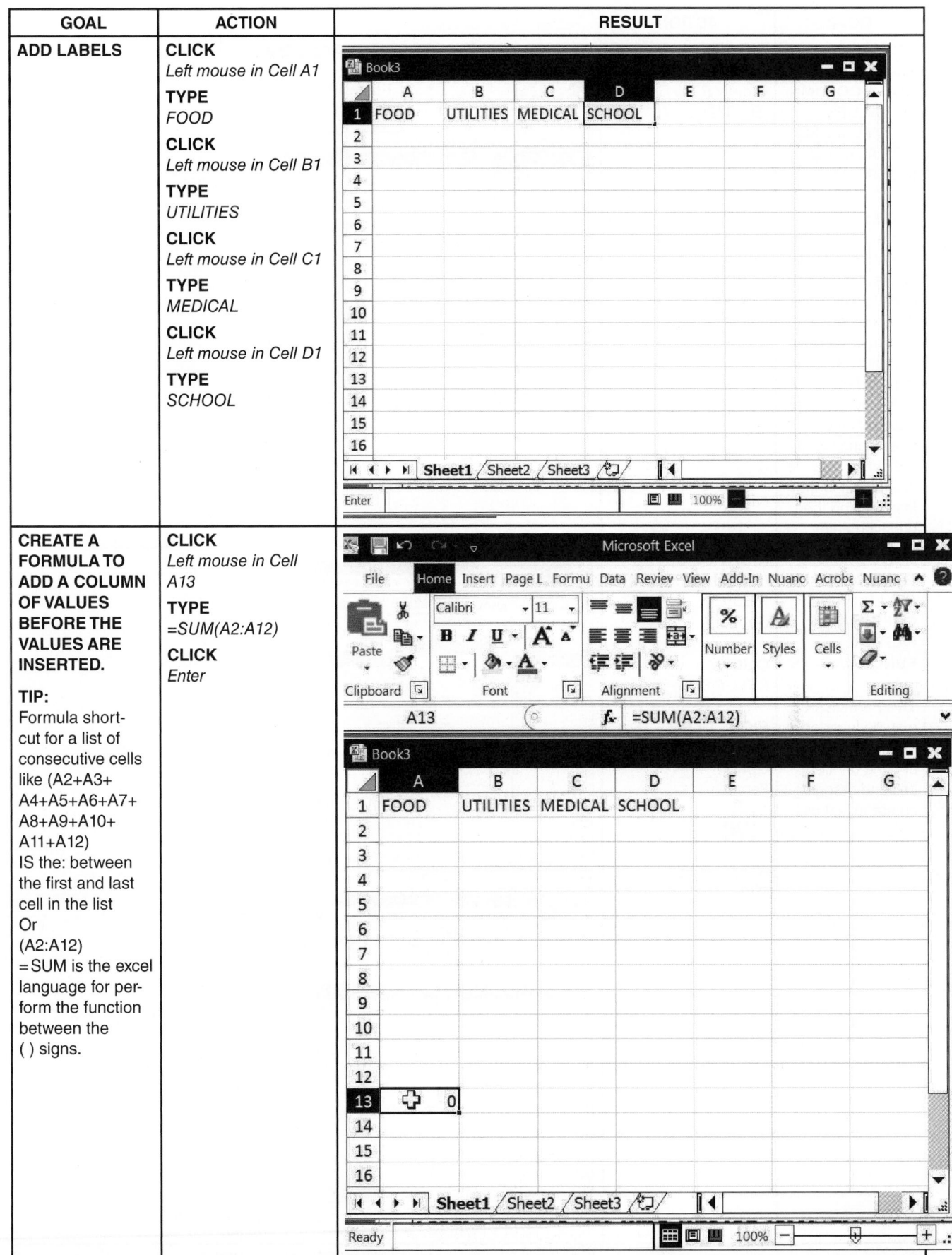
CREATE A FORMULA TO ADD A COLUMN OF VALUES BEFORE THE VALUES ARE INSERTED. **TIP:** Formula short-cut for a list of consecutive cells like (A2+A3+A4+A5+A6+A7+A8+A9+A10+A11+A12) IS the : between the first and last cell in the list Or (A2:A12) =SUM is the excel language for perform the function between the ( ) signs.	**CLICK** *Left mouse in Cell A13* **TYPE** *=SUM(A2:A12)* **CLICK** *Enter*	

(continued)

GOAL	ACTION	RESULT
CREATE A FORMULA TO ADD A COLUMN OF VALUES WHEN VALUES ARE ALREADY INSERTED. **NOTE:** When values exist a dotted line will appear to suggest the range of cells. This may be accepted by pressing the enter key, or by selecting a different range by highlighting the first cell in the range with the cursor and dragging it to the last cell and then pressing enter.	**ENTER** *Sample numbers in cells B2 to B12 (B2:B12)* **CLICK** *Cell B13* **CLICK** *Σ symbol in Home Tab Editing Group* **PRESS** *Enter Key*	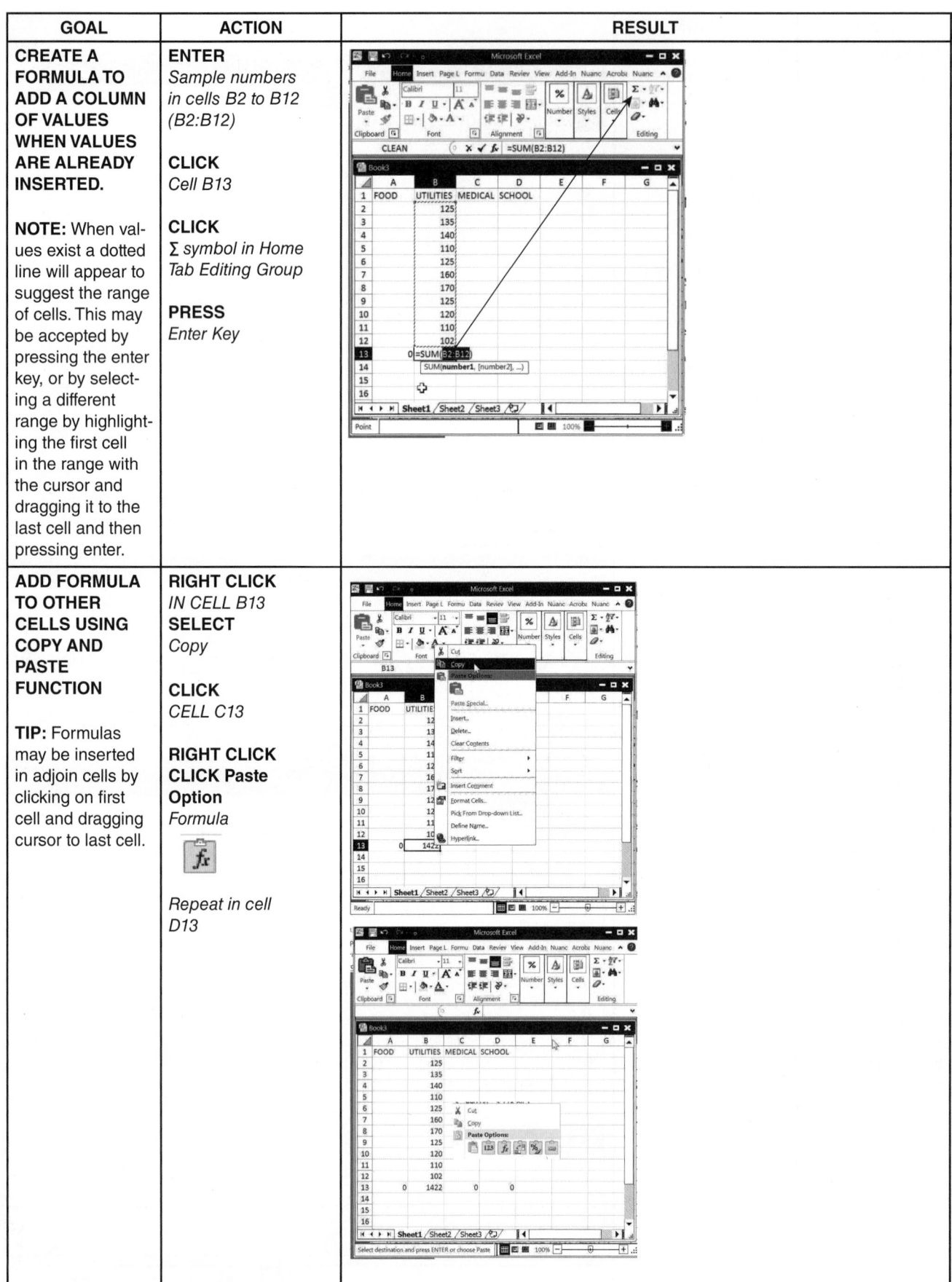
ADD FORMULA TO OTHER CELLS USING COPY AND PASTE FUNCTION **TIP:** Formulas may be inserted in adjoin cells by clicking on first cell and dragging cursor to last cell.	**RIGHT CLICK** *IN CELL B13* **SELECT** *Copy* **CLICK** *CELL C13* **RIGHT CLICK** **CLICK Paste Option** *Formula* *Repeat in cell D13*	

(continued)

GOAL	ACTION	RESULT
ADD A FORMULA TO A ROW	**ENTER** *VALUES IN CELLS*	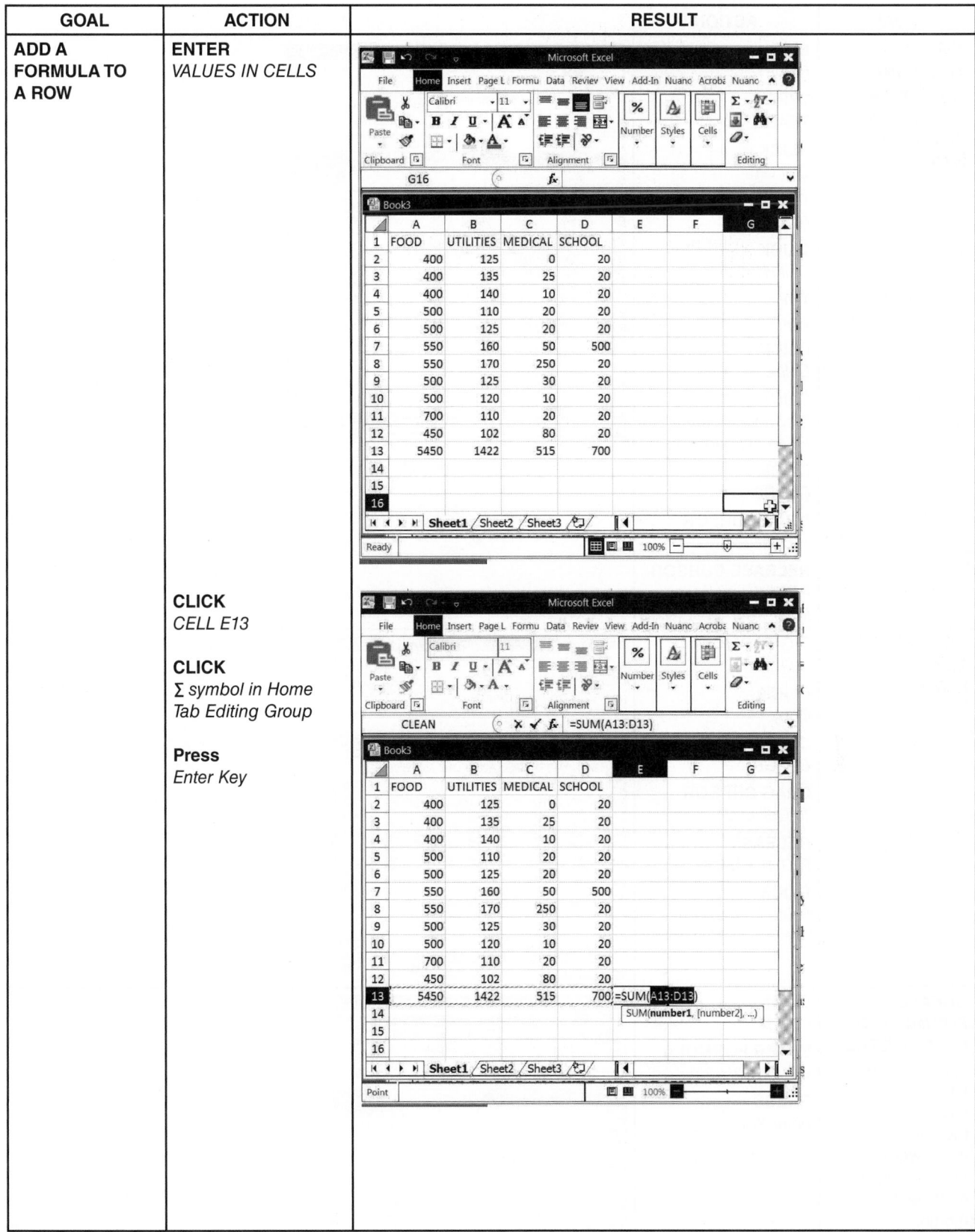
	CLICK *CELL E13* **CLICK** *Σ symbol in Home Tab Editing Group* **Press** *Enter Key*	

(continued)

GOAL	ACTION	RESULT
ADD ADDITIONAL LABELS AND TOTAL ROWS NOT CONTIGIOUS.	**CLICK** *Cell F1* **TYPE** *YEAR* **CLICK** *Cell G1* **TYPE** *Month* **CLICK** *Cell H1* **TYPE** *Week* **CLICK** *Cell G2* **CLICK** *Σ symbol in Home Tab Editing Group* **CLICK** *Cell B2* **DRAG CURSOR** *TO Cell E2* **RELEASE CURSOR PRESS** *Enter Key*	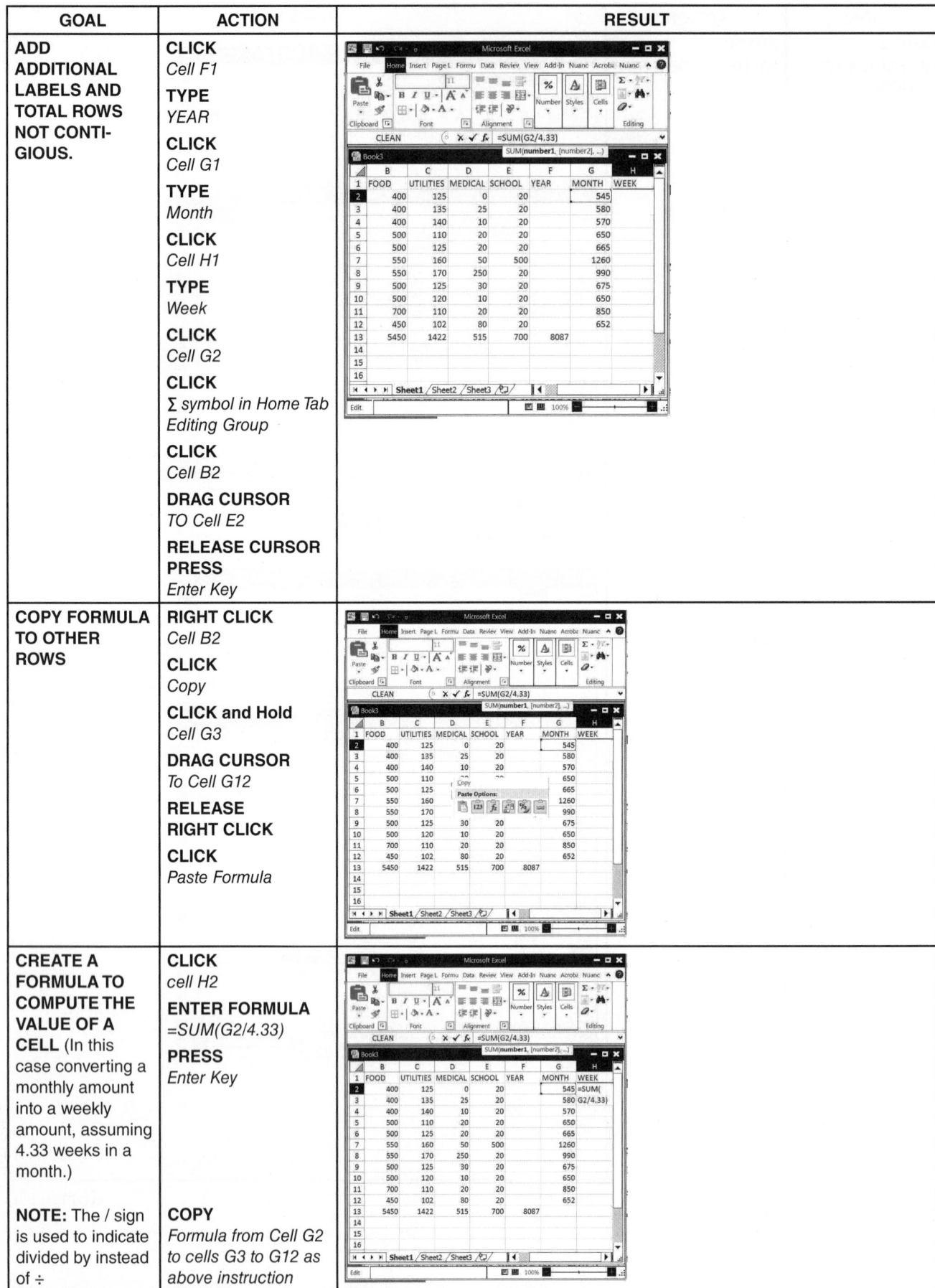
COPY FORMULA TO OTHER ROWS	**RIGHT CLICK** *Cell B2* **CLICK** *Copy* **CLICK and Hold** *Cell G3* **DRAG CURSOR** *To Cell G12* **RELEASE RIGHT CLICK** **CLICK** *Paste Formula*	
CREATE A FORMULA TO COMPUTE THE VALUE OF A CELL (In this case converting a monthly amount into a weekly amount, assuming 4.33 weeks in a month.) **NOTE:** The / sign is used to indicate divided by instead of ÷	**CLICK** *cell H2* **ENTER FORMULA** *=SUM(G2/4.33)* **PRESS** *Enter Key* **COPY** *Formula from Cell G2 to cells G3 to G12 as above instruction*	

(continued)

GOAL	ACTION	RESULT
CALCULATE AN AVERAGE	**CLICK** *Cell H13* **CLICK** *Formula Tab Function Library AutoSum* **CLICK** *AVERAGE* **PRESS** *Enter Key*	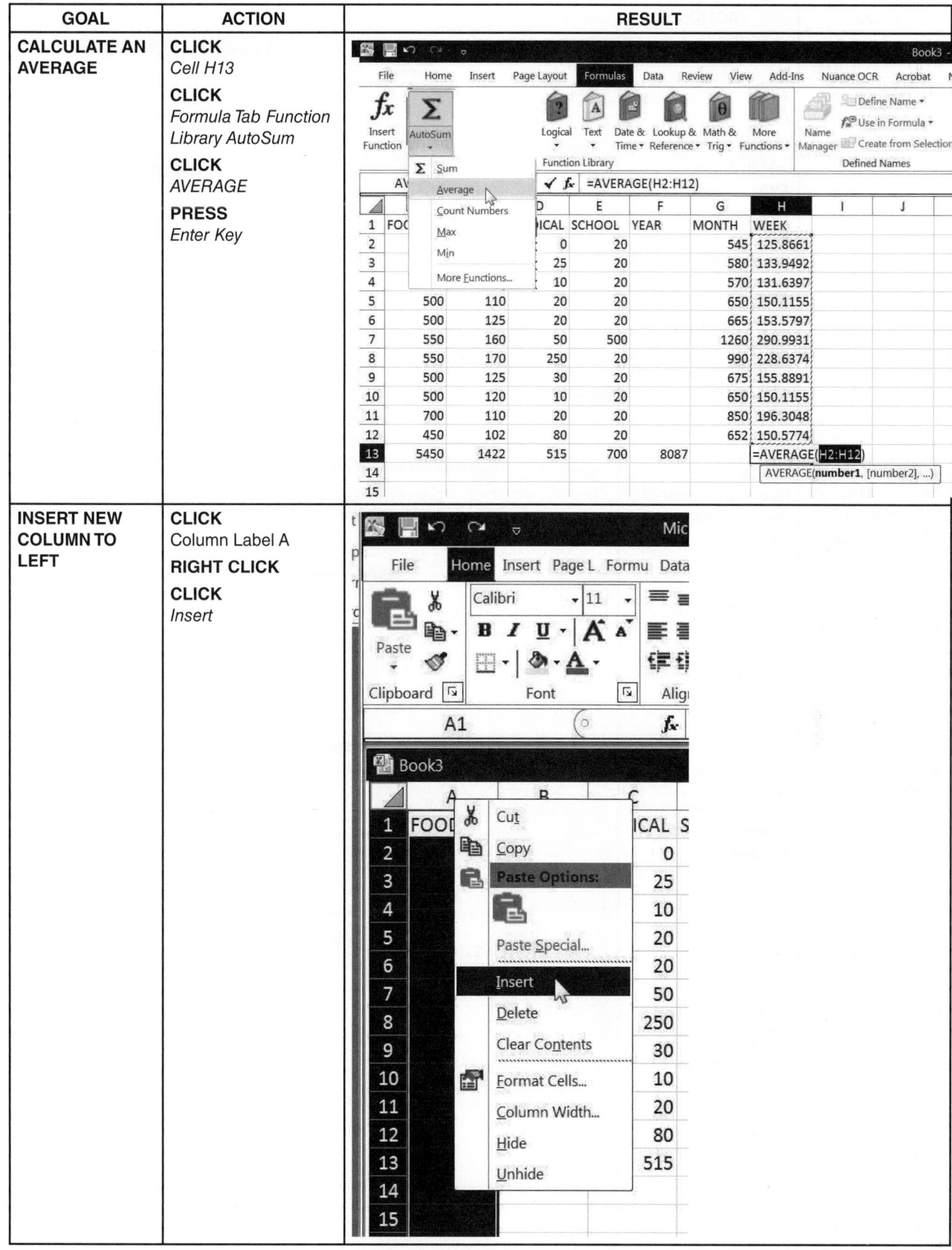
INSERT NEW COLUMN TO LEFT	**CLICK** Column Label A **RIGHT CLICK** **CLICK** *Insert*	

(continued)

GOAL	ACTION	RESULT
ADD LABELS AND RELOCATE FORMULA	**CLICK** *Cell A13* **TYPE** *TOTAL* **CLICK** *Cell A14* **TYPE** *WEEKLY AVERAGE* **Create Weekly Average** *for Cells H2:H12 as shown above Or Copy and Paste Formula or Value using Paste Functions*	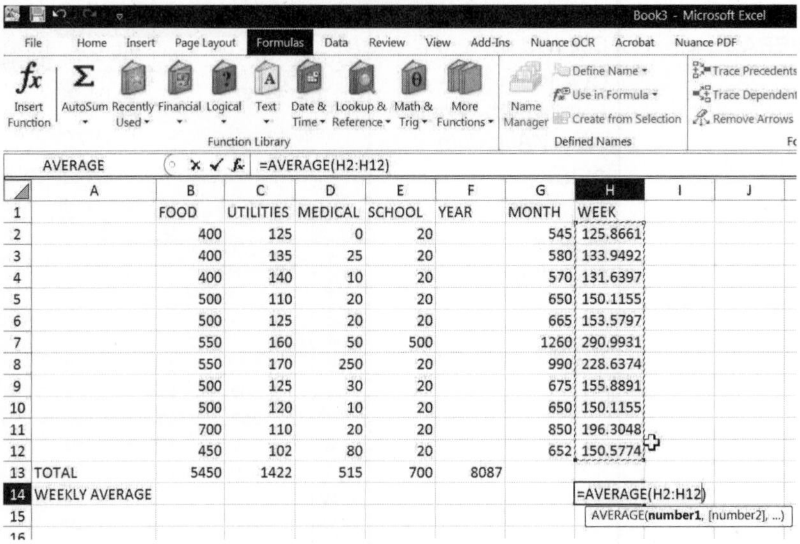
MAKE ALL CELLS CURRENCY VALUES USING STYLES GROUP OPTIONS	**CLICK** *Upper left Corner of Spreadsheet to select entire spreadsheet* **CLICK** *Home Tab Styles Group Cell Styles* **CLICK** *Currency*	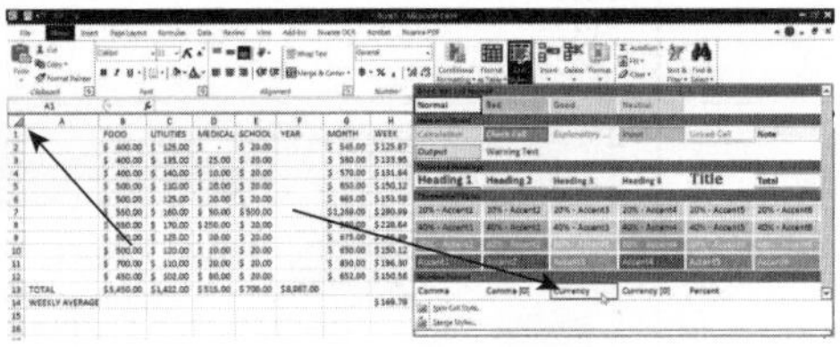
RENAME WORKBOOK SHEETS ADD ROW LABELS	**CLICK** *Sheet 1 label tab* **RIGHT CLICK** **CLICK** *Rename* **TYPE** *SUMMARY* **Rename Sheet 2** *INCOME* **CLICK** *Cell A15* **TYPE** *Annual Income* **CLICK** *Cell A16* **TYPE** *Weekly Income*	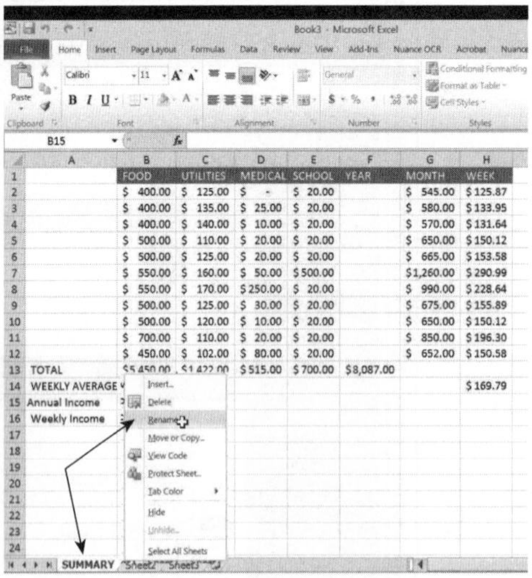

(continued)

GOAL	ACTION	RESULT
CREATE NEW SUPPORTING SPREADSHEET	USE INSTRUCTION FROM ABOVE TO CREATE THE INCOME SPREADSHEET AS SHOWN ASSUME 52 weeks in year to calculate Per Week Amount	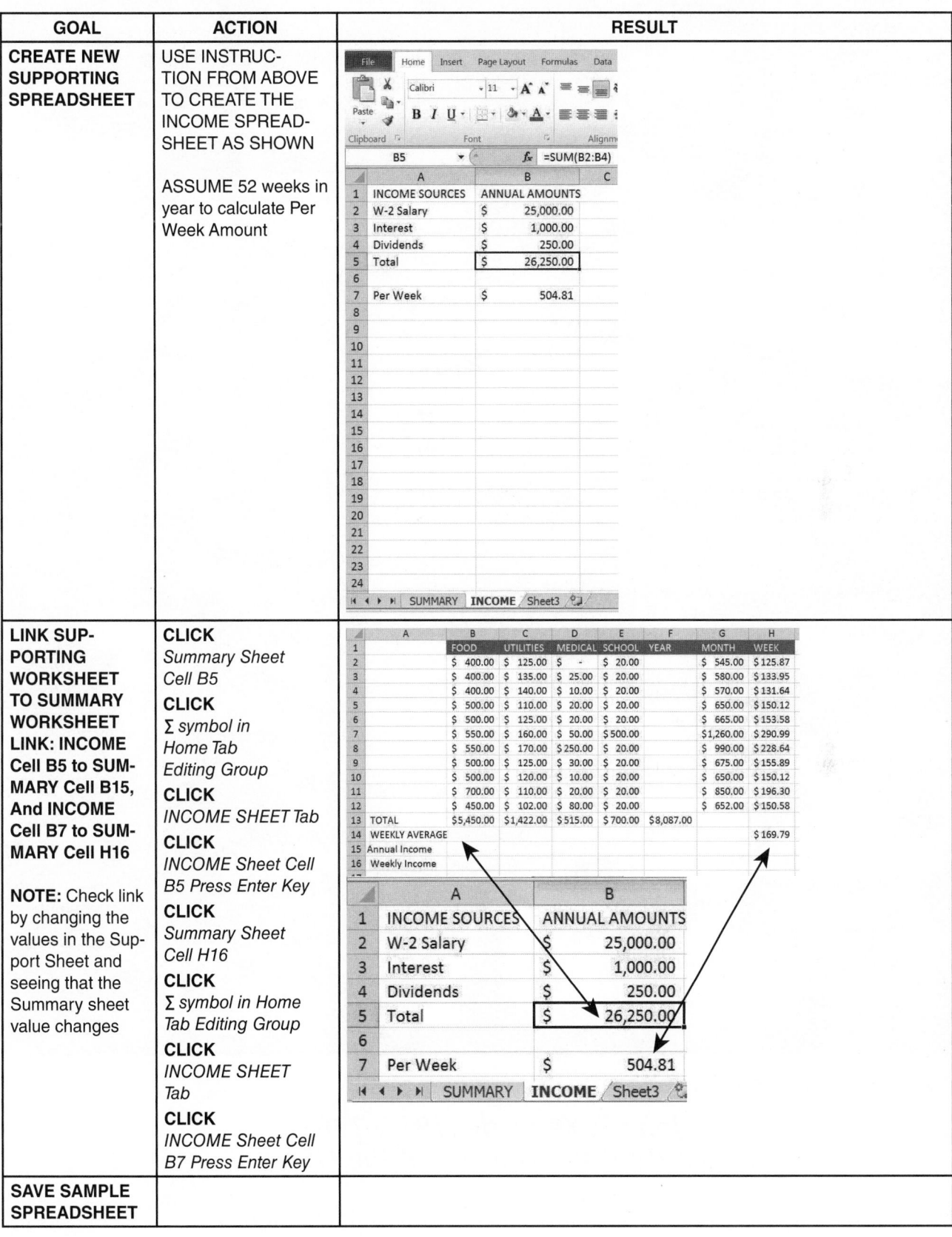
LINK SUPPORTING WORKSHEET TO SUMMARY WORKSHEET LINK: INCOME Cell B5 to SUMMARY Cell B15, And INCOME Cell B7 to SUMMARY Cell H16 **NOTE:** Check link by changing the values in the Support Sheet and seeing that the Summary sheet value changes	**CLICK** *Summary Sheet Cell B5* **CLICK** *Σ symbol in Home Tab Editing Group* **CLICK** *INCOME SHEET Tab* **CLICK** *INCOME Sheet Cell B5 Press Enter Key* **CLICK** *Summary Sheet Cell H16* **CLICK** *Σ symbol in Home Tab Editing Group* **CLICK** *INCOME SHEET Tab* **CLICK** *INCOME Sheet Cell B7 Press Enter Key*	
SAVE SAMPLE SPREADSHEET		

"Man is still the most extraordinary computer of all."
—*John F. Kennedy (1917–1963),*
Thirty-fifth President of the USA

Electronic Databases | CHAPTER 8

OPENING SCENARIO

Before taking the position with Owen Mason, Ethan had worked for a sole practitioner who had been practicing for thirty years. This attorney used somewhat outdated methods for scheduling and keeping track of client information. For example, he maintained a set of 3-by-5 cards, each containing all the personal information about a client. He also maintained a set of cards for opposing counsel and their clients, and copies with the names of the opposing parties that could be checked for conflicts of interest. In the scheduling system, a separate file was kept by Ethan, with the important dates for each case, that could be pulled out daily. The related file could then be recovered from the file room and put on the attorney's desk.

These systems were increasingly difficult to maintain accurately, which sometimes led to serious problems. In one incident, Ethan scheduled an appointment with a prospective client for one of the new associates in the office. The new client was suing someone who happened to be an existing client of the firm. However, the card for the existing client had been accidentally removed from the file. As a result, when Ethan searched the files, he did not discover the conflict, and informed the associate that the opposing party was not in the client card file. The associate accepted the case, reviewed all the case documents, and received a substantial retainer. But once the conflict was discovered, the firm was not able to represent either client.

LEARNING OBJECTIVES

After studying this chapter, you should be able to:

1. Describe the function of a database and identify its components.

2. Explain how databases may be used by the legal team.

3. Find resources for learning how to use a database program and its features.

4. Explain how to plan and set up a database.

5. Explain what can be done to protect data and computer systems.

VIDEO INTRODUCTION

Professor Thomas F. Goldman, Esq.

ELECTRONIC DATABASES
After watching the video in MyLegalStudiesLab, answer the following questions.

1. What is an electronic database?
2. How can databases be used in the law office?

■ INTRODUCTION TO ELECTRONIC DATABASES

A database is a repository of information that can be sorted and displayed in a meaningful manner. Some offices use a manual card system to keep track of the names of clients and opposing parties. These cards are searched to determine possible conflicts of interest in representing new clients. For the small firm, this system works adequately. But for the larger firm, with many attorneys and possibly multiple offices, this system is insufficient for entering and searching large amounts of information in a timely manner. Computerized database software, such as Microsoft Access and Corel DB, provides an alternative. These systems facilitate timely, accurate access to information by every authorized member of the legal team. For example, information may be stored on the law firm's server in an information database that includes the names, addresses, contact information, and personal data of every client. It may also contain every opposing party, witness, and opposing attorney with whom any member of the firm has ever had contact with in the course of the firm's business. With a few keystrokes, a search can be performed for any matter in which a name appears, or a list can be prepared for manually checking for conflicts of interest.

In addition to checking prospective clients for potential conflicts of interest, client information is frequently is used to maintain client relations. Many firms use the information to send updates on specific changes in the law for matters in which the client has previously consulted the firm. The information can also be used to send birthday and anniversary greetings.

Lawyers, paralegals, and legal assistants rarely create their own databases, but they use software databases all the time. Virtually every specialty application program for managing litigation is a database, such as LexisNexis CaseMap, shown in Exhibit 8.1.

Applications created for the legal community, such as AbacusLaw, have custom **form views** for inputting information specific to a law practice. The information typed into these forms is processed through algorithms that search the central database, as shown in Exhibit 8.2. A report or table is then generated to present the search results.

When a special application is required, many of the software vendors will create custom table and report generators. For example, a firm may want form views with input fields appropriate to a particular area of practice, such as estate planning.

Knowing what a database is and understanding database terminology makes working with software developers, in-house IT professionals, or outside consultants easier and more productive. And using an application that incorporates a database is easier if you know how a database works.

form views
An alternative way of viewing and presenting the information in a database.

Exhibit 8.1 LexisNexis CaseMap

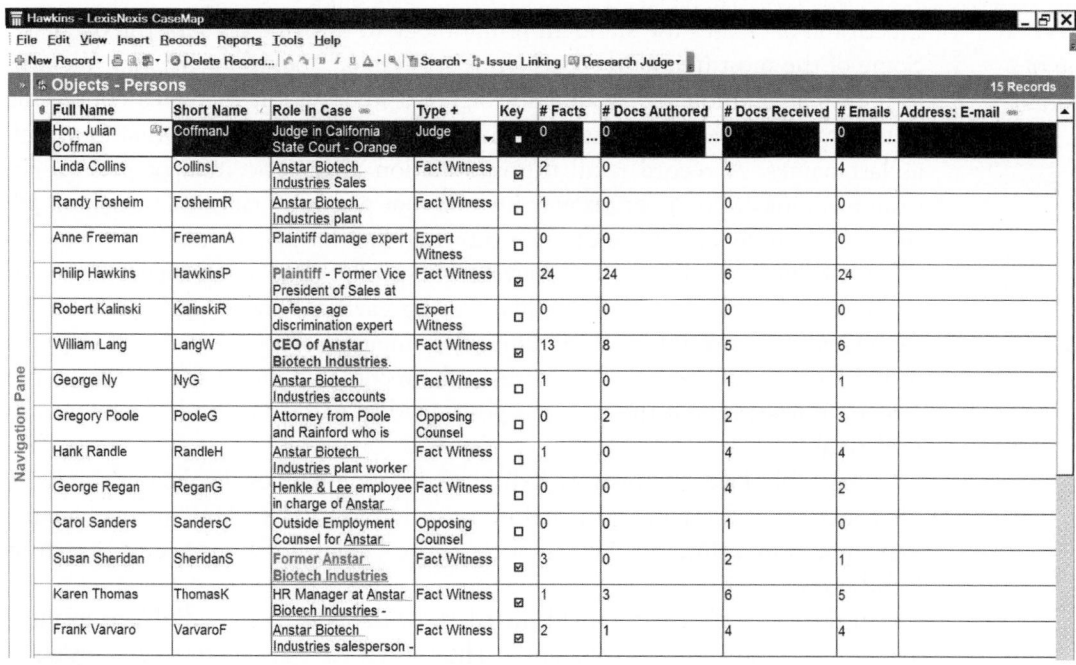

LexisNexis.

Exhibit 8.2 AbacusLaw Name screen

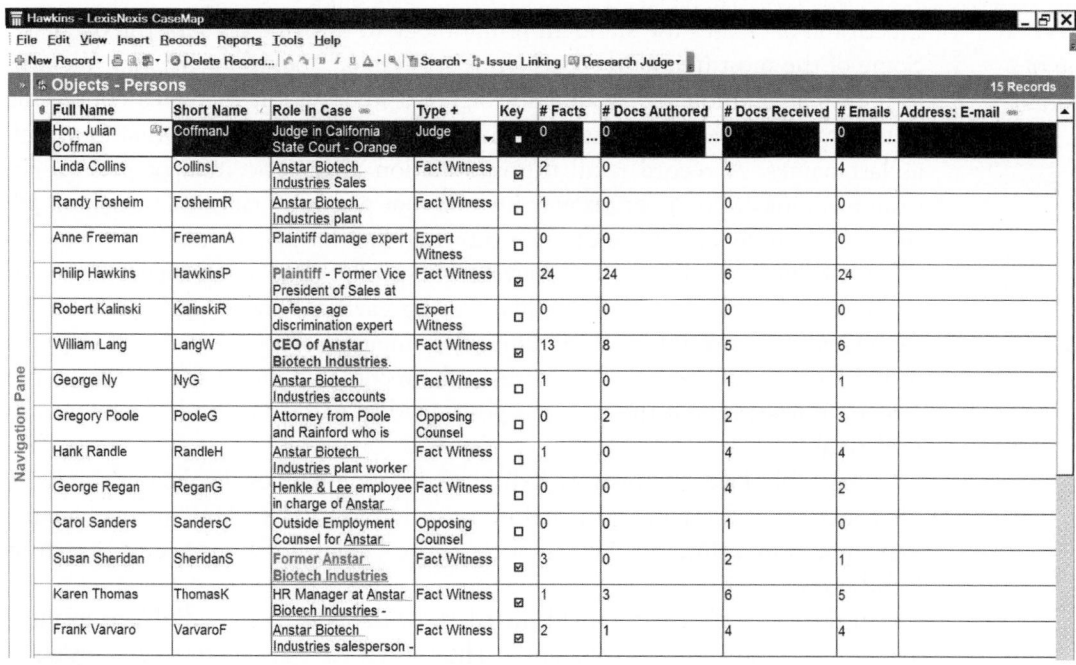

AbacusLaw.

■ NAVIGATING ELECTRONIC DATABASES

table
Data that is organized in a format of horizontal rows and vertical columns.

field
Information located in vertical columns.

record
In a database, the information in a horizontal row.

Electronic databases use standard terminology to describe parts of the database. Some of the most frequently used terms are "table," "field," "cell," and "record," as shown in Exhibit 8.3. Databases organize information in **tables** containing fields of information, or data. A **field** contains one type of information, such as last names. A **record** is all the information about one item or person. For example, a record of a person may include that person's first and last names, job title, phone numbers, and address, as shown in Exhibit 8.3. Think of the database as a file cabinet: a table is a file drawer for a specific class of information, such as employees; the records are individual files for each employee; and the fields are individual pieces of information about the employee. Note that in the example in Exhibit 8.3, the numeral 3 appears in the record window at the bottom of the screen, indicating that the cursor is positioned to enter the third of four records in this table.

The table layout shown in Exhibit 8.3 is one way of displaying the basic elements of a database—the fields, records, and cells. The same elements may appear in a different layout, such as the Design view in Access shown in Exhibit 8.4.

In the Design view, the fields listed vertically are the same fields as in table layout view, only oriented differently. The Design view also permits certain characteristics to be applied while designing the database. The user may specify the number of characters allowed in each field (called the field size or string length), and whether the information entered in a field will be text or numerical data.

Tables

Databases may organize data in two or more tables. Each table will contain data in a particular category of information. For example, a database used in a law office may have one table for employees of the firm, another for clients of

Exhibit 8.3 Parts of a database

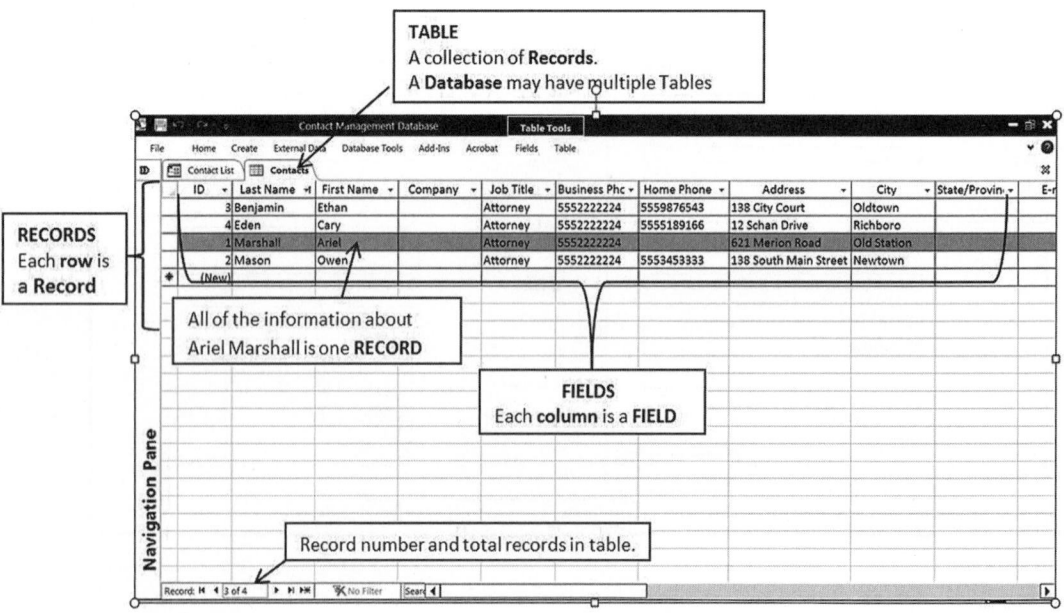

© 2011 Microsoft.

Exhibit 8.4 Access 2010 Design view

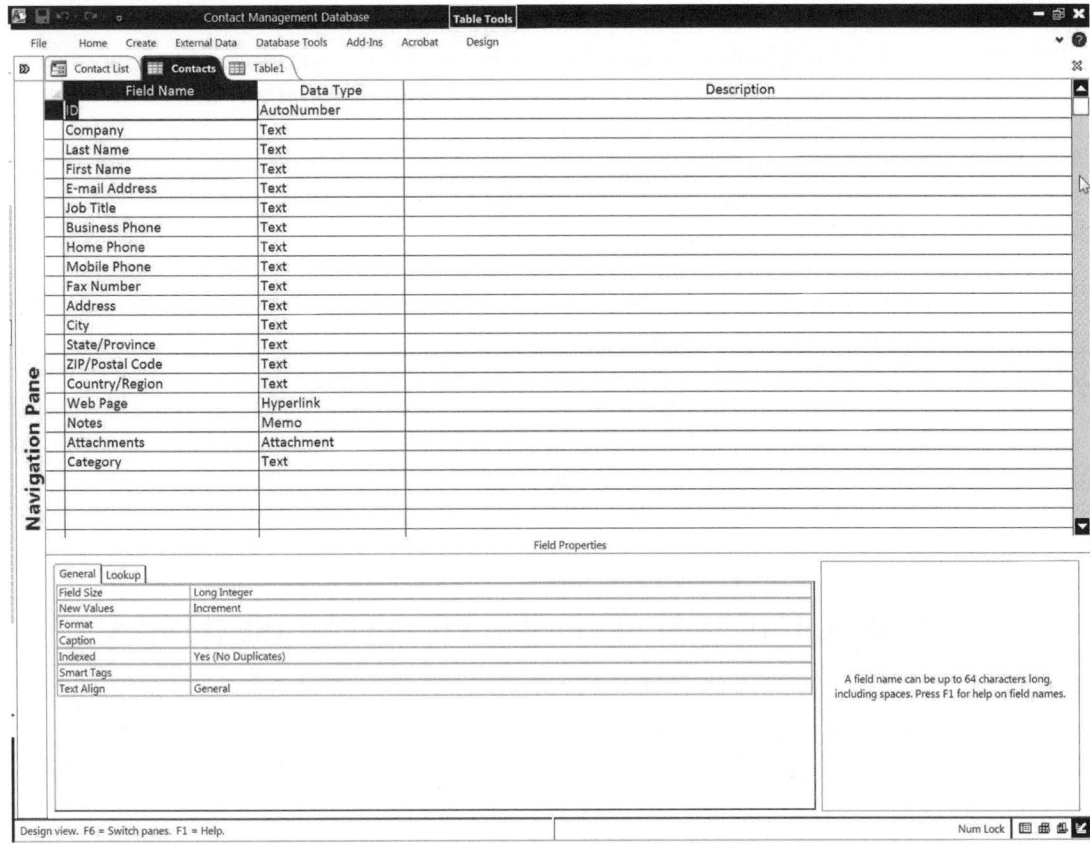

© 2011 Microsoft.

the firm, a third for opposing attorneys, and a fourth for the opposing parties in cases the firm has handled.

Reports

Reports present the data from the database in an organized, readable presentation. A report may present information from only one table or field, such as employee birthdays. A report may also show the results from searching multiple tables and display the relationships between the information. For example, a report could show all the employees that have worked for an opposing attorney in a case against a particular client.

▪ ELECTRONIC DATABASE BASICS

In the days before computers, law firms kept client information on cards kept in alphabetical order in boxes or drawers. Lawyers relied on these cards when they checked for conflicts of interest. Important dates were also maintained in a similar fashion. The dates were checked daily and a list was made up for the legal team concerning important events such as deadlines, statutes of limitations, and appointments. In some offices a card was prepared for all opposing parties. These "decks of cards" were analogous to the computer databases used today. However, trouble sometimes arose when cards were misfiled or out of alphabetical order and conflicts and important dates were missed as a result.

LEARNING OBJECTIVE 2
Explain how databases may be used by the legal team.

WEB RESOURCES
For complete listing of available tutorials and the Access http://office.microsoft.com/en-us/access

With an electronic database, information can be checked more quickly, accurately, and reliably. The data can also be searched using a set of criteria defined by the user, with the results presented in a report.

Exhibit 8.5 shows a template for input of information into a contacts management database. The contact record for Owen Mason is one of many records in the contacts table of the database.

Reports can be generated in one of the predefined reports listed in the Navigation panel introduced in the 2010 version of Excel, as shown in Exhibit 8.6.

One of the advantages of the modern database is the ability to search across a number of different sets of information and sort the data according to a predefined set of relationships, as shown in the Excel training video in Exhibit 8.7.

In most specialty software programs, predefined reports may be generated that search across different databases used within that program. For example, in LexisNexis CaseMap, a report can be generated that presents all the facts associated with a particular witness, along with the sources of those facts and their legal relevance to the case, as shown in Exhibit 8.8.

■ RESOURCES FOR LEARNING DATABASE BASICS

LEARNING OBJECTIVE 3
Find resources for learning how to use a database program and its features.

Step-by-step tutorials for learning to create and use databases are provided on the Microsoft Access Help and How-to website; see Exhibit 8.9.

Templates, like the Contact template shown above, have a "getting started" tutorial. It includes a video presentation, as shown in Exhibit 8.10.

A number of short videos of two minutes or less are available on a wide variety of topics from Brainstorm QuickHelp™, as shown in Exhibit 8.11.

Exhibit 8.5 Access Contact Details

Exhibit 8.6 Access 2010 directory report

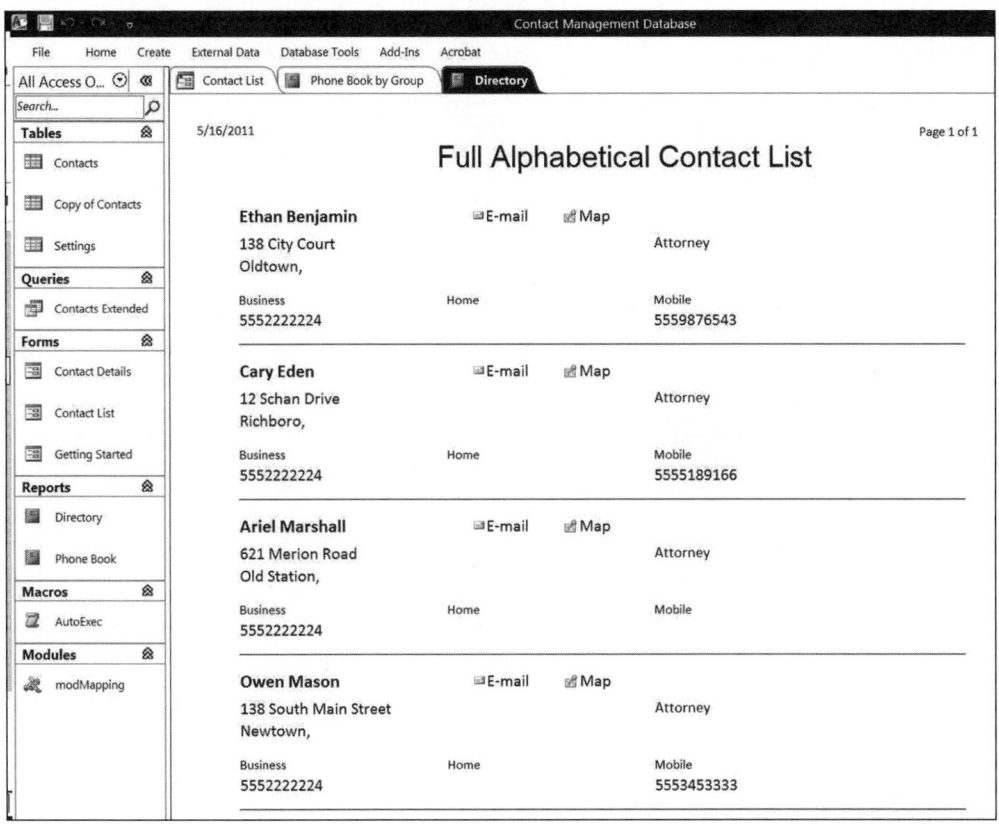

Exhibit 8.7 Relationships video tutorial

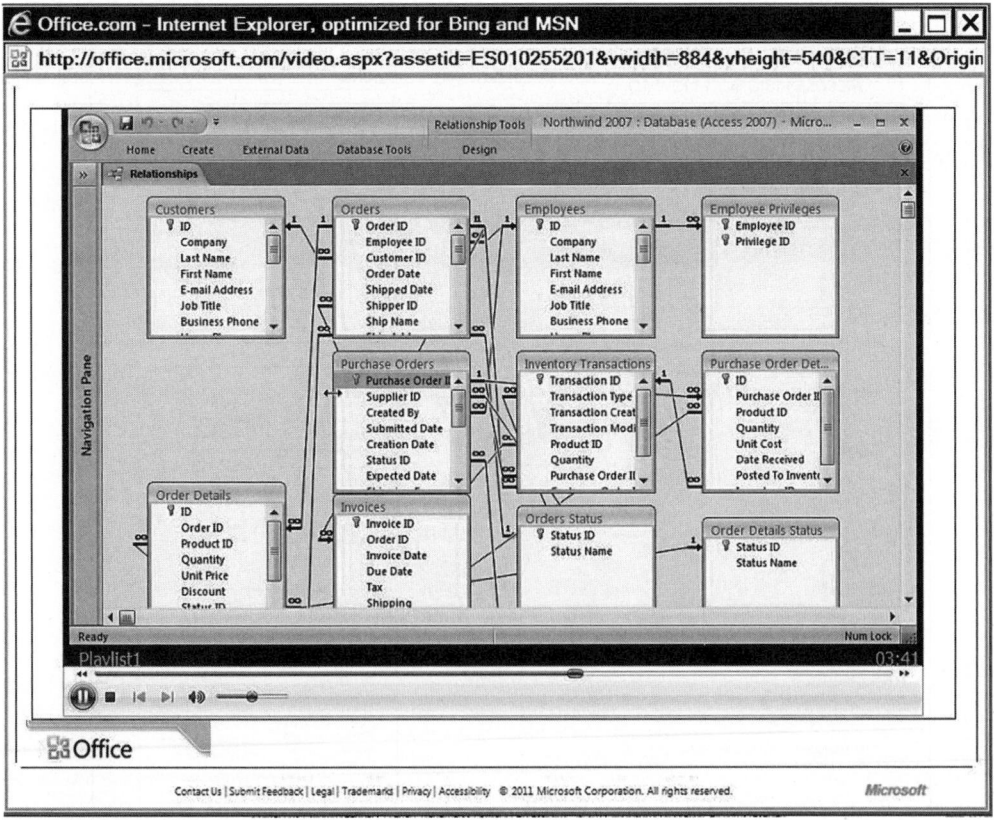

Exhibit 8.8 LexisNexis CaseMap report of Facts Grouped by Persons

Facts Grouped by Person

Continued: Facts linked to this Person:

Date & Time	Fact Text	Source(s)	Key	Status +	Linked Issues
**	**	Hawkins, 24:18	**	**	**
Tue 08/02/2005 #1	Philip Hawkins and William Lang meet.	????		Undisputed	Hawkins Specific
Tue 08/02/2005 #2	Philip Hawkins alleges that William Lang tells him "The old wood must be trimmed back hard."	Complaint, p. 8; Deposition of Philip Hawkins, 21:13; Hawkins Letter of 9/19/2005, Hawkins Letter of 8/2/2005	✓	Disputed by: Us	Hawkins Specific, Demotion
Thu 08/11/2005	Philip Hawkins transferred to Anstar Biotech Industries office in Fresno.	Deposition of Philip Hawkins, p.43, l18.		Undisputed	Transfer, Deserved Termination
Fri 08/12/2005	Frank Varvaro has lunch with Philip Hawkins.	Deposition of Philip Hawkins, 52:3-14		Undisputed	
Mon 09/19/2005	Philip Hawkins writes letter to William Lang complaining about the way he's being treated and alleging plan to eliminate older staff during reduction in force.	Hawkins Letter of 9/19/2005		Undisputed	Wrongful Termination, Hawkins Specific
Fri 11/11/2005	Reduction in force takes place. 55 Anstar Biotech Industries employees are let go including Philip Hawkins. Among others released were George Ny, and Hank Randle.		✓	Undisputed	Wrongful Termination, Hawkins Specific
Tue 11/15/2005	Philip Hawkins turns 51.	Deposition of Philip Hawkins, 56:11-23		Undisputed	Hawkins Specific
Tue 11/22/2005	Philip Hawkins files suit.	Complaint		Undisputed	
Wed 12/14/2005	Philip Hawkins turns down job offer from Converse Chemical Labs.	Rumor William Lang heard		Prospective	Failure to Mitigate
01/??/2006	Philip Hawkins is diagnosed as suffering Post Traumatic Stress Disorder.				Mental Anguish
01/??/2006	Philip Hawkins meets with Susan Sheridan	Rumor William Lang heard		Prospective	

Confidential Work Product. Do Not Reproduce.   12

LexisNexis.

Exhibit 8.9 Microsoft Access Help and How-to website

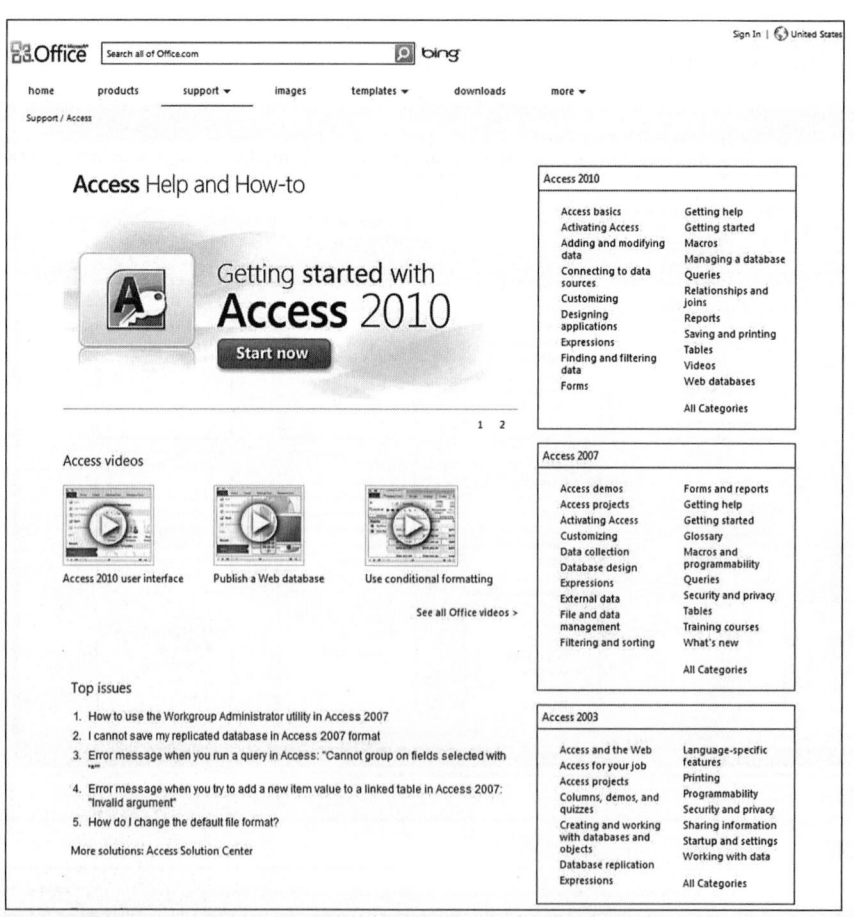

Exhibit 8.10 Template Getting Started tutorials

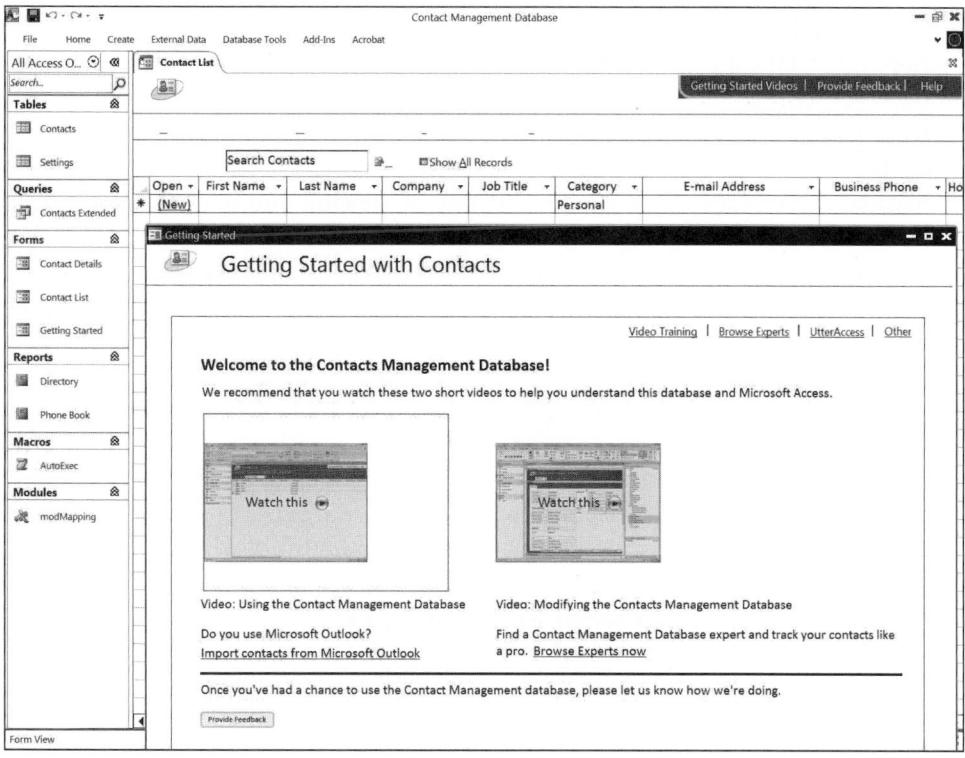

© 2011 Microsoft.

Exhibit 8.11 Free QuickHelp videos

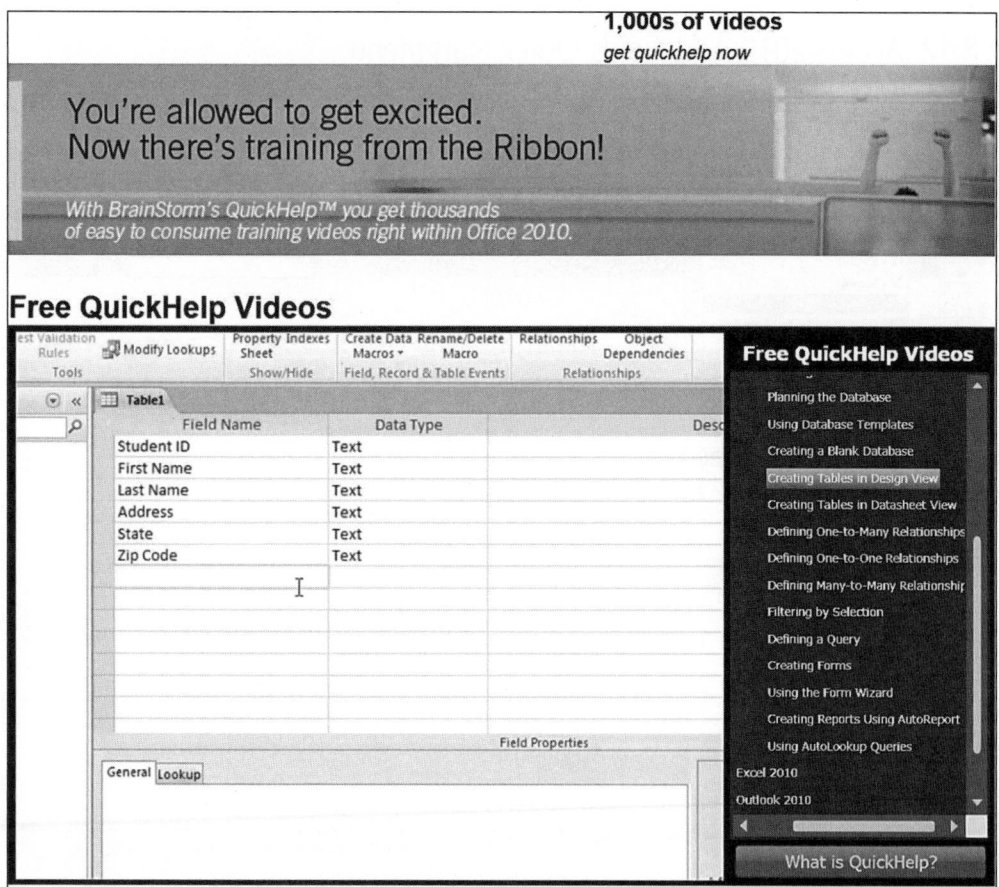

BrainStorm QuickHelp www.BrainStormInc.com/quickhelp.

◾ SETTING UP A DATABASE

At its most basic level, a database is a set of records that contain fields of information. But each database application has many options for displaying this information. The contact details in Exhibit 8.5 is an example of all the information in a record. In Access, this same information can be viewed in different arrangements, as shown in Exhibits 8.3 and 8.4. Both views contain the same basic field information. AbacusLaw also has a unique way of viewing information, as shown in Exhibit 8.2.

Access makes the setup of a database relatively simple. A database may be started by opening a Blank table, to which the desired fields are added by typing the field name in each field. Fields may also be added using the Fields tab and Add Fields Quick Start menu, as shown in Exhibit 8.12.

A database may also be created using one of the templates available in Access Backstage by selecting the New command. Additional templates may also be downloaded from the Microsoft website, as shown in Exhibit 8.13.

Each of the available selections includes a tutorial on setting up and using the selected database, such as the Contacts database in Exhibit 8.5.

Creating a Database from External Data

A database can also be created using a previously created spreadsheet. A database can be created from an Excel spreadsheet by selecting the External Data tab and Import group functions, as shown in Exhibit 8.14.

For example, the Investment Ledger from Chapter 7 can be imported into a database, as shown in Exhibit 8.15.

Exhibit 8.12 Access 2010 Add Fields Quick Start menu

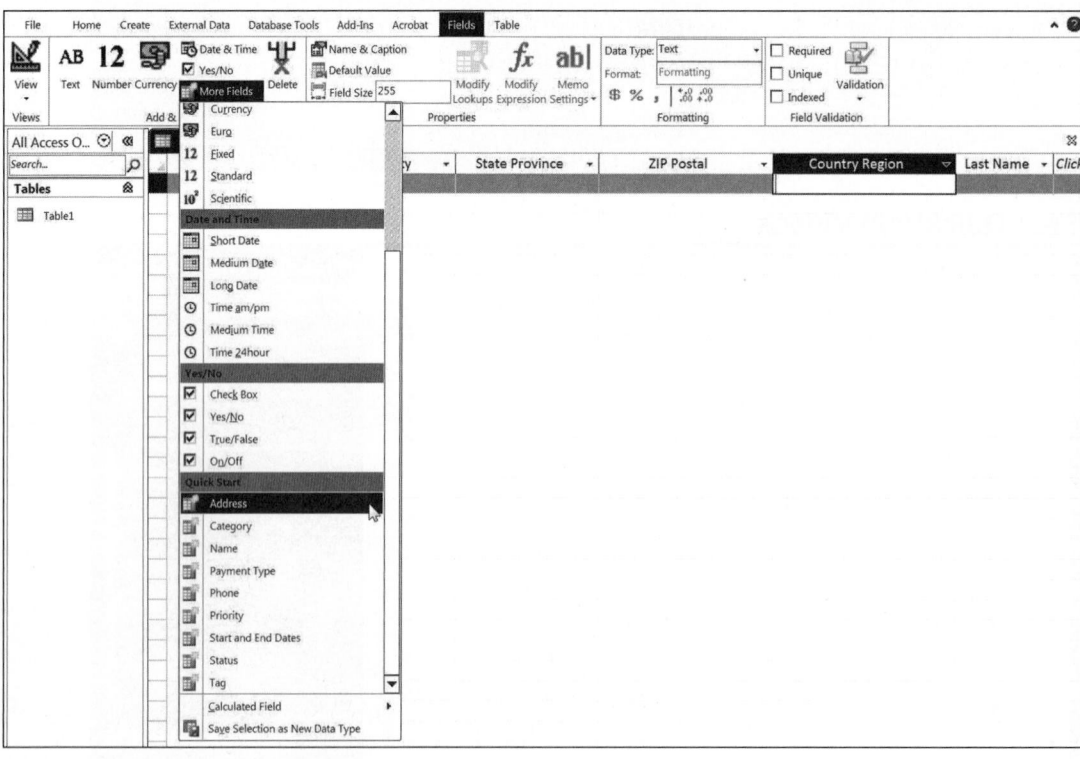

Exhibit 8.13 Access 2010 templates

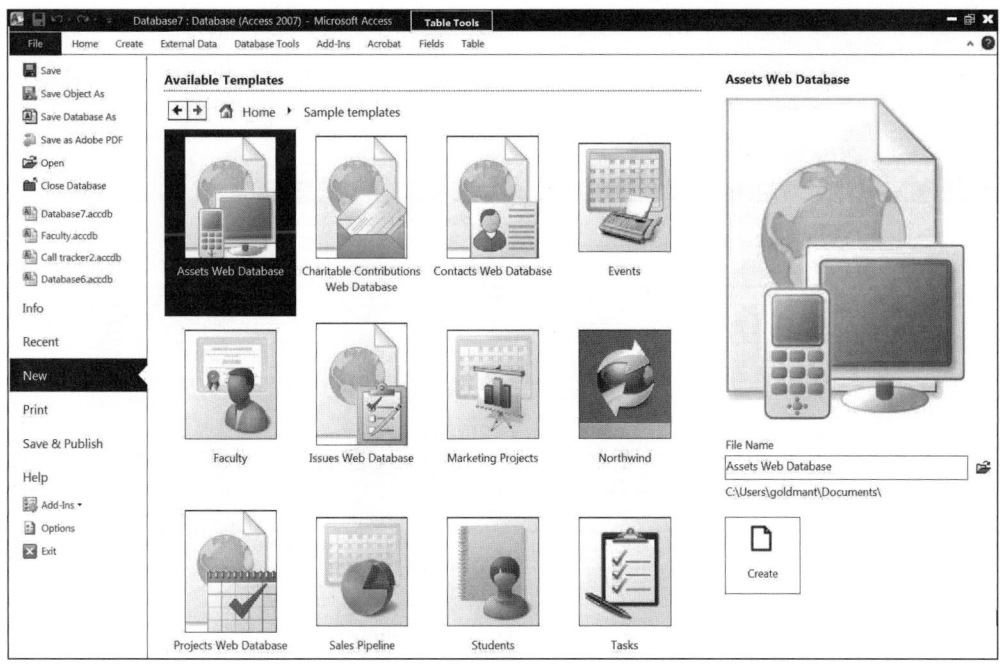

© 2011 Microsoft.

Exhibit 8.14 Access database in Design Sheet View created using external data, an Excel spreadsheet

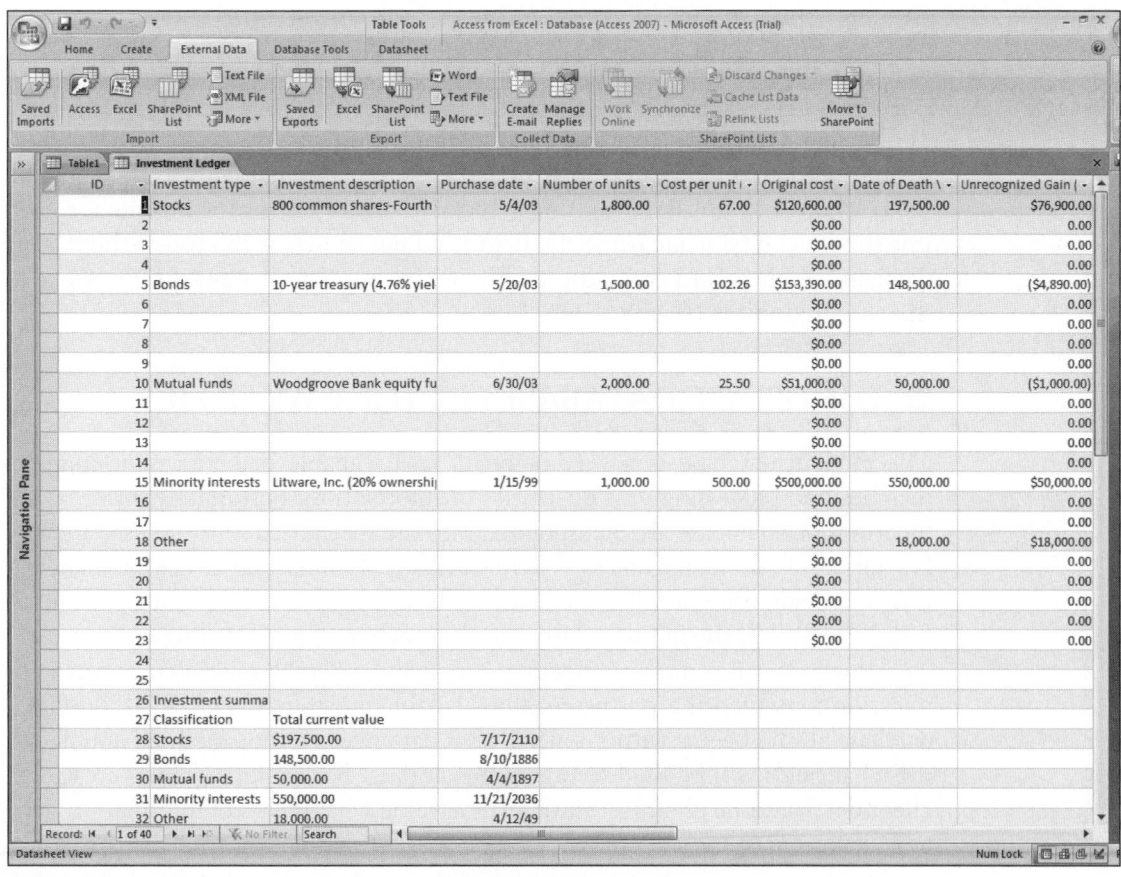

© 2011 Microsoft.

Exhibit 8.15 Excel spreadsheet imported as the external source of data

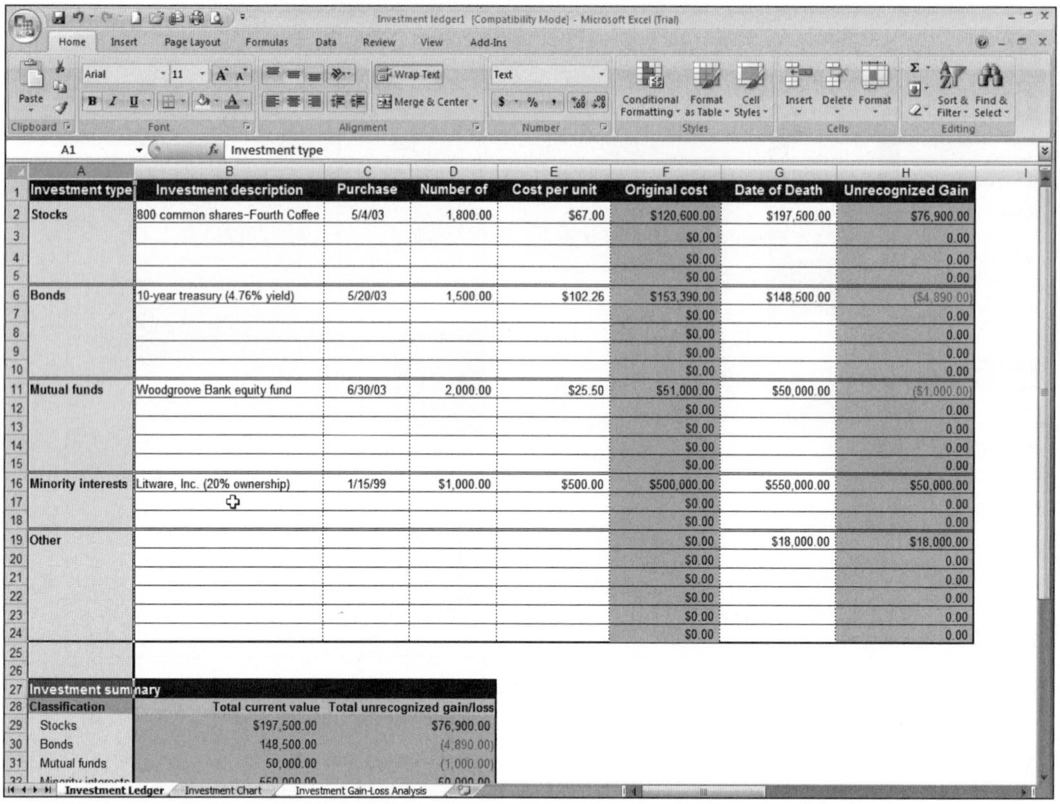

© 2011 Microsoft.

Note the change from the Button in 2007 to the File menu that opens the 2010 Backstage view.

By removing the extra information from the first few rows of the spreadsheet, the top row of the spreadsheet can be set up automatically as the database fields when they are imported into Access. Further entries of records for each investment can be made using the field headings shown at the top of the Access database. Each record from the database can be viewed in the form view, as shown in Exhibit 8.16.

■ THE USE OF DATABASES IN THE LAW OFFICE

The modern database is a very powerful tool, capable of performing complex searches and processing vast quantities of information. Fortunately, most of the functions of a database are incorporated into the specialized software used in most law offices. Case management, client contacts, billing, and litigation management programs are essentially databases. These programs are designed with input forms that search the fields of data records to prepare predefined reports.

However, it is sometimes necessary to create a database for a customized application for which there is no readily available program. Creating a customized database always begins with knowing what data needs to be organized and deciding what fields will be used to organize that data. For example, when creating a client database, the user must initially determine what pieces of information need to be collected in each client record. The goal is to produce a database that stores

Exhibit 8.16 Record #1 from the Investment Ledger database

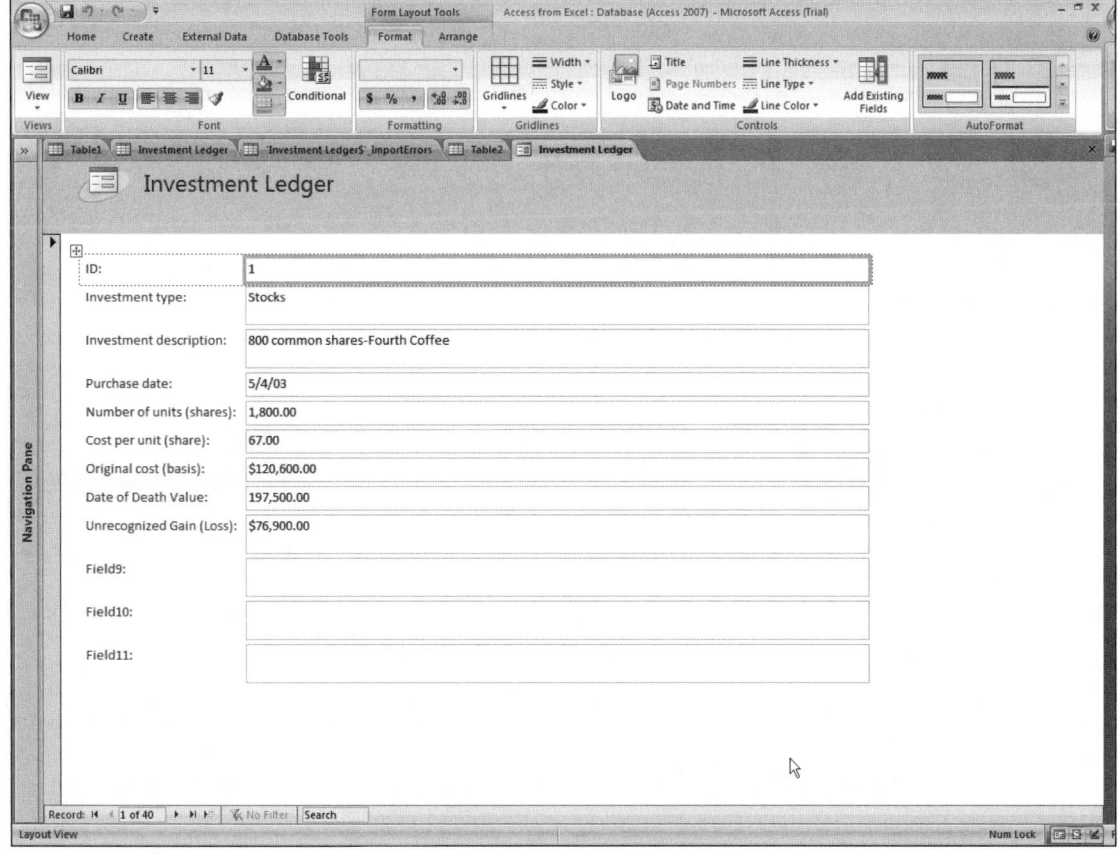

all the necessary data, can be searched using any combination of fields, and then reports the data in almost any form.

At a law firm, the actual design of the database is usually done by the IT staff or an outside database consultant. In order for the specialists to be able to create an effective database, the legal team must be able to identify what they need the database to accomplish. They can better communicate their needs if they can speak the same language as the IT person, and can use and understand such terms as "record," "field," and "report."

■ SPECIAL FEATURES OF ELECTRONIC DATABASE PROGRAMS

Security

Every law office database contains confidential information, such as the list of clients. These records may contain potentially privileged information—the reasons the clients are consulting the law firm. Protecting this information is an ethical obligation. But one of the main purposes of a database is to make the information easily accessible. Thus the need for access must be balanced with the need to protect the information.

Microsoft Access provides a number of options for restricting access, as shown in Exhibit 8.17.

LEARNING OBJECTIVE 5
Explain what can be done to protect data and computer systems.

Exhibit 8.17 Access 2010 Backstage view and Set Database Password menu

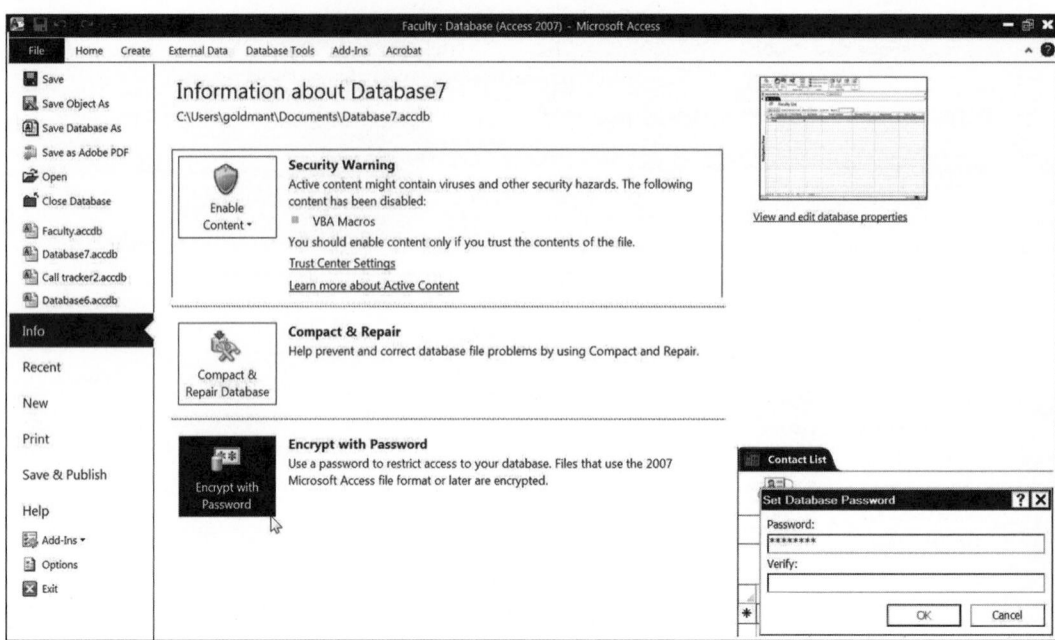

© 2011 Microsoft.

Passwords and other security options are found on most programs used in the legal community. As noted above, many specialty applications programs used in law offices are themselves database programs with input and report features. Where the data is of a confidential or privileged nature, the legal team should have a secure procedure for limiting access only to those who need the data.

CHAPTER REVIEW AND REINFORCEMENT

KEY TERMS

field 198	record 198
form views 196	table 198

CHAPTER SUMMARY

Introduction to Electronic Databases	A database program is a repository of information of all types that can be sorted and presented in a desired, meaningful manner. The reality is that legal team members, lawyers, paralegals, and legal assistants rarely create their own databases.
	Software vendors have created applications for the legal community with custom-designed views for input of information, query forms for generating the desired reports, and a setup of the search and presentation formulas for searching for data. Knowing what a database is and the associated terminology makes working with the software developer, in-house IT professional, or outside consultant easier and more productive in obtaining what is needed, wanted, and possible.

Navigating Electronic Databases	Electronic databases use standard terminology to describe parts of the database: table, field, cell, and record. Databases are collections of *tables*. Tables contain *fields* of information (data) (called a "column" in a spreadsheet); a field is one type of information, like last names; a *record* is all the information about one item or person (called a "row" in a spreadsheet); the intersection of a row and a column in a spreadsheet is a cell; in the database it is one field in a record.
Tables	Databases can and frequently do contain two or more tables.
Reports	Reports present the data from the database in an organized presentation.
Electronic Database Basics	A database is a collection of information, essentially an electronic card file with information that can be searched using a set of items to look for and is present in a predefined manner. An advantage of the database is the ability to search across a number of different sets of information and sort the data according to a predefined set of criteria.
Resources for Learning Database Basics	Step-by-step tutorials for learning to create and use databases are provided on the Microsoft website.
Setting Up a Database	A database at its most basic is a set of records that contain fields of information. The individual pieces of information, like the last name and the first name, are called fields. Databases may be set up using a blank form to which desired fields are added or using a database template that may be modified to meet specific needs.
Creating a Database from External Data	A database can also be created using a previously created spreadsheet.
The Use of Databases in the Law Office	The modern computer database is a very powerful tool, capable of performing complex searches and calculations. Creation starts with knowing what data needs to be manipulated and deciding on the fields and the total collection of fields of a single type.
Special Features of Electronic Database Programs	It is obvious that a database in a law office contains confidential information that ethically must be protected.
Security	Microsoft Access provides options for password and permissions-level setup that can be used to restrict access.

REVIEW QUESTIONS AND EXERCISES

1. What security features are available in Access? Choose one of these features and explain, in your words, how it can be used to prevent someone with a conflict of interest from accessing specific client information.

2. What steps may be taken to locate and use the resources for learning how to use the Access program?

3. Explain how a database organizes data, using the terms "table," "record," "field," and "report."

4. Think of one type of information that may be collected by a law firm about their clients. Describe how a database may be used by the legal team to organize, search, and report this information.

5. Imagine you are helping an attorney start a new law practice. Explain how to plan and set up a database for collecting data about new clients.
6. Explain why security features are vital when a law firm maintains a client database.
7. A database of information can be used in many ways by the legal team. Prepare a list of at least five reports that could be prepared using a database. What is the purpose of each report? What data will they contain?
8. How can a database be used to prevent a conflict of interest when a new client engages a law firm's services?
9. How can a properly maintained database of client information be used for marketing the firm's services? Give two examples of marketing strategies that would employ the law firm's database.
10. In a law office that has a network, everyone may have access to all the information on the network. If the firm's database is on the network, what, if anything, should be done to limit access? What levels of access should be set up and why?
11. Prepare a database of family and friends, including important dates such as birthdays and anniversaries. Sort the list by date.

BUILDING YOUR PARALEGAL SKILLS

INTERNET AND TECHNOLOGY EXERCISES

1. Complete the Microsoft Office "Hands-On Training for Access Forms I: Create a form to enter and view your data." After the training, explain in your own words how a form is created, as if you were explaining to the legal team.
2. Prepare a list of online tutorial topics for learning and using the Access database. Name at least five topics for tutorials.

CHAPTER OPENING SCENARIO CASE STUDY

Use the Opening Scenario for this chapter to answer the following questions. The setting is a law office with metal boxes full of hundreds of 3-by-5 cards containing client records.

1. Prepare a memo stating the reasons why the attorney should switch to an electronic database. Detail the potential ethical problems that could be avoided by using a database to keep client records.
2. Prepare a design for a client database table for a small office practice, listing the fields for each table.
3. Explain how the database designed in question 2 could be used in the practice. Detail at least three purposes.
4. How could the database designed in question 2 have prevented the conflict in the Opening Scenario?
5. Prepare a memo for the employee handbook about the procedure to be followed for entering client data and using the database to check for conflicts.

CONTINUING CASES AND EXERCISES

1. Prepare a database for the information in Case A in Appendix II.
2. Prepare a list of individual databases that should be set up with the records and fields to manage Case A in Appendix II.
3. Use the Contacts template in Access 2010 to create a database of the clients in Case A in Appendix II.

BUILDING YOUR PROFESSIONAL PORTFOLIO

1. Prepare a memo to law firm staff outlining a procedure for entering new client data into the firm's client database.

2. Prepare a presentation on the uses of a database as a productivity tool. Outline how a database can be used for such purposes as improving and expediting conflicts checks, or preparing for trial by sorting facts, sources, and witnesses.

"Technology means the systematic application of scientific
or other organized knowledge to practical tasks."
—*John Kenneth Galbraith*

Office Management Software | CHAPTER 9

When Owen Mason first hired Mrs. Hannah, most of her time was spent on the core functions of a paralegal—performing legal research and actively working on cases with clients. In the early days of their small practice, it was relatively easy for her to take care of the checkbooks, pay the bills, and prepare payroll tax forms. But as the practice grew and more staff was added, Mrs. Hannah saw her job expand as she took on a greater role in managing the office. She was now handling major accounting, payroll, and human resource functions—responsibilities that were often overwhelming. Time and billing management, which involved collecting everyone's time slips and preparing the bills for clients each month, usually took days to finish. The calculation of the monthly payroll, which had to be done manually, took almost a full day. Without some help, she would not be able to manage it all.

LEARNING OBJECTIVES

After studying this chapter, you should be able to:

1. Explain the basic functions of office management software.

2. Describe the function of calendaring software in the law office.

3. Explain the importance of timekeeping software.

4. Explain the importance of accounting records in a law office.

VIDEO INTRODUCTION

OFFICE MANAGEMENT SOFTWARE

After watching the video in MyLegalStudiesLab, answer the following questions.

1. What are some of the administrative functions in a law office for which computers can be used?
2. How can computers be used to avoid conflicts?

■ INTRODUCTION TO OFFICE MANAGEMENT SOFTWARE

There are certain administrative activities that are necessary for the successful management of most law offices. These tasks include timekeeping, calendar maintenance, and accounting. If timekeeping records are not managed adequately, fees may be lost for hours that were worked but not billed. If the calendar is not maintained accurately, a significant appointment, trial date, or statute of limitations deadline may be missed. And tracking expenses is particularly critical in a law office where attorneys have a fiduciary responsibility to maintain escrow accounts for client funds. They must frequently provide an accounting to the courts as well as to clients regarding these accounts.

A sole practitioner with relatively few clients can keep track of the most important office information using a paper calendar and two checkbooks. The calendar can be consulted on a daily basis for appointments, deadlines, and statute of limitations dates. Any disbursements for office expenses can be recorded in the office checkbook, and client funds can be deposited and disbursed using a separate checkbook.

But when the number of clients increases and additional personnel are added, it becomes increasingly difficult to record and access information. With busier schedules and more time spent out of the office, critical information may be delayed or lost. In addition, a paper system requires someone to physically look at the books, which is inconvenient if the offices are on different floors, and impossible if an attorney is in another town or at the courthouse.

Electronic office management systems allow access from anywhere over a computer network or an Internet connection. For example, important deadlines can be automatically sent by the software, eliminating the need to rely on a staff member, who may not always available, to pass along deadlines.

■ BASIC FUNCTIONS OF OFFICE MANAGEMENT PROGRAMS

LEARNING OBJECTIVE 1
Explain the basic functions of office management software.

Most office management functions can be divided into the following categories:

Calendar—personal appointments, case deadlines, statutes of limitations, and important reminder dates.

Contacts—names, addresses, phone numbers, email addresses, and other information for clients, opposing counsel, vendors, and networking contacts.

Files—individual files for cases, projects, and other client matters.

Accounting—timekeeping, billing, firm accounts, client escrow accounts, financial reports, and tax returns.

There are also a number of legal specialty office or practice management software programs available, of which AbacusLaw and Tabs3 are two of the most popular. These programs offer a number of **integrated functions** in a common package, like Office Suites. In the past, office managers have purchased and used one program for maintaining their calendars, another program for time and billing, and yet other programs for other functions like contact management. Today's programs integrate some or all of these functions into one **program shell.** These shells allow the use of one or more programs and the sharing of information across programs.

Office management software programs use databases to store information. As detailed in Chapter 8, a **database** is a collection of records that contain similar information. The user can search these collections for specific items by using a query such as "What are all the appointments for today?"

As an example, the AbacusLaw software program uses four main databases to store the information, as explained in its literature:

Names
Think of names as the contacts in your address book. This includes every person with whom your firm has contact: clients, prospects, vendors, defendants, judges, attorneys, expert witnesses, friends, relatives, and anyone you might want on your mailing list. Abacus gives you fast and easy access to information on anyone in your Names database. Notes for names are kept in a linked database so you can keep essentially unlimited notes about your contacts.

Events
Events are any appointments, tasks, reminders, or things to do that are scheduled for specific dates. Events can be entered into Abacus by many different methods. The events window is the primary data window, while the Daily Organizer and various calendar windows give you different views of your events.

Matters
Matters refer to any matter, case, file, or project that you need to track. Once entered, matters can be attached to any number of names. Notes for matters are kept in a linked database so you can keep essentially unlimited notes about your files.

Documents
In Abacus, **documents** are any previously saved word processing files, scanned images, pleadings, correspondence, or Internet Web pages. They can be files on disk or just printed documents stored in a box. Abacus keeps a list of these documents in a database so you can find or edit them right from the client's Name or Matter window.

Source: AbacusLaw.

These databases can be searched individually—for example, the Names list can be queried to present a report of all clients listed alphabetically. Or, the software can perform a more complex search that accesses several different databases simultaneously. The user can prepare a report of all documents, for one particular client, sorted by the individual matters being handled by the firm, and listing important dates and deadlines for each matter.

Some office management software may be categorized as "generic." These programs do not offer the depth and features of specialty programs for managing the office functions. However, some of these programs, such as Microsoft Outlook, do have a number of features common to the specialized programs, like calendaring, contact management, email, and appointment reminder features. Outlook also offers the ability to search email, as shown in Exhibit 9.1.

---

integrated functions
The sharing of data among different functions in a software program.

program shell
A software program containing a platform for using different software programs. See integrated functions.

database
A collection of similar records.

events
Any appointments, tasks, reminders, or things to do that are scheduled for specific dates.

matters
Any item, case, file, or project that you need to track.

documents
Previously prepared word processing, scanned images, and pleadings.

Exhibit 9.1 Microsoft Outlook personal organizer

© 2011 Microsoft.

CALENDAR PROGRAM OVERVIEW

LEARNING OBJECTIVE 2
Describe the function of calendaring software in the law office.

The law office calendar is a tool that can organize time-sensitive information about:

- Appointments with clients
- Litigation deadlines
- Filing deadlines
- Court appearance dates
- Statute of limitations dates
- Routine reminders

At one time, most law firms maintained a master office calendar on paper. In offices with more than one attorney, these calendars had multiple columns, each pertaining to a different attorney. An office assistant would print out or photocopy the calendar for each person in the office on a weekly basis. Diary reminders, such as statute of limitations dates, were recorded on cards in a file box. The reminders were filed by dates that were fixed periods of time before the deadlines, to allow enough time for action on the file. A legal assistant or paralegal was responsible for pulling out the deadline cards and reporting the deadlines to the responsible attorney, with a reminder attached to the outside of the file.

Now, all of these tasks can be handled by a calendar program. A calendar program is basically a database of dates and related information. Preset reporting criteria allow for presentation of the data in a number of ways, such as:

- Daily, weekly, monthly, or annual calendars for the whole office
- Daily, weekly, monthly, or annual calendars for each staff member
- Reports of important dates in a particular category, such as statute of limitations dates or reminders of deadlines.

Most calendar programs have an alert or alarm feature that signals when a preset time is reached. Typically, a specific time and date is set for a reminder or alert. In Microsoft Outlook, a popup window gives a reminder of an event that has been set up. In programs like Abacus, a specific time is set for each event, and a fixed time period is chosen in advance of the event for giving the alarm.

Specialized, Rules-Based Calendar Programs

As with all technology, calendar programs are constantly being improved. A calendar system may consist of a paper calendar, an electronic calendar (such as Outlook), or a complex, **rules-based calendaring** program. These programs automatically calculate deadlines based on the type of case, the type of event, and the court rules of the selected jurisdiction. Programs like AbacusLaw will count the days for items such as filing deadlines and hearing dates, and make the appropriate entries in the calendar, as shown in Exhibit 9.2.

rules-based calendaring
Custom dates or reminders created for a set period before or after a selected event.

Deadlines Set by Rules of Civil Procedure

A court's rules of civil procedure will establish the time limits for filing and responding to pleadings. For example, the rules may state that an answer to a complaint is due in twenty days. Generally, the time period for responding to a pleading begins the day after the pleading is received. If a defendant is served with a complaint today, day 1 is tomorrow, and the period includes all calendar days that follow, including Saturdays, Sundays, and holidays. If the due date falls on a Saturday, Sunday, or holiday, the due date is the court's next regular business day. The paralegal is usually responsible for entering the deadlines and reminders in the firm's central calendaring system.

Exhibit 9.2 AbacusLaw statute of limitations rules calculator

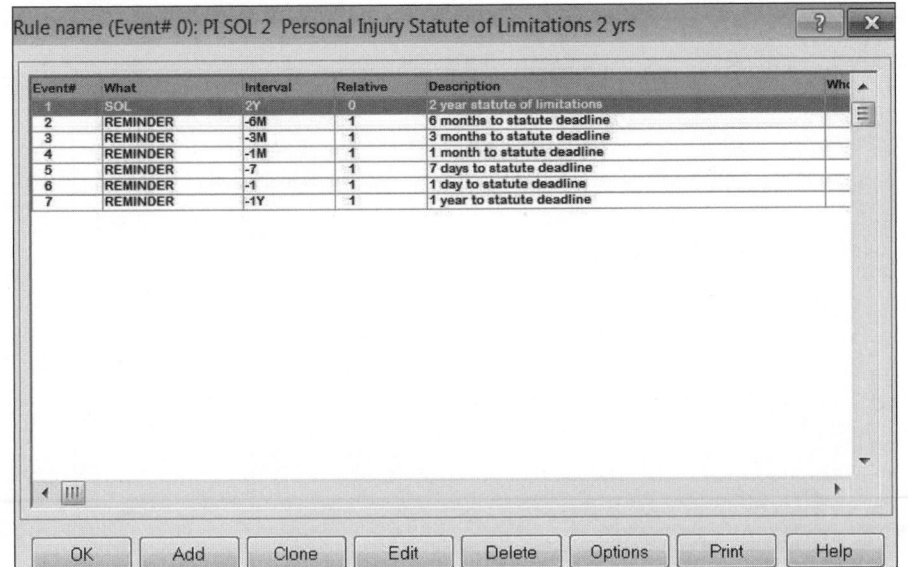

AbacusLaw.

Software for Calculating Deadlines

Calculating the important dates in a case requires a careful review of the specific court rules of the jurisdiction in which the case is filed. Among different jurisdictions, there may be variations in the timetables for proceedings. To address these differences, some programs, such as Abacus, have been pre-programmed with these schedules, and the deadlines for different jurisdictions are built into the program. Dates are automatically calculated based on the required intervals set by the court, as shown in Exhibit 9.2. Custom dates or reminders can also be created for a set period before or after a selected event. These dates may be used to send follow-up letters or to schedule routine case status conferences in the office.

The AbacusLaw program is used on a local network or personal computer, whereas CompuLaw offers a web-based, pay-per-use version of their software designed for small firms, called Deadlines.com. Exhibits 9.3 through 9.6 show the Deadlines On Demand service (www.deadlines.com).

Abacus and CompuLaw will synchronize events and reminders with Outlook and other calendaring software, and provide a single copy without the duplicate

Exhibit 9.3 CompuLaw Step 1: Select jurisdiction

```
⊞ 🗀 Mississippi
⊞ 🗀 Missouri
⊞ 🗀 Montana
⊞ 🗀 Nebraska
⊞ 🗀 Nevada
⊞ 🗀 New Hampshire
⊞ 🗀 New Jersey
⊞ 🗀 New Mexico
⊟ 🗀 New York
   ⊞ 🗀 State
   ⊟ 🗀 Federal
      ⊟ 🗀 U.S. District Courts - Civil Litigation
         ─ 🗋 Eastern District
         ─ 🗋 Northern District
         ─ 🗋 Southern District
         ─ 🗋 Western District
      ⊞ 🗀 Appeals
   ⊞ 🗀 U.S. Bankruptcy Courts
⊞ 🗀 North Carolina
⊞ 🗀 North Dakota
⊞ 🗀 Ohio
⊞ 🗀 Oklahoma
⊞ 🗀 Oregon
⊞ 🗀 Pennsylvania
⊞ 🗀 Puerto Rico
⊞ 🗀 Rhode Island
⊞ 🗀 South Carolina
⊞ 🗀 South Dakota
⊞ 🗀 Tennessee
```

Exhibit 9.4 CompuLaw Step 2: Select event

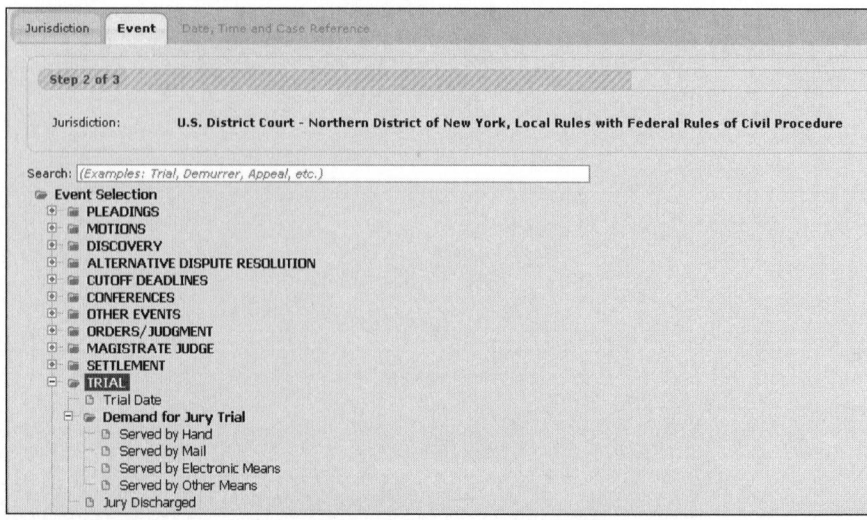

Exhibit 9.5 CompuLaw Step 3: Enter event date and case reference

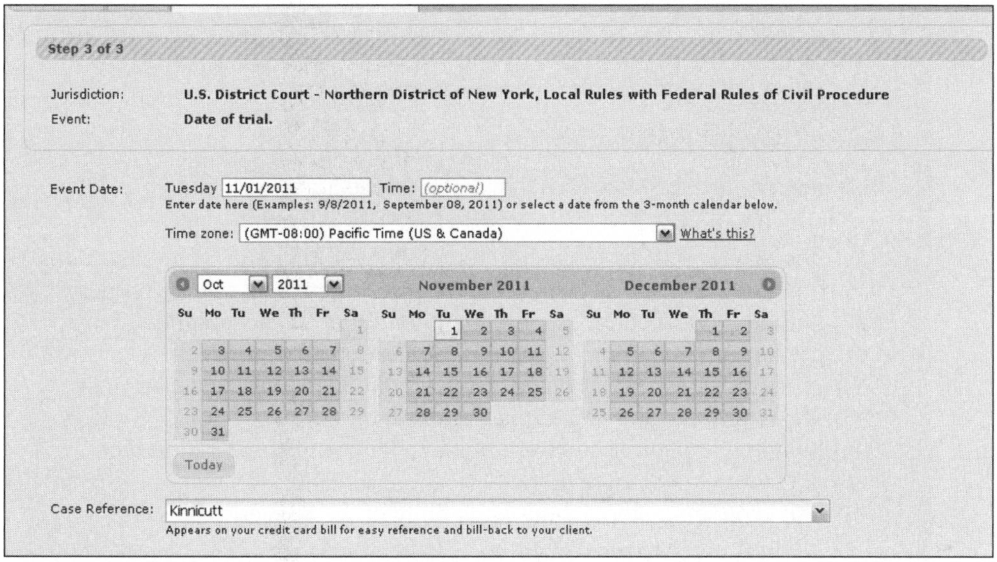

Exhibit 9.6 CompuLaw Review deadline results

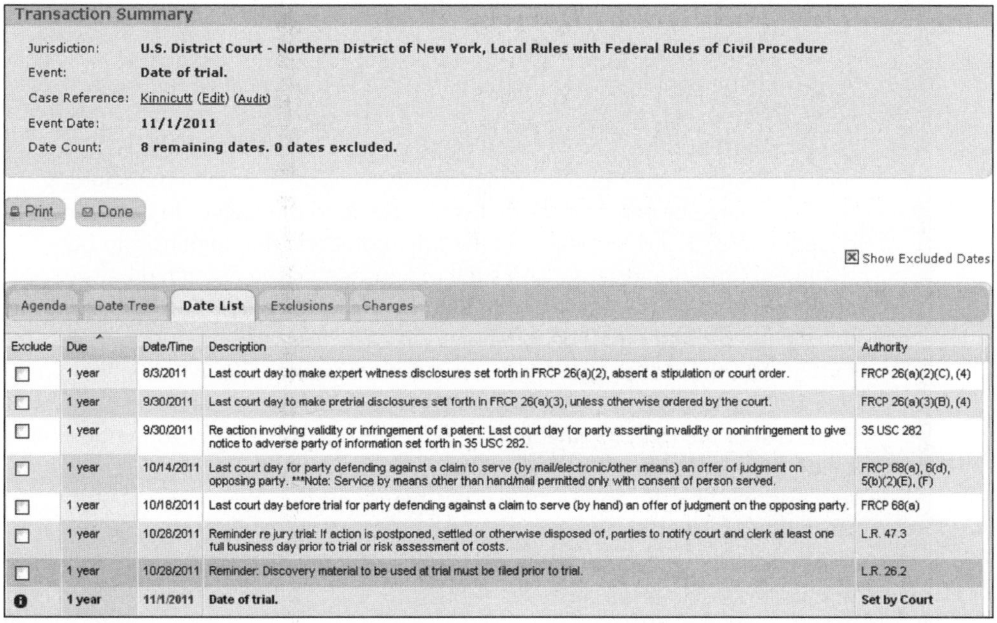

entries. This feature helps prevent errors that may result from entering the same information in more than one place. Errors may also be avoided by having a firm-wide, centralized system that provides advance notification of upcoming deadlines. But a calendaring program is only as good as the information entered. It is thus imperative to inform office staff of the importance of accurately entering deadline dates.

According to the American Bar Association's Profile of Legal Malpractice Claims 2004–2007, calendar-related errors are the leading cause of malpractice claims. Setting up an effective calendaring system is critical in avoiding these errors. Malpractice insurance carriers recognize this risk, and many offer discounts on insurance premiums for law offices that use an automated, rules-based system.

WEB RESOURCES

Contrast and compare Rule 1.5 of the Kansas Rules of Professional Conduct at http://www.kscourts.org/rules/Rule-Info.asp?r1=Rules+Relating+to+Discipline+of+Attorneys&r2=50 with the American Bar Association Model Rules of Professional Conduct at http://www.abanet.org/cpr/mrpc/mrpc_toc.html, and the ethical rules in your jurisdiction.

ETHICAL Perspectives

RULE 226

KANSAS RULES OF PROFESSIONAL CONDUCT

1.5 Client-Lawyer Relationship: Fees

(a) A lawyer's fee shall be reasonable. The factors to be considered in determining the reasonableness of a fee include the following:

   (1) the time and labor required, the novelty and difficulty of the questions involved, and the skill requisite to perform the legal service properly;

   (2) the likelihood, if apparent to the client, that the acceptance of the particular employment will preclude other employment by the lawyer;

   (3) the fee customarily charged in the locality for similar legal services;

   (4) the amount involved and the results obtained;

   (5) the time limitations imposed by the client or by the circumstances;

   (6) the nature and length of the professional relationship with the client;

   (7) the experience, reputation, and ability of the lawyer or lawyers performing the services; and

   (8) whether the fee is fixed or contingent.

(b) When the lawyer has not regularly represented the client, the basis or rate of the fee shall be communicated to the client, preferably in writing, before or within a reasonable time after commencing the representation.

(c) A lawyer's fee shall be reasonable but a court determination that a fee is not reasonable shall not be presumptive evidence of a violation that requires discipline of the attorney.

(d) A fee may be contingent on the outcome of the matter for which the service is rendered, except in a matter in which a contingent fee is prohibited by paragraph (f) or other law. A contingent fee agreement shall be in writing and shall state the method by which the fee is to be determined, including the percentage or percentages that shall accrue to the lawyer in the event of settlement, trial or appeal, and the litigation and other expenses to be deducted from the recovery. All such expenses shall be deducted before the contingent fee is calculated. Upon conclusion of a contingent fee matter, the lawyer shall provide the client with a written statement stating the outcome of the matter and, if there is a recovery, showing the client's share and amount and the method of its determination. The statement shall advise the client of the right to have the fee reviewed as provided in subsection (e).

(e) Upon application by the client, all fee contracts shall be subject to review and approval by the appropriate court having jurisdiction of the matter and the court shall have the authority to determine whether the contract is reasonable. If the court finds the contract is not reasonable, it shall set and allow a reasonable fee.

(f) A lawyer shall not enter into an arrangement for, charge, or collect:

   (1) Any fee in a domestic relations matter, the payment or amount of which is contingent upon the securing of a divorce or upon the amount of alimony, support, or property settlement; or

   (2) a contingent fee for representing a defendant in a criminal case; or

   (3) a contingent fee in any other matter in which such a fee is precluded by statute.

(g) A division of fee, which may include a portion designated for referral of a matter, between or among lawyers who are not in the same firm may be made if the total fee is reasonable and the client is advised of and does not object to the division.

(h) This rule does not prohibit payments to former partners or associates or their estates pursuant to a separation or retirement agreement.

■ TIMEKEEPING SOFTWARE

Timekeeping is the recording of all time spent performing activities during the work day. It is one of the principal administrative functions in a law office, since keeping track of billable time ensures that the law firm will be properly compensated for its advice and efforts on behalf of clients. In some offices, only time that may be billed to a client is recorded. In others, billable as well as non-billable time, such as pro bono or client development work, is recorded. Timekeeping is not limited to attorneys, but usually includes paralegals as well. In some cases, time spent by secretaries and file clerks is also included.

Fortunately, timekeeping has been automated by the use of software, such as Tabs3 by STI (Software Technology, Inc.). These applications accurately capture, store, and process this information and automatically prepare billing and timekeeping records, as shown in Exhibit 9.7.

LEARNING OBJECTIVE 3

Explain the importance of timekeeping software.

timekeeping
The recording of all time spent performing activities during the work day.

Exhibit 9.7 Tabs3 time and billing screens

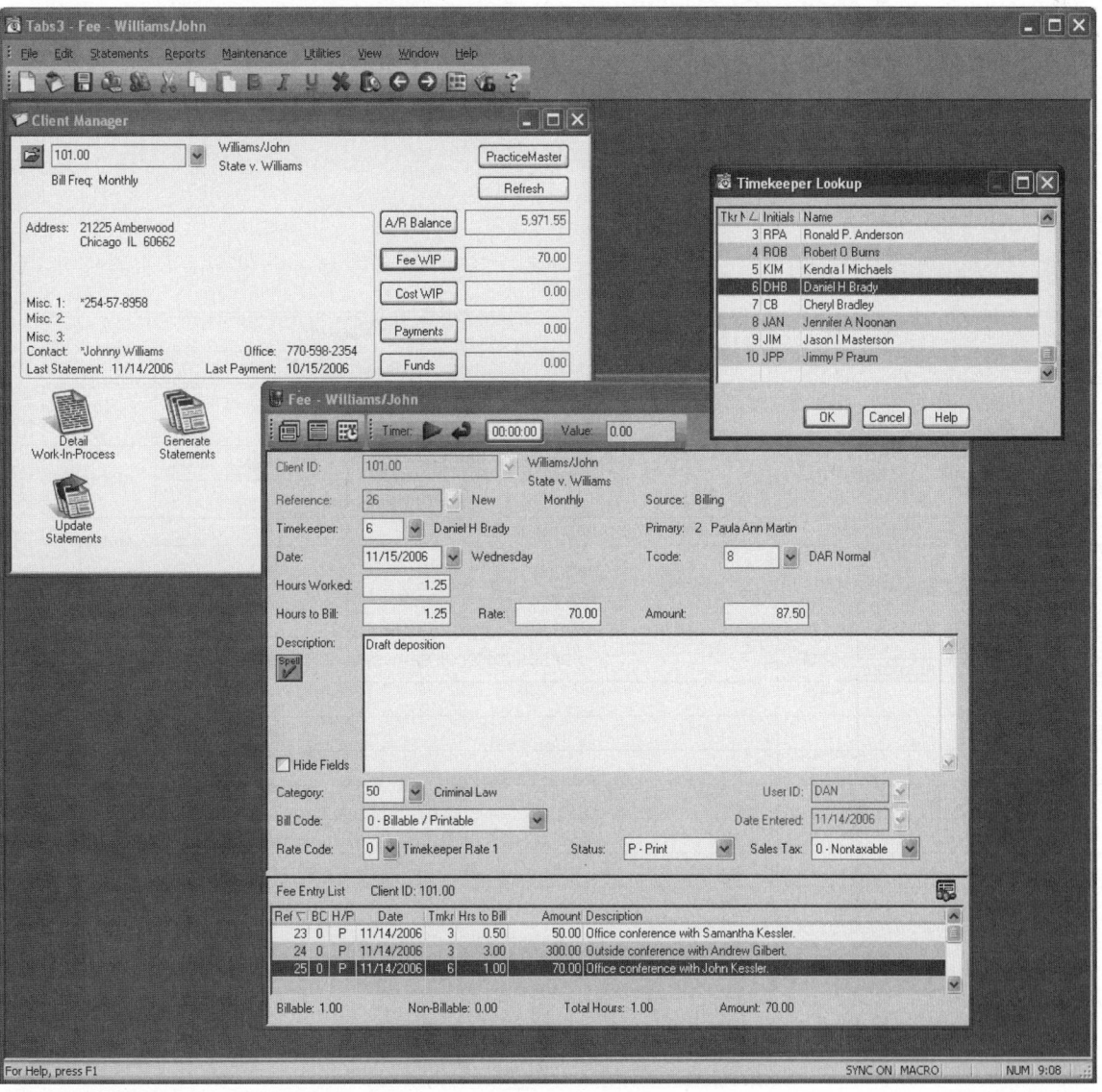

Software Technology, Inc.

Time records are often written down manually for later recording in the timekeeping software. One of the informal methods used by many lawyers and paralegals is to write the activity and the time spent directly on the inside or outside of the case file folder. One problem with this method, however, is that it leaves the client's potentially confidential information exposed. Recording on the inside conceals the information to some extent, but the information is still accessible to anyone who opens the file folder. Some firms use a form for recording time, as shown in Exhibit 9.8. The time entered on the form is later entered into the timekeeping system.

The form shown in Exhibit 9.8 is similar in many ways to the input screen used in programs such as Abacus Accounting, as shown in Exhibit 9.9. Time records are transferred from the paper forms into the software using this input screen.

ETHICAL Perspectives

PROOF OF SUPERVISION

Accurate, contemporaneously recorded time records for the paralegal and for the attorney may be used to show the level of supervision of the paralegal by the supervising attorney.

Exhibit 9.8 Weekly time report

ACCOUNT NUMBER	NAME OF CLIENT	HOURS WORKED								AMOUNT	
		MON.	TUE.	WED.	THUR.	FRI.	SAT.	SUN.	TOTAL		1
ACCOUNT NUMBER	NAME OF CLIENT	MON.	TUE.	WED.	THUR.	FRI.	SAT.	SUN.	TOTAL	AMOUNT	2
		HOURS WORKED									
DO NOT WRITE IN SHADED AREA BELOW											3
											4
											5

DATE	TIME			CODE	DESCRIPTION OF SERVICES PERFORMED	
	START	STOP	ELAPSED			
						6
						7
						8
						9
						10

CODE		NAME		
		CLIENT ⟶		11
		⟵ STAFF MEMB.		
		CLIENT ⟶		12
		⟵ STAFF MEMB.		

Exhibit 9.9 Abacus Accounting time ticket entry form

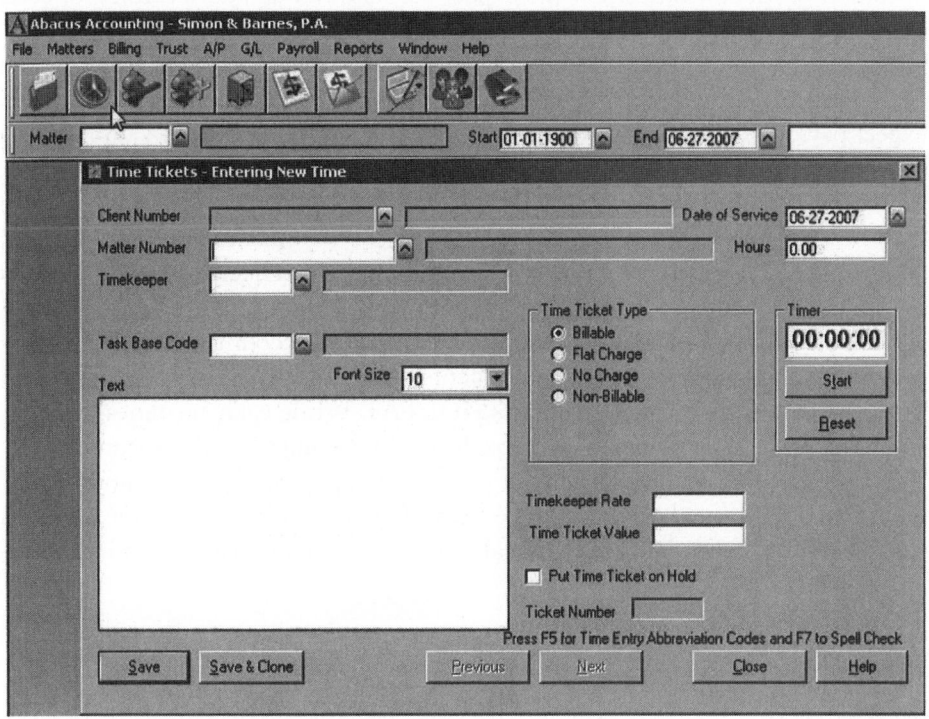

AbacusLaw.

ETHICAL Perspectives

BILLING FOR PARALEGAL TIME

The 11th Circuit Court of Appeals has said "...we have held that paralegal time is recoverable as 'part of a prevailing party's award for attorney's fees and expenses, [but] only to the extent that the paralegal performs work traditionally done by an attorney.'" Quoting from *Allen v. United States Steel Corp.*, 665 F.2d 689, 697 (5th Cir. 1982).... "To hold otherwise would be counterproductive because excluding reimbursement for such work might encourage attorneys to handle entire cases themselves, thereby achieving the same results at a higher overall cost." *Jean v. Nelson*, 863 F. 2d 759 (11th Cir. 1988).

■ ACCOUNTING SOFTWARE

Accounting software is used for recording and processing the financial transactions of the firm. Most general accounting software follows the general rules of accounting for recording financial information. This information falls into five major classifications: **assets, liabilities, equity, revenues,** and **expenses.** While every industry or profession uses the same five major classifications, each has its own **chart of accounts** that is specific to the industry or profession. A chart of accounts is a list of the individual categories under the five major classifications. For example, in a law firm, revenue would most likely be described as "Fees Received," whereas a retail business would use the description "Sales."

assets
Things that have value.

liabilities
Claims of outsiders to the assets of the entity.

equity
The value of the assets of an entity reduced by the claims of outsiders.

revenue
The increases in the owner's equity from the delivery of goods or services.

expenses
The decreases in the owner's equity caused by an outflow of assets from the entity in the delivery of goods and services.

chart of accounts
A listing of all the names of the accounts used in a particular financial entity.

LEARNING OBJECTIVE 4
Explain the importance of accounting records in a law office.

check register
A chronological record of disbursements of checks and deposits.

IOLTA
Trust accounts used for holding small amounts of client funds or that will be held for too short a period of time to generate income sufficient to allocate to the client. Interest is paid to state designated agencies to aid nonprofit legal aid providers. www.IOLTA.org

ledger
The individual records for each account.

journals
Chronological listings of financial transactions of a business.

Accurate financial record keeping and reporting is an essential part of the operation of the law office. Clients expect accurate billing and recording of costs expended on their behalf. The courts expect accurate reporting of escrowed client funds, such as the proceeds of settlements where court approval is needed. The employees, as well as the taxing authorities of federal, state, and local governments, expect payroll records to be maintained and reported accurately. In addition, vendors who sell goods and services to the firm expect prompt and accurate payment.

For many small firms, the checkbook, whether in paper or electronic form, is the accounting system for the office. Quicken is a popular example of a basic, computerized checkbook program. Generally used as a **check register,** it allows multiple bank accounts to be maintained in one program. For example, a firm generally will have an operating account, an escrow account for client funds, a petty cash account for small disbursements, a payroll account, and possibly an **Interest on Lawyers Trust Accounts (IOLTA).** While each account may be in a different bank, all are managed through the same computerized program.

Quickbooks is an alternative that provides computerized records more closely resembling traditional accounting records. This expanded version of Quicken provides subsidiary **ledgers** for **journals,** such as accounts payable and accounts receivable.

ETHICAL Perspectives

LOUISIANA RULES OF PROFESSIONAL CONDUCT
Rule 1.15. Safekeeping Property

(a) A lawyer shall hold property of clients or third persons that is in a lawyer's possession in connection with a representation separate from the lawyer's own property. Funds shall be kept in a separate account maintained in a bank or similar institution in the state where the lawyer's office is situated, or elsewhere with the consent of the client or third person. Other property shall be identified as such and appropriately safeguarded. Complete records of such account funds and other property shall be kept by the lawyer and shall be preserved for a period of five years after termination of the representation.

(b) A lawyer may deposit the lawyer's own funds in a client trust account for the sole purpose of paying bank service charges on that account, but only in an amount necessary for that purpose.

(c) A lawyer shall deposit into a client trust account legal fees and expenses that have been paid in advance, to be withdrawn by the lawyer only as fees are earned or expenses incurred. The lawyer shall deposit legal fees and expenses into the client trust account consistent with Rule 1.5(f).

(d) Upon receiving funds or other property in which a client or third person has an interest, a lawyer shall promptly notify the client or third person. For purposes of this rule, the third person's interest shall be one of which the lawyer has actual knowledge, and shall be limited to a statutory lien or privilege, a final judgment addressing disposition of those funds or property, or a written agreement by the client or the lawyer on behalf of the client guaranteeing payment out of those funds or property. Except as stated in this rule or otherwise permitted by law or by agreement with the client, a lawyer shall promptly deliver to the client or third person any funds or other property that the client or third person is entitled to receive and, upon request by the client or third person, shall promptly render a full accounting regarding such property.

(e) When in the course of representation a lawyer is in possession of property in which two or more persons (one of whom may be the lawyer) claim interests, the property shall be kept separate by the lawyer until the dispute is resolved. The lawyer shall promptly distribute all portions of the property as to which the interests are not in dispute.

(f) A lawyer shall create and maintain an interest-bearing trust account for clients' funds which are nominal in amount or to be held for a short period of time in compliance with the following provisions:

(1) No earnings from such an account shall be made available to a lawyer or firm.

(2) The account shall include all clients' funds which are nominal in amount or to be held for a short period of time except as described in (6) below.

(3) An interest-bearing trust account shall be established with any bank or savings and loan association or credit union authorized by federal or state law to do business in Louisiana and insured by the Federal Deposit Insurance Corporation or the National Credit Union Administration. Funds in each interest-bearing trust account shall be subject to withdrawal upon request and without delay.

(4) The rate of interest payable on any interest bearing trust account shall not be less than the rate paid by the depository institution to regular, non-lawyer depositors.

(5) Lawyers or law firms depositing client funds in a trust savings account shall direct the depository institution:

A. To remit interest or dividend, net of any service charges or fees, on the average monthly balance in the account, or as otherwise computed in accordance with an institution's standard accounting practice, at least quarterly, to the Louisiana Bar Foundation, Inc.;

B. To transmit with each remittance to the Foundation a statement showing the name of the lawyer or law firm for whom the remittance is sent and the rate of interest applied; and

C. To transmit to the depositing lawyer or law firm at the same time a report showing the amount paid to the Foundation, the rate of interest applied, and the average account balance of the period for which the report is made.

(6) Any account enrolled in the program which has or may have the net effect of costing the IOLTA program more in bank fees than earned in interest over a period of time may, at the discretion of the program's administrator, be exempted from and removed from the IOLTA program. Exemption of an account from the IOLTA program revokes the permission to use the administrator's tax identification number for that bank account. Exemption of a pooled clients' trust account from the IOLTA program does not relieve an attorney or law firm from the obligation to maintain the property of clients and third persons separately, as required above, in a non-interest-bearing account.

IOLTA Rules

Effective January 1, 1991

1. The IOLTA program shall be a mandatory program requiring the participation by attorneys and law firms, whether proprietorships, partnerships or professional corporations.

2. The program shall apply to all clients of the participating attorneys or firms whose funds on deposit are either nominal in amount or to be held for a short period of time.
3. The following principles shall apply to clients' funds which are held by attorneys and firms.

   (a) No earnings on the IOLTA accounts may be made available to or utilized by an attorney or law firm.
   (b) Upon the request of the client, earnings may be made available to the client whenever possible upon deposited funds which are neither nominal in amount nor to be held for a short period of time; however, traditional attorney-client relationships do not compel attorneys either to invest clients' funds or to advise clients to make their funds productive.
   (c) Clients' funds which are nominal in amount or to be held for a short period of time shall be retained in an interest-bearing checking or savings trust account with the interest (net of any service charge or fees) made payable to the Louisiana Bar Foundation, Inc., said payments to be made at least quarterly.

WEB RESOURCES

Contrast and compare Rule 1.15 of the Louisiana Rules of Professional Conduct at http://www.ladb .org/Publications/ropc2006-04-01.pdf with the American Bar Association Model Rules of Professional Conduct at http://www.abanet.org/cpr/ mrpc/mrpc_toc.html, and the ethical rules in your jurisdiction.

Does your jurisdiction have an IOLTA program?

Specialized Legal Accounting Software

In a larger law firm, volumes of financial information may be handled more efficiently using accounting software. While many computerized accounting programs are available, it may be easier for a law firm to implement software with input and output tailored to a law office. Abacus Accounting and Tabs3 are examples of programs designed specifically for the legal environment. They have preset input screens and output report functions for typical law office items, such as client fees and costs that are expended and reimbursed. In addition, they are designed to be integrated with their respective timekeeping programs, as shown in Exhibit 9.10.

As shown in Exhibit 9.11, the software created by Tabs3 provides user-friendly screens, which include icons of task folders. This makes it easy for the user, at a glance, to click on the task he or she needs instead of having to read text.

Exhibit 9.12 shows an example of a Tabs3 accounting chart of accounts and input screens.

Learning Resources

Information is available from most software vendors to help users learn the programs and their features. These resources, available within the program and from online software vendor websites, allow users to quickly begin to implement the programs and features without the need to attend classes or obtain books. Exhibit 9.13 is an example of one of the resources available.

Exhibit 9.14 is a sample page from the Tabs3 tutorial available for download from the Tabs3 website. It offers keystroke-by-keystroke lessons in using different functions of the program.

Exhibit 9.15 shows a tutorial screen demonstrating the depth and variety of the training available for each of the major functions of AbacusLaw.

Exhibit 9.16 shows a sample screen from the training materials.

Exhibit 9.10 Abacus Accounting input screens

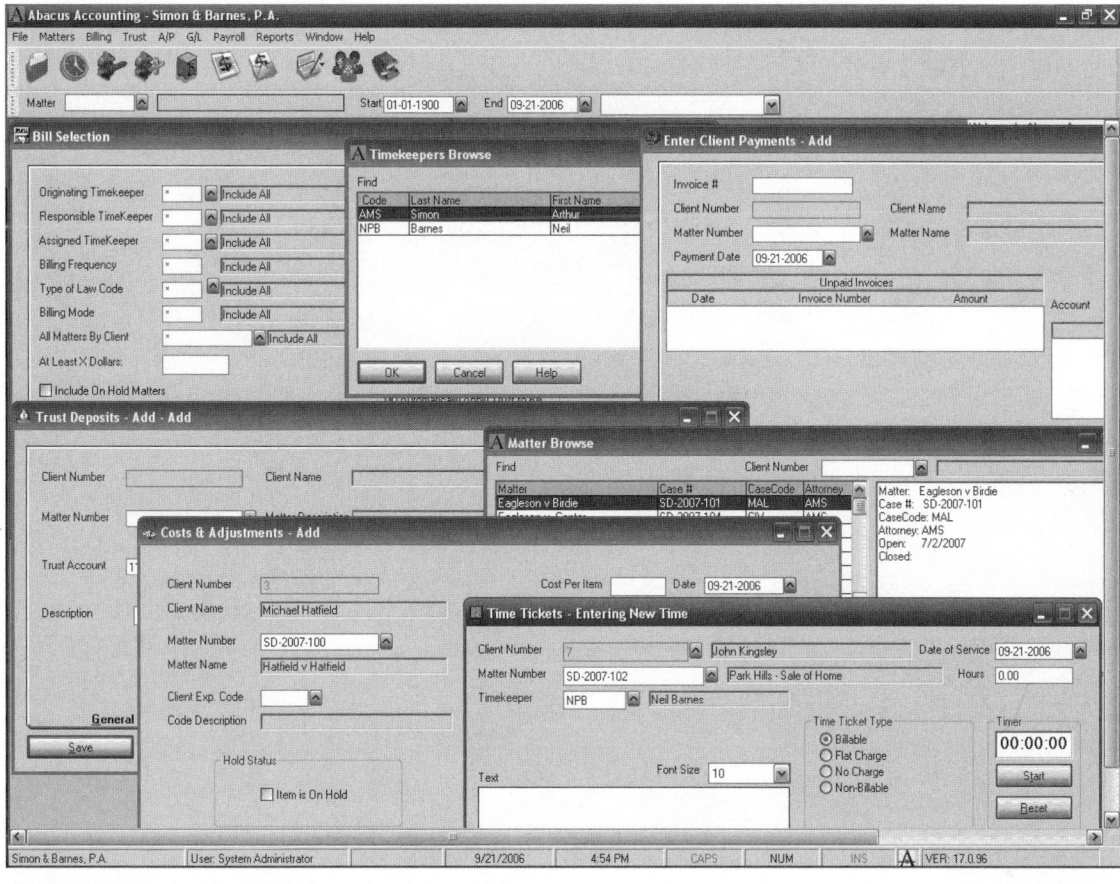

AbacusLaw.

Exhibit 9.11 Tabs3 window with task folders displayed

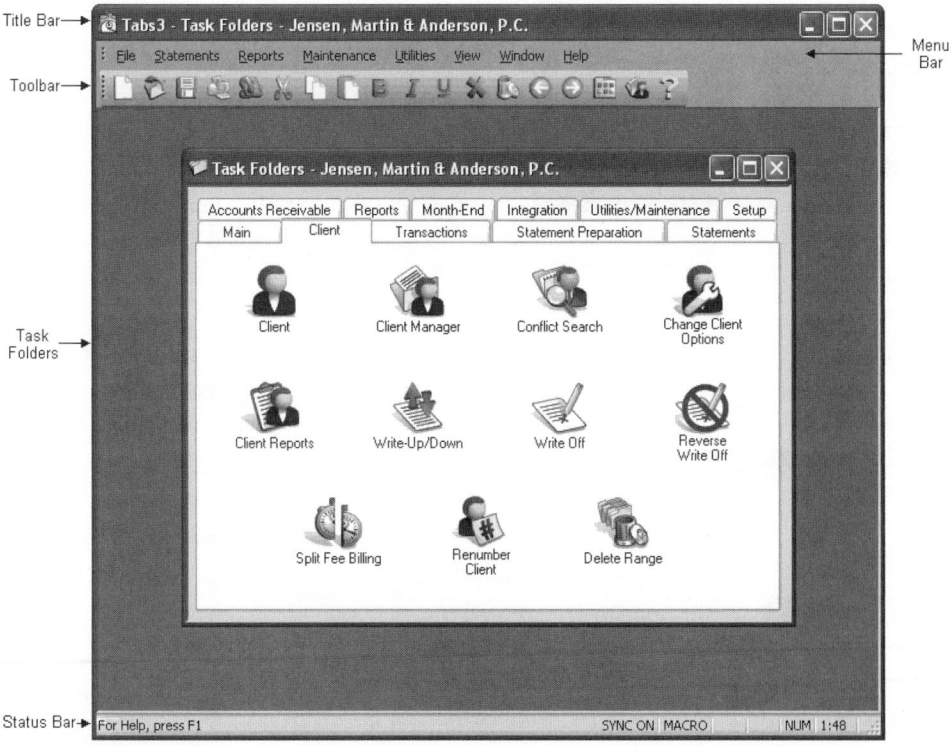

Software Technology, Inc.

Exhibit 9.12 Tabs3 Accounting Chart of Accounts and input screens

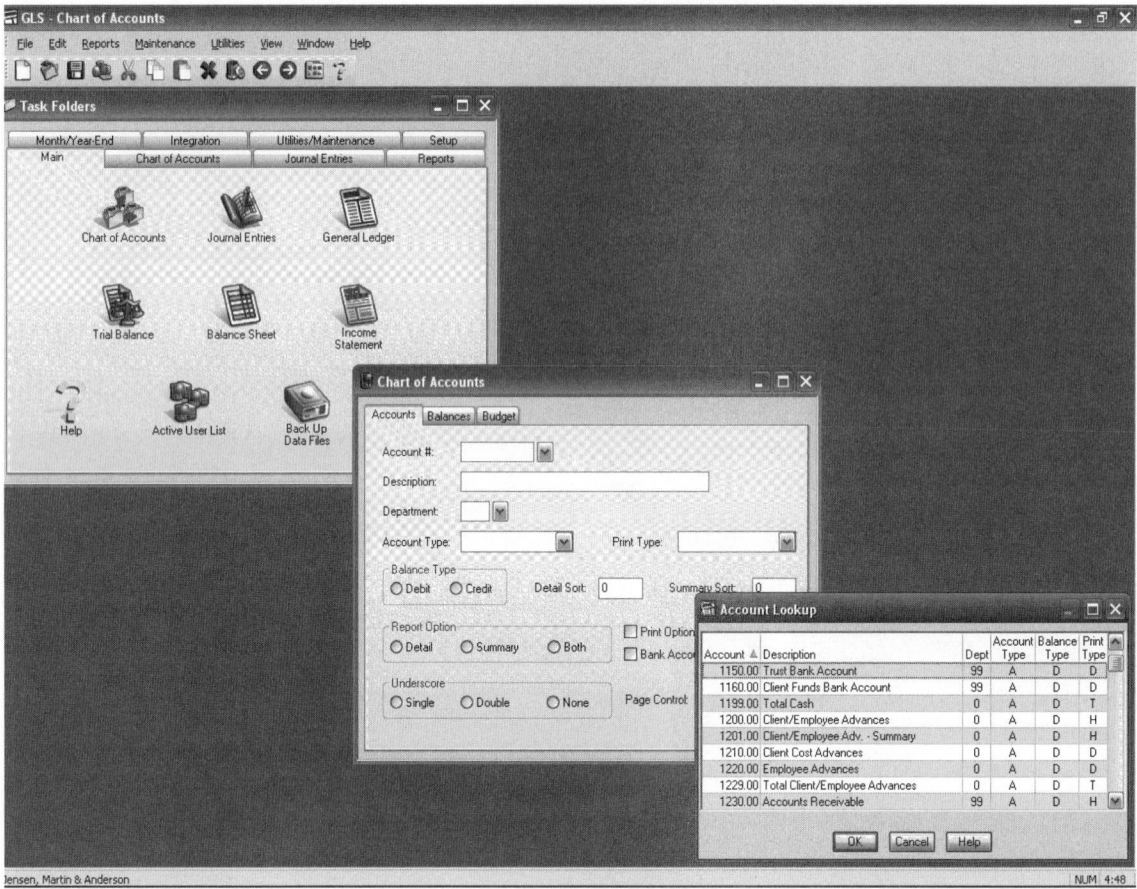

Software Technology, Inc.

Exhibit 9.13 Tabs3 online resources and tutorials

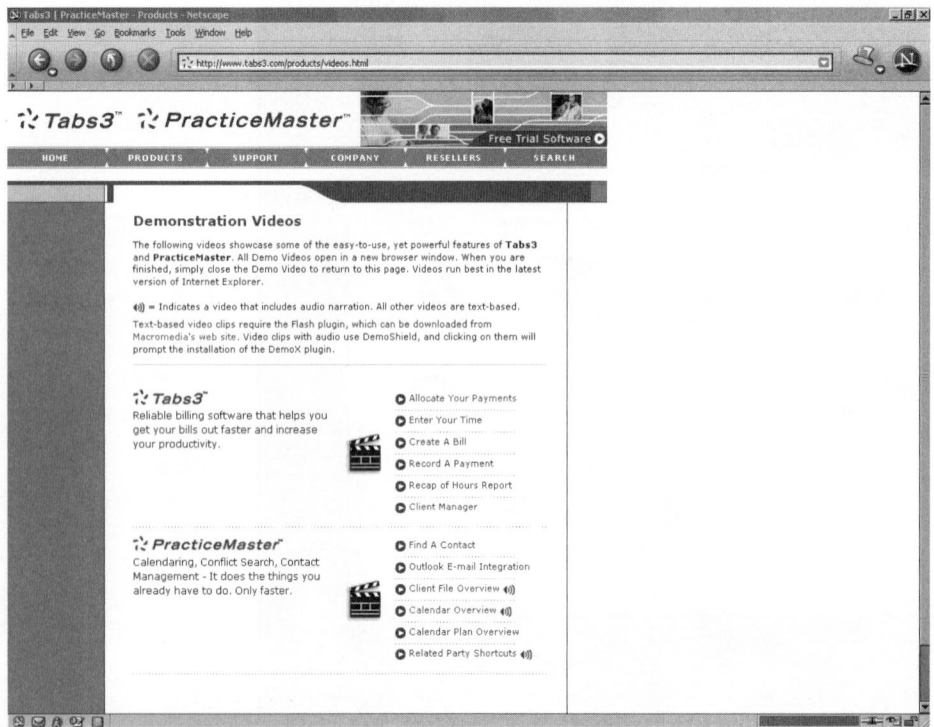

Software Technology, Inc.

Exhibit 9.14 Sample page from Tabs3 tutorial

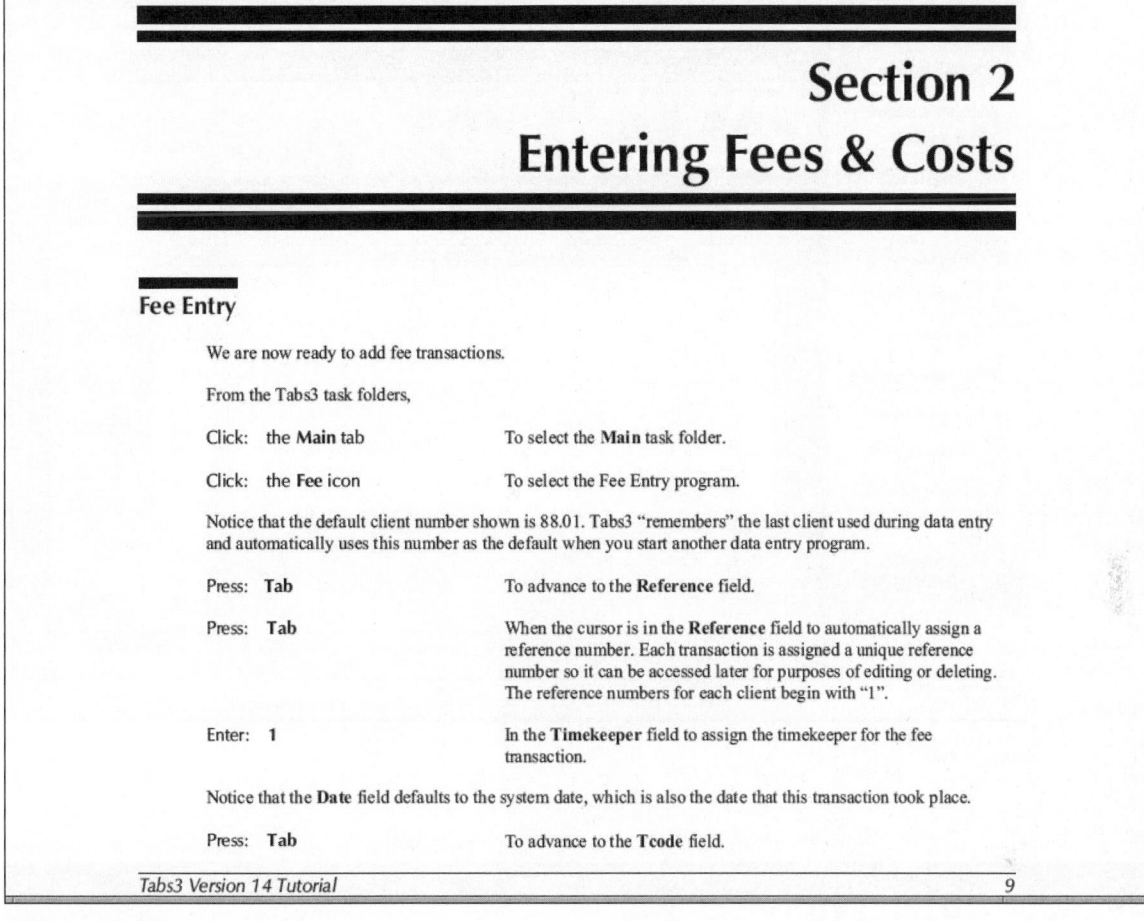

Section 2
Entering Fees & Costs

Fee Entry

We are now ready to add fee transactions.

From the Tabs3 task folders,

Click:	the **Main** tab	To select the **Main** task folder.
Click:	the **Fee** icon	To select the Fee Entry program.

Notice that the default client number shown is 88.01. Tabs3 "remembers" the last client used during data entry and automatically uses this number as the default when you start another data entry program.

Press:	**Tab**	To advance to the **Reference** field.
Press:	**Tab**	When the cursor is in the **Reference** field to automatically assign a reference number. Each transaction is assigned a unique reference number so it can be accessed later for purposes of editing or deleting. The reference numbers for each client begin with "1".
Enter:	**1**	In the **Timekeeper** field to assign the timekeeper for the fee transaction.

Notice that the **Date** field defaults to the system date, which is also the date that this transaction took place.

Press:	**Tab**	To advance to the **Tcode** field.

Tabs3 Version 14 Tutorial   9

Software Technology, Inc.

Exhibit 9.15 AbacusLaw online lessons for Accounting Management Training

AbacusLaw.

Exhibit 9.16 Sample AbacusLaw lesson

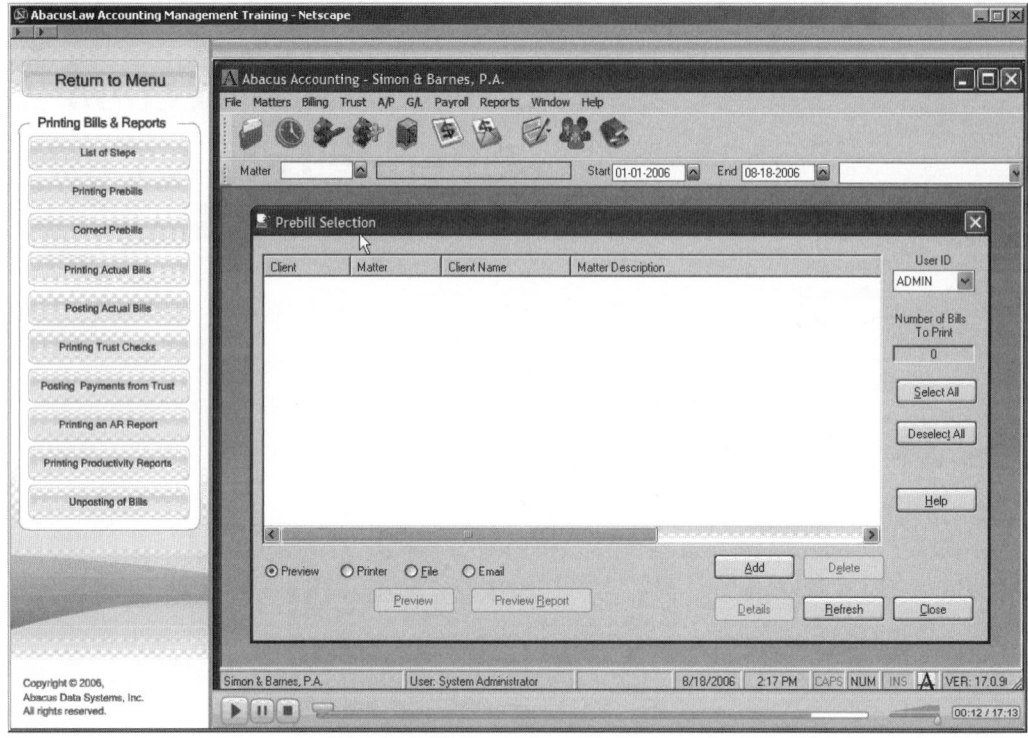

AbacusLaw.

ABACUS ACCOUNTING

How the Functions Fit Together

Abacus Accounting is an integrated product in which all of its specialized functions are closely linked together. This integration is demonstrated in the following scenario.

Imagine that you are the paralegal responsible for managing the accounts of the law firm of Anderson, Bascombe, and Clark (ABC). On March 1, your firm took on its first matter—a patent infringement matter for Xtrafine Yardgoods and Zippers, Inc. (XYZ). The client is to be billed at the end of each month until the matter is closed. The personnel who will be handling the matter are Joanne Brown, the responsible attorney, Chris Umber, the paralegal, and Nola Gray, the research clerk. Your firm has also hired Peter Sienna, a yard goods expert, as a consultant. You will use an outside vendor, CCC Printing, to photocopy the exhibits.

In Abacus, XYZ is set up as a client with a client code, and "patent infringement" is set up as a matter

with a matter number. Peter Sienna and CCC Printing are input as vendors. Joanne, Chris, and Nola are already set up in your system as timekeepers.

As Joanne, Chris, and Nola work on this matter, they record their time using the Time Ticket function. As invoices arrive from Peter and CCC Printing, you enter them in Accounts Payable as billable items for XYZ.

At the end of March, you use the Print Prebills function to preview the information before printing XYZ's bill. When you activate this function, the program searches for all time tickets with the XYZ client code and patent infringement matter number. It locates all the time tickets entered by Joanne, Chris, and Nola and calculates their hours. Since Joanne, Chris, and Nola are billed at different rates, the program multiplies their hours by their billing rates to calculate the total amount. It then locates any other billable costs to be added to the bill. In that search, the amount billed for

Peter and CCC Printing would be found. With all the calculations done, the system generates a prebill that shows the client billing address and the hours billed, along with the costs owed. If you have set up your system to calculate a percentage of the billed time as administrative overhead, the program will perform that calculation and state the amount on the prebill.

After you review the prebill and verify that everything is correct, you then activate the Print Bills function to print the bill for XYZ. When you post this bill, Abacus will update the client's ledger, along with all tables in the database that are affected by this transaction.

When you receive payment from XYZ, you enter it on the XYZ account. The program will update XYZ's account and your general ledger.

Now that your firm has money to pay Peter and CCC Printing, you activate the Print Check function in Accounts Payable to print the checks for Peter and CCC Printing. The system will then update your Accounts Payable and General Ledger tables in the database.

With a small number of entries, a few keystrokes, and very little time, you have completed all the financial transactions for this client.

Source: Courtesy of Abacus Data System

CONCEPT REVIEW AND REINFORCEMENT

KEY TERMS

assets 223	events 215	liabilities 223
chart of accounts 223	expenses 223	matters 215
check register 224	integrated functions 215	program shell 215
database 215	IOLTA 224	revenue 223
documents 215	journals 224	rules-based calendaring 217
equity 223	ledgers 224	timekeeping 221

CHAPTER SUMMARY

Introduction to Office Management Software	Certain administrative activities are necessary for the successful management of the business operation of the law office: timekeeping, calendar maintenance, and accounting.
Basic Functions of Office Management Programs	Most of the office functions can be divided into: Calendar Contacts Accounting These programs offer a number of integrated functions in a common package. Office management software programs use a database or sets of databases to record information.
Calendar Program Overview	The law office calendar is a source of information about: Appointments with clients Litigation deadlines Filing deadlines Court appearance dates Statute of limitations dates Routine reminders

Timekeeping Software	Timekeeping includes the recording of all time spent performing activities during the work day. Keeping track of billable time is a critical function to ensure that the law firm will be properly compensated for its advice and efforts on behalf of clients.
Accounting Software	Accounting software consists of specialty applications software for recording assets, liabilities, equity, revenues, and expenses.
Specialized Legal Accounting Software	Abacus Accounting and Tabs3 are typical of programs designed specifically for the legal environment. They have preset input screens and output report functions for typical law office items, such as client fees and costs expended and reimbursed.

REVIEW QUESTIONS AND EXERCISES

1. What resources are available for learning how to use office management software programs? Where are these resources located?
2. Explain, in your own words and as if you were explaining it to another member of the law firm staff, what office management software does and how it works.
3. What is the function of calendaring software in the law office? How can calendaring software help prevent malpractice claims?
4. What is the importance of maintaining accurate timekeeping records in a law office? How do timekeeping records benefit both the law firm and the client?
5. While inputting time records, a paralegal sees that the same law firm employee is billing two clients for the same time on the same task ("double billing"). What are the ethical obligations of the paralegal? Are there any ethical issues that the paralegal or law firm may face if the double billing is not corrected?
6. What potential ethical problems could result from recording time spent on a case on the outside of a client's file folder? How can these problems be avoided?
7. How can legal specialty software ensure compliance with the ethical obligations related to client funds?
8. What is the purpose of the IOLTA account program? Is it in use in your jurisdiction?
9. What are the ethical implications of attorneys using client funds?
10. How do IOLTA programs help the administration of justice?

BUILDING YOUR PARALEGAL SKILLS

INTERNET AND TECHNOLOGY EXERCISES

Prepare a list of companies offering law office management software. Then prepare a table listing and comparing the functions performed as well as the training resources available online. Based on the comparison, which products are the most useful or comprehensive? Which software is the most carefully tailored to a law practice?

CHAPTER OPENING SCENARIO CASE STUDY

Use the Opening Scenario for this chapter to answer the following questions. The scenario is that of a paralegal in an office that has grown from just herself and one attorney to a large firm of many attorneys, paralegals, and secretaries.

1. Name at least three tasks that can be automated in a firm of this size.
2. Use the Internet to find software solutions for performing the tasks you listed in your answer to question 1. What are the costs for software

licenses? What are the hardware requirements for the different software solutions?

3. What are the security and confidentiality issues that must be addressed in implementing these solutions? Explain fully, with suggestions for resolving the issues.

4. What are the advantages that can be presented to the partners to justify the cost of implementing the solution you recommend?

VIDEO CASE STUDIES

FEES AND BILLING—CONTEMPORANEOUS TIMEKEEPING

A paralegal must get his time records completed. He is trying to figure out how he has spent his day. Because he has trouble remembering what he did during a long day, he makes up time records to fill out his billable day.

Watch this video case study in MyLegalStudiesLab and answer the following questions.

1. What are the advantages and disadvantages of computerized timekeeping?
2. How would the use of computer software have prevented this ethical issue?
3. How can properly prepared time records be used to document proper supervision and diligent handling of a case?

CONTINUING CASES AND EXERCISES

1. Complete the AbacusLaw tutorial in the appendix to this chapter available on the Technology Resources Website, www.pearsonhighered.com/goldman. Describe at least two features that you find the most convenient. How do these features streamline a common task in a law practice?
2. Complete the Tabs3 tutorial available on the Technology Resources Website, www.pearsonhighered.com/goldman. Describe at least two features that

you find the most convenient. How do these features streamline a common task in a law practice?
3. Enter all of your calendar information and time slip information in AbacusLaw and Tabs3.
4. Enter the relevant information in each program from Case A in Appendix II.
5. Prepare an interim bill for your time spent in preparing for and attending class and print a draft copy for your instructor.

ADVANCED EXERCISES

1. What functions performed using Abacus and Tabs3 can be performed using the programs found in an Office Suite of programs? What additional work would need to be performed to tailor the Office applications to a law practice? Explain the advantages and disadvantages of Office versus using Abacus or Tabs3.

2. What features of Abacus and Tabs 3 are useful in a law firm of any size, including a small practice of two or three attorneys? What additional case management functions should be used, if any, for efficient management of the law office as it grows?

BUILDING YOUR PROFESSIONAL PORTFOLIO

Prepare a memo for the employee handbook on the procedures to be followed when using one of the software solutions discussed in this chapter. Explain the

reasons for each of the procedures, including the ethical duties associated with each.

■ HOW DO I DOWNLOAD ABACUSLAW FROM THE ABACUSLAW WEBSITE?

Some Internet browsers may give you a choice to **Save** or to **Run.**
You may download and **save** the **installer program** or immediately **run** it on your computer. Depending on the speed of your Internet connection, it may take from 1 to 10 minutes. It is recommended that you save the program and then run the program after closing your web browser and antivirus program. When you save the program, make a note where the program was saved so you can locate it and install it at a later time.

For example, the location where the program is saved includes

Drive designation**Folder** name**File** name

or

C :\\Downloads\\AbacusLaw2010ALL.exe

The location C:\\Downloads\\AbacusLaw2010ALL.exe is called the **path.**

When you download the program, record the path for your computer below.

Enter your Drive : _____: |
Enter your download folder : _____ \\
File name: AbacusLaw2010ALL.exe

DOWNLOADING AND INSTALLING ABACUSLAW FROM WEBSITE

GOAL	ACTION	RESULT
DOWNLOAD AND SAVE ABACUSLAW INSTALLER PROGRAM FROM ABACUSLAW WEBSITE	**START** Your Internet web browser **ENTER** http://media .pearsoncmg.com/ ph/chet/chet_ goldman_ techresources_1/ for120-daydemo or www.abacuslaw.com for 30-day demo **CLICK** *Save*	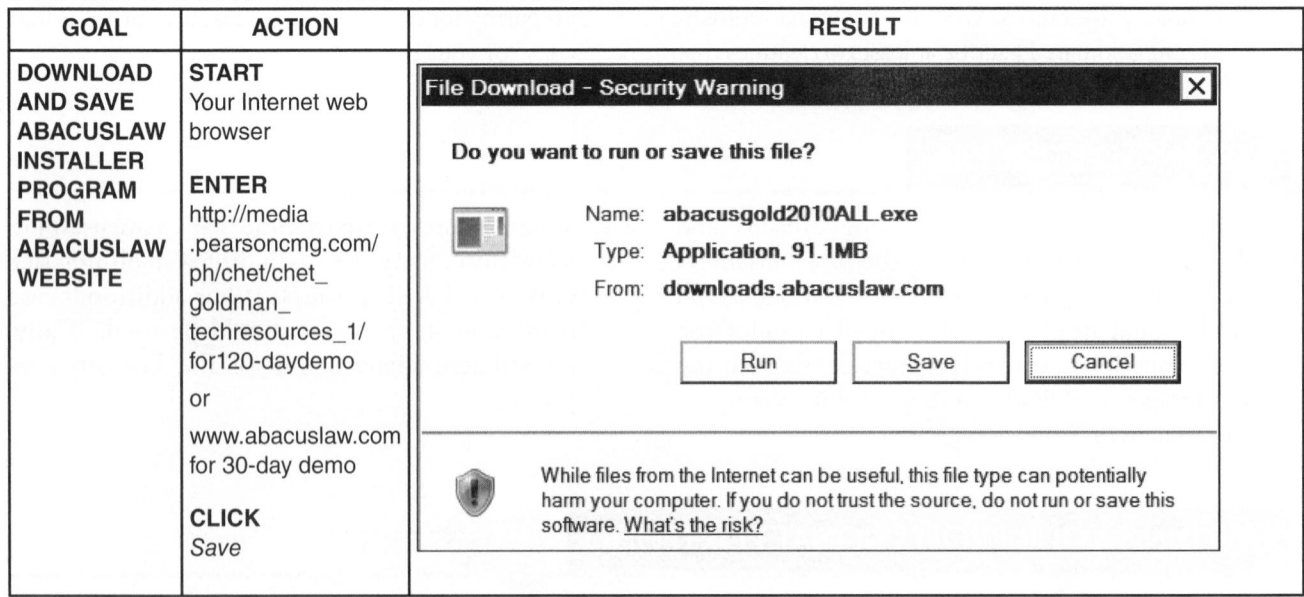

When you run the installer program, it installs the actual program files, sets up the necessary AbacusLaw folder, and adds necessary entries on your computer hard drive to allow it to run and function.

■ HOW DO I VERIFY MY FIRM INFORMATION?

Firm information is needed to use the Practice Manager. The basic firm information is entered as part of the AbacusLaw installation registration and verification process. The firm information is provided to AbacusLaw when the program is purchased, a demo version requested, or the academic version is preregistered. It is a good idea to check the accuracy of the information and make any necessary changes or update the information. Additional information about the firm may need to be entered during the Abacus Accounting installation and setup.

Verifying My Firm Information

GOAL	ACTION	RESULTS
VERIFY THE FIRM INFORMATION **NOTE:** The My Firm information comes from the registration information provided to AbacusLaw. You cannot change the information in this window. You will be able to change it in the next tutorial lesson.	**CLICK** *File menu* **SELECT** *Setup* **SELECT** *My Firm* **VERIFY** Firm Information **CLICK** *OK*	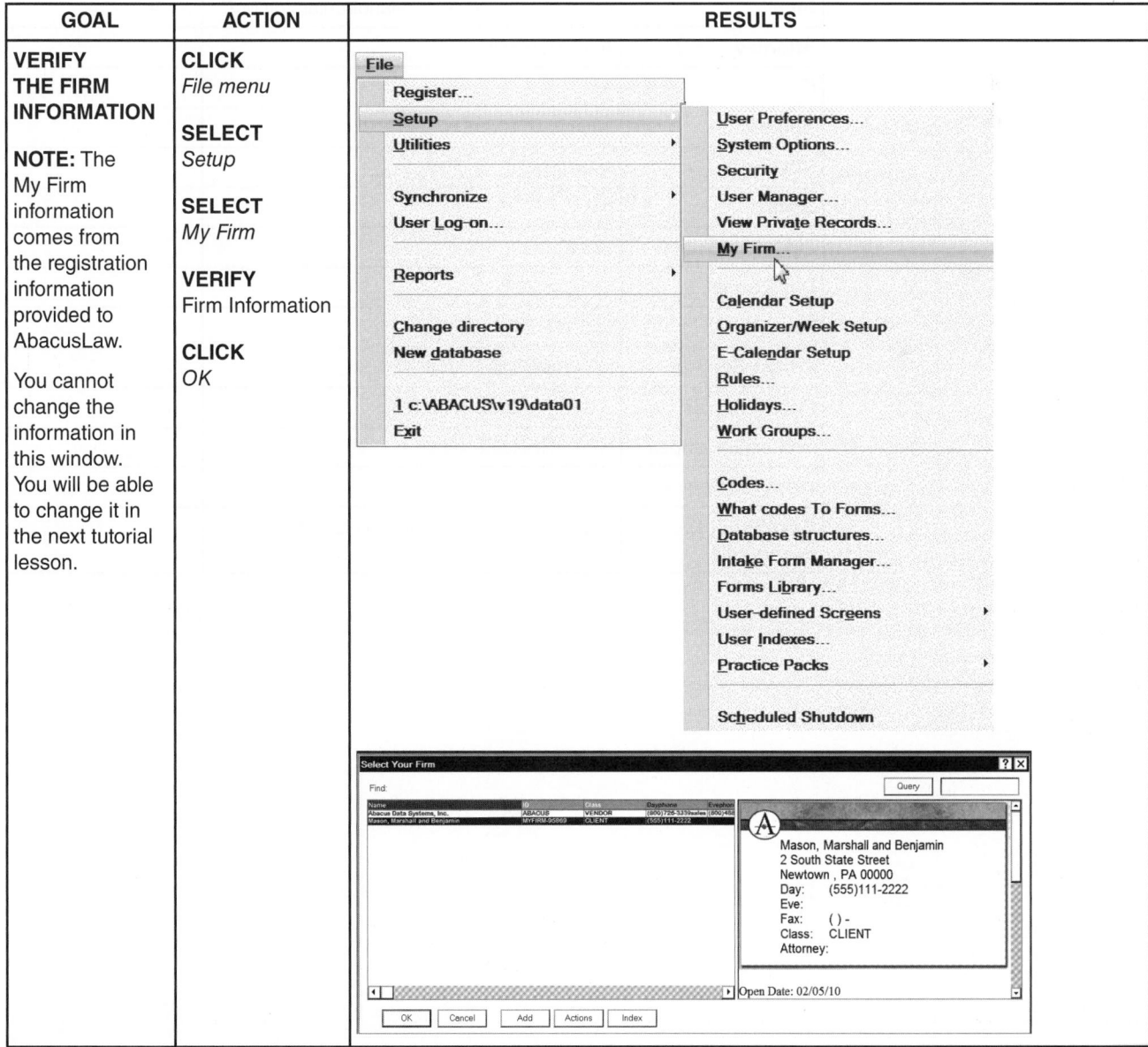

Continue with the following tutorial before exiting the program.

■ HOW DO I CHANGE THE FIRM INFORMATION?

Firm information is shown in a Names window like all contacts and names, including clients, vendors, opposing counsel, and parties. Names window can be accessed using the Names menu, Browse command, or the Names Browse window.

Substitute your personal information. Fill in the information before starting.

	TUTORIAL INFORMATION	YOUR INFORMATION
Firm Name	Mason, Marshall and Benjamin	
Attorney	Owen Mason	
ID	OM	
Email	mason@masonmarshallandbenjamin.com	
Attorney	Ariel Marshall	
ID	AM	
Address	138 North Street	
City	Newtown	
State	PA	
Zip	18940	
Day Phone	555 111 2222	
Fax	555 111 3333	
Printer Reports	HP LASERJET 4250	
Printer Labels	SMARTLABEL PRINTER	
Printer Envelopes	HP LASERJET 4050	
Word Processor		
Word Processor Executable	C:\programfiles\microsoft office\winword	

■ CHANGE FIRM INFORMATION
ON THE NAMES WINDOW

GOAL	ACTION	RESULT
START ABACUSLAW	**CLICK** *AbacusLaw icon* or **CLICK** *start* **SELECT** All Programs **CLICK** A AbacusLaw	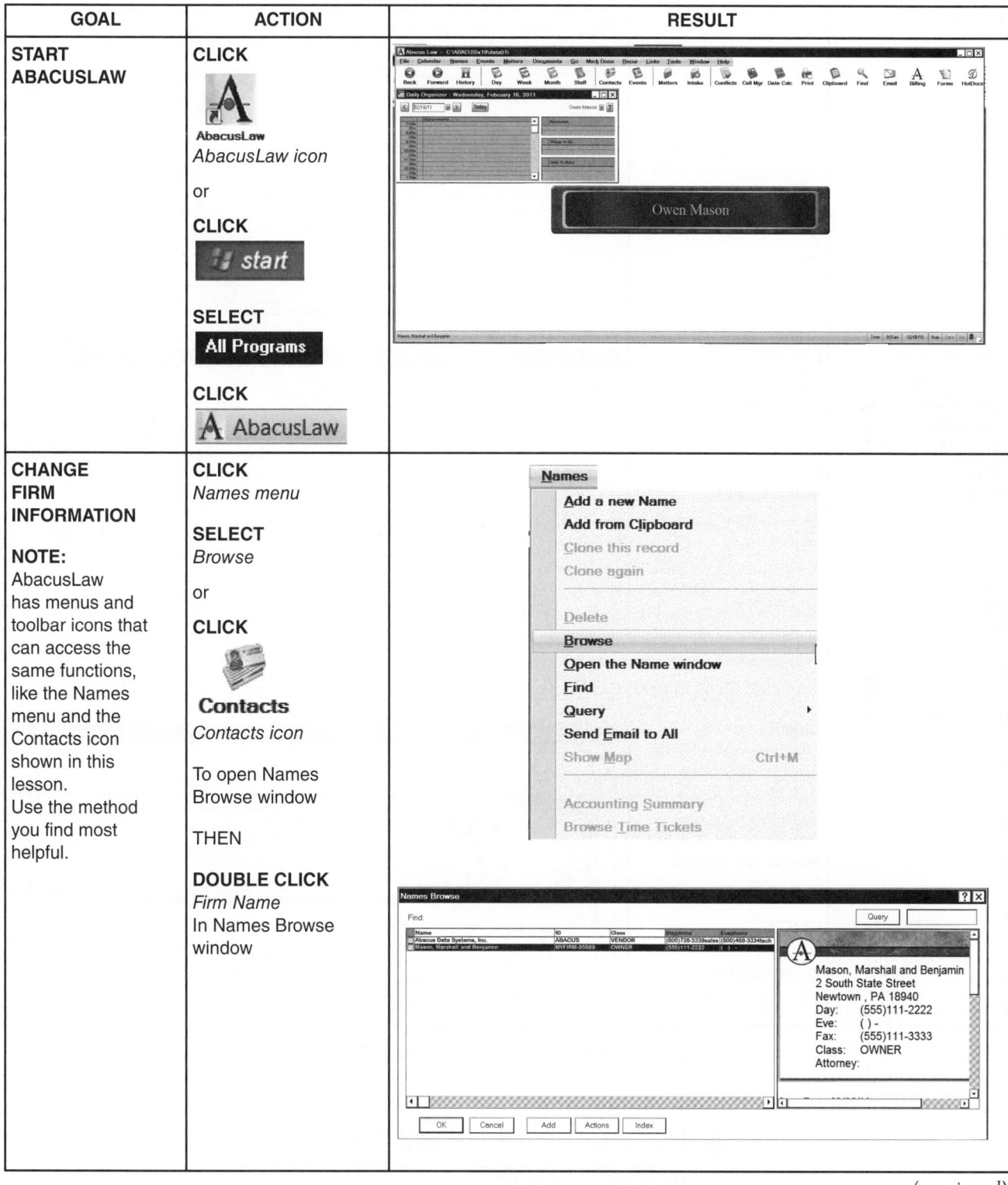
CHANGE FIRM INFORMATION **NOTE:** AbacusLaw has menus and toolbar icons that can access the same functions, like the Names menu and the Contacts icon shown in this lesson. Use the method you find most helpful.	**CLICK** *Names menu* **SELECT** *Browse* or **CLICK** **Contacts** *Contacts icon* To open Names Browse window THEN **DOUBLE CLICK** *Firm Name* In Names Browse window	

(*continued*)

GOAL	ACTION	RESULT
VERIFIY INFORMATION FOR FIRM	**VERIFY** Information	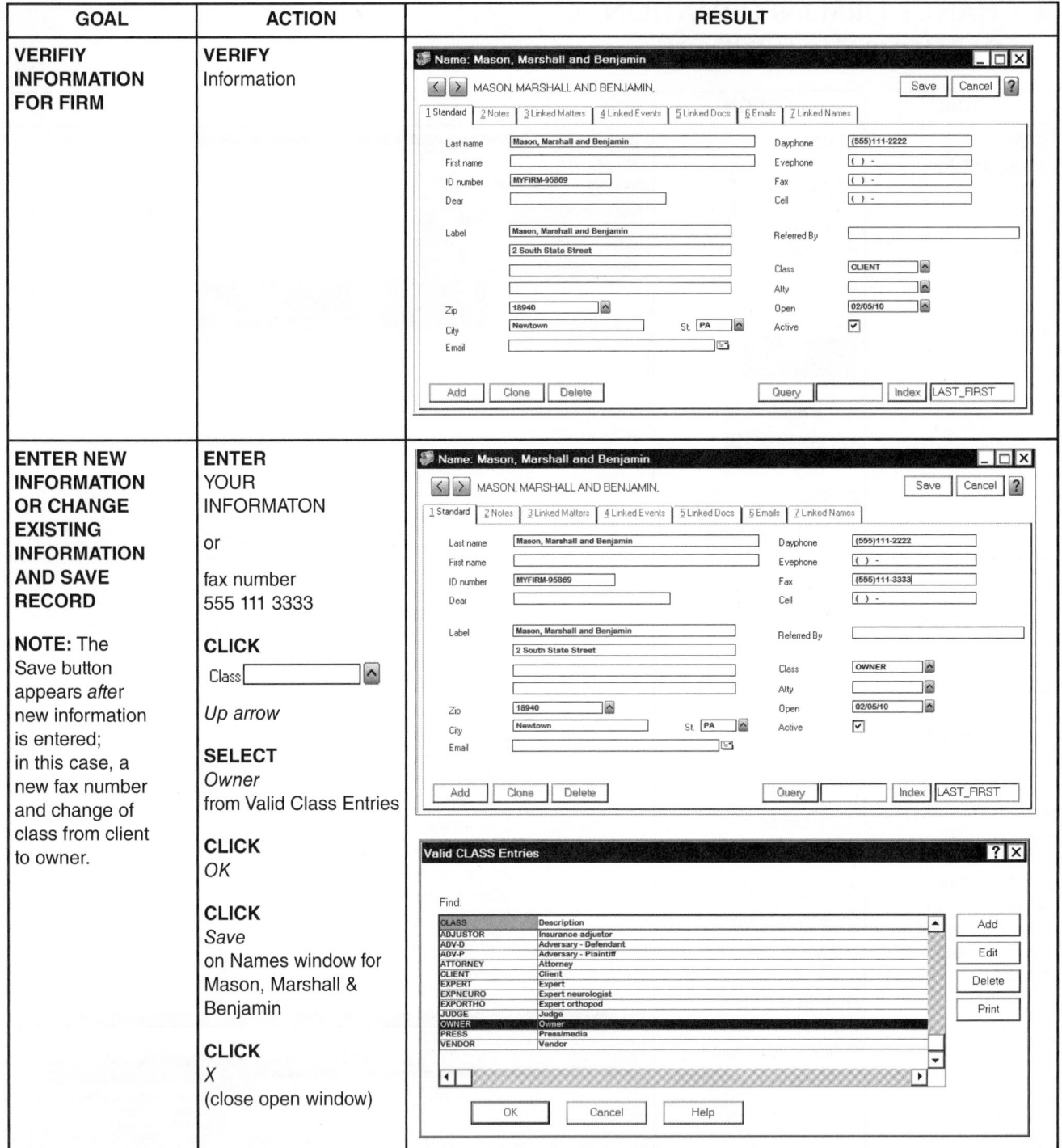
ENTER NEW INFORMATION OR CHANGE EXISTING INFORMATION AND SAVE RECORD **NOTE:** The Save button appears *after* new information is entered; in this case, a new fax number and change of class from client to owner.	**ENTER YOUR INFORMATON** or fax number 555 111 3333 **CLICK** Class *Up arrow* **SELECT** *Owner* from Valid Class Entries **CLICK** *OK* **CLICK** *Save* on Names window for Mason, Marshall & Benjamin **CLICK** *X* (close open window)	

Continue with the following lesson before exiting the program.

■ HOW DO I SET UP MY PERSONAL USER INFORMATION?

Each AbacusLaw user may enter his or her personal information, including ID initials used to log on to AbacusLaw, personal email address, and how the program will appear on the desktop when AbacusLaw is started (such as with or without a nameplate). Each user may have a different printer or word processor; these may also be customized for individual users' workstations. In some cases there may be different printers used for documents, labels, and envelopes.

The User Preference window has four tabbed screens for entering preferences: User Info, Appearance, Printing/Email Program, and Queries & Miscellaneous.

User Preferences

USER INFO TAB	APPEARANCE TAB	PRINTING/EMAIL TAB	QUERIES & MISCELLANEOUS TAB

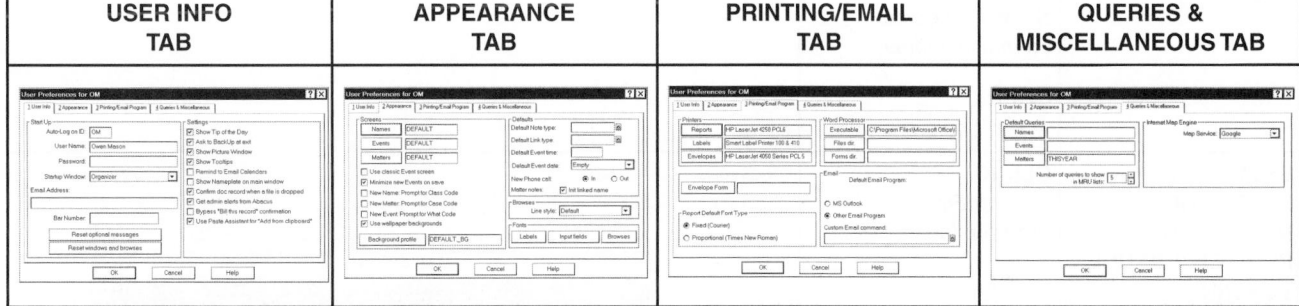

Setting Up Personal Preferences

GOAL	ACTION	RESULT
SET UP YOUR PERSONAL USER PREFERENCES	**CLICK** *File menu* **SELECT** *Setup* **SELECT** *User Preferences*	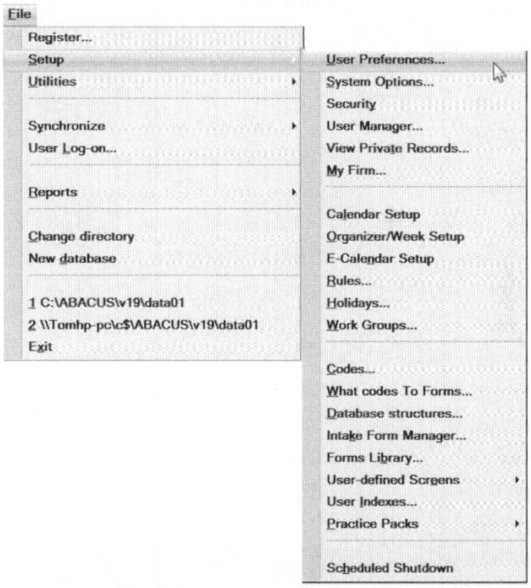
ENTER YOUR PERSONAL INFORMATION **NOTE:** You can change the settings at any time by checking or unchecking the settings boxes.	**ENTER YOUR PERSONAL INFORMATION** or *OM* In Auto-Log on ID **ENTER** *Owen Mason* in User Name	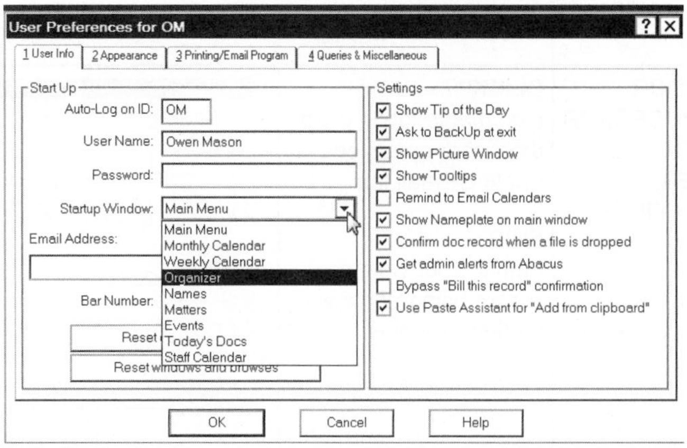

(continued)

GOAL	ACTION	RESULT
NOTE: You may personalize the look of the desktop by selecting one of the calendar options, such as organizer selected in this lesson.	**CLICK** Down arrow by Startup Window field **SELECT** *Organizer* **CHECK** *Show Nameplate* on *main window* **CHECK** *Ask to backup at exit*	
SELECT OR ENTER THE NAME OF THE PRINTER YOU USE TO PRINT DOCUMENTS AND REPORTS **NOTE:** Your **default printer** will appear as the Name on the **Print Setup** Window (HP LaserJet 4250PCL6 is shown only as an example). You must enter *your* printer to be able to print AbacusLaw report. Change this by selecting your printer in the Printing Setup window; click on the down arrow at the end of the Name. If you use a different printer for labels or envelopes, repeat the process of selecting the printer.	**CLICK** *Printing/Email Program* tab **CLICK** *Reports* tab In Printers **SELECT** *Your printer for reports* from the Print Setup window **CLICK** *OK* In Print Setup window	**User Preferences for OM** [?][X] 1 User Info 2 Appearance 3 Printing/Email Program 4 Queries & Miscellaneous Printers: Reports, Labels, Envelopes, Envelope For Word Processor: Executable Report Default F: ◉ Fixed (Courie, ○ Proportional **Print Setup** [X] Printer Name: HP LaserJet 4250 PCL6 ▼ Properties... Status: Toner low; 0 documents waiting Type: HP LaserJet 4250 PCL6 Where: 192.168.2.101 Comment: Paper Size: Letter ▼ Source: Automatically Select ▼ Orientation ◉ Portrait ○ Landscape Network... OK Cancel
SELECT YOUR WORD PROCESSOR FROM YOUR COMPUTER PROGRAM FILES **TIP:** Find your word processor on your computer using Windows Explorer.	**CLICK** *Executable* tab in word processor option on Printing/Email tab **FIND** Path to your word processor using Windows Explorer window	**User Preferences for OM** [?][X] 1 User Info 2 Appearance 3 Printing/Email Program 4 Queries & Miscellaneous Printers: Reports — HP LaserJet 4250 PCL6; Labels — Smart Label Printer 100 & 410; Envelopes — HP LaserJet 4050 Series PCL 5 Word Processor: Executable — C:\Program Files\Microsoft Office\; Files dir.; Forms dir. Envelope Form Report Default Font Type: ◉ Fixed (Courier); ○ Proportional (Times New Roman) Email — Default Email Program: ○ MS Outlook; ◉ Other Email Program; Custom Email command: OK Cancel Help

(continued)

GOAL	ACTION	RESULT
	SELECT Your word processor **CLICK** *Open* **CLICK** *OK*	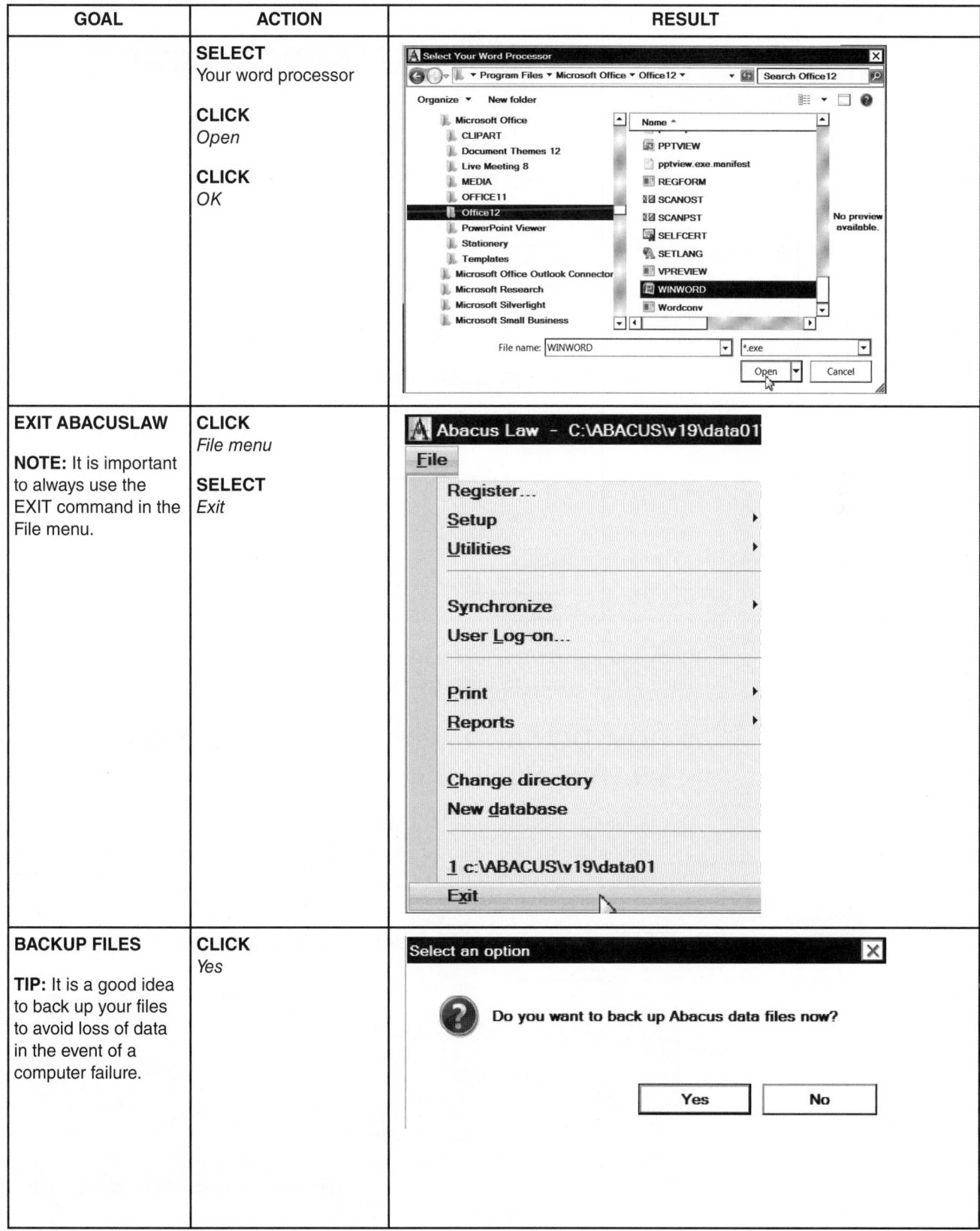
EXIT ABACUSLAW **NOTE:** It is important to always use the EXIT command in the File menu.	**CLICK** *File menu* **SELECT** *Exit*	
BACKUP FILES **TIP:** It is a good idea to back up your files to avoid loss of data in the event of a computer failure.	**CLICK** *Yes*	

(*continued*)

GOAL	ACTION	RESULT
SELECT THE DESTINATION FOR THE BACKUP **TIP:** You should back up to a removable storage device by indicating that device as the DESTINATION in the backup options window. To locate other storage devices connected to your computer, click the DESTINATION button.	**ENTER** Path to your removable backup device or *C:\Abacus* As destination **CLICK** *Start Backup*	**Backup Abacus Files**　　　　　　　　　　　**?** **X** Directories 　Destination　　C:\ 　Source　　C:\ABACUS\v19\data01\ 　Number of backup files to retain　　7 ▼ Include along with main data 　☐ Abacus MessageSlips 　☐ Forms .AF files (only recommended if you design forms) 　☐ Accounting data 　　☐ Saved PDF bills (may be huge!) Current file: File Compression Overall Progress Cancel　　　Start Backup　　☐ Send in email

When you restart AbacusLaw, the changes in user preferences, including the nameplate and daily organizer calendar, will appear on your personal desktop.

■ HOW DO I ADD APPPOINTMENTS (EVENTS) TO THE CALENDAR?

Appointments or events may be added for each person or item listed on a calendar. Items added to one calendar view, such as daily calendar, will also be added and shown on the other calendar views. Events may be entered for any person, place, or thing with a WHO code.

NOTE: Appointments or scheduled activity in the calendar are referred to as *events*.

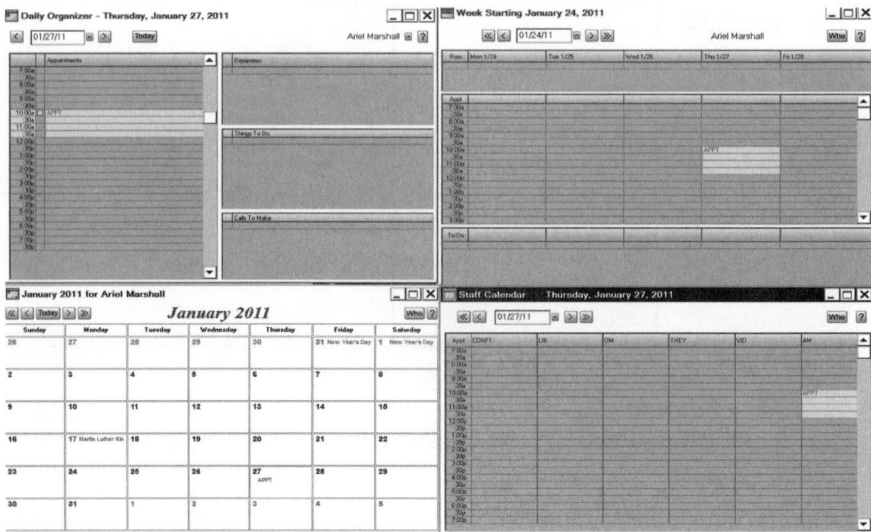

Add an Event to the Calendar for a Specific Person

GOAL	ACTION	RESULT
ADD NEW APPOINTMENT **TIP:** You can also bring up the Add a new Event window by double clicking on the calendar time.	**CLICK** *Events menu* **SELECT** *Add a new Event*	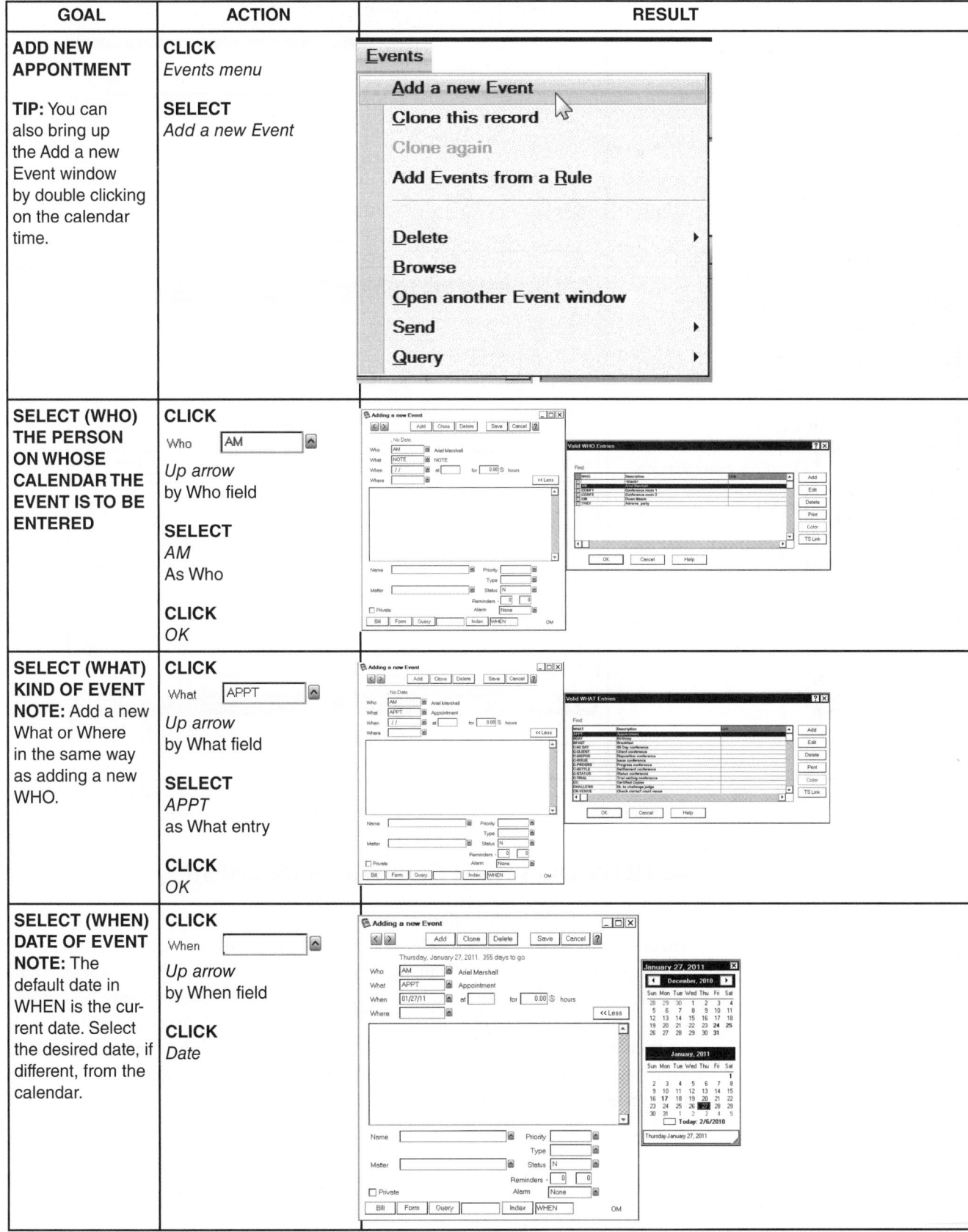
SELECT (WHO) THE PERSON ON WHOSE CALENDAR THE EVENT IS TO BE ENTERED	**CLICK** Who AM *Up arrow* by Who field **SELECT** *AM* As Who **CLICK** *OK*	
SELECT (WHAT) KIND OF EVENT **NOTE:** Add a new What or Where in the same way as adding a new WHO.	**CLICK** What APPT *Up arrow* by What field **SELECT** *APPT* as What entry **CLICK** *OK*	
SELECT (WHEN) DATE OF EVENT **NOTE:** The default date in WHEN is the current date. Select the desired date, if different, from the calendar.	**CLICK** When *Up arrow* by When field **CLICK** *Date*	

(continued)

GOAL	ACTION	RESULT
SELECT (WHERE) THE LOCATION OF EVENT	**CLICK** *Where* ⬛ *Up arrow* by Where field **SELECT** *Here* as Where entry **CLICK** *OK*	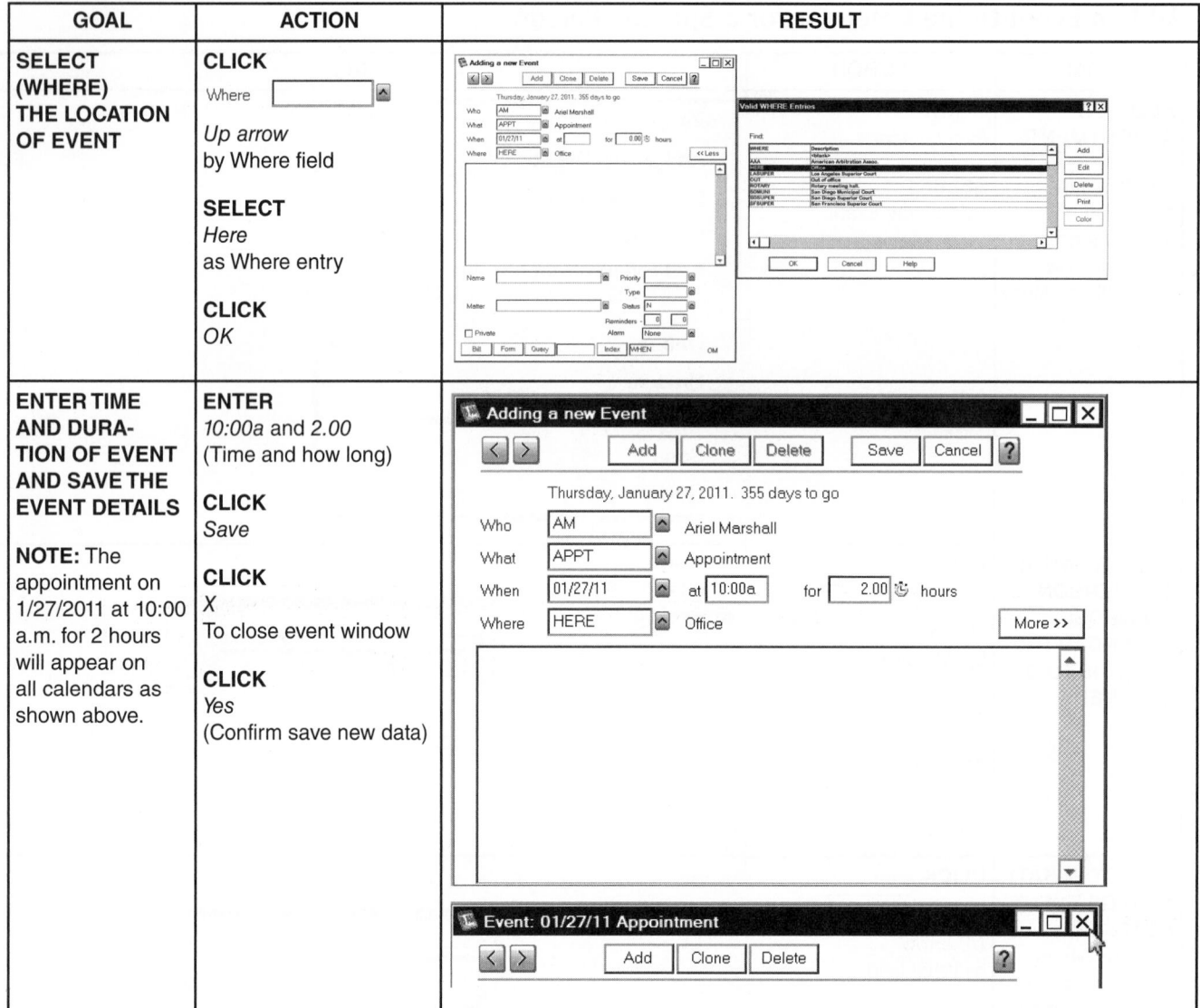
ENTER TIME AND DURATION OF EVENT AND SAVE THE EVENT DETAILS **NOTE:** The appointment on 1/27/2011 at 10:00 a.m. for 2 hours will appear on all calendars as shown above.	**ENTER** *10:00a* and *2.00* (Time and how long) **CLICK** *Save* **CLICK** *X* To close event window **CLICK** *Yes* (Confirm save new data)	

You may exit the program or continue the next tutorial.

■ HOW DO I ADD CONTACTS (NAMES)?

A contact (person, firm, client, or counsel) is any name in your address book, email list, or whose information you want to record for future use. It may be information that has been kept in the firm's or personal address book on individual index cards or in a paper conflicts file or note cards. It may be current clients, prospective clients, other attorneys and paralegals, or other professionals or friends. All of the contacts' names and information when entered into the AbacusLaw program is saved and stored in the Names database. You can add new names and contacts at any time or during the new matter setup.

Adding Contacts (Names)

GOAL	ACTION	RESULT
START ABACUSLAW	**CLICK** **AbacusLaw** *AbacusLaw icon* or **CLICK** **start** **SELECT** **All Programs** **CLICK** **A AbacusLaw**	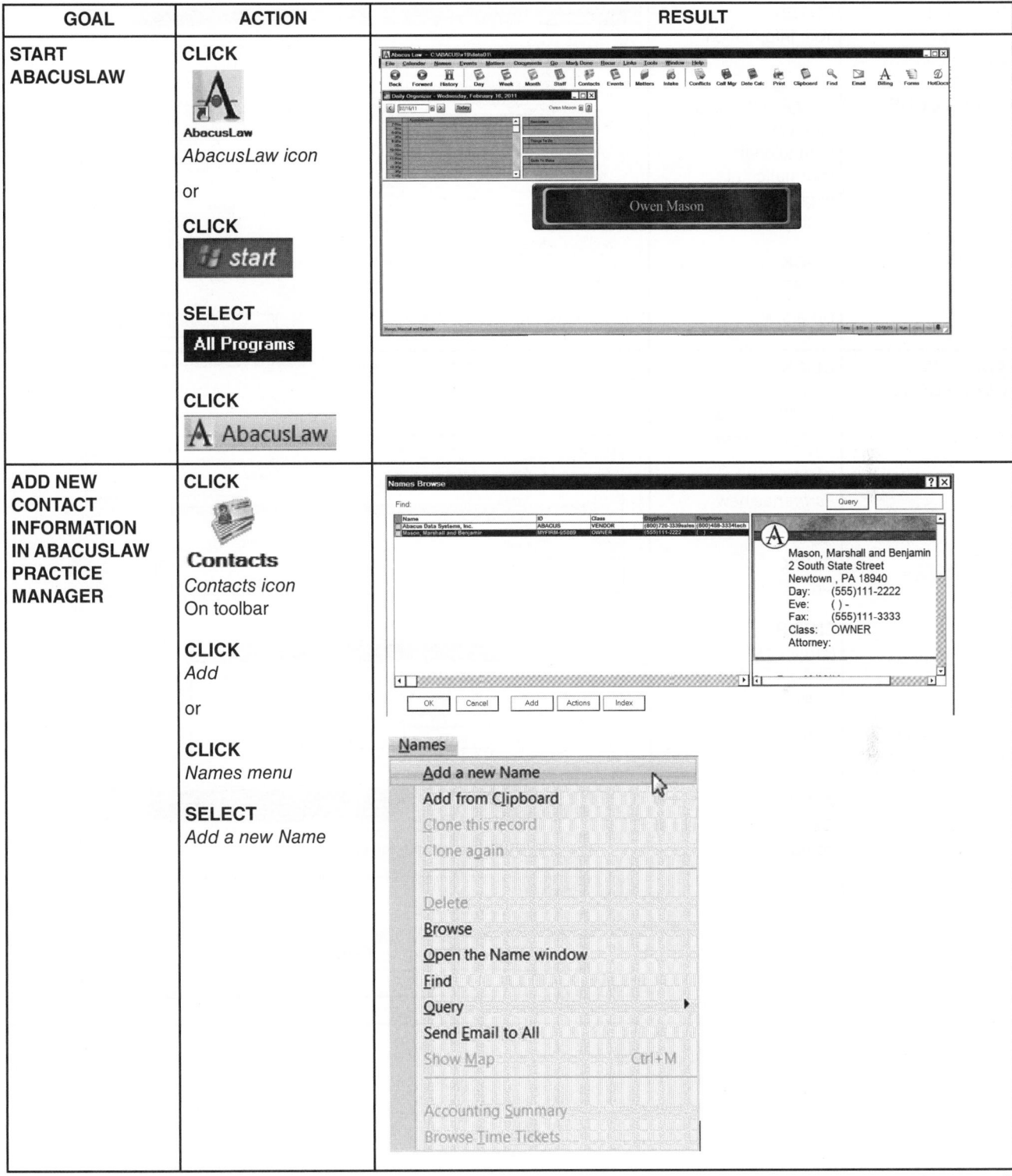
ADD NEW CONTACT INFORMATION IN ABACUSLAW PRACTICE MANAGER	**CLICK** **Contacts** *Contacts icon* On toolbar **CLICK** *Add* or **CLICK** *Names menu* **SELECT** *Add a new Name*	

(continued)

GOAL	ACTION	RESULT
ENTER NEW CONTACT INFORMATION AND ADD NEW CLASS CODE	**ENTER** Your information *or* *Contact information for OWEN MASON from tutorial information at beginning of section* **CLICK** Class ⌄ *Up arrow*	
ADD NEW CLASS CODE	**CLICK** *Add* in Valid CLASS Entries window **ENTER** *Partner* as new "CLASS" code **CLICK** *OK* **ENTER** *Partner* as CLASS Code Description **CLICK** *OK* **CLICK** *OK* (to add to class)	

(continued)

GOAL	ACTION	RESULT
SELECT RESPONSIBLE ATTORNEY, DATE ENTERED, AND SAVE **TIP:** You can use the shortcut CTRL + S to save the contact information entered.	**CLICK** Atty [ ] [▲] *Up arrow* **DOUBLE CLICK** *Owen Mason* or *Your Attorney ID from list* **CLICK** *Save*	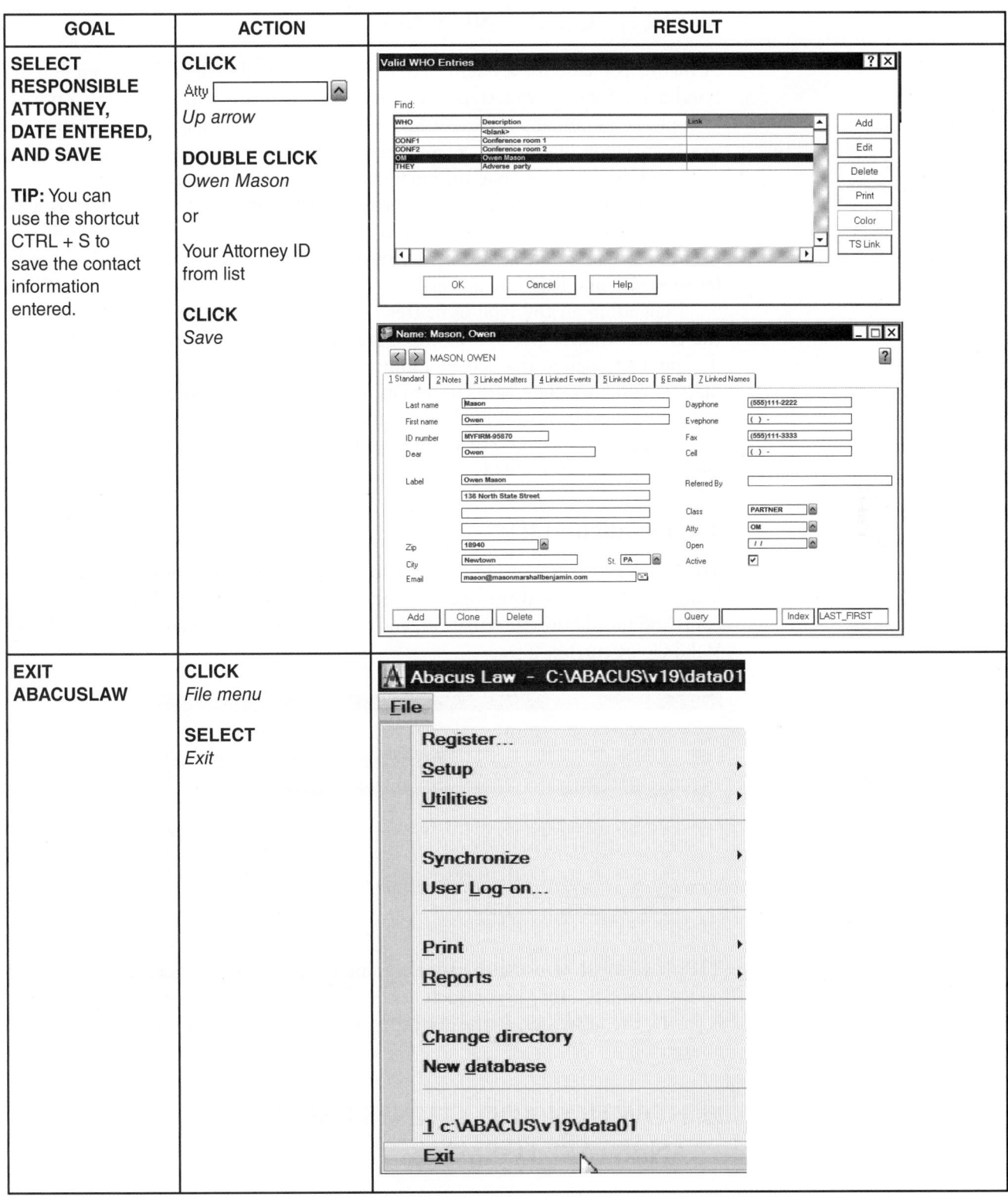
EXIT ABACUSLAW	**CLICK** *File menu* **SELECT** *Exit*	

■ SETTING UP A NEW MATTER

A matter is a case for a client. There may be a single client for whom you are handling a number of matters; for example, preparing a will, defending a breach of contract action, and representing the client seeking damages for a personal injury from a motor vehicle accident. You only need to input the client information once and then use the same information in each matter as it is set up.

All of the information about the case may be entered using the Matters window, including items related to the matter, like notes, people, documents, and events. These are referred to in AbacusLaw as *linked: linked notes, linked names, linked events,* and *linked documents.*

Depending on the type of matter (kind of case or area of law), you may use the generic Matter window to enter the information or use an AbacusLaw add-on product, such as the personal injury practice pack intake forms and specialty matters windows. The basic information is the same, but the specialty practice screens have additional linked information.

In this tutorial you will need to enter the information about the court in which the case will be filed.

The Jurisdiction ID

To be able to enter a code in the Jurisdiction ID, the court must be listed in the Valid Court entries. If the specific court is not listed, you will need to add the court and jurisdiction information, and then add the desired court from the list of Valid Court entries.

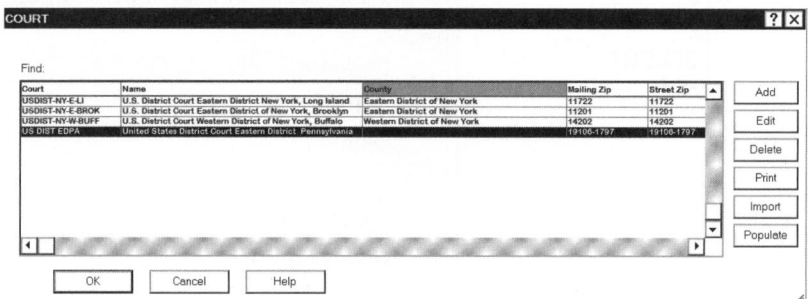

TIP: If you will be using the timekeeping functions, it is a good practice to set up the client or other party, such as the insurance company or corporation who is paying the legal fees, as the "bill to" party when setting up the individual case matter.

■ HOW DO I ADD CLIENTS USING AN INTAKE FORM?

Client information can be entered as contact information using the Names window or as part of a new case setup, as shown above. Information may be entered using a new contact or new matter intake form, which contains the basic contact information and details of the new contact or matter.

Adding Clients Using PI Case Intake Form

GOAL	ACTION	RESULT
ADD NEW MATTER AND CLIENT INFORMATION USING PI CASE INTAKE FORM **NOTE:** Many forms can be accessed in different ways including the menu bar or toolbar icon, as well as from within other forms.	**CLICK**  **Intake** *Intake icon* **CLICK** *PI Case Intake Form* or **CLICK** *Matters menu* **SELECT** *Intake Forms* **SELECT** *PI Case Intake Form*	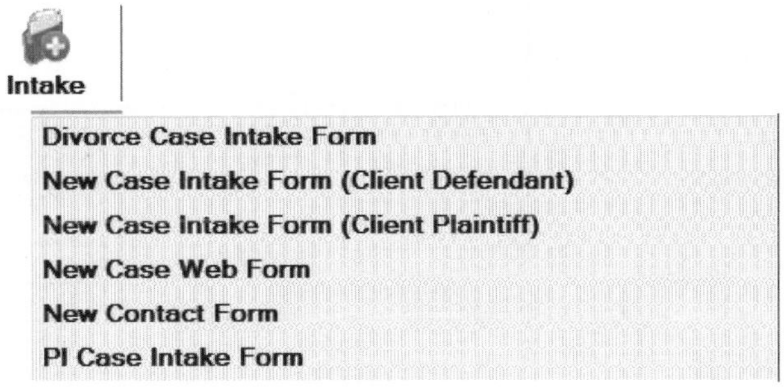 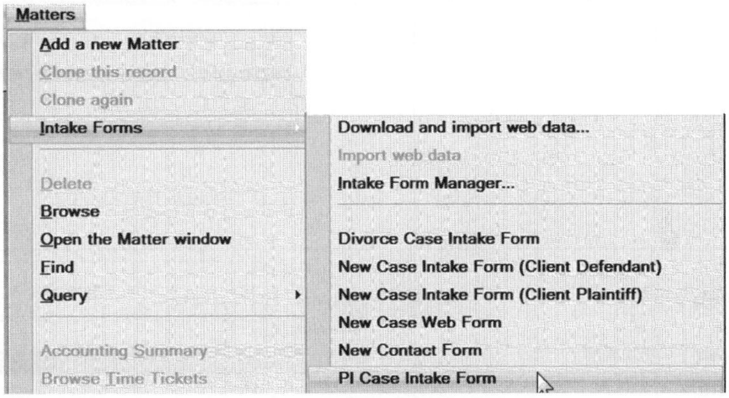
ENTER NEW CLIENT AND MATTER INFORMATION ENTER OPPOSING PARTY INFORMATION **NOTE:** The top half of the intake form is the same information entered in the New Matter screen and the New Names input screen. **NOTE:** After you save the intake form, a Billing Information screen will open, as shown below.	**ENTER** Information as shown **CLICK** *Save*	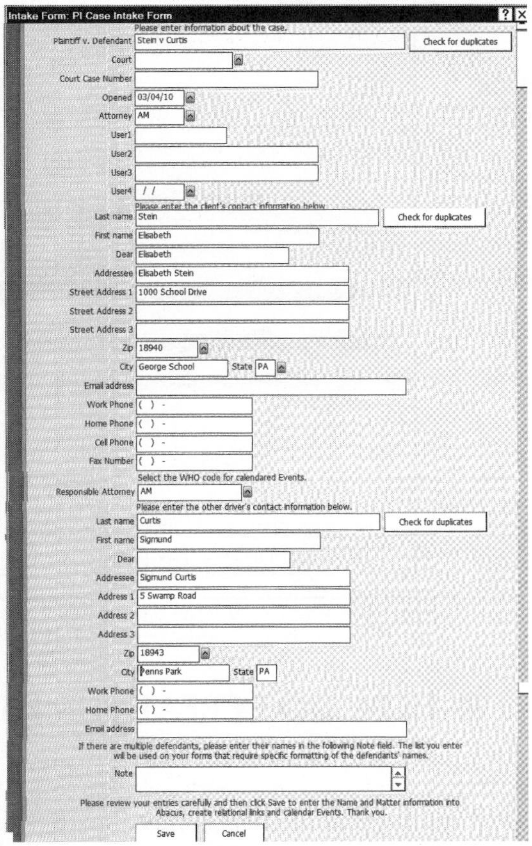

(continued)

GOAL	ACTION	RESULT
ENTER CLIENT BILLING AGREEMENT INFORMATION	**ENTER** Billing information **CLICK** OK	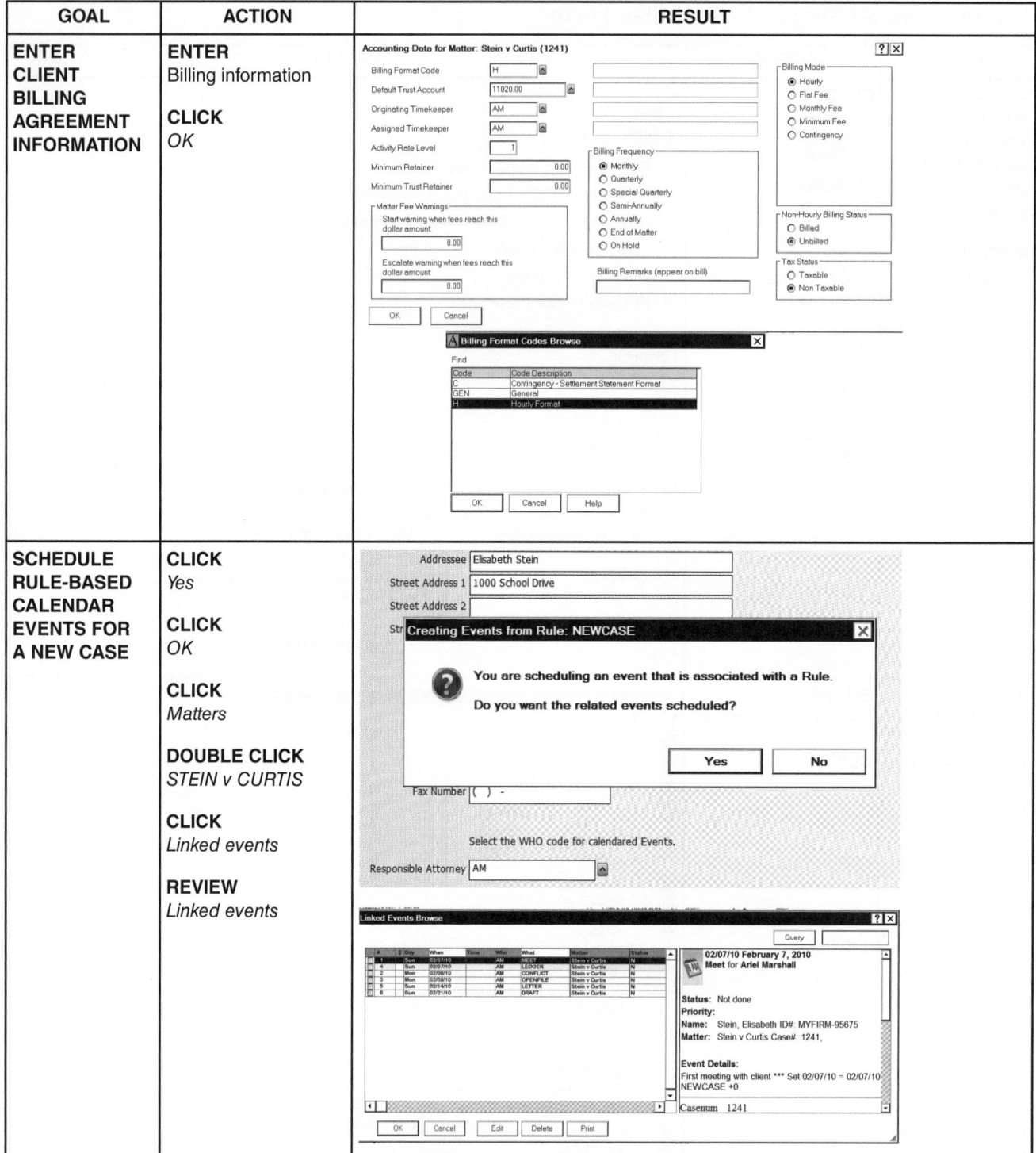
SCHEDULE RULE-BASED CALENDAR EVENTS FOR A NEW CASE	**CLICK** Yes **CLICK** OK **CLICK** Matters **DOUBLE CLICK** STEIN v CURTIS **CLICK** Linked events **REVIEW** Linked events	

■ HOW DO I CREATE TIME TICKETS IN ABACUS ACCOUNTING?

Time is billed to clients and to matters (cases) for events (things that happen). The linked events in matters are usually billable activities and can be set to be billed to that matter. A separate time ticket may also be created for each activity on each matter. This may be a result of entering paper time records or a record of time spent on a matter while out of the office and away from a computer.

NOTE: To enter a time ticket, you must identify the matter.

NOTE: *Task-based billing codes* were established by the American Bar Association (ABA) and are used to organize time entries by category to meet the ABA billing standards. Abacus Accounting is preloaded with the ABA task-based billing codes. You do not need to modify or delete these codes unless the ABA changes its code set.

Creating a Time Ticket in a Contingency Fee Case

GOAL	ACTION	RESULT
OPEN BLANK TIME TICKET IN ABACUS ACCOUNTING	**CLICK** Matter ☐ ▲ *Up arrow* **SELECT** *Bates v Howard* **CLICK** *OK* **CLICK** 🕐 *Time Tickets icon*	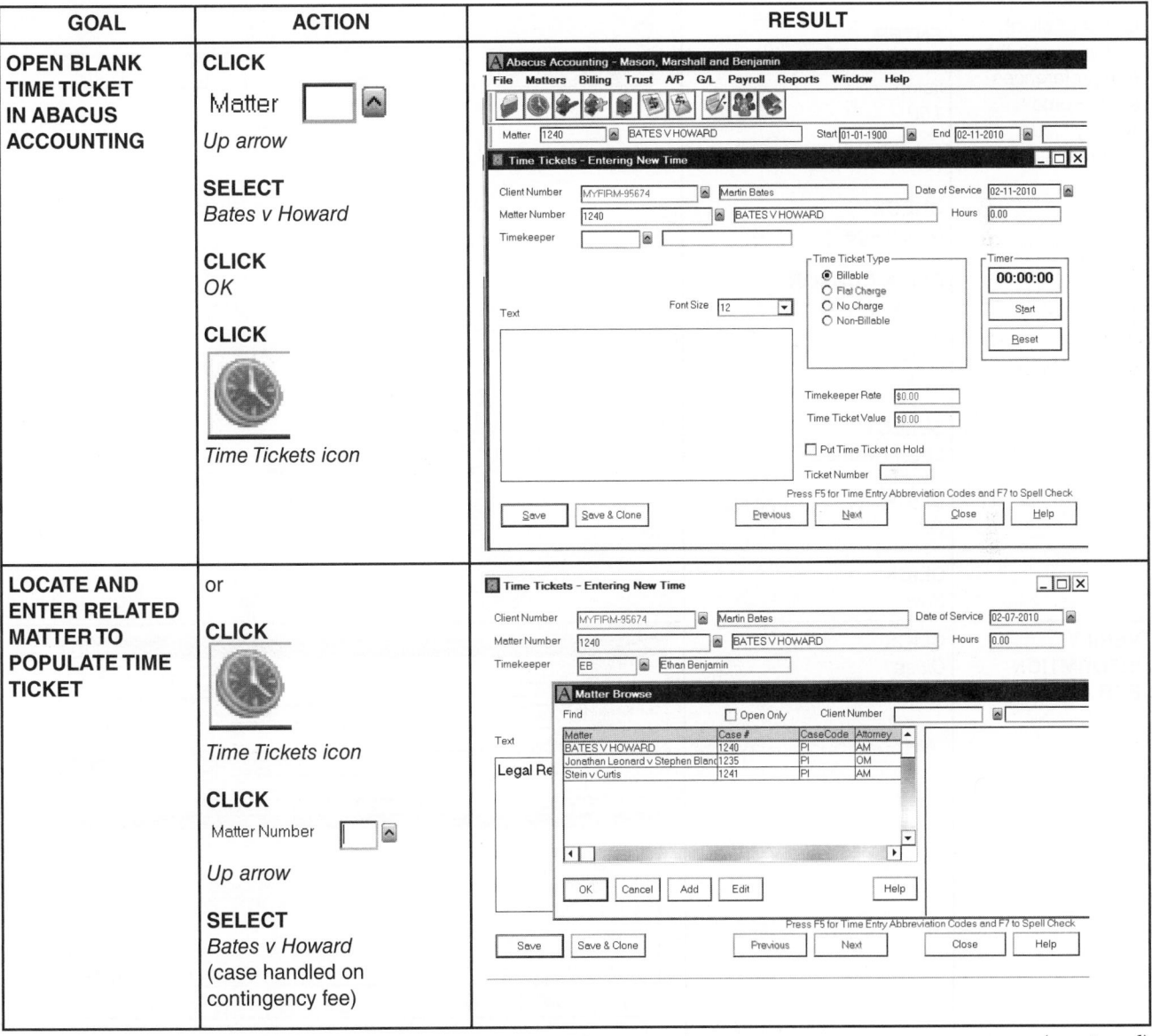
LOCATE AND ENTER RELATED MATTER TO POPULATE TIME TICKET	or **CLICK** 🕐 *Time Tickets icon* **CLICK** Matter Number ☐ ▲ *Up arrow* **SELECT** *Bates v Howard* (case handled on contingency fee)	

(continued)

GOAL	ACTION	RESULT
IDENTIFY NATURE OF CHARGE USING TIME TICKET CODES **NOTE:** Activity code will only appear if you have Task-Based Billing selected as the billing format for the selected matter or client, or if you have the firm preferences set to Force Activity Code on Time Tickets.	**CLICK** Timekeeper *Up arrow* **SELECT** *EB* *as Timekeeper* **CLICK** *OK* in Timekeeper Browse window **ENTER** *12-07-2010* (Date of Service field) *1.00* (Hours field) **CHECK** *No Charge* **CLICK CURSOR** In Text box **CLICK** *F5 key* **SELECT** *Legal Research* **CLICK** *OK* **CLICK** *Save*	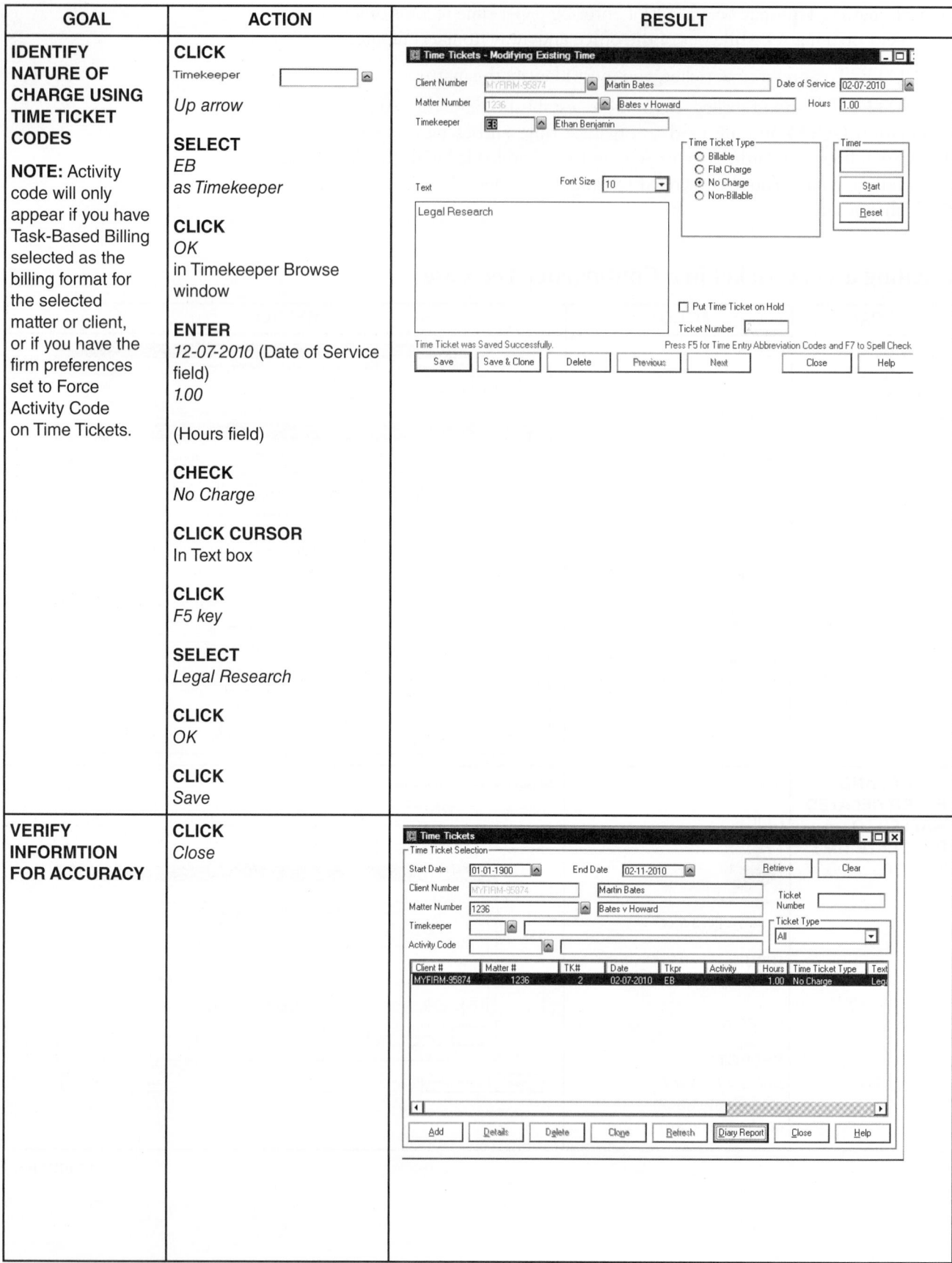
VERIFY INFORMTION FOR ACCURACY	**CLICK** *Close*	

Close Abacus Accounting.

■ HOW DO I ENTER TIME CHARGES FOR EVENTS FROM THE ABACUSLAW PRACTICE MANAGER?

Events within a matter may be set up as time tickets within the Practice Manager. Events include time spent working with a client or on a client case, including conferences, drafting, research, and other billable time. These events may be charged as time tickets using the same method as entering an event into a calendar.

Enter Chargeable Event in Practice Manager

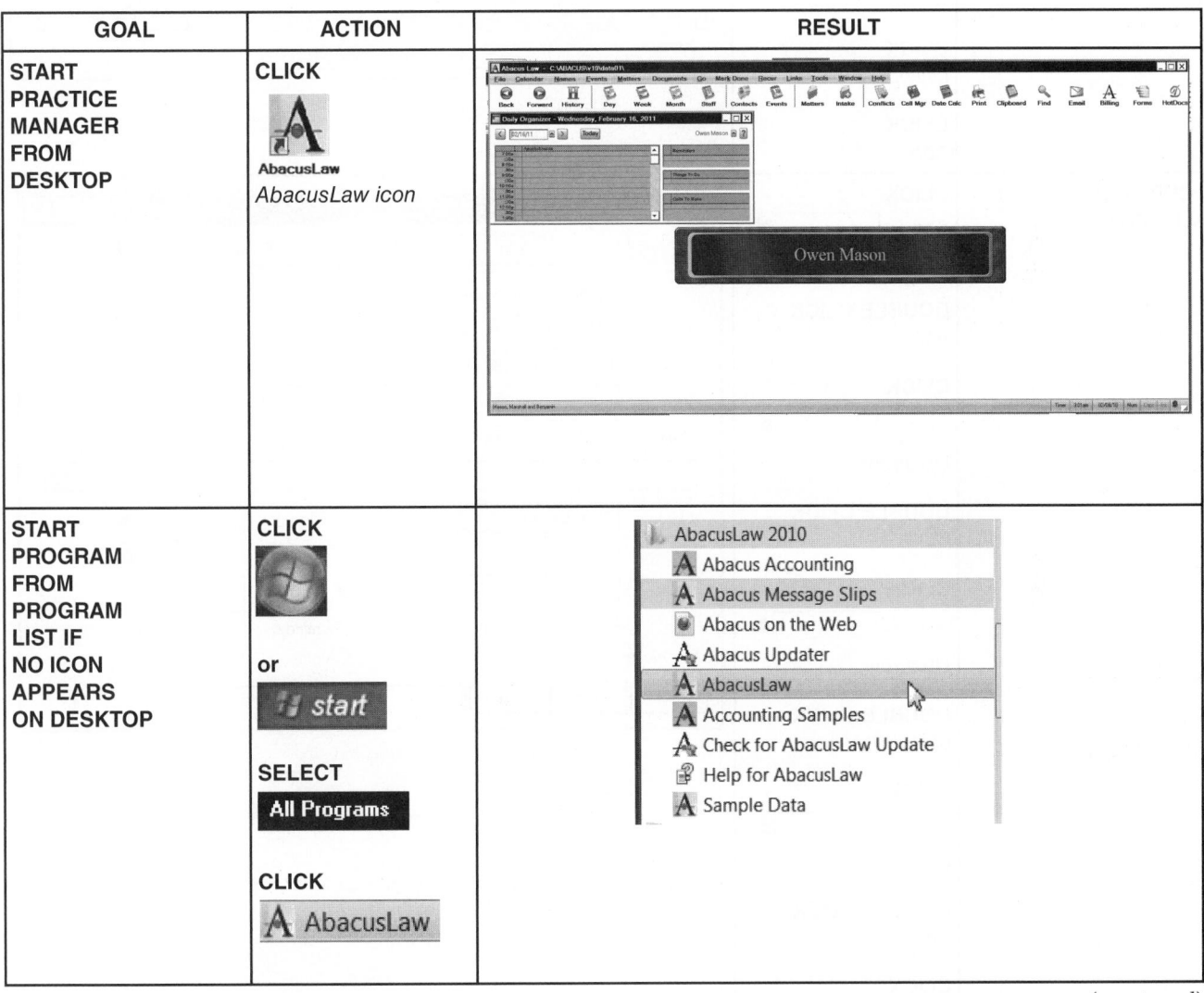

GOAL	ACTION	RESULT
START PRACTICE MANAGER FROM DESKTOP	CLICK AbacusLaw *AbacusLaw icon*	
START PROGRAM FROM PROGRAM LIST IF NO ICON APPEARS ON DESKTOP	CLICK or *start* SELECT All Programs CLICK A AbacusLaw	

(continued)

GOAL	ACTION	RESULT
OPEN LINKED EVENTS IN A MATTER	**CLICK** **Matters** *Matters icon* **SELECT** *Stein v Curtis* **CLICK** *OK* **CLICK** *Linked Events tab* **CLICK** *Add*	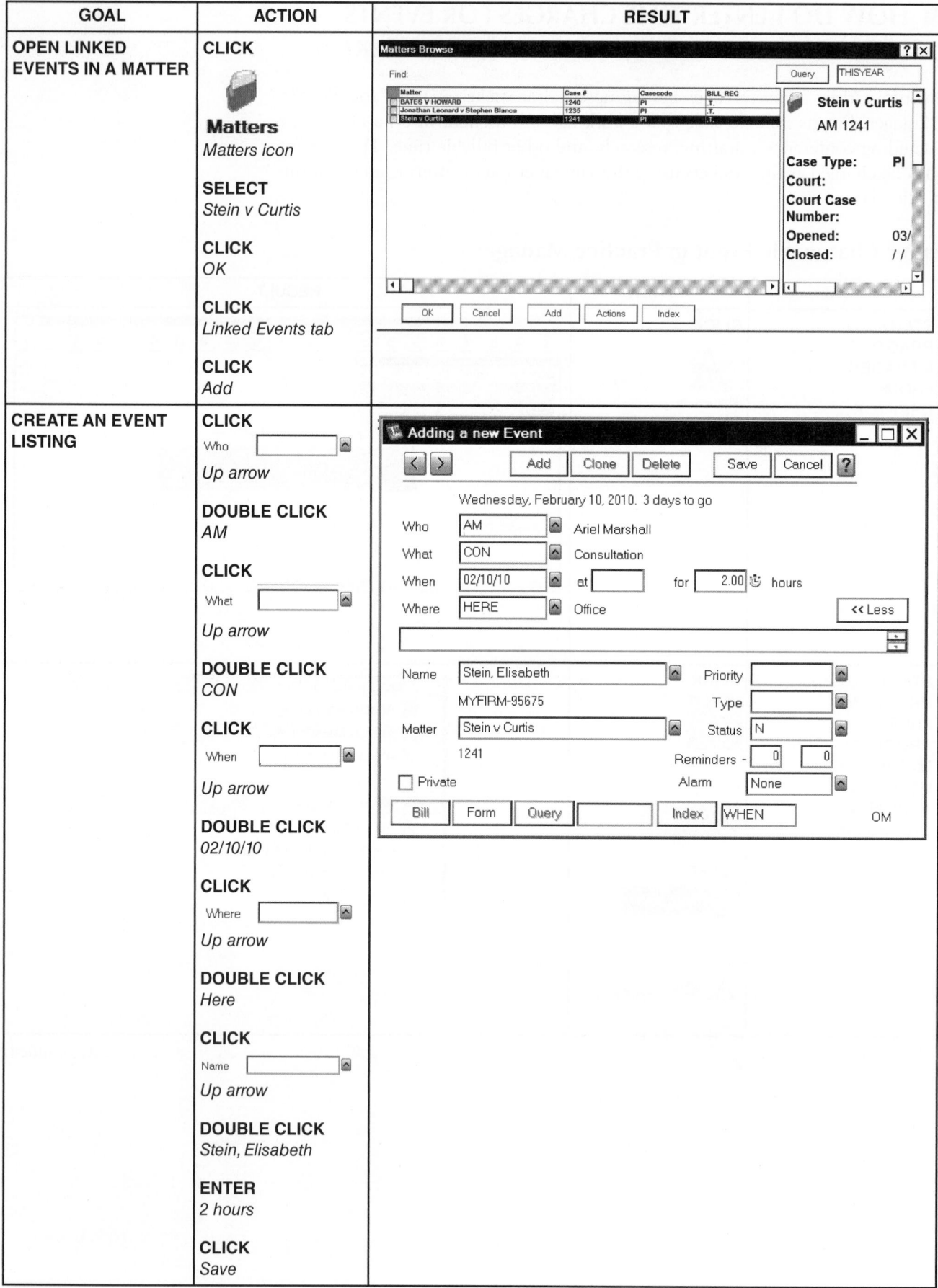
CREATE AN EVENT LISTING	**CLICK** Who *Up arrow* **DOUBLE CLICK** *AM* **CLICK** Whet *Up arrow* **DOUBLE CLICK** *CON* **CLICK** When *Up arrow* **DOUBLE CLICK** *02/10/10* **CLICK** Where *Up arrow* **DOUBLE CLICK** *Here* **CLICK** Name *Up arrow* **DOUBLE CLICK** *Stein, Elisabeth* **ENTER** *2 hours* **CLICK** *Save*	

(continued)

GOAL	ACTION	RESULT
ENTER A LINKED EVENT IN THE BILLING RECORDS	**SELECT** *CON* as item to bill **CLICK** *Bill* **CLICK** *Yes* in Send to Accounting window	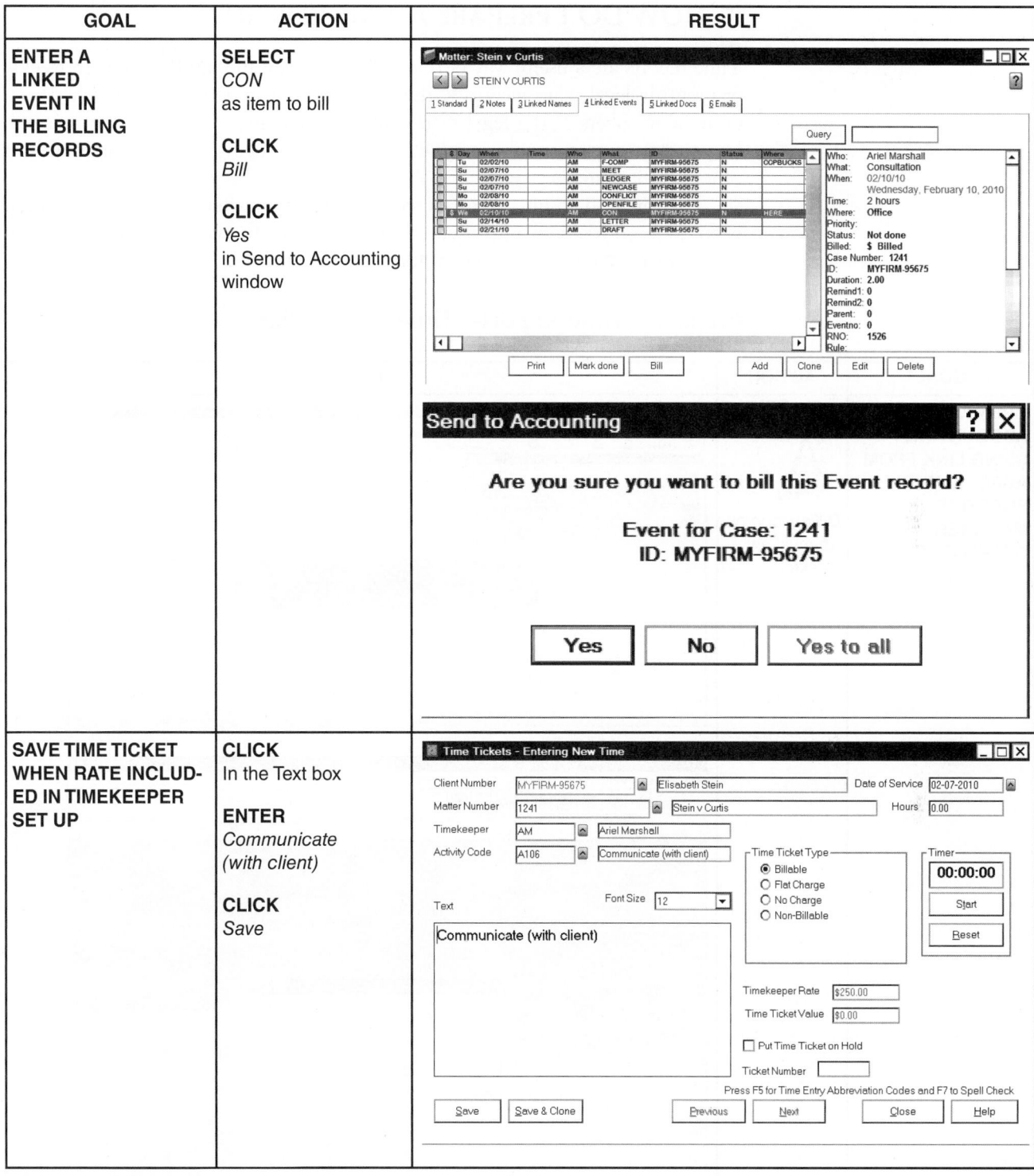
SAVE TIME TICKET WHEN RATE INCLUDED IN TIMEKEEPER SET UP	**CLICK** In the Text box **ENTER** *Communicate (with client)* **CLICK** *Save*	

Continue without closing and go on to next tutorial.

■ HOW DO I PREPARE A TIME REPORT?

Time reports are a useful way of tracking activity on files and matters. In weekly or monthly legal team meetings, they may be used to determine what has been done by members of the legal team and what remains to be done. Partners will frequently want to see the productivity or efforts being made by associates or others in the firm.

They are also an important source of information when a court asks what has been done on a case, to justify a billing request to the court for court-assigned cases, or to request reimbursement for paralegal time spent on a case.

Prepare a Time Report—Time Ticket Diary

GOAL	ACTION	RESULT
OPEN ABACUS ACCOUNTING USING LINK FROM ABACULAW PRACTICE MANAGER DESKTOP	**CLICK** Ⓐ **Billing** *Billing icon* on AbacusLaw Desktop	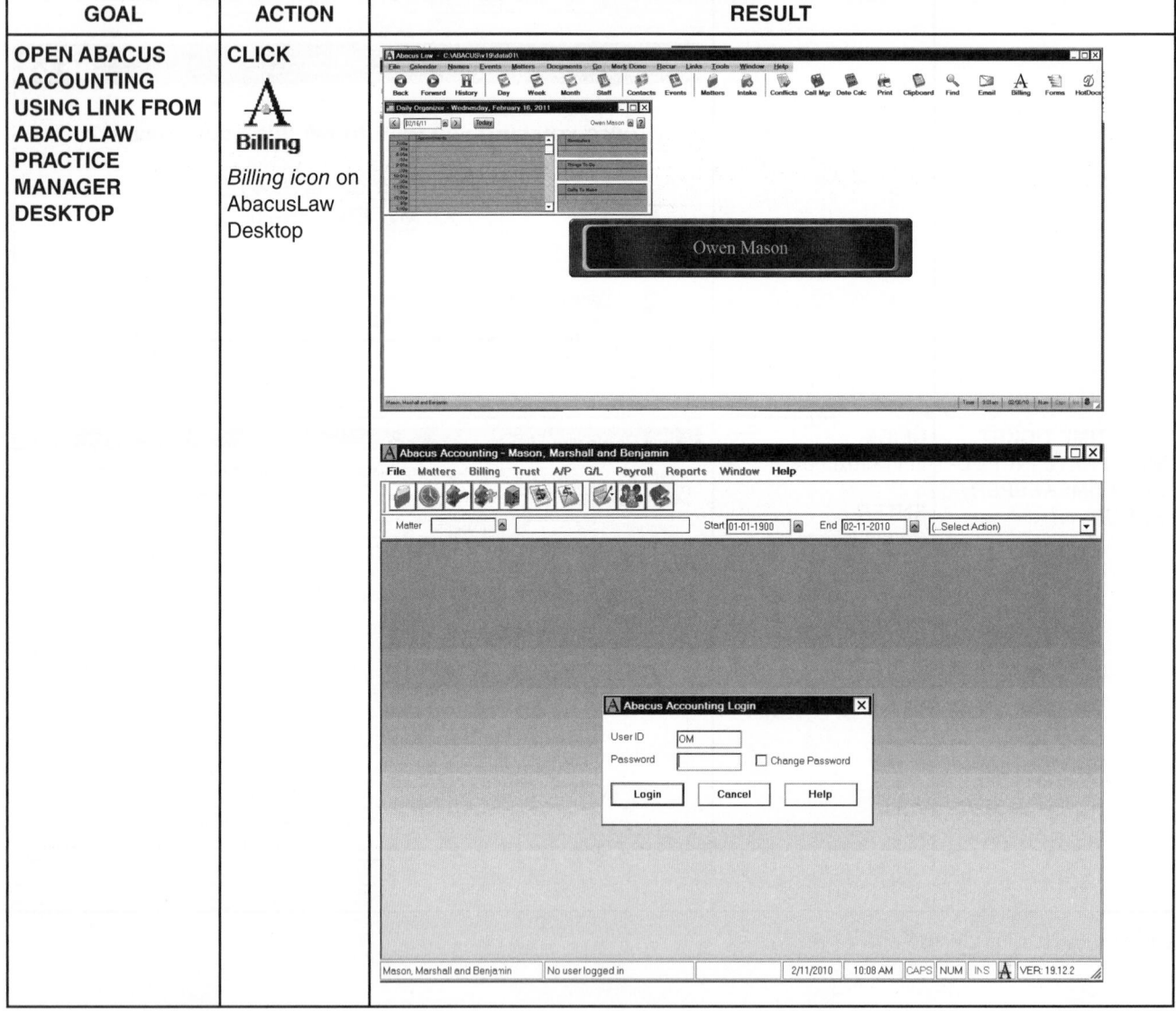

(continued)

GOAL	ACTION	RESULT
PREPARE A TIME TICKET DIARY REPORT IN ABACUS ACCOUNTING	**CLICK** *Billing menu* in Abacus Accounting **SELECT** *Time Ticket Diary* **ENTER** *02-27-2013* (in the End field in Date Range) **CLICK** *Preview*	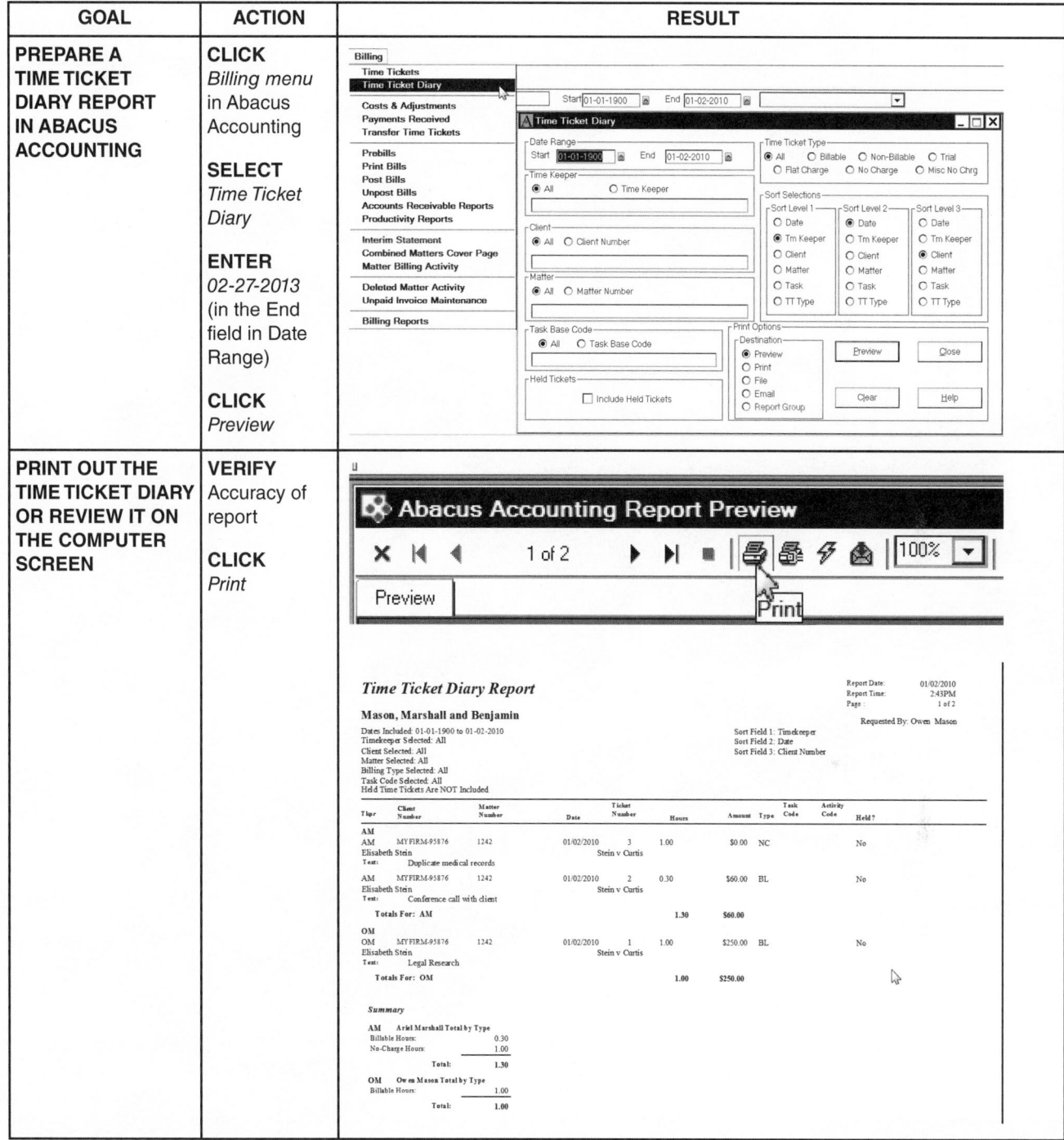
PRINT OUT THE TIME TICKET DIARY OR REVIEW IT ON THE COMPUTER SCREEN	**VERIFY** Accuracy of report **CLICK** *Print*	

Additional tutorial information is available at
http://media.pearsoncmg.com/ph/chet/chet_goldman_techresources_1/

or on the Technology Resources Website:
www.pearsonhighered.com/goldman

"I want people to understand the amazing, positive way our software can make leisure time more enjoyable, and work and businesses more successful."

—*Steve Ballmer, Microsoft*

Case Organization and Management Software

CHAPTER 10

OPENING SCENARIO

A number of children were injured when a school bus was struck by a tractor trailer. Preliminary investigation indicated that the cause of the accident was partly due to a defective brake system in the truck. However, the injuries to the bus passengers were also partly the result of seats breaking loose from the bus floor. Though the injuries were regrettable, the case was something every lawyer dreams of. It was Mr. Mason's first big case.

Based on a preliminary review, it was clear that even if the firm represented only a few of the passengers, there would be thousands of medical documents from multiple doctors and medical facilities. If the firm were hired by all of the passengers, there would be an overwhelming number of documents to track. In addition, there would be documents from the investigation of the brake failure and the seat design and installation. Mr. Mason, Mrs. Hannah, and Mr. Benjamin could handle most of the work of organizing the files, but they would clearly need to enlist the help of other investigators, attorneys, and paralegals. Fortunately, attorney Ariel Marshall had agreed to work on the case with Mr. Mason, as had a sole practitioner the firm had worked with on another federal case on the other side of town. With so many people using the files, there was a danger that the documents, file folders, and boxes would end up everywhere, and files might not be available when needed.

LEARNING OBJECTIVES

After studying this chapter, you should be able to:

1. Explain the reasons for the use of software in managing litigation cases.

2. Describe how case management programs are used.

3. Understand the functions of case analysis software, and explain its value to a law firm.

4. Describe the advantages of using time lines in litigation.

VIDEO INTRODUCTION

Professor Thomas F. Goldman, Esq.

CASE ORGANIZATION AND MANAGEMENT SOFTWARE
After watching the video in MyLegalStudiesLab, answer the following questions.

1. How can computers be used to find relevant documents?
2. How can computers be used to manage cases?

■ INTRODUCTION TO CASE ORGANIZATION AND MANAGEMENT SOFTWARE

The advent of the computer has been both a blessing and a curse. Computers can be used to search for specific language in a single document among thousands of pages, or save time by eliminating duplicates of the same document. However, it has become so easy to create electronic documents that computers have increased the volume of potentially relevant documents disclosed in discovery. Consider the number of emails generated each day in large organizations. In litigation, these emails may need to be reviewed to find relevant evidence. A few incriminating emails could prove that a large, multinational financial institution created a hostile working environment by allowing the sexual harassment of employees.

Managing Case Information

Effectively managing a case may involve reviewing, sorting, and marking for identification hundreds or even thousands of documents, photographs, and other evidence. Careful tracking and organizing of evidence should start at the beginning of a case. Good case management requires a thoughtful process for storing, handling, examining, evaluating, and indexing every page.

There are almost as many different approaches to setting up case files and managing cases as there are legal teams. One of the more common approaches is the use of a case notebook, or **trial notebook.** Summaries of information about the case are maintained in a single notebook with tabs for each major activity, party, expert, or element of proof needed. In addition to the notebook, case files are maintained along with file boxes or cabinets containing hard copies of documents, exhibits, and physical evidence. Someone on the litigation team must take responsibility for making sure there is no duplication of effort and that the most current activities are entered in the trial notebook and case files. If each member of the team has his or her own copy, then each trial notebook must be updated regularly.

The process may be simplified by using virtual trial notebooks. All of the case file information may be maintained on a single computer, network server, or cloud-based server, including copies of the documents in electronic form. Each member of the litigation team may, with proper access rights, access the information.

trial notebook
Summary of the case usually contained in a tabbed, three-ring binder with sections such as pleadings, motions, law, pretrial memo, and witnesses.

Integrating Software Functions

Office management and case management functions are closely related, and some of these functions overlap. For example, managing contact information for clients, parties, and others is a part of both office management *and* case management. Early versions of some software used separate applications for functions such as calendaring and file maintenance. Now, many specialty applications are designed to integrate these functions. The current trend is toward combining all of the desired functions of office and case management and organization into a single, integrated program, with modules for each of the functions needed in running a law office. Some of the advantages in using a single platform are reduced time for inputting information, a single interface for the user to learn, and a single software vendor point of contact.

■ CASE AND PRACTICE MANAGEMENT SOFTWARE

It is rare for a litigation team to work on one case at a time, from beginning to end. Instead, the legal team will often work on a number of cases simultaneously, with each case in a different stage of preparation for trial. Frequently, each member of the legal team will work on different aspects of the same case.

> **LEARNING OBJECTIVE 1**
> Explain the reasons for the use of software in managing litigation cases.

Thus each member of the team must be able to access case information. He or she also must know what the other members of the team have done and what still needs to be done. In a conventional case management system using paper files, the physical file is the repository of everything connected with the case, from interview notes to pleadings and exhibits. With so many people accessing and removing case material, it is not unusual for items to be "missing" because someone forgot to replace the documents, or forgot to put a note in the file saying where the documents are.

In cases with large volumes of documents and many days' or weeks' worth of deposition transcripts, software can be used to quickly locate relevant documents or portions of testimony. Electronic documents, including paper documents that have been scanned and converted to electronic form, can be stored and accessed using data storage devices. Case files may also be stored on Internet or cloud-based file servers in other states or countries. These remote storage systems are sometimes called **e-repositories** or *online document repositories*. Remote access to the e-repository is permitted only to those having authorization.

e-repositories
Web or cloud based services that store electronic information.

The use of computers for email and document storage by businesses and government has resulted in a massive increase in the number of potential documents that may have to be reviewed, tracked, and made available to opposing counsel in

Checklist ✓

A typical litigation case file contains the following items:

- the interview of the client;
- interviews of fact and expert witnesses;
- investigation reports;
- expert reports;
- documents;
- evidence;
- research memoranda;
- pleadings; and
- trial preparation material.

Exhibit 10.1 The steps in a typical personal injury case

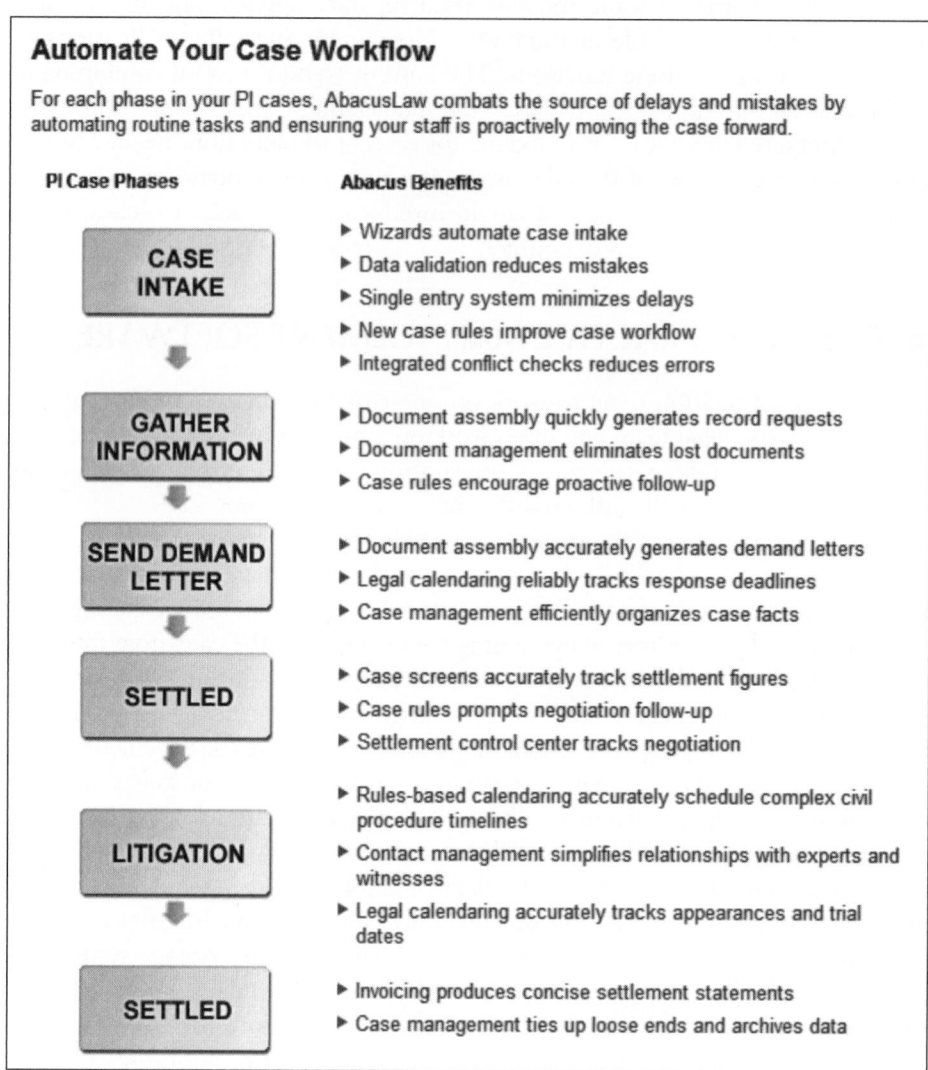

AbacusLaw.

a case. As a result, managing litigation with massive amounts of data has become increasingly difficult, and the size of the teams working on complex cases has grown. Computers are increasingly relied upon to manage the case files and the litigation process. Exhibit 10.1 shows the steps in a typical personal injury case and how an automated case management system can be used to avoid errors.

■ MANAGING THE CASE

case
Issues that a client has presented to a legal team to handle and resolve.

A "**case**" refers to a matter that a client has presented to a legal team to handle and resolve, and is sometimes referred to as the "client file" or the "client file on the [name of topic] matter." A file in a simple case such as the preparation of a power of attorney or a will may consist of only a few pages of information obtained from the client, a copy of an old will, and the final document prepared for the client's signature. In a more complex case like a tort claim involving a building under construction, or an employment discrimination class action, the case file may consist of thousands of documents, and hundreds of people may be involved as plaintiffs, defendants, witnesses, and experts. Also, a dozen or more members of the legal team may need access to the information.

Before computers were used in such complex cases, lawyers and their staff spent countless hours pushing papers around, moving file boxes, reviewing documents, creating indexes, cataloging files, and writing notes to others on the team. A case notebook was created that consisted of tabbed binders with a tab for each major element of the case. In some cases, an entire binder may be devoted to one topic, such as witnesses or documents.

The following is a representative listing of tabs and a sample of the form that might be used.

Things to Do

Date Due	What	Responsible Party
6-30-2007	Obtain accident report	J. L. Investigator
7-15-2007	Interview investigating police officer	J. L. Investigator

Parties—Witnesses

Name	Address	Home Phone	Work Phone	Comments
Nancy Smith	333 Main St	123-456-7890	987-654-3210	Passenger in other car
K. Lombardo	222 South St	555-111-2222	555-333-4444	School bus driver letting off passengers facing accident scene

Documents

Bates #	Document Name	Date	Comments	Author
P001–P003	Police accident report	5-15-2007	Shows citations issued to Def.	Officer Hannah
P002	Repair record	4-20-2006	Shows brake problem in Def. car	Newtown auto repair mechanic Ed

Research—Authorities

Name	Jurisdiction	Type	Citation	Description
Bell v. Farmers Insurance Exchange	Cal. Super. Ct	Case law	234 Cal. 456	Compensation issue
Driving too fast for conditions	Cal.	Statute	43 Ca. Code	Defines standards for...

A more complete list of tabs for the case notebook and the trial notebook is shown in Exhibit 10.2.

Now, each of the pages in the case or trial notebook can be created using the table feature of a word processing program, with headings added as shown in the previous samples. A trial notebook can also be created using a spreadsheet or database program, depending on whether the team will need to sort or extract information using database queries.

In the days before computers, preprinted forms were used instead of word processing tables. Contact information was written on individual cards. If the

Exhibit 10.2 Tabs for a physical case or trial notebook

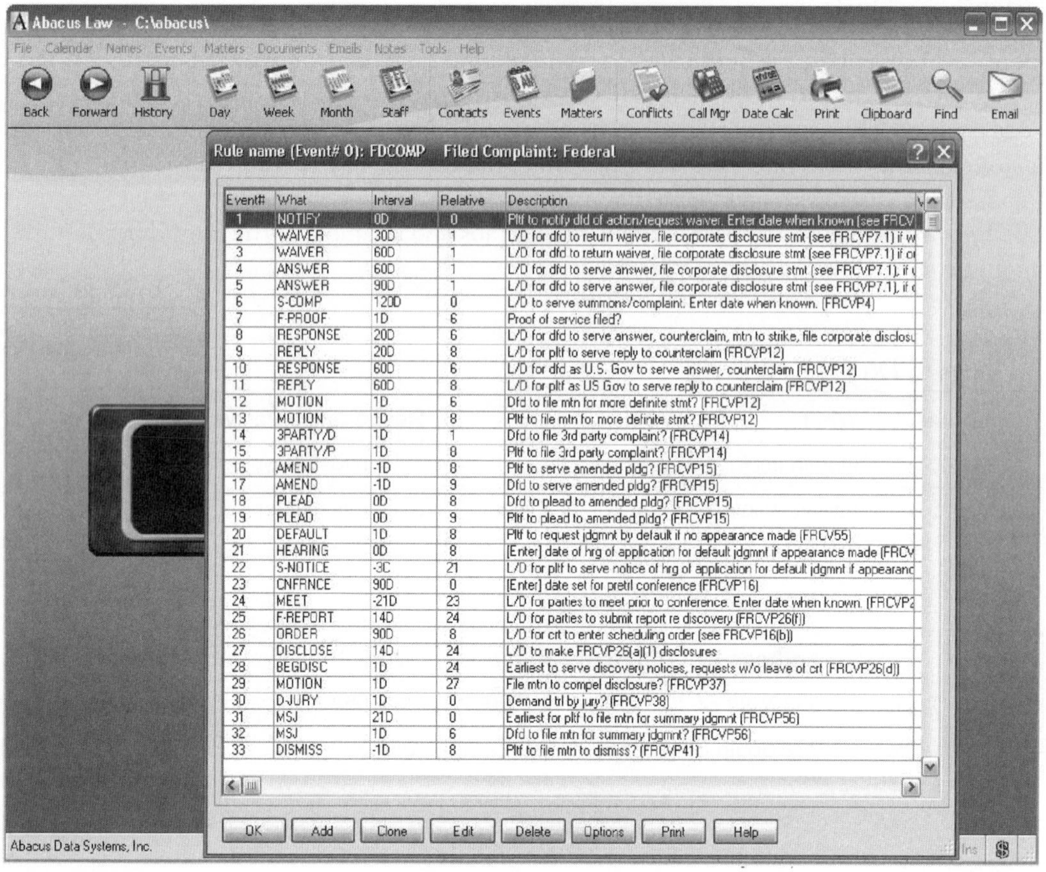

AbacusLaw.

case involved more than one attorney, the case file, or portions of it, were passed around the office, leading constantly to questions such as, "Who has the case file?" or "Who took home the evidence binder?"

However, case management software can now be used to organize the cast of characters in a case—documents, timetables, issues, legal authority, and other information—in a single system. Good case management software organizes this information and presents it in a readable manner to everyone working on the case. Individuals are able to input information in the areas for which they are responsible, along with the data from others, and everyone has access to the information over a large network.

The typical file or case starts with an interview with the client. In the pre-computer days, a client interview form was completed by the person who conducted the initial interview. Additional forms were also used for gathering and organizing information from fact witnesses and experts. The key information was written on the outside of the file folder or on a paper data sheet on the inside cover.

Forms such as those shown in Exhibit 10.3 are still used in many offices—not as a repository of the information, but as a method of recording information until it is inputted into the computerized case management system.

Some users may bypass the paper forms and enter the information directly into the system using a workstation, laptop, or tablet device. Some case management programs, like LexisNexis CaseMap, have tools that scan data directly from forms and templates. Exhibit 10.4 is a sample portion of the CaseMap form that is designed to be imported directly into the program database.

Exhibit 10.3a Paper-based interview form—Accident fact sheet

Accident Fact Sheet

CLIENT PERSONAL DATA

Client Name	Age, Date of Birth
Address	Home Phone
City, State, Zip	Work Phone
Place of Employment	Social Security No.
Job Description	Time Lost from Work

Date/Time of Accident

Location of Accident

Bodily Injuries

Name and Cost of Ambulance

Name and Address of Hospital

Names of Treating Physicians, including Physical Therapist

Exhibit 10.3b Paper-based interview form—Witness information

Witness Information

CLIENT PERSONAL DATA

Client Name	Case No.	File No.
Address	City, State, Zip	Phone

CASE DATA

File Label	Case Issue	Date

Responsible Attorney(s)

WITNESS DATA

Witness Name

Aliases, if any		US Citizen
		☐ Yes ☐ No

Current Address	City, State, Zip	Phone

Past Address(es)

Date & Place of Birth	Sex	Race	Age

Name of Spouse	Number/Former Marriages	Number/Children

Name of Children (natural & adopted)	Age	Name	Current Age

Exhibit 10.4 CaseMap input form

Persons

- Please list all people related to the case -- even people with a minor connection to it.
- List only one person in each row of the table below.
- In the Description cell for each person, please explain who the person is and how they are connected to the case. Your description can be any length -- the Description cells grow as you type in them.
- As mentioned above, you may need more horizontal rows than we've provided by default. When you're in the last cell of the Persons table, pressing the TAB key on your keyboard creates a new row.
- Again, please do not add or remove the vertical columns in this or any of the following tables.

Name of Person	Description of Person

LexisNexis.

As the members of the legal team obtain information, they can enter it into the case management software and update the case file as new information becomes available.

USING CASE MANAGEMENT SYSTEMS

LEARNING OBJECTIVE 2
Describe how case management programs are used.

case management system
Software for organizing the parts of a case in a central repository that can be shared by all members of the legal team.

A **case management system** allows all authorized members of the legal team to access the case information day or night. An effective system requires a central repository for information gathered by each of the team members, and the ability of team members to access the case information added by others. Depending on the available Internet access and connection speed, every member of the legal team should be able to access the same information from remote locations across town, across the country, or around the world.

Collaboration among members of the legal team is common, even in smaller law offices. This collaboration is often necessary to handle the increased complexity of cases and the shortened time in which to prepare for trial under new court rules. Some attorneys may even collaborate with attorneys in other firms. In many smaller, specialized practices, the resources or the expertise may not be available to handle the occasional large or complex case. For example, a small firm of tax attorneys with no trial experience may collaborate on a case with a small trial or litigation boutique. Each firm supplies the expertise in its specialty and shares all the case files and information. In a collaborative effort, each attorney may provide his or her own written assessment of the issues in the case. CaseMap provides a form for this individual assessment, shown in Exhibit 10.5, which then becomes available for other members of the team to review.

FILE ACCESS AND CONFIDENTIALITY

When clients seek legal advice, even their names and the subject matter of their cases must be kept confidential. The information handled by a case management system requires the same protection as any other source of confidential or privileged client information. Access to each case should be limited to the team members working on that particular case. Exhibit 10.6 shows the range of security and access settings for AbacusLaw, a typical case and office management system.

Exhibit 10.5 CaseMap form for individual legal team member assessment of the issues

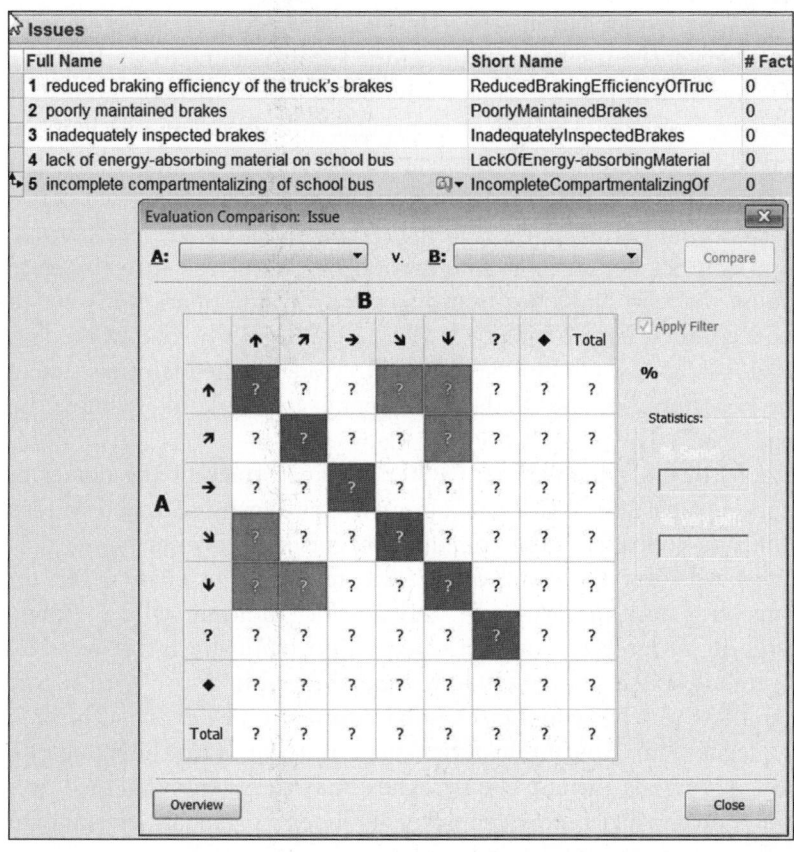

LexisNexis.

Exhibit 10.6 Security setting options

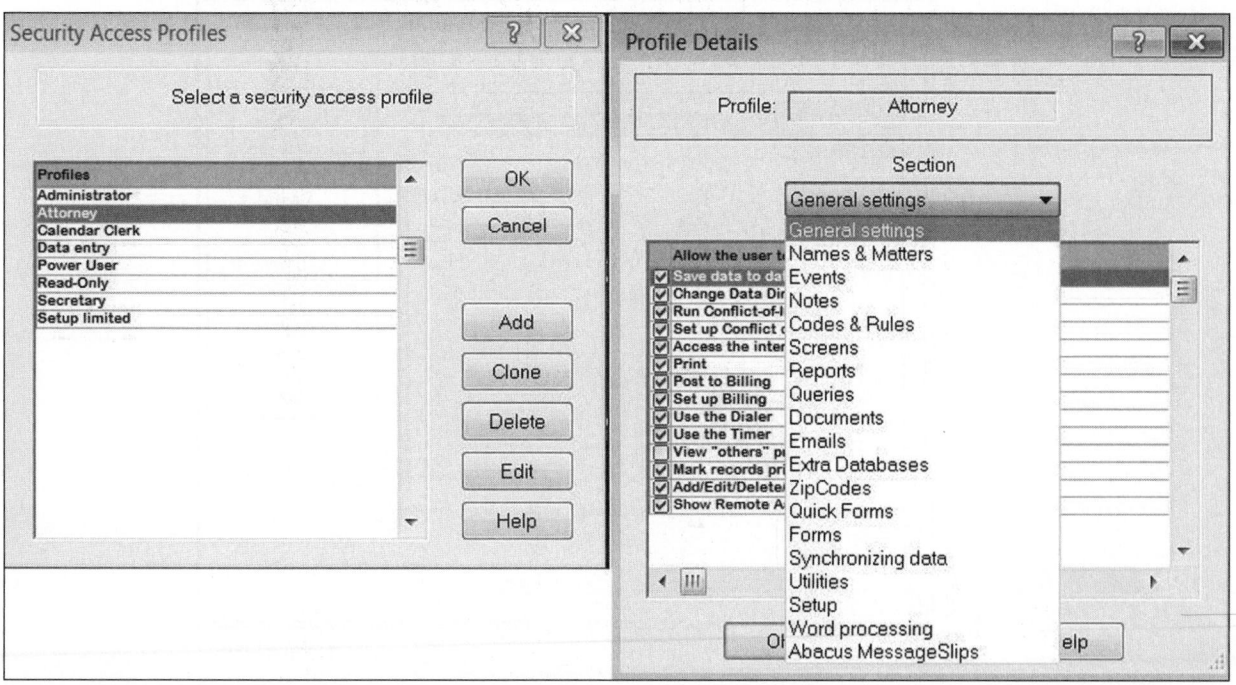

AbacusLaw.

■ CONFLICT OF INTEREST CHECKS

A case management system contains information about both current and former clients and cases. The system may also be used to collect information on previous clients that members of the legal team represented before coming to work for the firm. This information can be used to perform checks for conflicts of interest. It is not unusual for a prospective employee to provide a list of names of clients he or she has worked for so that the new firm can check its records and ensure that there will be no conflicts of interest. These lists are generally considered confidential, with access limited to senior firm management for the limited purpose of conducting a conflict check. This information will allow the firm to create a "wall" shielding the new employee from any access to information for which there might be a conflict. For example, a lawyer or paralegal who had worked on the defense team of a case would not be allowed to work on the plaintiff's side of the case at the new firm, because the lawyer or paralegal would likely know the defense strategy.

conflict report generator
A program for sorting names of parties and clients to identify similar names or cases.

Some offices still use a manual card system to keep track of the names of clients and opposing parties. These cards are then physically searched to find possible conflicts of interest before the firm accepts new clients or matters. This system may work for the small office with few cases or clients. But for the larger firm, with multiple attorneys and possibly multiple offices, timely entry and searching of large amounts of information manually is not feasible. A case management system may include a computerized database with report generators that allow timely, accurate access to information by every authorized member of the legal team. Routine searches, such as a search for the name of a potential client among all current client names, may be pre-programmed as a standard report. The **conflict report generator** included in AbacusLaw is shown in Exhibit 10.7.

Exhibit 10.7 Conflict of interest generator window

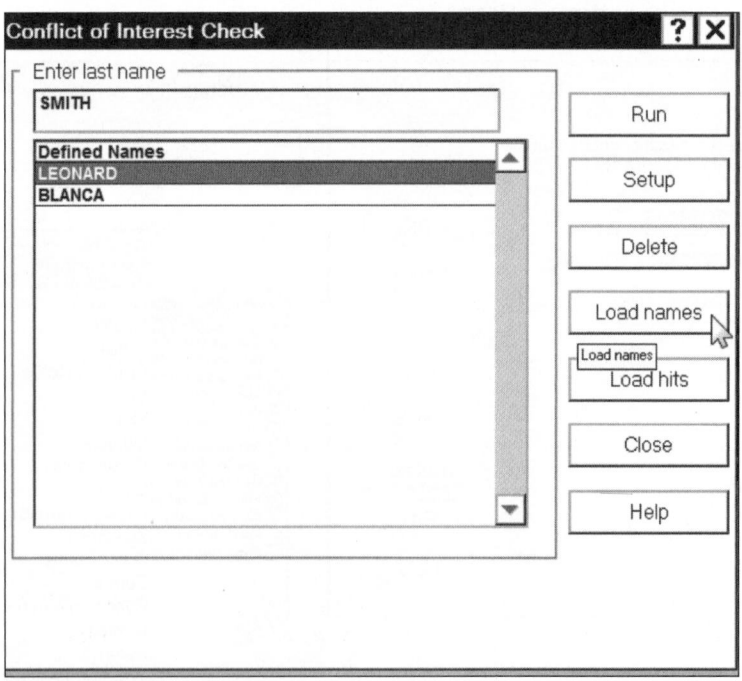

AbacusLaw.

Exhibit 10.8 Conflict report

```
CONFLICT.OM - Notepad                                                    _ □ X
File  Edit  Format  View  Help
2:44p                Mason, Marshall, and Benjamin        01/01/10
                          Conflict Check Report

  Checking these names:
     LEONARD
     BLANCA
     SMITH
-----------------------------------------------------------------
SEARCH NAME : BLANCA

   MATCHED FIELD: MATTERS->MATTER        Record# 4
   MATCHED DATA : Jonathon Leonard V. Steven Blanca
   Jonathon Leonard V. Steven Blanca                  1235      OM PI  / /

   MATCHED FIELD: MATTERS->MATTER        Record# 6
   MATCHED DATA : Stephan Blanca v. Jonathan Leonard
   Stephan Blanca v. Jonathan Leonard                 1236      OM PI  / /
   01/01/10  1:35p DEFS     OM
     Potential Conflict of Interest

   MATCHED FIELD: MATTERS->MATTER        Record# 8
   MATCHED DATA : STEPHAN BLANCA V. JONATHAN LEONARD
   STEPHAN BLANCA V. JONATHAN LEONARD                 1237      AM PI  / /

   MATCHED FIELD: NAMES->LAST            Record# 1
   MATCHED DATA : Blanca
   Blanca, Stephan             MYFIRM-95872 CLIENT   (609)555-9999
     01/01/10  1:17p backgrnd OM
   Client was a driver involved in an accident in which he
   suffered injuries and lost time from work.

   Matters: Stephan Blanca v. Jonathan Leonard        1236
            Stephan Blanca v. Jonathan Leonard        1236
            Jonathon Leonard V. Steven Blanca         1235
            Stephan Blanca v. Jonathan Leonard        1236
-----------------------------------------------------------------
SEARCH NAME : LEONARD

   MATCHED FIELD: MATTERS->MATTER        Record# 3
   MATCHED DATA : Jonathon Leonard V. Steven Blanca
   Jonathon Leonard V. Steven Blanca                  1235      OM PI  / /

   MATCHED FIELD: MATTERS->MATTER        Record# 5
   MATCHED DATA : Stephan Blanca v. Jonathan Leonard
   Stephan Blanca v. Jonathan Leonard                 1236      OM PI  / /
   01/01/10  1:35p DEFS     OM
     Potential Conflict of Interest
```

AbacusLaw.

With a few keystrokes, a list can be prepared to check for potential conflicts of interest, or a search can generate a printout of any matter or litigation where a name appears, as shown in Exhibit 10.8.

■ INPUT—ENTERING INFORMATION

Most case management programs provide a basic set of screens for entering different types of information, as shown in Exhibit 10.9. Some programs allow the user to create customized forms for practice specialties, such as the personal injury matter form shown in Exhibit 10.10. Fields may be created for entering information on a wide variety of people, including clients, opposing parties, fact witnesses, experts, and every opposing counsel with whom any member of the firm has ever had contact. At the start of a case, basic information about a client or the case may be entered using an **intake form,** shown in Exhibit 10.11. This form may be filled out by the legal staff or prepared by the client using a word processor, or in some cases, an Internet browser.

intake form
A form for obtaining information to enter into a computerized office or case management system.

PRACTICE TIP

In addition to being used to avoid potential conflicts of interest, client information is frequently used to maintain client relations. Many firms use the information to send birthday and anniversary greetings, and updates on specific changes in the law for matters in which the client has consulted the firm previously.

Exhibit 10.9 Blank matter window

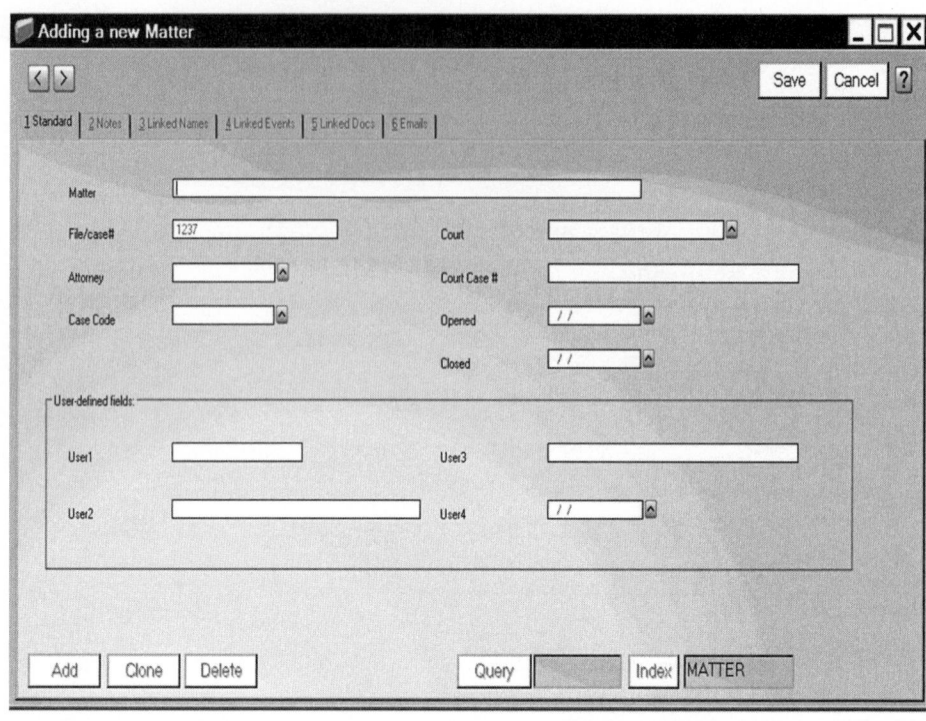

AbacusLaw.

Exhibit 10.10 Personal injury matter form

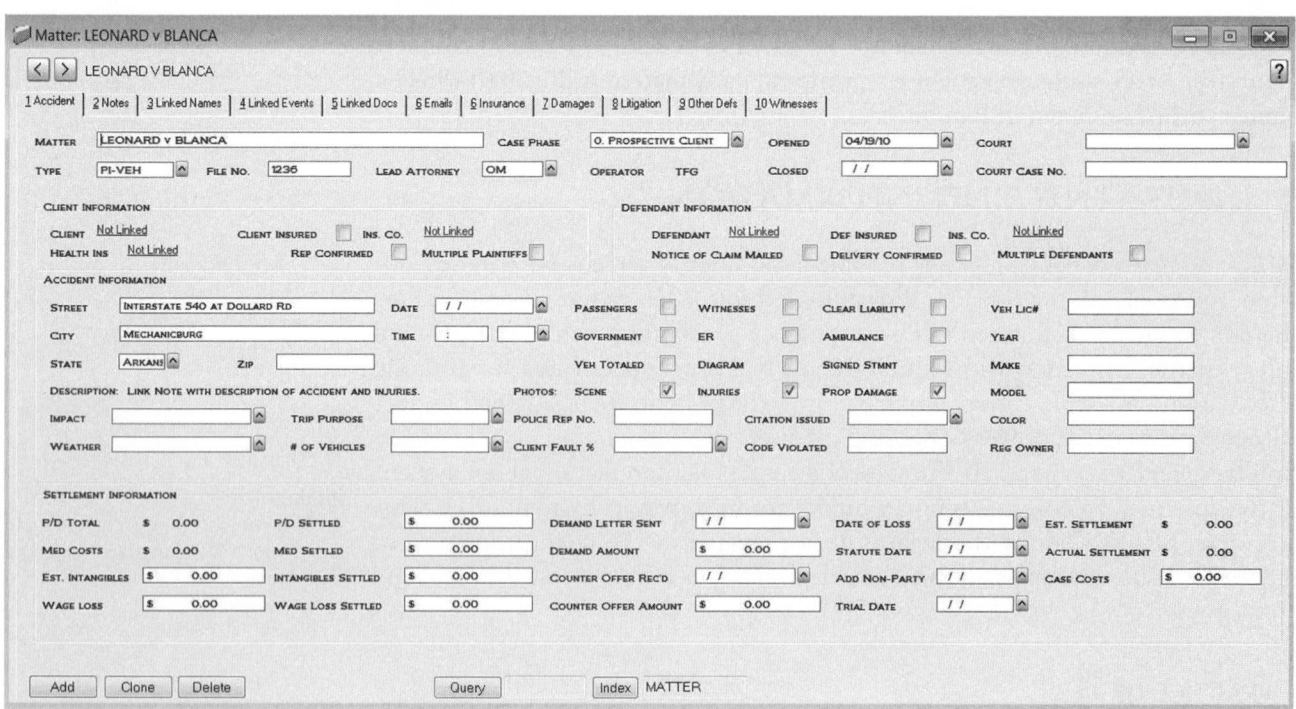

AbacusLaw.

Exhibit 10.11 Intake form for setting up a new matter

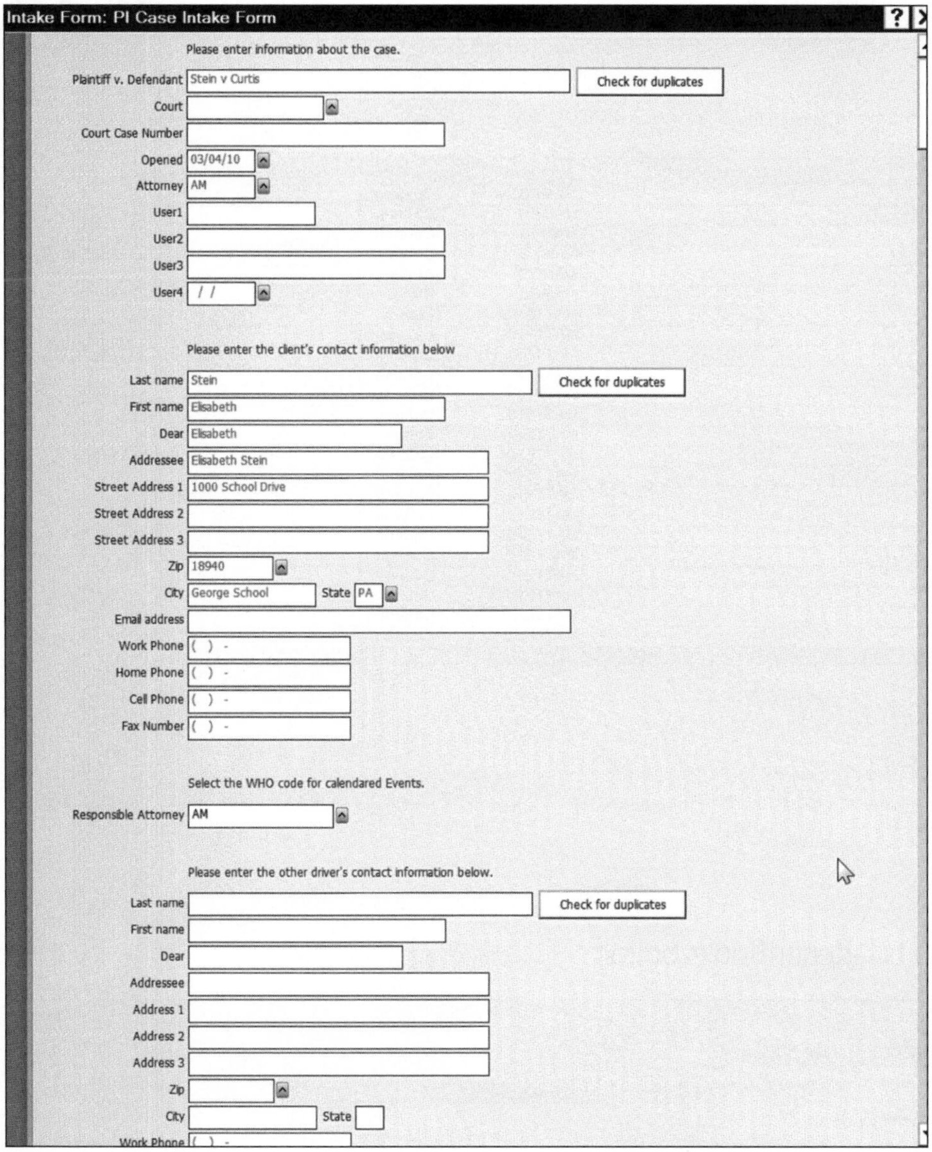

AbacusLaw.

■ OUTPUT—REPORTS

In programs that do not have preset or predesigned reports, a search or query screen may instead be used to identify the information or combinations of information desired in the report. A sample set of report formats for presenting information is shown in Exhibits 10.12 and 10.13. While most programs permit the user to modify or customize reports, some programs require the software vendor or other expert assistance to modify report formats. Among the specialty reports and documents in CaseMap are trial notebook information and privilege logs.

■ CASE ANALYSIS SOFTWARE

Unlike in television court dramas, the facts of real cases are rarely presented by clients in a perfect, well-organized, time-order sequence. Initially, the client may only be aware that an injury or loss has been sustained, or that a notice of

LEARNING OBJECTIVE 3
Understand the functions of case analysis software, and explain its value to a law firm.

Exhibit 10.12 AbacusLaw preset report list

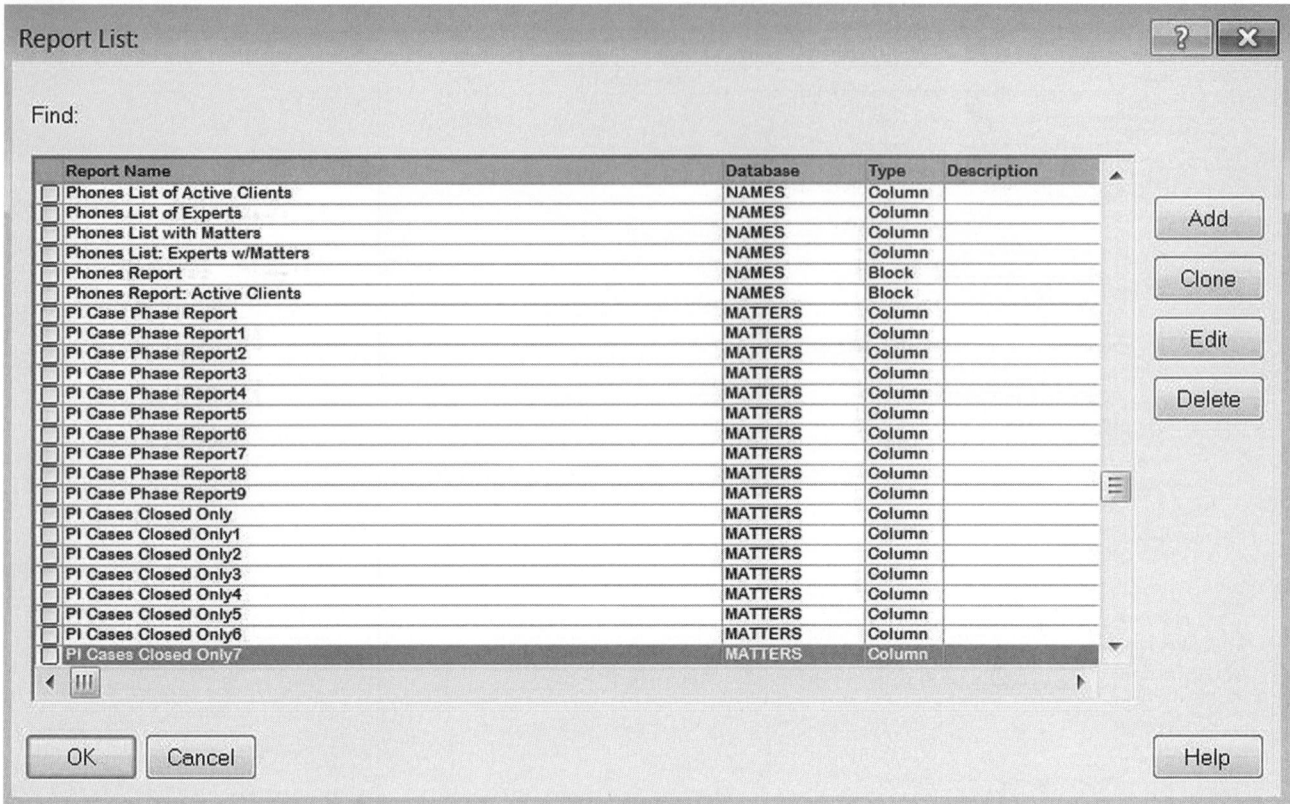

AbacusLaw.

Exhibit 10.13 CaseMap reports—ReportBooks option

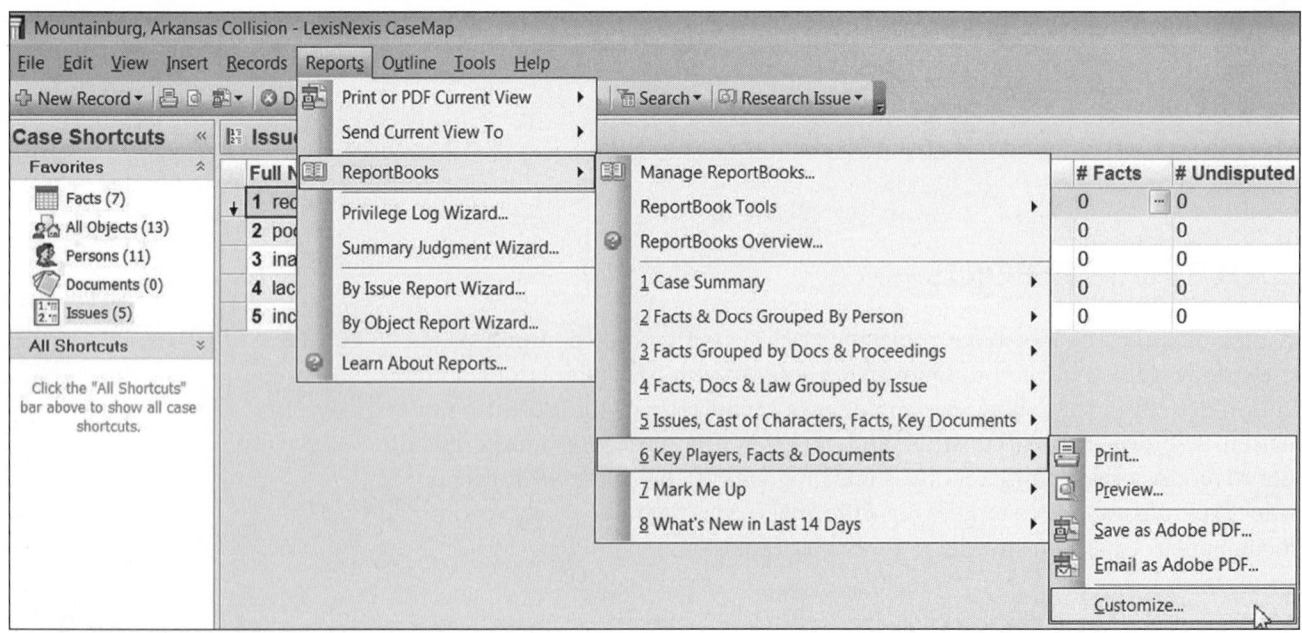

LexisNexis.

a lawsuit has been served on him or her. After a series of interviews and investigations, facts and events become clearer, and through the process of discovery, additional facts and potential evidence are found. From this information, the lawyers develop legal theories or defenses based on current case and statutory law.

Ideally, a small case is handled by one attorney who has no other cases to deal with, thus allowing him or her to retain all the facts and law for that case in his or her head. In actual practice, however, this is rarely the situation. Even seemingly simple cases may require efforts by paralegals, investigators, experts, and legal researchers, all of whom are working on a number of other cases at the same time. In larger cases, there may be a team of lawyers located in different cities, each with a support staff of other lawyers, paralegals, investigators, and information specialists.

Case analysis software, such as CaseMap™ from LexisNexis®, can assist in developing cases by providing a central repository for critical case knowledge. This information can be divided into categories—such as parties, witnesses, documents, case law, statutory law, and reports—that in a paper-based system might be kept in a folder or set of folders. As facts are gathered, parties are identified, and research is assembled, the data may be entered into the program. Once entered, the facts, the cast of characters, and the issues may be organized and explored by any member of the legal team, as shown in the sample case in Exhibit 10.14.

Exhibit 10.15 shows the flow of information in a typical case using CaseMap as the case management tool.

Setting Up a New Case in CaseMap

Exhibits 10.16 to 10.19 present an abbreviated sequence of screens showing the automated process for setting up a new case in CaseMap. For the purposes of these screens, the case study in Appendix II has been used.

Exhibit 10.14 CaseMap All Objects view

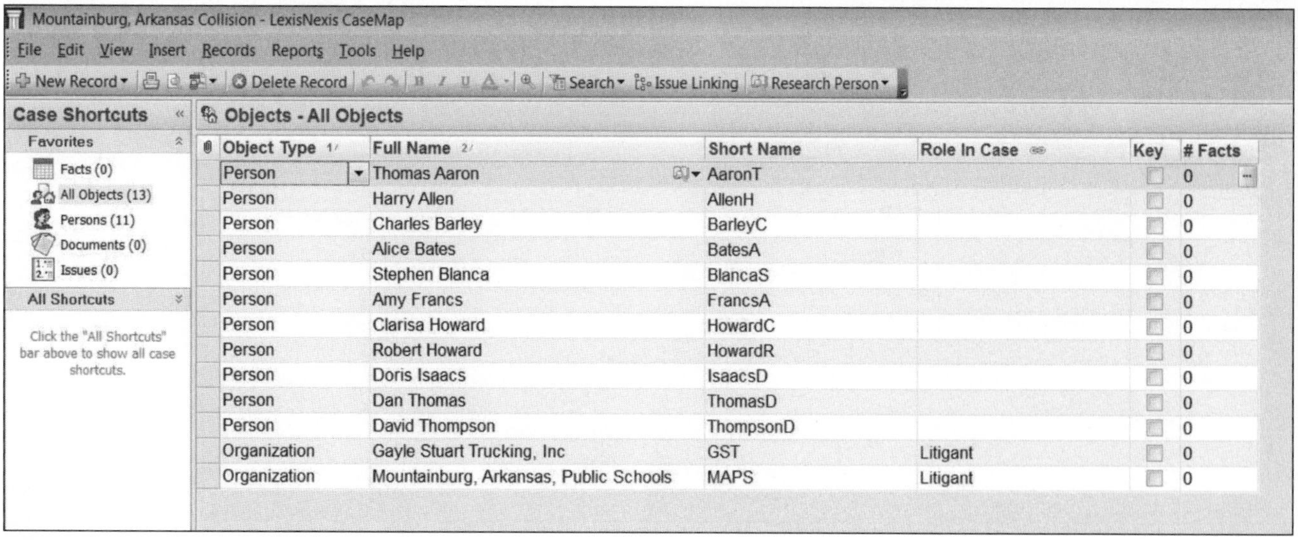

LexisNexis.

Exhibit 10.15 Case organization flowchart

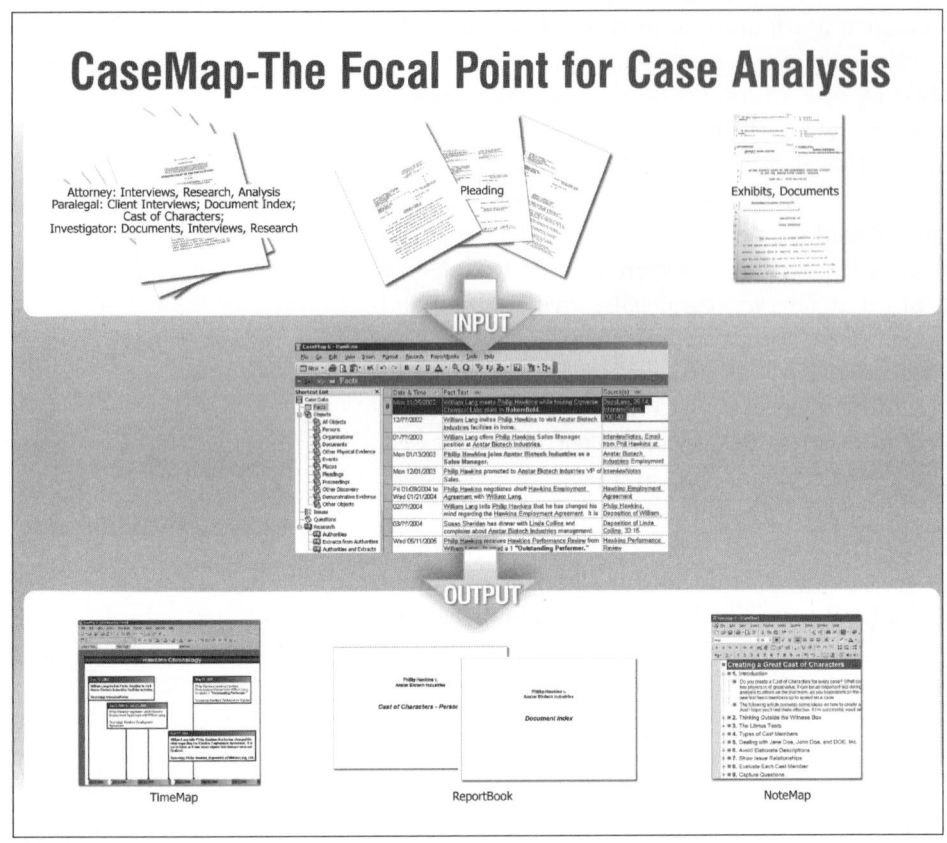

LexisNexis.

Exhibit 10.16 Getting started with CaseMap—New case wizard

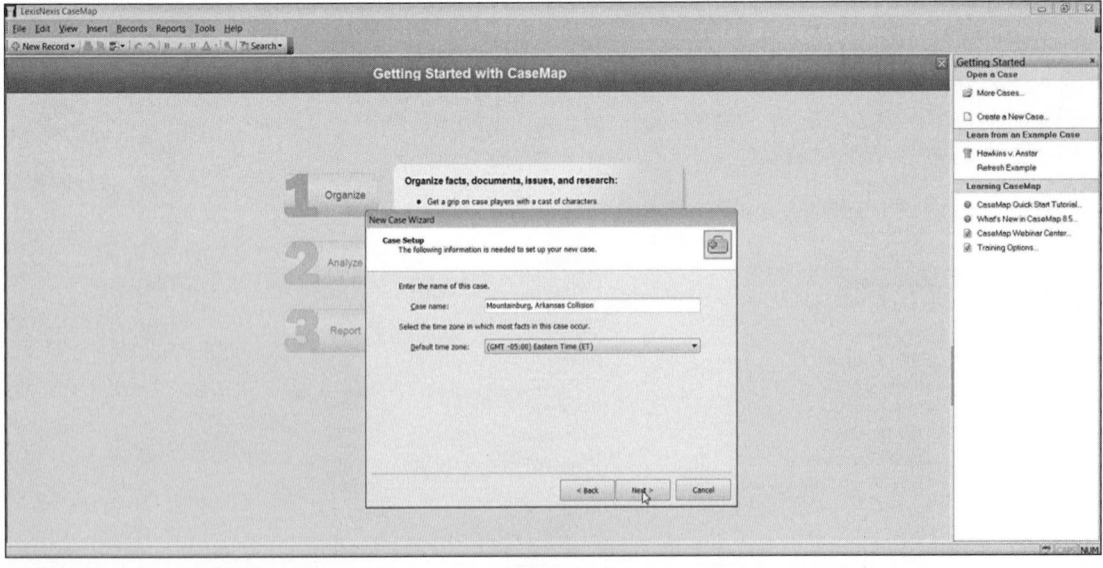

LexisNexis.

Exhibit 10.17 Entering the parties

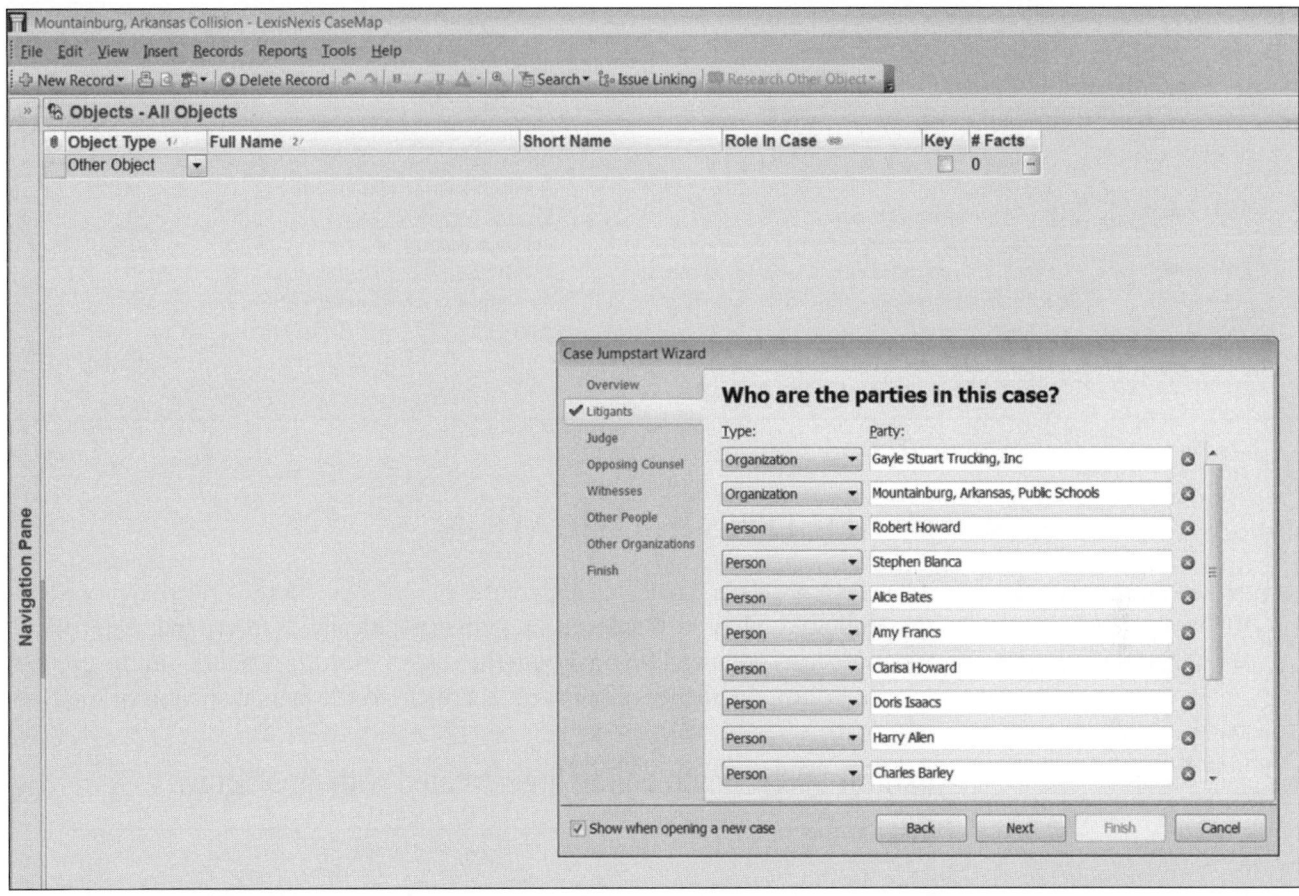

LexisNexis.

Exhibit 10.18 CaseMap object—All Objects view

Object Type	Full Name	Short Name	Role In Case	Key	# Facts
Person	Thomas Aaron	AaronT			0
Person	Harry Allen	AllenH			0
Person	Charles Barley	BarleyC			0
Person	Alice Bates	BatesA			0
Person	Stephen Blanca	BlancaS			0
Person	Amy Francs	FrancsA			0
Person	Clarisa Howard	HowardC			0
Person	Robert Howard	HowardR			0
Person	Doris Isaacs	IsaacsD			0
Person	Dan Thomas	ThomasD			0
Person	David Thompson	ThompsonD			0
Organization	Gayle Stuart Trucking, Inc	GST	Litigant		0
Organization	Mountainburg, Arkansas, Public Schools	MAPS	Litigant		0

Case Shortcuts

Favorites
- Facts (0)
- All Objects (13)
- Persons (11)
- Documents (0)
- Issues (0)

All Shortcuts

Click the "All Shortcuts" bar above to show all case shortcuts.

LexisNexis.

Exhibit 10.19 CaseMap Issues view

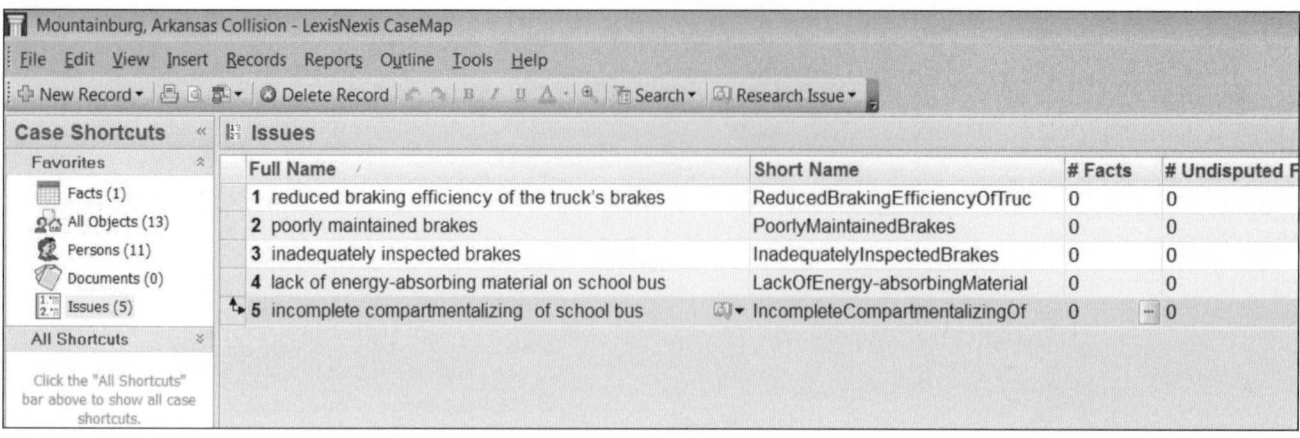

LexisNexis.

■ TIME LINES IN LITIGATION

LEARNING OBJECTIVE 4
Describe the advantages of using time lines in litigation.

time line
Chronological listings of the facts of a case.

Time lines are chronological listings of the facts of a case or the litigation procedures to be followed. They are frequently presented graphically, as shown in Exhibit 10.20.

Time lines are useful for analyzing the case or meeting deadlines in the process. In many cases, the sequence of events is critical to the factual analysis of the case,

Exhibit 10.20 Sample time lines created with SmartDraw

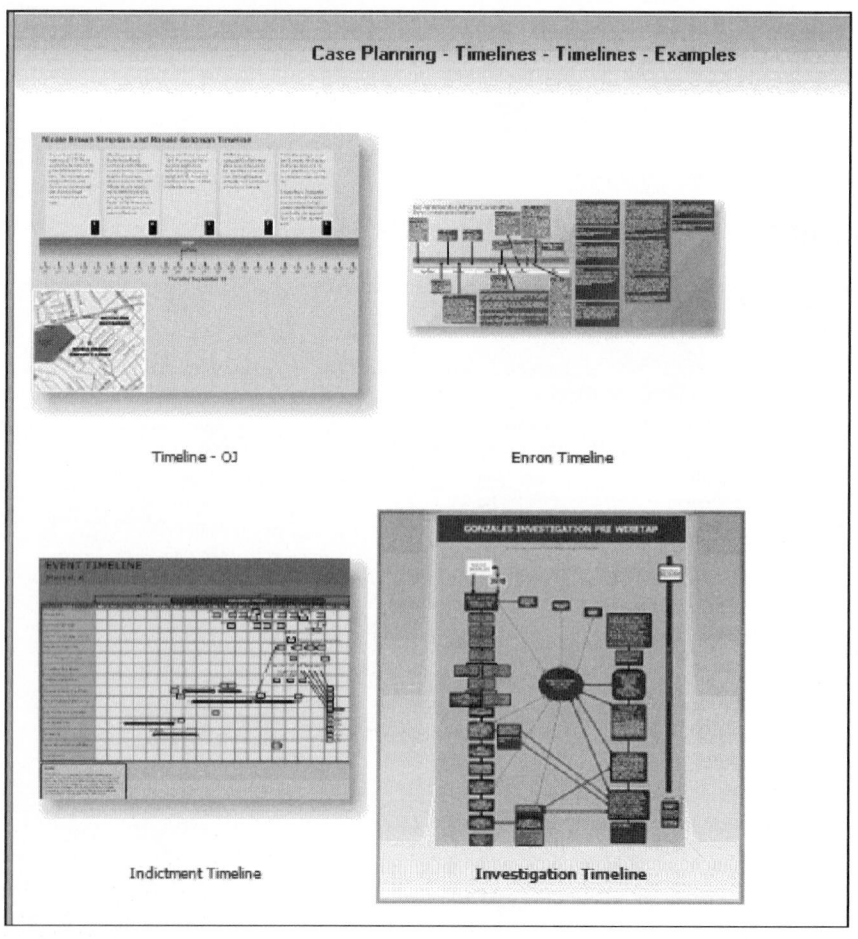

SmartDraw Software, LLC.

Exhibit 10.21 TimeMap time line of case

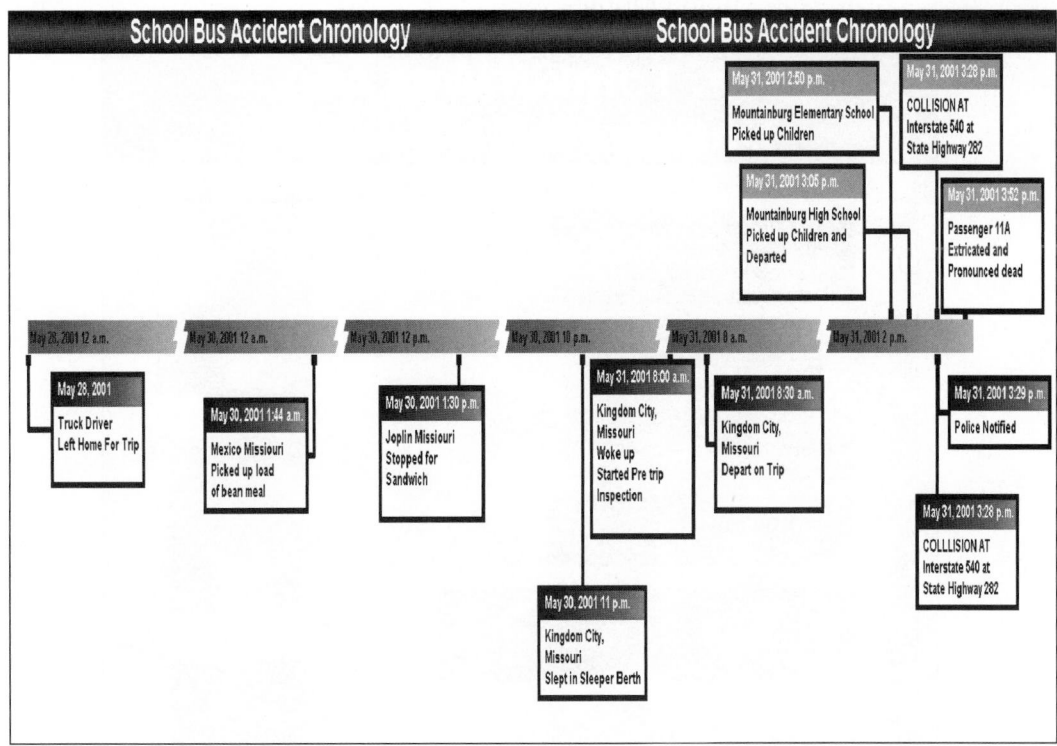

and the trial team must present evidence to support that sequence. At trial, the time line may be an effective tool in showing the jury the sequence of events leading to the injury or damage. Exhibit 10.21 is a time line created directly from the CaseMap file for the case study in Appendix II. Having a fact time line during depositions also helps ensure that questions are asked about every significant time-based event.

When attorneys are analyzing a new case, time lines offer them the opportunity to clarify their thinking about the case and make certain that all the facts and elements of the case line up. Using a comparative time line, which shows the sequence of facts from the perspectives of both plaintiff and the defense, can help the team focus on the strengths, weaknesses, and inconsistencies of a case. Time lines also help put facts in perspective for clients, juries, and opposing counsel.

In cases with accelerated trial schedules, the times for completing discovery and pretrial activities may be very short. A time line can thus provide the team with an effective reminder of crucial deadlines, and can help the team plan ahead or map out a litigation strategy.

With time-based statutes of limitations and deadlines for filing pleadings, motions, and appeals, it is important that an accurate time line be constructed that reflects the type of case and the specific jurisdiction.

Integration with Case Management Software

As in other integrated software applications, CaseMap allows seamless transfer of data among applications. With the click of a menu option, attorneys can transfer data from CaseMap into TimeMap, a time-line graphic program from LexisNexis. TimeMap can be used alone or integrated with CaseMap. Exhibit 10.21 shows how a comparative time line might be displayed horizontally. Exhibit 10.22 shows a vertical view with graphics.

Exhibit 10.22 A TimeMap time line in a vertical view
with graphics

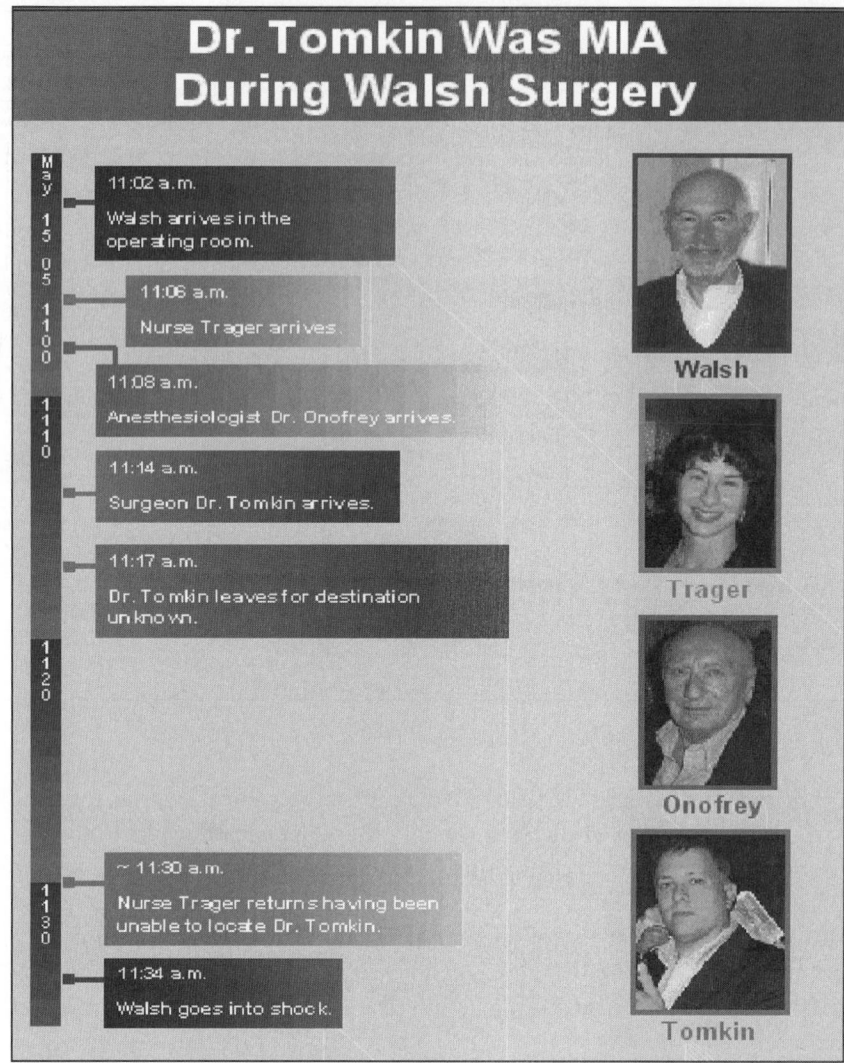

LexisNexis.

CaseMap

Creating a New Case File

Q: Any guidelines for naming my new case?

A: Only to note that you can use spaces, commas, and periods in the name, but you cannot use colons, quotation marks, slashes, or asterisks. The name you assign appears in CaseMap's title bar when you use the case.

Q: What does CaseMap do when I create a new case file?

A: When you create a case, CaseMap generates a new database that includes predefined fields for your facts, objects, issues, questions, and authorities. It then adds you to the Staff dialog box of the new case, sets your staff type to author, and creates for you the set of spreadsheet views, evaluation and link summary fields, and saves searches that authors have performed.

Case Template Overview

Q: Do I have to use the default CaseMap template when I create a new case file?

A: No. CaseMap lets you create case templates that you can use as the starting point for a new case.

Q: When I create a template, what information is retained from the case file that was used as the basis of the template?

A: Your case staff and any custom fields you've created in the case are always preserved. However, you can use options in the Template Wizard to determine whether facts, objects, issues, questions, or research records are kept as part of the template.

Q: When is it useful to create a custom template?

A: There are many circumstances where creating a custom case template can be of value. Here are two examples:

1. If you handle many cases of a particular type, create a custom case template that contains a standard outline of case issues, a standard list of initial questions, and any custom fields specific to that type of case.

2. If the same team of individuals works on every CaseMap case file, create a template that includes these persons as staff members. If you use this custom template as your default, you won't have to build the case staff each time you start a new case file.

Source: Copyright 2008 LexisNexis, a division of Reed Elsevier Inc. All Rights Reserved.

Learning Resources

LexisNexis CaseSoft provides extensive tutorial material for learning and using all of their programs. LexisNexis was among the first software vendors to use webinars for training (see Exhibit 10.23).

A **webinar** is a seminar produced and presented over the Internet for viewing at the user's computer (think web + seminar), in some cases with a separate

webinar
A program presented over the Internet for viewing at the user's computer.

Exhibit 10.23 CaseSoft webinar page

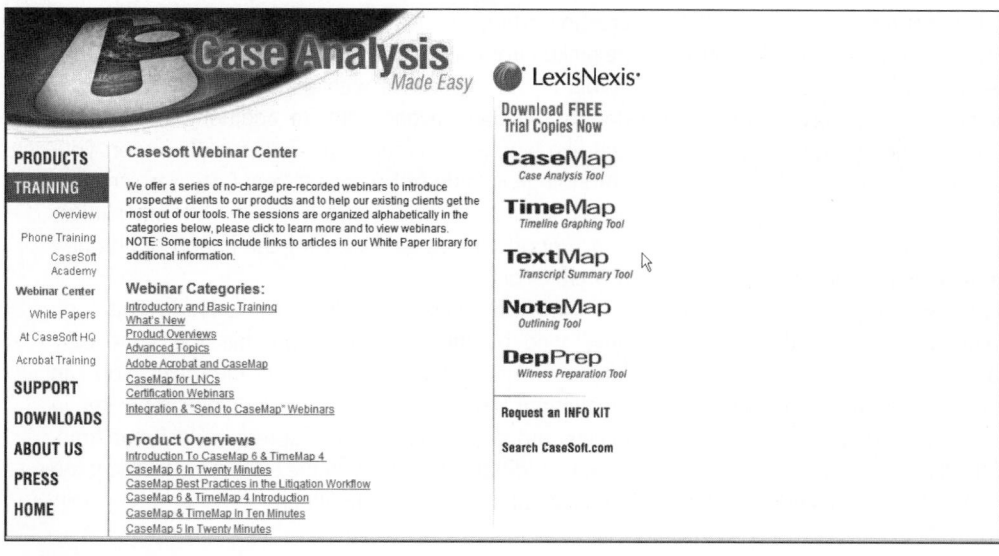

LexisNexis.

Webex viewer
A plug-in software program that allows the use of webinars.

telephone line for audio and feedback. CaseSoft has preserved all of its programs and made them available as webinars, as well as the needed Webex viewer. The **Webex viewer** is a plug-in specific to these programs.

ADVICE FROM THE FIELD

CREATING TIMELINES: POPULAR PRODUCT REVIEW
By Timothy A. Piganelli

In almost every case I work, the need for a timeline arises. Whether it is for the opening statement, a settlement conference or just a way to analyze the case amongst the trial team, a timeline is virtually always needed. Typically, a trial team creates a chronology of their case without realizing that they will eventually need to create a timeline visual. Whether it is the chronology of the documents in the case or a chronology of the facts in a case, a "chron" is always built. Similar to the way trial teams analyze cases, in chronological fashion, this is frequently the way the trial attorney introduces a case to a jury, or judge, or any tryer of fact. This visual representation is very important to the outcome of cases and as such, can become the underlying foundation for the flow of the case. It is very important that care be given in the creation of this important visual. Litigators struggle with how to create these timeline graphics in the most effective, easy and understandable way. How to create this visual and what to show on a timeline is critical. Here we will examine some of the do's and don'ts for creating these timelines, as well as visual aid tools that are available to assist with this very important task.

The first challenge is how to get a visual created. Having someone available to create a graphic timeline is the first step. Most legal professionals are not skilled at creating graphics. Many law firms rely on in-house graphic departments to assist with basic timeline graphics. The obvious choice is the in-house litigation support department, assuming one exists. They are usually the "go to person" for these needs. What if you don't have an in-house graphic expert? You can outsource the work, but that has an associated expense. That added expense might be more easily justified for the defense firms who can bill those services to the client, but for the plaintiff firms who must absorb these costs, trying to accomplish this task in-house is sometimes preferable.

Regardless of your situation, you still need to decide what you want the timeline to demonstrate and how you are going to integrate it into the presentation. Having a graphic is nice, but it must be tied to some oral presentation, either the opening statement, direct exam or in the closing argument. I am sure most of you will agree, a timeline is necessary for your case analysis and presentation. Bottom line, it is helpful to know how to generate these graphics on your own.

Creating Timelines—The Learning Curve

Fortunately, creating a timeline has been made easy by litigation support software developers and even a few non-legal applications. In my opinion, the easiest timeline software tool is TimeMap by CaseSoft. It remains one of the most popular tools on the market and at the top of any poll found in litigation support publications. CaseSoft has constantly improved this widely-used tool to keep up with the success of its litigation management tool, CaseMap.

This application is very easy to learn and to use. If you can type, you can use this tool. By simply adding dates and events to the New Fact Box, you can begin to create your timeline. As you key in dates and facts, your timeline automatically builds. TimeMap creates the base timeline for you and adjusts the time scale automatically. TimeMap is definitely a tool for the beginner. By picking a color scheme and template, you are on your way to creating a timeline. Most of your selections for style can be picked from pre-built templates. You can easily change colors and backgrounds with different gradients just by double clicking on an event. In addition, if you don't feel like typing, TimeMap will automatically import your chronological table or Fact Sheet from CaseMap, creating a timeline for you. It can also integrate with other litigation support applications allowing the import of chronology tables or lists.

TimelineExpress is equally easy to learn. This tool, developed by inData Corporation, has the same easy interface. Again, if you can type into the boxes, you can create your timeline. As shown below, you simply key in events and dates and TimelineExpress builds your timeline. In addition, as you key in the events and dates, it too automatically scales your timeline.

(continued)

PowerPoint, on the other hand, is really not timeline software, but rather a presentation software tool. Yet, it allows you to create practically any type of timeline you can conceive. The challenge is learning how to use PowerPoint to create these timelines. No question, PowerPoint is the more difficult timeline tool to learn, but the potential is almost limitless.

Attaching Exhibits to Timelines

Timelines used in court are frequently introduced during an opening statement. When presenting a timeline to a jury, it is important that the timeline, and any other graphic for that matter, have credibility. Each event depicted on the timeline should tie to a defensible source or have foundation behind the event. One of the best ways to show the founda-

tion behind each event is to tie the event with some sort of evidence in the case. In a timeline, a way to do this is to link the event with either a document exhibit or testimony.

Most of the tools mentioned above do an excellent job in allowing you to attach either images or multimedia. However, the best tool for this job is PowerPoint. Although it may not be the easiest tool to learn for this timeline application and the learning curve is greater, having exhibits zoom out from individual events on your timeline is very compelling....

About the Author: Timothy Piganelli is founder of Legal Technology Consulting, Inc. He is a nationally recognized speaker and author as well as one of the country's top trial consultants in the areas of trial strategies, trial presentation, courtroom technology, and computerized litigation support.

Source: The full article originally appeared in the *Litigation Support Today* November 2007/January 2008 issue. Reprinted with permission from Litigation Support Today magazine.

CONCEPT REVIEW AND REINFORCEMENT

KEY TERMS

case 261	e-repositories 261	trial notebook 260
case management system 266	intake form 269	Webex viewer 280
conflict report generator 269	time line 276	webinar 279

CHAPTER SUMMARY

Introduction to Case Organization and Management Software	Office management and case management functions overlap. Early versions of some software programs were individual applications, like calendar creation and maintenance programs. There is a trend toward integrating all of the desired functions of office and case management and organization into a single integrated master program. Effectively managing a case may involve reviewing, sorting, and marking for identification hundreds or even thousands of documents, photographs, and other graphics.
Case and Practice Management Software	Efficient use of a case management system provides all authorized members of the legal team with access to all the case information day or night. Computer systems today even permit members of the legal team to access the same information from remote locations. One of the tools in collaborative situations is the individual assessment of the importance of items in the case. Each member of the team must have the ability to input and use information for the tasks assigned to him or her.

Specialty Application Software Programs	Specialty applications programs combine different software programs to perform law office case and management functions. A case management software program offers a convenient method for organizing the parts of a case in a central repository that can be shared by all members of the legal team. CaseMap from LexisNexis CaseSoft is a case management and analysis software tool that functions as a central repository for critical case knowledge. Integrated software applications like CaseMap allow seamless transfer of data to other programs such as word processors.
Managing the Case	To the law office, cases are issues that a client has presented to a legal team to handle and resolve. A case file in a simple case may consist of only a few pages of information. In a more complex case, the case file may consist of thousands of documents and involve hundreds of people. Manual case management for the legal team may include the creation and use of a case notebook and a trial notebook. Case management software can be used to organize the cast of characters in a case, the documents, the relevant timetable, issues, legal authority, and other desired information. Different members of the legal team can obtain information and enter it into the case management software.
Using Case Management Systems	Complex litigation may involve millions of documents and hundreds of witnesses. The use of computers for email and document storage by businesses and government has caused a massive increase in the number of potential documents that may have to be reviewed, tracked, and made available. Case management systems permit collaboration among the members of the legal team.
Time Lines in Litigation	Time lines are chronological listings of the facts of a case and are frequently presented as a graphic representation.

REVIEW QUESTIONS AND EXERCISES

1. Describe how a trial notebook can assist a trial lawyer in preparing for trial. Give examples of three "tabs" that may be contained within the trial notebook.
2. What are some of the issues in using a "paper" trial notebook in a case in which more than one trial attorney is involved? How can using a "virtual" trial notebook avoid these issues?
3. What is the relationship between office management and case management software? What elements of office management software can be used to manage a specific case?
4. What is a data repository and how can it be used in litigation? Name three items of data that might be obtained from a data repository used in a case.
5. How were documents in complex litigation processed before the use of computers in litigation? How are paper forms still used today in connection with case management software?

6. Why is the maintenance of calendar dates critical to managing litigation? How can case management software help a team avoid missing deadlines?
7. How does a case management system aid in collaboration among the members of the legal team? What features can promote this collaboration?
8. How can a time line be used in the preliminary stage of a case? What information would be included in the time line?
9. How can a time line be used in the discovery or pleadings stage? What information would be included in the time line?
10. How can a time line assist an attorney in evaluating a case prior to settlement negotiations? How can a time line be used to present evidence to a jury?
11. What are the steps that may be taken in organizing a new case file? What information should be included initially? What information may be added later?

BUILDING YOUR PARALEGAL SKILLS

INTERNET AND TECHNOLOGY EXERCISES

1. Use a search engine to locate information on "case management software."
2. Prepare a list of the case management software programs that provide online tutorials for learning how to use the programs.
3. Visit the websites for the case management programs listed in this chapter. Determine the minimum operating requirements for a computer to run the software properly.
4. Locate information on companies that provide online document repository services.
5. Using LexisNexis TimeMap, create a time line using the facts in Case Study A in Appendix II.
6. Use LexisNexis CaseMap to set up a new file for Case Study A in Appendix II. Be sure to include all of the information that would be provided by a client interview and in a preliminary investigation of the case.

CHAPTER OPENING SCENARIO CASE STUDY

Use the Opening Scenario for this chapter to answer the following questions. A small law firm will be representing up to twenty plaintiffs in a school bus accident case where the defense will use product defect as a defense.

1. Prepare a memo for the lead attorney of the case explaining the issues in handling a case with many plaintiffs and potential witnesses. Explain how a case management program might be used to resolve these issues by helping to organize the case file.
2. What are the items that will need to be tracked using the case management program?

3. Answer the following questions raised by one of the attorneys. Explain your answers in a memo for the attorney's review.

   - "Can't we make our own database or spreadsheet to track the information and save money?"
   - "How will using a more expensive, pre-packaged specialty program be more cost effective?"
   - "How can using a program like CaseMap help in preparing for trial and during trial? What are the benefits of using this software in a case like this?"

CONTINUING CASES AND EXERCISES

Create a time line from the facts in Case Study A in Appendix II. Be sure to include every relevent fact in chronological order. Also include references to specfic documents that support each activity or event.

BUILDING YOUR PROFESSIONAL PORTFOLIO

Prepare a memo for the senior partner, using an informal memo format, explaining how a case management program might be used to organize a case. Specifically, explain how the program can help a trial attorney in each phase of the case:

- case intake
- investigation
- discovery
- settlement negotiations
- trial

"It's called fishing, man, not catching!"

—Denny Crane, Boston Legal

The Changing Face of Discovery and the Basics of E-Discovery

CHAPTER 11

OPENING SCENARIO

The partners and support staff of Mason, Marshall and Benjamin were having their weekly meeting. Following their usual agenda, new cases were discussed and follow-up assignments were made. Most of the work to date had concentrated on a few large federal court cases, each filed in a single forum. But a new case arrived that appeared to be much larger and more complex. After a discussion of the facts of the case, it appeared that jurisdiction existed in their state, in the adjacent state, as well as in federal court through diversity jurisdiction. The lawsuit involved product liability resulting from either an alleged manufacturing defect or an improper installation. The case would require extensive discovery of both the manufacturing records and the installation records. Each of the partners was admitted to the local and federal courts, as well as to the adjacent state court. Caitlin, the paralegal who was assigned to work on the case, indicated that she had never worked on any cases in either state court and asked if the rules were the same as those in the federal court she was accustomed to working in.

Owen Mason questioned whether Caitlin should work in a jurisdiction in which she had never handled a case. After some discussion, it was clear that everyone in the firm needed to understand the similarities and differences in the rules of the courts in which they practiced. Emily, the paralegal in the other office, suggested that it might be a good idea to put together a comparison of the differences in the rules, as well as the related opinions, to be sure the firm was choosing the correct jurisdiction to file suit.

LEARNING OBJECTIVES

After studying this chapter, you should be able to:

1. Define the term *discovery* and explain the purposes of discovery in litigation.

2. Describe how the federal rules have been changed to address the discovery of electronically stored information.

3. Describe the procedures and time periods for discovery under the federal rules.

4. Explain the purpose and the expected outcomes of the attorney "meet and confer" rule.

5. Explain the rules governing what information is discoverable.

6. Describe the function and use of depositions.

7. Explain how the litigation team can protect privileged or confidential information under the federal rules, and describe how the team can protect against the inadvertent disclosure of such information.

VIDEO INTRODUCTION

Professor Thomas F. Goldman, Esq.

THE CHANGING FACE OF DISCOVERY AND THE BASICS OF E-DISCOVERY
After watching the video in MyLegalStudiesLab, answer the following questions.

1. What is the fundamental purpose of discovery?
2. What new sources of evidence has technology created?

■ INTRODUCTION TO THE BASICS OF E-DISCOVERY

The fundamental purpose of discovery is to obtain evidence that may be used at trial, as well as information that may lead to evidence that may be used at trial. This purpose remains the same whether the legal team is dealing with paper or electronic documents. In the past, most documents produced in discovery were on paper. But today, the documents are increasingly in an electronic form. Initial changes in discovery practice were the result of the switch from paper to electronically stored information. As government, businesses, and individuals saved more of their records in electronic form, the discovery procedures had to be updated.

In the early days of personal computers, there were no standards for the creation and storage of electronic information. For example, some offices used WordPerfect for text documents, while others used Microsoft Word, and each program had its own electronic file format. In addition to these word processing programs were many lesser-known programs used in some major corporations. Added to these word processor variations were the many specialized formats used for the creation and storage of financial and other numerical data. Even today, there is still no universally accepted standard or common set of programs. Among the continuing issues is the inability of some programs to read the formats of other programs, or even different versions of the same program. In addition, there is no standard among the leading Apple, Microsoft, and Linux operating systems, which continue to compete for the personal computer market.

Advances in communication technology have created new sources of potential trial evidence in the form of video and sound recordings, emails, text messages, and social network data. Each type of media presents its own technical issues in locating, retrieving, and reviewing sources for evidence. As technology's playing field changes, the courts must establish rules for the discovery of electronically stored information. These rules must be crafted in a way that preserves affordable justice for all.

■ DISCOVERY IN THE TECHNOLOGICAL AGE

Discovery is a step in the litigation process where the plaintiff and defendant share information relevant to their dispute. The discovery process can be a time-consuming and sometimes frustrating phase in litigation, and managing that process requires a well-organized approach. Paralegals and litigation support specialists on the litigation team are often charged with coordinating discovery requests and responses from clients and opposing parties. If large volumes of electronic files are involved, they often need to work with information technology staff and outside technology experts.

PRACTICE TIP

Corel WordPerfect, unlike most of the other popular word processors, will open and save documents in virtually any format. In addition, documents may be opened in one format and saved in another.

discovery
A step in the litigation process where the plaintiff and defendant share information relevant to their dispute.

LEARNING OBJECTIVE 1
Define the term *discovery* and explain the purposes of discovery in litigation.

Successful discovery also requires a familiarity with the rules of court, and the rules relating to electronic files are becoming increasingly important. In December of 2006, e-discovery rules were added to the Federal Rules of Civil Procedure (Fed. R. Civ. P.). These new rules caused many in the legal field to look closely at how technology was changing traditional discovery practices.

If a document was originally created on paper, there may be only a single original copy of the document, or at most two or three copies. With electronic documents, however, it is easy to distribute hundreds of copies around the world with a single keystroke. These copies might in some cases be a rebroadcast of defamatory material, harassment, or other potentially incriminating information. They may be buried in a hard drive or a file server, waiting to be uncovered in the course of discovery.

The legal team must be prepared to address the issues associated with obtaining, retaining, preserving, and storing electronic information, whether representing a client in litigation or advising a client in general. This includes advising clients on the impact of the electronic discovery rules on business practices, especially electronic data retention policies. To facilitate this, the information technology (IT) professionals must be available to provide their expertise, and make available the necessary technology resources.

In order to be effective, the legal and IT staffs must be able to communicate with each other. Unfortunately, there is often a disconnect between lawyers and paralegals and the IT personnel that support them. Communication is sometimes impeded by the lack of clear legal standards or guidance in the rules pertaining to e-discovery.

■ PURPOSES OF DISCOVERY

Advances in technology have dramatically increased the availability and accessibility of information in discovery. But the basic purposes of discovery remain the same. Discovery is intended to help each litigant understand and evaluate the opponent's case, as well as the litigant's own. It is also meant to preserve testimony, and potentially facilitate settlement. For example, an attorney may learn information that may be used to impeach a witness because it shows inconsistencies in the witness's testimony.

The increased costs of electronic discovery are also forcing clients, attorneys, and the courts to look at ways of settling disputes more efficiently and economically. The benefits of settling earlier are given even greater consideration where the cost of the discovery phase alone can run into tens or hundreds of thousands of dollars.

ADVICE FROM THE FIELD _____

DISCOVERY LIFECYCLE AND BEST PRACTICES
©2006, Mark Lieb, *Ad Litem Consulting, Inc.*

Cost Codes

The discovery lifecycle is the lifeblood of the case. Every attorney should understand how their efforts, software and discovery will move the case forward from pleading to trial.

Every litigation technician should also understand how their own efforts and software benefit the legal team, helping to move the case forward. When both parties understand the full picture, the case has the greatest chance of success.

(continued)

(continued)

Planning

The attorney decides how to handle discovery during the pleading phase of a case based upon needs throughout the entire case. One must take the same approach to technical considerations. A technical treatment purchased during the pleading phase may only yield significant utility when the case reaches the deposition phase. Because each case follows the same case lifecycle, it is possible to create a technology plan that will address the needs of both the legal and technical worlds. Technical considerations extend to include software selection.

Non-Legal Considerations

Imagine litigating a case where a hot document cannot be moved from the review database to the exhibit program without involving a technician. This could mean a large turnaround time. Obviously it would be better to use software which allows the litigator and paralegal to perform this task with a few simple mouse clicks. This is a software lifecycle consideration.

About the Author: Mark R. Lieb is the President of Ad Litem Consulting and the author of the books *Litigation Support Department* and *Litigation Support Technical Standards*.

Source: Ad Litem Consulting, Inc.

Case Evaluation

By answering each other's questions, the parties share information about the facts, documents, statements, and expert witnesses related to the dispute. By openly sharing information that may be used at trial, each side is forced to evaluate its case and its opponent's case. Seeing all the available evidence allows each side to determine the ability to meet its respective burdens of proof. Drawing on prior experience or similar reported cases, each side can put a potential value on a trial outcome. In many instances, the decision to try or settle a case is a business decision. Thus the sides must ask whether the cost of a trial is outweighed by the potential recovery. If both sides are well prepared, their evaluations may be surprisingly close, and settlement may be within reach.

Preparing for Trial

If properly conducted, discovery can eliminate the potential for surprises in evidence presented at trial. Many of the "surprise" witnesses and evidence seen in television courtroom dramas would not be possible under actual court rules. Among these rules is the ethical obligation of fairness to opposing counsel and parties, which has been adopted in most states. Rules 3.4 of the Illinois Rules of Professional Conduct is set forth below.

ETHICAL Perspectives

ILLINOIS RULES OF PROFESSIONAL CONDUCT OF 2010
RULE 3.4: FAIRNESS TO OPPOSING PARTY AND COUNSEL

A lawyer shall not:

(a) unlawfully obstruct another party's access to evidence or unlawfully alter, destroy or conceal a document or other material having potential evidentiary value. A lawyer shall not counsel or assist another person to do any such act;

(b) falsify evidence, counsel or assist a witness to testify falsely, or offer an inducement to a witness that is prohibited by law;

(c) knowingly disobey an obligation under the rules of a tribunal, except for an open refusal based on an assertion that no valid obligation exists;

(d) in pretrial procedure, make a frivolous discovery request or fail to make reasonably diligent effort to comply with a legally proper discovery request by an opposing party;

(e) in trial, allude to any matter that the lawyer does not reasonably believe is relevant or that will not be supported by admissible evidence, assert personal knowledge of facts in issue except when testifying as a witness, or state a personal opinion as to the justness of a cause, the credibility of a witness, the culpability of a civil litigant or the guilt or innocence of an accused; or

(f) request a person other than a client to refrain from voluntarily giving relevant information to another party unless:

    (1) the person is a relative or an employee or other agent of a client; and

    (2) the lawyer reasonably believes that the person's interests will not be adversely affected by refraining from giving such information.

Adopted July 1, 2009, effective January 1, 2010.

Source: http://www.state.il.us/court/supremecourt/rules/art_viii/ArtVIII_NEW.htm#3.4

Facilitating Settlement

Properly conducted discovery facilitates settlements. Careful analysis of the evidence revealed through discovery enables the legal team to evaluate the client's case and that of the opposing side. Both sides are in a better position to evaluate their chances of success at trial based on the weight of evidence and the perceived credibility of witnesses.

Rules of Court and Rules of Evidence

Evidence that is permitted and evidence that is prohibited are both determined by the rules of procedure and the rules of evidence of each jurisdiction. In the federal courts, the Federal Rules of Civil Procedure (Fed. R. Civ. P.) provide the framework for conducting litigation. These rules may be supplemented by local court rules, as well as by any particular requirements and procedures of the assigned judge, such as those of U.S. District Judge Padova, shown in Exhibit 11.1.

The Federal Rules of Evidence (Fed. R. Evid.) are rules for determining what evidence may be introduced or admitted at trial. As stated by Judge Grimm below, admissibility "into evidence is determined by a collection of evidence rules." Some of these rules will also affect discovery, as will be discussed later in this chapter.

Civil litigation is a challenging and contentious business. But the rules of court, the ethical guidelines of the legal profession, and the rules of evidence are designed to create a level playing field. Like a professional baseball or football game, both sides need to know what the rules are and be able to expect the rules to be fairly applied. The judge is the interpreter and enforcer of the rules, similar to an umpire or referee. With a well-understood set of rules evenly and fairly applied, justice may be served, with both sides feeling they have had their day in court.

Exhibit 11.1 Policies and procedures of United States District Judge Padova

---

The Honorable John R. Padova
United States District Judge
Room 17613, U.S. Courthouse
601 Market Street
Philadelphia, PA 19106
215-597-1178
Fax: 215-580-2272

Deputies: **Gerrie Keane (Civil Case Management and Scheduling)**
Jenniffer Cabrera (Criminal Case Management and Scheduling)
Policies and Procedures

(Revised August, 2005)

. . . .

Discovery Conferences and Dispute Resolution
Judge Padova normally does not hold discovery conferences, but encourages the use of telephone conferences in lieu of motion practice to resolve discovery disputes. When a **discovery** *default* occurs, Judge Padova encourages counsel to file a motion to compel, which he will usually grant upon presentation pursuant to Local Civil Rule 26.1(g). When a **discovery** *dispute* occurs, and counsel have been unable to resolve it themselves or with Judge Padova's assistance by telephone, he requires a motion to compel. Judge Padova expects discovery to be voluntary and cooperative in accordance with the Federal Rules of Civil Procedure and the Plan.

Confidentiality Agreements
Parties may agree privately to keep documents and information confidential. The Court may enter an Order of Confidentiality only after making a specific finding of good cause based on a particularized showing that the parties' privacy interests outweight the public's right to obtain information concerning judicial proceedings. See Pansy v. Borough of East Stroudsburg, 23 F.3d 772, 786 (3d Cir. 1994).

Expert Witnesses
Counsel are required to identify expert witnesses and provide curriculum vitae and, as to all experts, voluntarily exchange the information referred to in Federal Rule of Civil Procedure 26(a)(2)(B) by expert report, deposition or answer to expert interrogatory in accordance with the dates outlined in the Court's scheduling orders. Except for good cause, expert testimony will be limited at trial to the information provided.

■ ELECTRONIC DOCUMENTS AND DISCOVERY

For hundreds of years, the documentation in legal cases was on paper. Documents were created by hand or with typewriters, and later on word processors, fax machines, or copiers. In a relatively short period of time, the computer and other electronic devices have enabled the creation of documents solely in electronic form. Documents that were formerly printed and placed in file folders in filing cabinets are now created and saved in electronic files and folders. Documents that were sent in paper form are now sent electronically, in some cases to hundreds of recipients, without anyone printing out a paper copy.

Requests for production and **interrogatories** are formal discovery requests. Requests for production seek the identification and physical location of relevant documents, or request copies of those documents. Interrogatories request written answers to questions, which in some cases may be substituted with the production of documents. In the age of paper discovery, the produced documents were

requests for production
Requests for production seek the identification and physical location of relevant documents, or request copies.

interrogatories
Interrogatories request written answers to questions, which in some cases may be substituted with the production of documents.

IN THE WORDS OF THE COURT...

Lorraine v. Markel American Insurance Company (Md. 5-4-2007)

Jack R. Lorraine and, Beverly Macke Plaintiffs v. Markel American Insurance Company Defendants.

CIVIL ACTION NO. PWG-06-1893.

United States District Court, D. Maryland.

May 4, 2007

Memorandum Opinion

PAUL GRIMM, Magistrate Judge

...Whether ESI is admissible into evidence is determined by a collection of evidence rules that present themselves like a series of hurdles to be cleared by the proponent of the evidence. Failure to clear any of these evidentiary hurdles means that the evidence will not be admissible. Whenever ESI is offered as evidence, either at trial or in summary judgment, the following evidence rules must be considered: (1) is the ESI **relevant** as determined by Rule 401 (does it have any tendency to make some fact that is of consequence to the litigation more or less probable than it otherwise would be); (2) if relevant under 401, is it **authentic** as required by Rule 901(a) (can the proponent show that the ESI is what it purports to be); (3) if the ESI is offered for its substantive truth, is it **hearsay** as defined by Rule 801, and if so, is it covered by an applicable exception (Rules 803, 804 and 807); (4) is the form of the ESI that is being offered as evidence an **original** or **duplicate** under the original writing rule, o[r] if not, is there admissible secondary evidence to prove the content of the ESI (Rules 1001-1008); and (5) is the probative value of the ESI substantially outweighed by the danger of **unfair prejudice** or one of the other factors identified by Rule 403....

relevant
That which tends to prove the existence of facts important to the resolution of a case or may lead to such evidence that is admissible.

usually photocopies, and often of poor quality. But in the electronic document world, the requests center on the sources, formats, and locations of the electronically stored documents.

The majority of litigation is small in scale, involving only a limited number of documents. But even in these cases, the handling and duplication of documents may be time consuming and costly. In some jurisdictions, local rules specify which party must pay the costs of duplication and delivery, or provide a formula for sharing costs. For example, the cost of a discovery request for a medical record from a medical provider may be shared, with each party paying half the total cost or paying for any copies each side requests.

With the increasing use of electronic alternatives for creating and storing documents, the number of paper copies has been reduced. However, the volume of documents has increased. For example, email is now the dominant form of written communication, and these messages are rarely reproduced as hard copy. In a large organization, such as a multinational corporation, the number of emails created and received daily may be in the thousands or tens of thousands. All of these communications may be discoverable, including all the messages received by persons that were copied on the emails. To give you an idea of the scope of this potential volume, Exhibit 11.2 shows the email patterns at Enron before its collapse.

Exhibit 11.2 Email patterns in Enron Corporation

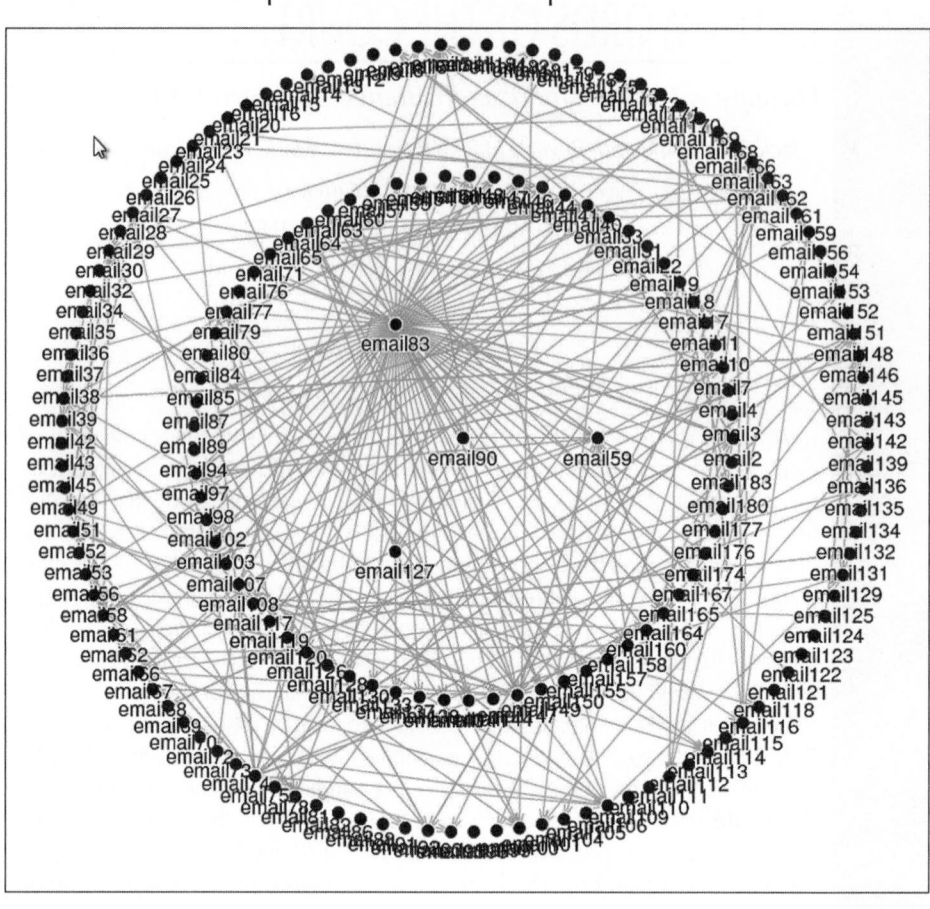

In major construction litigation, the conventional rolls of blueprints and other construction documents are being replaced by electronic files created with computer graphics programs and sent electronically to architects, builders, subcontractors, suppliers, and clients. When other items such as emails and word processor files are added to the body of documents, the number of items being handled in the litigation process may number in the thousands or more.

Discovery in Transition

The practice of law has long been based on tradition. Changes come slowly and are often accepted only as needed. Nevertheless, computer usage in business and in the law office has compelled a number of changes in the practice of law. In the view of some in the profession, computers have "burst" upon the scene—suddenly, everyone is sending emails and converting to paperless offices, and courts are requiring documents to be filed electronically. Businesses have come to depend on the computer for virtually every aspect of operation. Emails have replaced paper for most written communication, both in-house and with the outside. With computerized inventory systems, order placement and purchasing is done electronically, frequently without any paper being generated. Payments, too, are handled electronically by wire or electronic transfers between banks.

Many practitioners have been reluctant to recognize the importance of electronic documents, and those who did not grow up in the computer age have resisted change. But technology has evolved at an increasing pace and over a relatively short period of time. A few major cases have forced the profession to acknowledge that as electronic documents replace hard copies, procedures, policies, and methods must change. Because of the dominance of electronic documents, courts have also had to adapt to electronic discovery in order to maintain the orderly administration of justice.

■ AMENDMENTS TO THE FEDERAL RULES OF CIVIL PROCEDURE

The courts were initially slow in responding to technology. However, a few well-reasoned opinions of Judge Shira Scheindlin in the widely-reported *Zubulake* case, discussed later in this book, addressed the issues associated with **electronically stored information (ESI)** in discovery. These opinions offered a broad-based set of national standards for electronic discovery. In 2006, electronic discovery rules were finally adopted by the Federal Rules of Civil Procedure (Exhibit 11.3). These rules offered guidance on the issues surrounding discovery and provided a framework for requesting and satisfying requests for documents in electronic formats. These rules were further amended a year later to address new developments:

LEARNING OBJECTIVE 2
Describe how the federal rules have changed to address the discovery of electronically stored information.

electronically stored information (ESI)
Any type of information that can be stored electronically.

Rule 16 Pretrial Conferences; Scheduling; Management
...amendment to Rule 16(b) is designed to alert the court to the possible need to address the handling of discovery of electronically stored information early in the litigation if such discovery is expected to occur...

Rule 26 General Provisions Governing Discovery; Duty of Disclosure
...amended to direct the parties to discuss discovery of electronically stored information if such discovery is contemplated in the action....a party must disclose electronically stored information as well as documents that it may use to support its claims or defenses...

Rule 33 Interrogatories to Parties
...recognizing the importance of electronically stored information....the Rule 33(d) option should be available with respect to such records as well.
...Special difficulties may arise in using electronically stored information, either due to its form or because it is dependent on a particular computer system. Rule 33(d) allows a responding party to substitute access to documents or electronically stored information for an answer only if the burden of deriving the answer will be substantially the same for either party...

Rule 34 Production of Documents, Electronically Stored Information, and Things and Entry Upon Land for Inspection and Other Purposes
...amended to include discovery of data compilations, anticipating that the use of computerized information would increase...

Rule 37 Failure to Make Disclosures or Cooperate in Discovery; Sanctions
...absent exceptional circumstances, sanctions cannot be imposed for loss of electronically stored information resulting from the routine, good-faith operation of an electronic information system.

Rule 45 Subpoena
...amended to recognize that electronically stored information, as defined in Rule 34(a), can also be sought by subpoena....

Form 35 Report of Parties' Planning Meeting
...a report to the court about the results of this discussion. (under Rule 26)

Figure 11.3 Federal Rules of Civil Procedure- Numbering Scheme Reference Guide

Federal Rules of Civil Procedure –
Numbering Scheme Reference Guide

On December 1, 2007, the amendments to the numbering scheme of the Federal Rules of Civil Procedure (FRCP) became effective in an effort to improve the style of the rules, replacing long convoluted paragraphs with smaller subparts and headings.

The following chart summarizes the changes to the FRCP numbering scheme related to the electronically stored information (ESI) provisions.

Provision	Previous Rule	Current Rule
Contents of Pretrial Scheduling Order	16(b)(5)	16(b)(3)(B)
Initial Disclosures of ESI	26(a)(1)(B)	26(a)(1)(A)(ii)
Accessibility of ESI	26(b)(2)(B)	26(b)(2)(B)
Discovery Limitations – Nature and Extent	26(b)(2)(C)	26(b)(2)(C)
Claiming Work Product Privilege	26(b)(5)(A)	26(b)(5)(A)(i)-(ii)
Conference of the Parties – ESI Discovery Plan	26(f)(3)	26(f)(3)(C)
Production of ESI	34(a)(1)	34(a)(1)(A)
Party Requesting to Specify Form of ESI Production	34(b)	34(b)(1)(C)
Responding to Request for ESI	34(b)	34(b)(2)(D)
Producing ESI	34(b)	34(b)(2)(E)(i)-(iii)
Sanctions – Motion to Compel Disclosure	37(a)(2)(A)	37(a)(3)(A)
Sanctions – Motion to Compel Discovery Response	37(a)(2)(B)	37(a)(3)(B)
Sanctions – Payment of Expenses	37(a)(4)	37(a)(5)
Sanctions – Safe Harbor	37(f)	37(e)
Subpoena – Contents	45(a)(1)(C)	45(a)(1)(A)(iii)
Subpoena – Form of Production of ESI	45(a)	45(a)(1)(C)
Subpoena – Objections	45(c)(2)(B)	45(c)(2)(B)(i)-(ii)
Subpoena – Production of ESI	45(d)(1)	45(d)(1)(A)-(D)

TRIAL GRAPHIX
DISCOVERY • TRIAL CONSULTING • PRESENTATIONS

KROLL ONTRACK®

Kroll Ontrack.

PROCEDURES AND TIME LINES IN DISCOVERY

The federal rules provide a time line with a set of obligations that attorneys must follow. The discovery process starts with an attorney conference, and culminates in a meeting with the judge, as provided in Rule 16.

LEARNING OBJECTIVE 3
Describe the procedures and time periods for discovery under the federal rules.

Rule 16 Pretrial Conferences; Scheduling; Management

(a) Purposes of a Pretrial Conference.

In any action, the court may order the attorneys and any unrepresented parties to appear for one or more pretrial conferences for such purposes as:

(1) expediting disposition of the action;

(2) establishing early and continuing control so that the case will not be protracted because of lack of management;

(3) discouraging wasteful pretrial activities;

(4) improving the quality of the trial through more thorough preparation; and

(5) facilitating settlement.

(b) Scheduling.

(1) Scheduling Order.

Except in categories of actions exempted by local rule, the district judge—or a magistrate judge when authorized by local rule—must issue a scheduling order:

(A) after receiving the parties' report under Rule 26(f); or

(B) after consulting with the parties' attorneys and any unrepresented parties at a scheduling conference or by telephone, mail, or other means.

(2) Time to Issue.

The judge must issue the scheduling order as soon as practicable, but in any event within the earlier of 120 days after any defendant has been served with the complaint or 90 days after any defendant has appeared.

Insight on the significance of this rule may be found in the comments to the rules shown in Exhibit 11.4.

Exhibit 11.4 Comments of the judicial advisory committee on civil rules of practice and procedure

The Advisory Committee on Civil Rules of the Judicial Conference Committee on Rules of Practice and Procedure comments explain the reason for the change:

"The amendment to Rule 16(b) is designed to alert the court to the possible need to address the handling of discovery of electronically stored information early in the litigation if such discovery is expected to occur. Rule 26(f) is amended to direct the parties to discuss discovery of electronically stored information if such discovery is contemplated in the action. Form 35 is amended to call for a report to the court about the results of this discussion. In many instances, the court's involvement early in the litigation will help avoid difficulties that might otherwise arise."

Exhibit 11.5 Time line in federal court from filing the complaint to the scheduling conference

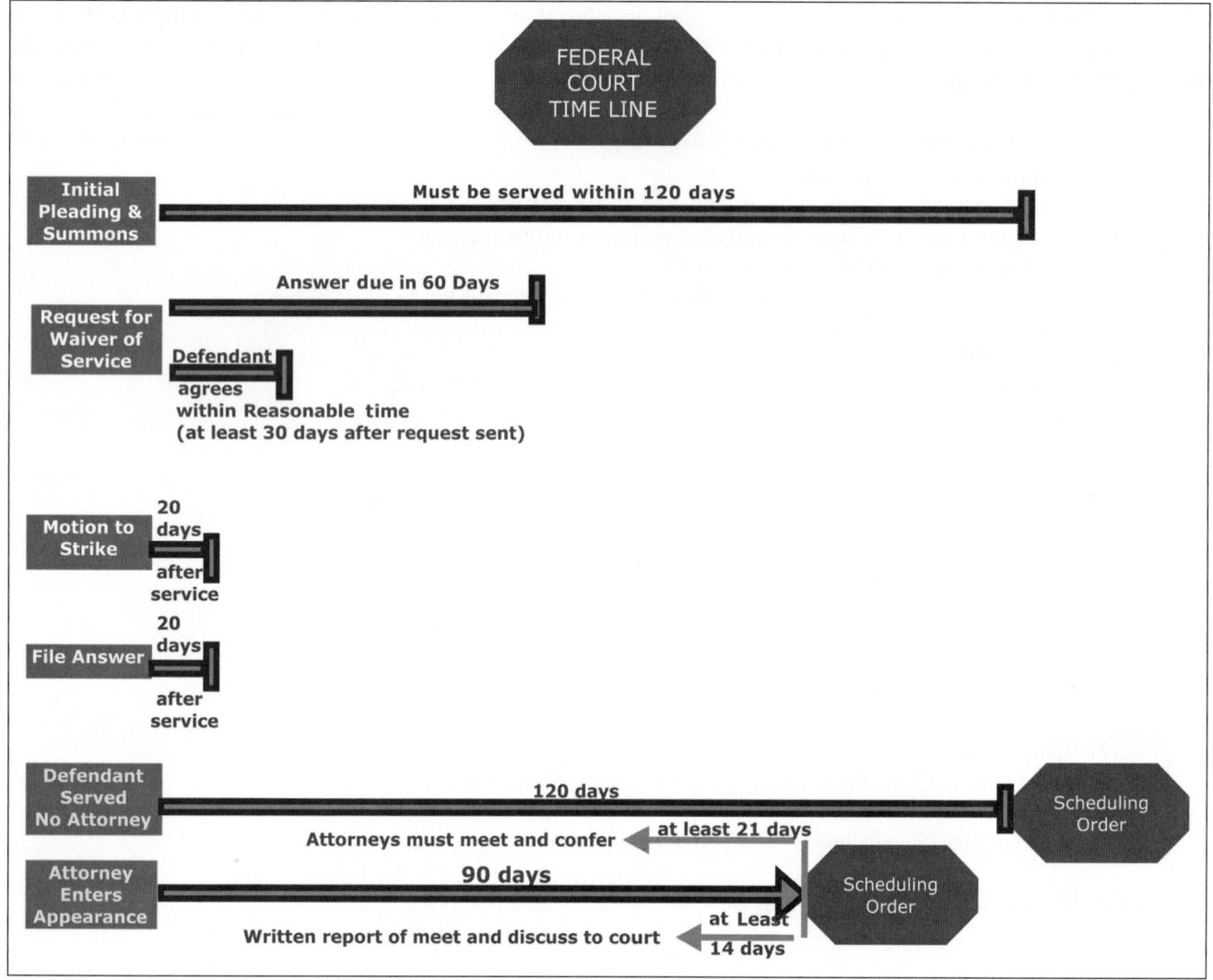

Attorney "Meet and Confer" Conference

The federal rules also set an initial time line for pretrial procedures, as shown in Exhibit 11.5.

Discovery may not begin until the lawyers have conferred and developed a proposed discovery plan, as required in Fed. R. Civ. P 26(f) and Fed. R. Civ. P 26(d). This "meet and confer" step is required before the scheduling conference with the assigned judge.

Fed. R. Civ. P. Rule 26. Duty to Disclose; General Provisions Governing Discovery

(d) **Timing and Sequence of Discovery.**

(1) Timing.

A party may not seek discovery from any source before the parties have conferred as required by Rule 26(f), except in a proceeding exempted from initial disclosure under Rule 26(a)(1)(B), or when authorized by these rules, by stipulation, or by court order.

(f) **Conference of the Parties; Planning for Discovery**

(1) Conference Timing.

Except in a proceeding exempted from initial disclosure under Rule 26(a)(1)(B) or when the court orders otherwise, the parties must confer as soon as practicable—and in any event at least 21 days before a scheduling conference is to be held or a scheduling order is due under Rule 16(b).

(2) Conference Content; Parties' Responsibilities.

In conferring, the parties must consider the nature and basis of their claims and defenses and the possibilities for promptly settling or resolving the case; make or arrange for the disclosures required by Rule 26(a)(1); discuss any issues about preserving discoverable information; and develop a proposed discovery plan. The attorneys of record and all unrepresented parties that have appeared in the case are jointly responsible for arranging the conference, for attempting in good faith to agree on the proposed discovery plan, and for submitting to the court within 14 days after the conference a written report outlining the plan. The court may order the parties or attorneys to attend the conference in person.

The scheduling conference occurs within 90 days after the **entry of appearance** by the attorney who will represent the defendant (or 120 days after the defendant is served with the complaint). The meet and confer must occur at least 21 days before the scheduling conference with the judge, thereby allowing 99 days for the meet and confer session. Following the meet and confer conference, a written statement memorializing the items discussed must be submitted to the court within 14 days.

The meet and confer conference is between the attorneys, without a judge present. The goal of the conference is to discuss the nature of the claims and likelihood of settlement, to arrange for mandatory disclosure under Rule 26(a), and to develop a discovery plan if one is necessary. It affords them the opportunity to amicably agree on a discovery schedule that can be submitted to the court. This process of discussing and planning discovery is particularly important in complex litigation and in those cases involving large volumes of electronically stored information.

The meet and confer meeting is closely linked to the Rule 16(b) scheduling conference with the judge. The judge will usually take an active role in setting a time line for discovery and trial, but the attorneys have an opportunity to be involved in that process by issuing the report of their conference and participating in the scheduling conference with the judge. The judge will usually give great deference to the recommendation of the attorneys in scheduling deadlines for discovery.

entry of appearance
An attorney for one of the litigants files papers officially identifying himself or herself as representing the client before the court.

■ ISSUES INVOLVING MEET AND CONFER

The meet and confer conference is supposed to result in a discovery plan as outlined in Fed. R. Civ. P. Rule 26, shown below.

LEARNING OBJECTIVE 4
Explain the purpose and expected outcomes of the attorney "meet and confer" conference.

Fed. R. Civ. P. Rule 26. Duty to Disclose; General Provisions Governing Discovery

(f) Conference of the Parties; Planning for Discovery

(3) Discovery Plan.

A discovery plan must state the parties' views and proposals on:

(A) what changes should be made in the timing, form, or requirement for disclosures under Rule 26(a), including a statement of when initial disclosures were made or will be made;

(B) the subjects on which discovery may be needed, when discovery should be completed, and whether discovery should be conducted in phases or be limited to or focused on particular issues;

(C) any issues about disclosure or discovery of electronically stored information, including the form or forms in which it should be produced;

(D) any issues about claims of privilege or of protection as trial-preparation materials, including—if the parties agree on a procedure to assert these claims after production—whether to ask the court to include their agreement in an order;

(E) what changes should be made in the limitations on discovery imposed under these rules or by local rule, and what other limitations should be imposed; and

(F) any other orders that the court should issue under Rule 26(c) or under Rule 16(b) and (c).

In a case that does not involve electronic documents, the attorney can prepare for a conference with opposing counsel by reviewing the client's records and the investigative file. The attorneys can then simply come to the conference with a list of parties to be deposed and records sought from the other side.

In cases with many electronic documents, preparation is not as simple. Demands for access and delivery of electronic data require a technological skill set that many lawyers do not possess. Lawyers for the most part are trained in the procedural and substantive areas of law, not in the science of computer data storage. Without an understanding of the methods of storage used by the client, the location and format of the files, and other technical issues, lawyers may find themselves agreeing to a document production plan that is either physically impossible or extremely costly. A growing number of skilled litigators will bring to the meet and confer conference a member of the IT or litigation support staff who is knowledgeable in the procedures and methods of e-discovery. This assistance can ensure that proper requests are made, and realistic plans agreed to. When clients have unique or complex computer systems, a person familiar with the technical aspects of the clients' system may also be brought in to offer insight and guidance.

Form 52 from the Fed. R. Civ., shown in Exhibit 11.6, may be used to complete the report to the court of the meet and confer meeting.

WEB RESOURCES

The form may be downloaded from the U.S. Courts website in WordPerfect or MS Word format at http://www.uscourts.gov/RulesAndPolicies/FederalRulemaking/RulesAndForms/IllustrativeCivilRulesForms.aspx

LEARNING OBJECTIVE 5

Explain the rules governing what information is discoverable.

■ THE SCOPE OF DISCOVERY

The documents that may be obtained in discovery are not limited to the items that will be used in trial. The general rule is that anything that may lead to relevant evidence is discoverable. In many cases, the actual items that will be used as evidence in trial may not be obvious at the outset of the case. The proverbial "smoking gun" evidence may be found indirectly after looking through a series of seemingly innocuous documents, one leading to another, and eventually pointing to the relevant, admissible document.

Under Rule 26 of the Federal Rules of Civil Procedure, information is discoverable if it is not privileged, and it is relevant or may lead to relevant evidence:

(b) **Discovery Scope and Limits.**

  (1) Scope in General.

      Unless otherwise limited by court order, the scope of discovery is as follows: Parties may obtain discovery regarding any nonprivileged matter that is relevant to any party's claim or defense—including the existence, description, nature, custody, condition, and location of any documents or other tangible things and the identity and location of persons who know of any discoverable matter. For good cause, the

Exhibit 11.6 Form 52, report of the parties' planning meeting

---

UNITED STATES DISTRICT COURT
for the
<_____> DISTRICT OF <_____>

<Name(s) of plaintiff(s)>,   )
)
Plaintiff(s)   )
)   Civil Action No. <number>
v.   )
)
<Name(s) of defendant(s)>,   )
)
Defendant(s)   )

REPORT OF THE PARTIES' PLANNING MEETING

1. The following persons participated in a Rule 26(f) conference on <Date> by <State the method of conferring>:
   <Name>, representing the <plaintiff>
   <Name>, representing the <defendant>

2. Initial Disclosures. The parties [have completed] [will complete by <Date>] the initial disclosures required by Rule 26(a)(1).

3. Discovery Plan. The parties propose this discovery plan:
   <Use separate paragraphs or subparagraphs if the parties disagree.>
   (a) Discovery will be needed on these subjects: <Describe>.
   (b) <Dates for commencing and completing discovery, including discovery to be commenced or completed before other discovery.>
   (c) <Maximum number of interrogatories by each party to another party, along with the dates the answers are due.>
   (d) <Maximum number of requests for admission, along with the dates responses are due.>
   (e) <Maximum number of depositions by each party.>
   (f) <Limits on the length of depositions, in hours.>
   (g) <Dates for exchanging reports of expert witnesses.>
   (h) <Dates for supplementations under Rule 26(e).>

4. Other Items:
   (a) <A date if the parties ask to meet with the court before a scheduling order.>
   (b) <Requested dates for pretrial conferences.>
   (c) <Final dates for the plaintiff to amend pleadings or to join parties.>
   (d) <Final dates for the defendant to amend pleadings or to join parties.>
   (e) <Final dates to file dispositive motions.>
   (f) <State the prospects for settlement.>
   (g) <Identify any alternative dispute resolution procedure that may enhance settlement prospects.>
   (h) <Final dates for submitting Rule 26(a)(3) witness lists, designations of witnesses whose testimony will be presented by deposition, and exhibit lists.>
   (i) <Final dates to file objections under Rule 26(a)(3).>
   (j) <Suggested trial date and estimate of trial length.>
   (k) <Other matters.>

Date: <Date>   <Signature of the attorney or unrepresented party>
                                      _____
                                      <Printed name>
                                      <Address>
                                      <E-mail address>
                                      <Telephone number>

Date: <Date>   <Signature of the attorney or unrepresented party>
                                      _____
                                      <Printed name>
                                      <Address>
                                      <E-mail address>
                                      <Telephone number>

Source: http://www.uscourts.gov/uscourts/RulesAndPolicies/Rules/Usable_Rules_Forms_Civil/CIV52-Report_of_the_Parties-_Planning_Meeting.wpd

IN THE WORDS OF THE COURT...

Louis H. Hopson, et al. Plaintiffs,

v.

The Mayor and City Council of Baltimore, A Municipal Corporation
of the State of Maryland, and

the Baltimore City Police Department, Defendants.

UNITED STATES DISTRICT COURT FOR THE DISTRICT OF MARYLAND

232 F.R.D. 228; 244–245

November 22, 2005, Decided

... as this case graphically demonstrates, it is no longer acceptable for the parties to defer good faith discussion of how to approach discovery of electronic records until they have complied with the briefing schedule in Local Rule 104.8. Rather, as the proposed changes to Rule 16(f) make clear, counsel have a duty to take the initiative in meeting and conferring to plan for appropriate discovery of electronically stored information at the commencement of any case in which electronic records will be sought. In the absence of any guidance in the court's scheduling order, or in the local rules of court, the parties are not without resources that will assist them in determining what to discuss at their meeting. Indeed, the newly revised Civil Discovery Standards for the American Bar Association Section on Litigation 40 contain detailed information about the issues that the parties should discuss in their effort to agree upon an electronic records discovery plan. At a minimum, they should discuss: the type of information technology systems in use and the persons most knowledgeable in their operation; preservation of electronically stored information that may be relevant to the litigation; the scope of the electronic records sought (i.e. e-mail, voice mail, archived data, back-up or disaster recovery data, laptops, personal computers, PDA's, deleted data); the format in which production will occur (will records be produced in "native" or searchable format, or image only; is metadata sought); whether the requesting party seeks to conduct any testing or sampling of the producing party's IT system; the burdens and expenses that the producing party will face based on the Rule 26(b)(2) factors, and how they may be reduced (i.e. limiting the time period for which discovery is sought, limiting the amount of hours the producing party must spend searching, compiling and reviewing electronic records, using sampling to search, rather than searching all records, shifting to the producing party some of the production costs); the amount of pre-production privilege review that is reasonable for the producing party to undertake, and measures to preserve post-production assertion of privilege within a reasonable time; and any protective orders or confidentiality orders that should be in place regarding who may have access to information that is produced.

It cannot be emphasized enough that the goal of the meeting to discuss discovery is to reach an agreement that then can be proposed to the court. The days when the requesting party can expect to "get it all" and the producing party to produce whatever they feel like producing are long gone. In many cases, such as employment discrimination cases or civil rights cases, electronic discovery is not played on a level field. The plaintiff typically has relatively few electronically stored records, while the defendant often has an immense volume of it. In such cases, it is incumbent upon the plaintiff to have reasonable expectations as to what should be produced by the defendant....

court may order discovery of any matter relevant to the subject matter involved in the action. Relevant information need not be admissible at the trial if the discovery appears reasonably calculated to lead to the discovery of admissible evidence. All discovery is subject to the limitations imposed by Rule 26(b)(2)(C).

The scope of information that may be obtained through the discovery process is considerably broader than that which may be admissible at trial under the Federal Rules of Evidence. Any item of information is **relevant** for purposes of discovery where it has a relationship to evidence about the litigation and is likely to lead to admissible evidence. For discovery purposes, an item of information need not meet the requirements of the Rules of Evidence for admission at trial. But in order to be admitted at trial, the information must survive additional scrutiny, such as the Requirement of Authentication or Identification under Fed. R. Evid. Rule 901.

> **Federal Rules of Evidence Rule 901. Requirement of Authentication or Identification**
>
> **(a) General provision.**
> The requirement of authentication or identification as a condition precedent to admissibility is satisfied by evidence sufficient to support a finding that the matter in question is what its proponent claims.

Mandatory Disclosure Requirements

Fed. R. Civ. P. Rule 26(a) makes mandatory the disclosure of certain basic information supporting a party's claims, information that for years was available only after a formal written discovery request was issued. Before the passage of this rule, no action was taken in many cases until one side moved the litigation forward with a formal discovery request. Under the current rule, everything the legal team intends to rely upon to prove its claims must be disclosed early in the litigation. Lack of time to investigate the claim is not a valid excuse for failure to comply. The benefits of mandatory disclosure are twofold:

1. to promote early evaluation and settlement of claims
2. to reduce the time and cost of formal discovery

While the new rules contemplate a specific time frame for mandatory disclosure, they do permit the attorneys to agree to some other time frame. The attorneys may agree to extend that time, but the judge at the scheduling conference may encourage them to conclude discovery at a faster pace.

From a practical standpoint, the plaintiff's legal team must be prepared for disclosure at or shortly after the filing of the complaint. The investigation that might have occurred after filing suit under prior rules must now be completed before filing suit. For the defense team, the time to investigate and comply is very short, and there is no time for procrastination in investigating and establishing defenses.

PRACTICE TIP

In criminal cases, the prosecution must turn over to the defense all exculpatory information in its possession. See *Brady v. Maryland,* 373 U.S. 83, 87 (1963).

Information Subject to Mandatory Disclosure

Almost anything relied upon in developing the claim must be disclosed, regardless of whether it is admissible at trial. This disclosure includes the identity of witnesses, copies of documents, a computation of damages, and a copy of any insurance policy that may be used to satisfy a judgment obtained in the litigation.

The computation of damages often reveals the plaintiff attorney's thought process, and under prior rules was not released as part of discovery pursuant to the work product doctrine. Under the current rule, however, the attorney's value on the case must be made known within months after the complaint is filed.

From the defense standpoint, the disclosure of insurance coverage is a significant change from the prior rule. Insurance information is not admissible at trial, and yet the existence of limits of insurance coverage is a key element in settling many cases. The chances of settlement are enhanced with both a realistic calculation of damages and the availability of insurance being known within months of filing the lawsuit.

Expert Witnesses

expert witness
A person qualified by education, training, or experience to render an opinion based on a set of facts that are outside the scope of knowledge of the fact finder.

Expert witnesses that either party expects to call at trial must be identified during discovery. A copy of the expert's qualifications must also be provided to the other side, as must a list of the expert's publications from the preceding ten years, a statement of compensation, and a list of other cases in which the expert has testified. The most critical element to be shared is the written report of the expert's opinion. This report reveals what the expert is expected to say at trial. The written report must include the opinion of the expert, the basis of that opinion, the information relied upon, and any assumptions made in rendering the opinion. These disclosures must be made at least ninety days prior to trial. Parties must also supplement the disclosures if the expert makes material changes or additions to the opinion, as set forth in Rule 26(e)(2) and shown in Exhibit 11.7.

Many lawsuits become a battle of the experts. If a party wishes to call an expert to rebut the opinion of his or her opponent's expert, that expert must be disclosed within thirty days of receipt of the opponent expert's report. The early disclosure of these experts and their opinions will often lead to early resolution of the case.

Limiting Provisions

There are some general limitations on discovery that are imposed by the federal rules. These provisions seek to eliminate duplicative, burdensome, and oppressive discovery requests. Requests are considered duplicative or burdensome when the information sought has already been provided or is more easily obtained from another source.

Duty to Supplement

Another obligation that continues throughout the litigation is the duty to supplement or revise responses should additional or different information become

Exhibit 11.7 Rule requiring the duty to supplement disclosures of expert opinions

> **Fed. R. Civ. P. Rule 26.**
> Duty to Disclose; General Provisions Governing Discovery
>
> (e) Supplementation of Disclosures and Responses.
>
> (2) Expert Witness.
>
> For an expert whose report must be disclosed under Rule 26(a)(2)(B), the party's duty to supplement extends both to information included in the report and to information given during the expert's deposition. Any additions or changes to this information must be disclosed by the time the party's pretrial disclosures under Rule 26(a)(3) are due.

PRACTICE TIP

To advise on trial preparation issues, some law firms hire independent experts (whom they do not intend to call as witnesses), in order to protect the information as work product.

Exhibit 11.8 Federal rule providing for the supplementation of discovery

---

Fed. R. Civ. P. Rule 26.
Duty to Disclose; General Provisions Governing Discovery
(e) Supplementation of Disclosures and Responses.
  (1) In General.
      A party who has made a disclosure under Rule 26(a)—or who has responded to an interrogatory, request for production, or request for admission—must supplement or correct its disclosure or response:
      (A) in a timely manner if the party learns that in some material respect the disclosure or response is incomplete or incorrect, and if the additional or corrective information has not otherwise been made known to the other parties during the discovery process or in writing; or
      (B) as ordered by the court.

---

known. A typical example is an answer to an interrogatory that indicates the identity and address of a witness. If it is learned that a witness has relocated, that information must be shared with opposing counsel. The duties to supplement discovery responses are set forth in Fed. R. Civ. P. Rule 26(e)(1), as shown in Exhibit 11.8.

Production of Documents or Things

Production of documents or things under Rule 34 makes available for discovery documents and other physical objects, like defective products, that are relevant to the lawsuit, as set forth in Exhibit 11.9. The party must respond in writing to each request. The response may also include a paper (hard copy) or electronic copy of the documents or the items requested. Examples include medical records

Exhibit 11.9 Rule providing for production of documents and physical objects

---

Rule 34. Producing Documents, Electronically Stored Information, and Tangible Things, or Entering onto Land, for Inspection and Other Purposes
(a) In General.

A party may serve on any other party a request within the scope of Rule 26(b):

(1) to produce and permit the requesting party or its representative to inspect, copy, test, or sample the following items in the responding party's possession, custody, or control:
    (A) any designated documents or electronically stored information—including writings, drawings, graphs, charts, photographs, sound recordings, images, and other data or data compilations—stored in any medium from which information can be obtained either directly or, if necessary, after translation by the responding party into a reasonably usable form; or
    (B) any designated tangible things; or

(2) to permit entry onto designated land or other property possessed or controlled by the responding party, so that the requesting party may inspect, measure, survey, photograph, test, or sample the property or any designated object or operation on it.

of an injured plaintiff, a copy of a liability insurance policy, a police accident report, or an employee personnel file.

Where the "thing" is not capable of delivery, such as a building or other large object, Rule 34 includes the right to enter onto the land of another for purposes of inspection. This discovery tool may also be used in cases where the volume of documentary evidence or electronic records is too large for practical delivery, such as a warehouse with thousands of cartons of paper files. Opposing counsel or their staff may be permitted to enter the facility to review the documents. If it is believed that discoverable information exists on a hard drive or file server, the rules also permit inspection of the device. If the opposing party believes that relevant information may have been erased or not delivered, a forensic expert may be used to inspect and search the storage media. An example of a Rule 34 request is shown in Exhibit 11.10.

Exhibit 11.10 Civil Form 50, Request to Produce Documents and Tangible Things, or to Enter onto Land Under Rule 34

UNITED STATES DISTRICT COURT
for the
<_____> DISTRICT OF <_____>

<Name(s) of plaintiff(s)>,
Plaintiff(s)   )   Civil Action No. <Number>
v.   )
<Name(s) of defendant(s)>,
Defendant(s)

REQUEST TO PRODUCE DOCUMENTS AND TANGIBLE THINGS,
OR TO ENTER ONTO LAND UNDER RULE 34

The plaintiff <Name> requests that the defendant <Name> respond within <____> days to the following requests:

1. To produce and permit the plaintiff to inspect and copy and to test or sample the following documents, including electronically stored information:

    <Describe each document and the electronically stored information, either individually or by category.>

    <State the time, place, and manner of the inspection and any related acts.>

2. To produce and permit the plaintiff to inspect and copy—and to test or sample—the following tangible things:

    <Describe each thing, either individually or by category.>

    <State the time, place, and manner of the inspection and any related acts.>

3. To permit the plaintiff to enter onto the following land to inspect, photograph, test, or sample the property or an object or operation on the property.

    <Describe the property and each object or operation.>

    <State the time and manner of the inspection and any related acts.>

Date: <Date>

<Signature of the attorney or unrepresented party>
_____

<Printed name>
<Address>
<E-mail address>
<Telephone number>

Source: http://www.uscourts.gov/RulesAndPolicies/FederalRulemaking/RulesAndForms/IllustrativeCivilRulesForms.aspx

■ DEPOSITIONS

Depositions allow parties to directly question parties and witnesses, under oath, without the limitation of carefully prepared, written answers to interrogatories. Depositions are, within the confines of court rules and procedures, opportunities to ask open-ended questions, obtain spontaneous responses, and follow up with additional questions. The costs of taking depositions can be significant. In addition to the fees of counsel and their assistants, a court reporter must be hired to transcribe the testimony. In videotaped depositions, the costs may also include one or more videographers or technicians, and in some cases the cost of videoconferencing connections. Depositions are provided for in Fed. R. Civ. P. Rule 30, set forth in Exhibit 11.11.

Videotaped depositions are used in many cases to preserve the testimony of a witness who might otherwise be unable to attend the trial. For example, a witness who is ill or of an advanced age may not be physically able to attend the trial, or an expert witness may not be able to wait to be called to testify because of personal or professional schedules.

Because of their potential use in trial, these depositions are conducted with the same formality of a trial proceeding, with the witness sworn in and the lawyers asking questions and making objections. However, unlike in trial, any objections are addressed by the court after the deposition is concluded but before presentation in court. The rules for the conduct of a deposition are shown in Exhibit 11.12.

LEARNING OBJECTIVE 6
Describe the function and use of depositions.

Exhibit 11.11 The federal rule providing for the taking of depositions

> **Rule 30. Deposition by Oral Examination**
> (b) Notice of the Deposition; Other Formal Requirements.
>   (1) Notice in General.
>   A party who wants to depose a person by oral questions must give reasonable written notice to every other party. The notice must state the time and place of the deposition and, if known, the deponent's name and address. If the name is unknown, the notice must provide a general description sufficient to identify the person or the particular class or group to which the person belongs.

Exhibit 11.12 Federal rules for the conduct of a deposition

> **Rule 30. Deposition by Oral Examination**
> (c) Examination and Cross-Examination; Record of the Examination; Objections; Written Questions.
>
>   (1) Examination and Cross-Examination.
>   The examination and cross-examination of a deponent proceed as they would at trial under the Federal Rules of Evidence, except Rules 103 and 615. After putting the deponent under oath or affirmation, the officer must record the testimony by the method designated under Rule 30(b)(3)(A). The testimony must be recorded by the officer personally or by a person acting in the presence and under the direction of the officer.
>
>   (2) Objections.
>   An objection at the time of the examination—whether to evidence, to a party's conduct, to the officer's qualifications, to the manner of taking the deposition, or to any other aspect of the deposition—must be noted on the record, but the examination still proceeds; the testimony is taken subject to any objection. An objection must be stated concisely in a nonargumentative and nonsuggestive manner. A person may instruct a deponent not to answer only when necessary to preserve a privilege, to enforce a limitation ordered by the court, or to present a motion under Rule 30(d)(3).

Rule 30(b). Deposition

In cases involving corporate or institutional defendants, it is critical to depose a representative of the organization who is actually knowledgeable about the issues of the case. Not every corporate officer or employee has the knowledge that may be needed. The problem for the opposing party is identifying the appropriate person with the required information. The person being deposed must be able to identify the sources of discoverable information and the methods used to create, store, and retrieve what may be needed. In the era of paper documents, the appropriate person may have been an office manager or records custodian. But in cases where electronically stored documents are involved, the proper person may be an IT specialist who has knowledge of the office network and file architecture.

The party responding to the deposition request may also have the burden of producing the correct person. As stated in the *Heartland Surgical v. Midwest Division*:

> For a Rule 30(b)(6) deposition to operate effectively, the deposing party must designate the areas of inquiry with reasonable particularity, and the corporation must designate and adequately prepare witnesses to address these matters. If the rule is to promote effective discovery regarding corporations the spokesperson must be informed. 2007 WL 1054279 (D. Kan. 2007)

Failure to properly present a responsive witness who can answer questions about the company's electronic filing systems can result in sanctions, including costs incurred by the requesting party.

IN THE WORDS OF THE COURT...

Covad Communications Company v. Revonet, Inc. (D.C. 3-31-2010)

Covad Communications Company, Plaintiff, v. Revonet, Inc., Defendant.

Civil Action No. 06-1892 (CKK/JMF).

United States District Court, D. Columbia.

March 31, 2010

...As I have stated before, one of the "primary purposes of the Rule 30(b)(6) deposition is to 'curb the 'bandying' by which officers or managing agents of a corporation are deposed in turn but each disclaims knowledge of the facts that are clearly known to the organization and thereby to it.'" Banks, 241 F.R.D. at 372-73 (citing Fed. R. Civ. P. 30(b)(6) advisory committee notes). Accordingly, upon receiving notice of the deposition that contains a description, with reasonable particularity, [of] the matters on which examination is requested, a corporation must: (1) designate a deponent knowledgeable on the topic; (2) designate multiple deponents if more than one is necessary to respond to all designated topics; and (3) prepare the deponent so that he or she can testify on matters both within his or her personal knowledge as well as those "reasonably known by the responding entity." Banks, 241 F.R.D. at 373 (citing *Alexander v. Fed. Bureau of Investigation,* 186 F.R.D. 137, 139-41 (D.D.C.1998)). A court "must guard against the gamesmanship of a company avoiding deposition topics by, for example, naming as a 30(b)(6) witness a person who knows nothing about the topics and does nothing to inform himself about them so that his deposition threatens to be a series of cynical 'I do not know' statements." Banks, 241 F.R.D. at 375 (citing In re *Vitamins,* 216 F.R.D. at 168)....

■ COMPLIANCE AND COURT INTERVENTION

Theoretically, the process of discovery should be accomplished in a cooperative fashion without court intervention. Often that is not the case. Whatever the reason, a response to discovery requests is often delayed—or, worse, forgotten. Thus the litigation team must be sure they have a system in place to comply with discovery deadlines. That means establishing an internal calendaring system and obtaining client cooperation. At those times when it is not possible to comply, the litigation team needs to know the steps to take to obtain an extension of the time. If the delay is due to the opposing party, they must also know how to seek court intervention to make their opponent comply.

VIDEO ADVICE FROM THE FIELD

Charlotte Harris—Manager of Litigation Support, Hess Oil
A discussion of the challenges of litigation support.
After watching the video in MyLegalStudiesLab, answer the following questions.

What are the personal skills required to be successful in litigation support?

Complying With Discovery Requests

The litigation paralegal or support staff will typically have primary responsibility for the preparation of responses within the specified time frame. It is crucial to develop a procedure that ensures client participation and cooperation in the preparation of responses. In cases involving e-discovery, a meeting with the client should be arranged to determine the client's file sources, locations, types, formats, and retention policies. Sufficient data must be obtained to allow the attorney to attend the meet and confer conference with enough information to properly work out a meaningful discovery plan and timetable.

Obtaining Compliance with Discovery Requests

It may be necessary to seek relief from the court when the responding party is not cooperative. In some cases, noncooperation may be due to the opponent's recalcitrance. But often, the party is not able to comply with the agreement made at the meet and confer conference because his or her attorney was unfamiliar with the client's system. Before granting any orders compelling compliance, the court will almost always ask whether a good faith attempt has been made. In many cases, counsel may demand delivery of documents that the opposing counsel considers confidential or work product. If the documents are not supplied in response to the request even after good faith attempts have been made, they often became the subject of motions to compel disclosure. A sample motion to compel and order is shown in Exhibit 11.13.

Most judges disfavor involvement in the discovery process. The mindset of the bench is that counsel should be able to resolve these issues without court

Exhibit 11.13 Sample motion to compel and order

UNITED STATES DISTRICT COURT NORTHERN DISTRICT OF NEW YORK

B.K., a minor by her

Parents and Guardians,
Janice Knowles and
Steven Knowles,   Plaintiff

v.

Harry Hart,
Kinnicutt Bus Company,
Charles Stanley, and
MVF Construction Company,
          Defendants

No.: _____

PLAINTIFF'S MOTION TO
COMPEL DEFENDANT
KINNICUTT BUS COMPANY
ANSWERS TO INTERROGATORIES

Attorney ID No. 124987

Plaintiff in the action files this Motion for relief and alleges as follows

1. On May 15, 2008, Plaintiff served by first class mail Interrogatories addressed to the Defendant Kinnicutt Bus Company.
2. Answers to the Interrogatories were due on June 17, 2008.
3. On June 20, 2008 counsel for plaintiff contacted defense counsel by telephone and follow-up letter to ascertain the reason for delay in response and to obtain a time frame within which answers would be provided. Defense counsel indicated an additional 30 days was required. A true and correct copy of the letter dated June 20, 2008 is attached as Exhibit A.
4. On July 25, 2008 more than 30 days had passed and still answers to Interrogatories were outstanding. Plaintiff counsel attempted to telephone and left numerous messages for defense counsel, none of which were returned.
5. On August 1, 2008 plaintiff's counsel issued a letter advising defense counsel of the intention to file the within Motion to compel. A true and correct copy of the letter dated August 1, 2008 is attached as Exhibit B.
6. To date, Defendant has neither answered nor objected to the Interrogatories.
7. To date, Defendant has filed neither a Motion for Enlargement of Time to Respond nor a Motion for a Protective Order.
8. Plaintiff has incurred costs in conjunction with seeking the compliance of Defendant Kinnicutt. Attached as Exhibit C is an affidavit of the time expended in informal means of contacting defendant as well as for the preparation, filing, service of the within motion.

WHEREFORE, it is respectfully requested this Honorable court enter an order compelling defendant to issue answers to interrogatories within 10 days and prohibiting objection to answer and awarding attorneys fees and costs in a reasonable sum.

Respectfully submitted,
Mason, Marshall and Benjamin
ATTORNEYS FOR PLAINTIFF

_____

Ethan Benjamin, Esquire
Attorney ID #
Mason, Marshall and Benjamin
Address,
Albany,
New York
Phone
Fax
Email

(continued)

Exhibit 11.13 Continued

UNITED STATES DISTRICT COURT NORTHERN DISTRICT OF NEW YORK

B.K., a minor by her	No.: _____
Parents and Guardians,	PLAINTIFF'S MOTION TO
Janice Knowles and	COMPEL DEFENDANT
Steven Knowles, Plaintiff	KINNICUTT BUS COMPANY
	ANSWERS TO INTERROGATORIES
v.	
Harry Hart,	
Kinnicutt Bus Company,	
Charles Stanley, and	
MVF Construction Company,	Attorney ID No. 124987
Defendants	

ORDER

AND NOW this _____ day of _____, 2008 the matter having been brought before the court on Plaintiff's Motion to Compel and after consideration of the Reply and the hearing on this matter it is hereby

ORDERED that Defendant KINNICUTT Bus Company shall within ten (10) days of the date hereof answer completely, fully and without objection the Interrogatories served upon it by the Plaintiff on May 15, 2008. Failure to comply with the terms of this order will result in the imposition of sanctions in accordance with Fed. R. Civ. P. 37;

FURTHER ORDERED Defendant Kinnicutt shall within ten (10) days of the date hereof pay to plaintiff the sum of $500, the reasonable attorney's fees and costs associated with obtaining compliance with the discovery request.

BY THE COURT

_____

---

intervention. Many practitioners find that court intervention is like a trip to the principal's office after a disagreement on the school bus—it is unpleasant, and leaves a bad impression on the authority figure. It is therefore advisabl e to anticipate problems that might arise in the discovery process, resolve them during the Rule 26(f) conference, and document the agreement as to discovery issues via the scheduling order.

▇ PROTECTING CONFIDENTIAL OR PRIVILEGED MATERIALS

The attorney has an ethical obligation to preserve the confidences of clients, as required by Rule 1.6 of the ABA Model Rules of Professional Conduct. Prior to disclosure, lawyers, paralegals, and law clerks routinely scan every document to find anything considered confidential, subject to the attorney–client privilege, or protected from disclosure under the work product doctrine. In litigation involving technology, some information may include trade secrets or proprietary processes. Additional protections must be sought to avoid delivering such documents.

Fed. R. Civ. P. Rule 26 specifically recognizes that parties may withhold information otherwise discoverable, and it provides within the rule a framework for the

LEARNING OBJECTIVE 7
Explain how the litigation team can protect privileged or confidential information under the federal rules, and describe how the team can protect against the inadvertent disclosure of such information.

Exhibit 11.14 Fed. R. Civ. P. 26(5)(A) and (B) procedures for claiming protection for privileged or work product materials

---

Rule 26. Duty to disclose; General provisions governing discovery

(b) Discovery Scope and Limits.

(5) Claiming Privilege or Protecting Trial-Preparation Materials.

(A) *Information Withheld*. When a party withholds information otherwise discoverable by claiming that the information is privileged or subject to protection as trial-preparation material, the party must:

   (i) expressly make the claim; and

   (ii) describe the nature of the documents, communications, or tangible things not produced or disclosed—and do so in a manner that, without revealing information itself privileged or protected, will enable other parties to assess the claim.

(B) *Information Produced*. If information produced in discovery is subject to a claim of privilege or of protection as trial preparation material, the party making the claim may notify any party that received the information of the claim and the basis for it. After being notified, a party must promptly return, sequester, or destroy the specified information and any copies it has; must not use or disclose the information until the claim is resolved; must take reasonable steps to retrieve the information if the party disclosed it before being notified; and may promptly present the information to the court under seal for a determination of the claim. The producing party must preserve the information until the claim is resolved.

---

process, as shown in Exhibit 11.14. Parties may also reach an agreement on how to handle privileged or confidential material that has been inadvertently disclosed. If the parties reach such an agreement on inadvertent disclosure, Fed. R. Civ. P. Rule 16 allows the court to make this agreement part of the court's scheduling order.

Privilege in Electronic Discovery

Withholding the document claimed to be privileged may sound as simple as not giving it to anyone. With paper documents, this may be true. However, in the age of electronics it is easy to accidentally send a privileged document by email or fax just by tapping "send" or pushing the wrong speed dial number. With vast quantities of data transferred electronically, the matter becomes even more complicated. How do you determine which of the thousands of potential documents are privileged?

Claim of Privilege

Privilege is not automatically invoked. The person claiming the privilege—usually the client—has the burden of establishing its existence by making a **claim of privilege.**

claim of privilege
The person claiming the privilege—usually the client—has the burden to establish its existence.

> "To sustain a claim of privilege, the party invoking it must demonstrate that the information at issue was a communication between client and counsel or his employee, that it was intended to be and was in fact kept confidential, and that it was made in order to assist in obtaining or providing legal advice or services to the client." *SR International Bus. Ins. Co v. World Trade Center* Prop No 01 Civ 9291 (S.D.N.Y. 2002), quoting *Browne of New York City, Inc v. Ambase Corp.*

privilege log
A list of documents claimed by the submitting party to contain material subject to privilege or work product exclusion.

To claim a document as privileged requires the submission of a **privilege log** identifying the item and the reason for the privilege, as shown in Exhibit 11.15.

Exhibit 11.15 Privilege log

Date	Author	Recipient	Document Description	Privilege
02/01/08	C. Fredeen. PDC Eng.	F. Bailey, GOV	6:59 am *E-mail re Request for Reappointment for Craig Freeden to AELS Board	Deliberative Process/Executive
01/24/08	D. Ogg	F. Bailey, GOV	9:21 am *E-mail re Education	Deliberative Process/Executive
02/01/08	D. Ogg	F. Bailey, GOV	8:32 am *E-mail re Education	Deliberative Process/Executive
02/01/08	S. Leighow, GOV	F. Bailey, GOV	8:46 am *E-mail re Appointment of member to the state Board of Game	Deliberative Process/Executive
02/01/08	S. Parnell, GOV	S. Palin, GOV	7:41 am *E-mail re Andrew Halcro	Deliberative Process/Executive
02/01/08	S. Parnell, GOV	F. Bailey, GOV K. Perry, GOV T. Palin	8:22 am *E-mail re Andrew Halcro	Deliberative Process/Executive
02/01/08	S. Palin, GOV	F. Bailey, GOV K. Perry, GOV T. Palin	8:28 am *E-mail re Andrew Halcro	Deliberative Process/Executive
02/01/08	S. Palin, GOV	F. Bailey, GOV K. Perry, GOV T. Palin	8:30 am *E-mail re Andrew Halcro	Deliberative Process/Executive
02/01/08	I. Frye, GOV	S. Palin, GOV F. Bailey, GOV K. Perry, GOV T. Palin	8:42 am *E-mail re Andrew Halcro	Deliberative Process/Executive
02/01/08	S. Palin, GOV	I. Frye, GOV K. Perry, GOV F. Bailey, GOV T. Palin	10:10 am *E-mail re Andrew Halcro	Deliberative Process/Executive
02/01/08	I. Frye, GOV	S. Palin, GOV F. Bailey, GOV K. Perry, GOV T. Palin	10:23 am *E-mail re Andrew Halcro	Deliberative Process/Executive

311

Exhibit 11.16 The claw-back provision in the federal rules

> **Rule 16. Pretrial Conferences; Scheduling; Management**
>
> **(3) Contents of the Order.**
>
> (A) *Required Contents.* The scheduling order must limit the time to join other parties, amend the pleadings, complete discovery, and file motions.
>
> (B) *Permitted Contents.* The scheduling order may:
>
> (iv) include any agreements the parties reach for asserting claims of privilege or of protection as trial-preparation material after information is produced....

Claw-Back Provisions

When vast numbers of electronic files are delivered as part of the discovery process, it may not always be possible, within the limited time frames required for compliance, to check each of the documents before handing them over to opposing counsel. Many times the documents will be part of an answer to a request for electronically stored documents that will be delivered on computer tape, CD, DVD, or other computer storage media. The electronic documents delivered may contain confidential material, like emails between attorney and client, work product materials, or a client's proprietary information or trade secret. Courts have recognized this problem, and some jurisdictions have rules providing for a **claw-backprovision** as part of the discovery plan. Exhibit 11.16 shows the claw-back provision in FRCP 16.

In theory, a claw back, or **non-waiver agreement,** allows a party to recover privileged or confidential material that is inadvertently disclosed, without waiver of privilege or confidentiality. The use of the claw-back agreement alone does not relieve the attorney of his or her obligations regarding confidential client information. The legal team must still take the necessary steps to protect the confidences of clients. The claw back is only a safety device in the event there

claw-back provision
A provision contained in the report of counsels' meet and confer and included in the court's scheduling order that describes what to do with privileged materials that are disclosed inadvertently through e-discovery. The provision should address return of the materials and waiver of the privilege.

non-waiver agreement
[Author to provide definition in pages]

IN THE WORDS OF THE COURT...

Victor Stanley, Inc., Plaintiff v. Creative Pipe, Inc., et al., Defendant
CIVIL ACTION NO. MJG-06-2662
UNITED STATES DISTRICT COURT FOR THE DISTRICT OF MARYLAND
2008 U.S. Dist. LEXIS 42025
May 29, 2008, Decided

... the Defendants initially sought to enter a non-waiver agreement such as discussed in *Hopson,* but then abandoned this effort. Should the issue of privilege waiver by inadvertent production of voluminous ESI be considered by the Fourth Circuit at some time in the future, it may be hoped that the court will be cognizant of the unique problems presented with regard to avoiding privilege waiver presented by ESI discovery, as well as the fact that the approval of Proposed Evidence Rule 502 by the Committee on the Rules of Evidence, as well as the Judicial Conference, recognizes a need to provide relief in this difficult area. The substantive law of privilege is not rigid and inflexible, *Hopson,* 232 F.R.D. at 240 (citing *Jaffee v. Redmond,* 518 U.S. 1, 8, 116 S. Ct. 1923, 135 L. Ed. 2d 337 (1996)), [*23] but is governed by principles of the common law as interpreted "by the courts of the United States in the light of reason and experience." *Fed. R. Evid. 501.* Experience has now shown that ESI discovery presents unique, heretofore unrecognized, risks of waiver of privilege or work-product protection even when the party asserting the privilege or protection has exercised care not to waive it. The approval of Proposed Evidence Rule 502 by the Judicial Conference, is a reasoned response to this new experience, but still pending in Congress. For those courts that have yet to decide which approach to follow regarding the inadvertent disclosure of privileged material during ESI discovery, the commentary to the proposed rule is worthy of consideration.

...As noted in *Continental Casualty Co. v. Under Armour, Inc.,* 537 F. Supp. 2d 761 (D. Md. 2008), if documents qualify as both attorney-client privileged and work-product protected, separate analysis is required to determine whether inadvertent production constitutes waiver. However, the majority view is that disclosure of work-product material in a manner that creates a substantial risk that an adversary will receive it waives the protection. *Id. at 772-73* [*24] (citing *Restatement (Third) of the Law Governing Lawyers § 91* (2000)). In this case, Defendants' voluntary, though inadvertent, production of the 165 documents directly to counsel for the Plaintiff waived any work-product protection they may have had. *Id....*

is inadvertent disclosure even after reasonable methods have been used to otherwise protect and preserve confidential material.

Limits on the Waiver of Privilege by Inadvertent Disclosure: FRE Rule 502

In large-scale e-discovery, it is often impossible for the litigation team to review every file for privileged or confidential information. **There is always a potential that privileged, confidential, or work product material may be inadvertently disclosed, regardless of the safeguards implemented by counsel.** To address the issue at the federal level, Congress passed an amendment to the Federal Rules of Evidence in 2008. The new rule, FRE Rule 502, has provided a framework for limiting the potential waiver of attorney–client privilege for inadvertently disclosed documents.

It was hoped that Rule 502 would resolve the issue and provide uniformity in the rules regarding inadvertant disclosure. However, it is not a complete solution, and the protection it affords is uncertain as courts continue to interpret this new rule. As with most laws and rules of court, it is now being challenged and tested by lawyers unsatisfied with the court's application of this rule to their particular case. However, acceptance of the new rule is growing among the litigation bar, and its philosophy and provisions are being incorporated in the langage of discovery scheduling orders. The text of the rule is shown in Exhibit 11.17.

Exhibit 11.17 Federal Rules of Evidence Rule 502

Fed. R. Evid. Rule 502. Attorney-Client Privilege and Work Product; Limitations on Waiver

(a) Scope of waiver.

In federal proceedings, the waiver by disclosure of an attorney-client privilege or work product protection extends to an undisclosed communication or information concerning the same subject matter only if that undisclosed communication or information ought in fairness to be considered with the disclosed communication or information.

(b) Inadvertent disclosure.

A disclosure of a communication or information covered by the attorney-client privilege or work product protection does not operate as a waiver in a state or federal proceeding if the disclosure is inadvertent and is made in connection with federal litigation or federal administrative proceedings—and if the holder of the privilege or work product protection took reasonable precautions to prevent disclosure and took reasonably prompt measures, once the holder knew or should have known of the disclosure, to rectify the error, including (if applicable) following the procedures in Fed. R. Civ. P. 26(b)(5)(B).

(c) Selective waiver.

In a federal or state proceeding, a disclosure of a communication or information covered by the attorney-client privilege or work product protection—when made to a federal public office or agency in the exercise of its regulatory, investigative, or enforcement authority—does not operate as a waiver of the privilege or protection in favor of non-governmental persons or entities. The effect of disclosure to a state or local government agency, with respect to non-governmental persons or entities, is governed by applicable state law. Nothing in this rule limits or expands the authority of a government agency to disclose communications or information to other government agencies or as otherwise authorized or required by law.

(d) Controlling effect of court orders.

A federal court order that the attorney-client privilege or work product protection is not waived as a result of disclosure in connection with the litigation pending before the court governs all persons or entities in all state or federal proceedings, whether or not they were parties to the matter before the court, if the order incorporates the agreement of the parties before the court.

(e) Controlling effect of party agreements.

An agreement on the effect of disclosure of a communication or information covered by the attorney-client privilege or work product protection is binding on the parties to the agreement, but not on other parties unless the agreement is incorporated into a court order.

(f) Included privilege and protection.

As used in this rule:

(1) "attorney-client privilege" means the protection provided for confidential attorney-client communications, under applicable law; and

(2) "work product protection" means the protection for materials prepared in anticipation of litigation or for trial, under applicable law.

IN THE WORDS OF THE COURT...

Ruling on Plaintiff's Motion to Compel and Motion for Protective Order

Breon v. Coca-Cola Bottling Company of New England, (Conn. 2005)

Civil No. 3:04-CV-00374(CFD)(TPS).

United States District Court, D. Connecticut.

November 4, 2005

Thomas Smith, Magistrate Judge

... B. Attorney-Client & Work-Product Claims

To protect from abuse, discovery must have limiting principles aside from the low threshold of relevance. One of these principles is that matters are not discoverable, under certain circumstances, if they are privileged. Fed. R. Civ. P.

26(b)(1). Here, the defendant claims that a number of requests for production are inappropriate because they ask for information protected by either the attorney-client privilege or work-product doctrine.

The attorney-client privilege prevents disclosure of a communication from a client to a lawyer, where that communication relates to a fact of which the attorney was informed (a) by his client (b) without the presence of strangers (c) for the purpose of securing primarily either (i) an opinion on the law or (ii) legal services or (iii) assistance in some legal proceeding, and not (d) for the purpose of committing a crime or tort; and (4) the privilege has been (a) claimed and (b) not waived by the client. *United States v. United Shoe Machinery Corp.,* 89 F.Supp. 357, 358 (D. Mass. 1950); *Colton v. United States,* 306 F.2d 633, 637 (2d Cir. 1962). The rationale behind the privilege is to foster open and honest communication between a client and his lawyer. *United States v. Schwimmer,* 892 F.2d 237, 443 (2d Cir. 1989). Because of this underlying rationale, communication running from the lawyer to the client is not protected unless it reveals what the client has said. *SCM Corp. v. Xerox Corp.,* 70 F.R.D. 508, 522 (D. Conn. 1976); *Clute v. Davenport Co.,* 118 F.R.D 312, 314 (D. Conn. 1988).

Completely distinct from the attorney-client privilege is the work-product doctrine. The work-product doctrine, as codified in the Federal Rules[,] states: a party may obtain discovery of documents and tangible things otherwise discoverable...and prepared in anticipation of litigation or for trial by or for another party or by or for that other party's representative (including the other party's attorney, consultant, surety, indemnitor, insurer, or agent) only upon a showing that the party seeking discovery has substantial need of the materials in the preparation of the party's case and that the party is unable without undue hardship to obtain the substantial equivalent of the materials by other means.

Fed. R. Civ. P. *26*(b)(3). "The work-product doctrine...is intended to preserve a zone of privacy in which a lawyer can prepare and develop legal theories and strategy with an eye toward litigation, free from unnecessary intrusion by his adversaries." *United States v. Adlman,* 134 F.3d 1194, 1196 (2d. Cir. 1998) (internal quotations omitted). As the rule itself makes clear, work-product enjoys only limited immunity from discovery. For "fact" work-product, that is[,] work-product that does not contain legal opinions or conclusions, the party seeking discovery must meet the "substantial burden" and "undue hardship" tests outlined in Rule 26. *Maloney v. Sisters of Charity Hosp.,* 165 F.R.D. 26, 30 (W.D.N.Y. 1995). Opinion work product, on the other hand, constitutes thoughts, strategies, legal opinions and conclusions by an attorney. *See Loftis v. Amica Mut. Ins. Co.,* 175 F.R.D. 5, 11 (D. Conn. 1997). Opinion work-product is given stronger protection and only discoverable in rare circumstances where the party seeking discovery can show extraordinary justification. *Id.; S.N. Phelps & Co. v. Circle K. Corp.,* 1997 U.S. Dist. LEXIS 713, No. 96 CV 5801 (JFK), 1997 WL 31197, at *7 (S.D.N.Y. 1997).

Under both the attorney-client privilege and work-product doctrine the party asserting the claim has the initial burden of showing it applies. *See Cornelius v. Consolidated Rail Corp.,* 169 F.R.D. 250, 253 (N.D.N.Y. 1996) (party claiming work-product protection must show three elements, "[f]irst, the material must be a document or tangible thing. Second, it must have been prepared in anticipation of litigation. Third, it must have been prepared by or for a party or its representative."); *In re Horowitz,* 482 F.2d 72, 82 (2d Cir.), *cert denied,* 414 U.S. 867 (1973) ("the person claiming the attorney-client privilege has the burden of establishing all essential elements").

To assist the court and counsel, both Federal and Local Rules require that the party asserting a privilege provide the court with a privilege log. Fed. R. Civ. P. *26*(B)(5); D. Conn. L.Civ. R. 37(a)(1) When a party withholds information

(continued)

otherwise discoverable under these rules by claiming that it is privileged or subject to protection as trial preparation material, the party shall make the claim expressly and shall describe the nature of the documents, communications, or things not produced or disclosed in a manner that, without revealing information itself privileged or protected, will enable other parties to assess the applicability of the privilege or protection.

Fed. R. Civ. Pro. *26*(B)(5). A party seeking to avoid discovery cannot hide behind bald statements of "privilege" and "work-product" and expect the court to supply the rational to support the claims. *See Obiajulu v. City of Rochester Dep't of Law,* 166 F.R.D. 293, 295 (W.D.N.Y. 1996). At the very least, the log should identify each document's author and recipient, as well as reasons why the information is claimed to be privileged. *See United States v. Construction Prod. Research,* 73 F.3d 464, 473 (2d Cir. 1996). The privilege log is not simply a technicality, it is an essential tool which allows the parties and the court to make an intelligent decision as to whether a privilege or immunity exists. *See Bowne v. Ambase,* 150 F.R.D. 465, 474 (S.D.N.Y. 1993). Preparation of a privilege log is a critical step in discharging one's burden of establishing the existence of a privilege.

ADVICE FROM THE FIELD

SAILING ON CONFUSED SEAS

Privilege Waiver and the New Federal Rules of Civil Procedure
John M. Facciola

VII. THE FUTURE

Lawyers and judges face a difficult future in dealing with privileged information stored in a computer's memory. As server space increases and the cost of memory decreases, the tendency of computer users to save everything and organize none of it will increase. As noted earlier, the new Federal Rules justify extremely limited relief in one situation, the "claw back," and leave other solutions, including "sneaking a peek" or agreements as to [a] waiver, where it found them. Furthermore, waiver agreements cannot bind the rights of strangers to the litigation and, therefore, are full of peril where third-person litigation against one of the parties to the agreement is even a remote possibility. Indeed, the Tenth Circuit recently rejected a claim that disclosure to a government agency of computer information, pursuant to a confidentiality agreement, was not a waiver of the privilege as to third parties. That result is sobering not only for its rejection of any notion of the legitimacy of any kind of "selective waiver," but also for

its insistence that the attorney-client privilege not be extended an inch further than necessary to accomplish its purposes and its niggardly reading of the circumstances under which waiving it can be avoided. Thus, it can be said that, without the dramatic intervention of a new rule adopted by Congress providing that disclosure pursuant to court-ordered agreements is not a waiver, lawyers will have to confront the reality that their clients either (1) authorize what may be a king's ransom to do a full-scale privilege review or (2) permit them to enter into an agreement that eliminates the need for such a detailed review and take the risk that the agreement will not prevent a third party from seeing privileged information.

Perhaps an answer may lie in the technology. Word processing is now dominated by two companies and one wonders why they have not sought to market a program that would prevent a user from saving a document unless the user indicated that it was privileged. Electronic marking of such documents and their segregation into a privileged file would, at least, narrow what must be reviewed.

Absent the technology, one wonders when American corporations will adopt records retention policies that are reasonable, applicable without exception in all departments, and enforced by a corporate manager with real

(continued)

power to discipline those employees who refuse to follow them. It is hard to imagine a greater waste of money than paying a lawyer $250 an hour to look at recipes, notices of the holiday party, and NCAA Final Four pool entries while doing a privilege review. A company that permits that situation to occur is wasting its shareholders' money as surely as if it were burning it in the parking lot.

In the meantime, the staggering costs of a privilege review will grow, driving the costs of litigation ever upward and probably increasing the tendency of parties to avoid the federal courts for other fora to resolve their disputes. One thing is certain: without relief from somewhere, that associate will never sail on the Chesapeake Bay.

About the Author: John M. Facciola is a United States Magistrate Judge in the United States District Court for the District of Columbia in re *Qwest Comm. Int'l, Inc.,* 450 F.3d 1179 (10th Cir. 2006).

Source: © The Federal Courts Law Review.

CONCEPT REVIEW AND REINFORCEMENT

KEY TERMS

CHAPTER SUMMARY

Introduction to the Basics of E-Discovery	The law of discovery has not changed with the adoption of electronically stored information; only the methods used to obtain the information have changed.

Amendments to the Federal Rules of Civil Procedure	Effective December 2006 and since amended in 2007 are six new rules and one new form or attitude toward the Federal Rules of Civil Procedure used to address the issues of electronic discovery, including:
	    Rule 16 Pretrial Conferences; Scheduling; Management
	    Rule 26 General Provisions Governing Discovery; Duty of Disclosure
	    Rule 33 Interrogatories to Parties
	    Rule 34 Productions of Documents, Electronically Stored Information, and Things and Entry Upon Land for Inspection and Other Purposes
	    Rule 37 Failure to Make Disclosures or Cooperate in Discovery; Sanctions
	    Rule 45 Subpoena
	    Form 35 Report of Parties' Planning Meeting

Procedures and Time Lines in Discovery	The federal rules provide a time line and a set of obligations including an initial conference between counsel and a report to the court in a meeting with the trial judge.
Attorney "Meet and Confer" Conference	The scheduling conference occurs within 90 days after the entry of appearance or 120 days after the defendant has been served with the complaint. Counsel must meet at least 21 days before the scheduling conference with the judge and submit a report to the court within 14 days.
Issues Involving Meet and Confer	A primary purpose of the meet and confer is to develop a discovery plan.
The Scope of Discovery	Under the federal rules, everything is discoverable that is not privileged and that is or may lead to relevant evidence.
Mandatory Disclosure Requirements	Federal Rule 26(a) makes disclosure of certain information mandatory.
Information Subject to Mandatory Disclosure	Disclosures include identity of witnesses, copies of documents, computation of damages, and copies of insurance policies.
Expert Witnesses	The names of expert witnesses expected to be called, together with their qualifications, lists of publications, statements of compensation, and cases on which they have testified, must be provided to the opposing counsel.
Production of Documents or Things	Production of documents is by written request addressed to a party to litigation. When things are not capable of being delivered, such as a building or other large object, discovery rules provide a right to enter onto the land of another for purposes of inspection.
Compliance and Court Intervention	Under ethical guidelines and court rules, the discovery process is to be conducted in a cooperative fashion without court intervention. Courts are reluctant to intervene in the discovery process and look to the litigation teams to resolve the issues among themselves.
Obtaining Compliance with Discovery Requests	Each side may seek court intervention when necessary to obtain information or to protect information.
Protecting Confidential or Privileged Materials	According to Rule 1.6 of the Model Rules of Professional Conduct, an attorney has an ethical obligation to preserve the confidences of clients. Under Rule 26 of the Federal Rules of Civil Procedure, parties may withhold confidential information by expressly making the claim and describing the nature of the documents or things not produced or disclosed in such a way as to enable the opposing party to understand the claim made. Counsel may seek to protect inadvertently disclosed information by agreement in a "claw-back provision" under Rule 16, which permits agreements by the parties for asserting claims of privilege or protection as trial preparation material is produced. These agreements may be included in the requested court scheduling order.

REVIEW QUESTIONS AND EXERCISES

1. What is the purpose of discovery? Name at least three goals that discovery attempts to meet.
2. How has electronically stored information changed the discovery process? What aspects of ESI make discovery easier? What issues can make it more of a challenge?
3. List some of the sources of potential evidence that are maintained in electronic format.
4. What is the duty of the litigation team regarding the disclosure of electronically stored information? What are the limitations on this duty?
5. For purposes of discovery, what is considered to be relevant and discoverable? How does this rule differ from the admissibility of evidence at trial?
6. What provisions exist for discovery of information that cannot be delivered in paper or electronic form? Describe at least three situations where discovery rules allow discovery that is not in the form of documents.
7. After a lawsuit is filed, how soon, under the federal rules, should counsel have their initial meeting? What is the purpose of this meeting?
8. When should the initial scheduling conference with the judge occur, under the federal rules? What is the purpose of this conference? What is the role of the judge in directing this conference?
9. What is included in a discovery plan? What are the principal methods of discovery, and how are they requested?
10. How is a meet and confer conference in a case involving electronically stored information different from one involving only paper documents? What additional safeguards and expertise may be necessary with ESI?
11. How have the mandatory disclosure rules changed the rules for discovery? What are the purposes of these rules?
12. What information must be disclosed regarding potential expert witnesses? What is the purpose of this disclosure?
13. What general limitations on discovery are imposed by the federal rules? Name at least two limitations.
14. Which of the Model Rules of Professional Conduct impact discovery? How does this affect the conduct of discovery?
15. What is the procedure for obtaining compliance when the opposing party fails to produce requested information?
16. What is the obligation of the litigation team to protect the confidences of clients? How can the potentially vast amount of ESI during discovery make the protection of privileged and confidential information a challenge?
17. What is the procedure under the federal rules for claiming privilege with respect to trial preparation materials?
18. What is the purpose of a claw-back clause? What provisions can be made to obtain court sanctions in the language of a claw-back clause?

BUILDING YOUR PARALEGAL SKILLS

INTERNET AND TECHNOLOGY EXERCISES

1. Locate and save as a favorite or bookmark an electronic version of the Federal Rules of Civil Procedure and the Federal Rules of Evidence.
2. Locate and save as a favorite or bookmark an electronic version of your local rules of procedure and evidence.
3. Use the "Search" function in your Internet browser to find specific rules in the web pages above pertaining to the waiver of privilege or confidentiality in discovery.

VIDEO CASE STUDIES

MEET AND CONFER ·

The attorneys are meeting as required under the Federal Rules of Civil Procedure. The defense counsel has recently taken over the case from another attorney. He wants more time to complete discovery. The meeting is conducted without anyone experienced in electronic discovery.

Watch this video case study in MyLegalStudiesLab and answer the following questions.

1. What is the purpose of the meet and confer under the Federal Rules of Civil Procedure?
2. How should trial counsel prepare for the meet and confer under the federal rules?
3. How important is it to have someone in the meet and confer who is knowledgeable in electronic discovery?
4. Is there any time limit on the completion of the meet and confer?

PRIVILEGE ISSUES—MISDIRECTED EMAIL

The paralegal has accidentally sent an email to opposing counsel containing a confidential memo to the client. The supervising attorney is obviously upset and instructs the paralegal on the steps the paralegal must take.

Watch this video case study in MyLegalStudiesLab and answer the following questions.

1. Who has the ultimate responsibility for the mistakenly sent email?
2. How does your jurisdiction treat the accidental sending of confidential material to opposing counsel? What are the steps that should be taken?
3. Should there be an office policy on the use of email to communicate with clients about confidential material?
4. How safe is the use of the Internet for sending email?

CHAPTER OPENING SCENARIO CASE STUDY

Use the Opening Scenario for this chapter to answer the following questions.

1. What policies or procedures should a litigation firm with practices in multiple jurisdictions have in place?

2. Why is it necessary for the litigation support staff to be kept current on the local practices and procedures in the various courts? What changes in the rules could affect discovery?

CONTINUING CASES AND EXERCISES

For the school bus–truck accident case, Case A in Appendix II:

After viewing the Video Attorney Meet and Confer, prepare the Report of the Parties' Planning Meeting using Form 35 for submission to the court.

BUILDING YOUR PROFESSIONAL PORTFOLIO

Policy

Prepare a policy for when an information or technology expert should attend the attorneys' meet and confer conference. Write a memo explaining the policy and describing the situations at which the expert's attendance would be necessary.

Forms

1. Prepare a checklist for use in a meet and confer conference that involves electronically stored information. Be sure the items on the checklist address all the potential concerns of the client, as well as the purposes of the meet and confer.
2. Prepare a motion to compel discovery. In this situation, the defendant has failed to turn over employee records located on a corporate file server.
3. Prepare a motion for a protective order in discovery. The motion should be designed to protect from disclosure any information pertaining to your law firm's representation of the client, including any advice rendered to the client prior to the lawsuit.
4. Download copies of the federal rules' forms on a storage device in both WordPerfect and Word formats for future use. Create a reference document that provides a brief abstract or description of the purpose of each form.

Procedures

1. List the procedural steps and requirements needed to obtain a motion to compel in your state and federal jurisdictions.
2. List the procedural steps and requirements needed to obtain a protective order in discovery in your state and federal jurisdictions.

"The litigants and their lawyers are supposed to want justice, but in reality there is no such thing as justice, either in or out of court. In fact, the word cannot be defined. So, for lack of proof, let us assume that the word "justice" has a meaning, and that the common idea of the definition is correct, without even seeking to find out what is the common meaning. Then how do we reach justice through the courts? The lawyer's idea of justice is a verdict for his client, and really this is the sole end for which he aims."

— *Clarence Darrow*

Evolving Issues in E-Discovery

CHAPTER **12**

OPENING SCENARIO

Owen Mason, Ariel Marshall, and Ethan Benjamin were having their monthly face-to-face, partners-only lunch meeting. These sessions allowed the partners to address matters they might not want to discuss in the weekly firm meetings. The first item on everyone's mind was the issue of practice in multiple jurisdictions. Ariel asked her partners whether they saw any ethical issues in their staff working on cases in a jurisdiction they had not worked in before. Ethan pointed out that it would be not much different from keeping current in the courts they were already working in. Each attorney took continuing legal education courses, and it was suggested that the support staff be required to accompany them to those courses.

Ethan confided that he felt the same uncertainty that members of the support staff sometimes expressed about the policies and procedures regarding electronically stored information. He pointed out that the federal courts were still gradually clarifying the rules and procedures on electronic discovery. Meanwhile, the state courts were often looking to the federal rules as the basis for their own rules and decisions. Ariel reminded Ethan that ultimately, it was their responsibility as lawyers to supervise the staff more closely to avoid any problems.

Owen acknowledged their general concern, but reminded them that in many areas of practice, there would never be absolute certainty—only guiding principles. For example, when advising clients on document management, it was a question of choosing between priorities: the importance of saving information versus the possibility of litigation. Ethan commented that it was not unlike the riddle "Which comes first, the chicken or the egg?" Everyone agreed that the new rules had not solved all the issues, and that everyone on the team needed

LEARNING OBJECTIVES

After studying this chapter, you should be able to:

1. Explain the purpose of a litigation hold, and the duty to preserve evidence.

2. Define spoliation and explain its significance in discovery.

3. Describe the potential sanctions for spoliation of evidence.

VIDEO INTRODUCTION

EVOLVING ISSUES IN E-DISCOVERY
After watching the video in MyLegalStudiesLab, answer the following questions.

1. Why are there no absolutes in electronic discovery?
2. Why is it important to monitor cases and court rules involving discovery?

to keep current on trends and decisions. They all acknowledged that it was the partners' responsibility to be vigilant in checking the rules and case law in each jurisdiction, especially since there did not seem to be any consistency among those rules and case laws. They also agreed that they would need to include this topic at every staff meeting to be sure the staff was kept current on rules and court decisions.

■ INTRODUCTION TO THE EVOLVING ISSUES IN E-DISCOVERY

There are no absolutes in the rules regarding electronic discovery. The law is still evolving, with each jurisdiction applying the rules as it sees necessary to promote justice. Decisions vary widely from jurisdiction to jurisdiction, even on cases that have similar sets of facts. It is therefore essential that the litigation team carefully monitor the changes in the rules of civil procedure and rules of evidence, and the case law interpreting them, in each jurisdiction in which the team practices. It is also important to monitor leading cases from other jurisdictions that may be persuasive to a local court, even if the local case law may not currently support the same positions.

There are some court opinions and judges that are looked to more than others for guidance. Among the most widely read are the opinions of Judge Shira Scheindlin in the widely reported *Zubulake* case. In the course of this litigation, Judge Scheindlin wrote a series of groundbreaking opinions.

Opinions in *Zubulake*

Zubulake I	May 13, 2003 217 F.R.D. 309
Zubulake II	May 13, 2003 230 F.R.D. 290
Zubulake III	July 24, 2003 216 F.R.D. 280
Zubulake IV	October 22, 2003 220 F.R.D. 212
Zubulake V	July 20, 2004 229 F.R.D. 422
Zubulake VI	February 2, 2005
Zubulake VII	March 6, 2005

These opinions were written before the 2006 amendments to the Federal Rules of Civil Procedure. However, many still look to these opinions as a well-reasoned approach to issues in electronic discovery.

Judge Scheindlin also wrote the opinion in what is now informally referred to as the *Pension Committee* case, which she entitled, "*Zubulake* Revisited: Six Years Later." This opinion is also widely read, and is an update on the issues and potential solutions to many of the problems that were not addressed by the 2006 amendments to the FRCP. While not everyone agrees with the holding or the proposals, they are often looked to for guidance, and are considered by many other courts to be persuasive.

Preserving Electronically Stored Information

The rise in the numbers of electronic documents used in society has dramatically increased the volume and scope of **e-discovery**—the discovery of documents created, disseminated, and stored via electronic means. Until the adoption of the 2006 Federal Rules of Civil Procedure, lawyers and the courts relied on conventional requests for production of documents to obtain paper copies and electronically stored information. However, the old rules were insufficient to address all the potential issues in e-discovery. The new rules address three specific concerns, namely: (1) preserving electronic materials, (2) producing electronic materials, and (3) destruction of electronic materials.

In many businesses, written documentation in the form of emails and word processor documents may number in the thousands or more. Because these documents could be the subject of e-discovery in a potential lawsuit, attorneys frequently advise clients on establishing **retention policies** for electronic data. Attorneys must be able to advise clients on how long to keep these documents. When litigation does actually occur, they must also know how electronic documents should be reviewed in response to a request for production, and which party should bear the cost of retrieval.

Document Management

Lawyers are often asked, "How long do I have to keep records or documents?" or "What happens if I destroy them?" With paper or other physical evidence, available storage is often an important issue, with file cabinets or boxes of paper taking up valuable space. There is also the concern about the flammability of paper records if not stored in fireproof or protected areas. The electronic era has changed some of these issues. With tape, CD, and hard drive storage of electronic documents, thousands of documents can be saved and stored on a pocket-sized storage device. Since storage space is no longer a major issue, the remaining question is how long these records should be kept. Theoretically, electronic records could be kept indefinitely. But as the volume of electronic documents increases, the cost of secure, environmentally acceptable storage again becomes an issue.

Other issues arise when information is stored on types of media that are no longer supported. For example, in the past some companies used floppy disks or magnetic tape to store data. However, as the technology has improved, some computers no longer have floppy drives. In addition, older magnetic tape may be subject to deterioration, and some of the companies that made the drives have gone out of business. Data on these tapes is costly to recover and convert to a readable format.

The answer to the retention issue may be a compromise between indefinite storage and the practical realities of economics and the need to preserve documents for potential litigation.

Litigation Hold

A client that is concerned about a potential lawsuit can easily destroy evidence contained in electronic files. It is sometimes as easy as hitting the delete key.

LEARNING OBJECTIVE 1
Explain the purpose of a litigation hold, and the duty to preserve evidence.

e-discovery
Discovery of documents created, disseminated, and stored via electronic means.

retention policy
A formal process for retaining and destroying files and electronically stored information.

Paper documents can also be "deleted," usually with the help of a good paper shredder. If a client knows a lawsuit is imminent, is it appropriate to destroy files?

The common law and amendments to the Federal Rules of Civil Procedure suggest that once a client has a reasonable belief that litigation may arise from a dispute, a duty arises to preserve all documents related to that dispute, both paper and electronic. A lawsuit need not have been filed or a complaint served for the duty to attach, only a reasonable belief that litigation may arise. But it has been left to the courts to determine what constitutes a "reasonable belief."

An emerging line of cases suggests that the duty to preserve information arises if the party knows or should have known of the possibility of litigation. Preservation may require placing a matter and all documents related to it on **litigation hold**. This term serves as a red flag to the company and its employees not to destroy or alter any documents related to the dispute, and to save them in their present forms. When litigation is filed, or when there is a reasonable expectation of litigation, the individual or company must cease any activity that will result in the destruction or loss of records.

When litigation is actually commenced, counsel must issue a litigation hold letter to the client. A sample letter is shown in Exhibit 12.1. Court opinions have held that lawyers have an affirmative duty to follow up with the client to ensure that the litigation hold procedures are implemented and followed. This burden applies to both inside and outside counsel.

litigation hold

A process whereby a company or individual determines that an unresolved dispute may result in litigation and, as a result, that documents should not be destroyed or altered.

Exhibit 12.1 Litigation hold letter

SAMPLE PRESERVATION LETTER—TO CLIENT

[Date]

RE: [Case Name]—Data Preservation

Dear:

Please be advised that the Office of General Counsel assistance believes electronically stored information to be an important and irreplaceable source of discovery and/or evidence in [description of event, transaction, business unit, product, etc.]. The lawsuit requires preservation of all information from [Corporation's] computer systems, removable electronic media and other locations relating to [description of event, transaction, business unit, product, etc.]. This includes, but is not limited to, email and other electronic communication, word processing documents, spreadsheets, databases, calendars, telephone logs, contact manager information, Internet usage files, and network access information.

[Corporation] should also preserve the following platforms in the possession of the [Corporation] or a third party under the control of the [Corporation] (such as an employee or outside vendor under contract): databases, networks, computer systems, including legacy systems (hardware and software), servers, archives, backup or disaster recovery systems, tapes, discs, drives, cartridges and other storage media, laptops, personal computers, internet data, personal digital assistants, handheld wireless devices, mobile telephones, paging devices, and audio systems (including voicemail).

Employees must take every reasonable step to preserve this information until further notice from the Office of General Counsel. *Failure to do so could result in extreme penalties against [Corporation].*

All of the information contained in the letter should be preserved for the following dates and time periods: [List dates and times].

(continued)

Exhibit 12.1 Continued

PRESERVATION OBLIGATIONS

The laws and rules prohibiting destruction of evidence apply to electronically stored information in the same manner that they apply to other evidence. Due to its format, electronic information is easily deleted, modified or corrupted. Accordingly, [Corporation] must take every reasonable step to preserve this information until the final resolution of this matter.

This includes, but is not limited to, an obligation to:

- Discontinue all data destruction and backup tape recycling policies;
- Preserve and not dispose of relevant hardware unless an exact replica of the file (a mirror image) is made

---

Kroll Ontrack.

The Duty to Preserve Evidence

In addition to the obligations imposed by the rules of procedure, there is also a well-recognized common law duty to preserve evidence:

> Case law has developed the rule that when it is reasonably foreseeable that a claim may be asserted, a party must preserve relevant information. (*Shamis v. Ambassador Factors Corp.*, 34 F. Supp. 2d 879, 888-889 (S.D.N.Y. 1999); *Wm. T. Thompson Co. v. General Nutrition Corp.*, 593 F. Supp. 1443, 1455 (C.D. Cal. 1984); *Carlucci v. Piper Aircraft Corp.*, 102 F.R.D. 472, 485-86 (S.D. Fla. 1984); *Bowmar Instrument Corp. v. Texas Instruments, Inc.*, 25 Fed. R. Serv. 2d (Callaghan) 423, 427, 1977 U.S. Dist LEXIS 16078, at *11 (N.D. Ind. May 2, 1977); . . . Advisory Committee on the Civil Rules of the Committee on Rules of Practice and Procedure of the Judicial Conference of the United States, 2-1-2001)

It is clear that when actual notice of litigation is received, the duty to preserve potential evidence exists. But it is less clear at what point before litigation the duty arises. The case law is not consistent, with some cases taking the position that any preliminary activity that may lead to litigation creates the duty. For example, in the *Pension Committee* case, the court found that the duty arose when two of the numerous potential plaintiffs hired counsel to look into the situation, even before the entire group of plaintiffs hired common counsel.

In a contrary view, one district court decided that the duty had not arisen even though a party had already had a litigation strategy in place that was part of a licensing strategy. The court further ruled that the routine destruction of documents pursuant to a document management policy was not a violation of the duty to preserve. *Rambus, Inc. v. Infineon Technologies*, 222 F.R.D. 280 (ED Va. 2004). However, in the later case *Micron Technology v. Rambus*, 255 F.R.D. 135 (D. Del 2009), the court ruled that the destruction of documents critical to eventual litigation was grounds for sanctions. That case involved a challenge to patents involving semiconductor technology. The relevant data was information from which the court could have determined whether a party's patents were valid. The court found that the destruction of that information violated the company's duty to preserve evidence and was grounds for a sanction declaring Rambus's patent unenforceable against Micron. The appeals court, in reviewing the actions of the trial court, sent the case back for a new hearing on the issue of bad faith, saying:

> ...Litigations are fought and won with information. If the district court finds facts to conclude that Rambus's goal in implementing its document retention policy was to obtain an advantage in litigation through the control of information and evidence, it would be justified in making a finding of bad faith. If, on the other hand, the district court determines that Rambus implemented its document retention policy for legitimate business reasons such as general house-keeping, a finding of bad faith would be unwarranted. Without a finding either way, however, "the opinion explaining the decision lacks adequate fact findings, [and] meaningful review is not possible." *Dennison Mfg. Co. v. Panduit Corp.*, 475 U.S. 809, 811 (1986). This court therefore remands for the district court to further assess the factual record in reaching a determination on bad faith. *Micron Technology Inc v. Rambus Inc*, US Court of Appeals, Federal Circuit 2009-1263 (May 13, 2011)

With no universal rule on the duty to preserve evidence, and until there is a national standard, the litigation team must be constantly aware of local court rules and findings. In some cases, it may be better to take a more conservative approach and err on the side of caution; in fact,what is reasonable under the circumstances may be the best test. If a party has knowledge of a potential lawsuit, or a lawsuit is reasonably foreseeable, there may be a potential claim for sanctions for the destruction of potential evidence. While the client may win if the destruction of evidence was not deliberate, prevailing is not a certainty, as such an outcome depends on the particular court and that court's review of the facts.

The opinions of Judge Scheindlin in the *Zubulake* and *Pension Committee* cases are among the most read and discussed. These opinions are used as the basis for suggested litigation hold letters to clients, such as that of the State Bar of Alaska shown in Exhibit 12.2.

Exhibit 12.2 Alaska Bar sample litigation hold letter

_____, Esq.   **ATTORNEY-CLIENT PRIVILEGED**
                                                        CONTAINS ATTORNEY WORK PRODUCT

[Title]
[Client Name]
[Client Address]

Re: *Case Caption*
      [Court No.]
      Our File No.
      Litigation Hold re Documents and Electronic Data

Dear ____:

This letter is to provide guidance with respect to the preservation and retention of all documents and electronic information relating in any way to this lawsuit and the allegations init. The recent Federal District Court decision in *Zubulake v. UBS Warburg, LLC*,[1] addressed the issues of evidence preservation with an emphasis on electronically stored information and the duties of the parties and counsel. Although it is a Federal decision from New York, the guidance and standards set out by United States District Judge Scheindlin may be deemed persuasive by our judge and therefore applied to documents, electronically stored information, and other materials that fall within the scope of discovery in this case.[2]

The *Zubulake* standards, in one form or another, are now being followed by other Federal and state courts. *See e.g., Housing Rights Center v. Sterling*, 2005 WL 3320739 at *4-5 (C.D. Cal. 2005) adopting the *Zubulake* standards.[3] This letter is, therefore,

---

(continued)

Exhibit 12.2 Continued

written to conform to the guidelines set out by Judge Scheindlin in the *Zubulake* case. Many of the guidelines may not seem to apply in this case, but as counsel retained to represent [Client] it is my duty to make sure that I have done everything possible to ensure the preservation of all evidence. Both Judge Scheindlin in *Zubulake*, and other courts,[4] not only place counsel's discovery duties in the context of the Rules of Civil Procedure, but also in terms of counsel's ethical duties.

Judge Scheindlin summarized what she described as a "litigant's preservation obligations"[5] as follows:

> Once a party reasonably anticipates litigation, it must suspend its routine document retention/destruction policy and put in place a "litigation hold" to ensure the preservation of relevant documents. As a general rule, that litigation hold does not apply to inaccessible back up tapes (e.g. those typically maintained solely for the purpose of disaster recovery), which may continue to be recycled in the schedule set forth in the company's policy. On the other hand, if back up tapes are accessible (i.e. actively used for information retrieval), then such tapes *would* likely be subject to the litigation hold.[6]

Judge Scheindlin's admonition also includes the following guidelines:

> A party's discovery obligations do not end with the implementation of a "litigation hold" – to the contrary, that's only the beginning. Counsel must oversee compliance with the litigation hold, monitoring the party's efforts to retain and produce the relevant documents. Proper communication between a party and her lawyer will ensure (1) that all relevant information (or at least all sources of relevant information) is discovered, (2) that relevant information is retained on a continuing basis, and (3) that relevant nonprivileged material is produced to the opposing party.[7]

In identifying the duties, Judge Scheindlin said that counsel not only has a duty to locate relevant information, but that there is also a continuing duty to "oversee compliance"[8] and ensure preservation. In accordance with these duties, counsel must make certain that all sources of potential, relevant information are identified and placed on hold. According to Judge Scheindlin:

> To do this, counsel must become fully familiar with the client's data retention architecture. This will invariably involve speaking with information technology personnel, who can explain the system-wide back up procedures and the actual implementation of the firm's recycling policy. It will also involve communicating with the "key players" in the litigation in order to understand how they stored information.[9]

Judge Scheindlin observed that if it is not possible for there to be actual verbal contact with the key players, other methods should be implemented to accomplish the same goal and that once all potential relevant information has been identified, there is a duty to retain that information and to produce it in response to an opposing party's discovery request. In addition, there is always a continuing duty to supplement discovery responses.

Accordingly, at a minimum, the following steps should be taken:[10]

1. All destruction of documents of any type, including electronic information, pertaining in any way to this matter must immediately stop, even if your document retention policy would otherwise call for routine destruction. All such documents and electronic information must be retained.

2. I need to have you identify for me the "key players" relating to your document retention and destruction policies, the creation, storage, and retention of electronic information, and your primary IT people.

3. Ideally, in keeping with the Zubulake guidelines, I should meet or confer with each such person to be fully briefed by them regarding document retention and destruction policies so that I am fully familiar with them and can effectuate my duty to insure proper retention and proper disclosure, as well as my continuing duty to monitor the litigation hold that has been placed on all such information. We can, however, discuss other ways that will provide the same level of assurance.

I presume that the manner in which [Client] normally operates diminishes the risk of improper document destruction and, therefore, the matters set out in this letter may appear unnecessary or "overkill." However, the rapidly developing doctrine of spoliation, which includes the negligent or intentional destruction of evidence, is being used by opposing counsel with greater frequency and with increasing success. Furthermore, opposing counsel are increasingly making discovery requests that attempt to "set up" companies for spoliation claims. It is this type of situation that can result in devastating consequences, including sanctions imposed upon the offending company, personnel within the company, and counsel. In addition, the courts have other mechanisms to punish for spoliation, including the striking of certain defenses and/or a jury instruction that the documents and evidence that were destroyed should be presumed to have been harmful to the party that destroyed them. These risks can be avoided or minimized if we work together to ensure the retention and preservation of documents and electronic information.

(continued)

Exhibit 12.2 Continued

If you have any questions, please advise.

Very truly yours,

[1] 2004 WL 1620866 (S.D.N.Y. 2004).

[2] Alaska has recognized a remedy for spoliation of evidence. "In tort law when a party has destroyed records, it is sometimes appropriate to employ a rebuttable presumption that the records would have established facts unfavorable to the party who destroyed the documents." *Starek v. Kenai Peninsula Borough,* 81 P.3d 268, 272 (Alaska 2003), citing *Sweet v. Sisters of Providence in Washington,* 895 P.2d 484, 492 (Alaska 1995).

[3] *Zubulake,* 2004 WL 1620866 at *2 (S.D.N.Y. 2004) (recognizing counsel's "common law duty to preserve relevant evidence…"). See also A.B.A. Civil Discovery Standards, Standard 10 Preservation of Documents (August 1999). *See also* Devin K. Isom, *Electronic Discovery Primer for Judges,* 2005 Fed.Cts.L.Rev.1 (2005).

[4] *Metropolitan Opera Association, Inc. v. Local 100, Hotel Employees and Rest. Employee Int'l Union,* 212 F.R.D. 178 (S.D.N.Y. 2003), prior opinion adhered to on reconsideration as clarified, 2004 WL 1943099 (S.D.N.Y. 2004).

[5] *Zubulake,* 2004 WL 1620866 at *7.

[6] *Id.* citing *Zubulake v. UBS Warburg, LLC,* 220 F.R.D. 212, 218 (S.D.N.Y. 2003).

[7] *Zubulake,* 2004 WL 1620866 at *7.

[8] *Id.*

[9] *Id.* at *8.

[10] Id. at *7.

IN THE WORDS OF THE COURT …

Rimkus Consulting Group, Inc., Plaintiff,
v. Nickie G. Cammarata, et al., Defendants.
CIVIL ACTION NO. H-07-0405
UNITED STATES DISTRICT COURT FOR THE SOUTHERN
DISTRICT OF TEXAS, HOUSTON DIVISION
2010 U.S. Dist. LEXIS 14573
February 19, 2010, Decided
February 19, 2010, Filed

OPINION BY: Lee H. Rosenthal

OPINION

MEMORANDUM AND OPINION

…

B. When Deletion Can Become Spoliation

Spoliation is the destruction or the significant and meaningful alteration of evidence. *See generally* The Sedona Conference, The Sedona Conference Glossary: E-DISCOVERY & DIGITAL INFORMATION MANAGEMENT (SECOND EDITION) 48 (2007) ("Spoliation is the destruction of records or properties, such as metadata, that may be relevant to ongoing or anticipated litigation, government investigation or audit."). Electronically stored information is routinely deleted or altered and affirmative steps are often required to preserve it. Such deletions, alterations, and losses cannot be spoliation unless there is a duty to preserve the information, a culpable breach of that duty, and resulting prejudice.

Generally, the duty to preserve arises when a party "has notice that the evidence is relevant to litigation or…should have known that the evidence may be relevant to future litigation." Generally, the duty to preserve extends to documents or tangible things (defined by Federal Rule of Civil Procedure 34) by or to individuals "likely to have discoverable information that the disclosing party may use to support its claims or defenses." *See, e.g., Zubulake IV,* 220 F.R.D. at 217-18 (footnotes omitted).

These general rules are not controversial. But applying them to determine when a duty to preserve arises in a particular case and the extent of that duty requires careful analysis of the specific facts and circumstances. It can be difficult to draw bright-line distinctions between acceptable and unacceptable conduct in preserving information and in conducting discovery, either prospectively or with the benefit (and distortion) of hindsight. Whether preservation or discovery conduct is acceptable in a case depends on what is *reasonable,* and that in turn depends on whether what was done—or not done—was *proportional* to that case and consistent with clearly established applicable standards.[8] As Judge Scheindlin pointed out in *Pension Committee,* that analysis depends heavily on the facts and circumstances of each case and cannot be reduced to a generalized checklist of what is acceptable or unacceptable.[9]…

[8] *See* THE SEDONA PRINCIPLES: SECOND EDITION, BEST PRACTICES RECOMMENDATIONS & PRINCIPLES FOR ADDRESSING ELECTRONIC DOCUMENT PRODUCTION 17 cmt. 2.b. (2007) ("Electronic discovery burdens should be proportional to the amount in controversy and the nature of the case. Otherwise, transaction costs due to electronic discovery will overwhelm the ability to resolve disputes fairly in litigation.").

[9] *Pension Comm. of the Univ. of Montreal Pension Plan v. Banc of Am. Sec., LLC,* No. 05 Civ. 9016, 2010 WL 184312, at *3 (S.D.N.Y. Jan. 15, 2010). For example, the reasonableness of discovery burdens in a $550 million case arising out of the liquidation of hedge funds, as in *Pension Committee,* will be different than the reasonableness of discovery burdens in a suit to enforce noncompetition agreements and related issues, as in the present case.

■ SPOLIATION

Destruction of Electronic Records

Courts often use the term **spoliation** to refer to the destruction of evidence pertaining to litigation. Many court opinions have addressed this issue. As defined by one court, spoliation is:

> the destruction or significant alteration of evidence or the failure to preserve property for another's use as evidence in pending or reasonably foreseeable litigation
>
> (*West v. Goodyear Tire & Rubber Co.,* 167 F.3d 776, 779 (2d Cir. 1999)).

Spoliation can involve almost any method of destroying evidence. It may be the shredding or burning of a letter or handwritten note confirming the existence of a promise or other obligation. In the electronic world, it may be the deleting of electronically stored documents on a computer or the erasing of the backup tapes containing critical emails. Spoliation can also refer to the destruction of evidence other than documents. For example, it might involve the crushing of a motor vehicle that had damage showing the cause of an accident.

As stated by Judge Rosenthal in the *Rimkus* case:

> Spoliation of evidence—particularly of electronically stored information— has assumed a level of importance in litigation that raises grave concerns. Spoliation allegations and sanctions motions distract from the merits of a case, add costs to discovery, and delay resolution. The frequency of spoliation allegations may lead to decisions about preservation based more on fear of potential future sanctions than on reasonable need for information. Much of the recent case law on sanctions for spoliation has focused on failures by litigants and their lawyers to take adequate steps to preserve and collect information in discovery.

LEARNING OBJECTIVE 2
Define spoliation and explain its significance in discovery.

spoliation
Destruction of records that may be relevant to ongoing or anticipated litigation, government investigation, or audit. Courts differ in their interpretation of the level of intent required before sanctions may be warranted.

IN THE WORDS OF THE COURT...

Pension Committee of the University of Montreal Pension Plan, et al

Against

Banc of America Securities, LLC, et al

05 Civ 9016 (SAS) January 11, 2010

Zubulake Revisited: Six Years Later

Shira A. Scheindlin, U.S.D.J.:

...II. AN ANALYTICAL FRAMEWORK AND APPLICABLE LAW

From the outset, it is important to recognize what this case involves and what it does not. This case does not present any egregious examples of litigants purposefully destroying evidence. This is a case where plaintiffs failed to timely institute written litigation holds and engaged in careless and indifferent collection efforts after the duty to preserve arose. As a result, there can be little doubt that some documents were lost or destroyed.

The question, then, is whether plaintiffs' conduct requires this Court to impose a sanction for the spoliation of evidence. To answer this question, there are several concepts that must be carefully reviewed and analyzed. The first is plaintiffs' level of culpability—that is, was their conduct of discovery acceptable or was it negligent, grossly negligent, or willful. The second is the interplay between the duty to preserve evidence and the spoliation of evidence. The third is which party should bear the burden of proving that evidence has been lost or destroyed and the consequences resulting from that loss. And the fourth is the appropriate remedy for the harm caused by the spoliation....

...A failure to preserve evidence resulting in the loss or destruction of relevant information is surely negligent, and, depending on the circumstances, may be grossly negligent or willful. For example, the intentional destruction of relevant records, either paper or electronic, after the duty to preserve has attached, is willful. Possibly after October, 2003, when *Zubulake IV* was issued, and definitely after July, 2004, when the final relevant *Zubulake* opinion was issued, the failure to issue a *written* litigation hold constitutes gross negligence because that failure is likely to result in the destruction of relevant information....

...The next step in the discovery process is collection and review. Once again, depending on the extent of the failure to collect evidence, or the sloppiness of the review, the resulting loss or destruction of evidence is surely negligent, and, depending on the circumstances[,] may be grossly negligent or willful. For example, the failure to collect records—either paper or electronic—from key players constitutes gross negligence or willfulness as does the destruction of email or backup tapes after the duty to preserve has attached. By contrast, the failure to obtain records from *all* employees (some of whom may have had only a passing encounter with the issues in the litigation), as opposed to key players, likely constitutes negligence as opposed to a higher degree of culpability. Similarly, the failure to take all appropriate measures to preserve ESI likely falls in the negligence category....

...The common law duty to preserve evidence relevant to litigation is well recognized. The case law makes crystal clear that the breach of the duty to preserve, and the resulting spoliation of evidence, may result in the imposition of sanctions by a court because the court has the obligation to ensure that the judicial process is not abused.

It is well established that the duty to preserve evidence arises when a party reasonably anticipates litigation. "[O]nce a party reasonably anticipates litigation, it must suspend its routine document retention/destruction policy and put in place a 'litigation hold' to ensure the preservation of relevant documents."

"A plaintiff's duty is more often triggered before litigation commences, in large part because plaintiffs control the timing of litigation...."

c. Burdens of Proof

The third preliminary matter that must be analyzed is what can be done when documents are no longer available. This is not an easy question. It is often impossible to know what lost documents would have contained. At best, their content can be inferred from existing documents or recalled during depositions. But this is not always possible. Who then should bear the burden of establishing the relevance of evidence that can no longer be found? And, an even more difficult question is who should be required to prove that the absence of the missing material has caused prejudice to the innocent party.

The burden of proof question differs depending on the severity of the sanction. For less severe sanctions—such as fines and cost-shifting—the inquiry focuses more on the conduct of the spoliating party than on whether documents were lost, and, if so, whether those documents were relevant and resulted in prejudice to the innocent party..., for more severe sanctions—such as dismissal, preclusion, or the imposition of an adverse inference—the court must consider, in addition to the conduct of the spoliating party, whether any missing evidence was relevant and whether the innocent party has suffered prejudice as a result of the loss of evidence....

In short, the innocent party must prove the following three elements: that the spoliating party (1) had control over the evidence and an obligation to preserve it at the time of destruction or loss; (2) acted with a culpable state of mind upon destroying or losing the evidence; and that (3) the missing evidence is relevant to the innocent party's claim or defense....

■ SANCTIONS FOR SPOLIATION

Spoliation of evidence is punishable by court-imposed sanctions against the party who destroyed the evidence. Sanctions can range from ordering additional discovery to monetary penalties. The judge may even give an adverse inference instruction to the jury in which the judge advises them of the destruction of documents, and tells them that they may infer that the documents would have been favorable to the other side or damaging to the party that destroyed the documents.

An example of such an adverse instruction is presented in the *Pension Committee* case.

LEARNING OBJECTIVE 3
Describe the potential sanctions for spoliation of evidence.

IN THE WORDS OF THE COURT . . .

University of Montreal Pension Plan, et al v Banc of America Securities, LLC, et al

05 Civ. 9016 U.S. Dist. Crt. S.N.Y. 2010 at 81-83

With respect to the grossly negligent plaintiffs—2M, Hunnicutt, Coronation, the Chagnon Plaintiffs, Bombardier Trusts, and the Bombardier Foundation—I will give the following jury charge:

The Citco Defendants have argued that 2M, Hunnicutt, Coronation, the Chagnon Plaintiffs, Bombardier Trusts, and the Bombardier Foundation destroyed relevant evidence, or failed to prevent the destruction of relevant evidence. This is known as the "spoliation of evidence."

(continued)

Spoliation is the destruction of evidence or the failure to preserve property for another's use as evidence in pending or reasonably foreseeable litigation. To demonstrate that spoliation occurred, the Citco Defendants bear the burden of proving the following two elements by a preponderance of the evidence:

First, that *relevant* evidence was destroyed after the duty to preserve arose. Evidence is relevant if it would have clarified a fact at issue in the trial and otherwise would naturally have been introduced into evidence; and

Second, that 2M, Hunnicutt, Coronation, the Chagnon Plaintiffs, Bombardier Trusts, and the Bombardier Foundation were grossly negligent in their failure to preserve the evidence.

I instruct you, as a matter of law, that each of these plaintiffs failed to preserve evidence after its duty to preserve arose. As a result, you may presume, if you so choose, that such lost evidence was relevant, and that it would have been favorable to the Citco Defendants. In deciding whether to adopt this presumption, you may take into account the egregiousness of the plaintiffs' conduct in failing to preserve the evidence.

However, each of these plaintiffs has offered evidence that (1) no evidence was lost; (2) if evidence was lost, it was not relevant; and (3) if evidence was lost and it was relevant, it would not have been favorable to the Citco Defendants.

If you decline to presume that the lost evidence was relevant or would have been favorable to the Citco Defendants, then your consideration of the lost evidence is at an end, and you will *not* draw any inference arising from the lost evidence.

However, if you decide to presume that the lost evidence was relevant and would have been unfavorable to the Citco Defendants, you must next decide whether any of the following plaintiffs have rebutted that presumption: 2M, Hunnicutt, Coronation, the Chagnon Plaintiffs, Bombardier Trusts, or the Bombardier Foundation. If you determine that a plaintiff has *rebutted* the presumption that the lost evidence was either relevant or favorable to the Citco Defendants, you will *not* draw any inference arising from the lost evidence against that plaintiff. If, on the other hand, you determine that a plaintiff has *not rebutted* the presumption that the lost evidence was both relevant and favorable to the Citco Defendants, you may draw an inference against that plaintiff and in favor of the Citco Defendants—namely that the lost evidence would have been favorable to the Citco Defendants.

Each plaintiff is entitled to your separate consideration. The question as to whether the Citco Defendants have proven spoliation is personal to each plaintiff and must be decided by you as to each plaintiff individually.

University of Montreal Pension Plan, et al v Banc of America Securities, LLC, et al 05 Civ. 9016 U.S. Dist. Crt. S.N.Y. 2010 at 81-83

Another sanction may deny the party an opportunity to defend the claims that arise out of the destroyed documents.

Record Retention

Such serious consequences for spoliation of evidence make it even more important to implement a standard operating procedure for document retention and destruction. The legal team should advise a client to put in place a procedure that will allow the destruction of records in a way that avoids claims of spoliation. **Record retention** is the practice of retaining documents for a certain period of time. Various terms are used to refer to document retention policies, such as *information management*, *document management*, and *record management*. Whether a

record retention
Keeping documents and electronically stored information for a period of time.

document will be retained and for how long depends on a number of factors such as governmental regulations, the need to defend against litigation, and the reasonable belief in the pendency of litigation. In some professions and businesses, the retention and destruction policies may be dictated by the laws regulating that industry, such as securities laws, the federal regulation of the pharmaceutical industry, and the regulation of the health care community. For example, federal regulation under HIPAA (Health Information Portability and Accountability Act) dictates that in a medical practice, all files with no activity for a period of three years be destroyed. Against these issues are balanced the costs of preservation, storage, and potential retrieval.

In a perfect world, all clients would have some system in place long before a dispute arises or a lawsuit is filed. If it can be shown that documents were destroyed in good faith, and in the ordinary course of business pursuant to a reasonable retention policy, courts are more likely to look favorably on a party's actions. Where there is good faith, it is unlikely sanctions will be imposed.

A record retention policy should include a litigation hold policy. The client needs to establish a set of rules for determining which matters may result in litigation and for ensuring that documents related to those matters are not destroyed. In a medical practice this might include the records of patients who have complained about their medical treatment or failed to pay their bills. Files that meet either of these criteria would be placed on a litigation hold and not destroyed until some later date, usually after the statute of limitations expires.

Checklist ✔   LITIGATION HOLD

Sedona Guideline 8 explains an organization's need to ensure that legal hold recipients receive "actual, comprehensible and effective notice of the requirement to preserve information." A legal hold is most effective and shows a good faith effort when it:

1. Is issued in writing by a person of authority who commands attention
2. Is worded with appropriate urgency and sensitivity
3. Clearly describes the scope of the hold (e.g., type of content, data repositories, and time frame)
4. Clearly articulates what actions are to be taken (instructions to recipient)
5. Clearly delineates how long the hold remains in effect (and if it is an ongoing duty)
6. Clearly defines any terminology (e.g., "ESI" or "record")
7. Requests acknowledgment (i.e., that the hold has been received is applicable to the recipient, that the recipient understands and agrees to comply with the notice)
8. Requests notification about other employees, departments or systems that may be responsive
9. Includes contact information regarding questions or concerns (now or in the future)
10. Clearly articulates expectations of compliance and the implications of failing to do so

Source: http://www.fiosinc.com/e-discovery-knowledge-center/electronic-discovery-whitepaper-data.aspx?id=458
Ensuring effective preservation for e-discovery—managing the legal hold process Fios, Inc.
921 SW Washington Street
8th Floor
Portland, Oregon 97205
(503) 265-0700
(877) 700-3467 Toll Free
www.fiosinc.com

Fios, Inc.

■ SPOLIATION REMEDIES

The court has the power not only to impose sanctions, but also to impose remedies for spoliation of evidence. The extent of the remedy can vary from a monetary penalty to an adverse instruction to the jury, or even to dismissal of the case. There is no national standard on sanctions or on the extent of the conduct that will elicit a sanction. Different jurisdictions and courts often apply different remedies in what appear to be the same circumstances, thus requiring the litigation team to carefully monitor the individual courts in which they practice.

IN THE WORDS OF THE COURT . . .

United States District Court, D. Minnesota.
3M Innovative Properties Company and
3M Company, Plaintiff,

v.

Tomar Electronics, Defendant.
Civil No. 05-756(MJD/AJB).

Sept. 18, 2006.

MICHAEL J. DAVIS, District Court

. . .

B. This Court's Authority to Impose Sanctions for Discovery Abuse

The authority of the court to impose sanctions for misconduct committed in the course of discovery arises from two distinct authorities. The Federal Rules of Civil Procedure expressly provides authority for this court to impose sanctions for abuse of the discovery process. *See* Fed.R.Civ.P. 37. The court may impose sanctions when, *inter alia*, a party fails to comply with an order from the court or when a party fails to amend or correct a response to a discovery request. *Id*. The court may also impose sanctions based on its inherent authority to control its own judicial proceedings. *Stevenson v. Union Pac. R.R. Co.*, 354 F.3d 739, 745 (8th Cir.2004) (citing *Chambers v. NASCO, Inc.*, 501 U.S. 32 (1991)); *see also Arctic Cat, Inc. v. Injection Research Specialists, Inc.*, 210 F.R.D. 680, 683 (D.Minn.2002) ("In assessing the need for sanctions, a Federal District Court has the inherent authority, and responsibility, to regulate and supervise the bar practicing before it.").

IN THE WORDS OF THE COURT . . .

Goodman v. Praxair Services, Inc. (**D. Md. 2009**)
632 F. Supp.2d 494
Marc B. Goodman, Plaintiff, v. Praxair Services, Inc., Defendant.
Case No. MJG-04-391.
United States District Court, D. Maryland.
July 7, 2009.
MEMORANDUM OPINION

PAUL W. GRIMM, United States Magistrate Judge.

. . . The lesson to be learned from the cases that have sought to define when a spoliation motion should be filed in order to be timely is that there is a particular need for these motions to be filed as soon as reasonably possible after discovery of the facts that underlie the motion. This is because resolution of spoliation motions are fact intensive, requiring the court to assess when the duty to preserve commenced, whether the party accused of spoliation properly complied with its preservation duty, the degree of culpability involved, the relevance of the lost evidence to the case, and the concomitant prejudice to the party that was deprived of access to the evidence because it was not preserved. *See, e.g., Silvestri*, 273 F.3d at 594-95. Before ruling on a spoliation motion, a court may have to hold a hearing, and if spoliation is found, consideration of an appropriate remedy can involve determinations that may end the litigation or severely alter its course by striking leadings, precluding proof of facts, foreclosing claims or defenses, or even granting a default judgment. And, in deciding a spoliation motion, the court may order that additional discovery take place either to develop facts needed to rule on the motion or to afford the party deprived of relevant evidence an additional opportunity to develop it from other sources. The least disruptive time to undertake this is *during* the discovery phase, not after it has closed. Reopening discovery, even if for a limited purpose, months after it has closed or after dispositive motions have been filed, or worse still, on the eve of trial, can completely disrupt the pretrial schedule, involve significant cost, and burden the court and parties. Courts are justifiably unsympathetic to litigants who, because of inattention, neglect, or purposeful delay aimed at achieving an unwarranted tactical advantage, attempt to reargue a substantive issue already ruled on by the court through the guise of a spoliation motion, or use such a motion to try to reopen or prolong discovery beyond the time allotted in the pretrial order....

The first issue mentioned by the court in the *Pension Committee* case is that of culpability. The opinion describes a scale of culpability for different actions related to spoliation, from simple negligence, to willful negligence, to gross negligence. The following chart is a summary from that opinion and order:

Conduct of Discovery	Level of Culpability
Failure to adhere to contemporary standards after a duty to preserve arises	Gross Negligence
Failure to issue written litigation hold	Gross Negligence
Failure to identify key players	Gross Negligence
Failure to ensure preservation of ESI of key players	Gross Negligence
Failure to cease deletion of email	Gross Negligence
Failure to preserve records of former employees in party's possession, custody, or control	Gross Negligence
Failure to preserve backup tapes when sole source of relevant information or relate to key players	Gross Negligence
Intentional destruction after duty attaches	Willful Negligence
Failure to obtain from ALL employees	Negligence
Failure to take all appropriate measures to preserve ESI	Negligence
Failure to assess accuracy and validity of selected search terms	Negligence

Cooperation in Discovery

The leading source of guidance on e-discovery is the Sedona Conference®, a nonprofit organization that regularly conducts conferences for litigators, academics, and judges. It produced a *Cooperation Proclamation* that, by the end of 2009, had the endorsement of almost one hundred judges, including Supreme Court Justice

Breyer. In his praise of the proclamation, Justice Breyer called on litigants to "act cooperatively in the fact finding process." With cooperation, counsel may be able to reduce discovery disputes by negotiating agreements on discovery—a trend that is supported by the judiciary.

As stated by Magistrate Judge Paul Grimm in *Hopson v. the Mayor of Baltimore*,

> ...The cost-benefit balancing factors listed in Rule 26(b)(2) provide useful analytical tools to enable a producing party to marshal the specific facts that would justify less than full pre-production privilege review. The amount of discovery of electronically stored information that should be permitted in a particular case will be a function of the issues in the litigation, the resources of the parties, whether the discovery sought is available from alternative sources that are less burdensome, and the importance of the evidence sought to be discovered by the requesting party to its ability to prove its claims. As this court noted in *Thompson v. HUD*, 219 F.R.D. 93 (D. Md. 2003), courts have nearly limitless ability under Rule 26(b)(2) to fashion reasonable limits to potentially burdensome discovery requests, but the parties must get beyond the posturing that all too often takes place and provide the court with particularized information and reasonable suggestions how to do so. 232 F.R.D. 228 at 244.

A number of other courts have also discussed the need for cooperation among counsel in discovery:

> In my view, the *Cooperation Proclamation* correctly recognizes that while counsel are retained to be zealous advocates for their clients, they bear a professional obligation to conduct discovery in a diligent and candid manner.... Cooperation does not conflict with the advancement of their clients' interests—it enhances them. Only when lawyers confuse *advocacy* with *adversarial conduct* are these twin duties in conflict.... Counsel are on notice that, henceforth, this court will expect them to confer in good faith and make reasonable efforts to work together[,] consistent with well-established case law and the principles underlying *The Cooperation Proclamation*. (*Cartel Asset management v Ocwen Financial Corp.*, 2010 WL 502721 (D. Colo. Feb 8 2010))

 # IN THE WORDS OF THE COURT...

IN THE UNITED STATES DISTRICT COURT

FOR THE NORTHERN DISTRICT OF CALIFORNIA

2009 WL 3009059 (N.D. Cal. Sept. 17, 2009)

Oracle USA, Inc., et al.,

Plaintiffs,

v.

SAP AG, et al.,

Defendants.

No. C-07-01658 PJH (EDL)

ORDER GRANTING DEFENDANTS' MOTION FOR PRECLUSION OF CERTAIN DAMAGES EVIDENCE PURSUANT TO FEDERAL RULES OF CIVIL PROCEDURE 37(C)(1) AND 16(f)

ELIZABETH D. LAPORTE

United States Magistrate Judge

...This Court has closely monitored discovery in this complex litigation, holding thirteen discovery conferences addressing the progress of discovery and providing guidance on the numerous complex issues that have arisen, and six contested hearings on discovery motions. The production of electronic data in this case has been huge. For example, Plaintiffs' production of a collection of databases relating to the Customer Connection database totaled two terabytes, and Defendants' production of their Data Warehouse contained over ten terabytes of data.... Discovery has already cost each party millions of dollars. For example, Defendants spent approximately $100,000 per custodian on document review and production alone, and the parties have agreed to a limit of 140 custodians....

From the first discovery conference that this Court held on May 6, 2008, the Court has repeatedly emphasized that the scope of this case require[s] cooperation in prioritizing discovery and in being mindful of the proportionality requirement of Federal Rule of Civil Procedure 26. Rule 26 requires the Court to limit discovery if "the burden or expense of the proposed discovery outweighs its likely benefit," after consideration of a number of factors. Fed. R. Civ. P. 26(b)(2)(C). Further, production of electronically stored information may be limited if the sources of the information are "not reasonably accessible because of undue burden or cost." Fed. R. Civ. P. 26(b)(2)(B). Thus, proportionality has required that both parties focus on the amount of damages at issue from the outset of the case....

■ PROPORTIONALITY

An emerging concept in the areas of preservation and e-discovery is that of **proportionality**. As the cost of preserving documents and e-discovery increases, the courts are becoming increasingly concerned that litigation will be available only to the wealthy. As stated by Magistrate Judge Facciola in a conference on e-discovery, "We have to use common sense." ABA e-discovery Conference, May 2010. Not everything that can be preserved or discovered is needed to resolve a case. What must be weighed is the cost in proportion to the benefit. If the potential evidence is only marginally relevant, is it worth the cost to obtain it? The wealthier client or the company with the deeper pockets may demand "everything" from "everyone." But is it relevant to the resolution of the case, or merely a tactic to drive the opponent out of the case or force a settlement to save costs associated with the discovery? The courts are increasingly looking at the issue and limiting the number of document custodians from whom electronically stored information may be obtained without permission of the court upon a showing of a good cause.

proportionality
Weighing the cost against the benefits of preserving and obtaining evidence.

IN THE WORDS OF THE COURT . . .

As stated by Judge Scheindlin in the *Pension Committee* case:

...The determination of an appropriate sanction for spoliation, if any, is confined to the sound discretion of the trial judge and is assessed on a case-by-case basis."[38]

Where the breach of a discovery obligation is the non-production of evidence, a court has broad discretion to determine the appropriate sanction.[39] Appropriate sanctions should "(1) deter the parties from engaging in spoliation; (2) place the risk of an erroneous judgment on the party who wrongfully created the risk; and (3) restore 'the prejudiced party to the same position [it] would have been in absent the wrongful destruction of evidence by the opposing party.'"[40] It is well accepted that a court should always

(continued)

impose the least harsh sanction that can provide an adequate remedy. The choices include—from least harsh to most harsh—further discovery,[41] cost-shifting,[42] fines,[43] special jury instructions,[44] prec1usion,[45] and the entry of default judgment or dismissal (terminating sanctions).[46] The selection of the appropriate remedy is a delicate matter requiring a great deal of time and attention by a court. *Pension Committee of the University of Montreal Pension Plan, et al v Banc of America Securities, LLC, et al* 05 Civ. 9016 U.S. Dist. Crt. S.N.Y. 2010 at 18-20.

[38] *Fujitsu*, 247 F.3d at 436.

[39] *See Residential Funding*, 306 F.3d at 107. *See also Fujitsu*, 247 F.3d at 436 (reiterating the Second Circuit's "case-by-case approach to the failure to produce relevant evidence" in determining sanctions); *Reilly*, 181 F.3d at 267 ("Trial judges should have the leeway to tailor sanctions to insure that spoliators do not benefit from their wrongdoing—a remedial purpose that is best adjusted according to the facts and evidentiary posture of each case.").

[40] *West v. Goodyear Tire & Rubber Co.*, 167 F.3d 776, 779 (2d Cir. 1999) (quoting *Kronisch*, 150 F.3d at 126).

[41] *See, e.g., Treppel*, 249 F.R.D. at 123-24 (ordering additional discovery, including forensic search of adversary's computer).

[42] *See, e.g., Green (Fine Paintings) v. McClendon*, No. 08 Civ. 8496, 2009 WL 2496275, at *7 (S.D.N.Y. Aug. 13, 2009) (awarding monetary sanctions to the movant).

[43] *See, e.g., United States v. Philip Morris USA, Inc.*, 327 F. Supp. 2d 21,25 (D.D.C. 2004) (ordering defendant to pay $2.75 million in fines).

[44] *See, e.g., Arista Records LLC v. Usenet.com, Inc.*, 608 F. Supp. 2d 409, 443-44 (S.D.N.Y. 2009) (ordering an adverse inference instruction as a sanction for defendants' spoliation of evidence).

[45] *See, e.g., Brown v. Coleman*, No. 07 Civ. 1345,2009 WL 2877602, at *4 (S.D.N.Y. Sept. 8, 2009) (precluding certain evidence from being introduced at trial).

[46] *See, e.g., Gutman*, 2008 WL 5084182, at *2 (granting a default judgment for defendants' intentional destruction of evidence).

CONCEPT REVIEW AND REINFORCEMENT

KEY TERMS

e-discovery 325	proportionality 339	retention policy 325
litigation hold 326	record retention 334	spoliation 331

CHAPTER SUMMARY

Introduction to the Evolving Issues in E-Discovery	There are no absolute answers in the area of electronic discovery. The law is still evolving, with each jurisdiction applying the rules as it sees necessary to promote justice. Decisions on similar fact patterns vary widely from jurisdiction to jurisdiction.
Document Management	Legal counsels are often asked: "How long do I have to keep records or documents?" The answer is somewhere between forever and the practical realities of business economics and the need to preserve documents for potential litigation.
Litigation Hold	The amendments to the Rules seem to suggest that once a client has a reasonable belief that litigation may arise from a dispute, a duty arises to preserve all documents, paper and electronic, related to that dispute. The requirement is not that a lawsuit has been filed or a complaint served, only that a reasonable belief exists that litigation may arise.

The Duty to Preserve Evidence	There is a well-recognized common law duty to preserve evidence. It is clear that when actual notice of litigation is received, the duty to preserve potential evidence exists.
Spoliation	Spoliation is "the destruction or significant alteration of evidence or the failure to preserve property for another's use as evidence in pending or reasonably foreseeable litigation." It may be the destruction of physical evidence such as the disposal, crushing, or other destruction of a motor vehicle showing evidence of the cause of an accident. It may be the shredding or burning of a letter or handwritten note confirming the existence of a promise or other obligation. In the electronic world it may be the deleting of electronically stored documents on a computer or the erasing of the backup tapes containing critical emails and documents.
Sanctions for Spoliation	Spoliation of evidence is punishable by sanctions against the party who destroyed the evidence. Sanctions may include giving a negative inference instruction to the jury by advising the jury of the destruction of documents that they may interpret as being documents that would have been favorable to the other side and unfavorable to the case of the party that destroyed or lost the documents. Sanctions may also include denying the party an opportunity to defend the claims that arise out of the destroyed document.
Record Retention	Record retention is the practice of retaining documents for a period of time. Various terms are used to refer to the organized policies of document retention: *information management, document management,* and *record management.* What needs to be retained and for how long depends on a number of factors including governmental regulations, the need to defend against potential action, and the reasonable belief in the pendency of litigation.
Spoliation Remedies	The court has the power to create and impose remedies for spoliation of evidence. The extent of the remedy can vary from monetary penalty to dismissal or adverse instruction to the jury. There is no national standard on sanctions or on the extent of the conduct that will elicit a sanction. Different jurisdictions and courts may apply different sanctions under what appear to be the same circumstances.
Cooperation in Discovery	Judges are calling on litigants to act cooperatively in the discovery process.
Proportionality	Not everything that can be preserved or discovered is needed to resolve a case. What must be weighed is the cost in proportion to the benefit. If the potential evidence is only marginally relevant, is it worth the cost to obtain it? The wealthier client or the company with the deeper pockets can demand "everything" from "everyone," but is it relevant to the resolution of the case or a tactic to drive the opponent out of the case and force a settlement? The courts are increasingly looking at this issue and limiting the number of document custodians whose electronically stored information may be obtained upon good cause without permission of the court.

REVIEW QUESTIONS AND EXERCISES

1. What is the impact of the new Federal Rules of Civil Procedure on e-discovery procedures? What issues do the Rules try to address?
2. Where can the litigation team look for guidance on the procedures for trying cases involving electronic documentation? What sources should they use?
3. Define "spoliation." Give three specific examples, including evidence other than documents.
4. What is the duty to preserve documents? Under what circumstances must documents be preserved?
5. Has the introduction of electronically stored documents changed the duty to preserve? What new problems arise when the documents are in electronic form?

6. What are the possible costs associated with electronic discovery? What factors can make e-discovery costly for a party faced with a request for production?
7. May a firm or client regularly destroy files and records? What standards or directives related to litigation should be included within a document retention policy?
8. Does an attorney have a duty to learn about the issues in e-discovery? What should be part of an attorney's continuing legal education regarding e-discovery?

BUILDING YOUR PARALEGAL SKILLS

INTERNET AND TECHNOLOGY EXERCISES

Use the Internet to locate a current version of the Federal Rules of Civil Procedure 16, 26, 33, 34, 37, and 45. What resources on the web provide this information? What other information do these resources provide?

VIDEO CASE STUDIES

SCHEDULING CONFERENCE WITH JUDGE DISCOVERY ISSUE RESOLUTION

Watch this video case study in MyLegalStudiesLab and answer the following questions.

1. What is the purpose of the scheduling conference?
2. How can the scheduling conference be used to facilitate electronic discovery?

DESTROYING EVIDENCE FOUND BY PARALEGALS

A paralegal discovers a document that is detrimental to the clients case. Only the paralegals working on the case are aware of its existance.

Watch this video case study in MyLegalStudiesLab and answer the following questions.

1. Would a court determine destroying evidence to be spoliation?
2. If the court considers the destruction spoliation of evidence, what are the potential penalties?
3. How might the opposing side learn about the destroyed evidence?

CHAPTER OPENING SCENARIO CASE STUDY

Use the Opening Scenario for this chapter to answer the following questions.

1. Prepare a motion that might be used if it is found that the opposing side has not preserved vital evidence after notice of the lawsuit. State exactly what documents have not been preserved, and specify exactly what sanctions or remedies should be imposed by the court. Suggest more than one alternative for the court to choose from.

2. Prepare a discovery plan proposal for use at the meet and confer. Incorporate in the proposal possible ways the parties could cooperate or reach an agreement without court intervention.

3. Prepare a memo outlining the potential sanctions that can be requested from the judge in the initial meeting with the court if it is decided that the opposing party has not honored discovery requests. Explain the implications of each type of sanction. List them in order of severity.

4. Prepare a memo from the IT staff to the trial team explaining what issues the trial team should be aware of and providing suggestions for obtaining and protecting the needed data in the meet and confer.

CONTINUING CASES AND EXERCISES

For the case study A from Appendix II:

1. Prepare a protocol for the litigation team to use in reviewing documents for a claim of privilege for the accident case, Case A, in Appendix II.

2. As defense counsel, prepare a list of expert and factual witnesses that you would call at trial.

3. List the other mandatory disclosures that must be made under the federal rules.

BUILDING YOUR PROFESSIONAL PORTFOLIO

Procedures

1. Prepare a protocol for the litigation team to follow to ensure that a litigation hold is instituted and complied with by a client. Explain the reasons for the protocol, and the possible implications if the hold is not followed.

2. Prepare a litigation hold letter to a client based on the above memo.

"Ignorantia juris quod quisque scire tenetur non excusat."
— (Ignorance of the law, which everybody is supposed to know, does not constitute an excuse.)
Legal maxim

E-Discovery—The Process

CHAPTER 13

OPENING SCENARIO

At first, the litigation team had what seemed to be a simple vehicle collision case between a school bus and a truck. However, the evidence obtained in discovery revealed the possibility of a defect in the truck, either because of faulty maintenance or defective parts. This new evidence in turn raised new issues and options, and it was becoming clear that new areas of discovery would have to be explored. At the very least, the truck had to be inspected by the plaintiffs' own experts, and the trucking company's records had to be reviewed for anything related to the truck, including its use, maintenance, and repairs.

Meanwhile, the team working on the new airplane crash case was concerned about a flood of new information. They worried that the mass of information and data from federal investigators and individual corporate defendants might potentially overwhelm them. In addition, they were representing only one of the plaintiffs in the case, with a number of other attorneys representing the families of the other victims. Thus all of the attorneys needed access to the same data, and all needed to be able to sift through it to find usable evidence to support their legal theory. This was the first case the firm had handled where the defendants were large national firms with massive amounts of electronically stored data. The team members would also be dealing with federal agencies, which had similarly large amounts of electronic information.

LEARNING OBJECTIVES

After studying this chapter, you should be able to:

1. Describe the electronic discovery process and the role of information management.

2. Describe the methods used to identify relevant information in e-discovery.

3. Explain the issues in locating evidence among electronically stored information.

4. Describe the issues that arise in using search queries in e-discovery.

5. Describe the role of a forensic examiner in e-discovery.

VIDEO INTRODUCTION

Professor Thomas F. Goldman, Esq.

E-DISCOVERY—THE PROCESS
After watching the video in MyLegalStudiesLab, answer the following questions.

1. Why is it important to understand how the opposing side views a case?
2. Who determines when a lawsuit is filed?

■ INTRODUCTION TO EVIDENCE AND DISCOVERY

Each case has at least two sides: that of the plaintiff and that of the defendant. There may also be other interested parties who are potential litigants or who have an interest in the litigation, such as governmental agencies. In addition, each side comes to the litigation process from a different perspective. It is thus important for the legal team to understand the perspective of every party, regardless of whose side the legal team is on. The plaintiff may view the case as simply a matter of a wrong for which compensation or vindication is demanded. But the plaintiff may not yet possess all of the evidence needed to support his or her case. The defendant will likely have a very different view of his or her liability, and may or may not anticipate litigation. Before a complaint is served, the defendant may not know if or when a suit will be brought, and therefore will not necessarily know what records to preserve or for how long.

The attorneys for the parties also have their own unique perspectives. The plaintiff's attorney must grapple with finding the evidence to support the case. There may also be a question of timing the action and choosing where to bring suit. Meanwhile, defense counsel must advise the client on his or her rights in the litigation process, and protect him or her against unwarranted claims and potential intrusion into their business process by opposing counsel seeking documents or other information. Corporate or in-house counsel is concerned not only with the costs of the litigation, but also with the preservation of documentation and the costs of document review.

For both plaintiff and defense counsel, there is also the issue of protecting confidential or privileged material from disclosure in discovery.

■ ELECTRONIC DISCOVERY—THE PROCESS

LEARNING OBJECTIVE 1
Describe the electronic discovery process and the role of information management.

Electronic Discovery Reference Model
A suggested model for the procedures in electronic discovery.

Electronic discovery, or e-discovery, should be thought of as a process rather than as a single event. As shown in the **Electronic Discovery Reference Model** in Exhibit 13.1, e-discovery involves a number of steps or individual processes:

- information management
- identification
- preservation and collection
- processing, review, and analysis
- production
- presentation

Exhibit 13.1 EDRM—Electronic Discovery Reference Model

The Electronic Discovery Reference Model was created to address the lack of standards and guidelines in the electronic discovery (e-discovery) market. The completed model was placed in the public domain in May 2006.

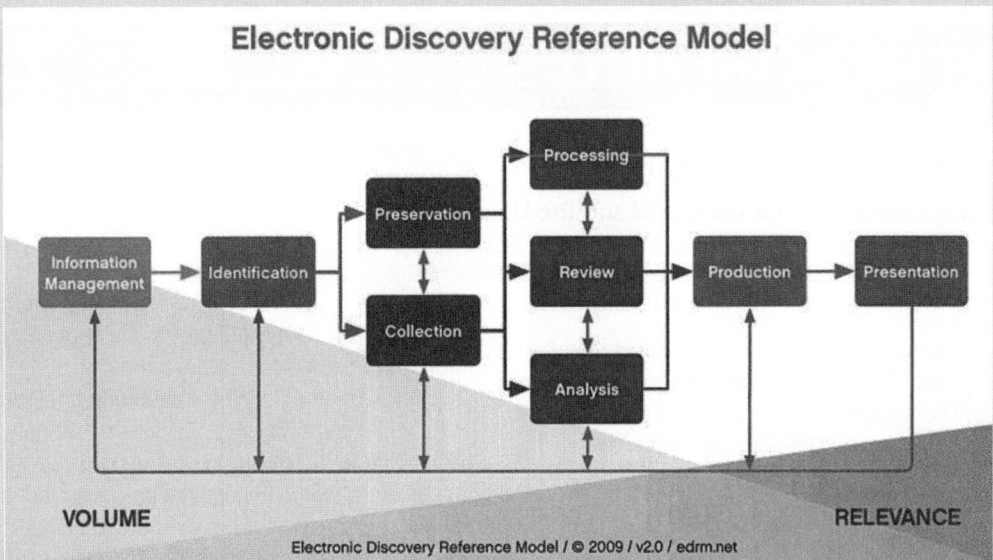

Information Management
Getting your electronic house in order to mitigate risk & expenses should e-discovery become an issue, from initial creation of electronically stored information through its final disposition.

Identification
Locating potential sources of ESI & determining its scope, breadth & depth.

Preservation
Ensuring that ESI is protected against inappropriate alteration or destruction.

Collection
Gathering ESI for further use in the e-discovery process (processing, review, etc.).

Processing
Reducing the volume of ESI and converting it, if necessary, to forms more suitable for review & analysis.

Review
Evaluating ESI for relevance & privilege.

Analysis
Evaluating ESI for content & context, including key patterns, topics, people & discussion.

Production
Delivering ESI to others in appropriate forms & using appropriate delivery mechanisms.

Presentation
Displaying ESI before audiences (at depositions, hearings, trials, etc.), especially in native & near-native forms, to elicit further information, validate existing facts or positions, or persuade an audience.

EDRM (edrm.net).

The ultimate goal is to reduce the total number of items and extract those that are relevant. Of the documents that are relevant, the attorneys must be sure those documents can meet the test of authenticity for presentation and admission in trial.

ADVICE FROM THE FIELD

ROLE APPRECIATION & PERSPECTIVE

Litigators, Litigation Support Professional and the Electronic Discovery Review Model

By Charlotte Riser Harris and Don Swanson

In the world of e-discovery there are two distinct teams—the legal team and the technical team—with two distinct perspectives. The technical team includes litigation support personnel and legal technology providers. The legal team includes attorneys and paralegals. These teams share goals. The goals are to get through the discovery stage of litigation as completely, quickly, efficiently, and painlessly as possible, while achieving the best possible result for their litigation client.

Members of each team often face challenges when they work together to collect, process, review, and produce electronically stored information (ESI) in litigation. These challenges create frustrations that are widely discussed in litigation support circles. There seems to be no dispute that technology is here to stay, that many legal teams are in the beginning stages of the transition to the full use of technology, and that this transition is painful for both the technical and the legal teams.

The difficult and frustrating management of this transition has become part of the job description of litigation support personnel, often implicitly. And many in this position are not trained or prepared to manage change and transition. Given this reality, taking the time to understand the differences in perceptions of each team might make the e-discovery process and the integration of technology into the practice of law easier.

Electronic Discovery Reference Model

The Electronic Discovery Reference Model (EDRM) is a flow chart and series of definitions designed to create a standard approach and common language for measuring the full range of electronic discovery activities. It was placed in the public domain in May 2006 after about three years of development. One of the goals of the EDRM was to codify the best practices and procedures for the e-discovery industry. The EDRM is widely accepted as a credible model for understanding the e-discovery process,

and it is now included in many presentations regarding e-discovery. It has continued to be expanded upon and improved since its first public release.

Work on the EDRM is continuing under the auspices of the "Evergreen Project," which is examining other aspects of the e-discovery process towards the goal of creating an even better understanding and standardization of additional aspects of e-discovery. Matters currently under consideration include metrics, an XML schema, and a code of conduct. Metrics refers to standardized methods to measure the time, effort and expenses associated with various electronic discovery activities. XML schema refers to the development of a standardized way to facilitate the movement of electronically stored information from one step of the electronic discovery process to the next, from one software program to the next and from one organization to the next; and the code of conduct effort focuses on the development of voluntary ethical guidelines for providers and consumers concerning electronic discovery.

Interestingly, the EDRM may provide a vehicle for understanding the perspectives of the technology and legal teams.

The Technical Team and Perspective

The EDRM describes the technical team's role in and view of the litigation process. Those working in the e-discovery industry understand the EDRM, and many who contributed to it are using it. It defines their scope of work and provides standards that can be followed to deliver services to legal teams.

However, it is unlikely that the content of the EDRM projects will reach—or should reach—the complete understanding and appreciation of most legal teams.

The Legal Team Perspective

The EDRM represents a small and largely unknown aspect of the legal team's role in and view of the litigation process.

(*continued*)

To most legal teams, discovery is a small part of the litigation process and ESI is a small part of discovery. This is partly because most pending legal actions do not have a smoking gun anywhere, much less lurking in the slack space of a hard drive. Many legal team members don't yet know what ESI is—except they know that email, Word, Excel and other electronic documents have to be produced. They have attended enough CLEs and read enough articles to be generally informed, but the terminology and process of e-discovery is not yet part of the legal team's daily jargon and instant recall.

Understanding the Differences

Much of the litigation work done by legal teams is not included in the EDRM chart of the e-discovery process. Although the steps outlined in the EDRM are critical and lay the foundation for the rest of the litigation process, they are but a small part of the litigation process from the legal team's perspective.

Between the production and presentation stages, and after the presentation stage, legal teams are focused on other phases of a litigation matter. For example, after a party has produced their documents, the legal team must create a privilege log; receive opposing party and non-party productions; incorporate those productions into the existing review application; review and analyze those productions; identify issues and fully address each one from both sides; prepare briefs, motions, and other legal materials; identify, hire and prepare expert witnesses; prepare witnesses; take and defend depositions; and much more.

While technical teams are focused on and have embraced litigation support applications and processes as modeled by the EDRM, many legal teams are still struggling in their daily practice to manage huge volumes of email and to use collaborative tools to share documents.

ESI has changed the landscape of discovery, and legal teams, for the most part, are overwhelmed by the change. When one is overwhelmed, often avoidance and denial are the first reactions. It is probably safe to say that many legal teams are actively avoiding and denying e-discovery!

The Practice of Law Does Not Require Technology But

The legal team's struggle is understandable. Think about it....the practice of law does not require technology. True, in today's world, technology provides tools of the trade that are required to get the job done. But if all electrical power was permanently lost, lawyers could and would continue to practice law. To litigate one only needs knowledge of the law with the appropriate licenses to practice, law books, a client, an opposing party with counsel, and a judge. In fact, there are probably many attorneys today who would welcome a return to that simplicity. Contrast that perspective with the technical team's love of technology—indeed, technology is the technical team's lifeblood and reason for being—at work anyway!

The reality is that technology is required in all phases and types of legal work. Legal teams who embrace and leverage the use of technology have a competitive edge, and the day is soon coming when legal teams simply will not be able to compete without the integration of technology into their practice. Because of the volume, complexity and nature of e-discovery, without the proper use of technology, it will be impossible to produce ESI of any significant volume, much less within the deadlines required by the courts.

That reality contrasts greatly with most legal teams' acceptance, understanding and use of computer technology today.

Technology in Law Schools and Paralegal Schools

Attorneys, especially litigators, generally attend law school because they love to debate and analyze, and want to change the world. This is also true for paralegals attending paralegal school. Few, if any, study the law in order to develop their use of computers and databases, or even consider the two to be linked.

The need for technology in the legal workplace has moved forward faster than most legal practitioners are ready, and traditional formal education programs have not kept up with the realities of the workplace. Consider the fact that most law school and paralegal school curricula do not include courses on the use of technology (other than computer-aided legal research) nor do they incorporate the use of applicable software tools into courses (other than perhaps the use of word processing and spreadsheet applications). The study of the production of ESI is certainly not universally included in coursework.

Many attorneys and paralegals are entering the workplace with little or no training and skill in the use of litigation technology, much less an awareness of the e-discovery process.

(*continued*)

(continued)

Responsibilities of Each Team

It is not necessary for technical team members to obtain law degrees or paralegal certificates; likewise, it is not necessary for legal team members to understand how the technology they use is programmed or all of the technical aspects of e-discovery. However, each team must have some basic knowledge about the work of the other team for projects to be successful. And the legal team must have a high level of trust in the technical team and the tools being used.

Each team has responsibilities in this process. However, the technical team can, and perhaps should, take the lead in managing the transition to the full use of technology by legal teams. By understanding the attorney or paralegal's level of acceptance of and comfort with technology, and gearing their interaction and information to that level, the technical team can be more effective.

Attorneys and paralegals must take the time and make the effort to gain the knowledge necessary to enable them to make informed decisions throughout the most visibly appealing and interactive timeline presentations. Either way, any of these tools can be used to create useful timelines so that the trial lawyer can effectively walk a jury or audience through the story and the evidence of their case.

About the Authors: Charlotte Riser Harris is Manager, Litigation Support at Hess Corporation; previously she was a Managing Consultant with Five Star Legal and Compliance Systems, Inc. and was the Manager of Practice Support at Vinson & Elkins LLP. Don Swanson is the President and Founder of Five Star Legal and Compliance Systems, Inc. Don is a recognized expert in litigation support computer systems and works with law firms and corporate and government clients across the country.

Information Management

As shown in the EDRM in Exhibit 13.1, the e-discovery process starts with information management, which is sometimes referred to as document management. Information management policies are concerned with how documents are created and stored, as well as with document destruction. The policy should be in effect before litigation occurs, and attorneys should counsel their clients on the importance of having an information management policy. Where there is an information management policy already in place, the first step for the litigation team is to learn the details and procedures of their client's retention policies and those of any third parties, such as suppliers who may have relevant supporting information.

Document retention policies that provide for the periodic or routine destruction of stored information are permissible. In the often quoted U.S. Supreme Court case of *Arthur Andersen v. U.S.*, the court said:

> Document retention policies, which are created in part to keep certain information from getting into the hands of others, including the Government, are common in business.... It is, of course, not wrongful for a manager to instruct his employees to comply with a valid document retention policy under ordinary circumstances. 544 U.S. 696 (2005)

With paper records, there is a very real need to periodically destroy files because of the physical space they require. In some cases, these documents may require the rental of an off-site warehouse space with secure, temperature- and humidity-controlled conditions. While it might be desirable to save everything indefinitely, the economics of retention frequently dictate a planned destruction program. Many document or information management systems thus have a timetable providing dates for removal to an off-site location, as well as dates for destruction. These dates are marked on the boxes in which the documents are stored.

Economic considerations notwithstanding, the time frames for destruction of documentation are frequently dictated by government regulations such as securities laws, tax regulations, or regulations governing health records. In some cases, the time frame is dictated by the statute of limitations for certain claims, such as a two-year statute of limitations for torts.

Initially, it was thought that the shift from paper to electronic storage would eliminate the need for any physical or off-site storage, thereby reducing the cost of data retention. However, experience has shown this to be an incorrect assumption. While the total space necessary to store items electronically is less than that for paper document storage, the cost may still be substantial. In addition to the cost of maintaining the computer systems for storage of items currently in use, there is also the cost of backup and archival storage for potential disaster recovery. Such backup schemes are required as part of information management or because of government regulation. In many cases, companies use multiple remote, off-site data storage services for disaster recovery and archival purposes, which significantly adds to the cost of information retention.

The use of technology has seen an explosion in the numbers of documents that is far greater than previously anticipated. For example, consider the growth in email and text messages: in the past, written communication took the form of letters and paper memos. Today, most written communication consists of email, text messages, and new forms of social networking such as Twitter and Facebook. Where a letter or memo might have gone only to one person, with a copy going to someone else, an email may be sent to multiple parties, many of whom send it on to several others—thus increasing the amount of storage required.

Email has become a major source of evidence and has spawned the need to archive emails. This archiving process itself requires additional computing power and increases cost. Because the use of computers makes saving documents easier, people save information of every type more than ever before, including every draft of every document, or every item they download from the Internet. These items may include still images, videos, and sound files, all of which use up large amounts of storage space. As a result, companies as well as individuals are saving and backing up more and more data.

A question clients frequently ask is, "Is it safe to routinely delete electronically stored information?" The federal rules, specifically Rule 37, provide a **safe haven** for routine, good faith destruction of electronically stored information (ESI):

safe haven
Procedures and circumstances under which a party will not be penalized.

Rule 37. Failure to Make Disclosures or to Cooperate in Discovery; Sanctions

(e) Failure to Provide Electronically Stored Information.
Absent exceptional circumstances, a court may not impose sanctions under these rules on a party for failing to provide electronically stored information lost as a result of the routine, good-faith operation of an electronic information system.

One factor that a court will consider in determining whether there is "routine, good-faith operation" of an electronic information system is whether there is a written company policy on information management. Such a policy should be monitored to ensure compliance by all employees on all the computer systems under the control of the company. It should be remembered, however, that this does not eliminate the company's obligation to suspend document destruction and preserve relevant documents when the company reasonably anticipates litigation. Clients must be properly notified of this obligation to impose a litigation hold. Moreover, the litigation team has the added ethical obligation to preserve evidence under Rule 3.4 of the Model Professional Conduct Code. That rule states that a lawyer shall not:

(a) unlawfully obstruct another party's access to evidence or unlawfully alter, destroy or conceal a document or other material having potential evidentiary value.

The rule also states that a lawyer shall not counsel or assist another person in destroying such material.

■ THE COST OF SAVING ELECTRONICALLY STORED INFORMATION

LEARNING OBJECTIVE 2
Describe the methods used to identify relevant information in e-discovery.

One of the biggest advantages provided by technology in the office setting is the efficient, economical creation and sharing of information. Initially, word processor files and some financial data files formed the bulk of electronically stored information. This information was maintained in formats that were relatively easy to store and save on backup tapes, and later on hard drives and other media. Recent advances in technology have resulted in new forms of ESI, including emails, text messages, and data from social networking sites, as well many other types of documentation used in business and government.

However, the adoption of these technologies does have its costs. Businesses are often uncertain about how much information to save, and for how long. Saving and archiving ESI in secure, multi-location storage facilities may be required by court action, company policy, or government regulation. Businesses incur significant costs in storing this data, which continues to increase in volume.

Information Management Reference Model (IMRM)
A proposed model for e-discovery that balances business and litigation needs.

Document retention policies are thus receiving close scrutiny as to what is economically reasonable. A balance must be reached between the need to save data and the costs of storing that data. The **Information Management Reference Model (IMRM)** shown in Exhibit 13.2 is an attempt to come to terms with the changes dictated by the needs of business and litigation.

■ IDENTIFICATION

The initial step in the discovery process is determining what documents are needed. It is also necessary to determine their location, their value to the case, their format, and the costs of retrieving them. All of this information is needed to prepare a proper discovery request. The request must also be tailored to the rules of the jurisdiction. A record, as defined by the court, may include many forms of information. In federal court, a "record" has been defined as:

a. As used in this Order, "record" means any book, bill, calendar, chart, check, compilation, computation, computer or network activity log, correspondence, data, database, diagram, diary, document, draft, drawing, e-mail, file, folder, film, graph, graphic presentation, image, index, inventory, invoice, jotting, journal, ledger, machine readable material, map, memo, metadata, minutes, note, order, paper, photograph, printout, recording, report, spreadsheet, statement, summary, telephone message record or log, transcript, video, voicemail, voucher, webpage, work paper, writing, or worksheet, or any other item or group of documentary material or information, regardless of physical or electronic format or characteristic, and any information therein, and copies, notes, and recordings thereof. *Jicarilla Apache Nation v U.S.* No. 02-25L U.S. Court of Fed. Claims (2004)

Exhibit 13.2 Information Management Reference Model (IMRM)

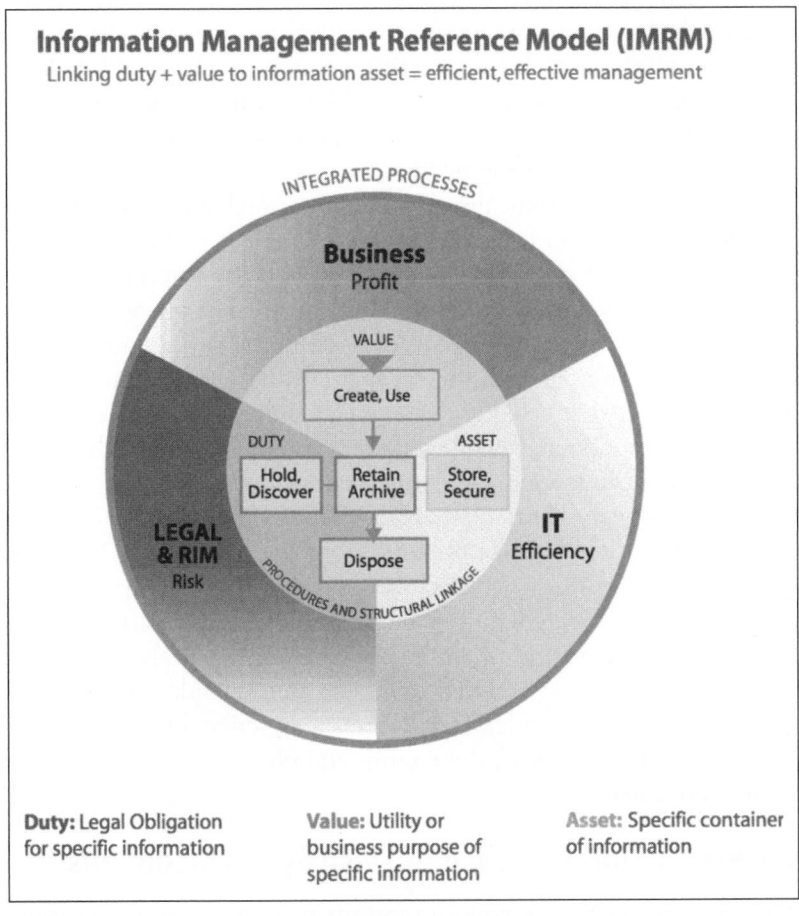

Information Management Reference Model (IMRM)
Linking duty + value to information asset = efficient, effective management

Duty: Legal Obligation for specific information

Value: Utility or business purpose of specific information

Asset: Specific container of information

EDRM (edrm.net).

VIDEO ADVICE FROM THE FIELD

Bill Dimm, Ph.D.—President, Neurons

A discussion of the methods used to search for information in electronic discovery. After watching the video in MyLegalStudiesLab answer the following questions.

1. What is the difference between an internet search and an e-discovery search?
2. What are some different approaches to searching?
3. What is the difference between concept search and Boolean search?

■ LOCATING EVIDENCE

Locating information begins with a good understanding of the location and types of documents needed, including documents kept by third parties. In a simple automobile property damage case, third-party documents might include the police report, tow truck dispatch log, auto body repair shop bill, rental replacement vehicle bill, and possibly a bill for the firefighters' response to clean up the gasoline or oil spill from the collision. Before computerization, all of these would have been paper documents. After a complete interview of the client, together with some intuition based on the legal team's litigation experience, the documents

LEARNING OBJECTIVE 3
Explain the issues in locating evidence among electronically stored information.

would have been requested from appropriate agencies or businesses, or from the opposing party through written discovery requests. If a personal injury was involved, the team might have added requests for medical records and bills for services by doctors or hospitals. In each case, a written request would have listed the names of the parties, the dates of the incident, and known treatment dates. Any misspelled names or incorrect dates would have required some human intervention to find out which person was being referred to.

In contrast, discovery of electronically stored information has for the most part eliminated the human element in retrieving data. In some cases, the requests are made by the litigation support staff using queries to search the Internet. Because only one database may be searched at a time, the searches must be very specific. The advantage of the electronic search is that there are no longer any missed documents resulting from misfilings or overlooked paper files. The disadvantage is the loss of the human assistance that could uncover a related document. For example, a person involved in the process may, while scanning manually through the paper files, find a second accident involving one of the parties.

When discussing discovery, particularly electronic discovery, there is a tendency to speak of electronic documents as generic, homogeneous items. One tends to forget the specialized nature of the documents when conducting computer search queries. Finding the desired document requires an appreciation of the types of records kept, and where and by whom they are kept. It is also important to understand the terminology used by those who created or indexed the documents. Every occupation has its own lexicon of terms to describe different types of documents. Without the knowledge of these terms and phrases, a search may not produce the desired documents.

Using Discovery to Find Evidence of Destroyed Documents

When seeking information, it may be as important to know what is routinely deleted from records as what has been preserved. If certain types of information are missing, it may be because they were deleted or destroyed as part of a company's document retention or information management system. Counsel should therefore make an effort to understand this system while attempting to meet its obligations, not only to the client, but also to opposing counsel and the courts.

The most basic use of the court system is to right a wrong. However, litigation or the threat of litigation is now used as a business tactic. It may be used as part of a marketing or licensing strategy, or to silence, intimidate, and censor critics in what is often referred to as a SLAPP (strategic lawsuit against public participation) suit. These are suits in which the plaintiff selects the timing and controls the evidence that may in the future be part of the lawsuit. For example, in *Micron v Rambus*, the court found:

> …because the document retention policy was discussed and adopted within the context of Rambus['s] litigation strategy[,] the court finds that Rambus knew[,] or should have known, that a general implementation of the policy was inappropriate because the documents destroyed would become material at some point in the future…. *Micron v Rambus* Civ. No. 00-792-SLLR US Dist. Crt. Dist. of Del. (2009)

In the *Micron* case, Rambus was punished by being prohibited from asserting its patents against Micron. To obtain this result, Micron had to prove "…that the document[s] destroyed were discoverable and the type of documents would be relevant to the instant litigation" (*Micron* at page 32). On appeal, the case was remanded for further proceedings on the issue of bad faith in the destruction of the documents.

As stated by Judge Scheindlin in another case:

…The innocent party must also show that the evidence would have been helpful in proving its claims or defenses—i.e. that the innocent party is prejudiced without the evidence.… In short, the innocent party must prove the following three elements: that the spoliating party (1) had control over the evidence and an obligation to preserve it at the time of destruction or loss; (2) acted with a culpable state of mind upon destroying or losing the evidence; and that (3) the missing evidence is relevant to the innocent party's claim or defense.… *Pension Committee, et al v Banc of America, et al* 05-Civ.9016 at page 14.

For the litigation team seeking electronically stored information during discovery, the task is not just to find existing documentation, but also to find evidence of any documents destroyed as part of a plan intended to lead to litigation. For example, in the *Micron* case, Rambus planned to "…establish a royalty rate and validate its patents.…" In this case, the "smoking gun" was a PowerPoint slide prepared for a Rambus board meeting that showed:

…that the [b]est route to IP credibility is through victory over a major DRAM manufacturer.… (*Micron* at pages 21, 30)

Using Interrogatories to Find Information

Interrogatories are written questions that must be answered by the opposing party. Because they are prepared in advance, and must be answered within a set time frame, these questions rarely result in any surprises, such as might be obtained in a face-to-face question session. The written requests are then submitted to opposing counsel, who reviews both the questions and the client's answers carefully to ensure that only required information is supplied. The answers do, however, provide a basic framework from which additional discovery will follow, including depositions and requests for production. The federal rules outlining the form and use of interrogatories are shown in Exhibit 13.3.

interrogatories
A form of discovery in which written questions are addressed to a party to a lawsuit and require written answers made under oath.

Exhibit 13.3 Rule 33 governing interrogatories

Rule 33. Interrogatories to Parties

(a) In General.

(1) Number.

Unless otherwise stipulated or ordered by the court, a party may serve on any other party no more than 25 written interrogatories, including all discrete subparts. Leave to serve additional interrogatories may be granted to the extent consistent with Rule 26(b)(2).

(2) Scope.

An interrogatory may relate to any matter that may be inquired into under Rule 26(b). An interrogatory is not objectionable merely because it asks for an opinion or contention that relates to fact or the application of law to fact, but the court may order that the interrogatory need not be answered until designated discovery is complete, or until a pretrial conference or some other time.

(continued)

Exhibit 13.3 Continued

(b) Answers and Objections.

(1) Responding Party.

The interrogatories must be answered:

(A) by the party to whom they are directed; or

(B) if that party is a public or private corporation, a partnership, an association, or a governmental agency, by any officer or agent, who must furnish the information available to the party.

(2) Time to Respond.

The responding party must serve its answers and any objections within 30 days after being served with the interrogatories. A shorter or longer time may be stipulated to under Rule 29 or be ordered by the court.

(3) Answering Each Interrogatory.

Each interrogatory must, to the extent it is not objected to, be answered separately and fully in writing under oath.

(4) Objections.

The grounds for objecting to an interrogatory must be stated with specificity. Any ground not stated in a timely objection is waived unless the court, for good cause, excuses the failure.

(5) Signature.

The person who makes the answers must sign them, and the attorney who objects must sign any objections.

(c) Use.

An answer to an interrogatory may be used to the extent allowed by the Federal Rules of Evidence.

(d) Option to Produce Business Records.

If the answer to an interrogatory may be determined by examining, auditing, compiling, abstracting, or summarizing a party's business records (including electronically stored information), and if the burden of deriving or ascertaining the answer will be substantially the same for either party, the responding party may answer by:

(1) specifying the records that must be reviewed, in sufficient detail to enable the interrogating party to locate and identify them as readily as the responding party could; and

(2) giving the interrogating party a reasonable opportunity to examine and audit the records and to make copies, compilations, abstracts, or summaries.

Discovery of documents usually starts with interrogatories seeking information not only about current documents, but also about the party's retention policies and the items or types of items that may have been destroyed. A good starting point is to submit an interrogatory asking the party to identify key persons who might have created or received any relevant electronically stored information. Exhibit 13.4 is a portion of sample interrogatories related to the discovery of electronic data.

Using Rule 30 Depositions to Find Information

deposition
A form of discovery available to ask questions and obtain oral answers under oath from a witness or party to a lawsuit. Questions and answers are recorded stenographically.

With the information from the interrogatories, the next step in obtaining information that may lead to existing or destroyed ESI is using a Rule 30 deposition. A **deposition** is an opportunity to question a witness out of court, and under oath. Rule 30 provides for the deposition of a person who is knowledgeable about the opposing party's information management system. The text of Rule 30 is given in Exhibit 13.5.

Exhibit 13.4 Sample interrogatories and requests for production

---

INTERROGATORIES AND REQUESTS FOR PRODUCTION

Interrogatory No. X:

Describe the computer system(s) including, but not limited to, network servers, workstations, laptops, backups/archives and hand-held computers (including, but not limited to, personal organizers) used by [PARTY] currently and at any time within [TIME PERIOD], including, but not limited to, for each such system, the brand and model; the amount of memory and capacity of the hard disk(s); the make, model and capacity of any removable media or near-line storage systems; the name and version of the operating system; the name and version of network software, if any; the brand and model of all peripheral devices including tape drives, external disk drives, other storage devices and modems; the brand and version of major software in use on the system(s) during such period (including, but not limited to, electronic mail programs, workgroup collaboration programs or groupware, and scheduling software); and the name of all online (electronic) services accessed with the system(s) during such period.

Response:

Interrogatory No. X:

Provide the name, employer, title, business and home addresses and telephone numbers for each person with operational or maintenance responsibility for the computer system(s) described above during [TIME PERIOD], including, but not limited to, the person(s) who maintain the hardware described above; the person(s) responsible for installing software on the system(s); the person(s) responsible for the day-to-day operation of the system(s); the person(s) responsible for making backups or archiving files and data on the system(s); and the person(s) who can provide any passwords that may be necessary to access the appropriate computer system(s) or files.

Response:

Interrogatory No. X:

If not the same person(s) as identified in your answer to the immediately preceding interrogatory, identify by job title, job description, and business address and telephone number, the person(s) employed by [PARTY] who is/are the most knowledgeable about the policies, procedures and actual practices for retention and destruction of documents at [PARTY].

Response:

Interrogatory No. X:

Describe all efforts and procedures taken by [PARTY] since the notice of this action to gather and secure documents, including, but not limited to, electronically generated or stored word processing files, spreadsheets or other electronic documents, electronic mail, and backup copies of information that may be relevant to the facts of this case. Describe the manner in which the notice of such efforts or procedures was communicated to [PARTY'S] employees.

Response:

Interrogatory No. X:

Has [PARTY] created any images of any computer since notice of this litigation? If so, identify each computer, the date the image was created, and the current location of the media containing the image.

LexisNexis.

Exhibit 13.5 Rule 30 regarding depositions

Rule 30. Deposition by Oral Examination

(6) Notice or Subpoena Directed to an Organization.

In its notice or subpoena, a party may name as the deponent a public or private corporation, a partnership, an association, a governmental agency, or other entity and must describe with reasonable particularity the matters for examination. The named organization must then designate one or more officers, directors, or managing agents, or designate other persons who consent to testify on its behalf; and it may set out the matters on which each person designated will testify. A subpoena must advise a nonparty organization of its duty to make this designation. The persons designated must testify about information known or reasonably available to the organization. This paragraph (6) does not preclude a deposition by any other procedure allowed by these rules.

A notice of deposition is a formal written request for a deposition. It provides the details of the questions that the deponent will be asked to answer, as shown in Exhibit 13.6.

Exhibit 13.6 Notice of Rule 30 deposition

UNITED STATES DISTRICT COURT
[XX] DISTRICT OF [STATE]

[NAME NAME], Plaintiff, v. [NAME NAME], Defendant.	No. XXX-XXXX NOTICE OF DEPOSITION PURSUANT TO FED. R. CIV. P. 30(b)(6)

TO: **[DEPONENT'S NAME]**
    AND TO: [ATTORNEY'S NAME], attorney of record

PLEASE TAKE NOTICE that the testimony of [DEPONENT] will be taken upon Oral Examination pursuant to Fed. R. Civ. P. 30(b)(6) at the request of the [PARTY] in the above-entitled and numbered action, before a Notary Public on [DATE] at [TIME] at the offices of [LOCATION, ADDRESS].

This deposition shall be subject to continuance or adjournment from time-to-time and place-to-place until completed, and will be taken on the ground and for the reason that this witness will give evidence material to the establishment of [PARTY'S] case.

Pursuant to Federal Rule of Civil Procedure 30(b)(6), [PARTY'S] corporate designee(s) shall be prepared to testify regarding the following subjects, all with respect to [PARTY'S] information technology systems:

I. SYSTEM PROFILE
1. Types of data processing and data storage devices used by company in the course of business.
2. Network architecture and usage policies.
3. Number, types, and locations of computers (including desktops, laptops, PDAs, cell phones, etc.) currently in use or in use at any time during the past [XX] years.
4. Brands and versions of software used on computer system(s).
5. File naming and saving conventions.
6. Identity of the person(s) responsible for the ongoing operation, maintenance, expansion, backup, and upkeep of computer systems and how frequently these activities occur (according to policy and actual practice).
7. Policies and practices for usage of home computers for business purposes.
8. Any modification of use of computers since notice of litigation.
9. Utility programs used to permanently "wipe files" from computer(s) in the company and date(s) used since notice of litigation.
10. Upgrades to computer hardware in the past [XX] months.
11. Upgrades or replacements to computer software in the past [XX] months.

II. BACKUP AND RETENTION
1. Electronic records management policies and procedures.
2. Steps taken to ensure preservation of electronic data.
3. Deletion of any documents since lawsuit commenced or since deponent received notification about litigation or pending litigation.
4. Instructions about preservation of electronic documents due to the lawsuit: Who provided notification? How was it disseminated? What procedures were in place for verification of receipt?
5. Backup software program(s) used (e.g., ARCserve, Backup Exec, StorageExpress, etc.).
6. Any modification of backup procedures since notice of litigation.
7. Information about disaster recovery plans in place currently and during past [XX] years.
8. Backup tape or archival disk naming/labeling conventions.
9. Location of backup tapes and other backup media.
10. Method and schedule used if files are ever deleted from the computer system(s).
11. Location(s), if any, where files are "archived" off the system.
12. Dates, if any, when data was restored from backup tapes within the past [XX] months. If so: What data was restored? Why was the data restored?

Exhibit 13.6 Continued

III. POLICIES AND PROCEDURES

1. Policy regarding purging of individual directories when an employee leaves the company (on desktop, laptop, and server systems).

2. Policy regarding reassigning workstations to incoming employees.
3. Policy regarding disposal/recycling/sale of hardware.
4. Procedures for handling used disks or drives before destruction or sale.
5. Policy and procedure for use of outside contractors to upgrade either hardware or software for system maintenance.

IV. DATABASES

1. Types of databases used (CRM, accounting, etc.).
2. Type(s) and names of database software used (e.g., Oracle, dBASE, Advanced Revelation, Access, proprietary, etc.).
3. The fields of information used in the database(s).
4. Identity of person(s) responsible for database design, database maintenance, report design, database backup.
5. Identity of person(s) who enter information into the database.
6. Ways and by whom the database is accessed.
7. Identification of any standard reports prepared on a routine basis.
8. Incidents and dates on which database files have been re-indexed, purged, repaired, or archived.
9. Protocol for using passwords or encrypted files are used on any of the computer systems, including name(s) of person(s) who manage this process.
10. Policy for changing/revoking passwords and access codes when an employee leaves the company.
11. Method used for those outside the company to access the computers (VPN or other).

V. EMAIL SYSTEMS

1. Identity of person(s) responsible for administering the email system(s).
2. Identification of all type(s) of email programs currently in use, including name(s) and version number(s), installation date(s), and number of users.
3. Location of users' email files (e.g., mail messages stored in a central location—a server—or locally on users' desktops, or both?).
4. Ways, if any, users can access their email remotely (e.g., from outside the office via BlackBerry or other wireless device, or via a web mail application).
5. Protocol for routinely changing email passwords.
6. Policy for running "janitorial" programs to purge email.
7. Identification of any other email systems used in the past [XX] years.
8. Details about email retention policies and practices (e.g., retention period, auto-delete features, deletion procedures, etc.)
9. Restoration of any mailboxes from backup tapes within the past [XX] months/years. If applicable, identify: What mailbox(es) was/were restored? Was the restoration operation successful? What resources were required to perform the restoration (labor hours, equipment, drive space, etc.).
10. Special active email retention settings.
11. Incidents and dates on which email databases have been re-indexed, purged, repaired, or archived.
12. Protocol for using passwords or encrypted files are used on any of the computer systems, including name(s) of person(s) who manage this process.
13. Policy for changing/revoking passwords and access codes when an employee leaves the company.
14. Method used for those outside the company to access the computers (VPN or other).

VI. MISCELLANEOUS

1. Information about production of electronic documents in other litigation or legal proceedings: Which cases were produced? What was produced, in what format?
2. Information about any persons who examined any of the company's computers since learning of this lawsuit, including details about reasons for examination and protocol utilized.

DATED this XX day of [MONTH, YEAR].

[LAW FIRM NAME]

By _____

[ATTORNEYS]

Attorneys for [PARTY]

This paragraph clarifies what is acceptable under the prior rule 30.

Rule 26. Duty to Disclose; General Provisions Governing Discovery.

(2) Limitations on Frequency and Extent.

(A) *When Permitted.* By order, the court may alter the limits in these rules on the number of depositions and interrogatories or on the length of depositions under Rule 30. By order or local rule, the court may also limit the number of requests under Rule 36.

(B) *Specific Limitations on Electronically Stored Information.* A party need not provide discovery of electronically stored information from sources that the party identifies as not reasonably accessible because of undue burden or cost. On motion to compel discovery or for a protective order, the party from whom discovery is sought must show that the information is not reasonably accessible because of undue burden or cost. If that showing is made, the court may nonetheless order discovery from such sources if the requesting party shows good cause, considering the limitations of Rule 26(b)(2)(C). The court may specify conditions for the discovery.

(C) *When Required.* On motion or on its own, the court must limit the frequency or extent of discovery otherwise allowed by these rules or by local rule if it determines that:

  (i) the discovery sought is unreasonably cumulative or duplicative, or can be obtained from some other source that is more convenient, less burdensome, or less expensive;

  (ii) the party seeking discovery has had ample opportunity to obtain the information by discovery in the action; or

  (iii) the burden or expense of the proposed discovery outweighs its likely benefit, considering the needs of the case, the amount in controversy, the parties' resources, the importance of the issues at stake in the action, and the importance of the discovery in resolving the issues.

■ COLLECTION

LEARNING OBJECTIVE 4
Describe the issues that arise in using search queries in e-discovery.

The collection phase is the part of e-discovery that involves finding and obtaining electronically stored information for review and analysis. The collection process may require retaining outside professionals who are experienced in searching databases. These specialists will need to understand the many different systems used for creating, storing, or archiving the ESI so that the data can be retrieved in a usable form. For example, some older information may have been stored on types of storage media that cannot be accessed by modern computers. In the 1970s, 15-inch floppy disks were used to store data, which were replaced with the 5-inch floppy in the 1980s. These were then replaced in the 1990s with the 3½-inch floppy. In the 2000s, floppies were replaced altogether by CDs and "thumb drives." Although no current computer systems have 15-inch disk drives, preliminary discovery may reveal the possibility of critical information on an old 15-inch floppy. A specialist should then be called in to access this information using a floppy disk drive and software that can read the original data.

Search Queries

search queries
Specific words used in a computerized search.

Boolean
[Author to provide definition in pages]

Finding information on a computer, database, or a website usually requires a **search query,** or a set of parameters that can narrow the data down to the relevant material. Lawyers and paralegals are trained to use queries with keywords to search legal literature. The most familiar method used for constructing a search query is the **Boolean** model. This model uses keywords with connectors such as

AND and OR. Selecting the right keyword and the right connectors is critical to obtaining good search results. However, those familiar with the process know that a Boolean search is not always reliable. If the wrong words are used, or word combinations are not properly structured, the computer may not find the desired information.

Often, a Boolean search is unsuccessful because the researcher was not familiar with the specific terms used in the particular industry or profession. Information may also be obscured through strategies designed to throw off anyone searching the recor ds. For example, the author of a document may use unrelated terms as identifiers. Or, companies like Apple and Microsoft may use code words to hide the existence of a new product under development.

Boolean search queries often do not provide the accuracy required for a particular purpose. A number of other search methods have thus been developed and are

IN THE WORDS OF THE COURT . . .

WILLIAM A. GROSS CONSTRUCTION   :
ASSOCIATES, INC.,

          Plaintiff,   :   07 Civ. 10639 (LAK) (AJP)

          -against-   :   **OPINION AND ORDER**

AMERICAN MANUFACTURERS MUTUAL
INSURANCE COMPANY,   :

ANDREW J. PECK, United States Magistrate Judge:

This Opinion should serve as a wake-up call to the Bar in this District about the need for careful thought, quality control, testing, and cooperation with opposing counsel in designing search terms or "keywords" to be used to produce emails or other electronically stored information ("ESI"). While this message has appeared in several cases from outside this Circuit, it appears that the message has not reached many members of our Bar.

Discussion

This case is just the latest example of lawyers designing keyword searches in the dark, by the seat of the pants, without adequate (indeed, here, apparently without any) discussion with those who wrote the emails. Prior decisions from Magistrate Judges in the Baltimore-Washington Beltway have warned counsel of this problem, but the message has not gotten through to the Bar in this District. As Magistrate Judge Paul Grimm has stated:

> While keyword searches have long been recognized as appropriate and helpful for ESI search and retrieval, there are well-known limitations and risks associated with them, and proper selection and implementation obviously involves technical, if not scientific[,] knowledge.

>   * * *

> Selection of the appropriate search and information retrieval technique requires careful advance planning by persons qualified to design effective search methodology. The implementation of the methodology selected should be tested for quality assurance; and the party selecting the methodology must be prepared to explain the rationale for the method chosen to the court, demonstrate that it is appropriate for the task, and show that it was properly implemented.

Victor Stanley, Inc. v. Creative Pipe, Inc., 250 F.R.D. 251, 260, 262 (D. Md. May 29, 2008) (Grimm, M.J.).

used by different search engines and electronic discovery software in an attempt to improve search accuracy. For example, in an algebraic search, a mathematical model is created to retrieve documents based on the proximity of certain words to others.

When using a search query, it is important to remember that words are not static—their meaning may change over time, or they may be applied to new areas. Consider the contemporary use of the word "head": to an automotive engineer, it is part of an engine; to a sailor, it is a bathroom. But a search may also miss some items because the search terms are too narrow. A topic or idea can often be described by a wide variety of words or expressions, yet the words contained in a query may be too limited to capture all of the items on the topic. A **concept search** can broaden the search by including similar or related terms in the query to stretch the net farther.

concept search
Using a list of terms statistically related to the words in a query.

Other search types include:

- Adaptive pattern recognition
- Associative retrieval
- Combined word search
- Full-text search
- Fuzzy search
- Indexing
- Keyword search
- Natural language search
- Numeric range search
- Phonic search
- Phrase search
- Proximity search
- Range search
- Similar document search
- Sound-alike search
- Stemming
- Synonym search
- Term search
- Topical search
- Variable weighted search
- Weighted relevance search
- Wildcard search

Accurate searches are essential to reducing the cost of electronic discovery. If searches are haphazard, or use poor techniques, they must be repeated. The more searches are run, the greater the cost. The need for search accuracy is not limited to the legal profession or for e-discovery—rather, it is a broad concern in every area of business and science. Although it is understood that no search will be 100 percent accurate, a high rate of success is important.

ADVICE FROM THE FIELD

THE U.S. HOUSE OF REPRESENTATIVES U.S. CODE OFFICE OF THE REVISION COUNSEL

Concept Search: Exploring A General Idea

Because of the richness of language, a topic or idea can be described with a wide variety of words or expressions. For this reason, a conventional search may be too limiting when you want to research a broad topic area. If other records discuss the desired topic but do so in terms other than those included in your query, they may not be retrieved.

Rather than formulating an all-encompassing query, you can perform concept searching.

In a concept search, PLWeb Turbo first generates a list of terms that are statistically related to the words in your query. This list is similar to the operation of the Relate Advisor. Those words that have a significant degree of co-occurrence with your query words are deemed related within the context of the current database. If you are searching a virtual database, related words will be identified for all open databases.

After generating the aforementioned list, the concept search operation then performs a conventional search using the original query words as well as the related terms. You will find that many of the records retrieved, while perhaps not having occurrences of your original query words, will nonetheless contain information that is relevant to your search interests.

Source: http://uscode.house.gov/search/help/htmlsrc/consrch.html

IN THE WORDS OF THE COURT . . .

UNITED STATES DISTRICT COURT
FOR THE DISTRICT OF COLUMBIA

United States of America,

Vs

Michael John O'Keefe, Sr.,

Sunil Agrawal,

Defendants.   v. Cr. No. 06-249 (PLF/JMF)

MEMORANDUM OPINION

3. Search Terms and Other Deficiencies

As noted above, defendants protest the search terms the government used.
Whether search terms or "keywords" will yield the information sought is a complicated question involving the interplay, at least, of the sciences of computer
technology, statistics and linguistics.... Indeed, a special project team of the
Working Group on Electronic Discovery of the Sedona Conference is studying
that subject and their work indicates how difficult this question is....

Given this complexity, for lawyers and judges to dare opine that a certain search term or terms would be more likely to produce information than
the terms that were used is truly to go where angels fear to tread. This topic
is clearly beyond the ken of a layman and requires that any such conclusion
be based on evidence that, for example, meets the criteria of Rule 702 of the
Federal Rules of Evidence. Accordingly, if defendants are going to contend
that the search terms used by the government were insufficient, they will have
to specifically so contend in a motion to compel and their contention must
be based on evidence that meets the requirements of Rule 702 of the Federal
Rules of Evidence.

Text Retrieval Conference

The issue of search accuracy has become the subject of an annual conference
to encourage research in large text collections. The Text Retrieval Conference
(TREC), co-sponsored by the National Institute of Standards and Technology,
seeks to increase the effectiveness of electronic research.

One of the conference sections is the Legal Track, which seeks to develop
search technology that meets the needs of lawyers who must pursue discovery
in digital document collections. As part of the annual meeting, a set of simulated complaints are used as the basis of a search query that will locate the
ESI needed in the case. The plaintiff and defense counsel must collaborate to
create each query. In Exhibit 13.7, an example is shown of the fictitious case
of *Jensen v Smokin' Cigarettes*. A number of topics are run to test the search systems. In this example, the topic "all documents concerning actual or projected
sales" is shown. The final search using a Boolean query resulted in an accuracy
of 55 percent.

Exhibit 13.7 A document search in a hypothetical case during the Text Retrieval Conference

PLAINTIFF'S REQUESTS FOR PRODUCTION OF DOCUMENTS

Pursuant to Rule 34 of the Federal Rules of Civil Procedure, Plaintiff Jenny Je[n]sen requests that Smokin' Cigarettes, Inc. and Jesse Winston (collectively, "Defendants") produce all responsive documents requested herein at the office of undersigned counsel as soon as practicable.

INSTRUCTIONS

1. These requests require the production of all responsive documents within the sole or joint possession, custody or control of the Defendants, including their agents, departments, attorneys, directors, officers, employees, consultants, investigators, insurance companies, or other persons subject to Defendants' custody or control.

2. All documents that respond, in whole or in part, to any portion of these Requests must be produced in their entirety, including all attachments and enclosures.

3. For purposes of these requests, the words used are considered to have, and should be understood to have, their ordinary, everyday meanings. Plaintiffs refer Defendants to any dictionary in the event Defendants assert that the wording of a request is vague, ambiguous, unintelligible, or confusing.

DEFINITIONS

4. The words "and," "or," "each," "any," "all," "refer," and "discuss," shall be construed in their broadest form and the singular shall include the plural and the plural shall include the singular whenever necessary so as to bring within the scope of these Requests all documents (defined below) that might otherwise be construed to be outside their scope.

5. The phrase "advertising, marketing or promotion" of cigarettes includes public relations activities involving smoking and health.

6. For present purposes, the term "defendants" includes Smokin' Cigarettes Inc. as well as those companies whose records are found in the Tobacco Master Settlement Agreement database.

7. Solely for the purpose of the TREC 2008 legal track, "document" means all text-searchable data, information or writings stored in the Tobacco Master Settlement Agreement database, including without limitation: any written, electronic or computerized files, data or software; memoranda; emails; correspondence; OCR scanned images; communications; reports; summaries; studies; analyses; evaluations; notes or notebooks; indices; spreadsheets; logs; books; pamphlets; binders; calendar or diary entries; ledger entries; press clippings; graphs; tables; charts; printouts; drawings; maps; meeting minutes; transcripts. The term "document" encompasses all metadata associated with the document. The term also includes all drafts associated with any particular document.

8. "Person" or "individual" means natural persons, corporations, firms, partnerships, unincorporated associations, trusts, and any other legal entity.

9. The term "plans" means tentative and preliminary proposals, recommendations, or considerations, whether or not finalized or authorized, as well as those that have been adopted.

10. The term "relating to" means in whole or in part constituting, containing, concerning, discussing, describing, analyzing, identifying or stating.

FIRST SET OF REQUESTS FOR PRODUCTION:

Plaintiffs request that Defendants produce all responsive documents on the following topics:

   [TOPIC 145] All documents concerning actual or projected sales.

Topic 145 (2008-H-4)

Request Text: All documents concerning actual or projected sales.

Initial Proposal by Defendant: "actual sales" OR "projected sales"

Rejoinder by Plaintiff: (estimate! OR anticipate! OR forecast! OR actual[!] OR project!) w/5 sales

Final Negotiated Boolean Query: (estimate! OR anticipate! OR forecast! OR actual[!] OR project!) w/2 sales

Sampling: 6910192 pooled, 2500 assessed, 419 judged highly relevant, 258 other judged relevant, 1816 judged non-relevant, 7 gray, \C"=5.60

Est. Rel.: 461322.3 (including 143094.7 estimated highly relevant)

Final Boolean Result Size (B): 40315, F1: 8.4%, (Precision: 55.0%, Recall: 4.6%)

Sampling

The accuracy of a search query can be tested using **sampling.** In this technique, the query is run against a limited set of documents to measure its accuracy. Consider a simple test in which information is sought about product defects in automobiles made by major manufacturers. Using words such as "car" or "automobile" would result in substantial numbers of records, most of which would probably not contain the desired information. In the context of litigation, the failure to place limits on a search during discovery can have disastrous consequences. One example is recorded in the Fannie Mae securities litigation, in which over four hundred search terms were used, covering 660,000 documents. As this case demonstrates, it can be a waste of time and money to search a large database of ESI using a query with terms and phrases that are not properly selected.

sampling
The testing of a search query by running it against a limited set of documents to measure the accuracy of the response to the search query.

 WEB RESOURCES
Sedona Conference® working group 1 documents on Electronic Document Retention and Production may be viewed at http://www.thesedona-conference.org/content/miscFiles/publications_html?grp=wgs110.

Computer Forensics

In some cases, critical data has been modified or deleted from documents produced in discovery, and dates of these modifications or changes may be very relevant and material. The metadata of these documents will usually show the dates of any changes. Qualified forensic experts can examine the original hard drive to determine if there were any changes or deletions of material. However, it is important to remember that each time a document is opened, the metadata changes. Therefore, in cases where forensic data collection is required, it is important to have an expert who can obtain the information without changing anything on the original storage media.

LEARNING OBJECTIVE 5
Describe the role of a forensic examiner in e-discovery.

 WEB RESOURCES
Review the efforts of the Legal Track at the websites for Information Technology Laboratory (ITL) and Intelligence Advanced Research Projects Activity (IARPA) at http://trec.nist.gov/overview.html.

 WEB RESOURCES
To learn more about computer forensics, go to http://searchsecurity.tech-target.com/sDefinition/0,,sid14_gci1007675,00.html.

 ## IN THE WORDS OF THE COURT . . .

United States Court of Appeals,
District of Columbia Circuit.

In re FANNIE MAE SECURITIES LITIGATION.

No. 08-5014.

Decided Jan. 6, 2009.

Pursuant to the stipulated order, the individual defendants submitted over 400 search terms, which covered approximately 660,000 documents. OFHEO objected on the grounds that the stipulated order limited the individual defendants to "appropriate search terms," but the district court disagreed, ruling on November 2, 2007 that the stipulated order gave the individual defendants sole discretion to specify search terms and imposed no limits on permissible terms. Although the district court made this ruling in an off-the-record chambers conference, the parties agree on its meaning.

OFHEO undertook extensive efforts to comply with the stipulated order, hiring 50 contract attorneys solely for that purpose. The total amount OFHEO spent on the individual defendants' discovery requests eventually reached over $6 million, more than 9 percent of the agency's entire annual budget.

ADVICE FROM THE FIELD

LEXISNEXIS APPLIED DISCOVERY TECH TIPS: UNDERSTANDING THE DIFFERENCE BETWEEN COMPUTER FORENSICS AND DATA GATHERING

As the field of electronic discovery has evolved over the past several years, there has been increasing confusion about the difference between computer forensics—a specialized application of scientific principles and practices—and data gathering, the process for collecting documents and other electronic evidence from computers. Without understanding the differences between these services, many attorneys have paid to retain "forensics experts" in cases involving electronic discovery, when all they really needed was some good advice or hands-on assistance with collecting electronic files from their clients' computers.

Think of computer forensics as taking an "autopsy" of a computer hard drive. The science of computer forensics can be of great value in certain circumstances. For example, allegations of attempts to delete incriminating documents from a computer may be confirmed or refuted with the assistance of a forensic expert. Similarly, information from computer equipment damaged in a fire or flood may be recoverable with the assistance of a forensic data recovery expert. A forensic investigation can take heroic efforts and many hours of an expensive consultant's time to find the electronic needle in the haystack. Fortunately, most cases involving electronic discovery do not warrant such a burdensome expenditure.

	Computer Forensics	**Data Gathering**
Goal	To locate hidden or deleted files.	To capture potentially responsive documents.
Tools Required	Highly specialized, expensive hardware and software.	Relatively inexpensive tools utilized by most client IT departments.
Expertise Required	Computer forensics experts.	IT staff trained by or assisted by electronic discovery service provider.
Relative Expense	Can cost thousands of dollars to analyze a single hard drive.	Cost efficient methods employed to leverage the client's own resources.

Many attorneys facing an electronic discovery request need only basic assistance with data gathering. While it is critical to employ forensically sound data collection practices, in many cases, this may be as simple as providing procedures for how to intelligently and safely copy data from a computer hard drive to a CD-ROM, tape, or other transportable media. These forensically sound practices will ensure that metadata is not altered when data is copied from its original location. They will also help attorneys understand how best to save and store the copied information for use with electronic discovery review tools.

In other cases, attorneys may need on-site assistance to collect data from multiple physical locations or to assist with chain of custody tracking. In these circumstances, chain of custody tracking would include detailed documentation of the data collection procedures, who had custody of the electronic data, who collected it from its original location, and where the data was located when collected. Further tracking measures should include application of bar codes to individual pieces of media and storage in a secured evidence room.

Electronic discovery often presents unique circumstances that depend on how well the client's documents are sorted and organized in the ordinary course of business. Your electronic discovery service provider should be able to advise you on how best to approach the particular circumstances of a given case.

Source: LexisNexis.

■ CHAIN OF CUSTODY

Those who have watched some of the current crime and forensic television shows have probably heard the term **"chain of custody"** regarding evidence. In a criminal case, the chain of custody begins with the paper or plastic bags used to collect and store evidence. Steps are then taken to ensure that the evidence is properly preserved, and that the possession of the evidence is properly documented at each step in the processing, pretrial, and trial phases of the case. Any failure to follow the prescribed protocol can result in the evidence lacking credibility at the time of trial.

chain of custody
A written record showing the identity of everyone accessing evidence and showing that the evidence was not altered while in possession of the law firm.

The chain of custody also plays a role in electronic evidence. Sources of electronic documents such as hard disk drives and other storage media must be properly handled, accessed, and preserved to ensure the integrity of the electronic files. Unless certain steps are taken, the metadata is updated electronically to reflect the change in the file's history—and this takes place every time an electronic file is opened or accessed. For example, each time you open a Word document and then save it, the metadata within the file keeps a record of the time and date you opened and saved it, even if you made no changes to the content of the document. If the date a file was created is relevant in a case, the original version must be preserved to prevent changes of any type occurring to the underlying metadata. Much like the preservation of physical evidence at a crime scene, electronic evidence may be preserved in sealed "digital evidence bags," as shown in Exhibit 13.8. In this way, a chain of custody of an electronic file is maintained to prove no changes have occurred. If a claim is made of spoliation, the legal team may offer proof that the forensic examination was properly conducted.

■ RESOURCES TO SUPPORT E-DISCOVERY

Service Companies

Law firms sometimes lack in-house expertise or have a workload that prevents them from being able to handle extensive e-discovery. In those situations, firms often retain a service bureau or consulting company to help in the electronic discovery process. Some full-service companies offer a range of services—from the basic, such as simply scanning paper documents into electronic form, to the complex, such as forensic recovery or investigation of lost, destroyed, or missing files. In some cases, allowing a specialist to prepare and deliver the documents may be a better allocation of resources. The trend for companies in this field is toward offering a complete range of products and services, from stand-alone software that may be used on the law firm's own computers to cloud computing systems that store and process ESI. A cloud system can allow any authorized member of the litigation team to access the ESI from anywhere in the world through the Internet.

AD Summation Software

As the number of documents in a case increases, the ability to locate relevant documents in a timely fashion becomes more and more critical, and managing the documents is crucial to successful litigation outcomes. In cases involving potentially millions of documents, it is essential for the legal team to be able to find the relevant information quickly, sometimes in the middle of the direct or cross-examination of a witness.

Exhibit 13.8 Digital Evidence Bags

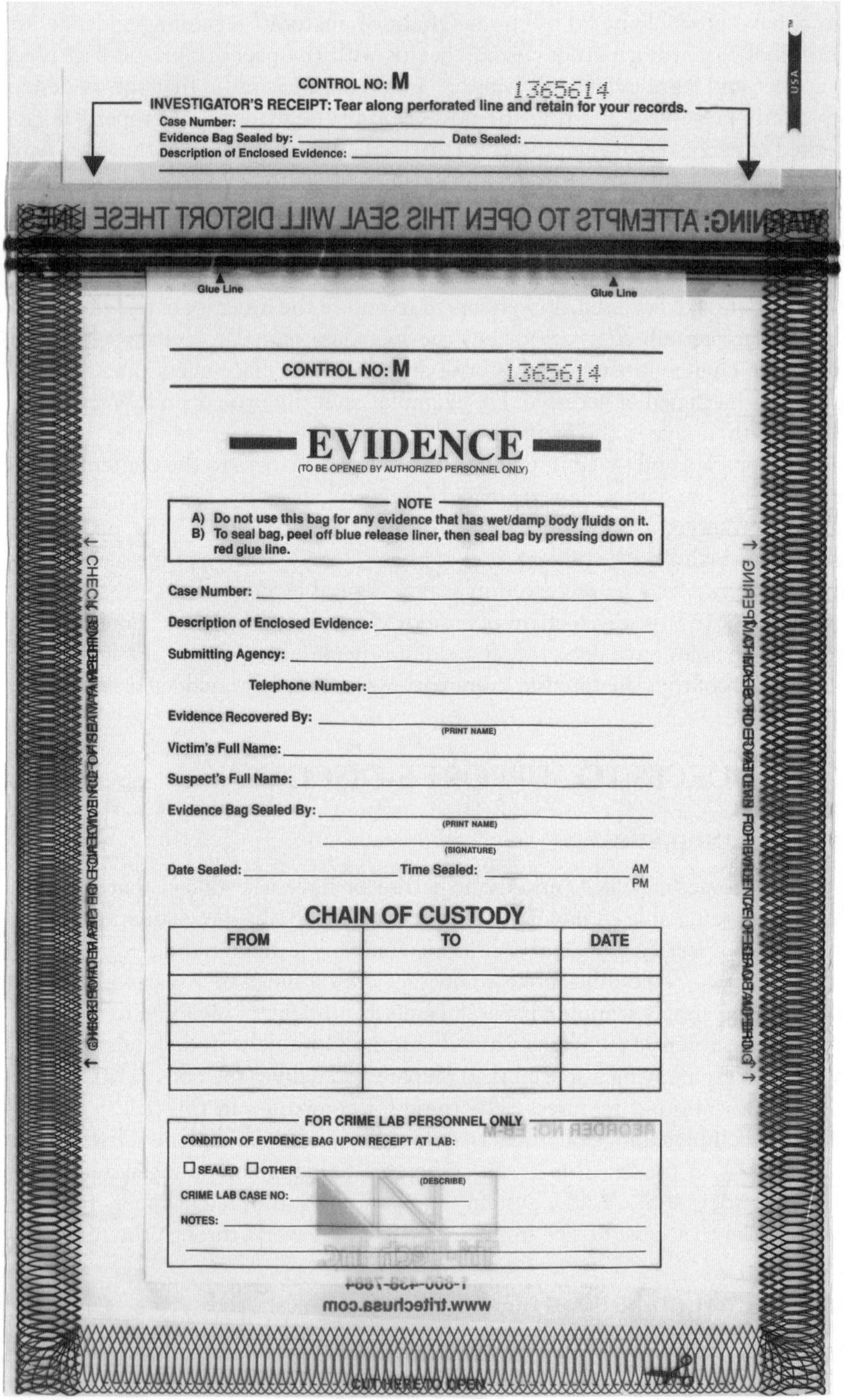

CONTROL NO: M 1365614

INVESTIGATOR'S RECEIPT: Tear along perforated line and retain for your records.

Case Number: ______

Evidence Bag Sealed by: ______ Date Sealed: ______

Description of Enclosed Evidence: ______

WARNING: ATTEMPTS TO OPEN THIS SEAL WILL DISTORT THESE LINES

Glue Line Glue Line

CONTROL NO: M 1365614

EVIDENCE

(TO BE OPENED BY AUTHORIZED PERSONNEL ONLY)

NOTE

A) Do not use this bag for any evidence that has wet/damp body fluids on it.
B) To seal bag, peel off blue release liner, then seal bag by pressing down on red glue line.

Case Number: ______

Description of Enclosed Evidence: ______

Submitting Agency: ______

Telephone Number: ______

Evidence Recovered By: ______ (PRINT NAME)

Victim's Full Name: ______

Suspect's Full Name: ______

Evidence Bag Sealed By: ______ (PRINT NAME)

______ (SIGNATURE)

Date Sealed: ______ Time Sealed: ______ AM PM

CHAIN OF CUSTODY

FROM	TO	DATE

FOR CRIME LAB PERSONNEL ONLY

CONDITION OF EVIDENCE BAG UPON RECEIPT AT LAB:

☐ SEALED ☐ OTHER ______ (DESCRIBE)

CRIME LAB CASE NO: ______

NOTES: ______

CUT HERE TO OPEN

ADVICE FROM THE FIELD

BLUEPRINT FOR CLOUD-BASED EDISCOVERY—ON DEMAND TECHNOLOGY
A Framework for eDiscovery Cloud Computing Security, Privacy, Control, Risk and Cost Concerns

Bringing eDiscovery in-house: eDiscovery cloud versus on-premise software

When considering a cloud-based eDiscovery application versus an on-premise application, one must consider not only the audience and focus for the application being delivered, but also the hardware, systems, data centers and human capital necessary to deliver the application. For corporations and law firms looking to bring eDiscovery in-house, cloud-based eDiscovery can be very attractive. Cloud-based eDiscovery is often less risky, less costly and more efficient than purchasing, installing and maintaining on-premise software. eDiscovery practitioners control the process, data and access without incurring the costs, risks and time delays[3,4] inherent in on-premise software deployments or the headaches involved [in] lobbying your IT department to modify your corporate firewall and security standards to allow outside parties to access on-premise eDiscovery software. Initial cloud computing application deployment is proven to be much faster and on-going maintenance

costs are proven to be much less expensive than on-premise software deployments.[3,4] Additionally, cloud-based eDiscovery software can provide highly predictable costs that eliminate the expense spikes typically associated with on-premise software, hardware, and human capital.

There has been a lot of misinformation equating "bringing eDiscovery in-house" with the purchase, installation and on-going management of on-premise software for various eDiscovery tasks. The true nature of bringing eDiscovery in-house is that corporate legal teams and their executives are trending toward retaining control of eDiscovery decision-making, creating and owning the overall eDiscovery process and acting as collaborative partners throughout the life cycle of a particular matter. The delivery model for eDiscovery software and services, cloud-based or on-premise, is not directly related to the notion of "bringing eDiscovery in-house."

According to Forrester Research, Inc.[3] the benefits of cloud-based applications include:

Dimension	Software-as-a-service helps by…
Reduced cost adoption	Reducing the licensing, training, and support costs of adding additional users.
Quicker adoption	Decreasing the time to ramp up new users, maximizing their productivity from using the application.
Improved adoption	Enabling more users to use the application.
On-premise cost avoidance	■ Eliminating maintenance costs. ■ Reducing full-time help desk and server support, and transferring staff to higher value, proactive roles.
Improved flexibility	Reducing spend on excess capacity.

Public Clouds and Private Clouds: Why public clouds are wrong for eDiscovery

The difference between public and private clouds is very important for those performing eDiscovery. A public cloud uses shared hardware, software and applications that are available to the public. Examples include Amazon EC2, AWS and Google Apps. This approach is very effective when used for consumer-based applications or business applications that do not have the same security and access control requirements or the level of legal and regulatory scrutiny that eDiscovery data has. A private cloud, whether

deployed by a company behind the firewall (aka "internal cloud") or deployed by a provider, uses hardware, software and applications only for subscribing users.

Private clouds have specific advantages over public clouds when it comes to eDiscovery: With a public cloud you don't know where (including what country, state or server) the files are stored, and don't know if you can really control document retention and destruction. And you may not be receiving the level of disaster recovery and business continuity that you require. Clients need to know that they are completely in control of their data, and a private, trusted cloud is the only way to do that.

(continued)

(continued)

As recently cited in the *Electronic Commerce & Law Report*, a non-private cloud pools resources to serve multiple clients, which "implies both an increased risk of inadvertent access to data by others in the cloud and an inability to pinpoint with any specificity where data resides at a given moment."

With private clouds, subscribers understand where their data resides, so their information aligns with proper jurisdiction, security and applicable document retention.[5]

[3] "The ROI of Software-as-a-Service," by Forrester Research, Inc., Liz Herbert and Jon Erickson, July 13, 2009

[4] "Talking To Your CFO About Cloud Computing," by Forrester Research, October 29, 2008

[5] Sotto, Lisa J., Bridget C. Treacy, and Melinda L. McLellan. "Privacy and Data Security Risks in Cloud Computing," *Electronic Commerce & Law Report,* February 3, 2010

Reproduced in part from Blueprint for Cloud-Based eDiscovery—On Demand Technology

The full article may be viewed at: www.CaseCentral.com/cloudblueprint.php
Courtesy of CaseCentral, Inc., www.CaseCentral.com

AD Summation software and other, competitive products allow for easy search and retrieval of all of the evidence—whether documents, testimony, photographs, or electronic files—with a single command. Documents associated with a case are stored on the computer in electronic folders. These folders may be set up to include transcripts, pleadings, and core databases. Some versions of these programs are designed to work on stand-alone systems such as a laptop carried into court. Others permit concurrent use by many users over a network, and some permit remote access over the Internet.

Concordance

Concordance, by LexisNexis, is a litigation support system that provides focused document management. According to LexisNexis,

> Concordance is a highly focused text database management program that features sophisticated text search and retrieval functions. Text database management differs substantially from traditional database management in that its focus is searching for, retrieving, and categorizing specific words, phrases, or combinations of words. The ability to perform detailed text searches is particularly important for individuals whose work is heavily text-concentrated, for example attorneys, scientific researchers, marketing researchers, librarians, and personnel managers for resume retrieval.

CaseCentral

CaseCentral provides secure, cloud-based e-discovery software. First created in 1994, CaseCentral's software was the industry's first web-based discovery management system to support clients throughout the various stages of litigation and e-discovery. Its e-discovery platform integrates early case assessment, processing, search, analysis, review, and production capabilities with a **private cloud** delivery model. This model allows users to log in through the Internet from anywhere, and create and load new cases almost immediately. It also provides the necessary technology infrastructure, thus eliminating the need for corporations and law firms to provide these resources in-house.

Users can perform early case assessment, review, and production in one online environment. They can also conduct advanced searches to cull and filter documents and identify specific groups for further review. Using the same system, documents

private cloud
An Internet-based service that allows restricted access to information stored on servers of a third-party host company.

Exhibit 13.9 Steps in CaseCentral's e-discovery process

> ### Step 1. Early Case Assessment
> Search and analyze large sets of data to quickly determine what ultimatelly needs active review
>
> ### Step 2. Integrated Review
> Evaluate and tag document and groups of documents in preparation for production
> • Responsiveness and Privilege review
> • Redaction and issue coding
> • Witness preparation and trial strategy
>
> ### Step 3. Post Review Utilization
> Utilize the work product to guide your litigation hold or preservation strategy for further ECA or case management

Courtesy of CaseCentral, Inc., www.CaseCentral.com.

may also be reviewed and prepared before sending them to opposing counsel. The steps in CaseCentral's e-discovery process are shown in Exhibit 13.9.

Using CaseCentral, litigation support and attorneys can also search, analyze, code, and prepare documents for production, as shown in Exhibits 13.10 to 13.12.

CaseCentral's unique multi-matter support allows hundreds or even thousands of cases to be managed within the same repository, sharing workflow,

Exhibit 13.10 Documents view and related review criteria tagging window

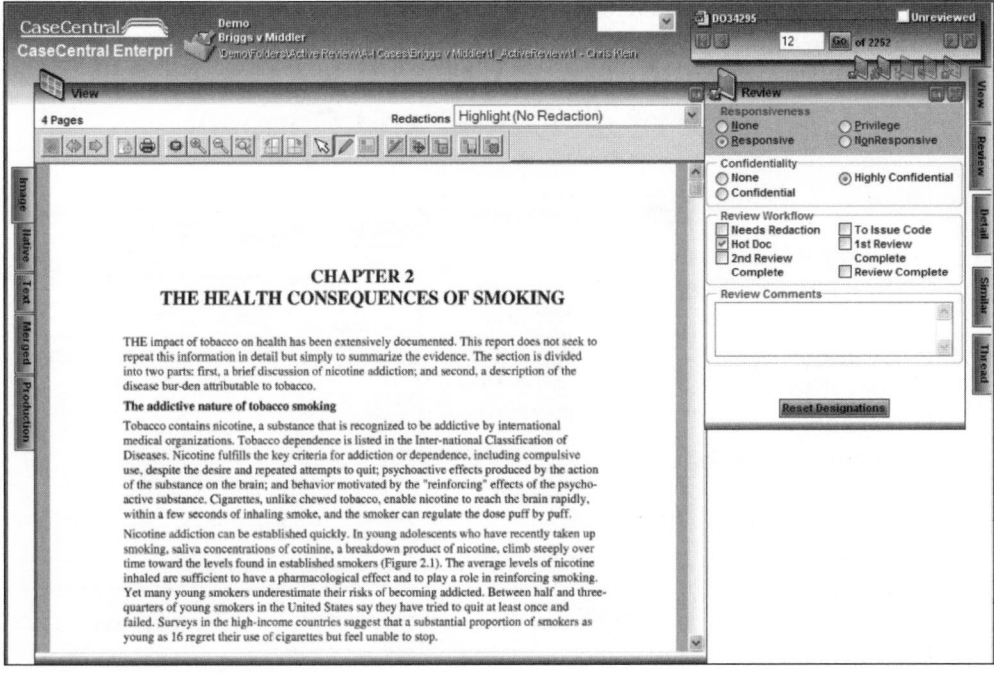

Courtesy of CaseCentral, Inc., www.CaseCentral.com.

Exhibit 13.11 CaseCentral's report on near-duplicate documents

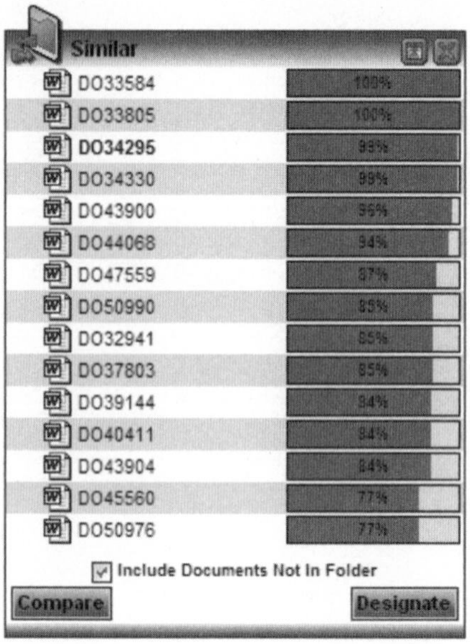

Exhibit 13.12 Related email threads of near-duplicate documents

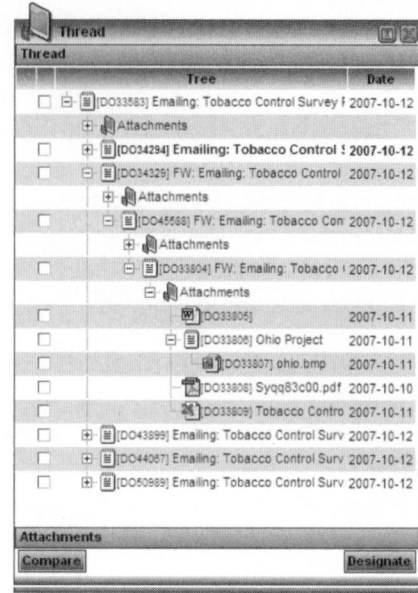

Courtesy of CaseCentral, Inc., www.CaseCentral.com.

Courtesy of CaseCentral, Inc., www.CaseCentral.com.

security roles, production processes, and even work product between cases. Prior to production, an administrator can even verify whether any documents have ever been withheld from any case. Exhibit 13.13 shows how all cases, reviewers, time lines, and counsel may be monitored from a single Administrator Dashboard.

Exhibit 13.13 CaseCentral's Administrator Dashboard monitor of all cases and counsel

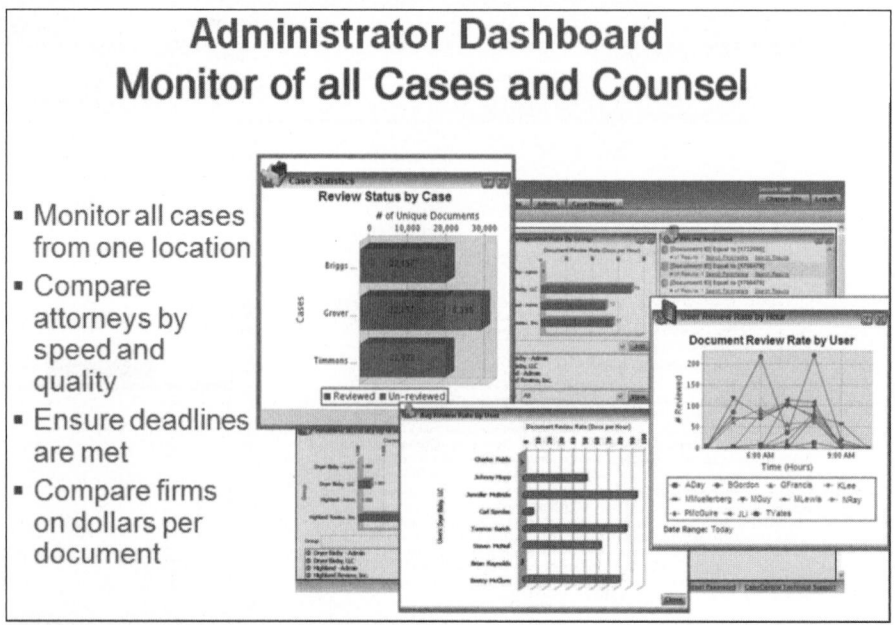

Courtesy of CaseCentral, Inc., www.CaseCentral.com.

CONCEPT REVIEW AND REINFORCEMENT

KEY TERMS

Boolean   360
chain of custody   367
concept search   362
deposition   356

Electronic Discovery Reference
   Model   346
Information Management Reference
   Model (IMRM)   352
interrogatories   355

private cloud   370
safe haven   351
sampling   365
search query   360

CHAPTER SUMMARY

Introduction to Evidence and Discovery	For the plaintiff's attorney, discovery is a matter of finding relevant evidence to present the case. For the plaintiff, it may also be a question of the timing of the action and where to institute suit. The defendant frequently is in the position of not knowing if or when a suit will be brought for which he or she will need a defense, and therefore not does necessarily know what records need to be preserved or for how long.
Electronic Discovery—The Process	Electronic discovery, or e-discovery, should be thought of as a process and not a single event. It consists of a number of steps or individual processes, as shown in the Electronic Discovery Reference Model in Exhibit 13.1: information management; identification; preservation and collection; processing, review, and analysis; production; and presentation.
Information Management	The first step for the litigation team is learning the details and procedures of each party's retention policy and that of any potential third parties, such as a supplier of the parties that may have relevant supporting information.
The Cost of Saving Electronically Stored Information	Technology has both advantages and disadvantages. One of the biggest advantages is the use of computer systems for the efficient, economical creation and sharing of information in electronic form. One of the disadvantages that the explosion of ESI has created is the business and legal issue of how much information to save and for how long. Saving and archiving ESI in secure, multi-location storage facilities as required by court action, company policy, and government regulation incurs a cost that increases as the volume of ESI increases.
Identification	The initial step in the discovery process, both traditional and electronic, is determining what documents are needed, who has those documents, what formats the documents are in, the value of those documents to the case, and the potential costs of retrieving those documents.
Locating Evidence	Finding the desired document requires an appreciation of the types of records kept, by whom they are kept, where they are kept, and the language used by the creators of the records and those indexing the records. Every occupation has its own lexicon of terms and types of documents used to record its activity. Without knowledge of the terms and phrases used, a search may not produce the desired documents.

Interrogatories and Depositions	Interrogatories are written questions that are required to be answered by the opposing party. These questions rarely result in any surprises, such as might be obtained in a face-to-face question session. They are submitted to opposing counsel, who reviews both the questions and the answers of the client carefully to ensure that only required information is supplied. With the information from the interrogatories, the next step in obtaining the needed information that may lead to existing or destroyed ESI is the Rule 30 deposition of a person knowledgeable in the opposing party's record retention system.
Collection	Collection is the part of the e-discovery process that includes finding and obtaining electronically stored information for review and analysis. The collection process may require retaining outside professionals who are experienced in the techniques of searching databases. Depending on the computer systems or programs used for creating, storing, or archiving the ESI, the specialist may be required to retrieve the data in a usable form.
Search Queries	A search query is a set of parameters that are used to search through electronic data to find relevant material. Lawyers and paralegals are trained to use keywords in conducting searches of legal literature. The most familiar search query is the keyword search method using the Boolean model. Boolean search queries, however, are acknowledged not to have the degree of accuracy needed. Thus a number of other search methods have been developed that are used by different search engines and electronic discovery software in an attempt to improve search accuracy.
Sampling	Sampling is the testing of a search query by running it against a limited set of documents to measure the accuracy of the response to the search query.
Computer Forensics	The goal of computer forensics is to perform a structured investigation while maintaining a documented chain of evidence to find out exactly what happened on a computer and who was responsible for those changes. There are times when one believes that documents have been modified or deleted. In these cases, the dates of the original creation and those of any modifications or changes may be very relevant and material. The metadata for documents will typically show these relevant dates of creation and changes.
Chain of Custody	Steps should be taken to ensure that evidence is properly collected and preserved, and that the possession of the evidence is properly documented and accounted for at all steps of the processing, pretrial, and trial phases.
Resources to Support E-Discovery	Law firms often retain a service bureau or consulting company to help in the electronic discovery process. There are many reasons for using an outside consultant, such as a lack of in-house expertise or a workload that will not permit another case to be handled in-house. Some full-service companies offer a range of services—from the basic, like scanning paper documents into electronic form, to the complex, like forensic recovery and investigation of lost, destroyed, or missing files.

REVIEW QUESTIONS AND EXERCISES

1. List three key elements of the electronic discovery process.
2. What is the goal of the electronic discovery process?
3. What is information management? What is an important priority of information management in the context of litigation or potential litigation?
4. Is the destruction of electronic documents permitted? Under what circumstances is it appropriate?
5. How has the development of electronic forms of information affected the number of documents created and stored?
6. What is meant by a "safe haven"?
7. Once a party becomes aware of litigation, what are its obligations regarding documents?
8. What are the costs to businesses of retaining documents?
9. During e-discovery, what are the key elements in identifying electronically stored documents?
10. How do the courts define a record for discovery purposes? List three types of items that are included in this legal definition but that are not ordinarily thought of as "records" by laypeople.
11. What information is needed to locate potential evidence in e-discovery? Name three types of information that can lead to electronic evidence.
12. Why is knowledge of the vocabulary of different professions and industries necessary for the litigation team? How can this knowledge aid in formulating a search query?
13. What is the purpose of interrogatories? Why are interrogatories usually only a preliminary form of discovery, and why must they be followed up by other methods?
14. What information can be obtained through interrogatories that will help in locating electronically stored information?
15. How can interrogatories be used in preparing for depositions?
16. What are the requirements for giving notice of the taking of a Rule 30 deposition?
17. What kind of information can be learned in a Rule 30 deposition that will aid in electronic discovery?
18. When might the litigation team need the help of outside consultants in collecting electronically stored information? What types of knowledge and expertise can a consultant contribute to the team?
19. What is the purpose of a search query in electronic discovery?
20. In electronic discovery, how effective is the Boolean model of searching? What factors can prevent it from being effective?
21. What are some examples of other types of search methods that might be used in electronic discovery? How are these different from a Boolean search?
22. What is the significance of the Legal Track of the Information Technology Laboratory's annual conference? How does the Legal Track simulation help our understanding of the e-discovery process?
23. Why is sampling an important element in reducing the cost of electronic discovery?
24. What is the role of computer forensics in electronic discovery? How can a forensic expert help the legal team?
25. Why is a properly maintained chain of custody important in e-discovery?
26. What role do service companies play in supporting electronic discovery?

BUILDING YOUR PARALEGAL SKILLS

INTERNET AND TECHNOLOGY EXERCISES

1. Locate the websites of companies that support electronic discovery and list the services that they offer.
2. Review the current information on the Electronic Discovery Reference Model at www.EDRM.net.
3. Use the Internet to locate ethics opinions with regard to electronic discovery in your jurisdiction.
4. Use the Internet to find other contexts where search queries are used by the legal profession. Locate at least three instances. What types of queries are used? What specific types of legal information are being sought? How is the chosen type of query appropriate to that form of information?

VIDEO CASE STUDIES

SECOND MEETING WITH BRAKE COMPANY PRESIDENT

The president of the Brake manufacturing company meet with her attorney and learns the company will be brought into a lawsuit.

Watch this video case study in MyLegalStudiesLab and answer the following questions.

1. Is the president of the company a suitable person to offer to the opposing side for a Rule 30b deposition?
2. What are the qualifications a person should have to be deposed under Rule 30b?
3. What is the purpose of a Rule 30b deposition?

CHAPTER OPENING SCENARIO CASE STUDY

1. Use the Opening Scenario for this chapter to answer the following questions.
   a. Prepare an electronic discovery plan for use in the school bus case Appendix II, Case A. At this stage, include further steps that apply to the new issues in the case regarding the potential product defect and possibly negligent truck maintenance.
   b. Prepare a discovery plan for use in a complex litigation case like the airplane crash in Appendix III, Case 7.

2. For the assigned case study:
   a. Prepare a set of interrogatories for use in this case. Craft questions designed to discover sources of relevant electronic files and information regarding the defendant's document management plan.
   b. Prepare a Rule 30 deposition notice for use in this case. The deposition will be of an appropriate records custodian at the defendant company.

CONTINUING CASES AND EXERCISES

For the school bus–truck accident case, Case A in Appendix II:
1. Prepare a list of potential items that might have been destroyed.
2. Prepare a list of interrogatories to identify potentially destroyed evidence and to identify sources

of existing records, including electronic records. Also include questions regarding the defendant's document retention policy.

BUILDING YOUR PROFESSIONAL PORTFOLIO

1. Prepare a standard set of interrogatories for use in a case involving electronic discovery.

2. Prepare a deposition notice for a corporation involving any federal Rule 30 deposition.

Contacts and Resources

1. Prepare a list, including website information and local contact information, of companies providing forensic services to the legal profession. Create a table comparing the services each offers.
2. Prepare a list of local companies that provide e-discovery support services to the legal profession. Create a table comparing the services each offers.

3. Prepare a list of companies, including their contact information, that provide cloud computing electronic discovery support. Create a table comparing the services each offers.

"The power of the lawyer is in the uncertainty of the law."

—*Jeremy Bentham, Philosopher*
and Activist, 1748–1832

Analysis and Review of E-Discovery

CHAPTER 14

OPENING SCENARIO

The litigation teams working on the school bus and airplane crash cases met with an information technology support specialist to discuss discovery issues. The IT specialist was asked to advise the team members on problems that could arise in the discovery process.

The school bus group said that since the defendant truck company was so small, they did not foresee any issues in the production or delivery of electronic documents. They planned to simply make a standard production request for all documents related to the truck and its maintenance and repair. However, the IT specialist told them that they should not assume there would no problems even though it was a small company. In her experience, some of the smaller companies used older or "legacy" computer systems with outdated software. With these systems, it was often difficult to replicate or read documents in their native form.

The specialist then turned to the air crash litigation team. She was very concerned about the overwhelming amounts of information that the team would have to deal with. This information would include documents generated in the investigation by the state and federal agencies in addition to the records that the airline was required to keep pursuant to government regulation. Owen Mason, the senior partner, worried that they might not have the resources in-house to handle large-scale electronic document discovery. He asked his litigation support paralegal to look into the options for outside help that might be available.

LEARNING OBJECTIVES

After studying this chapter, you should be able to:

1. Describe the issues in reviewing large volumes of material as part of e-discovery.

2. Describe techniques for filtering, reducing, and coding large volumes of documents.

3. Describe the purpose of privilege review and how items may be protected from disclosure.

4. Describe the process for authentication of documents.

ANALYSIS AND REVIEW OF E-DISCOVERY
After watching the video in MyLegalStudiesLab, answer the following questions.

1. Why is responding to a discovery request time consuming?
2. What are the potential effects of disclosure of client information?

■ INTRODUCTION TO ANALYSIS AND REVIEW OF E-DISCOVERY

Responding to an opposing party's discovery request is often a meticulous and time-consuming process. Once the discoverable information has been identified, it must be carefully reviewed by the litigation team to ensure that it is relevant to the discovery request and that all privileged or confidential information has been logged and removed.

It is generally agreed that the attorney review process is the most costly part of electronic discovery because it potentially requires the review of every document obtained in the collection phase of e-discovery. Because of the cost factors involved, efforts are made to reduce the total number of documents that must be reviewed by the attorneys. Where possible, computers are used to identify and remove documents that are duplicates, or are outside of the requested time range. In some cases, contract attorneys, law students, or paralegals are hired to review the documents.

But even after the most thorough document review, some items may be mistakenly released to the other side. Depending on the circumstances and the jurisdiction, an inadvertent release of a document may result in the waiver of the privileged or confidential status of the information.

■ REVIEWING ELECTRONIC DOCUMENTS

LEARNING OBJECTIVE 1
Describe the issues in reviewing large volumes of material as part of e-discovery.

review
Checking documents for confidential, privileged, or work product content.

Document **review** is one of the most costly parts of electronic discovery. All of the material obtained from clients must be reviewed to find information that is relevant to the request for production, and to identify privileged, confidential, or protected documents. In small cases with a limited amount of information, copies of the electronic files may be made by simply using the original software as if making a backup copy. The client delivers the file copies using portable storage media such as a CD, DVD, flash drive, or memory card. The attorneys then use the same software to review the files on-screen, or by printing a hard copy.

After obtaining the documents, decisions must be made about how to process the material. Nearly all business documents will be in an electronic format such as emails, spreadsheets, word processing documents, database files, or graphic images. The good news is that unlike paper documents, electronic files can be processed, searched, and reviewed using computers.

When documents are delivered in a number of different electronic file formats, the review process will require multiple programs to open and view the original files. When the number of documents is in the thousands (or, in complex cases, the millions), this process can be very time-consuming. Document review can some-times be done more efficiently by converting all of the different types of documents into a common format that can be searched and indexed with a single program.

VIDEO ADVICE FROM THE FIELD _____

Janet Laquintano—Vice President Document Review, Sanction Solutions

A discussion of the document review process, as well as the qualifications and skills required to perform document review.

After watching the video in MyLegalStudiesLab answer the following questions.

1. What is document review?
2. What are review platforms?
3. Who is qualified to perform document review?

■ THE DELIVERY OF ESI

Before responding to a discovery request, the documents provided by clients for review may be in several different formats. The files are usually converted to a single format before delivering them to the other side. One of the first decisions to be made by the litigation team is what format will be used.

Rule 34 of the Federal Rules of Civil Procedure allows the requesting party to specify the desired format for the delivery of the information. If no format is requested, Rule 34 states that unless an objection is raised and sustained by the court, the documents may be delivered in the form they are kept in the usual course of business or in another reasonably usable form.

> **Rule 34. Producing Documents, Electronically Stored Information, and Tangible Things, or Entering onto Land, for Inspection and Other Purposes**
> **(b) Procedure.**
>   (1) Contents of the Request.
>
>   **The request:**
>   (A) must describe with reasonable particularity each item or category of items to be inspected;
>   (B) must specify a reasonable time, place, and manner for the inspection and for performing the related acts; and
>   (C) may specify the form or forms in which electronically stored information is to be produced.
>
> **(b) (2) Responses and Objections.**
>   (E) *Producing the Documents or Electronically Stored Information.* Unless otherwise stipulated or ordered by the court, these procedures apply to producing documents or electronically stored information:
>   (i)   A party must produce documents as they are kept in the usual course of business or must organize and label them to correspond to the categories in the request;
>   (ii) If a request does not specify a form for producing electronically stored information, a party must produce it in a form or forms in which it is ordinarily maintained or in a reasonably usable form or forms; and
>   (iii) A party need not produce the same electronically stored information in more than one form.

As stated in the rule, delivery of the documents, if not otherwise requested, may be in the "form...in which it is ordinarily maintained or in a reasonably usable form." Although this rule seems fairly broad, there may be limits to what a court considers "ordinarily maintained" or "reasonably usable." These terms were interpreted by U.S. Magistrate Judge Facciola in *Covad v. Revonet*:

> ...I noted that the strips of spreadsheet were clearly not produced in the form that they were ordinarily maintained, nor were they produced in a reasonably usable form. Id. Revonet's suggestion that the documents be pasted together was pure impertinence and simply not acceptable to the Court; I found that it is improper to "take an electronically searchable document and either destroy or degrade the document's ability to be searched." Id. (citing *Dahl v. Bain Capital Partners, Inc.*, 655 F. Supp. 2d 146, 150 (D. Mass. 2009)) (requiring production of spreadsheets in native format); In re *Classicstar Mare Lease Litig.*, No. 07-CV-353, 2009 WL 260954, at *3 (E.D. Ky. Feb. 2, 2009) (production may not degrade searchability); *Goodbys Creek, LLC v. Arch Ins. Co.*, No. 07-CV-947, 2008 WL 4279693, at *3 (M.D. Fla. Sept. 15, 2008) (same; conversion of e-mails from native to PDF not acceptable); *White v. Graceland Coll. Ctr. for Prof'l Dev. & Lifelong Learning*, 586 F. Supp. 2d 1250, 1264 (D. Kan. 2008).... Earlier in this case, I found the production of 35,000 e-mails in hard copy to be unacceptable, because no reasonable person could believe that Revonet, in its day to day operations, prints out all of its electronic communications on paper and then preserves them. *Covad II*, 254 F.R.D. at 150-51. The conversion to paper was therefore a bit of gamesmanship that I was not obliged to tolerate.

Source: Covad v. Revonet civ action no 06-1892 at page 7-9.

As Judge Facciola pointed out, the Rule may be interpreted narrowly to prevent parties from abusing the discovery process to delay and frustrate an opponent.

■ METADATA IN DOCUMENT PRODUCTION

metadata
Information about a particular data set that may describe, for example, how, when, and by whom it was received, created, accessed, and/or modified and how it is formatted.

resource (system) metadata
Data such as file names, size, and location.

content (application) metadata
Information about the contents of a document.

native file format
An associated file structure defined by the original creating application of electronic documents.

TIFF
Tagged Image File Format, one of the most widely used formats for storing images. TIFF graphics can be black and white, gray-scaled, or color.

Every electronic document has **metadata,** which is simply information about the document. This information may include **resource (system) metadata,** which gives the location of the file, and **content (application) metadata,** which identifies the content and author of the file. For example, Exhibit 14.1 shows the metadata for this chapter as displayed in Microsoft Word 2010.

Having the metadata delivered with the document is not an issue when there is no question as to the authenticity and accuracy of the document. In addition, if the copies produced are those that the requesting party already has in her or his possession, there may not be any need for the metadata. However, metadata may contain critical information, such as in cases where the date a document was first authored indicates the time at which certain information was known to a party or witness.

The method used to create the electronic file can impact the metadata that is delivered. If the document is delivered in its **native file format** (the format in which the document was originally created), the metadata is part of the document. However, if the document is delivered in the format that the document was copied into, the hidden data or metadata is not part of the document as delivered. For example, a **TIFF** file is a document *image*. If a Word file is converted to a TIFF, it will not contain the metadata. This may

Exhibit 14.1 Microsoft Word 2010 metadata display

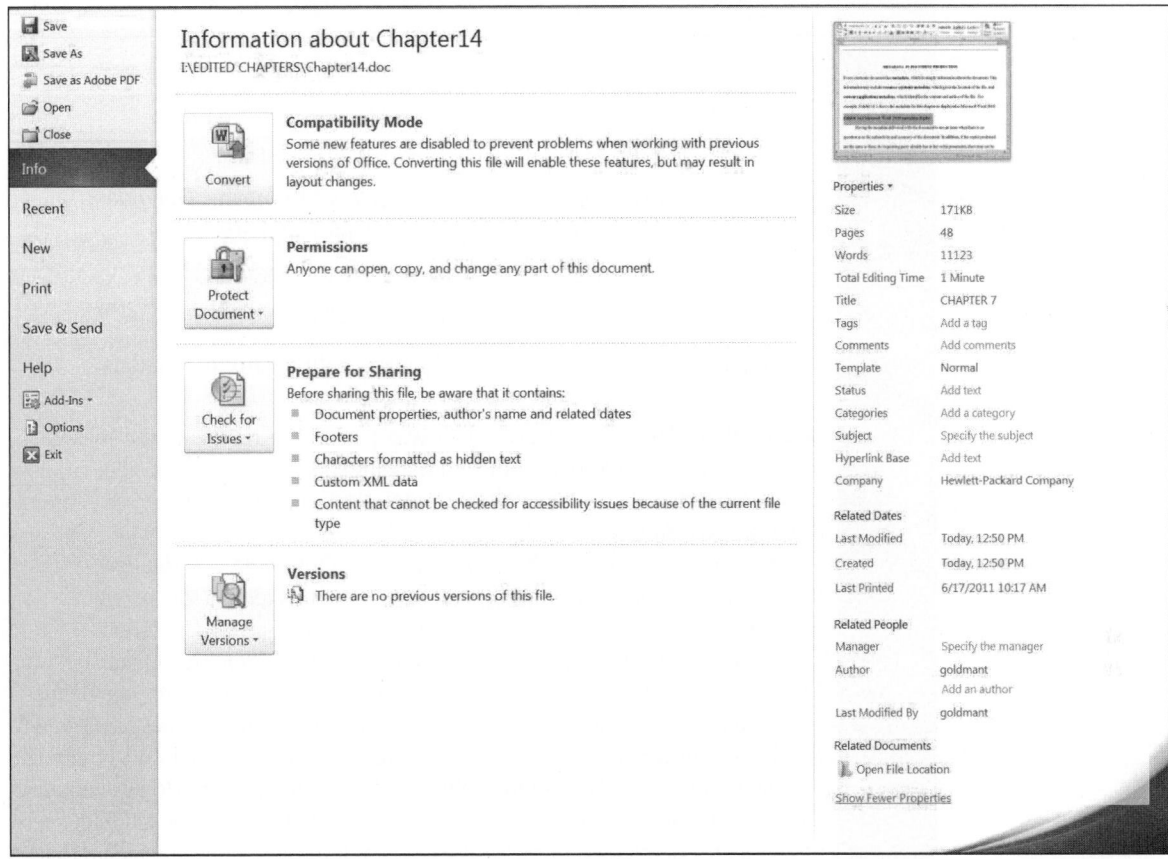

be an advantage or a disadvantage, depending on whether someone wants to conceal the metadata or wants to learn more about the creation of the original document.

As noted by Judge Facciola in *Covad*, it may not be absolutely necessary that documents produced pursuant to Rule 34 include the metadata:

> Covad, however, would like me to take the current case law a step further and determine that electronically stored data produced in hard copy is inherently unusable and unacceptable under the Rules, because it lacks the metadata available in the native format. Mot. Hr'g Tr. 121:18-23. Thus, Covad asks the Court to hold that only native production, with metadata, of electronically stored information, is reasonably usable under Rule 34(b) (2)(E)(ii). But, the rule itself permits production *either* in the format in which e-mail is ordinarily maintained, *i.e.* "native format," *or* another usable format. Thus, by its exact terms, the Rule provides an alternative to the native format, contradicting Covad's claim that native, electronic format is absolutely obligatory....
>
> *Source: Covad v. Revonet* civ action no 06-1892 at page 7-9.

Thus according to Judge Facciola's opinion, formats other than an email's native format can be considered a "usable format" under the rule.

IN THE WORDS OF THE COURT...

METADATA ETHICAL ISSUES

Williams v. Sprint/United Management Company,
(Kan. 2005) *Shirley Williams et al.,*
Plaintiffs, v. Sprint/United Management Company, Defendant.
Civil Action No. 03-2200-JWL-DJW.
United States District Court, D. Kansas.
September 29, 2005.

1. Emerging standards of electronic discovery with regard to metadata.

a. What is metadata?

Before addressing whether Defendant was justified in removing the metadata from the Excel spreadsheets prior to producing them to Plaintiffs, a general discussion of metadata and its implications for electronic document production in discovery is instructive.

Metadata, commonly described as "data about data," is defined as "information describing the history, tracking, or management of an electronic document."

Appendix F to *The Sedona Guidelines: Best Practice Guidelines & Commentary for Managing Information & Records in the Electronic Age* defines metadata as "information about a particular data set which describes how, when and by whom it was collected, created, accessed, or modified and how it is formatted (including data demographics such as size, location, storage requirements and media information.)" Technical Appendix E to the *Sedona Guidelines* provides an extended description of metadata. It further defines metadata to include "all of the contextual, processing, and use information needed to identify and certify the scope, authenticity, and integrity of active or archival electronic information or records."

Some examples of metadata for electronic documents include: a file's name, a file's location (e.g., directory structure or pathname), file format or file type, file size, file dates (e.g., creation date, date of last data modification, date of last data access, and date of last metadata modification), and file permissions (e.g., who can read the data, who can write to it, who can run it). Some metadata, such as file dates and sizes, can easily be seen by users; other metadata can be hidden or embedded and unavailable to computer users who are not technically adept.

Most metadata is generally not visible when a document is printed or when the document is converted to an image file. Metadata can be altered intentionally or inadvertently and can be extracted when native files are converted to image files. Sometimes the metadata can be inaccurate, as when a form document reflects the author as the person who created the template but who did not draft the document. In addition, metadata can come from a variety of sources; it can be created automatically by a computer, supplied by a user, or inferred through a relationship to another document.

Appendix E to *The Sedona Guidelines* further explains the importance of metadata: Certain metadata is critical in information management and for ensuring effective retrieval and accountability in record-keeping. Metadata can assist in proving the authenticity of the content of electronic documents, as well as establish the context of the content. Metadata can also identify and exploit the structural relationships that exist between and within electronic documents, such as versions and drafts. Metadata allows organizations to track the many

(continued)

layers of rights and reproduction information that exist for records and their multiple versions. Metadata may also document other legal or security requirements that have been imposed on records; for example, privacy concerns, privileged communications or work product, or proprietary interests.

The Microsoft Office Online website lists several examples of metadata that may be stored in Microsoft Excel spreadsheets, as well as other Microsoft applications such as Word or PowerPoint: author name or initials, company or organization name, identification of computer or network server or hard disk where document is saved, names of previous document authors, document revisions and versions, hidden text or cells, template information, other file properties and summary information, non-visible portions or embedded objects, personalized views, and comments.

It is important to note that metadata varies with different applications. As a general rule of thumb, the more interactive the application, the more important the metadata is to understanding the application's output. At one end of the spectrum is a word processing application where the metadata is usually not critical to understanding the substance of the document. The information can be conveyed without the need for the metadata. At the other end of the spectrum is a database application where the database is a completely undifferentiated mass of tables of data. The metadata is the key to showing the relationships between the data; without such metadata, the tables of data would have little meaning. A spreadsheet application lies somewhere in the middle. While metadata is not as crucial to understanding a spreadsheet as it is to a database application, a spreadsheet's metadata may be necessary to understand the spreadsheet because the cells containing formulas, which arguably are metadata themselves, often display a value rather than the formula itself. To understand the spreadsheet, the user must be able to ascertain the formula within the cell.

Due to the hidden, or not readily visible, nature of metadata, commentators note that metadata created by any software application has the potential for inadvertent disclosure of confidential or privileged information in both litigation and non-litigation setting[s], which could give rise to an ethical violation. One method commonly recommended to avoid this inadvertent disclosure is to utilize software that removes metadata from electronic documents. The process of removing metadata is commonly called "scrubbing" the electronic documents. In a litigation setting, the issue arises of whether this can be done without either the agreement of the parties or the producing party providing notice through an objection or motion for protective order.

IN THE WORDS OF THE COURT...

EMAIL METADATA

Wiginton v. CB Richard Ellis, Inc., (N.D. Ill. 2004) Amy Wiginton, Kristine Moran, Norma Plank Fethler, Andrea Corey and Olivia Knapp, individually and on behalf of all persons similarly situated, Plaintiffs, v. CB Richard Ellis, Inc., Defendant.

Case No. 02 C 6832. United States District Court, N.D. Illinois, Eastern Division. August 9, 2004.

…Plaintiffs filed this class action complaint against CBRE alleging a nationwide pattern and practice of sexual harassment at the CBRE offices. As evidence of the hostile work environment prevalent at the offices of CBRE, Plaintiffs seek discovery

(continued)

of pornographic material that they claim was distributed electronically (i.e., via e-mail) and displayed on computers throughout the offices.

CBRE initially produced 94 monthly e-mail backup tapes from 11 offices. The backup tapes consist of the e-mails that existed on a given server at the time the backup is made. They are not a complete depiction of every e-mail that existed on the CBRE system during a month.

…At this point, we note that discussing documents in terms of numbers is somewhat inexact. For example, an e-mail containing a search term that exists in a user's outbox, and also exists in another user's inbox, counts as two hits, even though it is really one document. A document containing a search term that is sent from one user to another, and returned under the "reply with history" option available on CBRE's e-mail system[,] counts as two hits. But, because of de-duplication, an e-mail that is present multiple times in one user's mailbox is not counted multiple times. So although talking about documents in terms of numbers is not entirely accurate, the search system was designed to get an idea of how frequently the documents containing search terms were being passed around by CBRE users within or between the offices. Because spam was eliminated, it means the picture does not present an entirely accurate view of any other pornographic e-mails that [may] have been available on the CBRE e-mail system, or how often users are opening such documents in view of other people. The numbers also do not reflect e-mails that were not captured on backup tapes.

PRACTICE TIP

Sometimes the most important information about a document is found not in the metadata but right on the face of the original document. Estate probate officials and Recorders of Wills frequently look at original documents to see if there is an excess number of staple holes, indicating that the document may have been taken apart after originally prepared—therefore raising the question of a removed or substituted page.

The color ink used in creating the document may offer important information as well. For example, in a paper medical record, such as a patient's chart, each nursing shift may have used a different-colored ink to make notes. Or, a person may have signed off on a document using a red pen, which appears black on a photocopy.

Such differences between originals and copies came to light in the case of *Robinson-Reeder v American Council on Education* 262 F.R.D. 41, where the court ruled:

> …Although ACE is correct that, in general, black and white copied documents satisfy a party's discovery obligations, here ACE has put a color or a mark on the original enrollment form at issue. Therefore, ACE must either arrange for Ms. Robinson Reeder to inspect the original enrollment form at counsel's office, or provide her with a color copy of the original form.

Obtaining Documents via Paper Discovery

Even today, some documents may not be available in electronic form. Many public agencies, such as police and fire departments, may still file reports on paper. Litigation that involves a time frame prior to the age of electronic documents may also include paper documents. These cases often involve a large volume of material that must be processed by the legal team. Converting the paper documents to an electronic format may be a solution.

The typical response to a paper document request is the delivery of a photocopy of the requested item. As with electronic discovery, the number of documents can be in the thousands or even millions (such as a class action suit involving tobacco companies). Before the computer era, these documents had to be reviewed manually, which provided work for many contract lawyers, law students, and paralegals. Now, however, computer technology allows these paper documents to be converted into electronic files that can be processed like other electronic files. Typically, the documents are copied, or scanned and saved, in some electronic file format.

Scanning Documents

When paper documents are scanned and converted to an electronic form, the format chosen may vary depending on how the files will be used. Most scanners have software that allows a choice of formats for viewing and saving the files. One of the most popular is the PDF format, which permits easy portability and sharing of files. It is also the required format for filing documents in many courts. A competitive format is TIFF, which has similar characteristics.

■ GRAPHIC IMAGE FILE FORMATS

In the e-discovery phase of litigation, *native files*, *PDFs*, or *TIFFs* are the formats most frequently used to convert documents. The native file format is the format in which a file was first created. These formats can be identified by their file suffixes, such as *.doc* for Microsoft Word, or *.wpd* for WordPerfect. If a production request asks a party to "deliver documents in native format," the files must be delivered in the same format that they were created and saved in originally.

TIFF is short for "tagged image file format." It is one of the most widely used formats for storing images. TIFF graphics can be black and white, gray-scaled, or color. Files in TIFF format often end with a .tif extension. **PDF** is short for "portable document format." It was created by Adobe, which had previously invented the TIFF format.

Portable Document Format or PDF
An open standard format for document exchange that enables a document to be processed and printed on any computer.

The PDF Format

One of the basic requirements of a system of electronic documentation is the ability to save documents in a format that cannot be easily changed. Anyone who has received a word processing file knows that the file can be changed, saved, and presented as an original unless access has been restricted by a password. Documents may now be saved in a graphic image format or portable document format or PDF. These files, in which text is converted to graphic images, may not be easily changed by the recipient.

The conversion or creation of documents in PDF format requires specialty software such as Adobe Acrobat, Nuance PDF Creator, or a built-in PDF-creation application within a word processing program. Once created, anyone can read the PDF-format document using free PDF-reading programs such as Nuance PDF Reader or Adobe Reader. The free availability of this software has increased the acceptance of the PDF format, and with this acceptance has come a willingness to scan and store documents electronically, which eliminates the need to retain the original paper copies.

Adobe Acrobat

Adobe Acrobat has become the standard software tool in many paperless offices for creating PDF files. With each new version or update to this program, additional features have been added to allow greater sharing of documents and a higher level of security. Acrobat is now a useful tool for collaboration in the preparing of documents.

In newer versions of Acrobat, the creator of a PDF document can, by applying a password to the file, limit the ability of the recipient to print the document. This password feature allows the legal team to send a document to others without permitting changes to be made to the original document, while at the same time allowing comments to be added to the file. As discussed in a previous chapter, digital formats for documents have evolved over time. The newest version of the PDF format is PDF/A, an archival format increasingly required for e-filing with the courts and government agencies that locks or freezes the content and precludes changes and is self contained with all fonts embedded for use in all viewing program. It is an international, open source format supported by many companies.

PDF Converters

Nuance PDF Converter (see Exhibit 14.2) is a lower-cost alternative to Adobe Acrobat. In addition to creating PDF documents, it can be used to convert PDF files into fully formatted Word, WordPerfect, and Excel documents.

The Professional and Enterprise versions of this program include a feature that converts documents into audio files that can be played back through a

Exhibit 14.2 Nuance PDF Converter

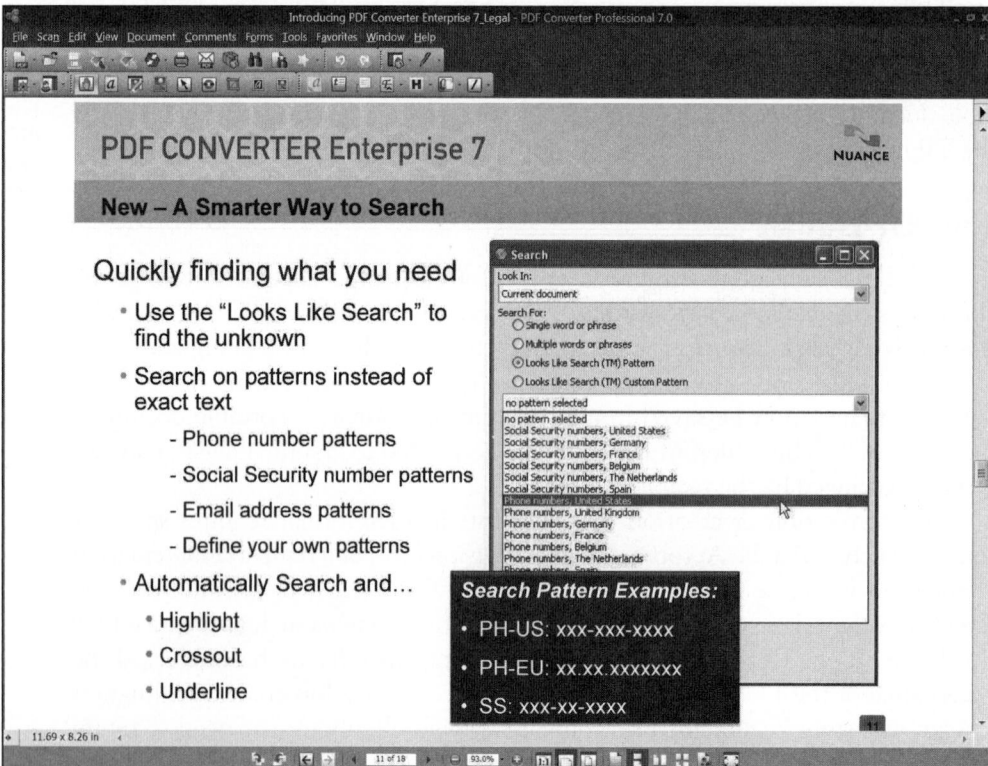

Nuance Communications.

Exhibit 14.3 Nuance PDF Converter Help screen

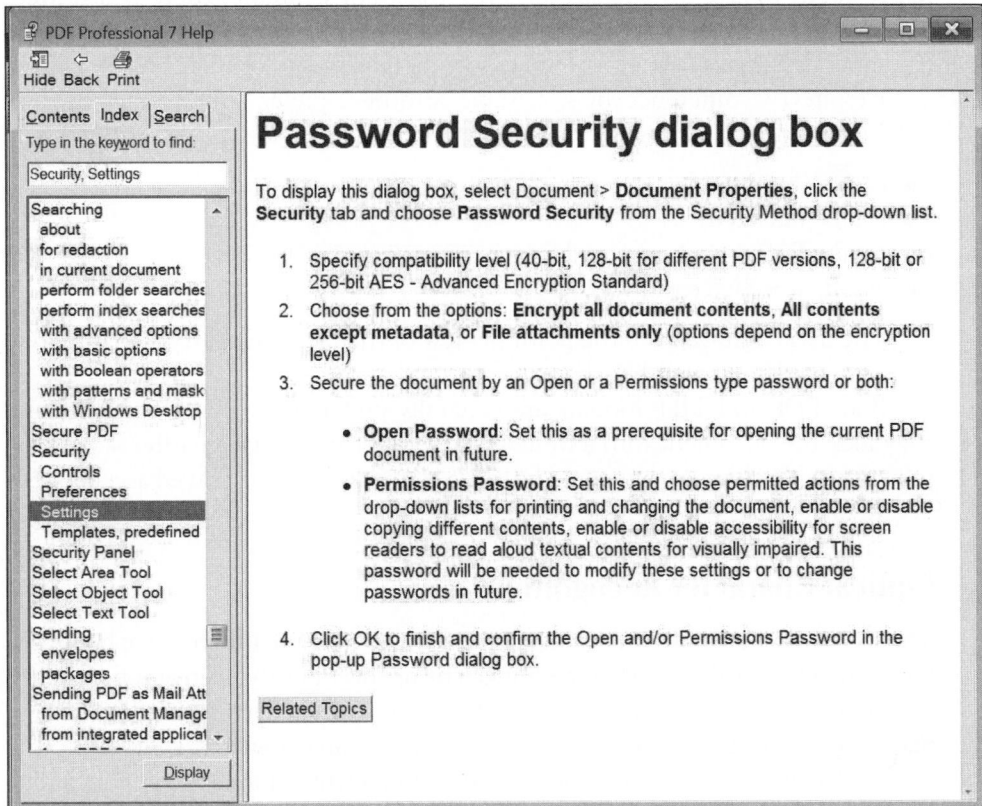

Nuance Communications.

computer or on an MP3 player such as an Apple iPod. Anyone who has tried to proofread technical or legal language, such as the legal description in a real estate agreement or deed, will appreciate the ability to have the language "read to" him or her while following the language in the document to verify accuracy.

Like Acrobat, Nuance PDF Converter has security settings such as password limitations for changing and printing documents. These settings are listed in the PDF Converter Help screen and the security menu options shown in Exhibit 14.3.

Comparison of PDF and TIFF

TIFF and PDF formats are both commonly used for large-scale cases. The upfront cost to change a native file format to TIFF is about the same as converting a native file format to PDF. Many programs used to create the original documents, such as WordPerfect and Word, have a built-in feature allowing files to be saved automatically as PDF files. In addition, most litigation support software programs, such as Summation and Concordance, support both TIFF and PDF formats. The advantage of conversion to either format is that the new files can be searched across the different file types, and indexes can be prepared.

One of the differences between TIFF and PDF is the amount of memory required to store one document. When saving a TIFF file, the actual file size will vary depending on which of the many compression methods is used.

Because of the built-in file compression of the PDF format, PDF files are normally about one-tenth the size of TIFF files. For example, there is a noticeable difference in the time it takes to email a TIFF file versus a PDF version of the same document.

Despite the difference in size, some attorneys prefer TIFF format because TIFF files:

- cannot be altered,
- can be redacted,
- can be Bates numbered, and
- can be searched easily.

The disadvantage from the point of view of the receiving party is that hidden data or metadata cannot be seen.

Both PDF and TIFF formats are generally preferred over any other because they lock the document into a format that cannot be changed easily, as opposed to the possible changes that could be made to the document if saved as a Word or WordPerfect file.

Optical Character Recognition

optical character recognition (OCR)
A technology that takes data from a paper document and turns it into editable text data. The document is first scanned, and then OCR software searches the document for letters, numbers, and other characters.

There are also times when documents need to be converted from a graphic image format to a format that allows for editing. The applications that can accomplish this type of conversion are often referred to as **OCR, or optical character recognition,** applications. Products such as OmniPage, by Nuance, can convert a PDF file, or other type of document file, into one of a number of different editable formats, including Microsoft Word or Corel WordPerfect. If used with a document scanner, paper documents may also be scanned and converted into a native word processor format for editing. OCR technology can also be used to create a full-text, searchable version of a graphic image document. Once converted into a full-text OCR document, you can search for words and phrases within its text.

Often, the information in a PDF document must be inserted into a file type other than that of a word processor file, such as a spreadsheet. Nuance PDF Converter converts PDF files into spreadsheets and other file types, retaining any original formatting and graphics as necessary.

Hidden Content in a PDF

The misconception persists that PDFs do not have metadata. Every document, including a PDF, has metadata—data about the document—as part of the document file. Exhibit 14.4 shows the basic metadata for a PDF copy of a chapter of this book, which is viewable by selecting the Document Properties tab. This feature is similar in appearance to the Document Properties tab in MS Word. Exhibit 14.5 shows additional detailed metadata for the same file using the Advanced settings in Acrobat.

As shown in Exhibit 14.6, one of the options in Acrobat X is to set a preference to "Remove Hidden Information" (1) when closing documents, or (2) when sending documents by email. Both practices might prevent information that is not intended for the recipient from being sent.

Some versions of Adobe Acrobat can be used to search documents and computer systems, as shown in Exhibit 14.7.

Exhibit 14.4 Basic metadata for a PDF

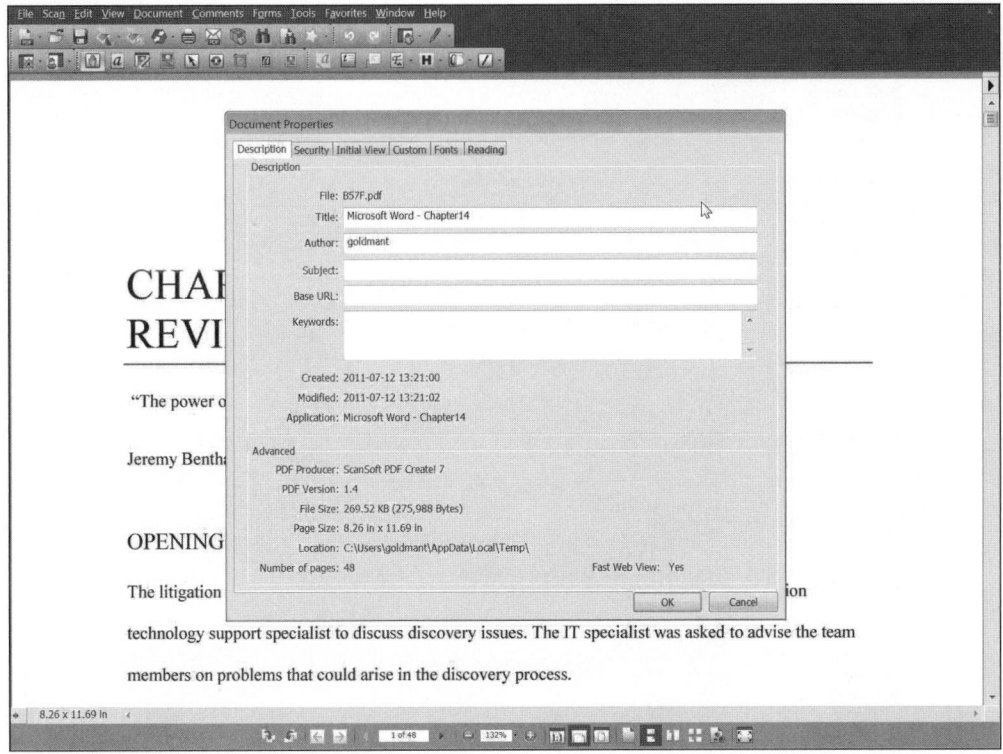

© 2011 Microsoft.

Exhibit 14.5 Detailed metadata for file using Advanced settings in Acrobat

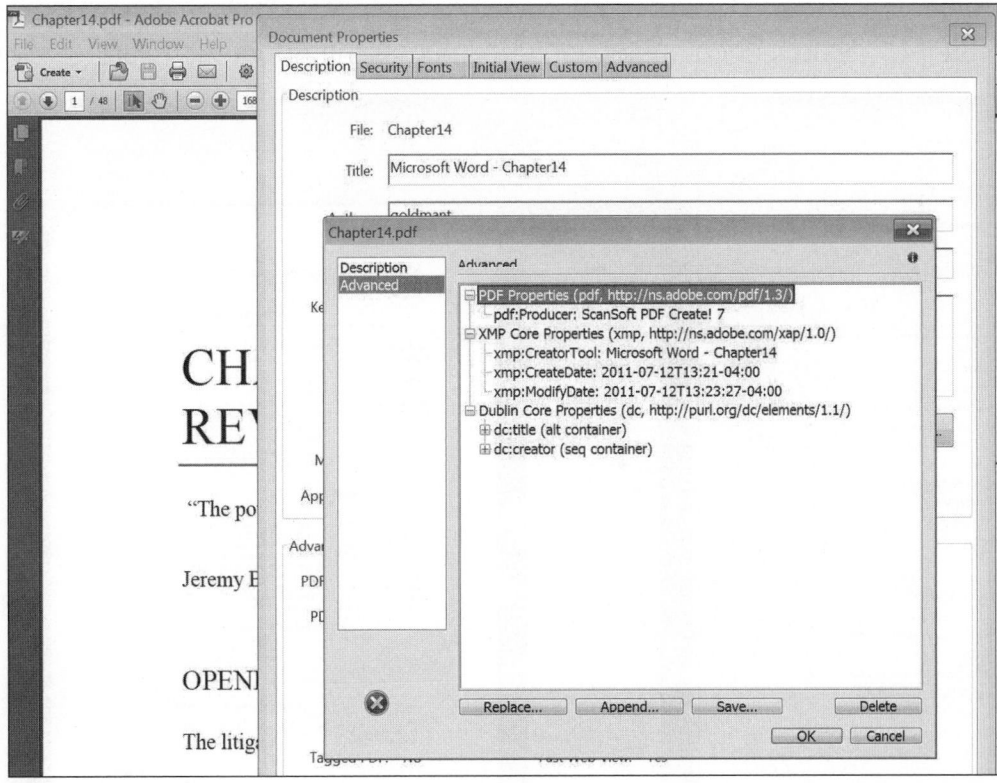

Source: Adobe Systems.

Exhibit 14.6 Acrobat X preference "Remove Hidden Information"

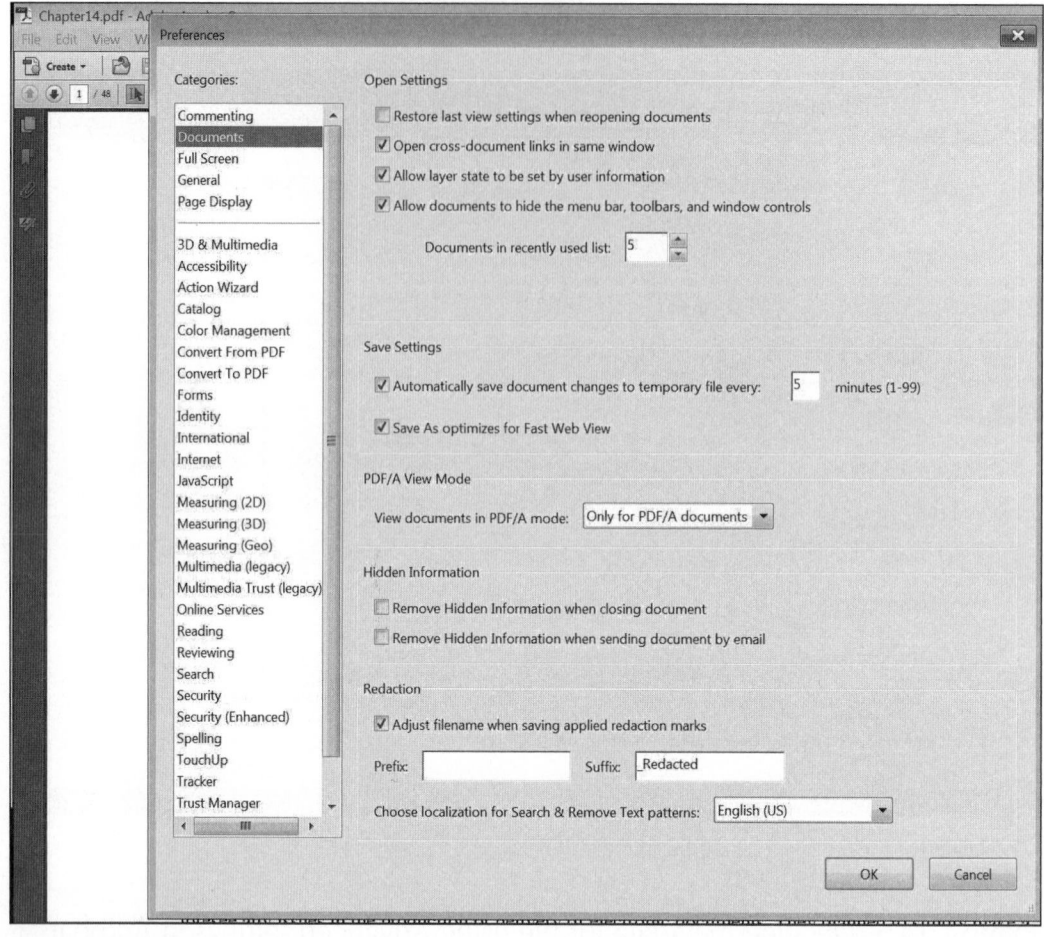

Source: Adobe Systems.

Exhibit 14.7 Search of computer and document using Adobe Acrobat

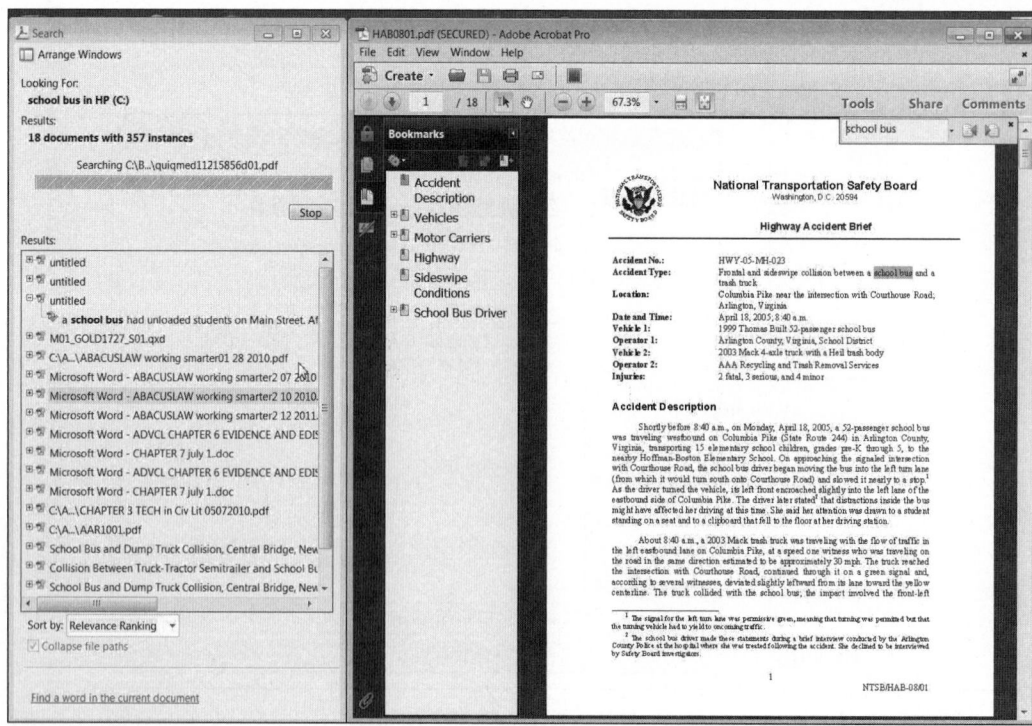

Source: Adobe Systems.

■ DOCUMENT PROCESSING

The number of electronic documents supplied in response to the discovery request may be in the hundreds, thousands, or millions. Some or most of the documents produced may not be relevant or may have little value as evidence in the litigation. When a high volume of documents is first received, the production can be made more manageable by using the processes of filtering, coding, and numbering the documents.

LEARNING OBJECTIVE 2
Describe techniques for filtering, reducing, and coding large volumes of documents.

Reducing ESI to Manageable Levels

In many cases, the quantity of documents may need to be reduced to a reasonable number. Two useful processes for doing so are filtering and de-duplication.

Filtering is the process of scanning or searching the documents for relevant terms in an attempt to narrow the documents' focus. For example, documents may be filtered to eliminate documents created before or after a certain date.

Many of the excess documents produced are simply duplicate copies of the same document. **De-duplication, or de-duping,** is the process of electronically eliminating the duplicates. This process may require more care and sophistication than is immediately apparent. For example, an email may have been sent to multiple recipients. All of the emails are identical, but it may be necessary in some cases to know the names of the parties who received copies. In a defamation or harassment case, for example, it may be necessary to prove that a manager was sending harassing or defamatory comments. In these types of cases, it would be important to know the names of recipients of the messages and the names of those to whom the recipients had forwarded the same message. The same situation may be true for invoices, letters, and similar documents. Although the content of the documents may appear the same, the metadata on each document might in some cases be important if there is a need to show changes, recipients, or similar information.

filtering
The process used to scan or search documents for relevant terms in an attempt to narrow the focus, such as by filtering to eliminate documents created before or after a certain date.

de-duplication/de-duping
The process of comparing electronic records based on their characteristics and removing duplicate records from the data set.

Document Coding

To be effectively sorted, retrieved, and identified for further review, each document must be identified by distinguishing characteristics, such as the date created or the author. This process is known as coding.

Coding is the process of capturing case-relevant information from a document—for example, the author, date authored, date sent, recipient, and date opened. The most basic type of coding is **objective coding,** also referred to as bibliographic indexing. This information includes the author, type of document, recipient, and date. **Subjective coding** captures more details about the document, such as keywords within the document or other criteria not related to bibliographic information.

Obviously the manual coding of this information is time-consuming and costly. To reduce coding costs, some companies offer outsourcing services from foreign locations where the labor rates are lower than in the United States. With modern scanning techniques and high-speed scanners, some companies provide **auto coding**—the electronic scanning and coding of documents by selected key terms and dates. In some cases, the documents are first auto-coded, and then selected documents are manually coded.

coding
The process of capturing case-relevant information (i.e., author, date authored, date sent, recipient, date opened, etc.) from a document.

objective coding
Also referred to as a bibliographic indexing. This includes the author, type of document, recipient, and date.

subjective coding
Identifies keywords within a document or other criteria not related to bibliographic information.

auto coding
The electronic scanning and coding of documents by selected key terms and dates.

ADVICE FROM THE FIELD

AUTOMATIC DOCUMENT CODING

By Lisa Rosen

Document coding has historically been the most expensive and time-intensive step of the entire process required for creating document production databases. On average, a coding professional can manually code approximately 20 documents (based on a five-page document) and 10 bibliographic fields per hour. In order to reduce the time and cost associated with manual coding, a movement began to send documents offshore to areas of cheap labor. However, many law firms and government agencies cannot or will not send their documents offshore for security reasons. The cost and time associated with manual document coding is significantly reduced with the use of document coding software, such as ALCoder, which allows the case team to focus efforts on the case at hand.

The new federal rules pertaining to ESI (Electronically Stored Information) [have] created an increased awareness of the need for coding and the need for auto-coding. ESI or native files/emails are often processed and imported into existing databases such as CT Summation and LexisNexis Concordance. During the extraction process, metadata (or data about the data) is identified and populated into those databases for searching and sorting purposes. Many believe that the metadata is accurate or complete, when that is often not the case. The metadata reflects the "profile" of a document, not the bibliographic information contained within the document. ALCoder goes into the native files, emails and attachments and extracts the bibliographic information from the document, supplementing the metadata with accurate bibliographic information. The improvement in Optical Character Recognition (OCR) technology in quality and price (through the availability of off-the-shelf software) has resulted in OCR frequently replacing slower and often prohibitively expensive manual document coding. The problem with searching databases limited to OCR is that critical information such as document dates and authors are not able to be searched and sorted. For example, if the documents need to be assembled in chronological order, they must be coded. Automatic coding software, like ALCoder, solve[s] the problem.

Courtesy of Rosen Technology Resources.

PRACTICE TIP

The pages in paper documents supplied in response to a request for production are frequently numbered sequentially to aid in review as well as for identification purposes in pleadings and at trial. Plaintiffs use the letter *P* before the document number, and the defense uses a *D*. The sequential numbering of documents is referred to as **Bates production numbering,** after the Bates numbering stamp, shown in Exhibit 14.8.

Bates production numbering
A Bates production number is a tracking number assigned to each page of each document in the production set.

Although page numbers are added to paper documents with a mechanical numbering device such as the Bates stamper, computer document management programs sometimes have a feature that electronically adds the sequential page numbers to the documents.

The same documents may be required in multidistrict litigation—for example, pages of an employer's policy manual that will be referenced in employment discrimination suits filed in different courts across the country. Using one set of identifying production numbers simplifies identification for the litigation team. With the same document numbers used in all the cases filed, the chance of confusion will be eliminated. These numbers also allow parties to inventory the documents. If a number is missing from the sequence, it is clear that someone has removed or failed to deliver all the documents. To maintain consistency, counsel in each case should be asked to agree to the same numbering system.

Exhibit 14.8 Bates stamper

■ PRIVILEGE REVIEW

Privilege review is the process of reviewing a client's documents to identify those that contain privileged or confidential information, or attorney work product. Protection against disclosure is provided in the federal rules, such as the Rule 26 protection for privileged matter and work product. It is generally agreed that privilege review is the most costly phase of the discovery process.

LEARNING OBJECTIVE 3
Describe the purpose of privilege review and how items may be protected from disclosure.

privilege review
A review of documents for privileged or confidential content or attorney work product.

Rule 26. Duty to Disclose; General Provisions Governing Discovery.

(b) Discovery Scope and Limits.

(1) Scope in General.

Unless otherwise limited by court order, the scope of discovery is as follows: Parties may obtain discovery regarding any non-privileged matter that is relevant to any party's claim or defense—including the existence, description, nature, custody, condition, and location of any documents or other tangible things and the identity and location of persons who know of any discoverable matter. For good cause, the court may order discovery of any matter relevant to the subject matter involved in the action. Relevant information need not be admissible at the trial if the discovery appears reasonably calculated to lead to the discovery of admissible evidence. All discovery is subject to the limitations imposed by Rule 26(b)(2)(C).

. . .

(3) Trial Preparation: Materials.

(A) *Documents and Tangible Things.* Ordinarily, a party may not discover documents and tangible things that are prepared in anticipation of litigation or for trial by or for another party or its representative (including the other party's attorney, consultant, surety, indemnitor, insurer, or agent). But, subject to Rule 26(b)(4), those materials may be discovered if:

(i) they are otherwise discoverable under Rule 26(b)(1); and

(ii) the party shows that it has substantial need for the materials to prepare its case and cannot, without undue hardship, obtain their substantial equivalent by other means.

(B) *Protection Against Disclosure.* If the court orders discovery of those materials, it must protect against disclosure of the mental impressions, conclusions, opinions, or legal theories of a party's attorney or other representative concerning the litigation.

Documents identified as privileged should be removed from the documents produced to the opposing side. The excluded documents must be identified on a privilege log that states the basis for the claim of privilege. Voluntary disclosure usually acts as a waiver of privilege, but the protection may also be lost if a privileged document is accidentally released. Even with a careful privilege review, documents that are considered privileged may still be overlooked and produced unintentionally, which is referred to as **inadvertent disclosure.**

inadvertent disclosure
An unintended disclosure of privileged, confidential, or work product information to the opposing side.

With larger and larger numbers of ESI being demanded as part of discovery, the time and costs of privilege review, as well as the incidents of inadvertent disclosure, are also increasing. Initial efforts to address inadvertent disclosure were included in the 2006 federal rules changes, which provide for a claw-back provision under Rule 26. This rule requires parties to consider and discuss "claw-back" or non-waiver agreements, and empowers the courts under Rule 16(b)(6) to include these agreements in the courts' scheduling order:

26(f)(3)(D)...any issues about claims of privilege or of protection as trial-preparation materials, including—if the parties agree on a procedure to assert these claims after production—whether to ask the court to include their agreement in an order....

Court rulings on the effect of inadvertent disclosure have varied based on the reasons for the disclosure and the steps taken by the disclosing party. Rule 502 of the Federal Rules of Evidence was passed in 2009 as a solution to the inconsistent application of the claw-back provisions in different jurisdictions. The new evidence rule seeks to offer, at least in federal court, protection when the disclosure is inadvertent, when:

- reasonable steps were taken to avoid inadvertent production,
- action is taken promptly to correct the inadvertent production, and
- there is the existence of a claw-back agreement.

What constitute "reasonable steps" and "prompt action" remain issues for court interpretation.

Even with claw-back agreements and the potential benefit of FRE 502, there is a duty to use reasonable efforts to protect confidential, privileged, or work product documents against inadvertent disclosure. Once an inadvertent disclosure is made, the recipient still has the information even if, in theory, he or she cannot use it, or if no further use can be made by a claim of waiver. When the information that was inadvertently disclosed is important enough to a party's case, an argument can almost certainly be expected that privilege has been waived. Even the provisions of the Federal Rules of Evidence have the qualifying word "reasonable." In addition, the federal rule does not apply in state courts, each of which may have its own standard and case law. For example, some jurisdictions still hold that any disclosure is an automatic waiver.

It should be noted that any waiver or claw-back agreement b etween the parties governs only their conduct, not the conduct of third parties, unless the court issues an order that contains the agreement and applies it to third parties. It is therefore good practice to reduce all non-waiver or claw-back agreements to writing and request their inclusion in the court's scheduling order.

Conducting the Privilege Review

Those conducting the actual document review must be familiar with not only the attorney–client privilege and work product rules, but also any definitive statutory privileges and rules of evidence that apply to attorney–client privilege. They should also be aware of conditional privileges, such as those that apply to trade secrets or other proprietary material, which could be damaging to a client if publicly disclosed. For example, the client may possess data on research or new technology for which patents have not yet been obtained.

Redaction

redaction
The removal of confidential information (or at least that which is claimed to be confidential) or material prepared for trial under the work product doctrine.

If only a portion of a document contains privileged or confidential information, the sensitive material may be redacted. **Redaction** is the removal of confidential information, or material prepared for trial under the work product doctrine. With paper documents, a black marker is used to block out the sensitive material before making copies. Although the process is not as simple with electronic documents, material can be redacted using a program that electronically blacks out the information and applies the redaction permanently to any electronic or hard copy.

Claims of improper redaction or failure to disclose a document frequently result in motions to the court for orders to disclose. The federal rules specifically address the process for the protection of this type of information. The party seeking to exclude a document from production to the other side because of a claim of privilege must make an objection in a timely manner and identify the items and the reason for the objection in a privilege log.

RULE 37. Failure to Make Disclosures or to Cooperate in Discovery; Sanctions

(a) Motion for an Order Compelling Disclosure or Discovery.

(1) In General.

On notice to other parties and all affected persons, a party may move for an order compelling disclosure or discovery. The motion must include a certification that the movant has in good faith conferred or attempted to confer with the person or party failing to make disclosure or discovery in an effort to obtain it without court action....

(3) Specific Motions.

(A) *To Compel Disclosure.* If a party fails to make a disclosure required by Rule 26(a), any other party may move to compel disclosure and for appropriate sanctions.

(B) *To Compel a Discovery Response.* A party seeking discovery may move for an order compelling an answer, designation, production, or inspection. This motion may be made if:

(i) a deponent fails to answer a question asked under Rules 30 or 31;

(ii) a corporation or other entity fails to make a designation under Rule 30(b)(6) or 31(a)(4);

(iii) a party fails to answer an interrogatory submitted under Rule 33, or

(iv) a party fails to respond that inspection will be permitted—or fails to permit inspection—as requested under Rule 34.

(4) Evasive or Incomplete Disclosure, Answer, or Response.

For purposes of this subdivision (a), an evasive or incomplete disclosure, answer, or response must be treated as a failure to disclose, answer, or respond.

Privilege Logs

A **privilege log** is a list of documents claimed by the submitting party to contain material subject to a privilege or work product exclusion. Exhibit 14.9 shows a sample privilege log.

privilege log
A list of documents claimed by the submitting party to contain material subject to privilege or work product exclusion.

Rule 26. Duty to Disclose; General Provisions Governing Discovery

(5) Claiming Privilege or Protecting Trial-Preparation Materials.

(A) *Information Withheld.* When a party withholds information otherwise discoverable by claiming that the information is privileged or subject to protection as trial-preparation material, the party must:

(i) expressly make the claim; and

(ii) describe the nature of the documents, communications, or tangible things not produced or disclosed—and do so in a manner that, without revealing information itself privileged or protected, will enable other parties to assess the claim.

(B) *Information Produced.* If information produced in discovery is subject to a claim of privilege or of protection as trial preparation material, the party making the claim may notify any party that received the information of the claim and the basis for it. After being notified, a party must promptly return, sequester, or destroy the specified information and any copies it has; must not use or disclose the information until the claim is resolved; must take reasonable steps to retrieve the information if the party disclosed it before being notified; and may promptly present the information to the court under seal for a determination of the claim. The producing party must preserve the information until the claim is resolved.

Exhibit 14.9 Privilege log

Public Records Request	Privilege Log Ivy Frye's and Frank Bailey's February 2008 E-mails			July 18, 2008
Date	**Author**	**Recipient**	**Document Description**	**Privilege**
02/01/08	C. Fredeen, PDC Eng.	F. Bailey, GOV	6:59 am *E-mail re Request for Reappointment for Craig Freeden to AELS Board	Deliberative Process / Executive
01/24/08	D. Ogg	F. Bailey, GOV	9:21 am *E-mail re Education	Deliberative Process / Executive
02/01/08	D. Ogg	F. Bailey, GOV	8:32 am *E-mail re Education	Deliberative Process / Executive
02/01/08	S. Leighow, GOV	F. Bailey, GOV	8:46 am *E-mail re Appointment of member to the state Board of Game	Deliberative Process / Executive
2/1/2008	S. Parnell, GOV	S. Palin, GOV	7:41 am *E-mail re Andrew Halcro	Deliberative Process / Executive
2/1/2008	S. Parnell, GOV	F. Bailey, GOV K. Perry, GOV T. Palin	8:22 am *E-mail re Andrew Halcro	Deliberative Process / Executive
2/1/2008	S. Palin, GOV	F. Bailey, GOV K. Perry, GOV T. Palin	8:28 am *E-mail re Andrew Halcro	Deliberative Process / Executive
2/1/2008	S. Palin, GOV	F. Bailey, GOV K. Perry, GOV T. Palin	8:30 am *E-mail re Andrew Halcro	Deliberative Process / Executive
2/1/2008	I. Frye, GOV	S. Palin, GOV F. Bailey, GOV K. Perry, GOV T. Palin	8:42 am *E-mail re Andrew Halcro	Deliberative Process / Executive
2/1/2008	S. Palin, GOV	I. Frye, GOV K. Perry, GOV F. Bailey, GOV T. Palin	10:10 am *E-mail re Andrew Halcro	Deliberative Process / Executive
2/1/2008	I. Frye, GOV	S. Palin, GOV F. Bailey, GOV K. Perry, GOV T. Palin	10:23 am *E-mail re Andrew Halcro	Deliberative Process / Executive

IN THE WORDS OF THE COURT...

In Re *Grand Jury Subpoena*, 274 F.3d 563 (1st Cir. 2001)

In re *Grand Jury Subpoena* (*Custodian of Records, Newparent, Inc.*), *A. Nameless Lawyer* (*A Pseudonym*) *et al., Intervenors, Appellants.*

No. 01-1975.

United States Court of Appeals, First Circuit.

Heard September 14, 2001.

Decided November 8, 2001.

1. *Individual Attorney-Client Privilege Claims.* The attorney-client privilege protects communications made in confidence by a client to his attorney. *See, e.g., United States v. Mass. Inst. of Tech.,* 129 F.3d 681, 684 (1st Cir. 1997)

. . .

3. *The Work Product Privilege.* The claim of work product privilege raises a similar set of issues anent joint privilege. The work product rule protects work done by an attorney in anticipation of, or during, litigation from disclosure to the opposing party. *E.g., Sealed Case,* 29 F.3d at 718. The rule facilitates zealous advocacy in the context of an adversarial system of justice by ensuring that the sweat of an attorney's brow is not appropriated by the opposing party. *Hickman v. Taylor,* 329 U.S. 495, 511, 67 S.Ct. 385, 91 L.Ed. 451 (1947)

(continued)

B. *Fed.R.Civ.P. 45(d)(2).*

As an alternate ground for our decision, we note that the motion to quash was properly denied because the intervenors failed to present sufficient information with respect to the items to which their claim of privilege attaches. The Civil Rules specifically provide that:

> When information subject to a subpoena is withheld on a claim that it is privileged or subject to protection as trial preparation materials, the claim shall be made expressly and shall be supported by a description of the nature of the documents, communications or things not produced that is sufficient to enable the demanding party to contest the claim.

Fed.R.Civ.P. 45(d)(2). The operative language is mandatory and, although the rule does not spell out the sufficiency requirement in detail, courts consistently have held that the ru§ *see also Avery Dennison Corp. v. Four Pillars,* 190 F.R.D. 1, 1 (D.D.C. 1999) (describing privilege logs as "the universally accepted means" of asserting privilege claims in the federal courts); *cf. Vaughn v. Rosen,* 484 F.2d 820 (D.C.Ct.App. 1973) (articulating the justifications for requiring privilege logs in the context of the FOIA). A party that fails to submit a privilege log is deemed to waive the underlying privilege claim. *See Dorf & Stanton Communications, Inc. v. Molson Breweries,* 100 F.3d 919, 923 (Fed. Cir. 1996) (holding that failing "to provide a complete privilege log demonstrating sufficient grounds for taking the privilege" waives the privilege). Although most of the reported cases arise in the context of a claim of attorney-client privilege, the "specify or waive" rule applies equally in the context of claims of work product privilege. *See, e.g., Smith v. Conway Org., Inc.,* 154 F.R.D. 73, 76 (S.D.N.Y. 1994).

In a somewhat indirect fashion, the intervenors suggest that they were hampered in their ability to present a list of privileged documents by the district court's refusal to hold an evidentiary hearing. This suggestion does not withstand scrutiny. After all, the intervenors were not without knowledge of the communications to which the subpoena pertained; Lawyer originally had possession of them and turned them over to Smith & Jones only when Newparent decided to change counsel. Despite this knowledge, the intervenors made no effort to prepare a privilege log. That omission is fatal.

Privilege logs do not need to be precise to the point of pedantry. Thus, a party who possesses some knowledge of the nature of the materials to which a claim of privilege is addressed cannot shirk his obligation to file a privilege log merely because he lacks infinitely detailed information. To the contrary, we read Rule 45(d)(2) as requiring a party who asserts a claim of privilege to do the best that he reasonably can to describe the materials to which his claim adheres.

■ DOCUMENT AUTHENTICATION

A recurring theme in nearly all cases is the **authentication of documents.** Before a document may be admitted into evidence, it must be authenticated, meaning that sufficient supporting evidence must be introduced to verify that the document is what the proponent says it is. For a checklist of electronic evidence admissibility see Exhibit 14.10. In federal courts, Rule 901 of the Federal Rules of Evidence provides the groundwork for authentication:

(a) General Provision. The requirement of authentication or identification as a condition precedent to admissibility is satisfied by evidence sufficient to support a finding that the matter in question is what its proponent claims. F.R.E. 901 (a)

LEARNING OBJECTIVE 4
Describe the process for authentication of documents.

Exhibit 14.10 Admissibility of Electronic Evidence

ADMISSIBILITY OF ELECTRONIC EVIDENCE

Paul W. Grimm & Kevin F. Brady

Checklist of Potential Authentication Methods

E-MAIL

- Witness with personal knowledge (901(b)(1))
- Expert testimony or comparison with authenticated examples (901(b)(3))
- Distinctive characteristics including circumstantial evidence (901(b)(4))
- Trade inscriptions (902(7))
- Certified copies of business record (902(11))

INTERNET WEBSITE POSTINGS

- Witness with personal knowledge (901(b)(1))
- Expert testimony or comparison with authenticated examples (901(b)(3))
- Distinctive characteristics including circumstantial evidence (901(b)(4))
- Public records (901(b)(7))
- System or process capable of proving a reliable result (901(b)(9))
- Official publications (902(5))

TEXT MESSAGES, TWEETS, AND THE LIKE

- Witness with personal knowledge (901(b)(1))
- Circumstantial evidence of distinctive characteristics (901(b)(4))
- Expert testimony or comparison with authenticated examples (901(b)(3))

COMPUTED STORED RECORDS AND DATA

- Witness with personal knowledge (901(b)(1))
- Expert testimony or comparison with authenticated examples (901(b)(3))
- Distinctive characteristics including circumstantial evidence (901(b)(4)
- System or process capable of proving a reliable result (901(b)(9))

COMPUTER ANIMATIONS AND COMPUTER SIMULATIONS

- Witness with personal knowledge (901(b)(1))
- Expert testimony or comparison with authenticated examples (901(b)(3))
- System or process capable of proving a reliable result (901(b)(9)

DIGITAL PHOTOGRAPHS

- Witness with personal knowledge (901(b)(1))
- System or process capable of providing reliable result (901(b)(9)

CONNOLLY BOVE LODGE & HUTZ LLP
ATTORNEYS AT LAW

2010 Paul W. Grimm & Kevin F. Brady

Exhibit 14.10 Continued

1. PRELIMINARY RULINGS ON ADMISSIBILITY

■ Before evidence goes to jury, judge must determine whether proponent has offered satisfactory foundation (preponderance of the evidence) from which jury could reasonably find that evidence is authentic (104(a)) (FRE, except for privilege, do not apply)

■ When relevance of evidence depends on a disputed antecedent fact being established ("conditional relevance"), judge determines whether a reasonable jury could find that the fact has been proved, then submits the question to jury to decide. If jury finds that the antecedent fact has been proved, it considers the evidence. If not, it does not consider it. Example: dispute on authenticity.

2. IS EVIDENCE RELEVANT?   FRE 401

Does it have a tendency to make some fact that is of consequence to the litigation more or less probable than it otherwise would be?

YES

FRE 401

ADMISSIBLE - Go to FRE 402

FRE 402
Does Constitution, Statute or Rule Require Exclusion?
Yes - Inadmissible
No - Admissible - Go to FRE 403

FRE 403
Is probative value substantially outweighed by:
1) Danger of unfair prejudice?
2) Confusion of the issues?
3) Misleading the jury?
4) Undue delay?
5) Waste of time?
6) Needless presentation of cumulative evidence?

NO — ADMISSIBLE

YES — INADMISSIBLE

NO

FRE 401   INADMISSIBLE

3. IF RELEVANT, IS IT AUTHENTIC? FRE 901– 902

■ **FRE 901(a)** Is the evidence sufficient to support a finding that the matter in question is what proponent claims?

Determining the degree of foundation required to authenticate electronic evidence depends on the quality and completeness of the data input, the complexity of the computer processing, the routines of the computer operation and the ability to test and verify the results.

■ **FRE 901(b)**
Non-exclusive list of examples includes:
   (1) Testimony of witness with knowledge;
   (3) Comparison by trier or expert witness;
   (4) Distinctive characteristics and the like (e-mail address, hash values, "reply" doctrine);
   (7) Public records or report; and
   (9) Process or system capable of producing a reliable result.

■ **FRE 902**
Methods by which information may be authenticated WITHOUT EXTRINSIC EVIDENCE:

Ways to authenticate e-records:
   - 902(1)-(4) Public Records/Documents
   - 902(5) Official publications
   - 902(6) Newspapers, Magazines, Similar Publications
   - 902(7) Trade inscriptions
   - 902(11) Certified domestic records of regularly conducted activity (authenticate business records under FRE 803(6)).

Exhibit 14.10 Continued

4. IS EVIDENCE HEARSAY?   FRE 801 (a-c)

YES

1. Is it a statement (written/spoken assertion, non-verbal/non-assertive verbal conduct intended to be assertive)?

2. Is statement made by "Declarant" (person, not generated by machine)?

3. Is statement offered for proving truth of assertion?
   NOTE: Statement is not offered for substantive truth if offered to prove:
      a. Communicative/comprehension capacity of declarant;
      b. Effect on the hearer;
      c. Circumstantial evidence of state of mind of declarant;
      d. Verbal acts/parts of acts;
      e. Utterances of independent legal significance.

4. Is statement excluded from definition of hearsay by 801(d)(1) and (2)?

Prior witness statements – 801(d)(1)
- Prior testimonial statement 801(d)(1)(A)
- Prior consistent statement 801(d)(1)(B) to rebut allegations of recent fabrication
- Statement of identification 801(d)(1)(C)

Admission by party opponents – 801(d)(2)
- Individual admission 801(d)(2)(A)
- Adoptive admission 801(d)(2)(B)
- Admission by person with authority 802(d)(2)(C)
- Admission by agent/employees 802(d)(2)(D)
- Co-conspirator statements 801(d)(2)(E)

If HEARSAY, then it is INADMISSIBLE unless covered by a recognized exception:

HEARSAY EXCEPTION

NO

Availability of Declarant Irrelevant – 803
- Present Sense Impression 803(1)
- Excited Utterance 803(2)
- State of Mind Exception 803(3)
- Statements for Purposes of Medical Diagnosis or Treatment 803(4)
- Past Recollection Recorded 803(5)
- Business Records 803(6)
- Absence of an entry in records kept in the regular course of business 803(7)
- Public Records or Reports 803(8)
- Records of Vital Statistics 803(9)
- Absence of public record or entry 803(10)
- Records/ Documents affecting interest in property 803(14) & (15)
- Statements in Ancient Documents 803(16)
- Market Reports, Commercial Publications 803(17)
- Learned Treatises 803(18)
- Character Reputation Testimony 803(21)
- Record of Felony Convictions 803(22)

Residual "Catchall" Exception -- 807

Declarant Unavailable – 804
- Unavailability – 804(a)(1-5)   (privilege, refused to testify, lack of memory, death/illness beyond subpoena power)

- Unavailability Exceptions – 804(b)
  – Former Testimony 804(b)(1)
  – Dying Declaration 804(b)(2)
  – Statement Against Interest 804(b)(3)
  – Statement re family history 804(b)(4)
  – Forfeiture by wrongdoing 804(b)(6)

Exhibit 14.10 Continued

6 ORIGINAL WRITING RULE – FRE 1001 – 1008

- Is the evidence "original", "duplicate", "writing", "recording" (1001)

- Rule 1002 requires the original to prove the contents of a writing, recording or photograph unless "secondary evidence" (any evidence other than original or duplicative) is admissible. Rules 1004, 1005, 1006, 1007.

- Duplicates are co-extensively admissible as originals unless there is a genuine issue of authenticity of the original or circumstances indicate that it would be unfair to admit duplicate in lieu of original (1003)

- Permits proof of the contents of writing, recording or paragraph by use of "secondary evidence" – any proof of the contents of a writing, recording or photograph other than the original or duplicate (1004) if:
    i. Non-bad faith loss/destruction of original/duplicate
    ii. Inability to subpoena original/duplicate
    iii. Original/duplicate in possession, custody, control of opposing party

    iv. "Collateral record" (i.e., not closely related to controlling issue in case)

- Admission of summary of voluminous books, records or documents (1006)

- Testimony or deposition of party against whom offered or by that party's written admission (FRCP 30, 33, 36) (1007)

- If admissibility depends on the fulfillment of a condition or fact, question of whether condition has been fulfilled is for fact finder to determine under 104(b) (1008)

- But, the issue is for the trier of fact, if it is a question:
    (a) whether they asserted writing ever existed;
    (b) whether another writing, recording or photograph produced at trial is the original; or
    (c) whether other evidence of contents correctly reflects the contents, the issue is for the trier of fact.

7 PRACTICE TIPS

1 Be prepared. Start with a defensible and comprehensive records management program.

2 Think strategically about the case and the evidence from the beginning of the case.

3 Memorialize each step of the collection and production process to bolster reliability.

4 Use every opportunity during discovery to authenticate potential evidence.

Examples:
a) For pretrial disclosures under F.R.C.P. 26(a)(3), you have 14 days to file objections or possible waiver;

b) Documents produced by opposing party are presumed to be authentic – burden shifts

c) F.R.C.P. 36 Requests for Admissions

d) Request stipulation of authenticity from opposing counsel

5 Be prepared to provide the court with enough information to understand the technology issues as they relate to the reliability of the evidence at hand.

6 Be creative and consider whether there are case management tools that might assist the court and the other parties in addressing evidentiary problems concerning some of the more complex issues (such as "dynamic" data in a database or what is a "true and accurate copy" of ESI).

7 Keep your audience in mind... will this be an issue for the judge or the jury? (e.g., Rule 104(a) or (b).

For more information contact:
Kevin F. Brady at: KBrady@cblh.com

The Honorable Paul W. Grimm and Kevin F. Brady, Esquire.

Some records have inherent authenticity, such as public records. These documents are authenticated by proof of custody, even when they consist of data stored electronically. For example, section 1530 of the California Evidence Code states:

> (a) A purported copy of a writing in the custody of a public entity, or of an entry in such a writing, is prima facie evidence of the existence and content of such writing or entry if:
>
> (1) The copy purports to be published by the authority of the nation or state, or public entity therein in which the writing is kept....

Other types of documents are also considered self-authenticating under Rule 902 of the Federal Rules of Evidence:

1. Domestic public documents under seal
2. Domestic public documents not under seal
3. Foreign public documents
4. Certified copies of public records
5. Official publications
6. Newspapers and periodicals
7. Trade inscriptions and the like
8. Acknowledged documents
9. Commercial paper and related documents
10. Certified domestic records of regularly conducted activity
11. Certified foreign records of regularly conducted activity

Original documents, while preferable, are not required if the originals cannot be obtained or if they have been lost or stolen, unless, as stated in FRE 1004, "the proponent lost or destroyed them in bad faith."

For the most part, the great body of law on authentication developed during the time when most documents were on paper. Under these rules, a party may challenge the authenticity of documents based on their physical characteristics. Handwriting experts and forensic specialists in paper, ink, and aging characteristics may be called in if there is a question of authenticity. Such challenges sometimes arise when a will is challenged, and the date of execution or signature of the testator is questioned.

Electronically stored documents, when reproduced in printed form, do not have the same physical characteristics of original paper documents. Thus, challenges to their authenticity are not based on the physical characteristics of the material on which they are created, but on the electronic characteristics of their creation and storage—the metadata.

authentication of documents
The process of determining that the proposed evidence is what it is purported to be and is genuine.

 # IN THE WORDS OF THE COURT...

Lorraine v. Markel American Insurance Company (Md. 5-4-2007)Jack R. Lorraine and, Beverly Mack Plaintiffs v. Markel American Insurance Company Defendants.
CIVIL ACTION NO. PWG-06-1893.
United States District Court, D. Maryland.
May 4, 2007
Memorandum Opinion
PAUL GRIMM, Magistrate Judge

(continued)

Whether ESI is admissible into evidence is determined by a collection of evidence rules that present themselves like a series of hurdles to be cleared by the proponent of the evidence. Failure to clear any of these evidentiary hurdles means that the evidence will not be admissible. Whenever ESI is offered as evidence, either at trial or in summary judgment, the following evidence rules must be considered: (1) is the ESI relevant as determined by Rule 401 (does it have any tendency to make some fact that is of consequence to the litigation more or less probable than it otherwise would be); (2) if relevant under 401, is it authentic as required by Rule 901(a) (can the proponent show that the ESI is what it purports to be); (3) if the ESI is offered for its substantive truth, is it hearsay as defined by Rule 801, and if so, is it covered by an applicable exception (Rules 803, 804 and 807); (4) is the form of the ESI that is being offered as evidence an original or duplicate under the original writing rule, o[r] if not, is there admissible secondary evidence to prove the content of the ESI (Rules 1001-1008); and (5) is the probative value of the ESI substantially outweighed by the danger of unfair prejudice or one of the other factors identified by Rule 403.

CONCEPT REVIEW AND REINFORCEMENT

KEY TERMS

CHAPTER SUMMARY

Introduction to Analysis and Review of E-Discovery	Once the information needed has been identified and made available to a client's attorney, it must be reviewed for relevancy to the request and for privileged or confidential information and attorney work product, which must be identified, logged, and removed.
Reviewing Electronic Documents	One of the biggest costs in electronic discovery is incurred in review. Initially, the review is of the material obtained from clients to find relevant items and to identify privileged, confidential, or protected documents. After obtaining the documents, decisions must be made about how to process the material supplied.

The Delivery of ESI	The response to a discovery request may be in electronic form or in paper form or a combination of both. Documents from clients provided for a review before sending them to the other side may be in various formats. One of the first issues to be considered is the format for document delivery to the opposing side after review.
Metadata in Document Production	Every electronic document has metadata, which is simply information about the document. This information may include the location of the file, referred to as resource (system) metadata, and content (application) metadata, which is the content and author.
Obtaining Documents via Paper Discovery	Not all documents are in electronic form. Many public agencies, like police and fire departments, may still file paper-based reports. Litigation that involves a time frame prior to the age of electronic document preparation also requires paper-based documents. These cases often involve a large volume of material that must be processed by the legal team. Converting the paper documents to electronic forms may shorten the processing time.
Scanning Documents	Paper documents can be scanned to convert them to an electronic form. The format in which they are saved may vary depending on the use and the purpose of the scanning process. Most scanners have a software program that allows a choice of format. One of the most popular graphic image–scanning formats is the PDF format.
Graphic Image File Formats	Native file format is the format used by a program to save the data produced by the program. TIFF is short for "tagged image file format." It is one of the most widely used formats for storing images. PDF is short for "portable document format."
Document Processing	Each document must be identified by certain characteristics to allow it to be effectively sorted, retrieved, and identified for further review. This process is known as coding. The most basic type of coding is objective coding, also referred to as bibliographic indexing. This includes the author, type of document, recipient, and date. Additional coding may include subjective coding, which identifies keywords within the document or other criteria not related to bibliographic information.
Reducing ESI to Manageable Levels	It is clear that there are now more documents available that are relevant. The documents need to be reduced to a reasonable number. Filtering is the process used to scan or search the documents for relevant terms in an attempt to narrow the focus, such as by eliminating documents created before or after a certain date. De-duplication, or de-duping, is the term used to describe the process of electronically eliminating duplicates of the same document.

Privilege Review	Privilege review is the process of reviewing documents to identify those that contain privileged communication, confidential information, or attorney work product. Documents identified as privileged can then be removed from the documents produced to the opposing side. But, the protection may be lost if steps are not taken to safeguard the information against disclosure. Voluntary disclosure traditionally acts as a waiver of the various privileges. Even with careful privilege review, sometimes documents that are considered privileged are still produced to the opposing side; this is referred to as inadvertent disclosure. Rule 502 of the Federal Rules of Evidence was passed in 2009 as a solution to the inconsistent application of the claw-back provisions based on the reasons and steps taken after the disclosures. It seeks to offer, at least in federal court, protection when the disclosure is inadvertent, when reasonable steps were taken to avoid inadvertent production, when steps are taken promptly to correct the inadvertent production, and when there is the existence of a claw-back agreement.
Conducting the Privilege Review	Those conducting the actual document review must be familiar with not only the attorney–client privilege and work product rules, but also any definitive statutory privileges, such as in the attorney–client privilege under statute and federal laws or rules of evidence, and the conditional privileges for such items as trade secrets or other confidential material the public disclosure of which could be damaging to a client, such as pharmaceutical research or new cell phone technology for which patents have not yet been obtained.
Redaction	In documents that contain confidential information, privileged material may be redacted. Redaction is the removal of confidential information, or at least that which is claimed to be confidential, or material prepared for trial under the work product doctrine.
Document Authentication	Before a document may be admitted into evidence, it must be authenticated. Some records have inherent authenticity, such as public records, which are authenticated by proof of custody even when they are comprised of data stored electronically. Other documents are considered self-authenticating under Rule 902 of the Federal Rules of Evidence. Original documents, while preferable, are not required if the originals cannot be obtained or have been lost or stolen, "… unless the proponent lost or destroyed them in bad faith…" F. R. E. 1004.

REVIEW QUESTIONS AND EXERCISES

1. What is the purpose of document review? What are the stages in the process, and what are the goals of each?
2. How is document review complicated by different file types and formats? Describe a solution to this problem.
3. What file format is often required by courts for producing documents in discovery? Why is this format desirable in discovery?
4. If the requesting party does not specify a format for production of the documents, what form may the producing party use? What rules govern the format for production?
5. What is metadata? What is the difference between content and resource metadata?
6. Why might metadata be relevant in litigation? Can metadata be removed from documents?
7. Does metadata always need to be produced with a document? How do courts view the production of metadata?
8. How is metadata used to determine the authenticity of an electronic document?
9. Why might paper documents be converted to electronic form during discovery? Give at least three reasons. How is this conversion accomplished?
10. What are the advantages to having documents in electronic form? Give at least three reasons.
11. What is meant by native format? How is the native format different from a graphic image format?
12. What is the purpose of filtering in discovery? Give an example of a filtering term that might assist a party in discovery during an employment discrimination suit.
13. What is the purpose of de-duplication? Why is this an important process in e-discovery?
14. What is the purpose of coding documents? How does coding assist parties during the processing of documents?
15. What is the difference between objective and subjective coding?
16. What is auto coding? What are its advantages? What further steps may be necessary after auto coding is accomplished?
17. What is privilege review? Why is careful privilege review necessary in almost every case?
18. What types of documents need not be provided to the other side?
19. What is inadvertent disclosure? What is a possible effect of inadvertent disclosure?
20. What is a claw-back clause? What purpose does it serve?
21. What is the purpose of redaction?
22. Why must documents be authenticated? How is the authentication of electronic documents different from the authentication of paper documents?
23. Do any documents have automatic authenticity? Give three examples.
24. How is the claim of privilege made? What is a consequence of failing to make a claim of privilege?
25. What is the purpose of a privilege log?

BUILDING YOUR PARALEGAL SKILLS

INTERNET AND TECHNOLOGY EXERCISES

1. Locate information about removing metadata from word processor documents.
2. Use the Internet to find redaction software. Create a table comparing the features of each.

CHAPTER OPENING SCENARIO CASE STUDY

Use the Opening Scenario for this chapter to answer the following questions.

1. In what form should each team request the documents be produced to them?
2. What are the potential problems with not specifying a format for production?
3. How can software programs or outside consultants be of advantage in either case?
4. What are the firm's options in discovery? How will these options make discovery more efficient or effective?

CONTINUING CASES AND EXERCISES

1. Review the issues that must be considered in each case as it relates to e-discovery and trial preparation. Prepare a list of the issues.
2. Use the list of issues to prepare instructions to the client from initial inception of each case. Be specific as to how documents are to be prepared for turning over to the legal team.
3. Use the Comprehensive case assigned or the school bus–truck accident case, Case A in Appendix II, to:
   a. Prepare a litigation hold letter to your client. Explain the reasons and the penalties.
   b. Prepare a memo to members of the firm on the necessary steps and actions they must take regarding litigation hold procedures.
   c. Instruct your client on what documents you wish to review and the reasons for the review, including instructions and the reasons for the requested file format of the files.
   d. Prepare a template for use in preparing a privilege log.
   e. Prepare a list of witness you will need to authenticate documents that will be admitted as evidence.

BUILDING YOUR PROFESSIONAL PORTFOLIO

Procedures

1. Locate any rules of procedure or evidence in your jurisdiction on requirements for producing privileged material.

2. Prepare a checklist of the steps that must be taken in your jurisdiction to prevent inadvertent disclosure of confidential information from being treated as a waiver of the privilege.

"It's impossible to move, to live, to operate at any level
without leaving traces, bits, seemingly meaningless
fragments of personal information."

—*William Gibson*

The Electronic Courtroom | CHAPTER 15

OPENING SCENARIO

It had been a very eventful six months for the firm. In the school bus accident case, twenty-five clients were now seeking damages. The basic facts of the case were not in dispute, but it would be a challenge to figure out how the jury would receive the presentation of the physical evidence. The team would need to determine the best way to demonstrate how the defects in the truck and the bus contributed to the severity of the injuries.

They knew they were lucky to get the case into a federal courtroom with electronic capabilities, as the local state courthouse, by contrast, did not even have TV monitors to present video depositions. The court's technical support staff assured the litigation team that all they had to do was bring a laptop to court and hook it up. Despite these assurances, however, they knew they would have to master the technology in order to present their case effectively to the jury.

The lead attorney, Owen Mason, was getting nervous about how he would manage the trial presentation. He was unsure whether he could effectively present the case to the jury while simultaneously operating the laptop and controlling the graphics. There was a lot of documentation supporting their theory of liability, including the electronic documents they had obtained during discovery that provided the "smoking gun" to prove their case.

The biggest question they had yet to answer was whether they should present the case electronically or use photographic enlargements. The multimedia tools were all available (if a little costly), but which method would make the best impression on the court and the jury?

Another major problem was presenting the testimony of their expert witnesses. The engineering expert they were counting on would be out of the country the

LEARNING OBJECTIVES

After studying this chapter, you should be able to:

1. Describe the elements of the electronic courtroom.

2. Describe how court staff can assist the legal team with using electronic resources in the courthouse.

VIDEO INTRODUCTION

THE ELECTRONIC COURTHOUSE
After watching the video in MyLegalStudiesLab, answer the following questions.

1. How has technology changed courtroom procedures?
2. What are the potential problems in working in an electronic courtroom?

week the trial was scheduled. And getting the individual treating physicians to appear at the last minute was also a challenge. The firm anticipated the difficulty of having all of their medical experts appear at trial, and had incurred considerable expenses in videotaping their depositions.

The hope was that technology would help them overcome all of these challenges. By using a high-technology electronic courtroom in federal court, the entire case could be presented with graphics and videotape.

■ INTRODUCTION TO THE ELECTRONIC COURTROOM

Increasingly, judges are embracing the use of technology and computer systems for presentations in the courtroom. The initial reluctance to allow these systems is giving way to acceptance, as judges realize that these tools can enhance the speedy administration of justice.

One of the earliest uses of technology in the courtroom was the playing of videotaped depositions of expert witnesses on TV monitors in court. Getting experts to testify is often difficult because of the uncertainty of trial schedules. Many experts, such as noted surgeons and medical forensics experts, have active, lucrative practices, and demand compensation for the time lost while waiting to testify. These fees can run to the thousands of dollars per hour, and the average litigant can rarely afford this litigation cost. However, a video recording of a deposition can be a cost-effective method of presenting expert witnesses, or witnesses who for reasons of health or distance would not otherwise be available to testify personally at a trial.

Courtrooms are now being outfitted with computers and audiovisual presentation systems, as judicial budgets will allow. Exhibit 15.2 shows the new Corpus Christi Federal Courthouse technology courtrooms for the Honorable Hayden W. Head and the Honorable Janis Graham Jack.

Computerized courtrooms can be seen frequently on Court TV trials, in which computer terminals are present at each lawyer's table, on the judge's bench, for each of the court support personnel, and for the jury.

VIDEO ADVICE FROM THE FIELD

Debra Weaver—Certified Real-Time Court Reporter
A discussion explaining Real-Time Reporting.
After watching the video in MyLegalStudiesLab answer the following questions.

1. What is Real-Time Reporting?
2. What are the advantages of using a real-time reporting transcript?

Exhibit 15.1 Transcript and deposition display in Sanction

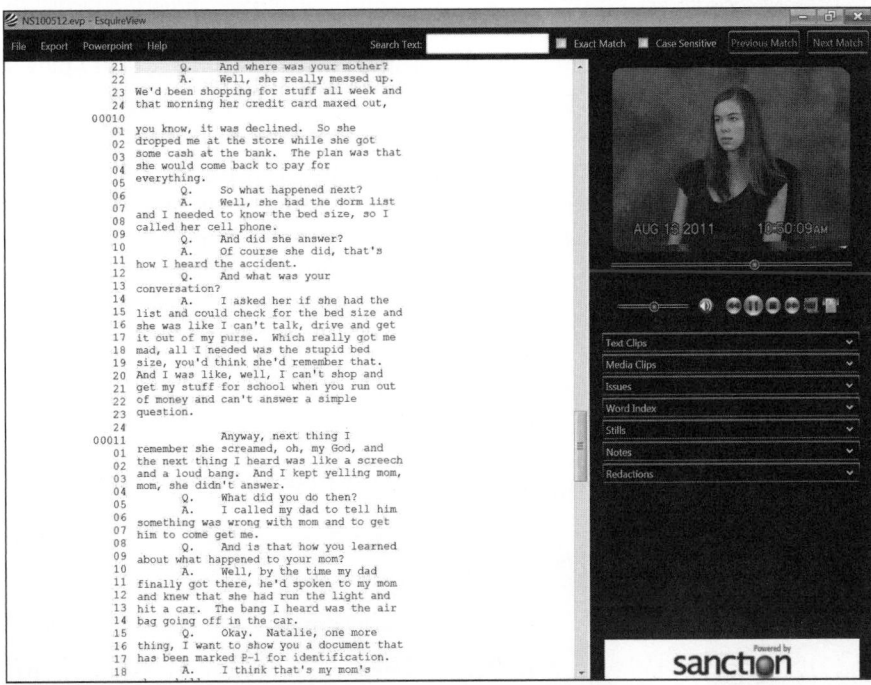

Litigation support software can be used to display documentary evidence, graphic presentations, and computer simulations of accident cases. Relevant portions of documents can be displayed as the witness identifies the document during his or her testimony. Everyone in the courtroom can see the document at the same time, without the need to distribute paper copies. Lawyers can rapidly search thousands of pages of depositions and documents from their laptop computers to find pertinent material for examination or cross-examination of witnesses. Software can also display part of a transcript of a deposition while the video of the deposition is running, as shown in Exhibit 15.1.

■ THE ELECTRONIC COURTROOM

The types of electronic equipment available can vary, even among rooms within the same courthouse. These differences may occur because of budgetary issues or the personal preferences of the jurists using each courtroom. Just as some trial attorneys are not comfortable using multimedia presentation tools, some judges may feel that multimedia technology detracts from the ultimate task of reviewing the facts to make a judgment. The trial team thus has to be prepared to make the best presentation of their client's case, whether in a traditional courtroom or in a contemporary, multimedia courtroom.

In most traditional courtrooms, litigants use easels or display boards, blackboards, or erasable whiteboards. These may be used to display exhibits, list items, or provide a space for witnesses to draw diagrams.

In some contemporary courtrooms, these basic tools have given way to more modern technology such as the overhead projector, the video screen, and the computer projector. In more complex arrangements, computer monitors are located at the counsel's table, on the judge's bench, and in some cases in the jury

LEARNING OBJECTIVE 1
Describe the elements of the electronic courtroom.

box or witness stand, as shown Exhibits 15.3–15.5. The courtroom may also have a large-screen monitor for viewing by everyone in the room, as shown in Exhibit 15.6. As technology has advanced, some courts have installed multimedia podiums for lawyers to use that include special projection devices like a DVD player or the popular Elmo document projector, as seen in Exhibit 15.7.

In some cases, judges who do not have a multimedia-equipped courtroom will permit the attorneys to bring in their own equipment. Typically, such permission is granted when both sides can afford the shared cost. If one litigant is better financed than the other, the judge may permit him or her to bring his or her own equipment if he or she agrees to give the other side full access to it.

Exhibit 15.2 Electronic courtroom visual presentation system, Corpus Christi Federal Courthouse

Exhibit 15.3 Counsel tables

Exhibit 15.4 The judge's bench

Exhibit 15.5 The jury box

Exhibit 15.6 Large screen and projector

Exhibit 15.7 Attorney lectern with
document camera

Learning how to use the different types of equipment is not difficult, but may take a little practice. Everyone on the trial team should be comfortable with the operation and use of the equipment before the start of trial.

> **PRACTICE TIP**
>
> All of the equipment used in the electronic courtroom is similar in type and purpose to that used in today's classrooms. Most teachers' colleges offer courses in the operation and use of multimedia equipment. In some cases, these courses are required for teaching certification. Litigation team members may learn the use and techniques of electronic equipment by taking these courses.

The Wired Courtroom

The most basic courtroom setup includes a projector with a projection screen, positioned for viewing by the court and the jury, to which each litigation team may hook up a multimedia device, such as a laptop or DVD player. This setup allows both defense and plaintiff to simultaneously share the projector using

Exhibit 15.8 Courtroom Setup A, a basic setup

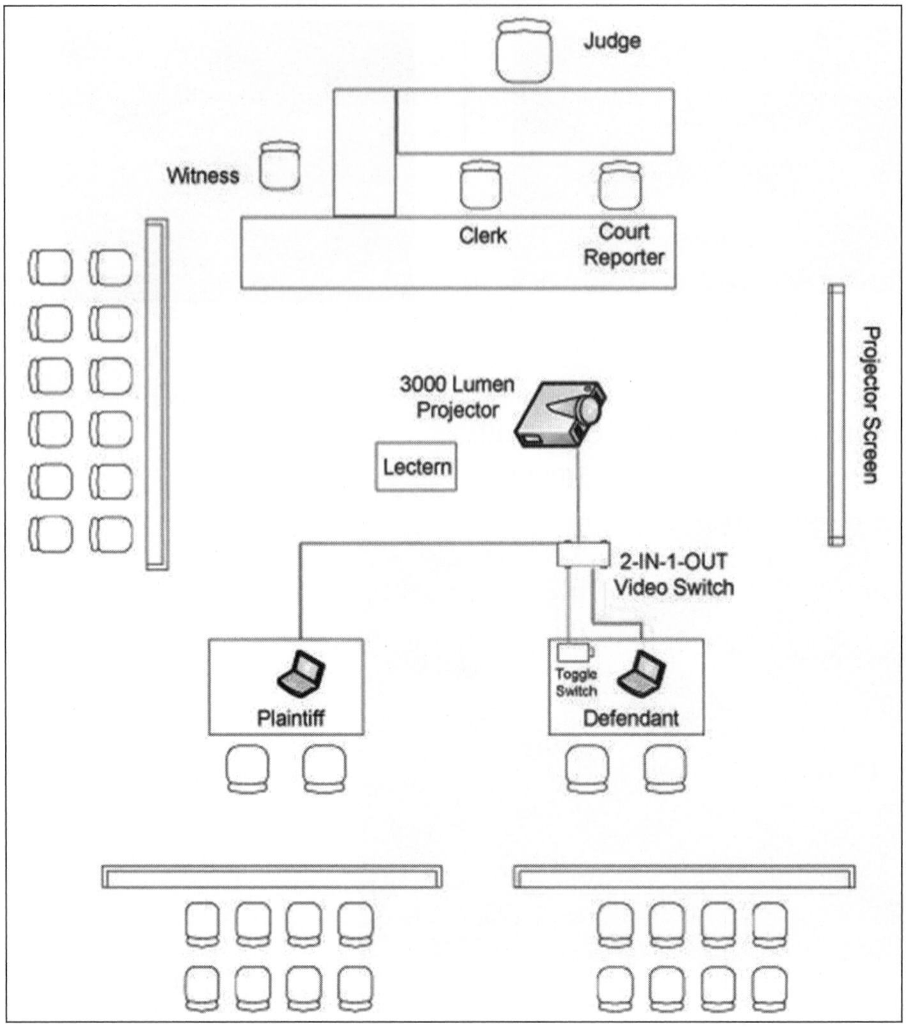

a 2-input, 1-output video connector switch, as shown in Exhibit 15.8. With each side's laptop plugged into an input, the video switch controls which laptop image is projected onto the screen. Audio can be played back using the courtroom's sound system or played from speakers plugged into the laptop computer.

Judge Control of Multimedia During Trial

At an initial meeting with trial counsel, the trial judge may determine what, if any, multimedia may be used during trial. This determination may take place during the same meeting at which they discuss motions or objections on the use of certain items of evidence. For example, they may discuss objections to photographs that are claimed to be prejudicial, objections raised in depositions, or motions to allow videotaped depositions. Such issues may need to be resolved before allowing the presentation of this evidence at trial.

In some cases, the judge may be concerned that additional objections will be raised during a video presentation at trial. If so, a "kill switch" can give the court the ability to cut off the video display by temporarily blacking it out. This is set up by introducing a second video switch between the main video switch and the projector, as seen in Exhibit 15.9. This is the same basic configuration as in Exhibit 15.8, except that the judge has ultimate control over whether or not an image is sent to the projector.

Some courtrooms now have more complex setups, with monitors at counsel's table, on the judge's bench, at witness stands, and in jury boxes, as shown in the schematic in Exhibit 15.10. This type of arrangement builds on the basic components shown in Exhibits 15.8 and 15.9. An additional connector allows multiple outputs. In this drawing, there is one input and six outputs.

The arrangement shown in Exhibit 15.11 adds a projector in conjunction with flat-panel screens for the jury to view. Notice that the feed to the jury monitors comes after the judge's kill switch, thus giving the judge the power to control what the jury sees.

Exhibit 15.9 Courtroom Setup B with judge-controlled kill switch

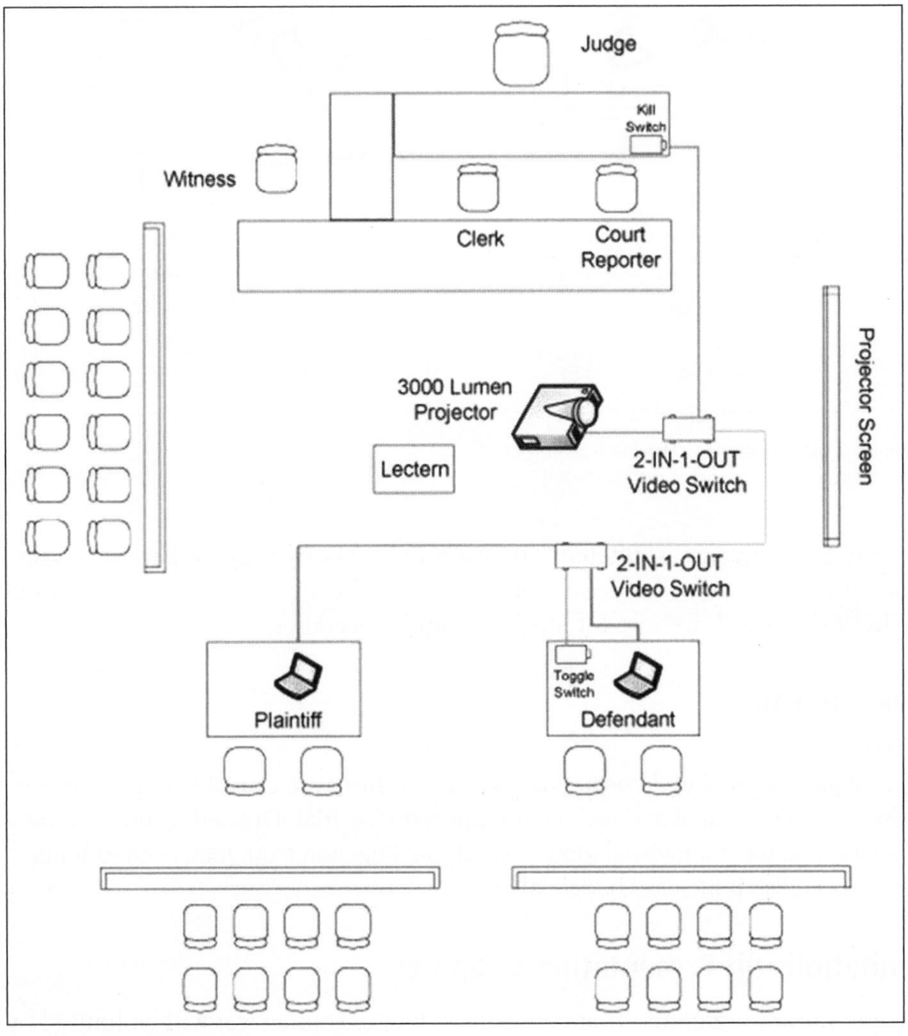

Exhibit 15.10 Courtroom Setup C

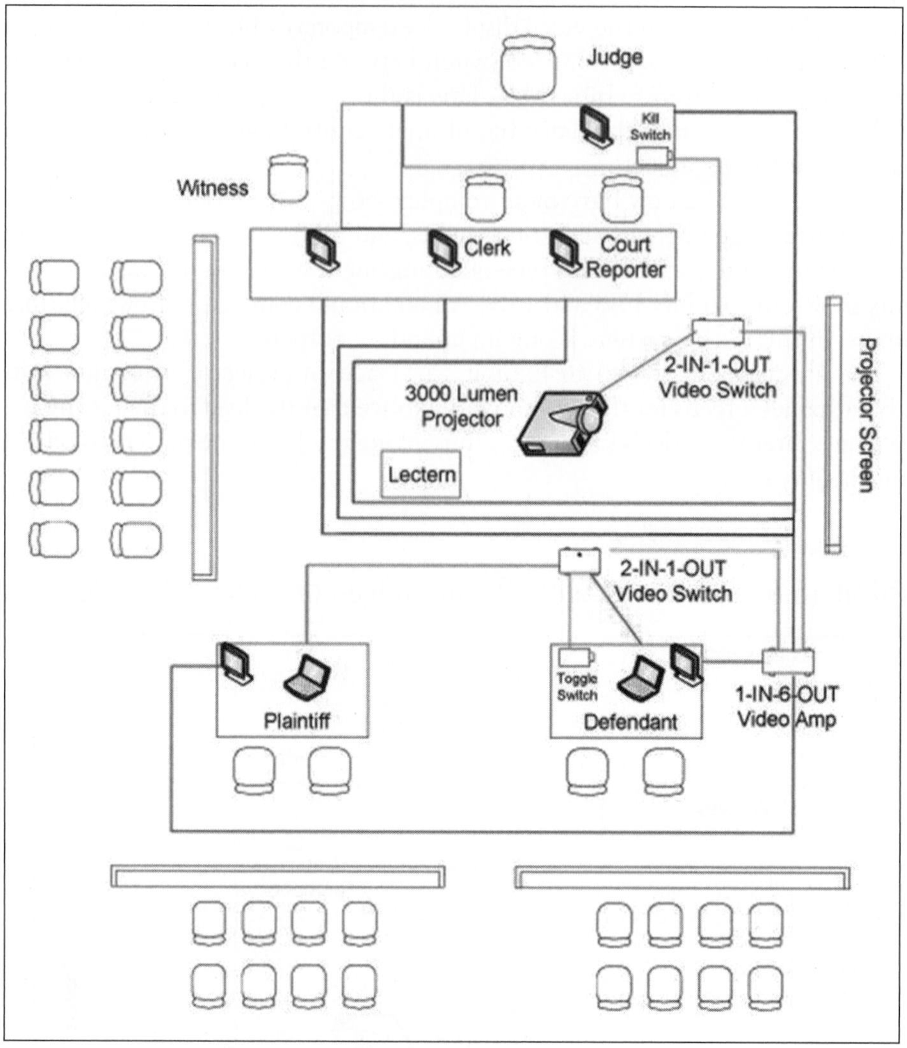

Copyright © AG/Sanction LLC. Used with permission.

Since every court is different and each judge controls his or her own court-room, it is essential for the legal team to consult the appropriate court personnel or check the court's website for local rules and procedures.

PRACTICE TIP

Trial

Local and national trial consulting and support firms are available to provide the necessary equipment and technical support during trial. Depending on the type of case and the audiovisual tools needed, the litigation team may need to bring in a specialist, if the case budget allows.

Limitations on Presentation Graphics

The presentation graphics that can be used by the trial lawyer will be limited by the equipment available in the courtroom. If the courtroom is not set up with

WEB RESOURCES

For complete informa-tion and documenta-tion on the Matthew J. Perry, Jr. Courthouse in Columbia, South Carolina, go to http://www.scd .uscourts.gov/

Exhibit 15.11 Courtroom Setup D

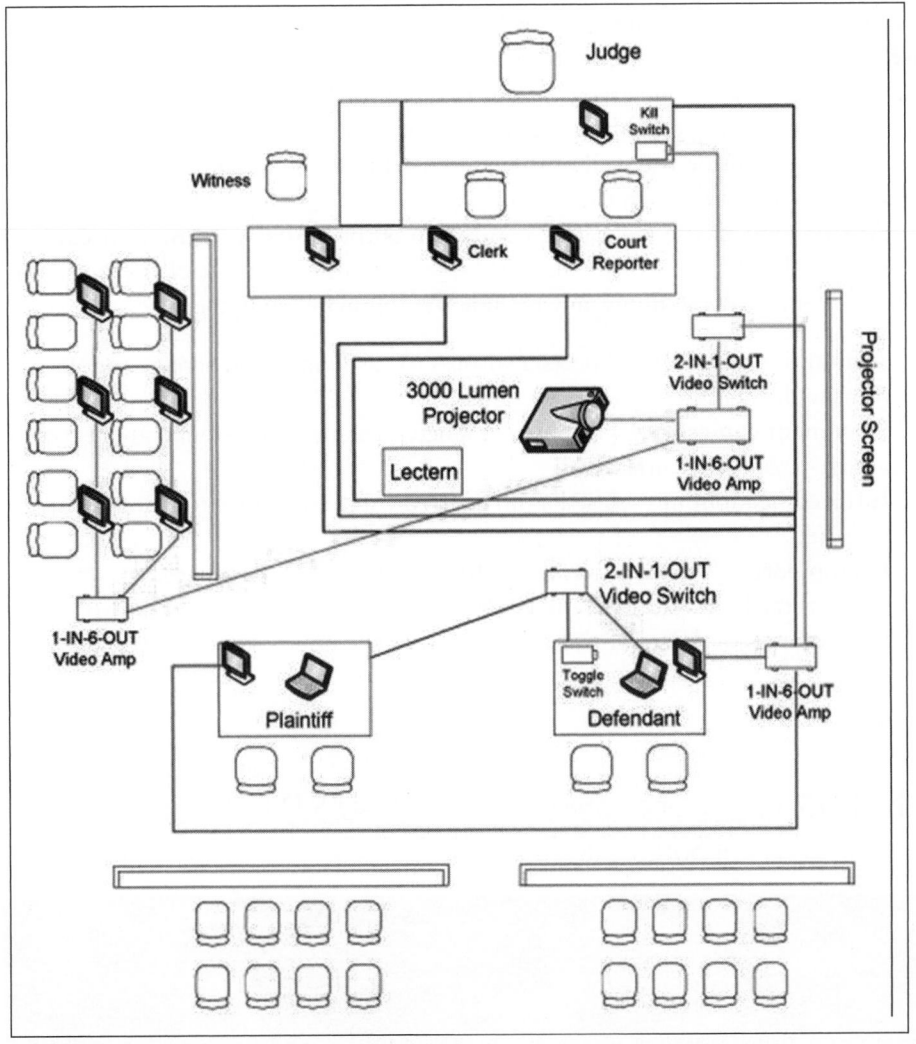

appropriate power sources, screens, or monitors, some computer presentations will simply not work, and print media may still be needed.

Legal support staff must determine the availability of technical resources in the courtroom well in advance of trial. If the courtroom is not equipped for computer presentations, the court may not allow the installation and use of additional equipment. And, if all of the equipment must be supplied by the team, the client may not be willing to pay for the costs associated with acquiring and installing the needed hardware. In cases like the notorious O. J. Simpson prosecution, if the courtroom had not been wired for computer use, the defendant certainly could have paid the cost of the equipment if he had been advised of its benefits by counsel and if it were allowed by the court.

The U.S. District Court for the District of South Carolina, which has opened fully electronic courtrooms at the Matthew J. Perry, Jr. Federal Courthouse in Columbia, South Carolina, provides a glimpse into the features and equipment that may be found in many courtrooms and courthouses. In these courtrooms,

electronic courtroom
Courtroom equipped with electronic equipment for use in trial presentations.

large-screen monitor
A video monitor conveniently located in the courtroom that is large enough for all to see the graphics displayed.

visual presentation cart
Media center located in the courtroom.

annotation monitor
Monitor that allows a witness to easily make on-screen annotations with the touch of a finger.

document camera
A portable evidence presentation system equipped with a high-resolution camera.

infrared headphones
An assisted listening device for the hearing impaired.

laptop port
A connection into which a laptop may be plugged.

interpreter box
Routes language translations from an interpreter to the witness/defendant's headphones or the courtroom's public address system.

video monitors are strategically placed around the courtroom. The judge's bench, the witness stand, the courtroom deputy, the counsel tables, and the jury box have video monitors to view the evidence, as shown in Exhibits 15.3–15.5. The jury box has one flat-panel monitor placed between every two juror chairs.

There are also **large-screen monitors** for displaying evidence using a document camera or other electronic media, as shown in Exhibit 15.6. These monitors are located just inside the well of the court so that those in the gallery may view evidence displayed through the system.

At the heart of the electronic courtroom is the **visual presentation cart,** as shown in Exhibit 15.12, or media center, which contains most of the presentation electronics. These items may include the following equipment:

Annotation monitor—Allows a witness to easily make on-screen annotations with the touch of a finger.
Document camera—A portable evidence presentation system equipped with a high-resolution camera.
Infrared headphones—Used as an assisted listening device for the hearing impaired.
Laptop port—A connection into which a laptop may be plugged.
Interpreter box—Routes language translations from an interpreter to the witness's or defendant's headphones, or the courtroom's public address system.

Exhibit 15.12 Evidence presentation cart—U.S.D.C. District of South Carolina

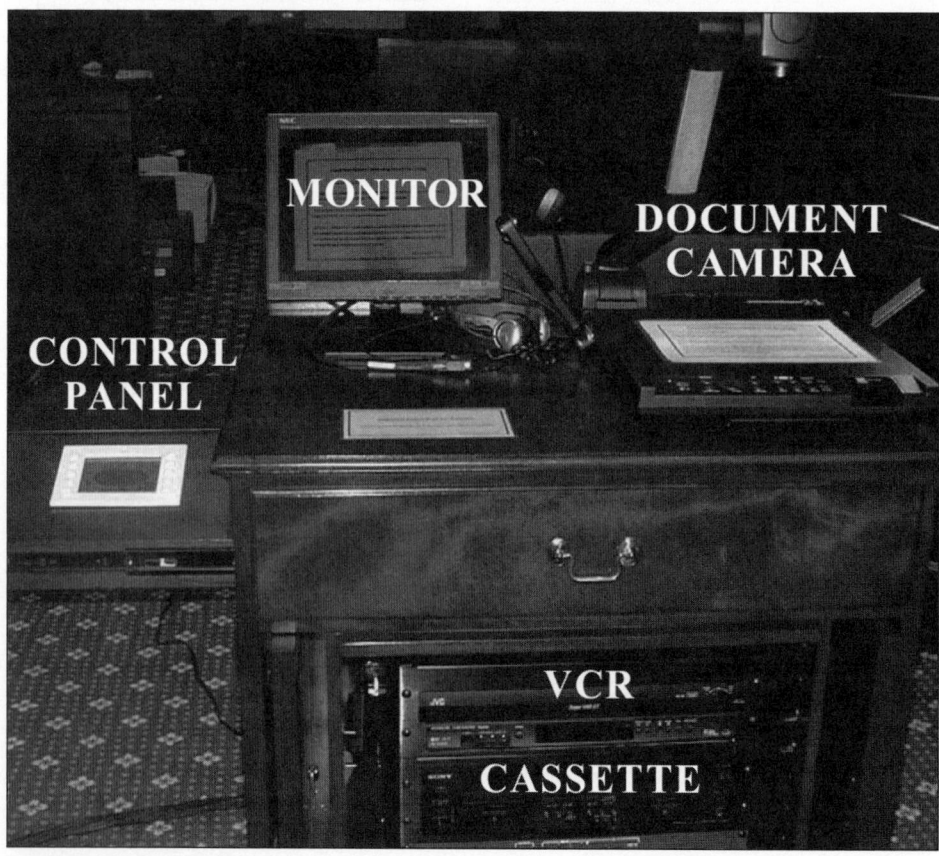

ADVICE FROM THE FIELD _____

TRIAL SUPPORT

LONE STARS: Enron trial support and the SPECIALISTS who made it happen

By Hillary Easom

Anyone who's stepped onto a dance floor knows that a waltz, a tango, and a two-step all require partners to move in sync. Working together, partners move smoothly and gracefully, creating a perfect rhythm. The relationship between attorneys and trial support specialists is another dance, demanding careful choreography, smooth movements, and excellent communication both before and during the trial.

In recent years, technology has helped make the trial dance less cumbersome. At the same time, glitches with technology can trip up one or both partners, creating awkward moments in the courtroom. The job of trial technology specialists is to develop a method of seamless presentation, supporting the attorneys without the need to count out each and every step.

A classic example of this vital "choreography" was the recent Enron criminal trial (*U.S. vs. Kenneth Lay and Jeffrey Skilling*). Over the course of several months, attorneys and support personnel had to practice their moves so as not to step on each other's toes during trial. One misstep in the litigation support process on either side could have been a serious factor in the trial's outcome.

Similar to a dance, the key to courtroom success can be summed up in one word: Preparation.

Expect the Unexpected

Scott Parreno knows the importance of careful pretrial groundwork. Parreno, from the Los Angeles office of O'Melveny & Myers, was the lead defense paralegal in the Enron case. He and four other paralegals acted as middlemen between the defense attorneys and other support personnel, ensuring that witness preparation binders and exhibits were complete and reproduced for relevant parties.

A 16-week trial with 56 witnesses inevitably presents surprises. "One thing that was constantly changing was the witnesses that were going to testify," says Parreno. This could be frustrating, as the team would put in a lot of time and effort in preparation to cross-examine a witness called by the prosecution, and suddenly the witness would be dropped and replaced by an alternate. "We'd be right back at square one preparing for a witness. The Judge maintained that each side had to know five witnesses ahead of time who the other side planned to call, but how important that witness was to either side really affected how much work we all would put into preparing."

In addition, preparations had to be made in advance for witnesses the defense believed might possibly be called further into the case. "For instance," says Parreno, "we thought that the government would be calling Richard Causey at some point during the trial, so we not only had to compile prep materials for him in case he was called, but we also had to work on the other five witnesses that the government had already disclosed."

Sounds pretty high-stress. But Parreno maintains that the team got along famously. "Sort of like sailors in a submarine, we learned to depend on each other," he says. "We really did have a great crew, and we all thought of each other as family."

One of those "family" members was Pam Radford, a trial consultant with Houston-based Legal Media Inc. Radford and her colleague Trevor Brock ran all of the trial presentations for the defense.

A Stitch in Time

Skilling's attorneys required more help with preparation than Lay's due to the greater number of securities and wire fraud counts being tried—28 versus 6. On a typical day, Radford and Brock arrived at Skilling's office at 6:30 AM. By 7:45 or 8:00 they were in the courtroom preparing for the day's events. After a full day of presenting evidence, they adjourned to Skilling's office to prepare for the next day. Despite the long hours, the attorney-support relationship was positive. "They were some of the best attorneys in the country, by far," says Radford....

Similarly, the Legal Media Inc. team was structured so that they could take over for each other if necessary. This alleviated some of the stress that could otherwise come with such a long, drawn-out trial. Radford and Brock were able to take turns meeting late into the night with the attorneys, preparing for the next day's proceedings.

The pair created all demonstratives for the Skilling team and a small portion for the Lay team. Thanks to technology's growing presence in the courtroom, Radford and Brock needed only two laptop computers. Radford used Trial Director to organize document[s], and Brock used Sanction to present video and audio evidence in court.

Exhibits included between 800,000 and 1 million pages of documents, stored on two external hard drives. Almost a terabyte of video evidence was stored on additional hard drives. Every day during this trial, some 200 documents were added to the cache.

(continued)

(*continued*)

Courtroom Tech 101

Technology in the courtroom was limited. "Judge Lake was very strict about not bringing additional monitors in," says Radford. The courtroom had one large monitor, and at the Judge's insistence the federal courts brought their own additional monitors. *Legal Media Inc. needed only to provide additional audio mixers and filters, equipment to help regulate sound in the courtroom.*

"We did have some glitches with their system because of the way it was wired," says Radford. For example, sometimes the audio would get out of sync after a recess. However, learning how the system functioned made these problems easy to fix.

The Enron Broadband case, which tried five former Enron Broadband Services executives, presented a different set of technological hurdles. Unlike the one used in the criminal trial, this courtroom was not equipped for technology, and cables had to be installed for video distribution during the trial. This was no easy task, as there were almost 20 video outputs used in the trial.

Arizona-based Verdict Systems (Sanction) handled technology support for this case under the direction of Dan Bowen, acting COO of the company. "The source set of data was somewhere in excess of 100 million pages," Bowen recalls. "At the trial site, we had access to 25 million pages of paper. We ultimately went into trial every day with over 4700 exhibits that made up almost 75,000 pages of paper, and over 500 video clips. And that was a subset."

Whereas in the past these documents would have to be lugged back and forth each day to court, modern technology helps prevent countless backaches: a single laptop with additional external hard drives is all that's needed. This was unheard of as recently as 5 or 6 years ago....

"In a case of this complexity, there was literally so much volume that things got pushed right up until almost the day of trial," Bowen says. "We were doing a lot of data management trying to not just identify from the client what their exhibit lists were going to be, but then convert those lists down into usable electronic data so that it could be used in Sanction for the electronic presentation." This required months of pre-trial preparation. "We literally worked around the clock writing custom applications to strip out the pertinent data and create it into a usable format."

The efforts proved worthwhile, however, once the trial started, allowing the attorneys to think about the law and not have to worry about the technology. "Because of the way that the [Enron Broadband trial] database was structured, with very simple naming conventions," says Bowen, "the attorneys were able to say something as simple as, 'Let me show you Exhibit 4000,[']" and the technology support specialist was able to quickly pull up the document. A labeling system that used the defendant's initials followed by a 4-digit number simplified the process; Exhibit 4000 was labeled "JH4000" and could be retrieved by typing 6 keys and hitting "Enter." This, in addition to prepping with the attorneys and trial team, helped greatly facilitate communication in court.

Room for Error

Still, no matter how well a team prepares, there is always room for a glitch. "We had hard drives fail," says Bowen, stressing that backups are essential in any trial situation. Radford agrees and adds, "Always have it somewhere else inside the courtroom with you."

Experienced support personnel know to have extra hard drives on hand with backups of all documents and video or audio evidence, in case the primary computer should fizzle. But what good does this equipment do if it's not there when an emergency strikes?

During the Lay/Skilling Enron trial, Radford tried to power up her computer with the opening statements, and the machine refused to boot. Fortunately, she was prepared with another machine containing the same information, and when she pulled out the mirrored backup everything went smoothly.

In another instance during the trial, an attorney accidentally kicked a plug out under a table. "When we went to test the audio, it wasn't playing," says Radford. "It had been playing 30 minutes before." This emphasizes the importance of testing equipment ahead of time; Radford and Brock were able to troubleshoot before the trial resumed. They also had backup speakers and computers on hand in case of emergency; fortunately, none of these had to be used.

For Radford and Brock, working the Enron case required stopping work on all other cases 2-1/2 months before the trial began....

Most pre-trial work was done via e-mail between the support specialists and the attorneys. Pre-trial work for Brock included digitizing and synchronizing video and audio evidence—a daunting task—and organizing all media exhibits. Radford's time was spent meeting with attorneys to work on demonstrative ideas, exhibit structure, and graphic design.

And in this corner...

Technology in the courtroom, for the prosecutors, was a new bag. This required some special choreographing by CACI, Inc.–Commercial, the firm providing litigation support for the government, to facilitate communications between the person in the hot seat and the attorneys.

(continued)

Brian Katz was CACI, Inc.–Commercial's Technical Support Services Manager at the time of the trial. "Some of these attorneys had never used technology or used it very little," he says. "This was a technology-driven case. Some attorneys would turn to the person in the hot seat and say, 'Could you zoom in to paragraph 2?'" Others simply mention an exhibit, and the technology support specialist must take the cue.

It is critical, notes Katz, to understand how each attorney operates. "They're going to blame you at the end of the day if a document didn't come up quick enough."

Chris Sasso, Michael Denault, and Matthew Mehler made up Katz's team, working with attorneys and running presentations during the trial. Katz's job was to ensure that the other three were able to get into a rhythm.

Sasso and Denault were in the hot seat running trial presentations, while Mehler worked behind the scenes, preparing and scanning documents and exhibits to be passed on for review. He essentially built the case in the "war room" and passed it on to his teammates to present in the courtroom....

The team prepared for over a year before the trial began, processing e-mails and documents for exhibits. This came to a head about 2-1/2 weeks before the trial, as they honed in on detailed preparations. Though another company prepared and presented opening statements, CACI, Inc.–Commercial, continued to work with the prosecution for the extent of the trial....

About the Author: Hillary Easom is a freelance writer and photographer whose work has appeared internationally in various print and online publications including *Better Investing, Marie Claire, Cruise Magazine,* and *American Fitness.* Ms. Easom lives in Bethesda, Maryland, with her husband, son, and lop-eared rabbit. Her interests include travel, yoga, and pop culture.

Reprinted with permission from Litigation Support Today magazine.

In addition to these electronic courtroom capabilities, videoconferencing technology is also available in any courtroom at the Matthew J. Perry, Jr. Courthouse.

PRACTICE TIP

Check the multimedia equipment and connectors on the courtroom media cart in advance. Many courts have installed the latest multimedia equipment. Older equipment such as VCRs are still found in some courtrooms; and the trial team may not be allowed to disconnect the courtroom equipment to use their own DVD players, or the correct interface connectors may not be available in the media cart control panel for newer devices like USB plugs.

VIDEO ADVICE FROM THE FIELD

Richard Manfredi—Videographer

A videographer discusses the role of the videographer in video depositions. After watching the video in MyLegalStudiesLab, answer the following question.

What is the role of the videographer in the deposition?

◼ ELECTRONIC EQUIPMENT IN THE COURTROOM

Document Camera

The document camera, shown in Exhibit 15.13, functions as a portable, easy-to-operate system for presenting evidence. A typical unit is equipped with a high-resolution camera, and features a 12:1 magnification zoom lens with an auto-focusing system.

Exhibit 15.13 Document camera

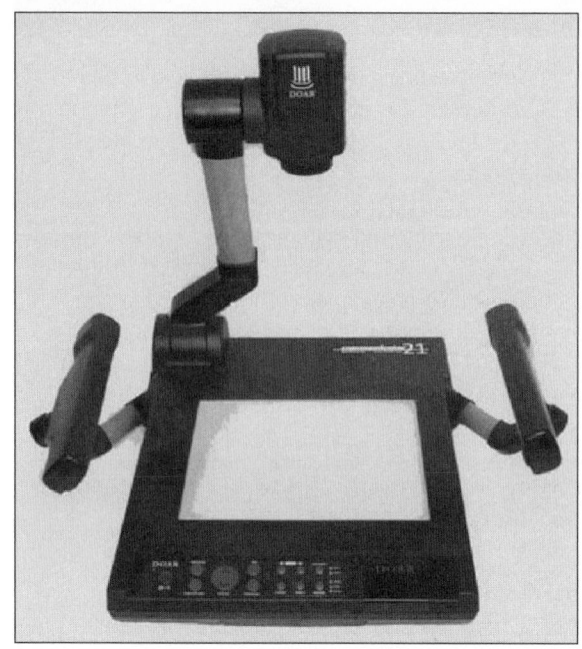

The document camera can present evidence such as 3-D objects, paper documents, transparencies, and X-rays for display on monitors throughout the courtroom.

Annotation Monitor

Annotation monitors, such as the one shown in Exhibit 15.14, allow a witness to easily make on-screen annotations with the touch of a finger. Annotations can be made by pressing lightly and dragging your finger as you would a pen.

Interpreter Box

The interpreter box, shown in Exhibit 15.15, routes language translations from an interpreter to a witness's or defendant's headphones, or to the courtroom's public address system.

Infrared Headphones

Infrared headphones, shown in Exhibit 15.16, are used as assisted listening devices for the hearing impaired. The Americans with Disabilities Act requires that this type of device be available for any individual needing it. It can also be used in conjunction with the interpreter box for language interpretations.

Many courts provide online information on the technology available in their courtrooms. For example, information from the website of the U.S. District Court for the Middle District of Pennsylvania can be viewed at http://www.pamd.uscourts.gov/docs/elec-cr.pdf, and is shown in Exhibit 15.17.

Exhibit 15.14 Annotation monitor

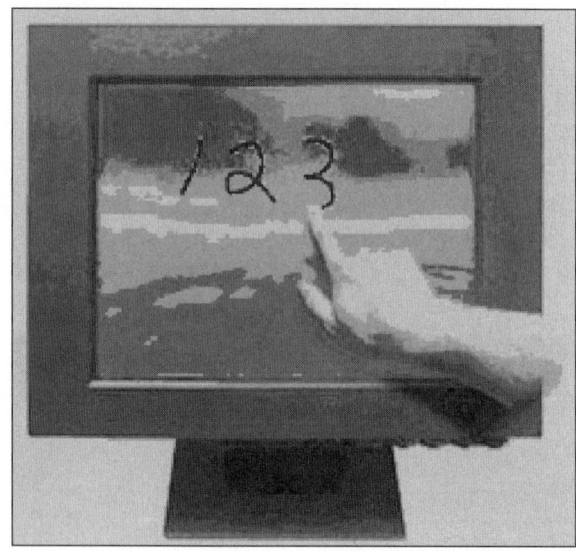

Exhibit 15.16 Infrared headphones

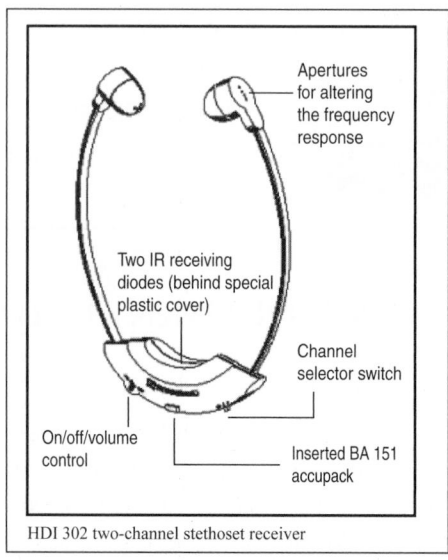

Exhibit 15.15 The interpreter box

■ WORKING WITH COURTHOUSE TECHNOLOGY STAFF

LEARNING OBJECTIVE 2
Describe how court staff can assist the legal team with using electronic resources in the courthouse.

Within each courthouse and each courtroom are numerous people who are more than willing to help the legal team if properly approached and consulted. They have specialized knowledge that has developed from working in their area of expertise on a daily basis. Because they are familiar with the idiosyncrasies peculiar to their own courthouses, they can make the process flow smoothly and help solve the problems that inevitably occur.

Exhibit 15.18 shows how the U.S. District Court for the Northern District of Illinois helps users become familiar with electronic support in the courtroom. The technical support office should be the first place to contact if any technology will be needed in the courthouse. The first step is to find out what the procedures are in each courtroom. Members of the support staff may also know how the different judges view the use of technology. Some judges may not approve of any large-screen displays, while others may think a single large-projection screen is appropriate. Some may have individual monitors throughout the courtroom, yet not want them used for specific events like presenting a video deposition, preferring instead a single monitor placed for the judge and the jury to view.

Getting all of the gear into the building, setting it up, and testing it can be stressful and time-consuming. The technical support person at the courthouse can help clear the team's hardware through security, saving time and stress on the day of trial. It is also important to remember that members of the courtroom's IT staff are usually the ones with the master keys to unlock the courtroom. It is also an advantage for the legal team to have someone who speaks the same technical jargon and can interface with the staff at the same knowledge level. A little goodwill can go a long way.

Exhibit 15.17 The Electronic Courtroom Brochure for the U.S.D.C. Middle District of Pennsylvania

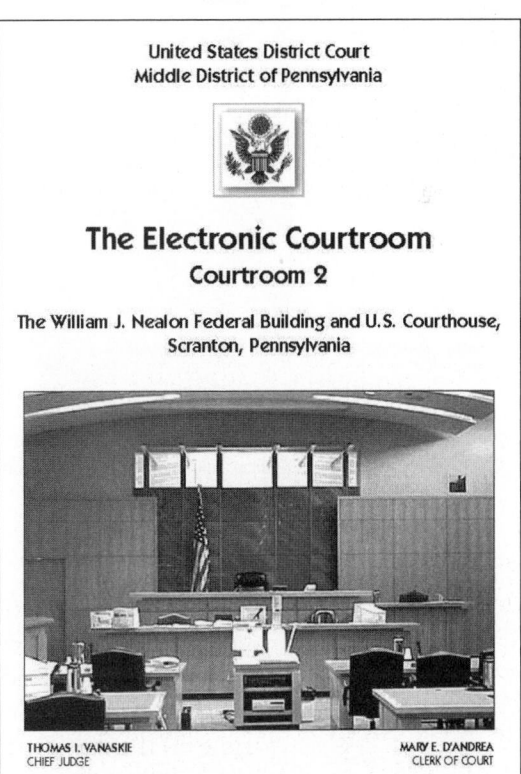

United States District Court
Middle District of Pennsylvania

The Electronic Courtroom
Courtroom 2

The William J. Nealon Federal Building and U.S. Courthouse, Scranton, Pennsylvania

THOMAS I. VANASKIE
CHIEF JUDGE

MARY E. D'ANDREA
CLERK OF COURT

Clearing Equipment with Security

Anyone who has been in a courthouse is aware of the elaborate security measures in place. Everyone entering the building must be subjected to metal scanners, X-ray machines, and briefcase searches. Anything out of the ordinary, particularly electronic equipment, can result in special scrutiny. In the ideal setting, where all the equipment is provided by the courthouse, the only thing the legal team needs to bring is a CD, DVD, or other electronic storage media. If that were all that was necessary, passing through security would not be an issue.

Rarely does getting through security work out so smoothly, though. Most attorneys carry the electronic files on their laptops, which are then connected to the courtroom equipment with a cable. But if the court system is not compatible with the team's system, or the presentation equipment is not provided, the legal team must bring the needed gear into the courthouse. It is highly recommended

Exhibit 15.18 Electronic courtroom technology website

Source: http://www.ilnd.uscourts.gov/home/CourtRoomTechnology.aspx

that the security office be contacted ahead of time to learn the courthouse's policy and procedures for bringing equipment in and setting it up. In a number of courthouses, a loading dock or alternate entrance must be used, and the team must wait for clearance. Clearing the equipment in advance can save valuable time on the day of trial, not to mention the stress and worry over whether everything will work out as planned.

WHAT HAPPENS WHEN THE LIGHTS GO OUT

Even the best plans can be sidetracked when the equipment fails or when there is a loss of power. In many parts of the country, excess power demand can result in a reduction in voltage, or a "brownout." Some equipment will work at a lower-than-optimum voltage, while other items must have a constant power supply. For example, the refrigerators in many homes have stopped working after a brownout because the motors burned out due to the lower voltage. A brownout can have similar repercussions for multimedia equipment. While there are safeguards available, such as battery-powered backup systems, these may not be practical in some situations. It is thus wise to anticipate worst-case situations, and have hard copies of graphs and charts as a backup.

Many legal teams bring a backup of important files and software on extra laptop computers, just in case. Well-prepared legal teams check all equipment in advance and bring spare parts, such as extra projection bulbs for the computer projector. Some even bring backup projectors, monitors, and printers. It is best to assume that if anything can go wrong, it will. Sometimes, equipment failure can happen at the worst possible moment—in the middle of trial.

Checklist

Getting Technology to Work
in the Courtroom
A Presentation Approach

- Try it out ahead of time.
- Have backup equipment.
- Have a separate operator.
- Have the passwords.

CONCEPT REVIEW AND REINFORCEMENT

KEY TERMS

annotation monitor   420
document camera   420
electronic courtroom   419

infrared headphones   420
interpreter box   420
laptop port   420

large-screen monitors   420
visual presentation cart   420

CHAPTER SUMMARY

Introduction to the Electronic Courtroom	Increasingly, judges are embracing the use of technology and computer systems for presentations in the courtroom as judges realize that these tools can enhance the speedy administration of justice.
The Electronic Courtroom	The basic electronic courtroom uses a computer projector, a projection screen, and a laptop computer. More complex arrangements include computer monitors at counsel's table, on the judge's bench, and in some cases in the jury box and witness stand, and possibly a large-screen monitor to replace the computer projector and projection screen.
The Wired Courtroom	Courtrooms are being wired with technology ranging from the very basic to high-technology monitors and computers at every workstation for lawyers, the judge, and the jury.
Working with Courthouse Technology Staff	Courtrooms generally have support personnel who are available to assist the members of the litigation team in the use of the technology available in the courtroom or the courthouse. They are also the key contact for obtaining a right to bring equipment into the courthouse on the day of trial. Good working relations with the technical support staff can be invaluable when everything goes wrong and backup equipment is needed on an emergency basis.

REVIEW QUESTIONS AND EXERCISES

1. List and explain some of the advantages to the use of technology in making courtroom presentations. Give three examples of how technology can make evidence clearer to a jury and increase the evidence's impact.
2. What functions can a litigation presentation program serve? Give three tasks at trial that this software can make easier or more effective.
3. How may the legal team use presentation graphics programs? Give examples of the ways graphics can be used by both litigation and nonlitigation legal teams.
4. Explain how a judge can maintain control over the presentation of evidence when multimedia equipment is used at trial.
5. How can some multimedia technology enhance videos of depositions? How can this technology help a jury understand the testimony?
6. What problems can arise with courthouse security when technology is used by a trial team? What can be done to avoid these issues?
7. What can be done to prepare for situations when the power fails during trial presentations?
8. Why is the courthouse technology team important to the legal team? Explain three ways these personnel can be essential to the legal team.

BUILDING YOUR PARALEGAL SKILLS

INTERNET AND TECHNOLOGY EXERCISES

1. Use the Internet to find information on the electronic courthouse and courtroom in your federal and state jurisdictions. List the specific resources that are available in each venue. Prepare a table showing what resources are available in different categories, such as video, projection, audio, and translation services.
2. Prepare a list of contact information of technology staff available at each venue.

CHAPTER OPENING SCENARIO CASE STUDY

Use the Opening Scenario for this chapter to answer the following questions.

1. What equipment will the trial team need to display the photographs electronically? What are their options for displaying the photographs?
2. What are the advantages and disadvantages of using video to display the images, versus using conventional enlargements?
3. How should the team plan to present the evidence of the medical experts and treating doctors? What equipment or arrangements will need to be made for video testimony? What systems or software can enhance these presentations?

CONTINUING CASES AND EXERCISES

1. Prepare a list of the electronic equipment available in the federal and state courts in your jurisdiction where you may be assigned to try a case.
2. Prepare a memo to the trial team explaining the local rules for bringing in and using multimedia equipment in trial.
3. Contact the staff in your federal and local courts to find out what the security protocols are for bringing multimedia equipment into the court-houses. What arrangements are needed to make setting up for trial faster and less stressful?
4. Prepare a list of the potential multimedia exhibits you would use in the school bus–truck accident case, Case A in Appendix II, or in the assigned comprehensive case. Create a table listing the technology and software that would be used for each, along with the advantages and disadvantages.

BUILDING YOUR PROFESSIONAL PORTFOLIO

Procedures

1. Prepare a memo explaining what multimedia resources are available in the federal, state, and local courts in your immediate jurisdiction.
2. Prepare a checklist of the steps needed to set up multimedia equipment at each court in your area.

Include steps for clearing security, gaining access to existing courtroom equipment, and gaining the cooperation of judges in each courthouse.

"A picture shows me at a glance what it takes dozens of pages of a book to expound."

—*Ivan Turgenev (1818–1883)*

Presentation and Trial Graphics

CHAPTER 16

OPENING SCENARIO

The legal team had worked hard for the past six months preparing the case for trial. It was a big case for a small firm. A large part of their resources had been invested in the case, and success was essential. The firm had been notified by the court that the trial was scheduled to begin in three weeks. They already knew it was a great case—they just needed to get the jury's attention with all the facts and evidence that the legal team had prepared.

They had been assigned to the new electronic courtroom, which was equipped with individual monitors and large projection screens. All members of the legal team agreed that the photos would help the jury understand where and how the accident happened. High-quality graphics would also be essential to gaining the jury's sympathy and obtaining a good verdict. The lead attorney, Owen Mason, and his partners were adamant that they not make the same mistakes in presentation that they had seen other lawyers make. They had observed trials in which poor graphics actually hurt the case, or were excluded by the trial judge for lack of veracity. Mason and his team would try to make the best presentation possible, but with limited additional resources, they knew they had to prepare the graphics in-house.

LEARNING OBJECTIVES

After studying this chapter, you should be able to:

1. Explain how graphics created with ordinary office suite applications and presentation graphics programs may be used in litigation.

2. Create a basic PowerPoint presentation.

3. Create an accident scene exhibit using graphics software.

VIDEO INTRODUCTION

PRESENTATION AND TRIAL GRAPHICS

After watching the video in MyLegalStudiesLab, answer the following questions.

1. What is the advantage of graphics creation software to the legal team?
2. What are the uses of graphics in the litigation process?

SMARTDRAW

After watching the video in MyLegalStudiesLab, answer the following question.

How can graphic creation programs be used in the litigation process?

■ INTRODUCTION TO PRESENTATION AND TRIAL GRAPHICS

It has been said that a picture can be worth a thousand words, and this old adage is particularly relevant in trial presentation. Properly prepared graphics are an excellent way of telling a story and expressing a key point, whether to a jury or a client. On the other hand, poorly prepared graphics can be boring, or can distract from the main message. For example, an effective PowerPoint presentation can send an audience a powerful message, with audience members requesting copies of the slides after the presentation is concluded. But if done poorly, such a presentation can at best convey a confusing message or, at worst, provide the audience with a few minutes of sleep.

More people are using graphics in presentations as graphics software has become more affordable and easier to use. Among the most accessible presentation graphics programs are those that are part of office suites, such as Microsoft PowerPoint, WordPerfect Presentation, and Quattro Pro. They can be used to create high-quality slide shows and drawings that include text, data charts, and graphic objects.

■ GRAPHICS AND PRESENTATIONS IN LITIGATION

LEARNING OBJECTIVE 1
Explain how graphics created with ordinary office suite applications and presentation graphics programs may be used in litigation.

In the days before electronic media, an attorney would arrive at the courtroom on the day of trial carrying an armload of photos and other images mounted on poster board, followed by easels carried by the legal support staff. Photos are one of the most common types of courtroom exhibits, but their impact often depends on their size and visibility. Although some lawyers have been known to use photos that are 8 × 10 inches or smaller, it may be prudent to follow the words of a wise old judge to a novice trial attorney: if it's important enough to use a picture, make sure that the judge and the last person in the jury box can see it at the same time. Hence, attorneys in the past have often used costly photo enlargements that could be seen by everyone in the courtroom. Now, however, with the availability of computer projectors, the size of images is limited only by the size of the screen or wall. Drawings and diagrams may also be projected easily.

Most think of litigation graphics as being useful only in courtroom presentations. However, graphics now play an important role not only during trial, but also in the stages leading up to trial. Using photographs, videos, computer simulations, time lines, and other graphics, the litigation team can get a better understanding of the facts and legal theories that support a case. Once these factors are understood and clarified by both parties, settlement is more likely. Thus, settlement

Exhibit 16.1 Sample settlement brochure created using a word processor

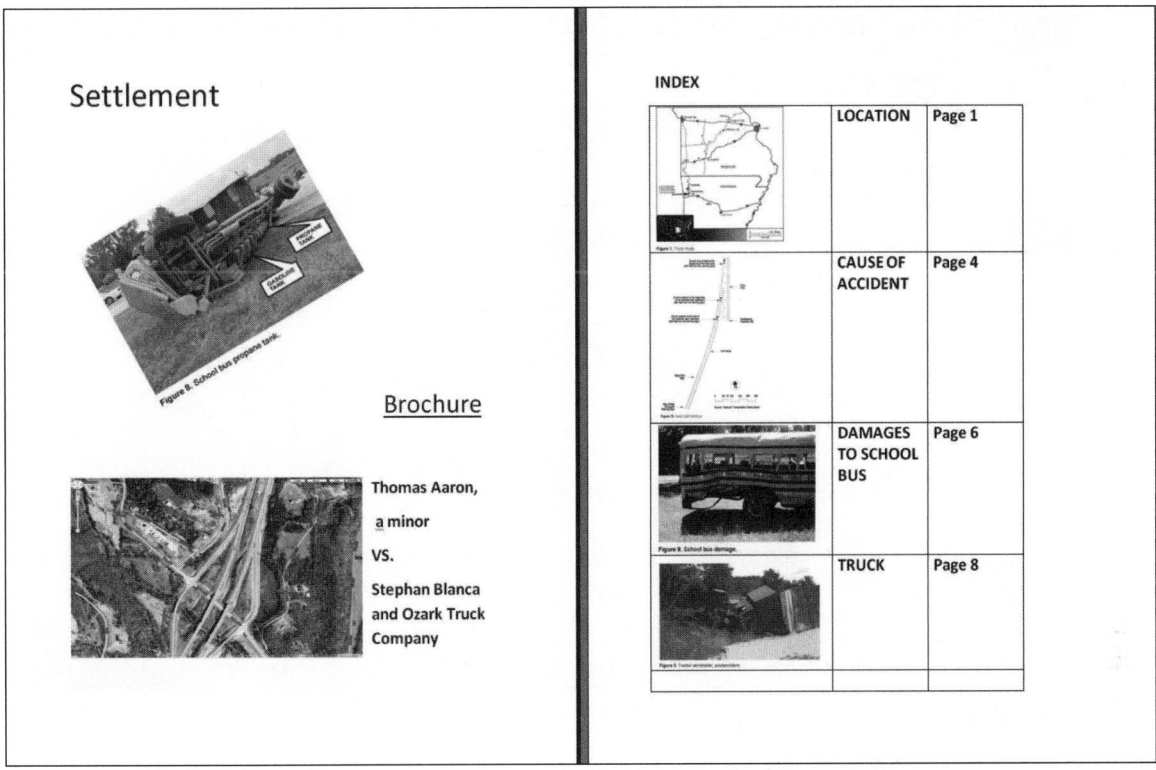

brochures that are sent to the opposing side now include graphics to illustrate the theory of liability, the damages, and the potential evidence that will be used if the case goes to trial. An example of such a brochure is shown in Exhibit 16.1.

If the case does not settle before trial, the graphics created in the pretrial process may be used as trial exhibits. In a larger case with a potentially high verdict, the settlement brochure may even include a video of a day in the life of the victim, showing the impact the accident had on the person. For example, in an extreme case, the video might show what daily life is like for a formerly able-bodied person who was so seriously injured that he or she must now spend the rest of his or her life in a wheelchair.

◼ USING OFFICE SUITE APPLICATIONS

The management of every case, whether big or small, must be well-organized from its inception. The legal team must keep careful records of all information about the case, including the activities of each person working on the case, and the items that need to be completed. Even if case management or office management software is not being used, the information still needs to be captured using time records, to-do lists, contact lists, and lists of investigative or discovery items. Sample forms for each of these types of items are available in the Microsoft and WordPerfect office suites, as shown in Exhibits 16.2 and 16.3. While technically not part of litigation graphics, they nevertheless illustrate the types of graphic tools that are available without purchasing additional pieces of software. The applications that were used to create these forms can also be used to create charts and tables in written communications, a presentation, or as an exhibit at trial.

Exhibit 16.2 Sample Excel spreadsheet templates

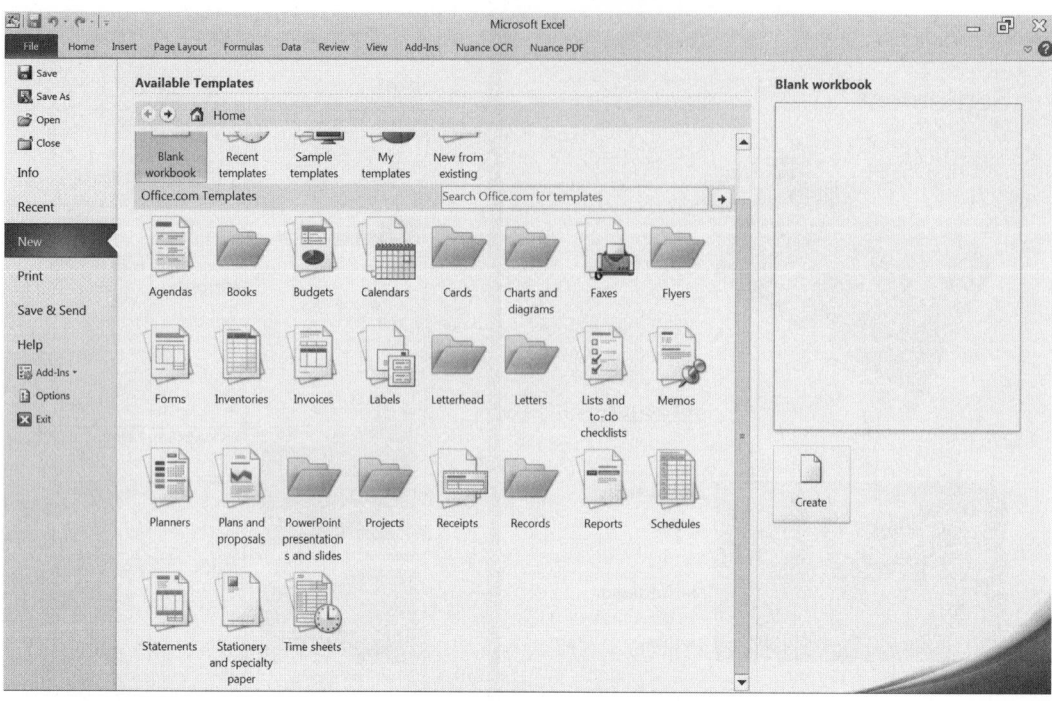

© 2011 Microsoft.

Exhibit 16.3 Sample Corel WordPerfect Suite spreadsheet templates

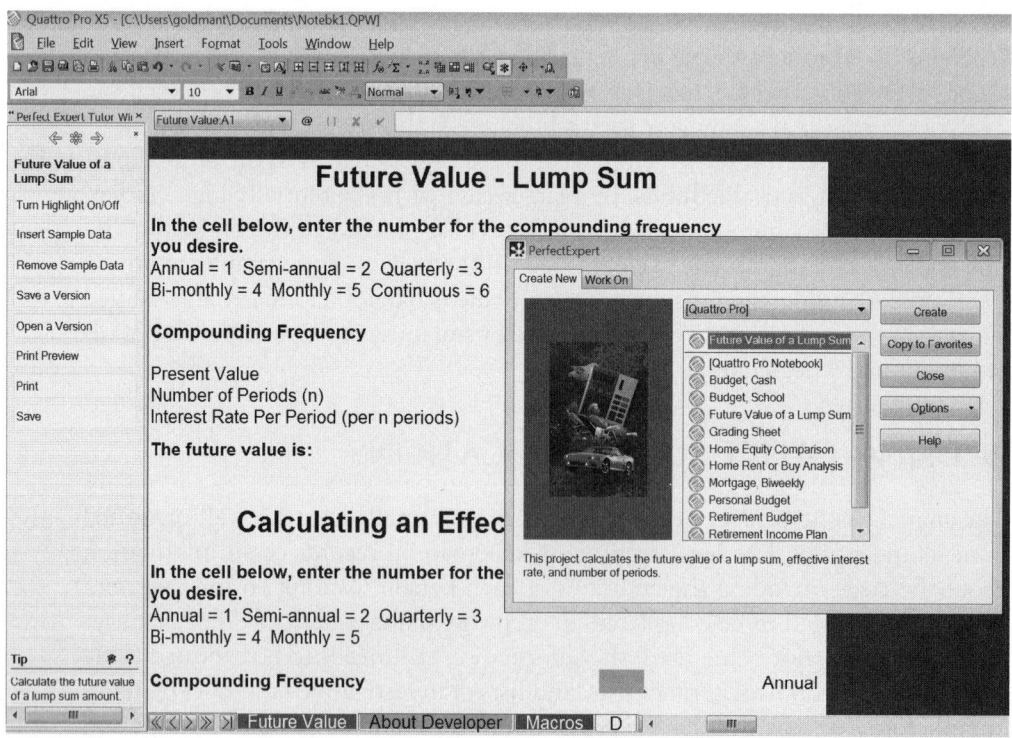

© Copyright 2012 Corel Corporation and Corel Corporation Limited, reprinted by permission.

spreadsheet
A computer software program with rows and columns in which primarily numeric data may be manipulated using formulas. Also sometimes called electronic accounting worksheets.

Spreadsheets

A **spreadsheet** can be used to display data in an easy-to-read format. For example, a spreadsheet might be used in a medical malpractice case to show the jury the level of pain the client suffered, as illustrated in Exhibit 16.4. This example is

Exhibit 16.4 Sample Excel spreadsheet downloads

a preset spreadsheet that may be downloaded from the Microsoft Office Excel application. The same type of spreadsheet can also be set up with columns that identify and track expenses, individual client medical expenses, or any other set of data for which keeping track of the items and amounts is important.

The information tracked, or any portion of the information in the spreadsheet, may be imported to a Word document using the copy and paste method, as shown in Exhibit 16.5. This can be a time-saver when information needs to be included in demand letters sent to the opposing side.

Exhibit 16.5 Excel information imported to Word

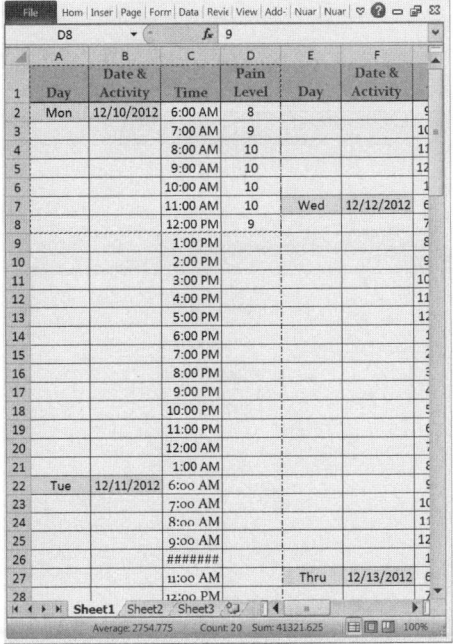
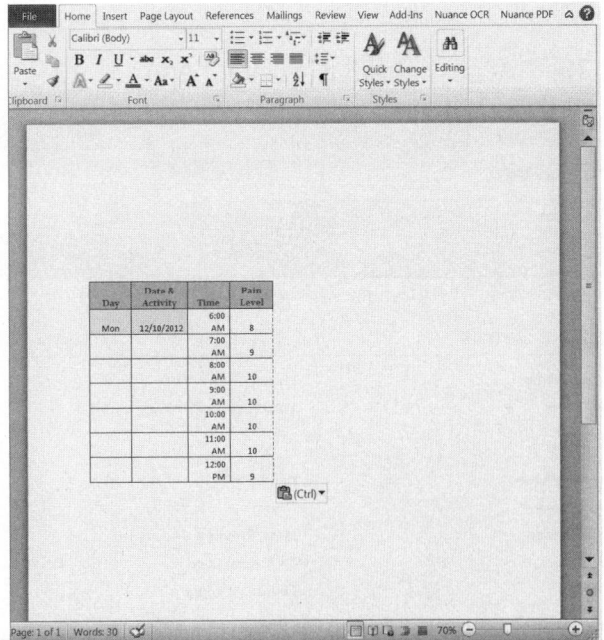

Electronic Databases

electronic database
An electronic repository of information of all types that can be sorted by a computer program and presented in a meaningful manner.

Task lists, otherwise known as "to-do lists," can be created using the **electronic database** in the office suite. For example, a task list may be created with Microsoft Access, as shown in Exhibit 16.6, by choosing a sample task list from the Access start menu. The information for each task is captured as a record called "Task Details." In the particular database shown in Exhibit 16.7, the program also allows contact information to be included.

Exhibit 16.6 Access Task List database

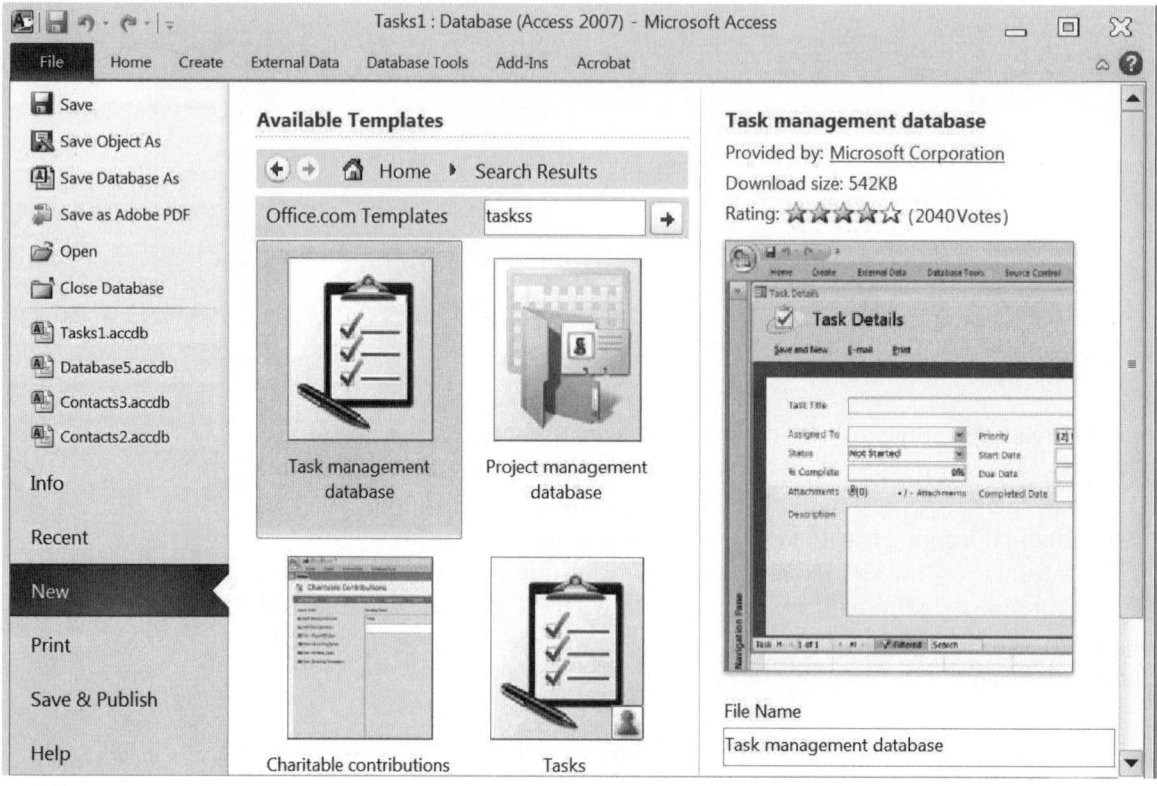

© 2011 Microsoft.

Exhibit 16.7 Access Task List contact entry

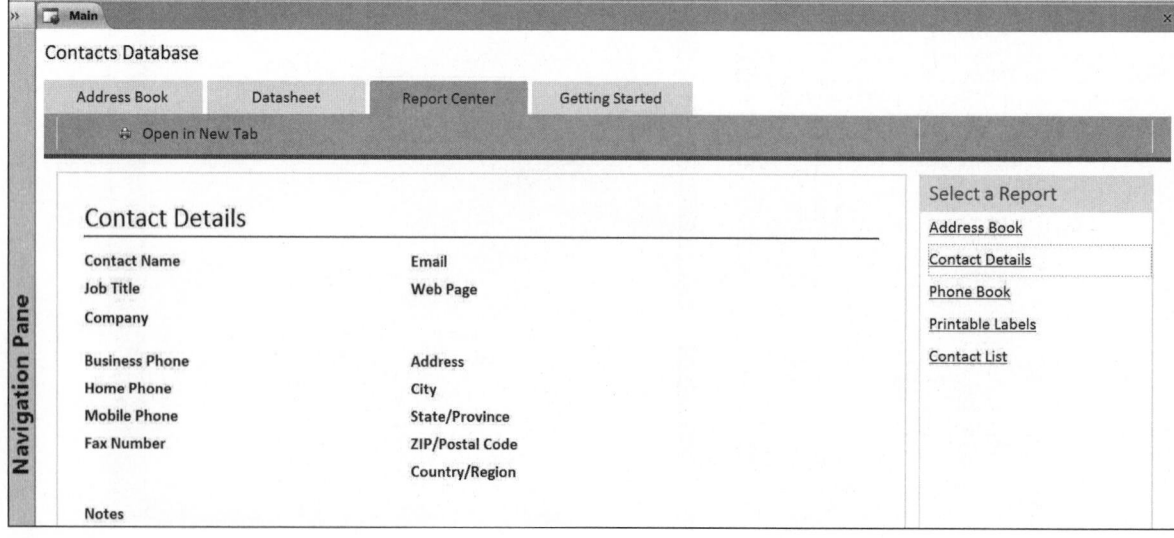

© 2011 Microsoft.

Word Processor

A **word processor** in a modern office suite can be used for more than just writing letters and memos. Among its features are the ability to vary text characteristics, making it possible to create letterheads with different fonts, colors, and sizes, as shown in Exhibit 16.8. Images and pictures can be inserted when needed, in addition to spreadsheet information, as shown above.

Using the various office suite tools, settlement brochures can be created in-house. The literature can be printed in color with low-cost color printers and high-quality paper, saving the cost of outside media services. Poster-size prints can also be made of any of the images, and each page of the settlement brochure can be used in face-to-face settlement conferences. If authenticated and permitted by the court, they may also be used in trial as part of the opening statement, during the trial as individual exhibits, or in the closing argument.

word processor
A computer software program for creating, editing, and producing word documents in various formats.

Exhibit 16.8 Word processor–created letterhead and letter with image inserted

Mason, Marshall and Benjamin
Attorneys and Counselor at Law
152 South State Street
Newtown, YS. 12345

October 15, 2011

Paul Smith
Other Peoples Insurance Company
345 Main Street
Anywhere, YS 98765

Dear Mr. Smith

As you can see from the photograph of the school bus after the accident, it rolled over and our client was thrown from the bus sustaining severe injuries.

Figure 4. School bus, postaccident.

Program Integration

Many of the applications within office suites provide options or links to import or export files. Sometimes these links are added automatically to other programs already installed on the computer. For example, the PDF Converter Pro link used in Exhibit 16.9 was added to PowerPoint (a previously installed program on the computer) when PDF Converter Pro was installed. Exhibit 16.9 shows the result of using the Import/Export link. Each page of the original document has been converted into a usable format by PDF Converter, and then imported into PowerPoint. Within the PowerPoint presentation, each individual page is a separate screen or slide.

Program integration is a time-saver when using different presentation and case management tools. Integration allows a single mouse click or keystroke to start a process that can transfer information from one application to another, a task that would otherwise require the user to start up multiple programs and use multiple functions within each program.

The import/export function within an office suite can be used to transfer drawings and other graphic images as well as text and data. For example, Exhibit 16.10 shows how a link can automatically export a SmartDraw graphic directly into

Exhibit 16.9 PDF images created from a single PDF file using PDF Converter

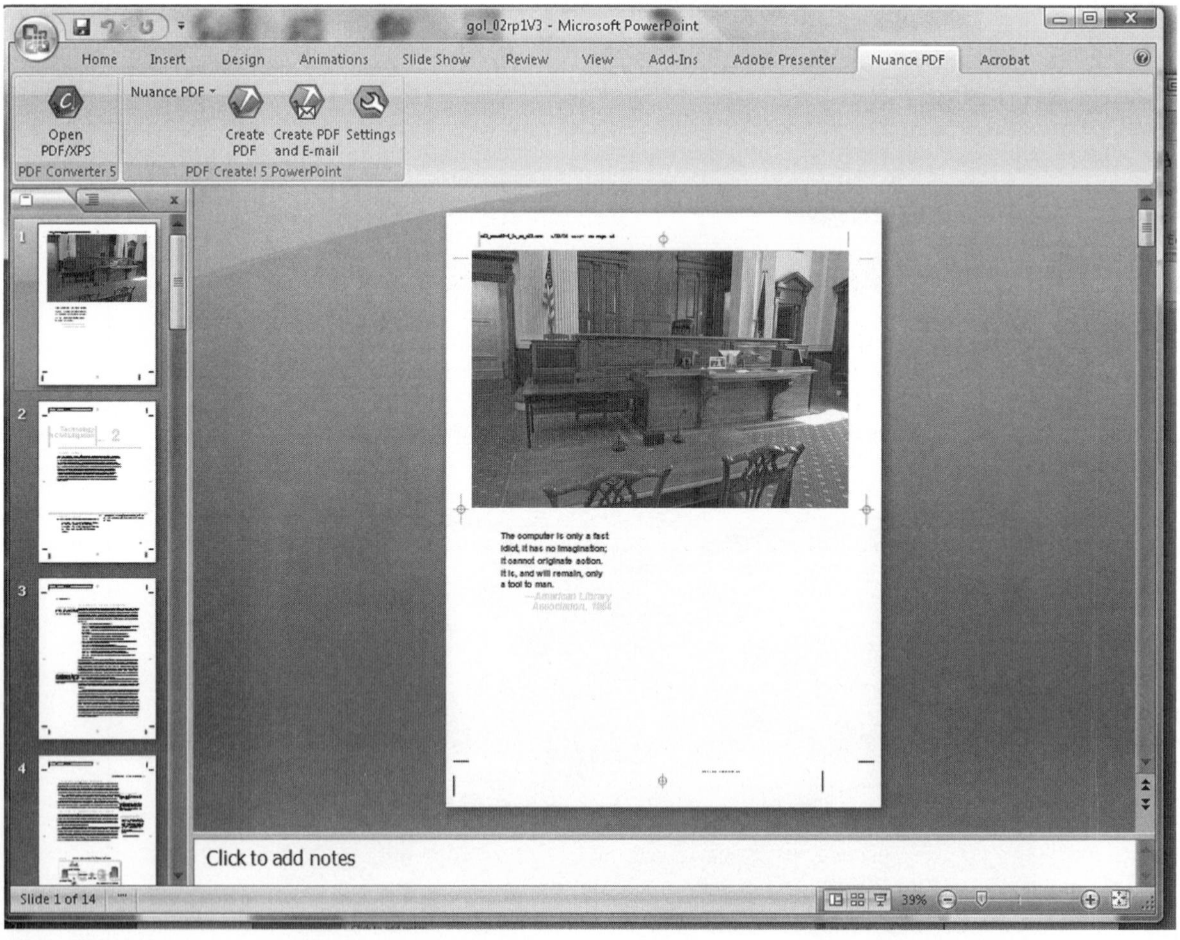

Exhibit 16.10 SmartDraw export options

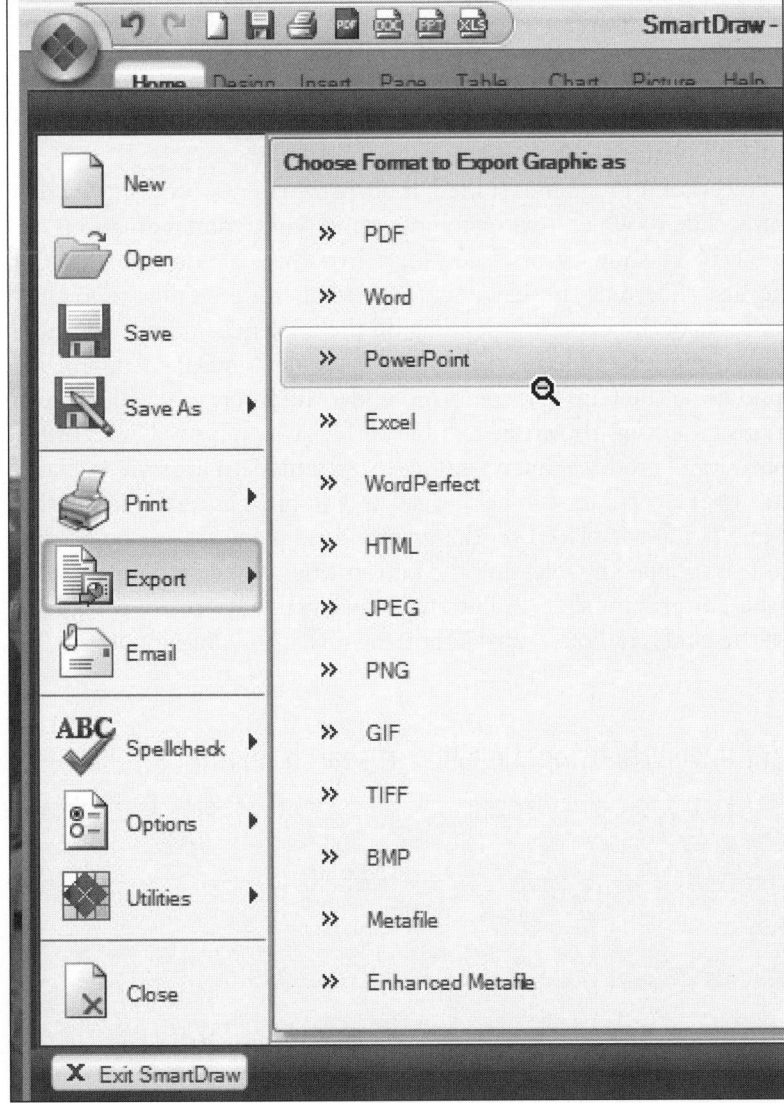

SmartDraw Software, LLC.

PowerPoint with a single mouse click. The user also has the choice of showing a separate slide per entry, or a combined single-entry slide showing multiple time points, all with one keystroke.

■ CREATING A POWERPOINT PRESENTATION

Presentations in the legal community are typically used to reinforce the ideas, concepts, and thoughts that the presenter wants to emphasize. A good presentation can enhance and highlight the speaker's ideas and concepts, whereas a poor presentation can undermine all the hard work that went into it.

PowerPoint has become the standard for making electronic presentations to all types of audiences, from grade-schoolers to courtroom juries. If used appropriately, PowerPoint can emphasize the speaker's main ideas and aid an audience's

LEARNING OBJECTIVE 2
Create a basic PowerPoint presentation.

understanding. Creating slide presentations in PowerPoint is made easier with the wide variety of available templates and content slides. A new presentation can be made using the templates provided in the program, or can be downloaded from the Microsoft website. Graphics and documents created in other applications can also be imported into the PowerPoint presentation or other programs. Files may be imported from such programs as LexisNexis TimeMap, SmartDraw, Adobe Acrobat, and Nuance PDF Converter.

When the PowerPoint program is started, it opens with a new working window and a single blank slide to which text, graphics, sound, video, and animations can be added. Exhibit 16.11 shows a first slide for a hypothetical trial presentation. The text of the first slide tells the judge and jury what the presenter is going to tell them—the "Facts of the Case." Depending on the audience and the attorney's approach, a graphic might be added—in this case, the scales of justice. Graphic images can be found using the Clip Art command under the Insert tab, which is part of the Illustrations groups, as shown in Exhibit 16.11. A search for "scales of justice" in "all collections" produces many options, from a modern art style to classic black and white. The selected art can be dragged and dropped using the left button of the mouse. The pointer is placed on the graphic, and dragged over by holding the left button. It is dropped by releasing the button when the graphic is correctly positioned on the PowerPoint slide. Additional adjustments to size are possible by selecting one of the circles or boxes surrounding the image and dragging it.

Exhibit 16.11 PowerPoint first slide using the Clip Art search feature

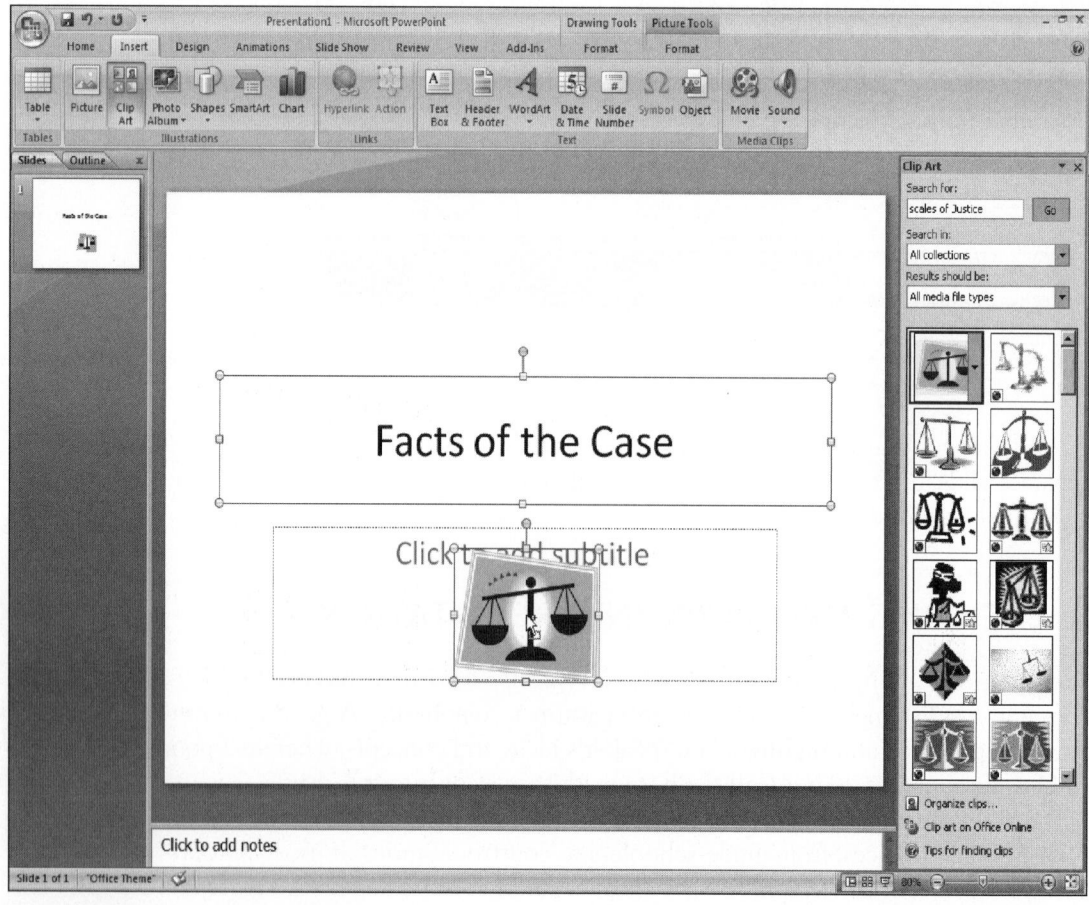

PRACTICE TIP

A few pointers on presentations using PowerPoint:

- *Viewability*—Use background and color combinations that can be seen by everyone in the room. Using color variations can be very effective—pastel colors can be soothing, while vivid colors can have a "wake-up" effect. However, some colors can "wash out" or disappear within others. Also be aware that some jury members may be colorblind.

- *Density*—Slides should support ideas in as few words as possible; no one wants to read a full page of text.

- *Sounds*—Sounds can be very effective, when used appropriately. However, if overdone, the impact is lost. Inappropriate sound effects used in a courtroom, like gunshots, may not be permitted.

- *Stand aside*—Even the best presentation is ineffective if the presenter is standing in front of the screen, blocking the audience's view.

- *Imagery*—One good picture is worth a thousand words—but choose the picture wisely. What impression do you want to leave in the mind of the jury when they go into deliberations? Among the most effective pictures in a personal injury case are those of the victim sitting in a wheelchair or lying in a hospital bed. In those cases, no words are necessary.

Slide Transitions

PowerPoint allows many enhancements to a slide presentation, such as slide transitions. For example, slides can be made to fade in or out, or transitions can be accompanied by sounds. The standard transitions are selected from the Animations tab on the PowerPoint Ribbon, and the sounds that may be used are found in the Transition to This Slide group, as shown in Exhibit 16.12.

Inserting Graphics and Sound

The Insert menu displays a number of options for inserting graphics. An easy way to include graphics is to insert clip art. The Clip Art search menu opens as a panel with a search feature for finding available clip art.

Presentations may also be enhanced, when appropriate, by the introduction of sound. Sound clips may also be found in the Clip Art panel by selecting audio media from the "Results should be" menu. The sounds may be added by clicking "Insert" in the Items options menu. They may be programmed to play automatically when the slide opens or upon clicking the mouse or a key.

Editing Graphic Elements

Multiple graphic elements may be used in a single slide. For example, both a taxi and a telephone pole can be added from clip art. Any graphic element can be moved in front of or in back of another graphic in the slide to allow one graphic to appear to overlay another. When an object has been selected, a dotted line appears around the object with corner and midline markers. These markers may be used to expand or contract the size of the selected object by holding the left mouse button. The marker in the middle of the line below the arrow may be used to rotate the object, as shown in Exhibit 16.13.

Exhibit 16.12 PowerPoint sound selections for enhancing a slide transition

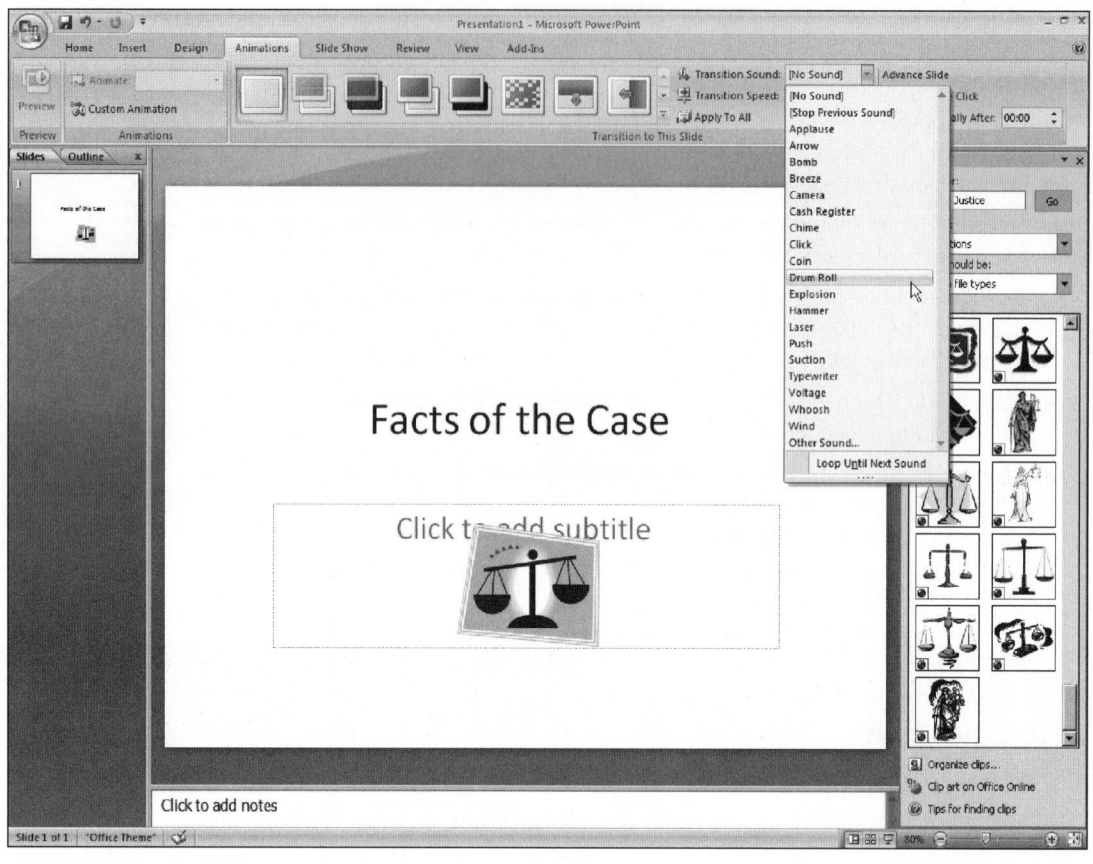

© 2011 Microsoft.

Exhibit 16.13 Graphic feature, corner markers
and rotation marker

© 2011 Microsoft.

PowerPoint Tutorials

Microsoft provides a number of web-based tutorials for learning how to use the different features in PowerPoint. It also provides sample presentations within the application that may be used as templates or as learning tools. A selection of these is shown below in Exhibits 16.14–16.16. A short tutorial is also included in the end

Exhibit 16.14 Microsoft PowerPoint 2010 Classic Photo Album Template with Slide View Option

© 2011 Microsoft.

Exhibit 16.15 Microsoft PowerPoint 2010 Widescreen Presentation Template with outline and notes View Option

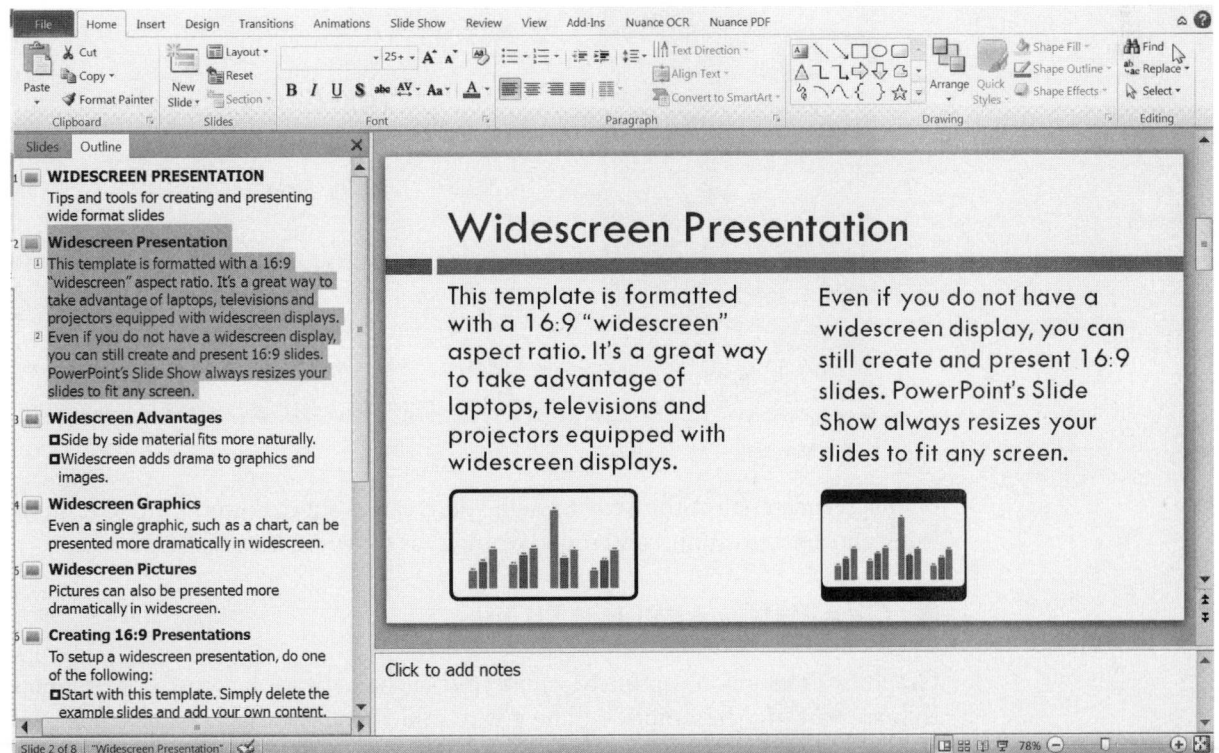

© 2011 Microsoft.

Exhibit 16.16 Microsoft PowerPoint 2010 Welcome Template with Slide View Option

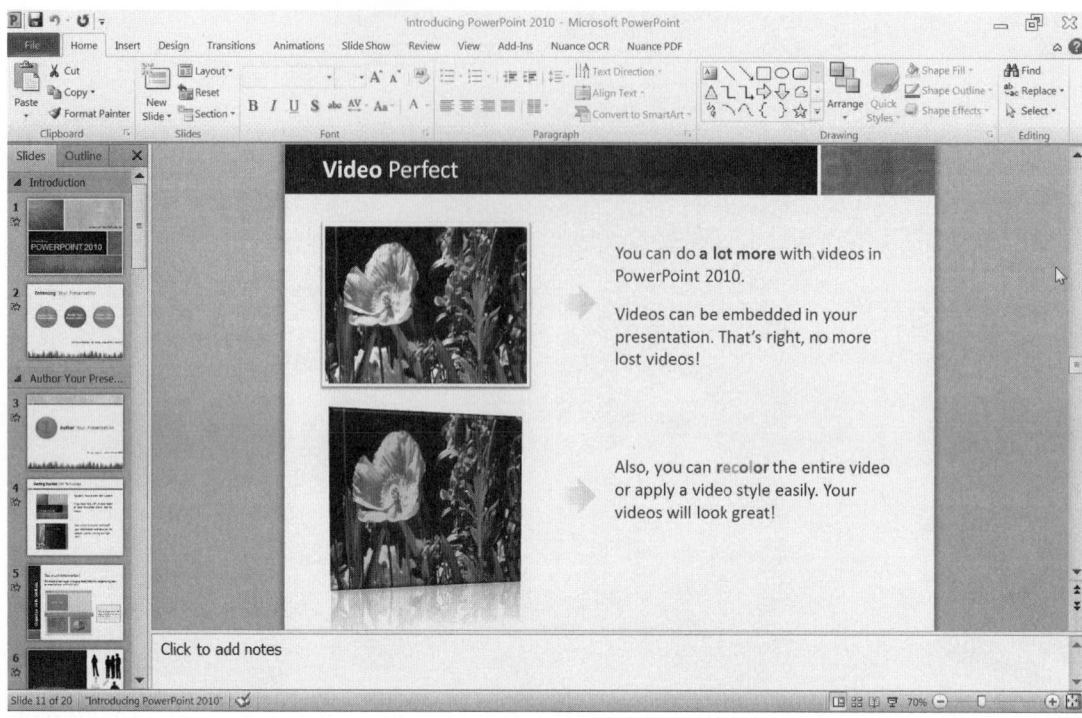

© 2011 Microsoft.

Exhibit 16.17 Microsoft PowerPoint 2010 slide show

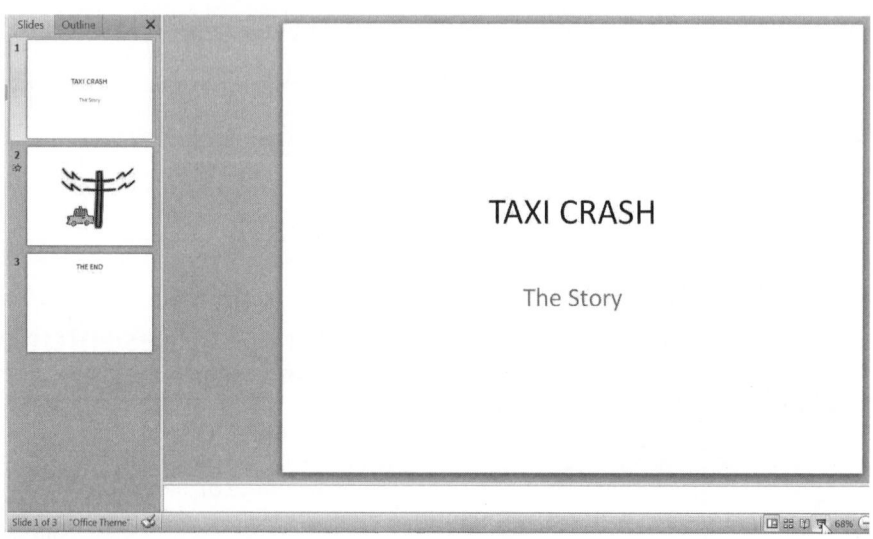

© 2011 Microsoft.

of chapter material of this text to help you create a short PowerPoint slide show using clip art, transitions, and sound features, as shown in Exhibit 16.17.

■ GRAPHICS APPLICATIONS

Graphics programs are used to create either stand-alone graphics or graphics that are part of a presentation. The greatest advantage of this class of software is the ability to create graphics without needing to hire graphic artists and outside consultants. The software may also be used to quickly create graphics on an ad hoc basis. For example, it is possible for the legal team to create trial graphics in court on a laptop computer to meet an unexpected factual twist, and then display the image using the laptop and projection unit. The software also provides an electronic backup if the large display boards are damaged, delayed in transit, or destroyed by an overzealous cleaning staff.

Microsoft Visio

Microsoft Visio is a popular graphic drawing program that is often used to display engineering and architectural design elements, such as drawings of buildings and roadways. The application can be used to illustrate these same elements in court-room presentations. It also provides many of the elements necessary to create time lines and other common business graphics. A sample of the work screen for Visio is shown in Exhibit 16.18.

SmartDraw

SmartDraw is a graphics program that provides thousands of predesigned objects and elements, including specialty features for different professions and businesses. It can be used to create stand-alone graphic images, both in print form and for

Exhibit 16.18 Microsoft Visio sample work screen

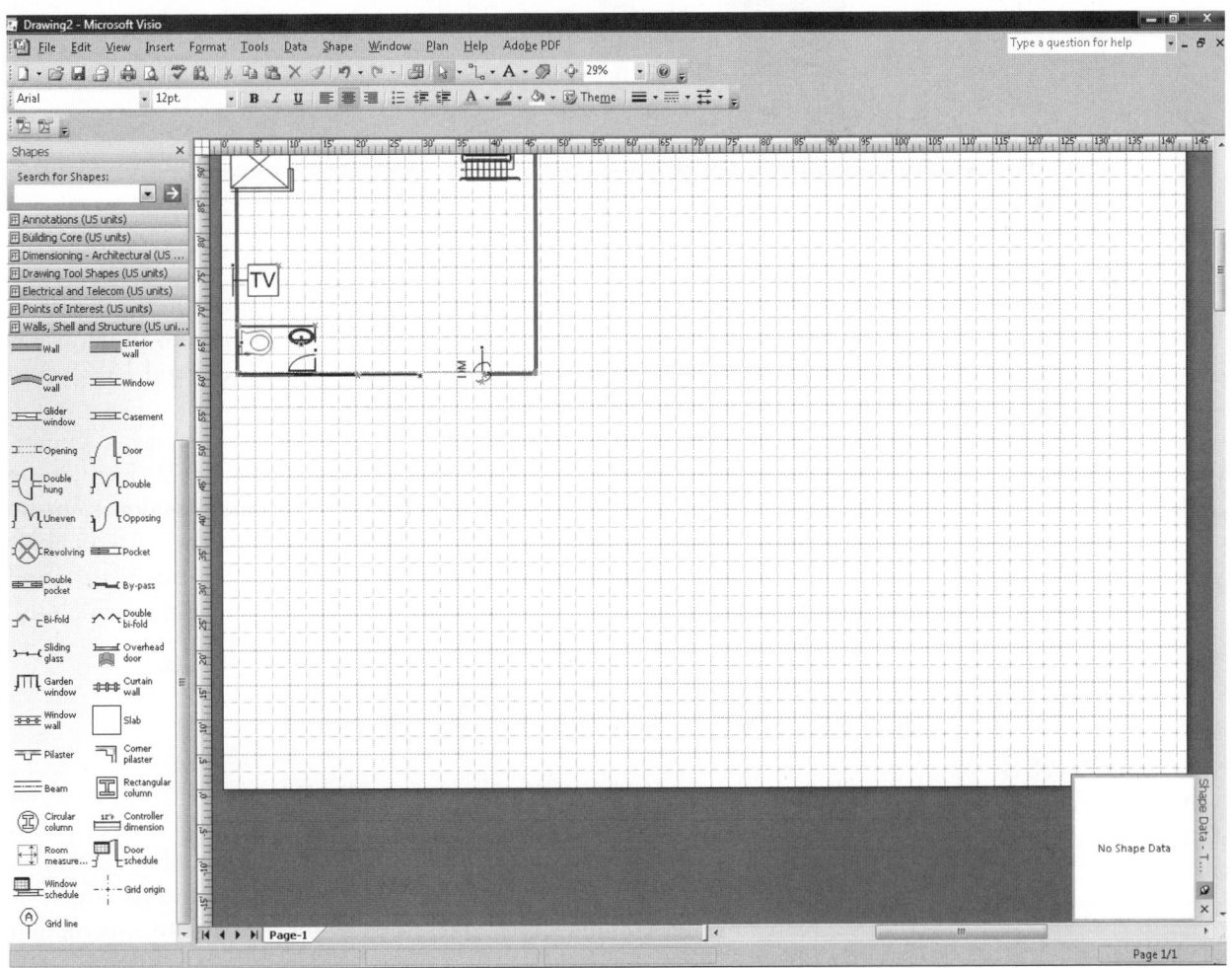

Exhibit 16.19 Sample accident reconstruction graphic

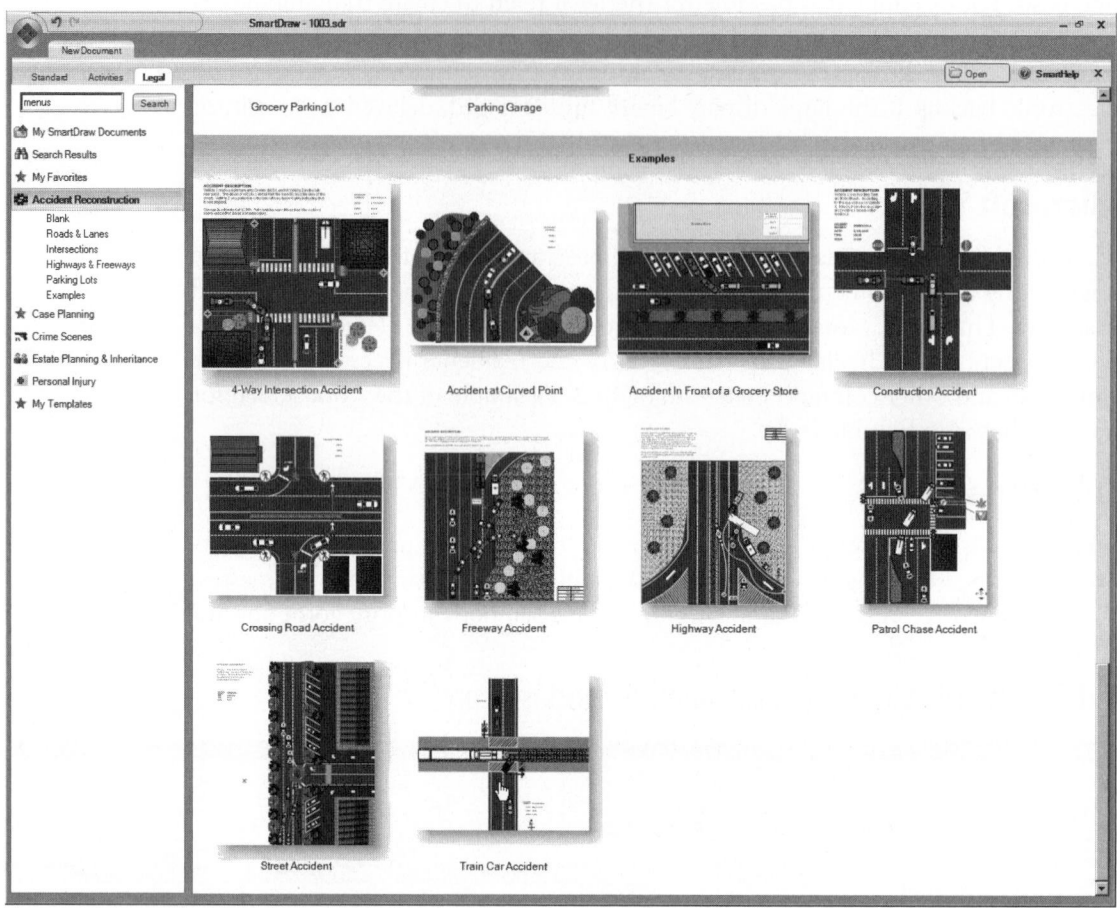

SmartDraw Software, LLC.

computer slide presentations. In addition to its intuitive user interface, one of SmartDraw's biggest advantages for the legal team is the thousands of templates and icons available for creating graphics quickly. Exhibits 16.19 and 16.20 show examples of graphics prepared for trial using SmartDraw.

Many of the predesigned graphics anticipate the needs of the legal community and require only minor modification, as shown in Exhibit 16.21. Each of the examples can be modified using the drag-and-drop technique common to many applications. Additional symbols can also be added easily from the stock symbols in the left panel of the SmartDraw user screen. Finished graphics can be exported from SmartDraw by using the Export tab and selecting the program to which the image is to be sent, such as PowerPoint, as shown in Exhibit 16.22.

■ CREATING A SMARTDRAW GRAPHIC

LEARNING OBJECTIVE 3
Create an accident scene exhibit using graphics software.

SmartDraw provides a number of templates of graphs and diagrams that are useful in litigation, some of which are shown in Exhibit 16.23.

The starting point for creating a graphic is selecting the template or sample that most closely resembles the actual image. For example, an automobile accident at a four-way intersection can be represented by the accident reconstruction SmartTemplate, as shown in Exhibit 16.24.

Exhibit 16.20 Intersection of accident scene created
with SmartDraw

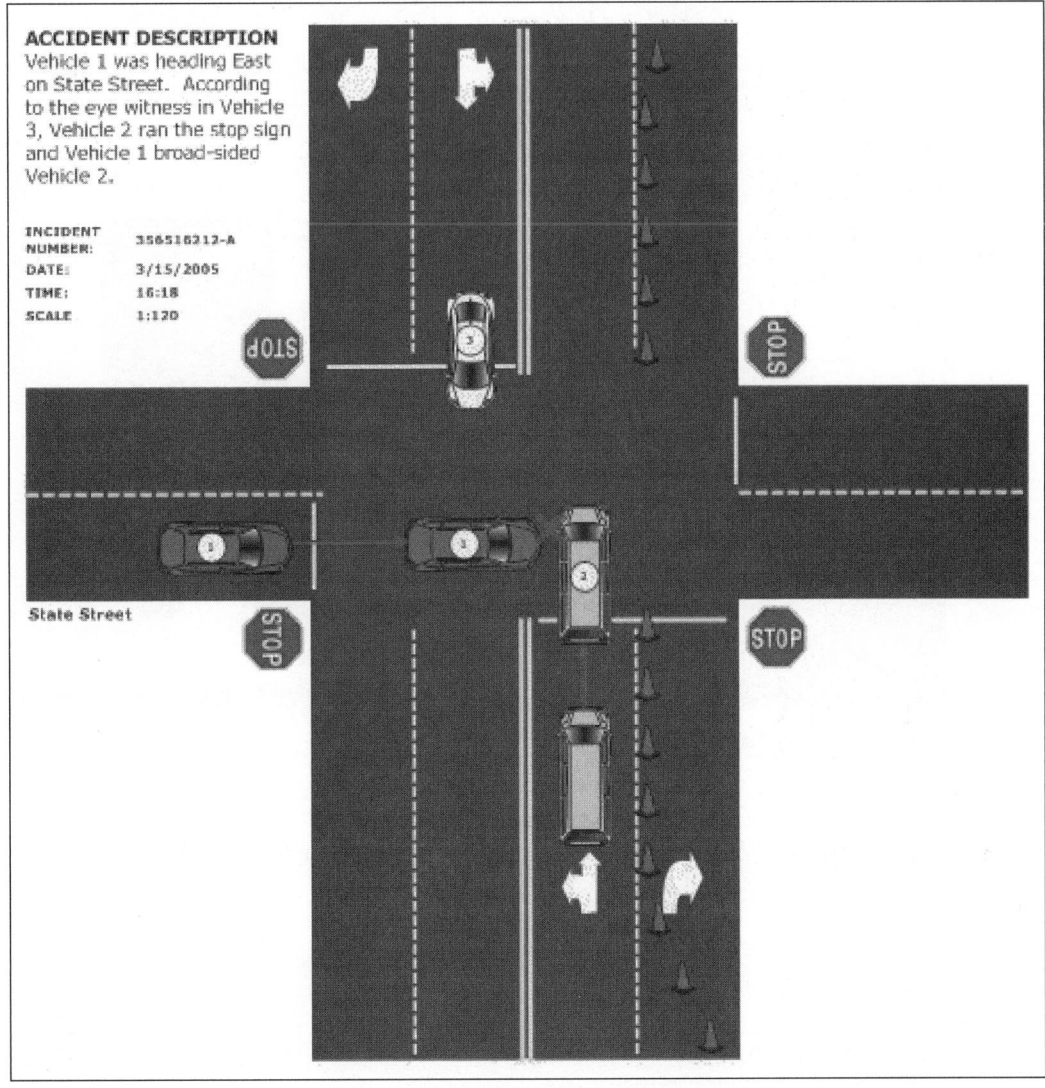

ACCIDENT DESCRIPTION
Vehicle 1 was heading East
on State Street. According
to the eye witness in Vehicle
3, Vehicle 2 ran the stop sign
and Vehicle 1 broad-sided
Vehicle 2.

INCIDENT
NUMBER: 356516212-A
DATE: 3/15/2005
TIME: 16:18
SCALE   1:120

State Street

SmartDraw Software, LLC.

Each of the items shown in the main panel of the graphic can be moved, re-moved, or edited.

The right panel contains SmartHelp for using the specific functions and also contains the library of graphics that may be used in creating or modifying the graphic. For example, a fire engine may be added from the SmartPanel to the graphic by the drop-and-drag method (Exhibit 16.25).

In Exhibit 16.25, Vehicle number 1 has been dragged on top of the fire truck graphic. Selecting the fire truck by a left mouse click highlights the selected graphic element. The selected element is indicated by corner boxes surrounding it. Selecting the option "Bring to Front" changes the view so that the car appears to be under the truck, as shown in Exhibit 16.26.

Graphic elements may be further modified by adding text and color fill using the Ribbon Tabs and Menu items. Completed graphics may be saved in a variety of formats, such as PDF, and exported directly to PowerPoint and other applications.

Exhibit 16.21 Export tab in SmartDraw

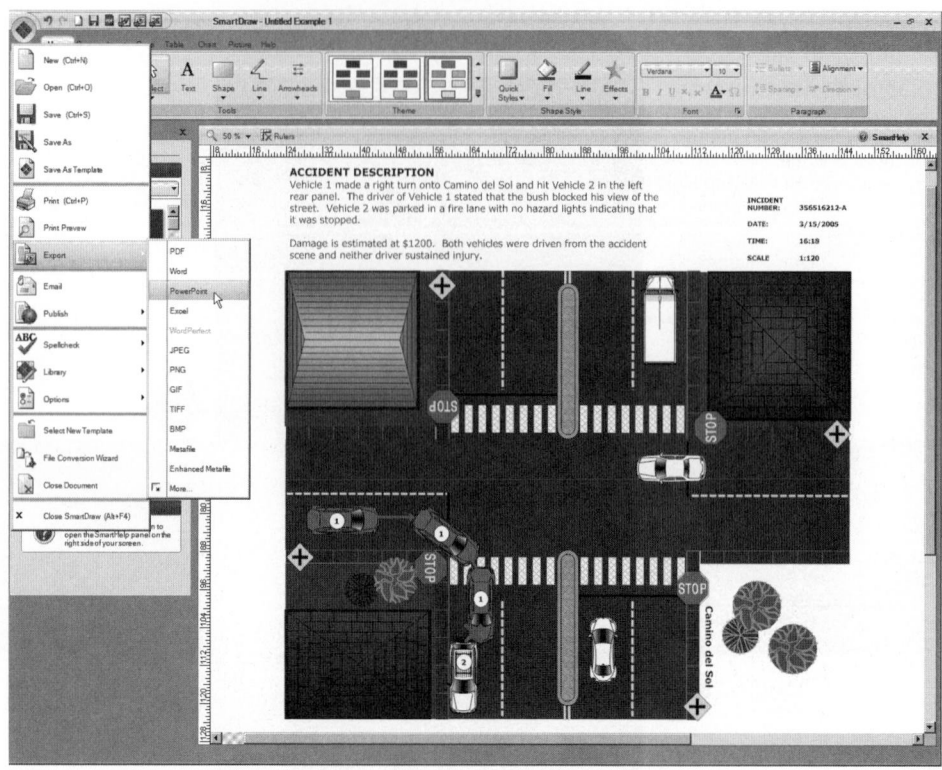

SmartDraw Software, LLC.

Exhibit 16.22 SmartDraw graphic exported to a PowerPoint presentation

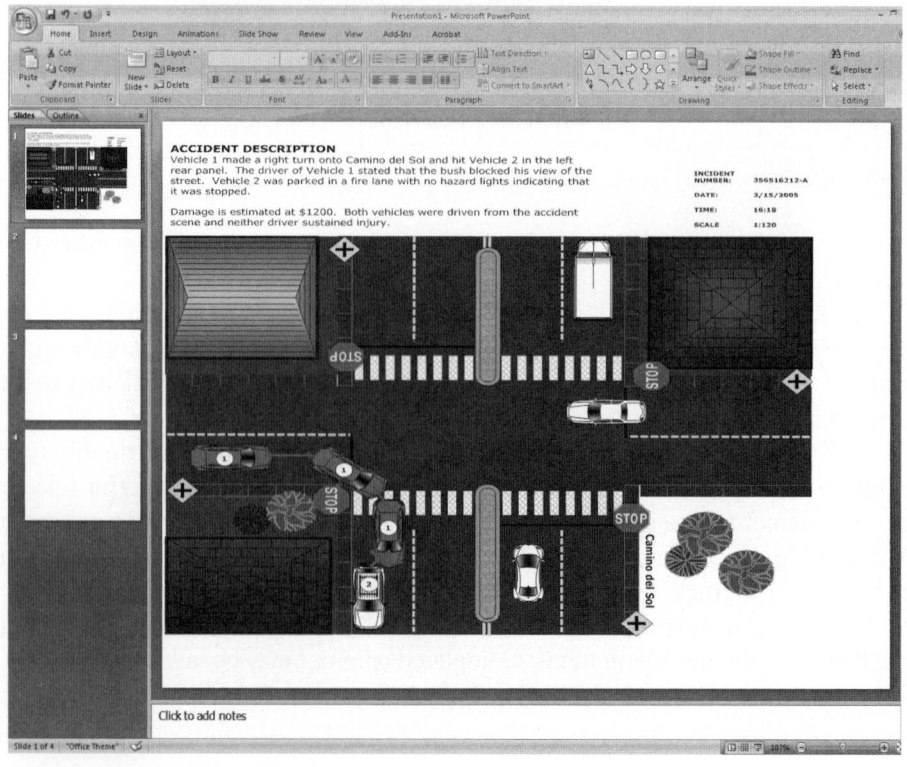

SmartDraw Software, LLC.

Exhibit 16.23 SmartDraw templates and sample graphics

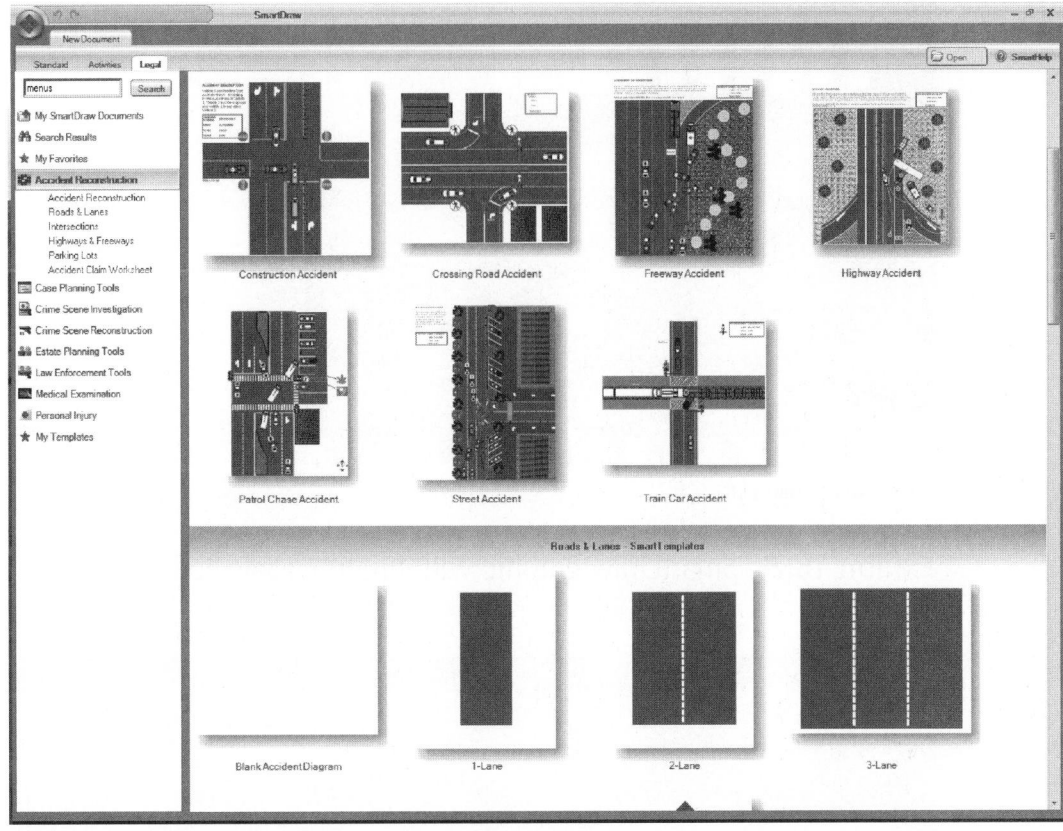

SmartDraw Software, LLC.

Exhibit 16.24 Accident reconstruction graphic created using SmartDraw

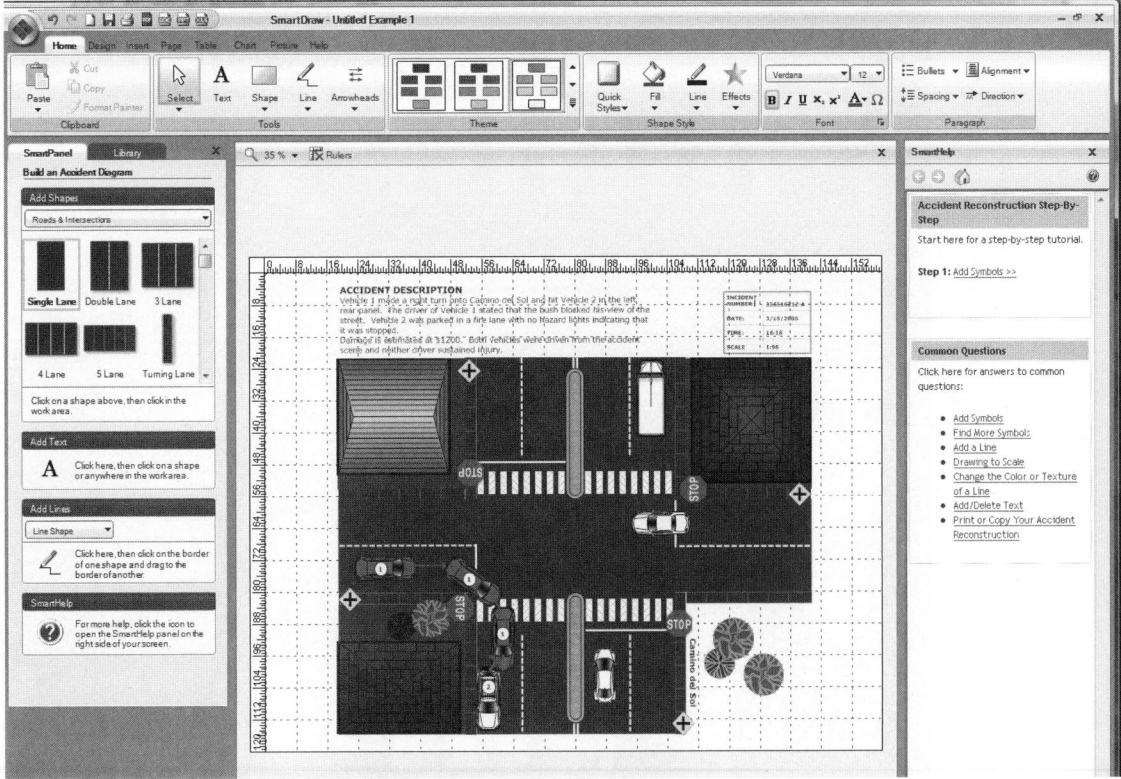

SmartDraw Software, LLC.

Exhibit 16.25 SmartDraw graphic with car
on top of fire engine

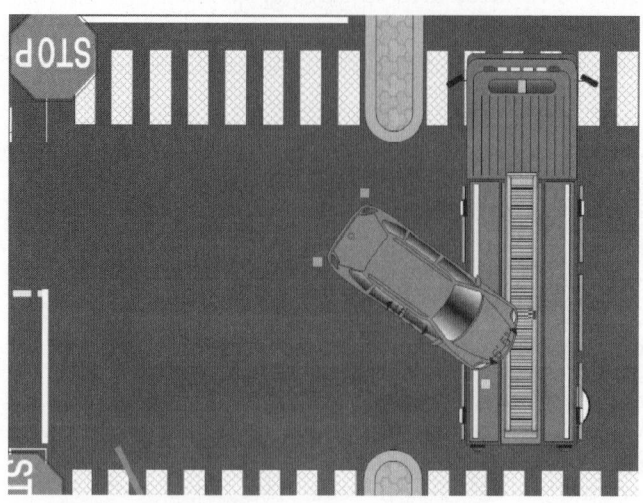

SmartDraw Software, LLC.

Exhibit 16.26 SmartDraw graphic with fire truck selected
and brought to front

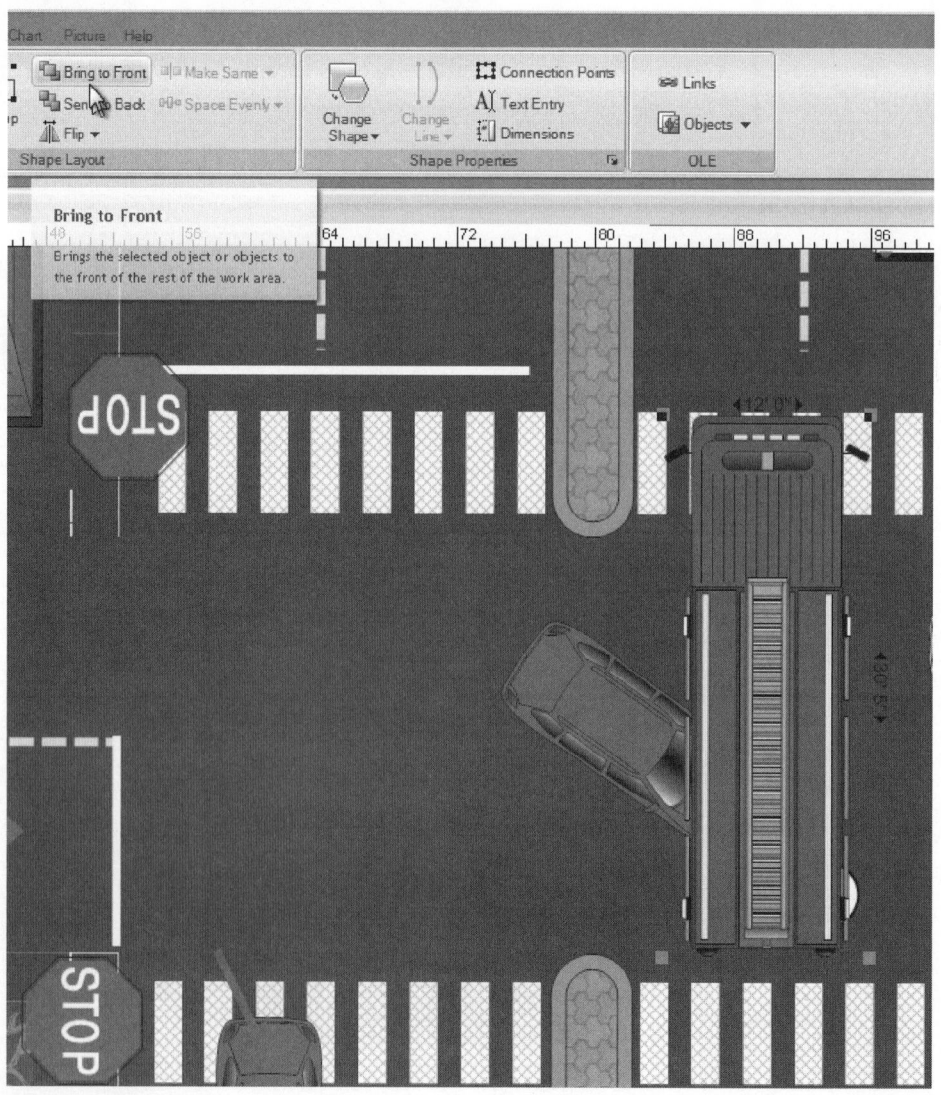

SmartDraw Software, LLC.

ADVICE FROM THE FIELD

THE "BUM" RULE—HOW TO CREATE EFFECTIVE DEMONSTRATIVE EVIDENCE

By John Cleaves

Remember Justice Potter Stewart's famous observation: "I shall not today attempt further to define the kinds of material I understand to be embraced...[b]ut I know it when I see it..."? This statement applies to effective demonstrative evidence just as well as it does to the original subject Justice Stewart had in mind.

What is effective demonstrative evidence? Nearly anything. Physical items, such as weapons, car bumpers, and computer chips; video shot at the scene of an accident, or showing the process by which an item is manufactured are typical examples. Other demonstratives include graphics illustrating events along a timeline, animation of a patent drawing, or diagrams of a medical procedure.

Attorneys occasionally fall into the trap of using bullet points to list their facts and arguments. But bullet points rarely help explain the facts and seldom convince jurors of the merits of the case. They do, however, bore everyone to tears as the attorney reads one after another. Bullet points are not effective demonstrative evidence.

As a Litigation Support professional you may be called upon to assist or manage the creation of demonstratives within your firm or corporate legal department. As trial time approaches the attorney team may be focusing on finalizing their exhibits and preparing witnesses. The creation of demonstratives may fall through the cracks or be a last minute detail left to you or your staff. Follow these tips to ensure you or you're (sic) staff create demonstratives that capture the attention of the jury and/or judge.

Believe, Understand and Remember

When considering that demonstrative evidence can be nearly anything (bounded by the rules of evidence, of course)—and often is an "I know it when I see it" type of thing—how do you as a litigation support professional come up with a demonstrative that is truly effective? One way is by using the "BUM" criteria: is the demonstrative believable, understandable and memorable?

A demonstrative is believable if it appeals to the jurors' common sense, is straight-forward, and is honest. For example, in a case where a company was accused of fraud for selling "vaporware," the defense attorney used the product in [the] opening. Not an image or photograph, but the actual item, putting it to the use it was intended. It is difficult to argue an item does not exist when it is sitting in court on counsel's table doing what it was supposed to do.

A demonstrative is understandable if it makes sense to the jurors without a long explanation. Attorneys often use clichés, logic and fundamentals (such as 2 + 2 = 4) to create understandable demonstratives. For example, in a breach of contract case[,] a graphic showing a man with his fingers crossed behind his back was used to demonstrate that one of the parties had ulterior motives.

By referencing the simple childhood cliché of crossing one's fingers when making a promise[,] the jury immediately understood the point made in the demonstrative.

An exhibit is memorable when it sticks with the jurors throughout the trial and deliberations. Unfortunately it is difficult to know what jurors will find memorable; jury research often shows jurors remembering items the attorneys find insignificant and missing points the attorneys stress repeatedly. One method to overcome this problem is to force the jurors to use several senses to process the information. Jurors typically rely on sight and sound, but adding touch to the mix helps fix the information in their minds. For example, in a patent infringement case involving the manufacture of computer chips, counsel distributed silicon wafers to the jurors as the expert explained the process by which they were made....

Overcoming the Problems and Pitfalls of Demonstratives

Two kinds of problems tend to come up when using demonstratives. The first is procedural: are they legally relevant, was a proper foundation laid, or are they argumentative? These are important questions [for Litigation Support professionals] to keep in mind as they consider and use the demonstratives.

The second type of problem is substantive. Demonstratives work best when they are straight-forward, clear of piles of money saved by the defendants by not enacting safety measures are often used to sway jurors['] feelings.

Another good source of demonstratives is to give jurors visual displays of the sheer volume of evidence, on the theory that a lot of evidence on one side probably means that is the party that should prevail, even if the small amount of evidence on the other side is very effective.

Seeing From the Jurors' Point Of View

When selecting physical items as demonstrative evidence, consider if the item is relevant, if it adds to the story, or if it is something a layperson would be curious to see. In civil

(continued)

(continued)

cases it may be difficult to come up with an item, often and concise. When full of information, perhaps lots of text or images, they can become confusing and even intimidating to jurors. If jurors are overwhelmed with a tidal wave of data[,] they may simply tune out. At the same time, it can be difficult for attorneys to avoid this pitfall because they are so intimately informed about every aspect of the case and have only a short time to teach and convince the jurors about a case they have been working on for months or years.

There are several ways to avoid these risks. One is to be very conscientious about limiting the number of words in a graphic. Most billboards['] ads are effective because they have very few words. The same is true of demonstratives— the fewer words the better.

Next, remove all extraneous information. This can be as simple as removing the decimal points if every number in a chart ends in .00, or cropping a photo to center it on the primary subject, or showcasing only the portion of a machine that's at issue rather than an entire piece of equipment. When jurors are first exposed to a new demonstrative[,] they do not necessarily know what is most important. If it is cluttered with extra information, they may be distracted or confused and miss your crucial point.

Finally, build slowly. Introduce the components of the demonstrative one at a time so they can be explained individually. If the jurors are presented with information in small bites[,] it is more likely they will understand and follow along. Even though it may be tempting to put the multi-variable formula or the hyper-detailed flowchart up all at once, if it causes even one juror to stop paying attention[,] it has not helped the case.

There are rewards for the attorney who effectively uses demonstrative evidence. In addition to showing common sense is on their side—which is one of the keys to consistent success in trial—effective demonstratives help entertain, and therefore engage[,] the jurors in the proceedings. Think back to those warm spring days in high school science class when the professor would show a video instead of dryly lecturing. Weren't those classes more interesting and memorable?

Demonstrative evidence can also speed up the trial by teaching the jury the facts in a more concise and therefore quicker way. One example is a timeline which ties together various facts into a chain of events. Another could be a theme signpost[,] which can help add structure to the disjointed way in which facts are presented in a case and can help jurors fit the facts together in a way that is logical and makes sense.

Finally, demonstrative evidence can be a very effective way of showing the other sides' motive. This is a key piece of information for jurors. Whether it is a physical item, as in a criminal case, or a smoking gun document in a civil case, showing the item or document repeatedly and reminding the jurors of the motive again and again will help cement it in their memories.

Andy Warhol once said, "I'm afraid that if you look at a thing long enough, it loses all its meaning." The same can be true of the evidence in a case. Documents, testimony and other exhibits can be spun one way or the other. They can be forgotten or ignored by a jury. Or, worst of all, they can be misinterpreted in favor of the opposition. But by using demonstratives [that] the jurors will believe, understand and remember to add meaning to the evidence, the chances of success are dramatically improved.

About the Author: John Cleaves is the Director of Forensic and Litigation Consulting at FTI Consulting.

Source: Reprinted with permission from Litigation Support Today magazine.

CONCEPT REVIEW AND REINFORCEMENT

KEY TERMS

spreadsheet   430

electronic database   432

word processor   433

CHAPTER SUMMARY

Introduction to Presentation and Trial Graphics	Properly prepared graphics are an excellent way of telling a story and making a point. The most accessible presentation software program is Microsoft PowerPoint.

Graphics and Presentations in Litigation	Graphic creation programs are used to create either stand-alone graphics for presentations or graphics that are part of a presentation. An advantage of this class of software is the ability of the legal team to create their own graphics without the need of graphic artists and outside consultants.
Creating a PowerPoint Presentation	Microsoft PowerPoint is standard for making electronic presentations. Templates and content slides are available for download from the Microsoft website when creating a new PowerPoint presentation. PowerPoint allows many enhancements to a slide presentation, including transitions, animation, and sounds. A good PowerPoint presentation can reinforce and highlight the speaker's ideas and concepts. PowerPoint presentation pointers: Use color combinations that can be seen by everyone in the room. Use as few words per slide as possible. Use sounds only when appropriate. Don't block the slides during the presentation. Choose pictures wisely.
SmartDraw	SmartDraw is a graphic creation program that provides thousands of templates and icons for creating graphics quickly. Template examples can be modified using the drop-and-drag technique.

REVIEW QUESTIONS AND EXERCISES

1. How can the legal team use presentation graphics programs? Give examples of ways that graphics may be used by both litigation and nonlitigation legal teams.

2. Create an accident scene exhibit using SmartDraw. How will the exhibit help the jury understand how the accident occurred? What features should be included to accomplish this?

3. Create a graphic of a room using Microsoft Visio. The graphic will be used to create a diagram of a crime scene. A client will use this diagram to explain to a defense team his version of the events leading up to an alleged homicide. How will the diagram help the client explain the facts?

4. Explain how trial presentation programs can help a trial team prepare for and conduct a trial. Describe three tasks in which an application can assist.

5. Create a basic PowerPoint presentation on the use of PowerPoint in litigation. Include a detailed explanation of how to create a slide. Create at least ten different slides on separate subtopics. Use graphics, such as clip art, to provide effective visuals. Use transitions to make the slides flow together.

6. Deliver the above PowerPoint presentation to a group. After the presentation, ask the group to give you feedback. Describe the positive and negative reactions to the presentation. What changes would you make if you were to give it again?

7. Use TimeMap to create a time line of at least ten time elements such as birthdays, anniversaries, or course-related deadlines. Export the time line to PowerPoint, with each item on a separate slide. Create a second PowerPoint presentation with all the time line elements on one slide.

BUILDING YOUR PARALEGAL SKILLS

INTERNET AND TECHNOLOGY EXERCISES

1. Use the Internet to locate resources for learning how to use Microsoft PowerPoint. List the topics available and the web addresses for accessing this information.

2. What Internet resources are available for obtaining maps and aerial views that might be used for trial preparation?

3. Locate resources for learning SmartDraw online. What resources are available that specifically pertain to using SmartDraw in litigation? Create list of at least five features in SmartDraw that you were not previously aware of, and explain how each is used.

VIDEO CASE STUDIES

FINAL PRETRIAL EVIDENTIARY ISSUES

 Trial attorneys are meeting with the judge prior to the trial. The attorneys on each side have opposing views of the use of graphics as demonstrative evidence. The court agrees to take the use of graphics under consideration.

Watch this video case study in MyLegalStudiesLab and answer the following questions.

1. How important is the use of photographs and graphics in a trial? How can they enhance a trial presentation?
2. Are there any issues that should be reviewed regarding the use of videotaped depositions?
3. Is the final pretrial conference an appropriate time to determine the judge's willingness to allow multimedia presentations?

CHAPTER OPENING SCENARIO CASE STUDY

Use the Opening Scenario for this chapter to answer the following questions.

1. Prepare a memo for the attorneys of the firm on the issues involved in using outside sources for the preparation of trial graphics. Explain alternatives for creating trial graphics in-house. Explain the advantages of creating the graphics in-house, particularly cost considerations.
2. How can graphics be used in the trial? List three different types of litigation in which graphics may be useful, such as construction litigation, an auto accident, or products liability. Write a memo to your firm explaining how graphics can be used in each type of case. Identify specific applications that can be used in each situation.
3. What cautions should the trial attorney consider in using graphics at trial? How can graphics actually hurt a trial attorney's trial performance?
4. What pretrial measures should be taken if trial graphics are going to be used? How should a trial team plan ahead when considering the use of trial graphics?

CONTINUING CASES AND EXERCISES

For the assigned case study A from Appendix II:

1. From the Technology Resources Website, www.pearsonhighered.com/goldman, download and install on your computer the demo version of SmartDraw.
2. If you do not have PowerPoint or Visio on your computer, download a demo version from the Microsoft Office link at www.pearsonhighered.com/goldman or directly from the Microsoft website.
3. Prepare a diagram of the case study accident scene using SmartDraw and showing the vehicles:
   a. Before the impact.
   b. After the collisions and all of the vehicles had come to rest.
4. Prepare a settlement brochure using SmartDraw.
5. Prepare a PowerPoint presentation for use in trial using the exhibits in the comprehensive accident case study, Case A in Appendix II, and the graphics prepared using SmartDraw and TimeMap.

POWERPOINT TUTORIAL

■ HOW DO I DOWNLOAD POWERPOINT DEMO FROM THE MICROSOFT WEBSITE?

NOTE: If you do not have Microsoft Office Suite or PowerPoint, you may download a 60-day trial version to use in completing this tutorial. The PowerPoint website is a good source of additional information and answers. You may want to save the link address for future reference.

DOWNLOADING AND INSTALLING 60-DAY TRIAL VERSION OF MICROSOFT OFFICE

GOAL	ACTION	RESULT
DOWNLOAD AND SAVE 60-DAY TRIAL VERSION OF MICROSOFT OFFICE	**START** *Your Internet web browser* **ENTER** http://office.microsoft.com/en-us /powerpoint *for 60-day demo* **MOVE** *Mouse over Get PowerPoint window* **CLICK** *Download a free trial*	

(continued)

GOAL	ACTION	RESULT
SELECT VERSION OF MICROSOFT OFFICE 2010 and **REGISTER FOR DOWNLOAD**	**CLICK** *Try it free*	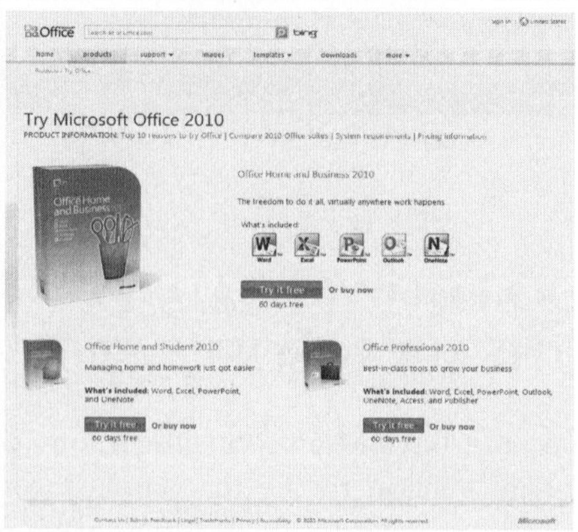 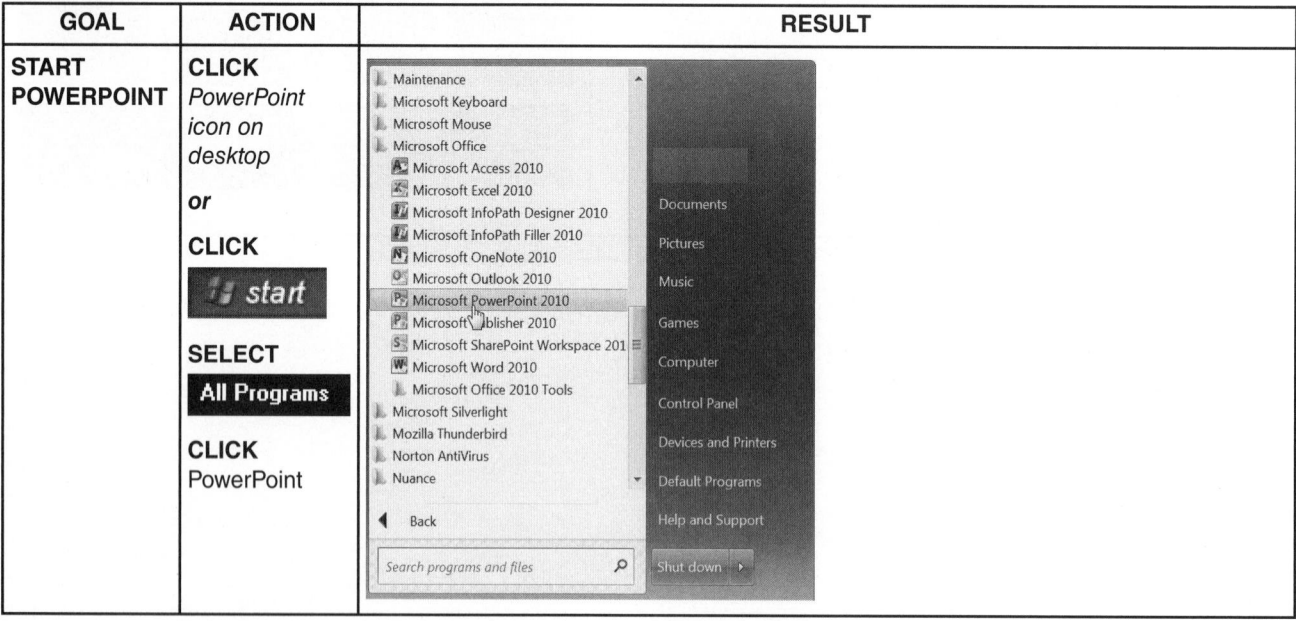
	COMPLETE *Registration*	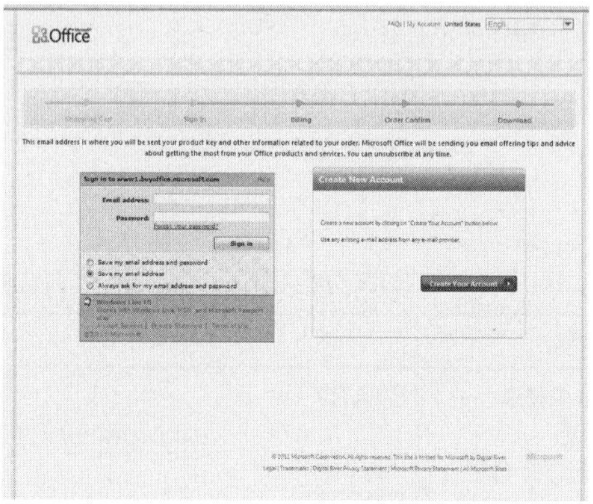

■ HOW DO I CREATE A POWERPOINT PRESENTATION?

GOAL	ACTION	RESULT
START POWERPOINT	**CLICK** *PowerPoint icon on desktop* **or** **CLICK** start **SELECT** All Programs **CLICK** PowerPoint	Maintenance Microsoft Keyboard Microsoft Mouse Microsoft Office 　Microsoft Access 2010 　Microsoft Excel 2010 　Microsoft InfoPath Designer 2010 　Microsoft InfoPath Filler 2010 　Microsoft OneNote 2010 　Microsoft Outlook 2010 　Microsoft PowerPoint 2010 　Microsoft Publisher 2010 　Microsoft SharePoint Workspace 201 　Microsoft Word 2010 　Microsoft Office 2010 Tools Microsoft Silverlight Mozilla Thunderbird Norton AntiVirus Nuance ◀ Back *Search programs and files* Documents Pictures Music Games Computer Control Panel Devices and Printers Default Programs Help and Support Shut down ▶

(continued)

GOAL	ACTION	RESULT
ADD TITLE AND **SUBTITLE TO POWERPOINT SLIDE**	**CLICK** *Cursor in top box* **TYPE** *Taxi Crash* **CLICK** *Cursor in bottom box* **Type** *The Story*	
ADD NEW BLANK SLIDE	**CLICK** *New Slide in Home tab* **CLICK** *Blank*	

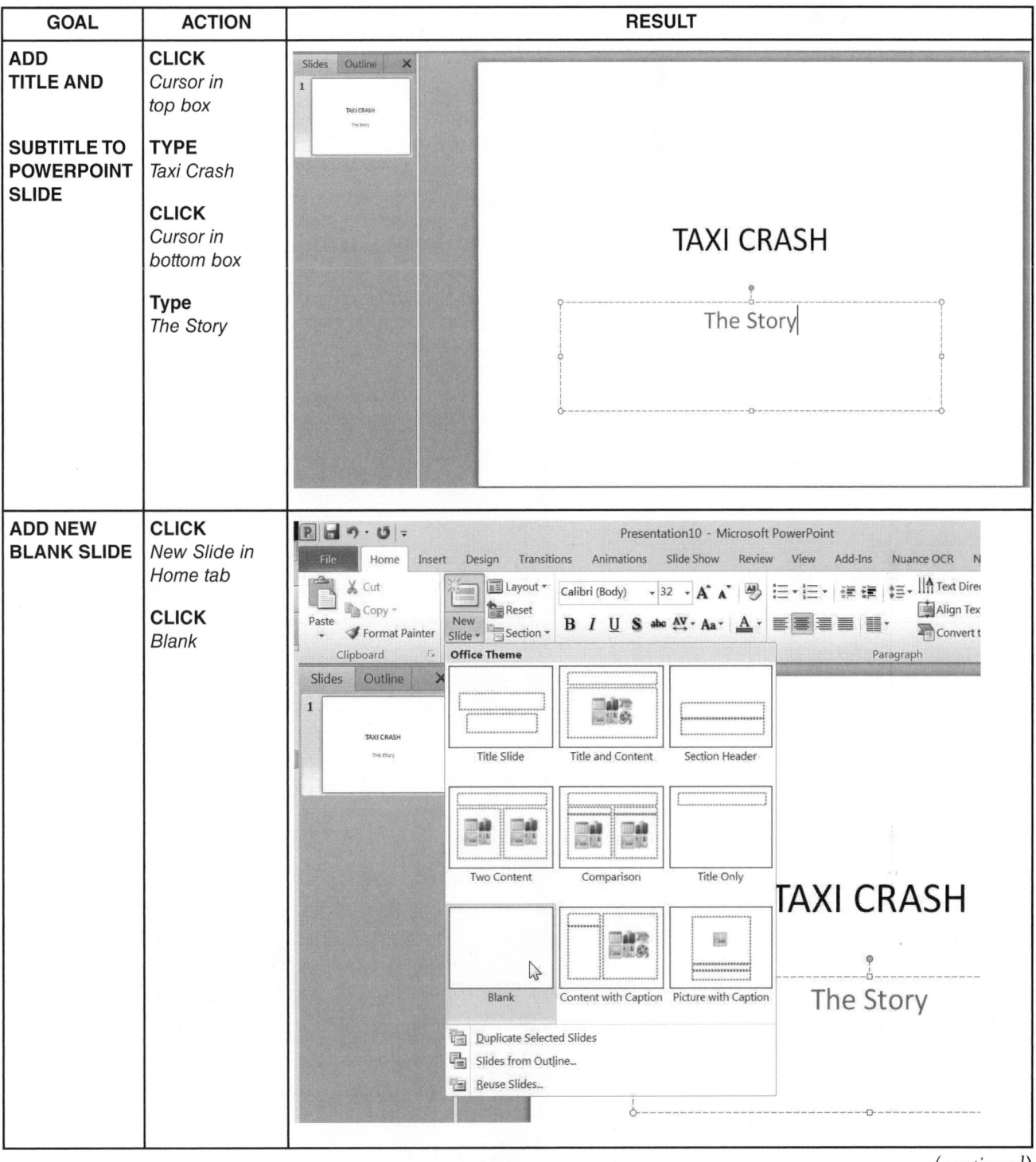

(*continued*)

GOAL	ACTION	RESULT
ADD CLIP ART	**CLICK** *Clip Art in Insert tab* **CLICK** *in Search for box* **TYPE** *Taxi* **CLICK** *Go* **CLICK** *Down arrow along right side of clip art* **CLICK** *Insert*	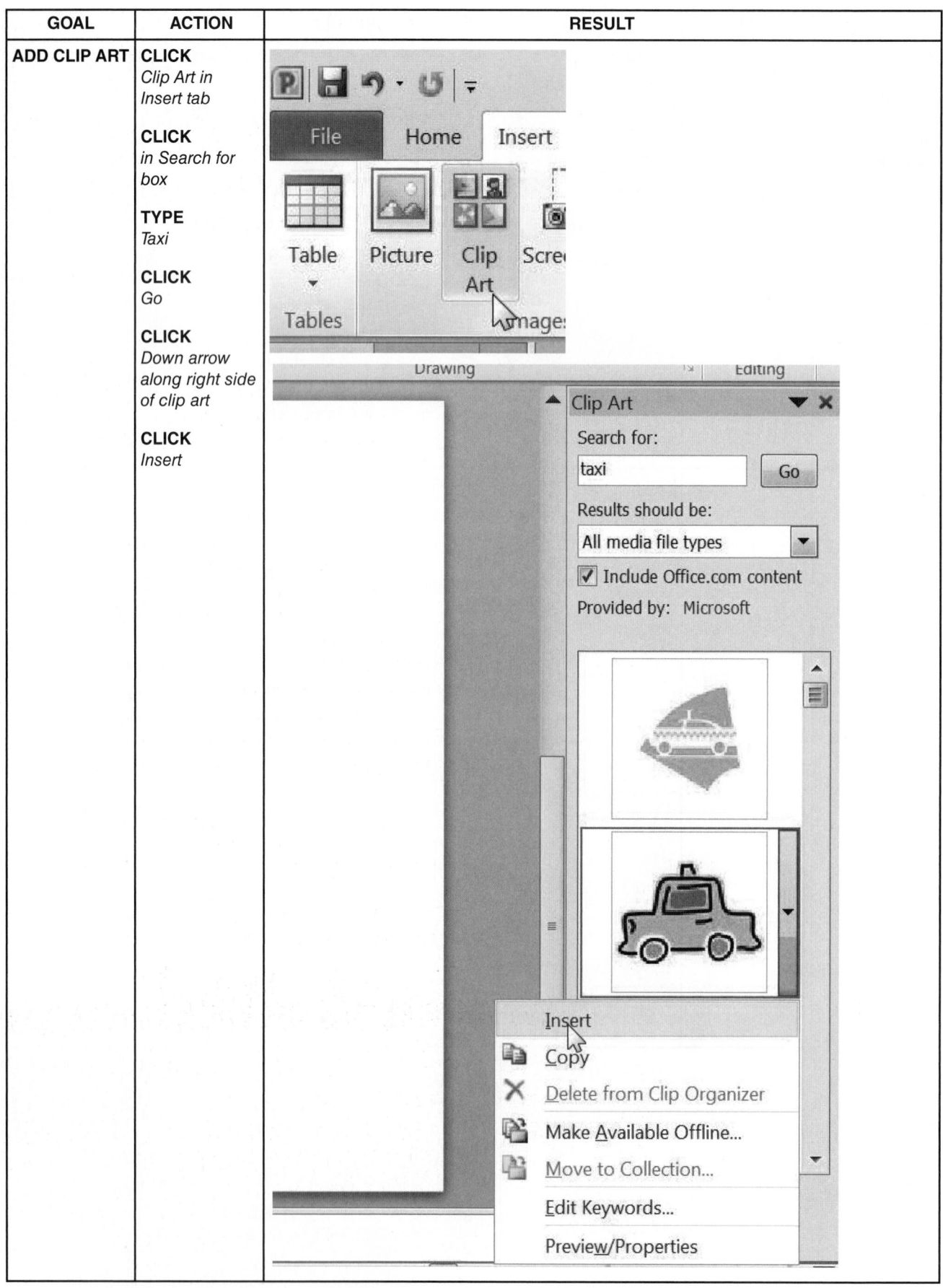

(continued)

GOAL	ACTION	RESULT
ADD ADDITIONAL CLIP ART AND ADJUST SIZE OF CLIP ART IMAGES **TIP:** Either image may be moved to appear on top of or under the other.	**CLICK** *in Search for box* **TYPE** *Telephone pole* **CLICK** *Go* **CLICK** *Down arrow along right side of clip art* **CLICK** *Insert* **CLICK** *on image* **CLICK and HOLD** *left Mouse button* **DRAG MOUSE** *To desired size* **REPEAT** *For other image* **POSITION** *as desired*	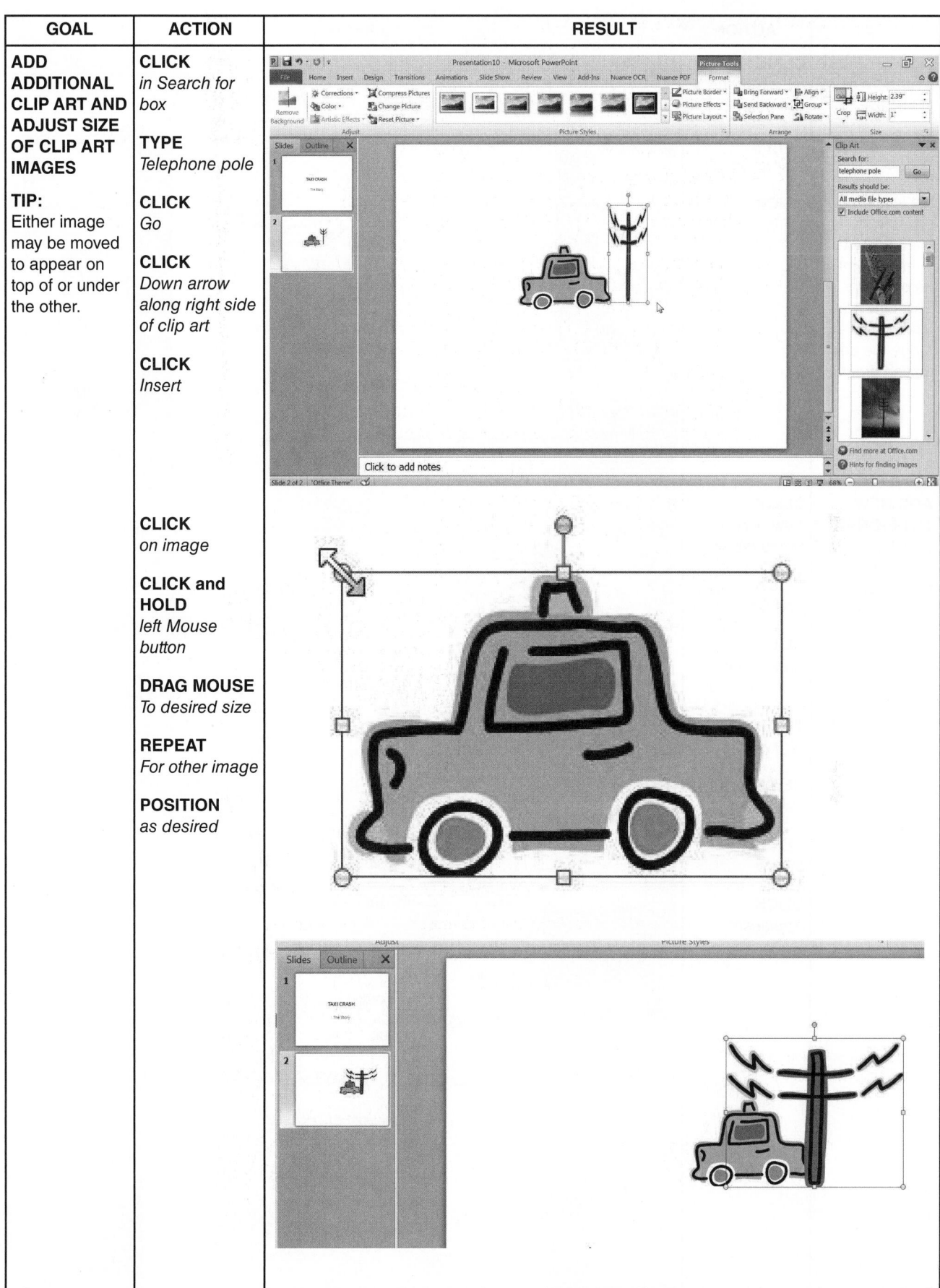

(continued)

GOAL	ACTION	RESULT
ADD ANIMATION TO SLIDE **NOTE:** Animation pane that shows the selected image and the selected animation may be opened. This may be used to rearrange the animation order.	**CLICK** *on telephone pole image* **CLICK** *Animation tab* **CLICK** *Fly In*	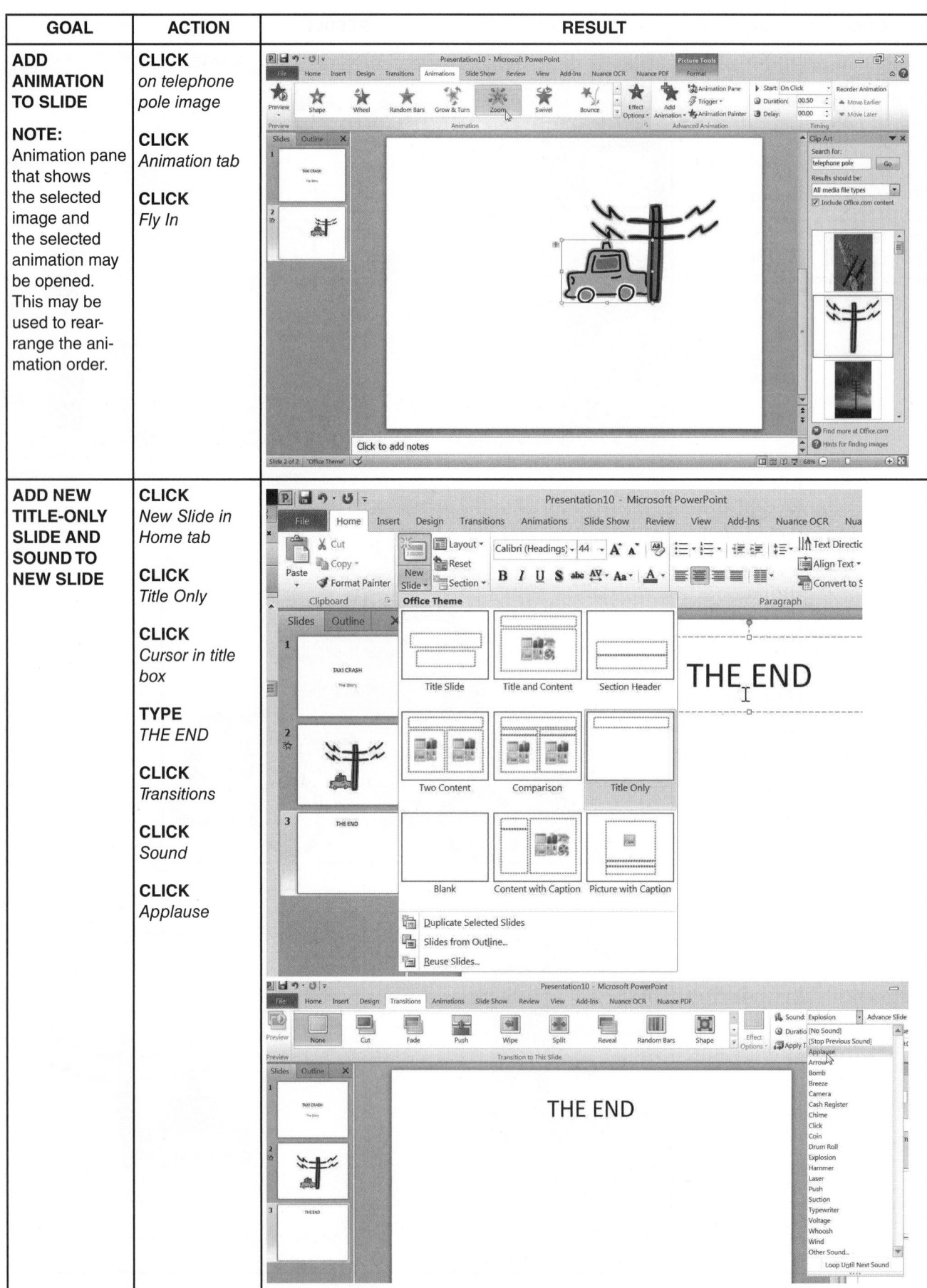
ADD NEW TITLE-ONLY SLIDE AND SOUND TO NEW SLIDE	**CLICK** *New Slide in Home tab* **CLICK** *Title Only* **CLICK** *Cursor in title box* **TYPE** *THE END* **CLICK** *Transitions* **CLICK** *Sound* **CLICK** *Applause*	

(continued)

GOAL	ACTION	RESULT
RUN POWERPOINT SLIDE SHOW	**CLICK** *First slide in left column* **CLICK** *Slide Show button* **LEFT-CLICK MOUSE** *To change slides*	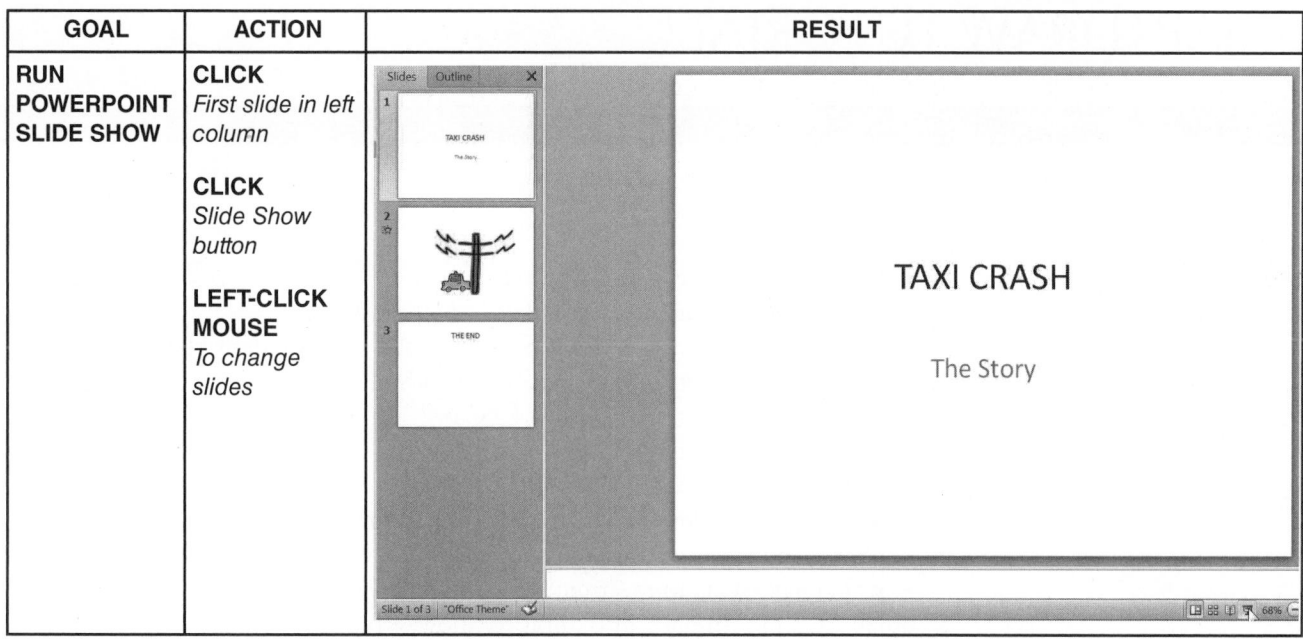

Using the File tab's Save As option, you can save the PowerPoint presentation to a selected file folder or removable memory device. PowerPoint slide shows may be saved as:

PowerPoint Presentation—Showing these requires PowerPoint to be loaded on the computer.

PowerPoint Show—Runs using a free PowerPoint Viewer even if PowerPoint is not loaded on the computer you are using.

The PowerPoint Viewer may be downloaded from the Microsoft Download Center: http://www.microsoft.com/downloads/en/details.aspx?displaylang=en&FamilyID=cb9bf144%2D1076%2D4615%2D9951%2D294eeb832823

PowerPoint Formats

POWERPOINT 2010	POWERPOINT 97–2003
PowerPoint Presentation (.pptx)	A PowerPoint 97–2003 Presentation (.ppt)
XPS Document Format (.xps)	A PowerPoint 97–2003 Presentation (.ppt)
PowerPoint Template (.potx)	A PowerPoint 97–2003 Template (.pot)
Office Theme (.thmx)	A PowerPoint 97–2003 Template (.pot)
PowerPoint Show (.ppsx)	A PowerPoint 97–2003 Show (.pps)

Additional tutorial information is available at www.microsoft.com or www.microsoft.com/powerpoint

OR

Create your first PowerPoint 2010 Presentation at http://office.microsoft.com/en-us/powerpoint-help/create-your-first-powerpoint-2010-presentation-RZ101848193.aspx?CTT=1

SMARTDRAW TUTORIAL

- How Can I Create Map Exhibits?
  - *Tutorial—Creating Map Exhibits Using Live Maps*
- How Can I Create an Exhibit Showing How the Accident Happened?
  - *Tutorial—Creating Map and Photo Exhibits*
- How Can I Create a Timeline of a Case?
  - *Tutorial—Creating a Case Timeline*
- How Can I Annotate a Timeline to Make It More Dramatic?
  - *Tutorial—Adding Pictures and Maps to a Timeline*
- How Can I Change the Line Directions of Labels?
  - *Tutorial—Changing Arrow Directions and Shapes*
- How Can I Animate an Exhibit to Show What Happened?
  - *Tutorial—Animating an Accident Presentation*
- How Can I Use SmartDraw to Create a Settlement Brochure?
  - *Tutorial—Creating a Settlement Brochure*

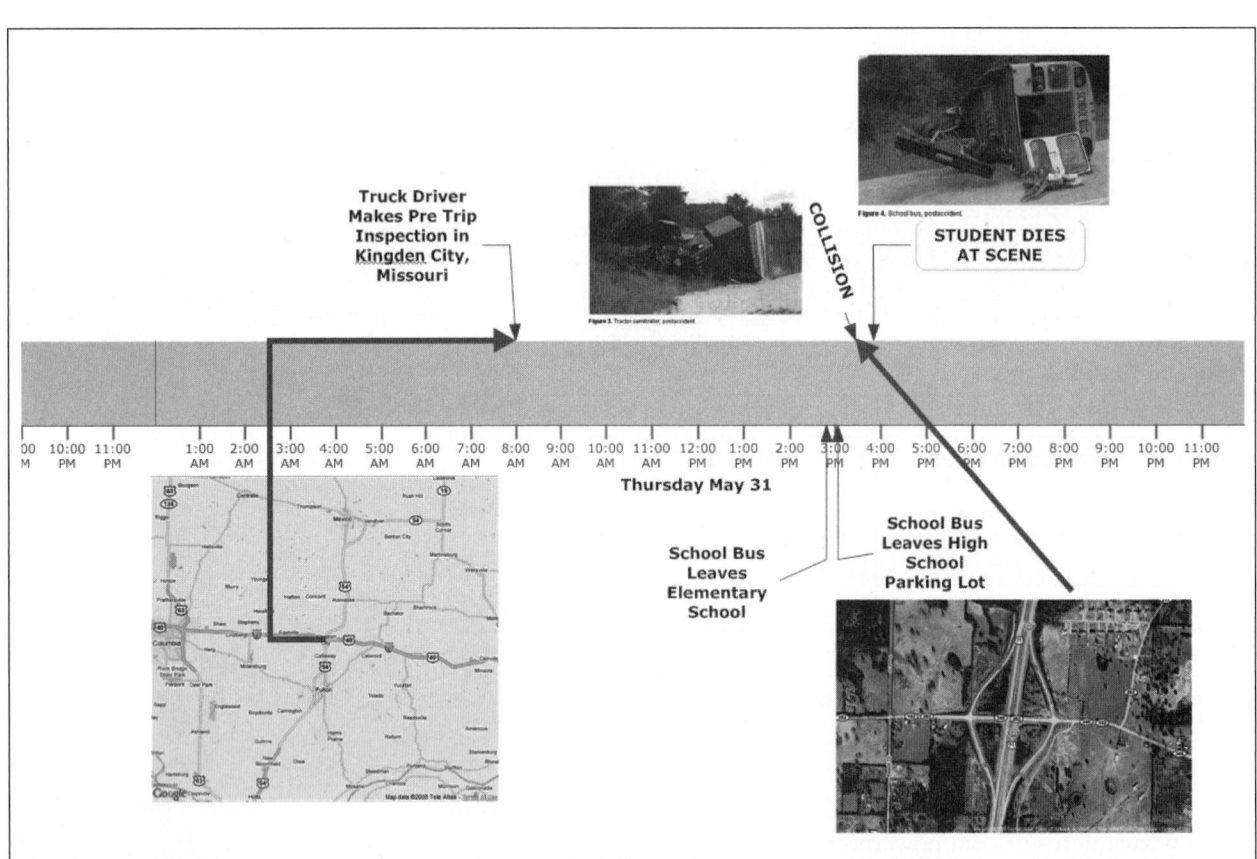

Source: Timeline created with SmartDraw.

Reproduced from: *SmartDraw: A Hands-On Tutorial and Guide*, by Thomas F. Goldman, Pearson/Prentice Hall, copyright 2012.

■ HOW CAN I CREATE MAP EXHIBITS?

SmartDraw provides a full set of traditional international, national, and local maps. SmartDraw also provides direct access to Google maps through an Internet connection. The Maps category in the Document Browser has a category of Live Maps; these show a specific area, such as a state and the surrounding area. A mouse click on a highlighted area connects to the Google map for that area over the Internet. Other maps can be created using the Blank Map template and the Map tool in the Insert tab.

An actual accident case reported by the National Transportation Safety Board is used for purposes of this tutorial. The same fact pattern, dates, and location will be used in the following group of legal application tutorials.

CREATING MAP EXHIBITS USING LIVE MAPS

GOAL	ACTION	RESULT
OPEN MAP OPTIONS MENU **IMPORT MAP TO SMARTDRAW DOCUMENT** **Note:** You can move around the map window with the cursor to locate and center a specific location. LEFT CLICK and HOLD the mouse and move the map.	**OPEN** *Map category in Document Browser* **CLICK** *USA-Live Map* **CLICK** *your state map* **DOUBLE CLICK** *on state map*	
SELECT SPECIFIC LOCATION BY ZOOM CONTROL	**CLICK** *Road Map option in Map Type* **ZOOM IN** *Using zoom slider to specific location* **CLICK** *Import to SmartDraw*	

(continued)

GOAL	ACTION	RESULT
CUSTOMIZE MAP	**ADD** *symbols and arrows to show locations and directions*	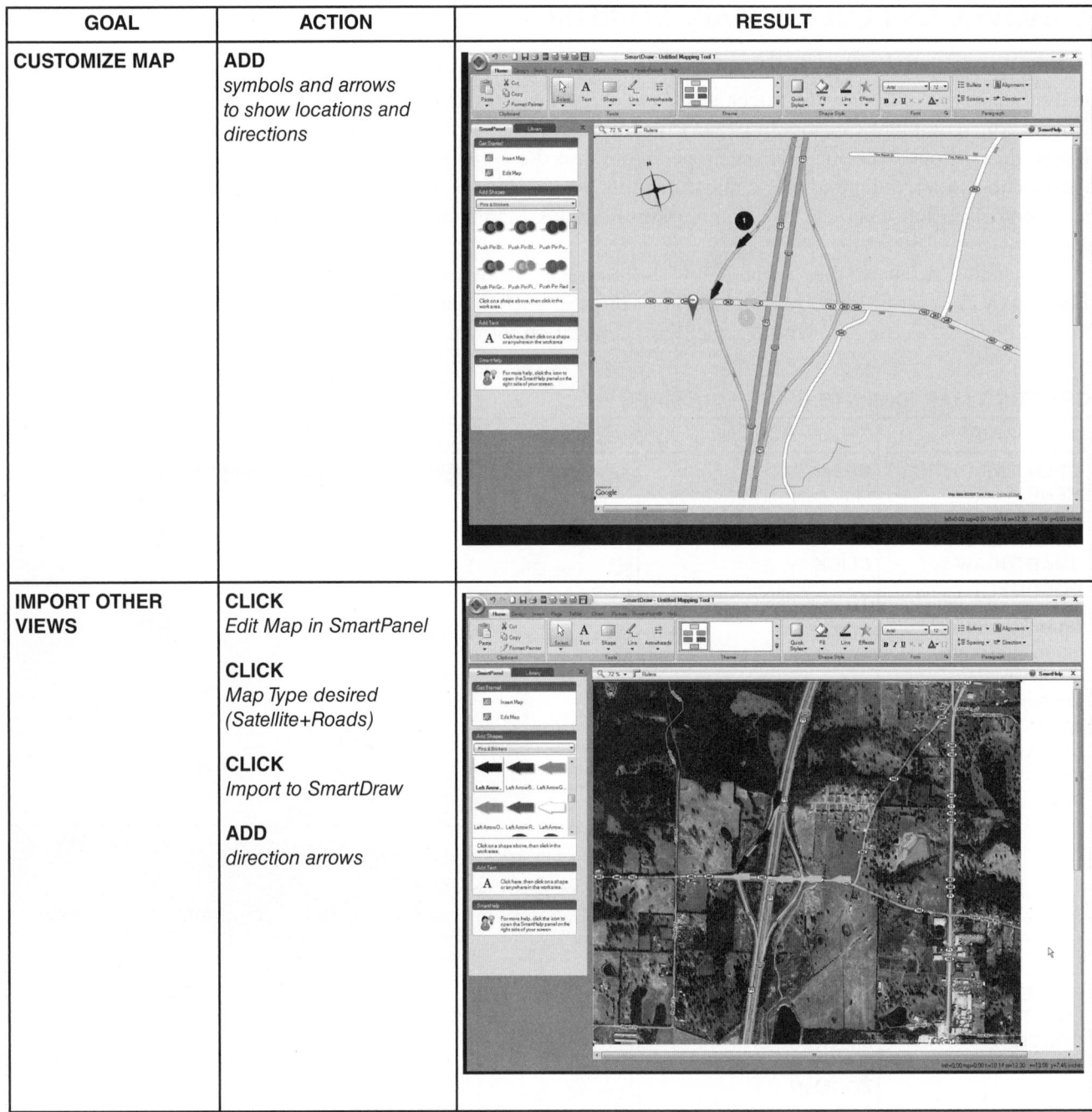
IMPORT OTHER VIEWS	**CLICK** *Edit Map in SmartPanel* **CLICK** *Map Type desired (Satellite+Roads)* **CLICK** *Import to SmartDraw* **ADD** *direction arrows*	

■ HOW CAN I CREATE AN EXHIBIT SHOWING HOW THE ACCIDENT HAPPENED?

Annotated maps and photos are frequently used as exhibits in pretrial activities and in trial. Visual representations of how an accident occurred can be easily prepared using the SmartDraw Accident Reconstruction SmartTemplates. In many cases you will be able to find an example of a scene close enough to the one you need in the Accident Reconstruction SmartTemplates.

Creating Map and Photo Exhibits

GOAL	ACTION	RESULT
DOWNLOAD AND ANNOTATE MAP **NOTE:** When the cursor is on the map, a left click changes its appearance to a hand, which can be used to move the map in the map window.	**OPEN** *Blank Interactive Map in Document Browser* **CLICK** *Insert Map in SmartPanel*	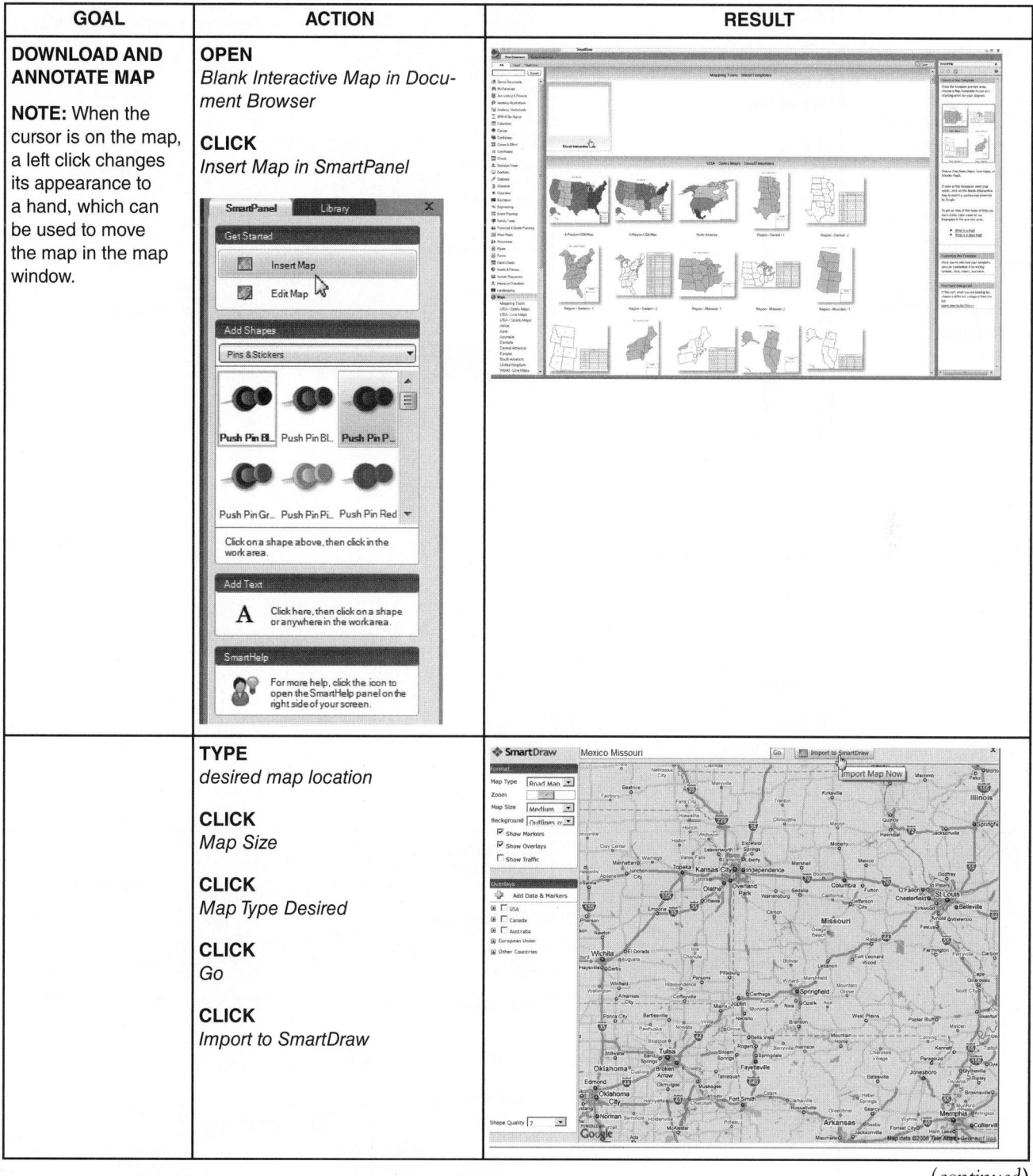
	TYPE *desired map location* **CLICK** *Map Size* **CLICK** *Map Type Desired* **CLICK** *Go* **CLICK** *Import to SmartDraw*	

(continued)

GOAL	ACTION	RESULT
EDIT MAP **TIPS:** The Pan and Zoom tools can be used to "lasso," and then zoom in on a desired area of a map. Save your work as a SmartDraw file for future use and to print as an exhibit poster or a settlement brochure.	**SELECT** *Map* **CLICK** *Picture tab* **CLICK** *Pan and Zoom* **LASSO and ZOOM** *desired map area* **CLICK** *Trim to Shape* **CLICK** *Continue*	
ANNOTATE MAP	**SELECT and MOVE** *symbols from SmartPanel to annotate* **CLICK** *Add Text In SmartPanel* **TYPE** *descriptive text*	

(continued)

GOAL	ACTION	RESULT
SAVE	**CLICK** *SmartDraw Button* **CLICK** *Save As* **SELECT** *SmartDraw Document (SDR)*	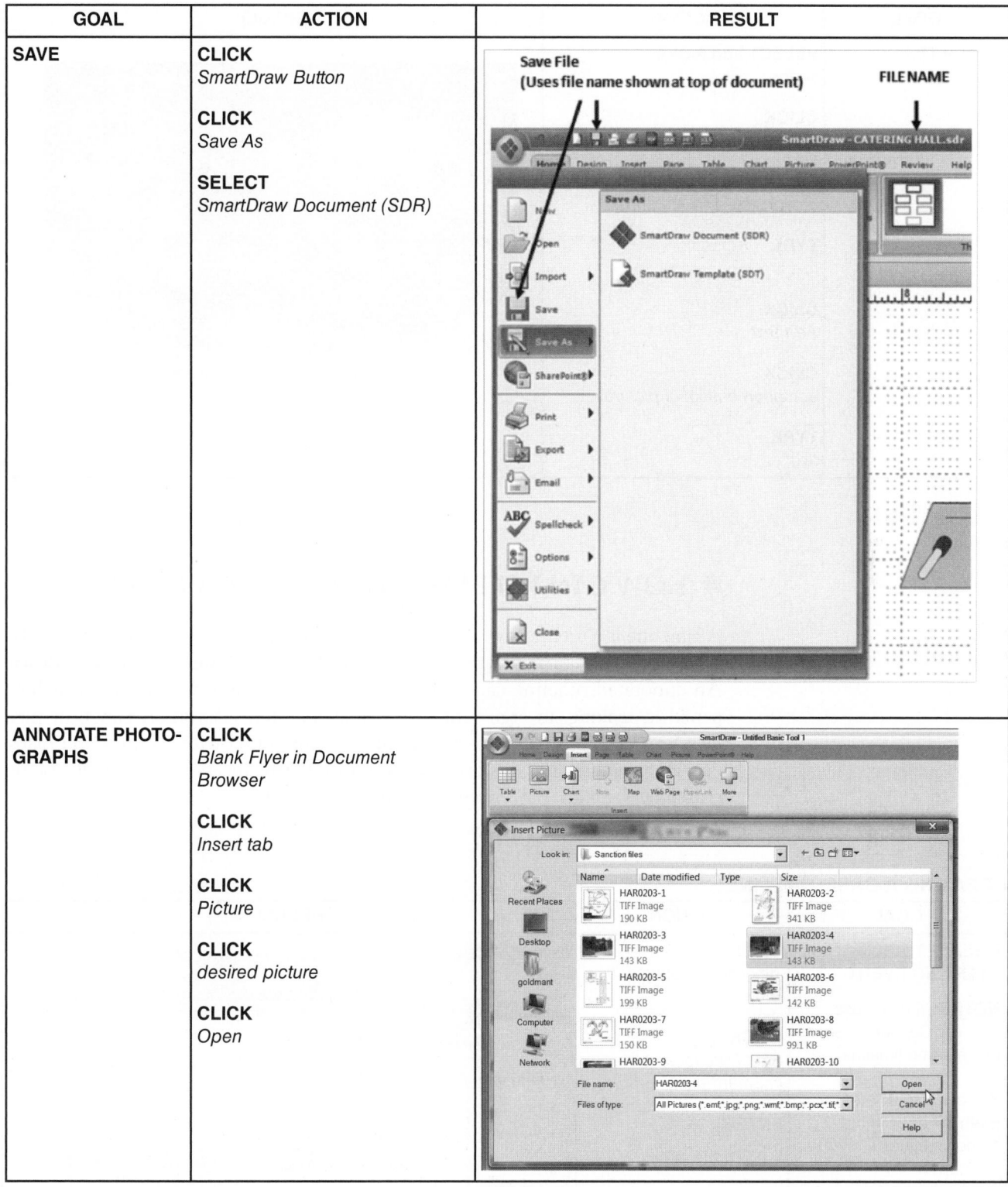
ANNOTATE PHOTO-GRAPHS	**CLICK** *Blank Flyer in Document Browser* **CLICK** *Insert tab* **CLICK** *Picture* **CLICK** *desired picture* **CLICK** *Open*	

(continued)

GOAL	ACTION	RESULT
ENTER TEXT	**SELECT and MOVE** *shape* **CLICK** *Add Text in SmartPanel* **CLICK** *cursor inside shape and* **TYPE** *text* **CLICK** *Add Text* **CLICK** *cursor on bottom of picture* **TYPE** *text*	 **SCHOOL BUS AFTER ACCIDENT**

■ HOW CAN I CREATE A TIMELINE OF A CASE?

A timeline is a useful way to quickly present a full sequence of events. It can also be used to summarize a series of events leading to a claim for injury or death. An annotated timeline can be used to show what happened and when it happened in making an argument to a claims adjuster, arbitration panel, or jury. The SmartDraw timeline templates may be annotated with pictures and maps. As mentioned earlier, the case used to illustrate this tutorial is an actual case reported by the National Transportation Study Board.

CREATING A CASE TIMELINE

GOAL	ACTION	RESULT
CREATE TIMELINE STARTING EVENT **NOTES:** You can use different Connector Styles in the same timeline. You can use different Event Shapes in the same timeline.	**CLICK** *Timeline in Document Browser* **CLICK** *Start Date for timeline in SmartPanel* **ENTER** *date*	

(continued)

GOAL	ACTION	RESULT
CREATE TIMELINE ENDING EVENT **TIPS**: One way of placing events on a timeline is to include the plaintiff's version on the top and the defendant's version on the bottom. Save your work as a SmartDraw file for future use and to print as an exhibit poster or a settlement brochure.	**CLICK** *End Date for timeline in SmartPanel* **ENTER** *date*	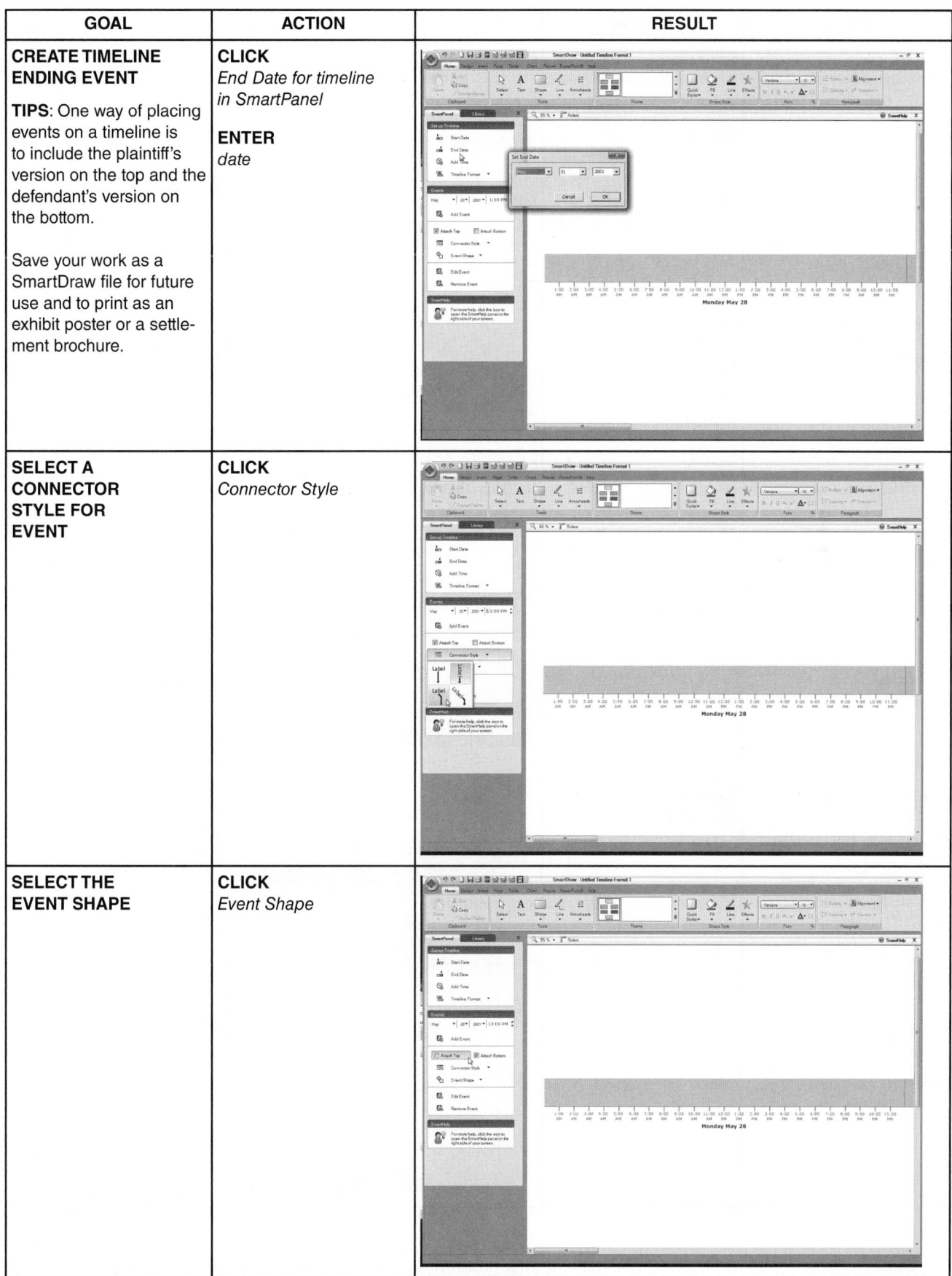
SELECT A CONNECTOR STYLE FOR EVENT	**CLICK** *Connector Style*	
SELECT THE EVENT SHAPE	**CLICK** *Event Shape*	

(continued)

GOAL	ACTION	RESULT
SELECT LOCATION ON TOP OR BOTTOM OF TIMELINE FOR EVENT	**SELECT** *location of event on top or bottom* **SELECT** *event time and* **CLICK** *Add Event*	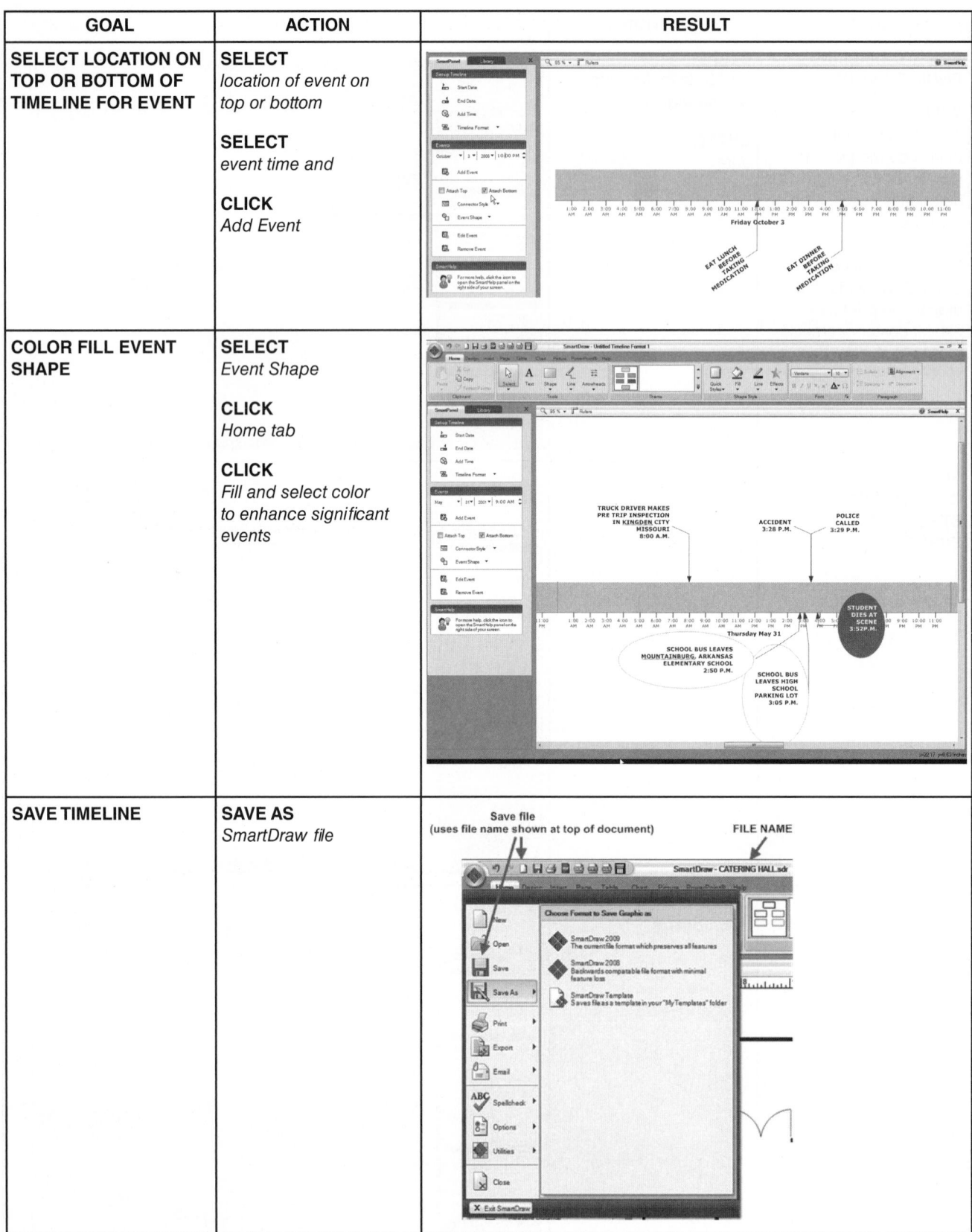
COLOR FILL EVENT SHAPE	**SELECT** *Event Shape* **CLICK** *Home tab* **CLICK** *Fill and select color to enhance significant events*	
SAVE TIMELINE	**SAVE AS** *SmartDraw file*	

You may use this timeline in the next tutorial or start a new one.

■ HOW CAN I ANNOTATE A TIMELINE TO MAKE IT MORE DRAMATIC?

A basic timeline can be very useful in showing facts. But a timeline annotated with pictures and maps, when permitted in court or in pretrial settlement activities, can communicate the story even more effectively. The timeline used in the previous tutorial is used in the following tutorial with the addition of maps and pictures. This tutorial provides the steps to add pictures. Before you start, locate a few sample pictures on your computer that you can use to practice inserting pictures in a timeline.

Adding Pictures and Maps to a Timeline

GOAL	ACTION	RESULT
INSERT PICTURE IN TIMELINE	**CLICK** *Insert tab* **CLICK** *Picture* **CLICK** *Add a New Picture*	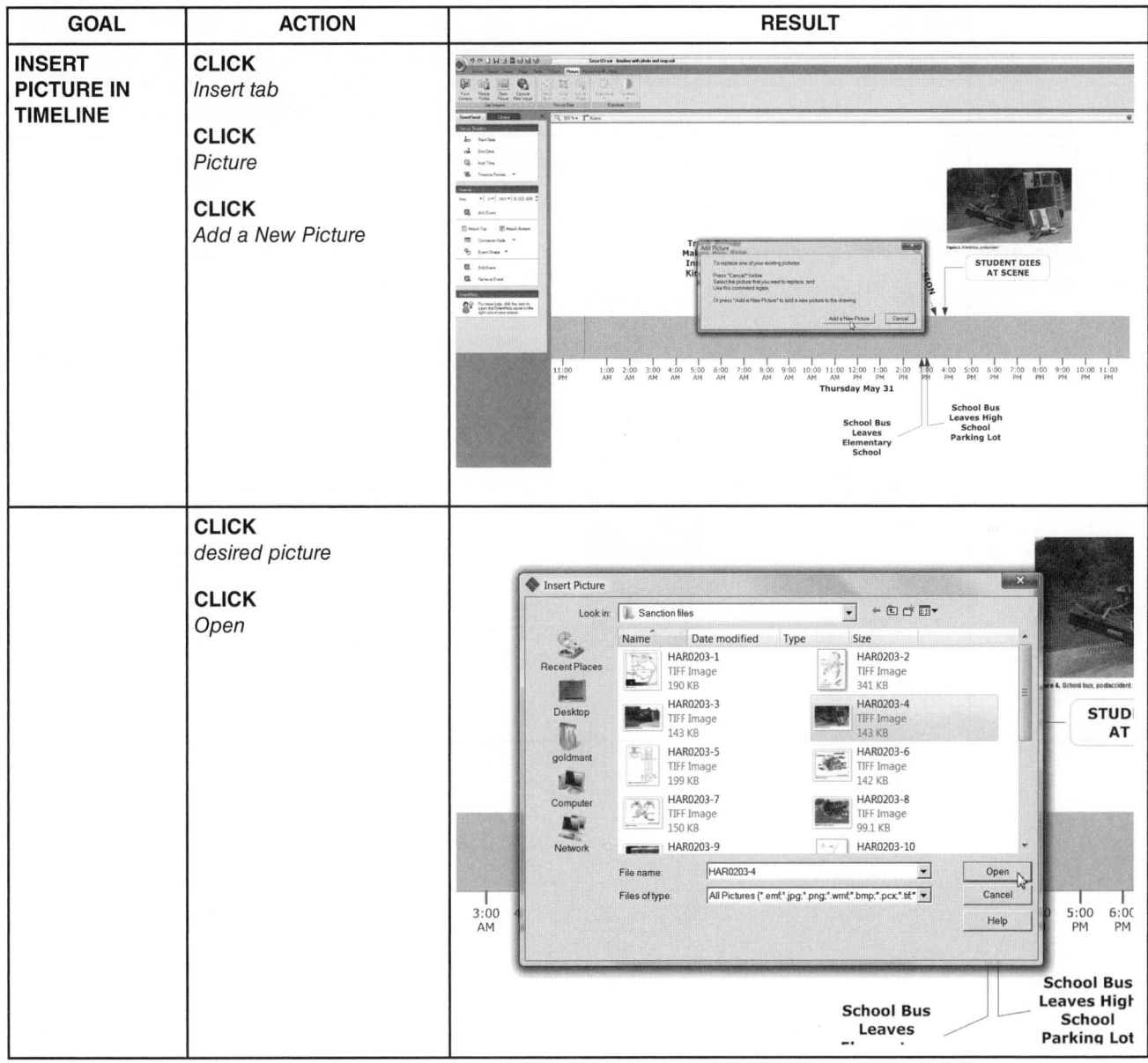
	CLICK *desired picture* **CLICK** *Open*	

(continued)

GOAL	ACTION	RESULT
DOWNLOAD AND INSERT MAP IN TIMELINE	**CLICK** *Insert tab* **CLICK** *Map* **TYPE** *desired map location* **CLICK** *Go* **CLICK** *Import to SmartDraw* **RESIZE** *and place as desired*	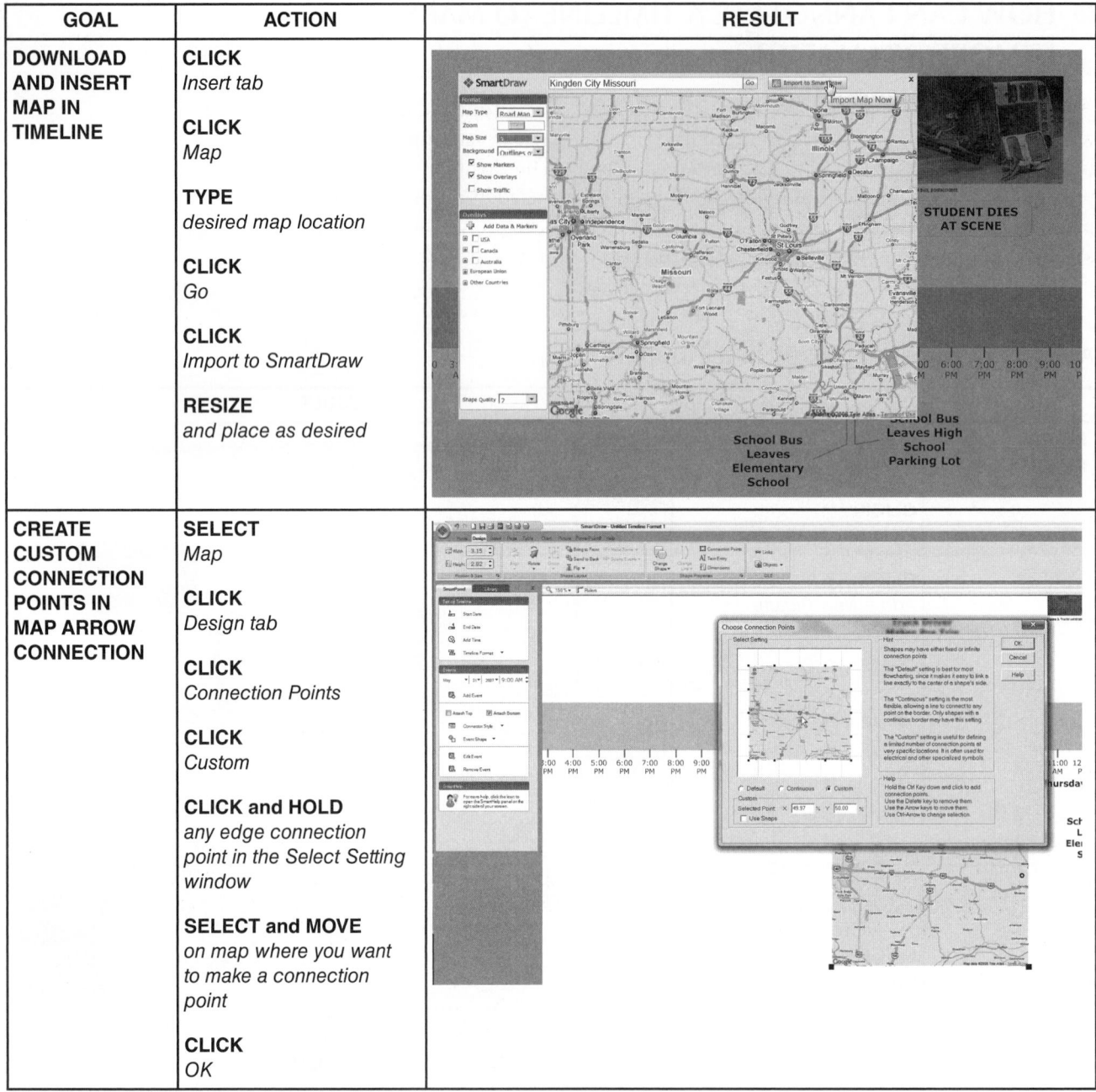
CREATE CUSTOM CONNECTION POINTS IN MAP ARROW CONNECTION	**SELECT** *Map* **CLICK** *Design tab* **CLICK** *Connection Points* **CLICK** *Custom* **CLICK and HOLD** *any edge connection point in the Select Setting window* **SELECT and MOVE** *on map where you want to make a connection point* **CLICK** *OK*	

(continued)

GOAL	ACTION	RESULT
DRAW LINE FROM MAP TO TIMELINE	**CLICK** *Home tab* **CLICK** *Arrowheads* **CLICK** *Right* **CREATE** arrow from map to timeline **SELECT** *Arrow* **RIGHT CLICK** to open menu **CLICK** *Color* **CLICK** *Line Thickness*	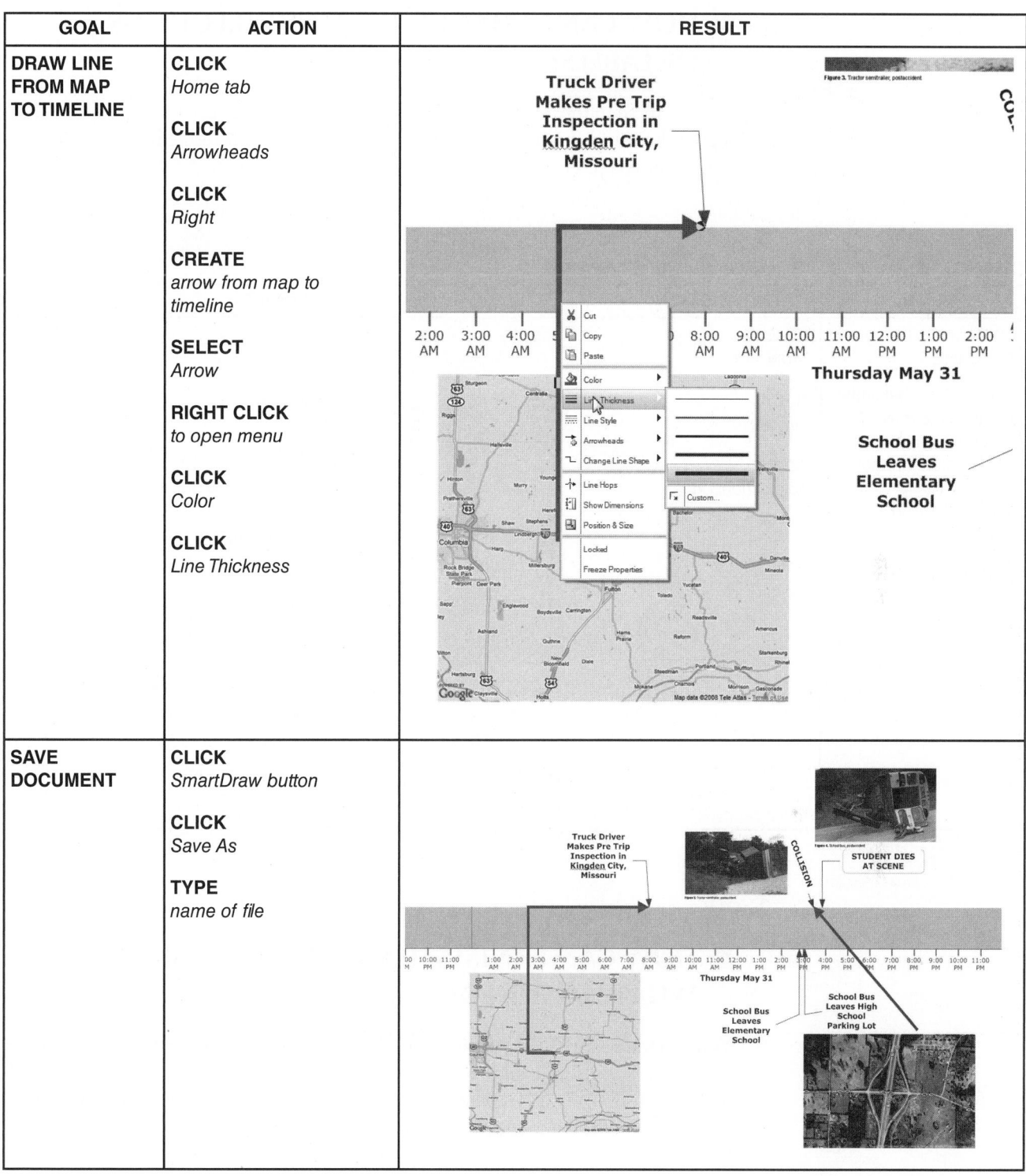
SAVE DOCUMENT	**CLICK** *SmartDraw button* **CLICK** *Save As* **TYPE** name of file	

■ HOW CAN I CHANGE THE LINE DIRECTIONS OF LABELS?

Arrows in timelines have selection handles. Depending on the type of label selected these may be fixed as a straight arrow, or have intermediate handles that can be moved to change direction or shape.

CHANGING ARROW DIRECTIONS AND SHAPES

GOAL	ACTION	RESULT
EDIT LINES IN TIMELINE NOTE: The label lines in a timeline may be edited by using the end or middle handles to move, rotate, or bend the line.	**SELECT** *Arrow* **CLICK** *handles* **MOVE** *to new location*	

■ HOW CAN I ANIMATE AN EXHIBIT TO SHOW WHAT HAPPENED?

Your client says the other car struck her car while it was parked. Creating an animated recreation would be nice, but the case does not justify the cost of a full-scale animation. SmartDraw enables you to create a step-by-step presentation of the position of the vehicles based on testimony or depositions.

Animating an Accident Presentation

GOAL	ACTION	RESULT
CREATE ANIMATION SHOWING ACCIDENT FROM ACCIDENT SCENE VISUAL **NOTE:** This tutorial requires SmartDraw VP or the previous version of SmartDraw (legal version).	**CLICK** *Legal tab* **CLICK** *Auto accident reconstruction* **CLICK** *4 way Intersection Accident* **CLICK** *PowerPoint® tab*	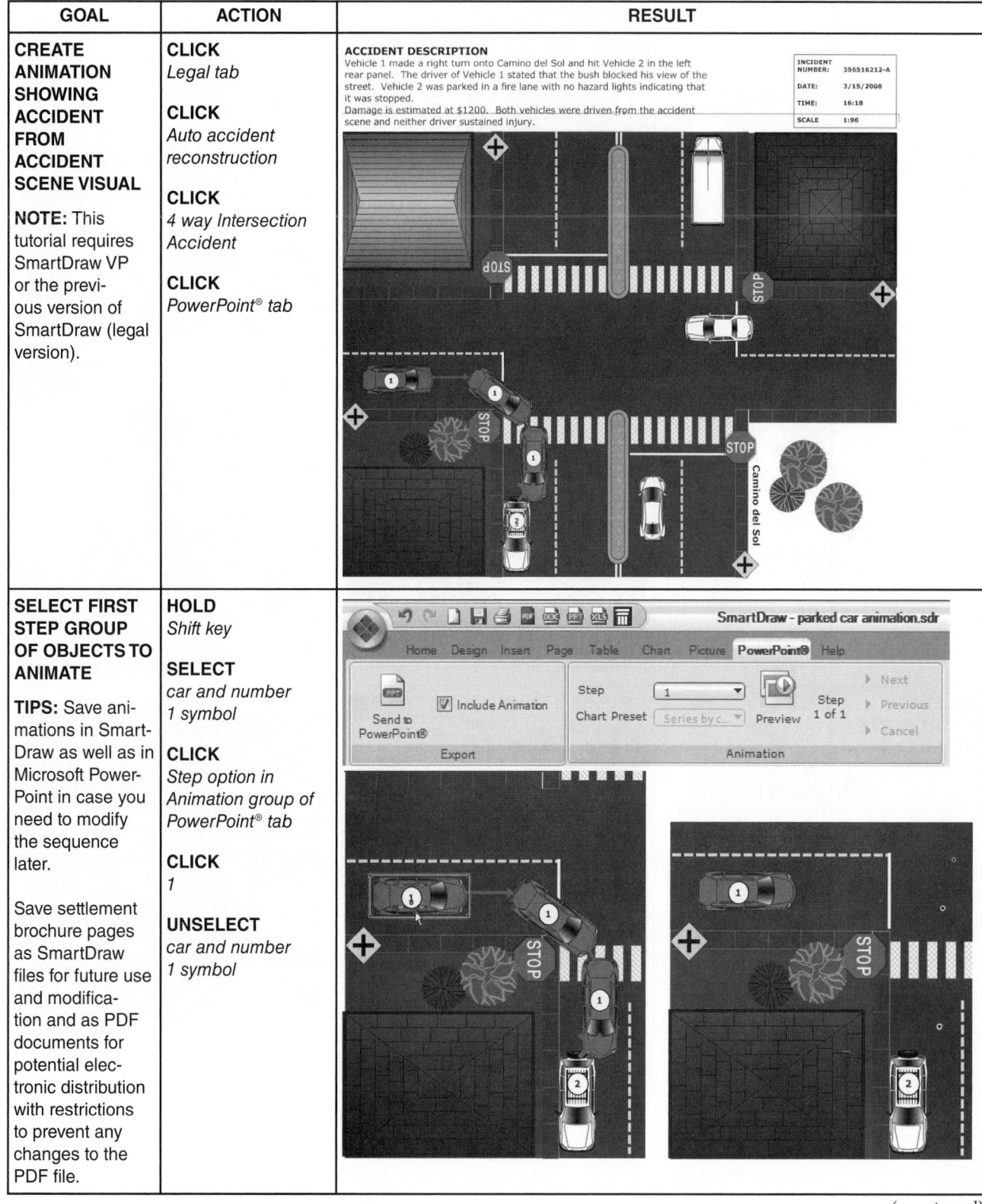
SELECT FIRST STEP GROUP OF OBJECTS TO ANIMATE **TIPS:** Save animations in SmartDraw as well as in Microsoft Power-Point in case you need to modify the sequence later. Save settlement brochure pages as SmartDraw files for future use and modification and as PDF documents for potential electronic distribution with restrictions to prevent any changes to the PDF file.	**HOLD** *Shift key* **SELECT** *car and number 1 symbol* **CLICK** *Step option in Animation group of PowerPoint® tab* **CLICK** *1* **UNSELECT** *car and number 1 symbol*	

(*continued*)

GOAL	ACTION	RESULT
SELECT SECOND STEP OBJECT TO ANIMATE	**SELECT** *arrow symbol* **CLICK** *Step option in Animation group of PowerPoint® tab* **CLICK** *2* **UNSELECT** *Arrow symbol*	
SELECT THIRD STEP GROUP OF OBJECTS TO ANIMATE	**SELECT** *car and number symbol* **CLICK** *Step option in Animation group of PowerPoint® tab* **CLICK** *3* **UNSELECT** *car and number symbol*	
SELECT FOURTH STEP OBJECT TO ANIMATE	**SELECT** *arrow symbol* **CLICK** *Step option in Animation group of PowerPoint® tab* **CLICK** *4* **UNSELECT** *arrow symbol*	

(continued)

GOAL	ACTION	RESULT
SELECT FIFTH STEP GROUP OF OBJECTS TO ANIMATE	**SELECT** *car and number symbol* **CLICK** *Step option in Animation group of PowerPoint® tab* **CLICK** *5* **UNSELECT** *car and number symbol*	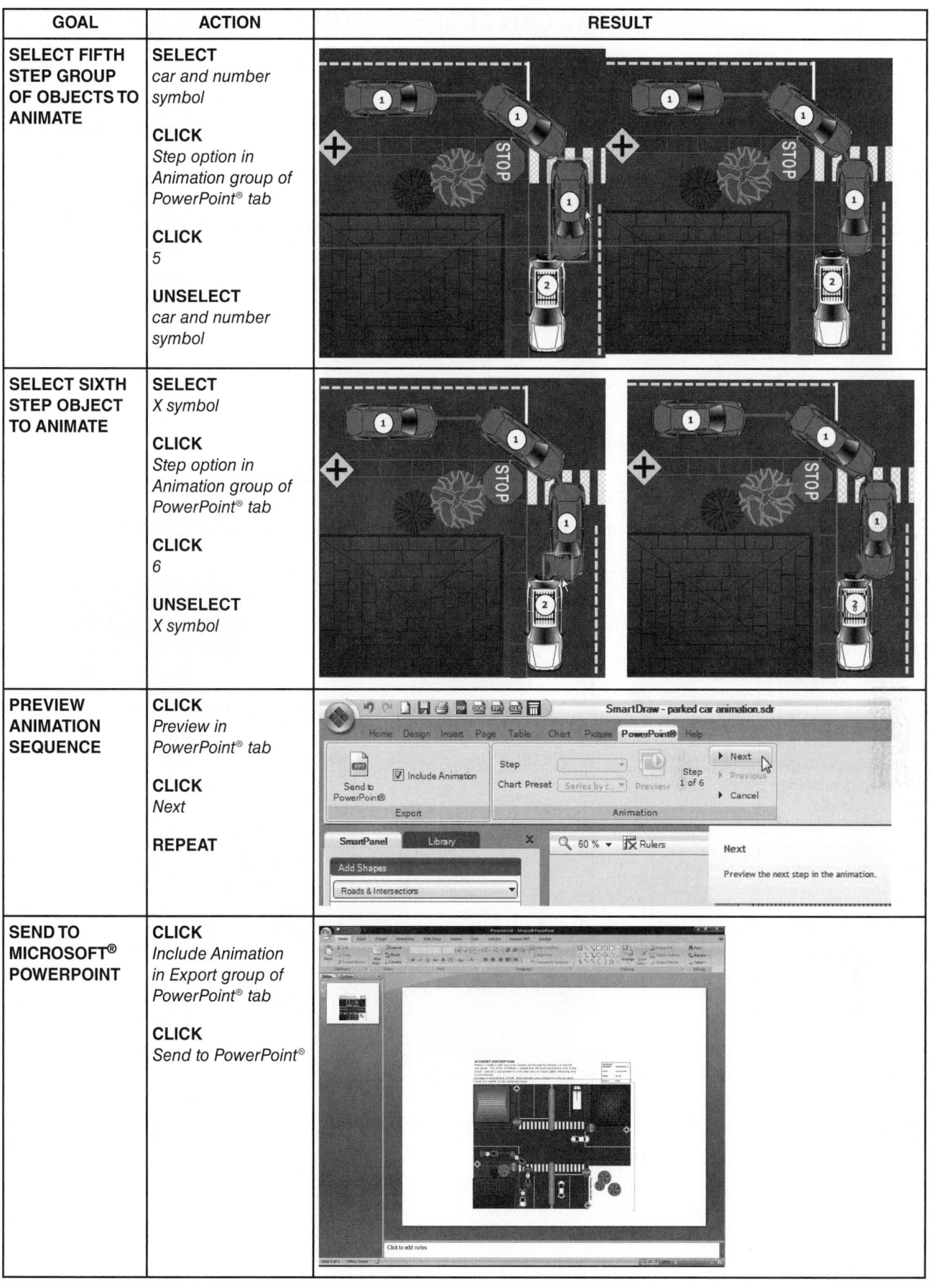
SELECT SIXTH STEP OBJECT TO ANIMATE	**SELECT** *X symbol* **CLICK** *Step option in Animation group of PowerPoint® tab* **CLICK** *6* **UNSELECT** *X symbol*	
PREVIEW ANIMATION SEQUENCE	**CLICK** *Preview in PowerPoint® tab* **CLICK** *Next* **REPEAT**	
SEND TO MICROSOFT® POWERPOINT	**CLICK** *Include Animation in Export group of PowerPoint® tab* **CLICK** *Send to PowerPoint®*	

■ HOW CAN I USE SMARTDRAW TO CREATE A SETTLEMENT BROCHURE?

A properly prepared settlement brochure can be an effective way to obtain the best possible settlement before trial. The exhibits in the brochure can also be enlarged and used as trial exhibits if the case does not settle. Photographs of injuries can show the visible signs of an injury, but not the underlying cause of the pain and suffering. An anatomically correct exhibit can show the specific body part affected by the injury, such as a spinal injury. SmartDraw Healthcare includes a wide assortment of medically accurate drawings that can be submitted in a brochure to the insurance company or opposing counsel, or enlarged for use as exhibits in trial. One of the obvious advantages of creating brochures is avoiding the cost of buying large exhibits or storing a collection.

CREATING A SETTLEMENT BROCHURE

GOAL	ACTION	RESULT
CREATE COVER **TIP:** Exhibits in a brochure can also be printed poster size or used in electronic format in trial as exhibits. Exhibits in brochures can also be printed poster size or used in electronic format as exhibits in trial. Local printer companies can provide the desired file format for large-scale printing.	**SELECT** *Blank Flyer template* **OR** **OPEN** *SmartDraw document* **IMPORT** *photographs and images*	 SETTLEMENT BROCHURE

(continued)

GOAL	ACTION	RESULT
PERSONALIZE	**ADD** *text*	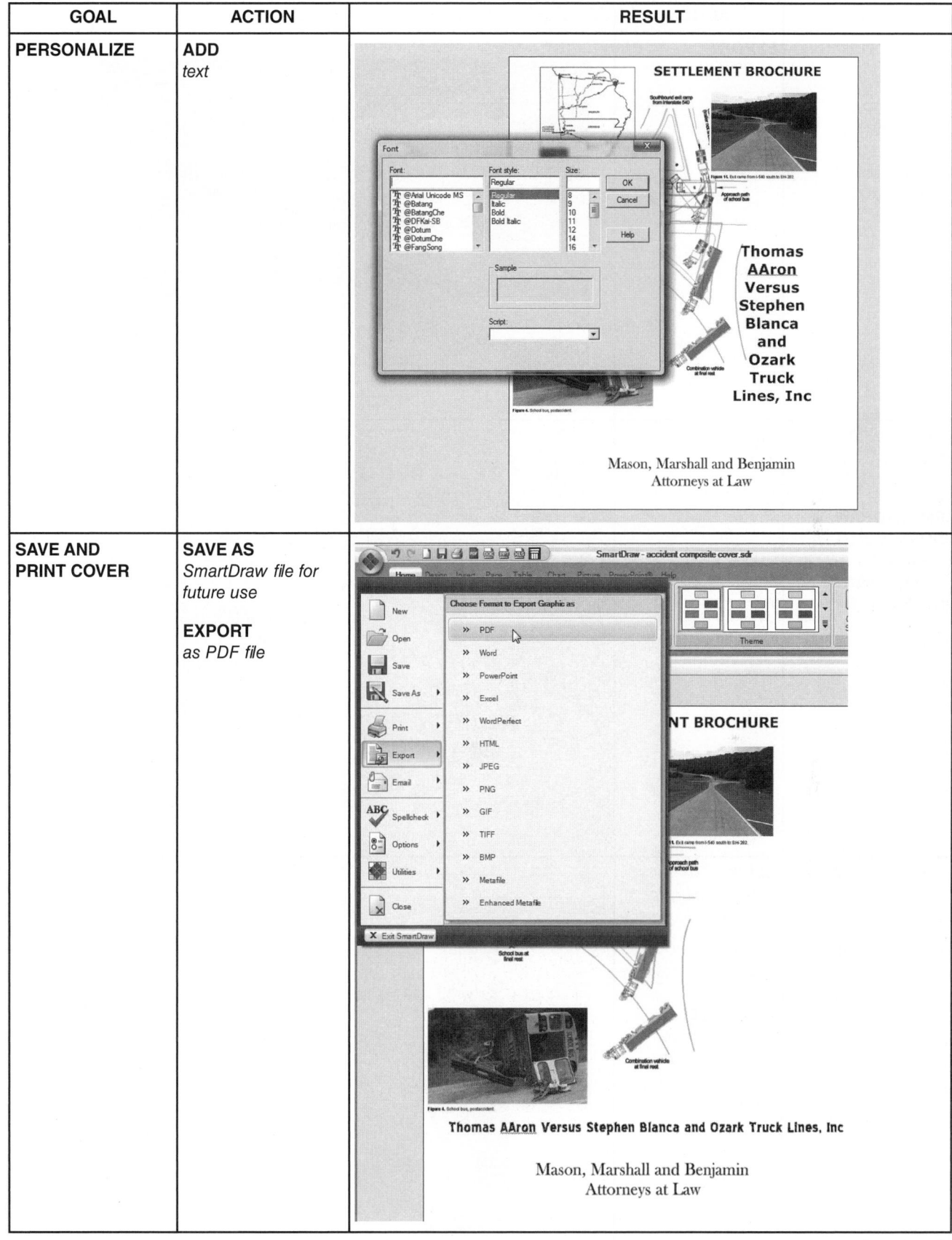
SAVE AND PRINT COVER	**SAVE AS** *SmartDraw file for future use* **EXPORT** *as PDF file*	

(continued)

GOAL	ACTION	RESULT
ADD PICTURES **EXPORT SMARTDRAW DOCUMENTS TO ADD TO SETTLEMENT BROCHURE**	**EXPORT** *as PDF file*	 **SCHOOL BUS AFTER ACCIDENT**
ADD ANNOTATED MAPS **EXPORT SMARTDRAW DOCUMENTS TO ADD TO SETTLEMENT BROCHURE**	**EXPORT** *as PDF file*	
CREATE EXHIBITS **EXPORT SMARTDRAW DOCUMENTS TO ADD TO SETTLEMENT BROCHURE**	**CLICK** *Personal Injury in Document Browser* **CLICK** *Spine* **ANNOTATE** *by adding arrow symbols and text showing area of injury*	

(continued)

GOAL	ACTION	RESULT
CREATE EXHIBITS **EXPORT SMARTDRAW DOCUMENTS TO ADD TO SETTLEMENT BROCHURE**	**ANNOTATE** *by adding arrow symbols and text showing area of injury*	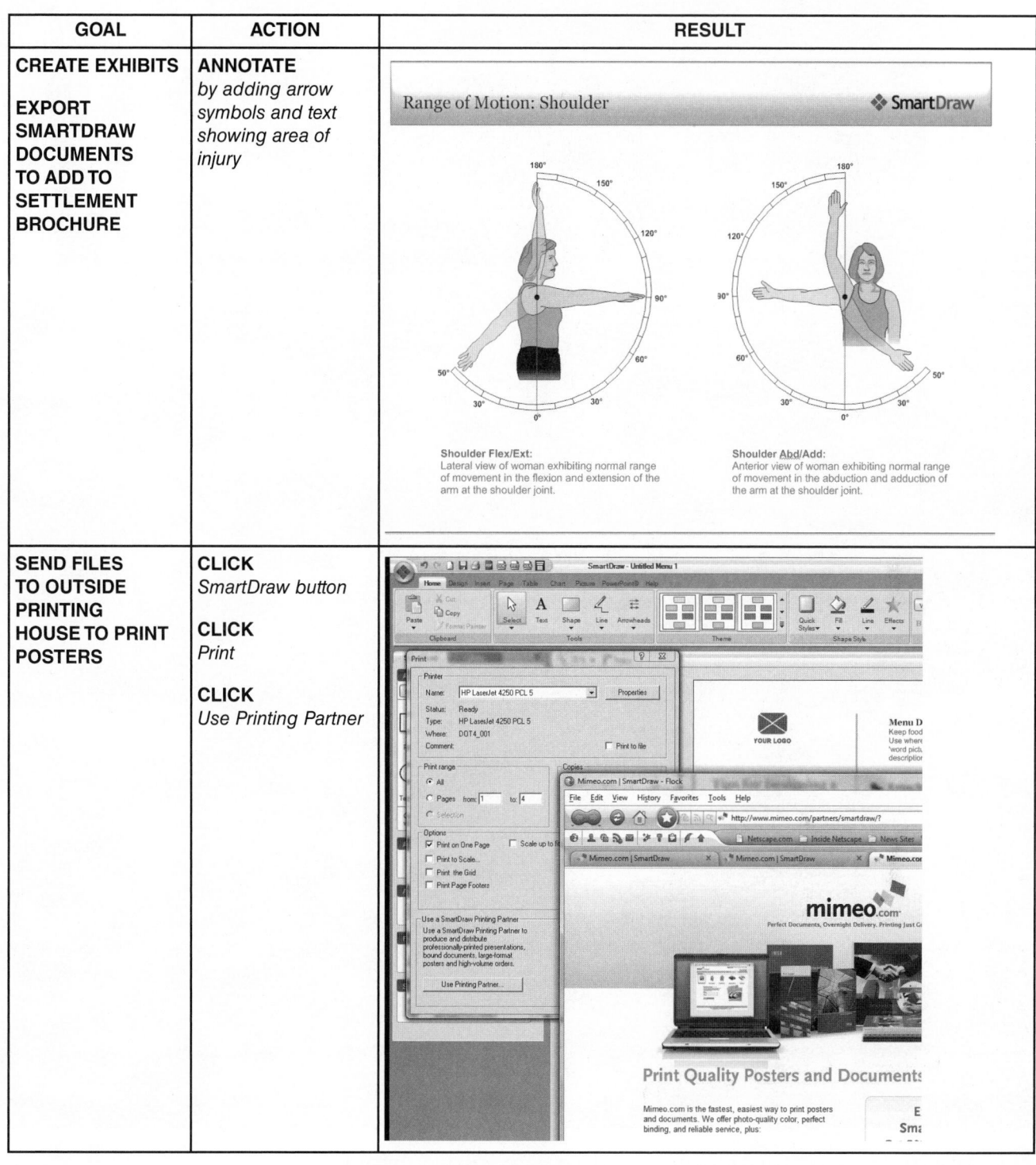
SEND FILES TO OUTSIDE PRINTING HOUSE TO PRINT POSTERS	**CLICK** *SmartDraw button* **CLICK** *Print* **CLICK** *Use Printing Partner*	

"Simplicity means the achievement of maximum effect
with minimum means."

—*Dr. Koichi Kawana, Architect*

Electronic Trial Presentation

CHAPTER 17

OPENING SCENARIO

The trial teams handling the school bus and airplane crash cases were having their regular meeting to discuss common issues in preparing the cases for trial. Efforts to settle the cases had not yet met with any success, and it was time to finalize the trial materials. Owen Mason informed everyone that the school bus case had been assigned to the new, high-tech courtroom. This assignment left Owen both relieved, and concerned.

The technology consultant who had been sitting in on the case meeting warned that the electronic courtroom was both a blessing and a curse. Shocked, Ethan Benjamin looked at her and asked, "How could having the latest technology be a problem?" She calmly told him that while it is nice to have the latest toys, the jury would expect the toys to entertain them, like the court cases they see on television. Owen mentioned that he had been meeting with another technologist to determine the cost of using the multimedia equipment. With a small trial budget and potentially a lot of evidence, it might be more than they could afford, especially with two major cases coming to trial at the same time. Ariel Marshall, the third partner, commented, "At least I don't have that problem with my case, because they put us in the large courtroom where the only electronic equipment is the wall outlets."

LEARNING OBJECTIVES

After studying this chapter, you should be able to:

1. Explain how presentation software is used in litigation.

2. Create a case presentation.

VIDEO INTRODUCTION _____

fessor Thomas F. Goldman, Es

ELECTRONIC TRIAL PRESENTATION

After watching the video in MyLegalStudiesLab, answer the following questions.

1. How can trial presentation programs help the trial attorneys achieve their primary goal?
2. What are trial presentation programs?

■ INTRODUCTION TO ELECTRONIC TRIAL PRESENTATION

Growing numbers of courts are allowing litigants to use computer-based display systems at trial. Some courts provide these systems for the litigants. Modern trial presentations frequently include videotaped depositions, photos, videos, and computer simulations. These may be shown on projection screens, personal monitors, or large-panel displays. Some view these multimedia presentations as nothing more than the logical outgrowth of older display technology such as overhead projectors, slide projectors, and films.

trial presentation programs
Computer program that organizes and controls documents, depositions, photographs, and other data as exhibits for trial, and displays them.

Managing the hundreds of individual multimedia elements in the courtroom can be a nightmare unless they are organized and easily accessible. Sanction by Sanction Solutions, TrialDirector by inData, and similar **trial presentation programs** allow the legal team to organize and manage the documents, depositions, photographs, and other data, and then display them when needed during depositions or trial.

VIDEO ADVICE FROM THE FIELD _____

Mike Hahn—Managing Director, Sanction Solutions
A discussion on the use of trial presentation software.
After watching the video in MyLegalStudiesLab answer the following questions.

1. What is trial presentation software?
2. Should every case presentation use multimedia presentations?
3. Can trial presentation software be used by the litigator without any support in court?

PRACTICE TIP

SUPPORTED FORMATS

Not all native file formats can be used with all trial presentation programs, just as not all music files can be played on every brand of portable music player. It is thus wise, early in trial preparation, to confirm that all the file formats being used are compatible with the chosen trial presentation program so as to avoid a rush to convert or find suitable replacements as the trial date nears.

■ USING TECHNOLOGY TO PRESENT THE CASE

LEARNING OBJECTIVE 1
Explain how presentation software is used in litigation.

The primary goal of every trial attorney is to make the best possible presentation of the case and obtain a favorable verdict. The most effective method may be a simple handwritten chart that counsel creates during the trial to show the evidence supporting each individual element of the case. At the end of the trial, this chart provides a summary of the evidence.

More frequently, however, effective presentation requires the use of photographs, videos, computer simulations, and other multimedia elements that will appeal to a jury of citizens who have been raised in the television era. They will expect to see in the courtroom what they have seen in the real or fictitious cases they have watched on television.

Presentation Programs

Trial presentation programs allow different types of media—including still photographs, text documents, video and sound clips, and computer simulations—to be organized and displayed using a single program. Consider the different types of potential evidence and the number of programs that would be needed to show all of these media types. For example, word processor documents would need the original word processor program; videos would require a multimedia player like Windows Media Player; and PDF files would need Nuance or Adobe Reader. Trial presentation programs provide all the necessary viewers in one package.

These presentation programs, such as Sanction by Sanction Solutions and TrialDirector by inData, are multifaceted. As exhibit management tools, they provide a single point of access for exhibits of different types, much like Microsoft Explorer allows access to different items on a computer or network. This capability is shown in the Tree View of available files in Exhibit 17.1. These programs allow existing files to be presented with no more effort than copying them into the program data file and making a selection for presentation.

Selected files can then be previewed on the attorneys' personal computer monitors before projecting the items onto the court's presentation system, as

Exhibit 17.1 Sanction with case file images

Exhibit 17.2 Preview and presentation screens with annotated document

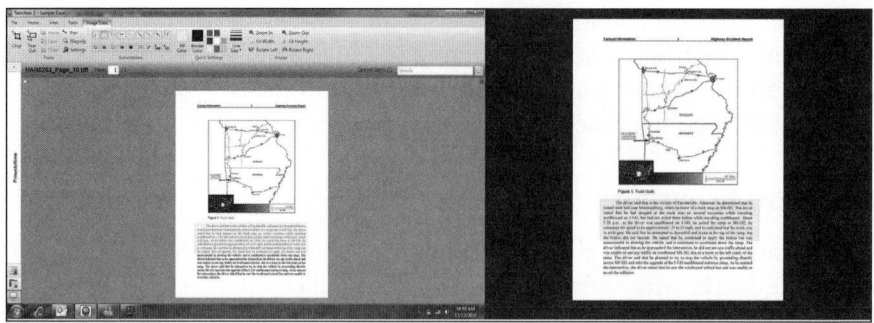

shown in Exhibit 17.2. Documents can then be annotated using highlighting, arrows, or underlining.

The advantage of these advanced presentation programs is their ability to work with a variety of file types, including video, which is an increasingly popular tool in the courtroom. Video presentations provide a convenient method of showing prerecorded depositions of witnesses, particularly experts who might not be available on short notice to appear in a trial. They are also used for elderly and very young witnesses who cannot travel or for whom the trial itself might be too emotionally upsetting. A videotaped deposition of a witness may be presented with a written transcript displayed simultaneously in a split screen, as shown in Exhibit 17.3. The transcript may be highlighted to focus on specific questions and answers, or it may be annotated. For example, the transcript may be used to point out what the witness has said in previous testimony.

Exhibit 17.3 Sanction video transcript screen

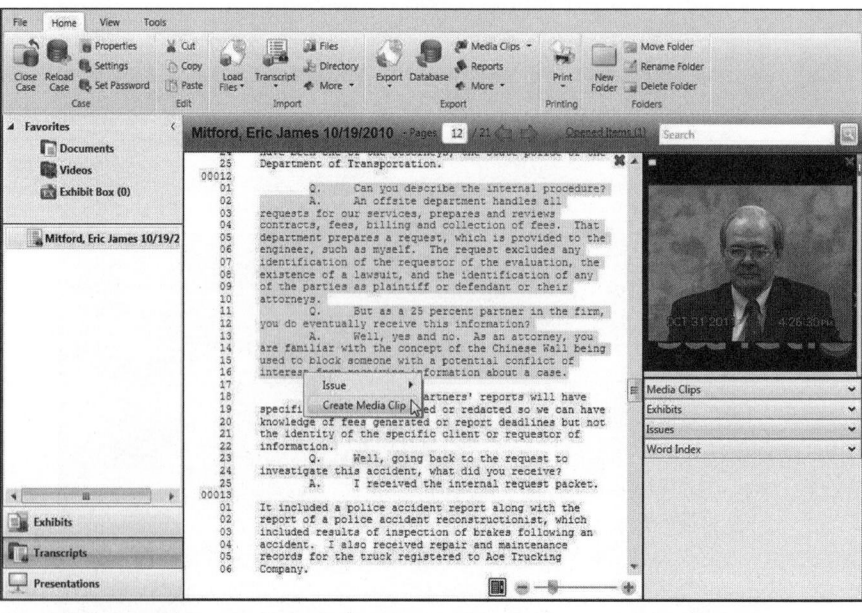

Bringing It All Together

Presentation programs like Sanction and TrialDirector allow the legal team to assemble all of the electronically storable evidence in one program. Photographs, video, document images, transcripts, and sound files can all be preloaded into the program for use in trial. In courtrooms equipped with display equipment, it is as simple as hooking up the laptop to the system.

With everything stored electronically, it is not difficult to find and show almost anything at a moment's notice when testimony or strategy changes. With coordination between the trial attorney and the litigation support team, the presentation may appear flawless.

VIDEO ADVICE FROM THE FIELD

Jennifer McCoy—National Litigation Support Coordinator
Discusses the role of paralegal in trial presentations.
After watching the video in MyLegalStudiesLab answer the following questions.

What is the role of the paralegal in trial presentation?

However, using presentation software, as with using any software, requires some training and practice. When used in a public forum like the courtroom, it is best to take advantage of available training and refresher courses to stay up to speed. In some cases, it may be appropriate to bring in a trial support consultant to manage the system and free up the litigation support staff for other trial functions.

Another advantage of these programs is their flexibility. They can be used to prepare and deliver the graphic presentation electronically using a computer, with or without a projector, and to print out paper copies for distribution.

PRACTICE TIP

Before creating a case, make sure all of the items you wish to use are in formats that are supported by the selected presentation program. Make copies or move all the items into a separate folder or groups of folders for easy access and use.

◼ CREATE A COURT PRESENTATION

Setting up a basic presentation requires an understanding of a few basic Windows tools, such as creating new folders, copying and pasting files, and "dragging and dropping" files and folders from one location to another. In Windows, using the copy and paste functions leaves the files in the original location and pastes a copy of the file in the new location—the original is not moved or deleted. On the other hand, the drag-and-drop method moves the file from one location to another, deleting the file from the original location.

When using Windows, it is always recommended that the copy and paste method be used, just as it is always recommended that the Save As function be used instead of the Save function to avoid overwriting or erasing the original files. In Sanction, either method (copy and paste or drag and drop)

LEARNING OBJECTIVE 2
Create a case presentation.

leaves the original file in its original location. Documents, images, videos, and transcripts can thus be safely added to the Sanction case by dragging and dropping them from a folder on the computer or memory media, because the drag-and-drop feature in Sanction sets up a link to the original location rather than actually removes the file. This is similar to the way document management programs set up links to the document, or the way a web address in a search engine tells the program where to look, without changing the file or its location.

PRACTICE TIP

Making backups is critical for safety and security. Remember this author's adage: "If anything can go wrong, it will, and at the worst possible moment—in the middle of a trial." Many attorneys will bring a complete backup system to trial, including extra copies of electronic files or even extra computers. In smaller cases, files may be backed up using removable media cards and thumb drives. In larger cases, they may be backed up on relatively inexpensive portable hard drives.

The first step in creating a presentation is to create a new case, as shown in Exhibit 17.4.

Items for each category may be dragged from their original folder on the computer. In this case, items are dragged from the Sanction Demo Folder on a removable thumb drive to a location in the program, as shown in Exhibit 17.5. Documents are then dragged from a folder on the computer to the Documents category in Sanction or imported using the import function in Sanction.

PRACTICE TIP

Multiple files can be selected in Windows Explorer by holding down the Crtl (control) key and pointing and clicking on each desired file with the left mouse button.

Again, dragging the individual files to a Sanction case does not actually move them; it only creates a link to the location for the program to use when

Exhibit 17.4 Creating a new case

Exhibit 17.5 Adding multiple documents from Windows folder on computer to new case in Sanction

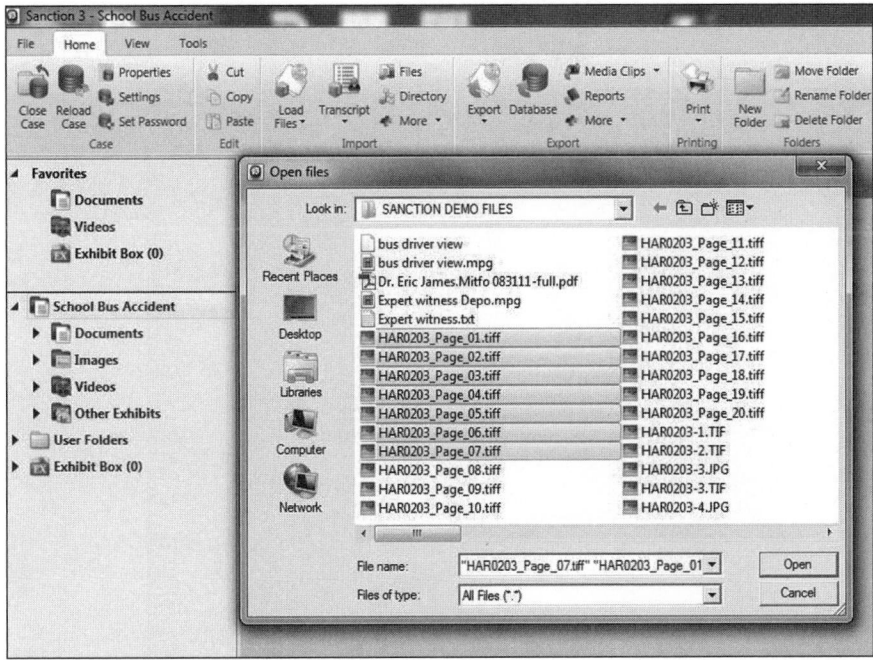

you want to view those items. In this sample case, all the desired items that will be used have been moved to one folder on a removable memory device. When the Sanction program is run, the memory media must be in the computer for the program to access the link to the files.

When items have been entered into the program, they can be previewed by highlighting the item in the Sanction Tree View, as in Exhibit 17.6, which shows the cover page of the NTSB report of the school bus–truck accident in the preview screen and a thumbnail view.

Organizing Files in Sanction

A presentation may contain any of the various files loaded into Sanction. To create a presentation in Sanction, desired items from the exhibits listed in the Tree View may be selected and dragged and dropped to the desired presentation using the mouse. Items that are needed for a particular presentation can be set up in advance as an individual collection of presentation items by dragging the items to the presentation folder. Depending on the case, a number of different presentations may be created—for example, a presentation may be created for a specific witness, a particular legal theory, or the opening and closing statements.

Special Features and Tools

As with all sophisticated programs, Sanction has numerous tools and features. For example, Sanction has a set of tools for marking up and annotating items, as shown in Exhibit 17.7. This image shows a number of potential annotations and the menu (selected with a right mouse click) used to select and change an annotation.

PRACTICE TIP

The optimal process is to have the data files on an internal hard drive on the computer, *not* on the flash drive. This prevents data being left behind.

Exhibit 17.6 Sanction Tree View with document and thumbnail view

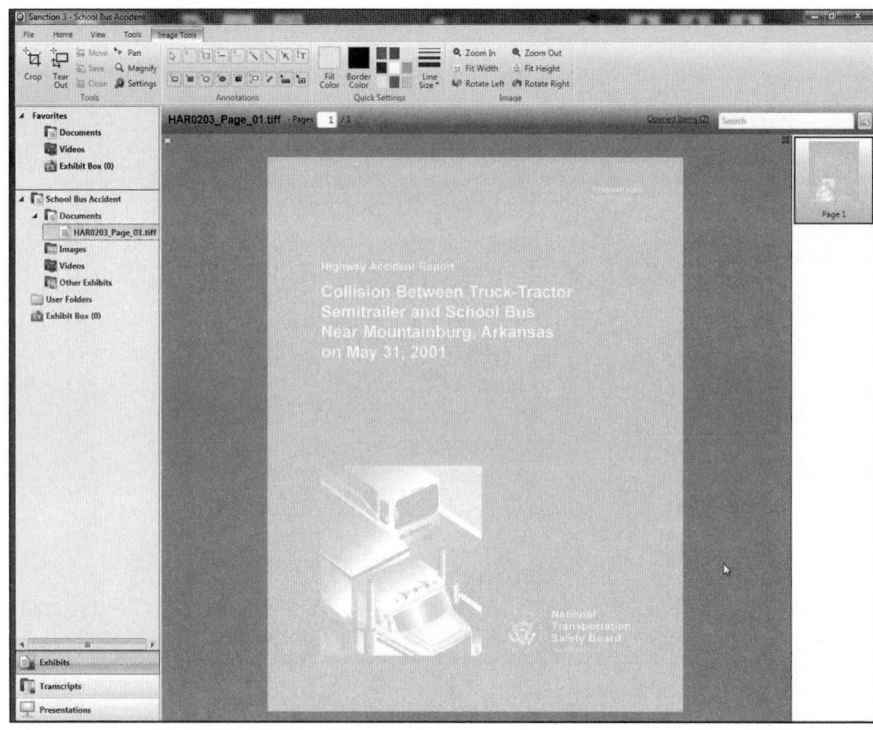

Exhibit 17.7 Annotation tools and menus

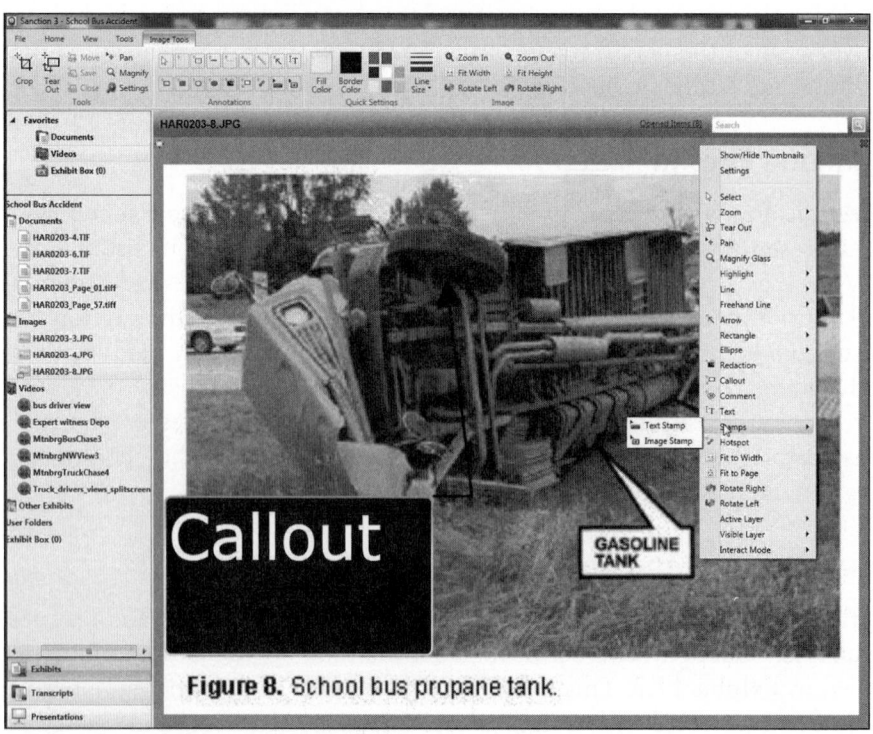

CONCEPT REVIEW AND REINFORCEMENT

KEY TERM

trial presentation programs 480

CHAPTER SUMMARY

Introduction to Electronic Trial Presentation	More and more courts are providing, or allowing litigants to bring into the courtroom, computer-based electronic display systems for use in trial.

Using Technology to Present the Case	Litigation presentation programs, like Sanction by Sanction Solutions and TrialDirector by inData, are multifaceted trial presentation programs that offer a comprehensive approach to presenting all types of exhibits in the courtroom, including documents, photographs, graphic images, video presentations, and recorded depositions.
	    Not all native formats can be used in all trial presentation programs.
	    It is wise, early in the preparation process, to check the formats supported by the trial presentation program selected for trial to ensure compatibility.

Bringing It All Together	Presentation programs like Sanction and TrialDirector allow the legal team to assemble all of the electronically storable evidence in one program. Photographs, video, document images, transcripts, and sound files can all be preloaded into the program for use in trial. In courtrooms equipped with display equipment, it is as simple as hooking the laptop up to the system.
Create a Court Presentation	Setting up a basic presentation requires an understanding of a few basic Windows tools, including the use of Windows Explorer to find files, create new folders, copy and paste, and "drag and drop" to move files from one folder to another. Dragging the individual files to a Sanction case does not actually move them, but only creates a link to the location for the program to use when you want to find those items.
Preparing a Presentation	A presentation may contain any of the case items (data) in the program. Items that are desired for a particular presentation can be set up in advance as an individual collection of presentation items.

REVIEW QUESTIONS AND EXERCISES

1. Who determines what equipment or systems may be used in a particular courtroom? How can any conflicts with this person be avoided prior to trial?
2. What are some factors to be considered in bringing a technology expert into a trial to help with the presentation? How can this expert help the trial attorney work more efficiently and effectively?
3. What is required in order to use existing images and documents with a trial presentation program? Why is it useful to have an integrated trial presentation program?
4. What is the advantage of using video as part of a trial presentation? What features of a trial presentation program can enhance a video deposition and aid the jury's understanding of the testimony?

5. How can a trial presentation program help an attorney manage objections to evidence being presented?

6. What is the advantage of having a trial consultant handle the trial presentation program?

7. Why is copy and paste preferred over drag and drop in Windows Explorer?

8. What happens to files that are dragged and dropped into the Sanction program? How does this feature help to safeguard data?

9. Why is it important to have backups of trial materials? Why do some trial lawyers carry backup equipment to trial?

10. How are individual presentation sets created in Sanction? How is this feature useful to a trial attorney?

11. How can annotation tools be used in Sanction? Give three examples of annotations that may be made to three different kinds of evidence.

BUILDING YOUR PARALEGAL SKILLS

INTERNET AND TECHNOLOGY EXERCISES

1. Search the Internet for your local court's website on trial technology. What information is provided on the website? What suggestions would you make to improve the website?

2. Locate any website for local judges' rules on technology in their courtrooms. What technology is permitted? What advice would you give to an attorney preparing to try a case in one of those courtrooms?

3. Conduct a search of the Internet for multimedia trial consultants. Create a table to compare the services provided by each.

VIDEO CASE STUDIES

EXPERT WITNESS DEPOSITION

Watch this video case study in MyLegalStudiesLab and answer the following questions.

1. How can the testimony of the expert witness be presented to the jury using trial presentation software?

2. What feature of the trial presentation program can be used to highlight significant testimony for the jury?

CHAPTER OPENING SCENARIO CASE STUDY

Use the Opening Scenario for this chapter to answer the following questions.

1. Prepare an outline of the potential multimedia elements that might be used in trial. Provide a list of options for presenting each piece of evidence.

2. Prepare a memo explaining how a trial presentation program might be used to present the case. Give a recommendation to the trial team as to whether they should adopt a particular system.

3. What are the items that will be needed in order to use a presentation program? What training resources are available?

4. Answer this question raised by one of the attorneys: "Can we present the case without a presentation program?" Explain how using separate applications or software for different types of files creates additional complications for the trial team.

5. How can using a program like Sanction help manage information during a trial? How can it be used to adapt to changes in evidence or legal theories in the middle of a trial?

CONTINUING CASES AND EXERCISES

1. For the assigned case study from Appendix II:
   a. From the website www.pearsonhighered.com/goldman, download and install on your computer the demo version of Sanction.
   b. Download the Sanction Demo Files to a removable memory device.
   c. Use Sanction to set up a new case.
   d. Prepare a presentation for Case Study A in Appendix II.

BUILDING YOUR PROFESSIONAL PORTFOLIO

Prepare a policy on access to the information in the trial presentation program. Cite any local case law or ethics opinions on confidentiality, privilege, and work product.

Forms

1. Obtain any forms necessary to preauthorize or bring audiovisual equipment into the courthouse.
2. Prepare a template for a trial equipment checklist.

Procedures

Prepare a step-by-step procedure for bringing trial presentation equipment into your jurisdiction's federal and state courts.

Contacts and Resources

1. Prepare a contact list with email addresses, phone numbers, physical addresses, and mailing addresses of the technology contacts in the federal and state courts in your jurisdiction.
2. Prepare a contact list with email address, phone number, physical address, and mailing address of each individual judge's contact person who can advise on the judge's rules and procedures for that court.
3. Prepare a contact list with email addresses, phone numbers, physical addresses, and mailing addresses of the local trial presentation consultants in your area.
4. Prepare a contact list with email addresses, phone numbers, physical addresses, and mailing addresses of the local companies that rent or repair audiovisual equipment or computers.

sanction™

■ CREATING A TRIAL PRESENTATION

Trial presentation programs may be used to display different types of evidence and trial exhibits including photographs or written documents, videotaped depositions of witnesses not present in the courtroom, computer simulations, or videos showing how an accident happened, on large screens or multimedia monitors for identification by a witness or to the court.

Sanction is used to assemble all of the potential items to be presented: paper-based exhibits, text transcripts of depositions, video depositions, and simulation videos. It may also be used to annotate on the screen passages in documents, or show enlarged sections of documents for emphasis.

The school bus–truck accident case presented in the text and detailed in Appendix II is used in this short tutorial. The sample files of the related exhibits, computer simulations, videotaped deposition, and transcript may be download from MyLegalStudiesLab, www.mylegalstudieslab.com.

■ TUTORIAL DEMONSTRATION FILES

Before starting the tutorial: create a folder such as C:\Sanction Files on your computer, or on a removable storage media, for the sample files; then download all of these materials to that folder from MyLegalStudiesLab.

Files may be downloaded individually or using the compressed file that contains all the files. To open the compressed file requires an unzip program be installed on your computer, such as WinZip.

Tutorial Requirements

Minimum Hardware Requirements

PC Users.

	Minimum Configuration	Optimal Configuration
Processor	2GHz or faster Single Core	2GHz or faster Core2 Duo
Processor Memory	1GB RAM	4GB RAM
Operating System	Windows XP (Service Pack 3)	Windows XP or Windows 7
Data Storage	80GB Internal Hard Drive	160GB Internal Hard Drive
Video	128MB Video Display Card	256MB Video Display Card

MAC Users. To use this program on a MAC requires a Mac computer that can run PC software.

■ HOW DO I DOWNLOAD SANCTION FROM THE SANCTION SOLUTIONS WEBSITE?

When downloading the demo program your Internet browser may ask if you want to **save** the **program** first and later run it, or immediately **run** it on your computer. Depending on the speed of your Internet connection, the download may take from 1 to 10 minutes. It is recommended that you save the program and then run the program after closing your web browser and antivirus program. When you save the program, remember where you saved the program so you can locate it and install it at a later time.

For example, the location where the program is saved includes

Drive designation\Folder name\Filename

or

C: \Downloads\Sanction 3.exe

The location: C:\Downloads\Sanction 3.exe is called the **path.**

When you download the program, record the path for your computer below.

*Enter Drive:*_____: |

Enter download folder: _____\

File name: Sanction 3.exe

When you run the program it installs the actual program files, sets up a Sanction Solution folder in the Program folder of the computer, and adds necessary entries on your computer hard drive to allow it to run.

The program will run more efficiently if the sample files are also saved in a folder on the computer on which the Sanction program is installed.

However, if you are going to use Sanction with the sample case files on a removable storage media, it must be plugged into the computer each time you use the program. When you set up a case in Sanction, such as the School Bus–Truck case study, the program creates a path to the source of the sample files. For example, if you are using a Toshiba portable hard drive, Sanction will setup the path to the sample files on that device. Every time you use Sanction to review this School Bus–Truck case, the Toshiba portable hard drive would need to be accessible.

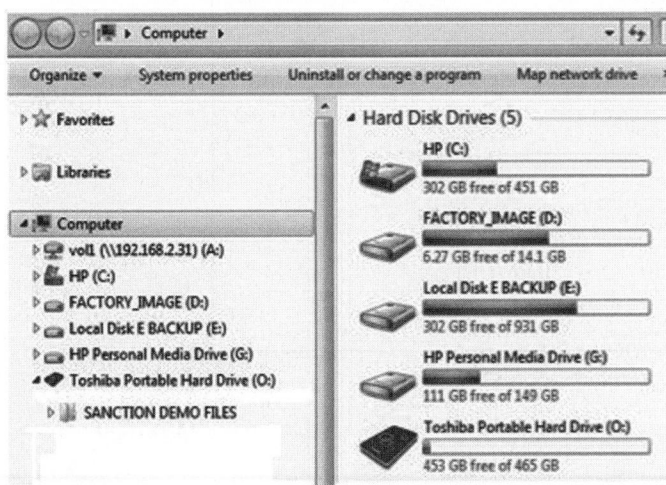

Downloading and Installing Sanction from Website

GOAL	ACTION	RESULT
DOWNLOAD SANCTION DEMO PROGRAM FROM THE SANCTION SOLUTIONS WEBSITE	**START** *Your Internet web browser* **ENTER** http://media.pearsoncmg .com/ph/chet/chet_goldman _techresources_1/ **CLICK** *Sanction icon tab* Follow instructions onwebsite	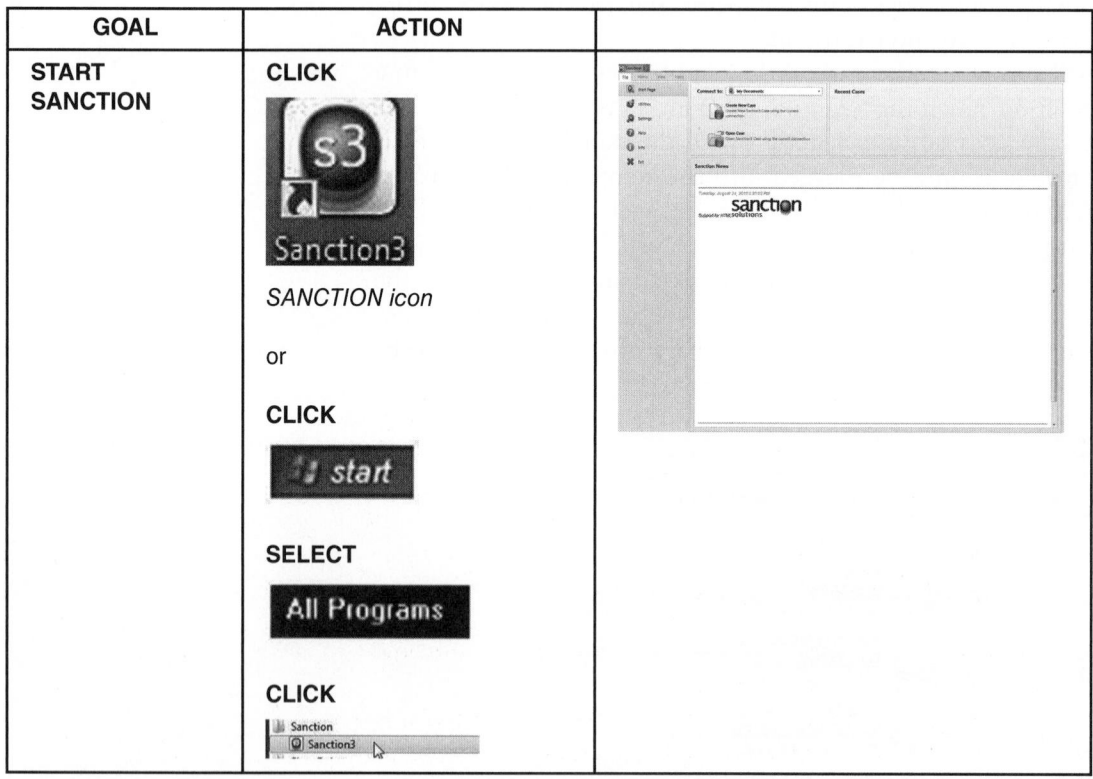

■ STARTING SANCTION

GOAL	ACTION	
START SANCTION	**CLICK** *SANCTION icon* or **CLICK** start **SELECT** All Programs **CLICK** Sanction Sanction3	

■ CREATING A NEW CASE

GOAL	ACTION	RESULT
CREATE A NEW CASE FILE IN SANCTION	**CLICK** *Open Case*	
ENTER NAME OF NEW CASE FILE	**TYPE** *School Bus* **CLICK** *Create*	

Exhibit 1 New case created in Sanction

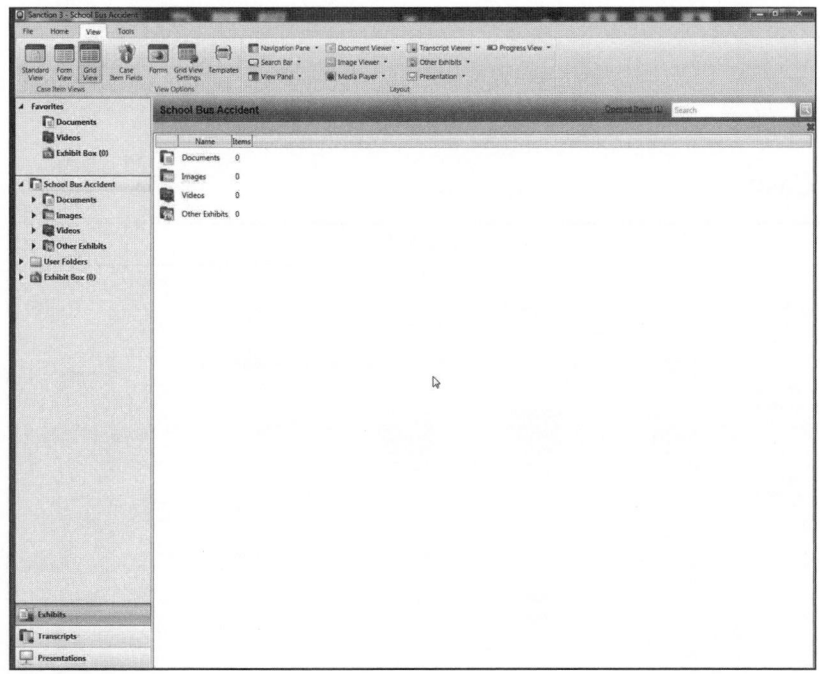

Adding Items to a Sanction Case for Presentation

Sanction divides the presentation elements into three main category folders: Exhibits, Transcripts, and Presentations.

Exhibits include documents, images, video, and other exhibits. Transcripts of deposition and trial are imported into the Transcripts folder. After adding exhibits and transcripts to a Sanction Case File they may be added to the specific Presentation folder for later use. Presentations folders are just convenient folders for sorting the different items that may be used in specific presentations such as that for a specific witness, an opening statement, or closing argument.

There are a number of different ways to add items to a Sanction case including the use of tab menu options and traditional Microsoft file selection, drag and drop.

You can add documents, images, videos, transcripts, and other exhibits that are in a computer format recognized by Sanction. Like other computer programs, Sanction must be able to recognize the file format to access it within the program. Sanction supports the following file formats:

Document types supported:	TIF, PDF
Image types supported:	JPG, GIF, BMP, PNG
Media types supported:	MPG, WAV, MP3

TIP
The Open Files window may be set to show the same files in detail or in icons. It may be easier to set your option to icons to locate files.

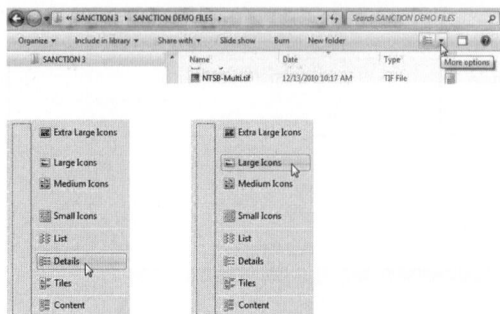

Adding Documents to a Sanction Case

GOAL	ACTION	RESULT
ADD DOCUMENT TO SANCTION SCHOOL BUS CASE	**CLICK** *Files* in the import options on the Home Tab **BROWSE** *Open files* window to folder containing Sanction sample files **CLICK** *Desired document* **CLICK** *Open*	

(continued)

Adding Images to a Sanction Case

GOAL	ACTION	RESULT
SELECT AND ADD IMAGES TO SANCTION SCHOOL BUS CASE	**CLICK** *Files* in the import options in the Home Tab **BROWSE** *Open files* window to foldercontaining image files **CLICK** *Desired image* **CLICK** *Open*	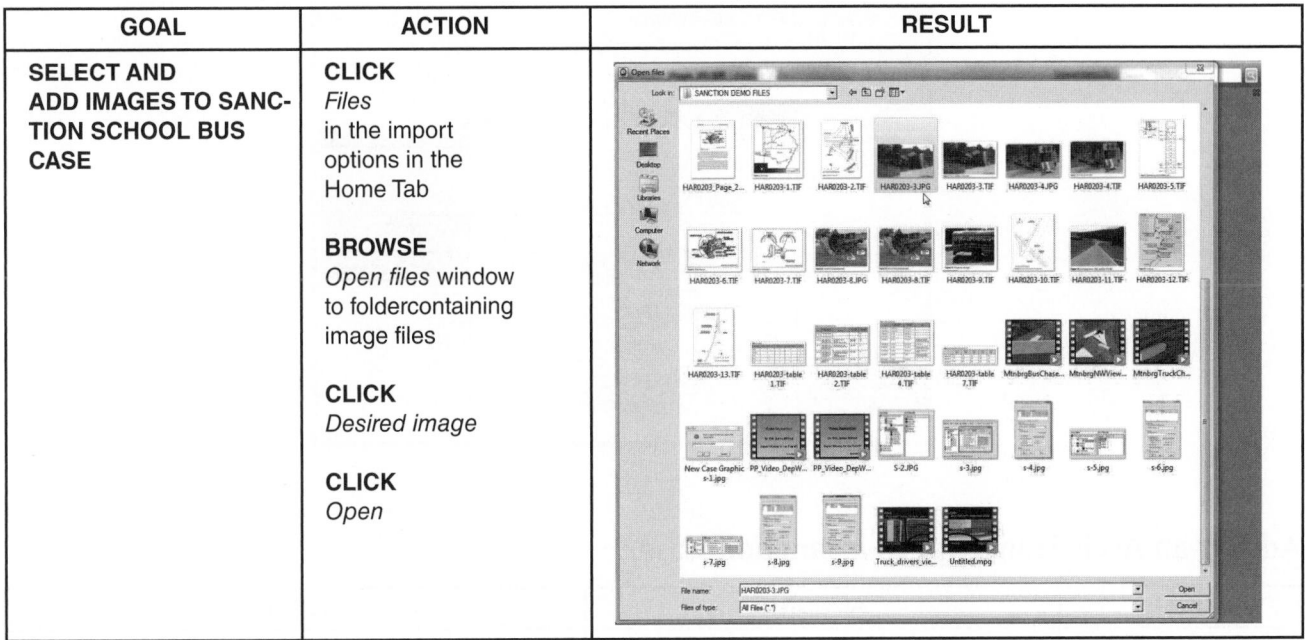

Adding Video Simulations to a Sanction Case

GOAL	ACTION	RESULT
ADD A VIDEO FILE TO SANCTION SCHOOL BUS CASE	**CLICK** *Files* in the import options in the Home Tab **BROWSE** *Open files* window to folder containing video files **CLICK** *Desired video* **CLICK** *Open*	

Adding Transcripts

Transcript may be provided in different formats. Typical is the ASCII or text file format. When a deposition is videotaped, the deposition may be provided with a linked text file and the video file. In Sanction this may be in a proprietary format that allows video and text to scroll together. For demonstration purposes you have been provided with the coordinated file (Esquireview Deposition) and the traditional text file.

Exhibit 2 Sanction video transcript screen

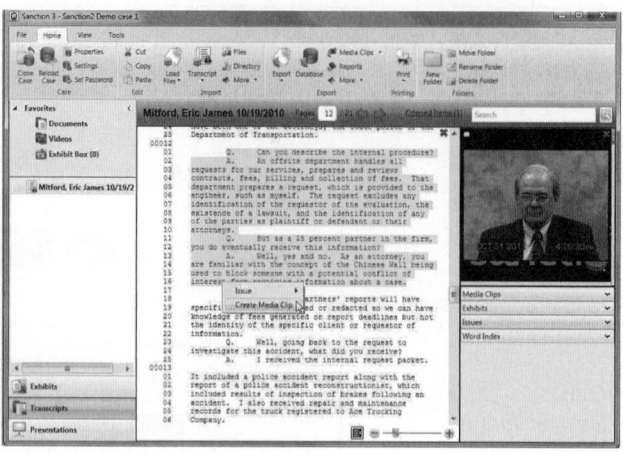

Adding an Ascii Transcript to a Sanction Case

GOAL	ACTION	RESULT
ADD TRANSCRIPT TO SANCTION	**CLICK** *Transcript* in the Import options in the Home tab **CLICK** *ASCII text* in the transcript option **BROWSE** *Open Transcript text file* window to folder containing text transcript files **CLICK** *Expert witness .txt file* **CLICK** *Open*	

Items are managed in a folder of similar type items—Exhibits, Transcripts and Presentations—shown on the bottom of the left panel-Tree. Selecting the folder shows the items in that category, which may then be displayed in the viewing area.

Viewing Items in the Preview Screen

GOAL	ACTION	RESULT
OPEN CATEGORY AND EXPAND LIST OF ITEMS	**CLICK** *Exhibits* **RIGHT CLICK** with cursor on *Documents* **CLICK** *Expand*	
SELECT FILE TOOPEN INTO THE VIEWING AREA	**RIGHT CLICK** *Documents* **CLICK** *Open*	

■ PRESENTATION ON THE COURT MONITOR

Presentations in Sanction are collections of documents, images, videos, and other exhibits that may be organized in individual presentation folders. The Presentation Mode allows the items in the individual presentation folders to be displayed on the court monitor. All of the items may be previewed in the viewing area of the legal team monitor before presentation.

Exhibit 3 Working screen with viewing area and Presentation Mode Screen

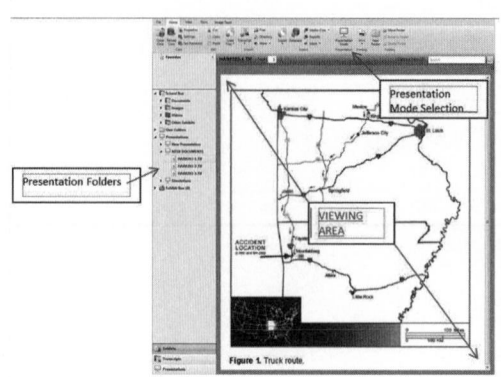

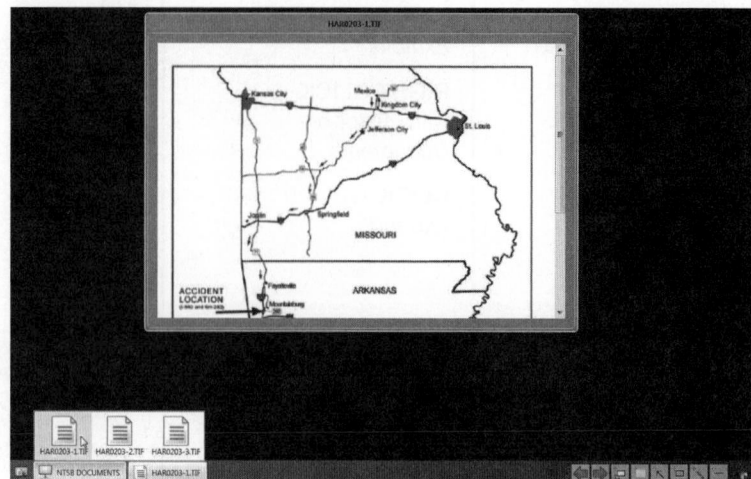

Presenting Items on the Court Monitor

GOAL	ACTION	RESULT
CREATE PRESENTATION FOLDERS WITH EXHIBITS FORUSE IN PRESENTATION MODE **NOTE:** This requiresa two monitor display-system.	**RIGHT CLICK** with cursor on *Presentations* **CLICK** *Create New Presentation* rename the folder **RIGHT CLICK** with cursor on *Documents* **CLICK** *Expand* **CLICK and Hold Mouse button** on document drag it to new presentationfolder **RELEASE CURSOR**	

(continued)

GOAL	ACTION	RESULT
OPEN PRESEN-TATION MODE SCREEEN	**CLICK** *Presentation Mode* in Home tab on ribbon	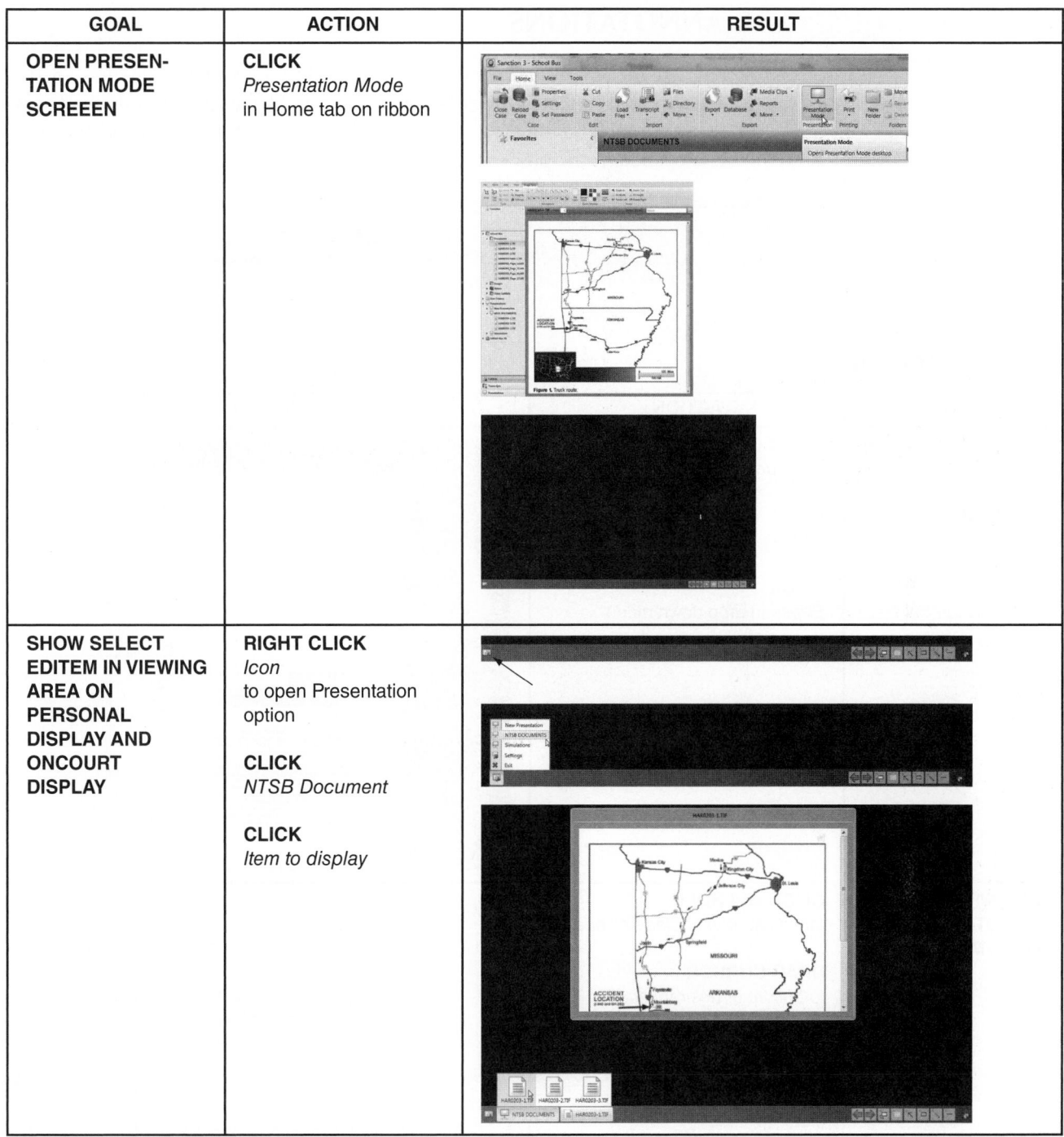
SHOW SELECT EDITEM IN VIEWING AREA ON PERSONAL DISPLAY AND ONCOURT DISPLAY	**RIGHT CLICK** *Icon* to open Presentation option **CLICK** *NTSB Document* **CLICK** *Item to display*	

■ ANNOTATIONS

A complete set of annotations tools can be used to mark up documents. The annotation tools are located in the Image Tools tab on the ribbon as shown below. An annotation menu is also accessible by a right click of the mouse when a document is opened in the preview area.

Adding Annotations

GOAL	ACTION	RESULT
OPEN ANNOTATION TOOLS MENU SELECT ANNOTATION TOOL	**RIGHT CLICK** *with cursor on document* **CLICK** *Ellipse* **CLICK** *Ellipse* in drop down menu	
INSERT ANNOTATION IN DOCUMENT	**CLICK and HOLD** *top of location to place ellipse* **DRAG CURSOR** *to bottom of desired location* **RELEASE CURSOR**	

(continued)

GOAL	ACTION	RESULT
SELECT ANNOTATION TOOL FROM IMAGE TOOLS TOOLBAR	**CLICK** *Highlight tool* **Position cursor** *at desired startingpoint* **DRAG** *cursor to ending position* **Release Mouse button**	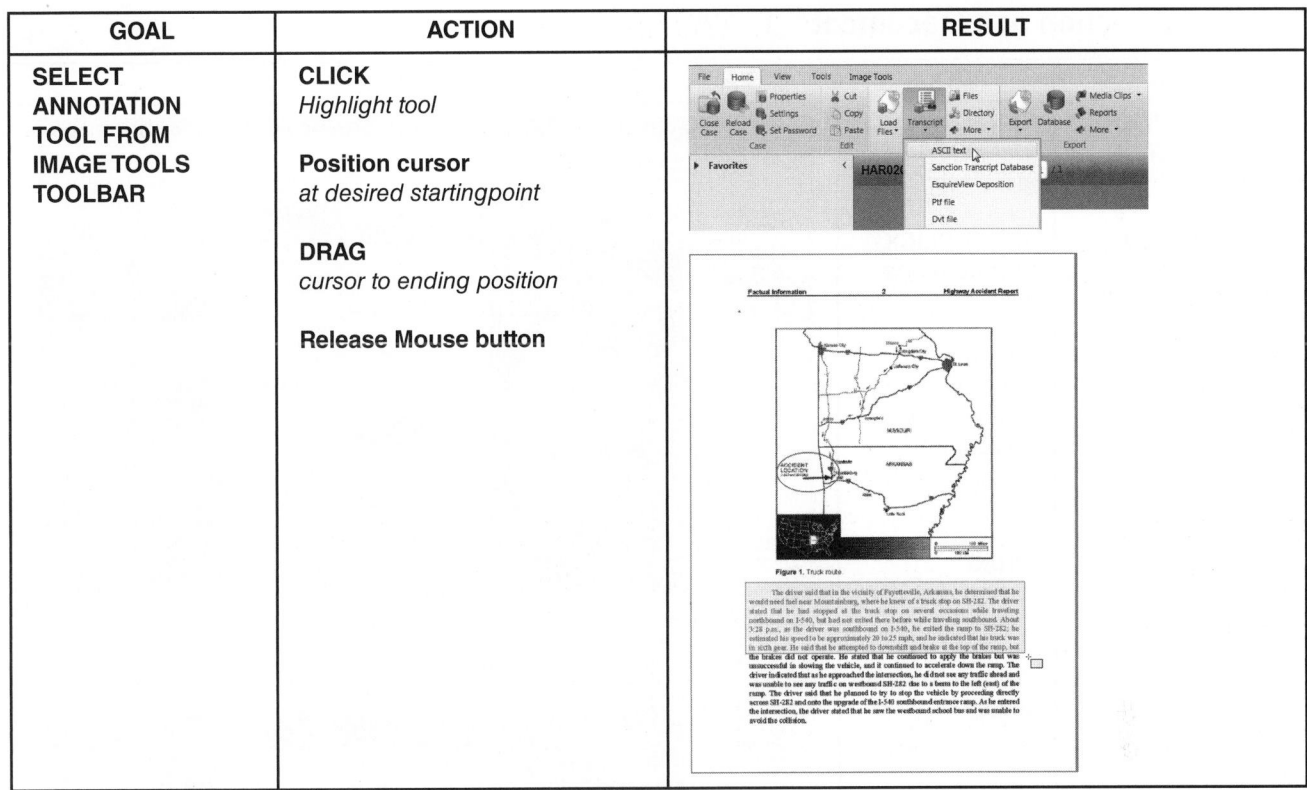

■ TEAR OUT A SECTION OF A DOCUMENT

There are portions of documents that may need to be shown clearly and in a larger view than the rest of the document of which it is a part. The tear out feature allows selected text to be shown in a larger separate window on top of the original document.

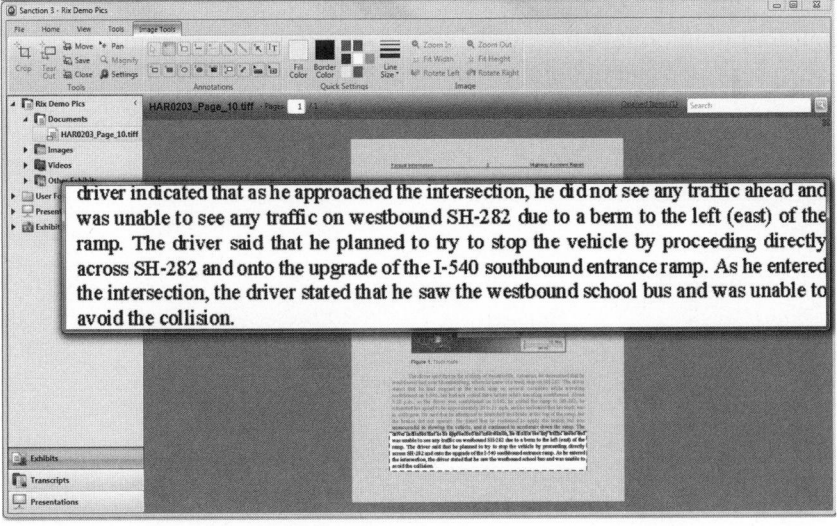

Tear out a Section of a Document

GOAL	ACTION	RESULT
OPEN DESIRED DOCUMENT **SELECT A SECTION OF A DOCUMENT TO HIGHLIGHT AND "TEAR OUT" FROM ORIGINAL DOCUMENT**	**OPEN** *Desired document* **RIGHT CLICK** *With cursor on document* **SELECT** *Tear out option Place cursor inupper left cornerof desired area* **DRAG** *Cursor to select desired area* **Release Mouse button**	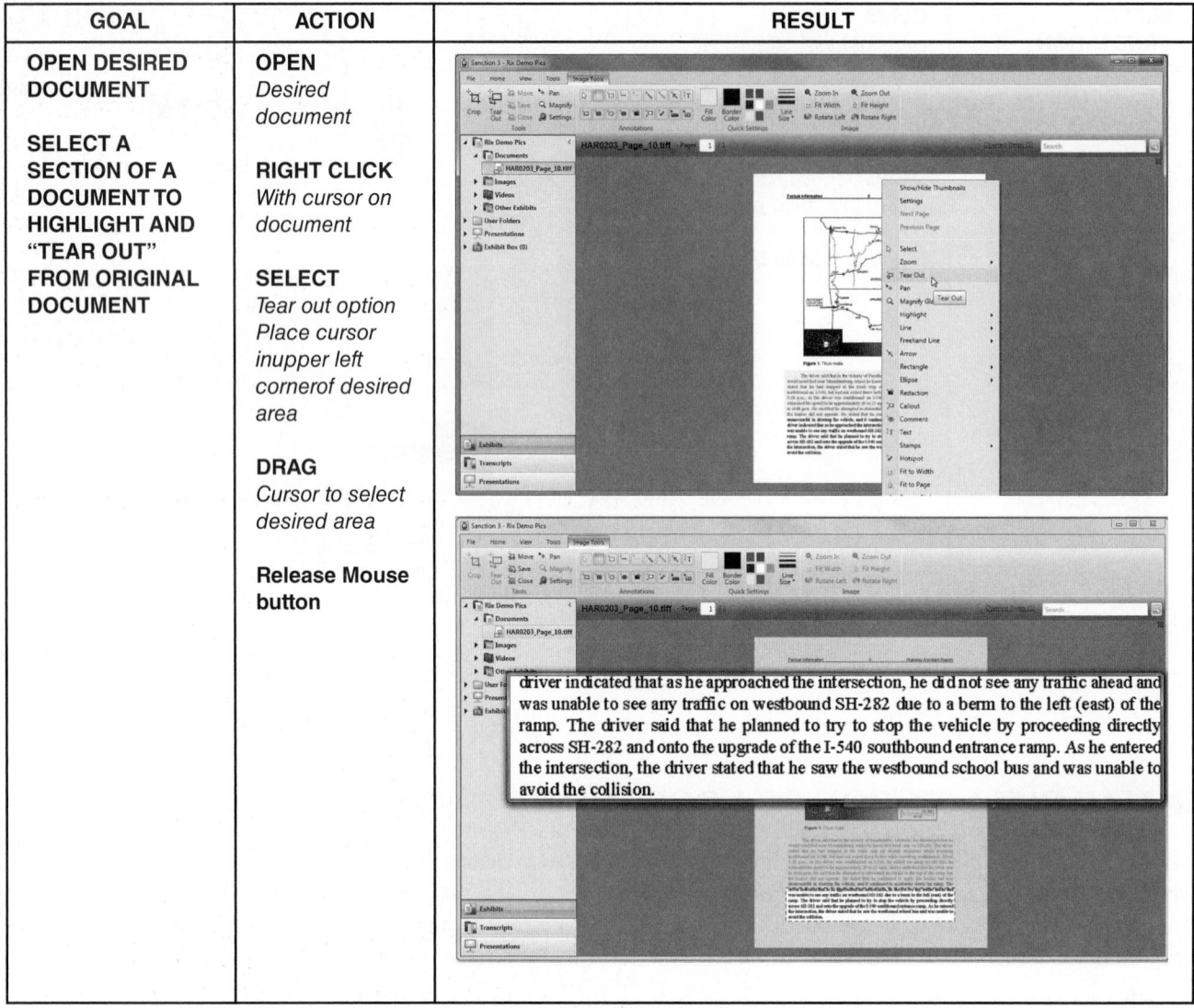

Additional tutorial information is available at
http://media.pearsoncmg.com/ph/chet/chet_goldman_techresources_1/

or on the Technology Resources Website:
www.pearsonhighered.com/goldman

APPENDIX I

CHAPTER OPENING CASE STUDY

Each chapter has an Opening Scenario that focuses on the issues presented in the chapter. The scenarios follow the activities of the law firm of Mason, Marshall and Benjamin, Attorneys and Counselors at Law. The firm started in a small town near the local state courthouse. With the increased volume of litigation cases, it was determined that a satellite office in the city of Oldtown was essential to service the cases in federal court. A new location was established across the street from the federal district court with Ethan Benjamin, Esq., as the office's managing partner. Benjamin, a former litigation paralegal for the suburban office, graduated from law school, passed the state bar, and was admitted, on the motion of the senior partner, Owen Mason, Esq., to the federal district court. Owen Mason had been a law clerk to a federal judge in the same court.

Edith Hannah, an experienced paralegal from a prestigious downtown law firm, was the first employee hired by Mr. Mason to run the original office in the suburban town of Newtown across from the local state trial court building. Ariel Marshall, a former prosecution attorney, and her litigation support paralegal, Emily Gordon, joined the firm shortly after its formation, after they had worked a major multiparty tort action. Ms. Marshall became a partner of Mr. Mason. With the growth of both offices, Mrs. Hannah became the office manager for both offices, and soon hired Emily's twin sister, Caitlin, as an additional paralegal to work in the center city office with Mr. Benjamin. Cary Eden, Esq., was hired by Mr. Benjamin as an associate in the center city office to assist him in federal court litigation.

■ LAW OFFICE INFORMATION

Mason, Marshall and Benjamin
Attorneys and Counselors
at Law
Newtown Office
2 South State Street
Newtown, Your State
Office Phone 555-111-2222

Oldtown Office
1 Federal Street
Oldtown, Your State
Office Phone 555-222-1111

Owen Mason, Esquire
138 South Main Street
Newtown, Your State
Social Security Number 123-45-6789
Office Phone 555-111-2222
Home Phone 555-345-3333
Date of Birth 08-19-1961

Ariel Marshall, Esquire
621 Merion Road
Old Station, Your State
Social Security Number 123-45-6792
Office Phone 555-222-2224
Home Phone 555-432-5673
Date of Birth 08-06-1968

Ethan Benjamin, Esquire
138 City Court
Oldtown, Your State
Social Security Number 555-22-7890
Office Phone 555-222-1111
Home Phone 555-987-6543
Date of Birth 06-23-1968

Cary Eden, Esquire
12 Schan Drive
Richboro, Your State
Office Phone 555-222-1111
Home Phone 555-518-9166
Date of Birth 08-12-1964

Mrs. Hannah
43 Washington Avenue
Newtown, Your State
Social Security Number 123-45-6790
Home Phone 555-453-3134
Date of Birth 01-12-1960

Emily Gordon
2916 Boulevard Avenue
Forest Park, Your State and Zip
Social Security Number 123-45-6793
Home Phone 555-468-3335
Date of Birth 01-28-1984

Caitlin Gordon
76 Medford Road
Lawnview, Your State
Social Security Number 999-11-0000
Home Phone 555-444-8888
Date of Birth 01-28-1984

Billing Rates

Owen Marshall, senior partner, attorney—$350 hour
Ariel Marshall, partner, attorney—$300 hour
Ethan Benjamin, managing partner, attorney—$250 hour
Cary Eden, associate attorney—$200 hour
Mrs. Hannah, paralegal—$90
Emily Gordon, litigation paralegal—$90 hour
Caitlin Gordon, paralegal—$90 hour

YOUR HOURLY BILLING RATE $40 Hour

COMPREHENSIVE CASE STUDIES

The comprehensive case studies are based on actual facts as reported in a National Transportation Safety Board (NTSB) report. Content has been edited and reproduced in the words of the report to provide as much authenticity as possible. Figures are reproduced from the same report. Some liberty has been taken with the identity of the parties, and no names used represent or are actual parties involved in the tragic accident reported. We use an actual incident to allow you to perform basic legal and factual research that will present actual information that would be found in a real case on which you might work in the future.

CASE A

Multi-Vehicle Collision between Truck and School Bus
Near Mountainburg, Arkansas
May 31, 2001

NTSB Abstract

On May 31, 2001, near Mountainburg, Arkansas, a Gayle Stuart Trucking, Inc., truck-tractor semitrailer collided with a 65-passenger school bus operated by the Mountainburg, Arkansas, Public Schools. Three school bus passengers were fatally injured; two other passengers received serious injuries. Four passengers, the school bus driver, and the truck driver sustained minor injuries.

Passengers

Refer to seat numbers on National Transportation Safety Board (NTSB) seating chart:

1A Alice Bates	9C Charles Barley
2A Amy Francs	10A Dan Thomas
2C Clarisa Howard	10E David Thompson
2E Doris Isaacs	11A Thomas Aaron
9A Harry Allen	

Other Drivers and Parties

Note: Names are fictional and not actual passenger names.

School Bus Driver:	Robert Howard
Tractor-Trailer Driver:	Stephen Blanca
Trucking Company:	Gayle Stuart Trucking, Inc

Highway Accident Report

■ NTSB EXECUTIVE SUMMARY

On May 31, 2001, about 3:28 P.M. central daylight time, a southbound Gayle Stuart Trucking, Inc., truck-tractor semitrailer exited Interstate 540 at State Highway 282 near Mountainburg, Arkansas. The driver was unable to stop at the stop sign at the bottom of the ramp. The 79,040-pound combination unit was traveling approximately 48 mph when it entered the intersection and collided with the right side of a westbound, 65-passenger, 1990 Blue Bird Corporation school bus operated by the Mountainburg, Arkansas, Public Schools. The school bus rotated approximately 300 degrees clockwise and overturned; the body, which partially separated from the chassis, came to rest on its right side on the eastbound shoulder of State Highway 282. The tractor semitrailer continued across the roadway, rotated about 60 degrees clockwise, overturned, and came to rest on its left side.

Three school bus passengers seated across from the impact area were fatally injured; one was partially ejected. Two other passengers, one of whom was seated in the impact area, received serious injuries, and four passengers had minor injuries. The school bus driver and the truck driver both sustained minor injuries.

The Safety Board determines that the probable cause of the accident was the truck driver's inability to stop the tractor semitrailer at the stop sign at the bottom of the ramp due to the reduced braking efficiency of the truck's brakes, which had been poorly maintained and inadequately inspected. Contributing to the school bus passengers' injuries during the side impact were incomplete compartmentalization and the lack of energy-absorbing material on interior surfaces.

NOTE: The complete National Transportation Safety Board report is available and may be downloaded from the Technology Resources Website, www .pearsonhighered.com/goldman, together with selected exhibits and accident simulations.

▓ INVESTIGATOR'S REPORT FOR EDUCATIONAL USE

School Bus Accident

Near Mountainburg, Arkansas, May 31, 201x

Abstract

On May 31, 201x, near Mountainburg, Arkansas, an Ace Trucking, Inc., truck-tractor semitrailer collided with a 65-passenger school bus operated by the Mountainburg, Arkansas, Public Schools. Three school bus passengers were fatally injured; two other passengers received serious injuries. Four passengers, the school bus driver, and the truck driver sustained minor injuries.

The accident occurred in midday when the weather was clear and dry. Post-accident inspection of the school bus revealed no mechanical problems. Results of post-accident drug and alcohol tests for both the truck driver and the bus driver were negative. Both drivers held valid commercial driver's licenses and medical certificates. The roadways were in good condition; the interstate and ramp signing was in compliance. Emergency response was timely and adequate. The school bus was traveling about 50 mph at the time of the collision; the speed limit on SH-282 was 55 mph. The truck driver admitted that he had falsified his logbooks to appear to be in compliance with federal hours-of-service rules, and he later described his actual work and rest times to Safety Board investigators. Until May 28 (3 days before the accident), he was off duty at home for 3 days, where he said he maintained a normal work-rest cycle, that is, awake and active during daylight hours and resting during nighttime hours. During the 3 days before the accident, he said he slept in the truck's sleeper berth each night, maintaining a normal work-rest cycle. Investigators compared data available from fuel receipts and bills of lading for the accident vehicle against travel times between locations on the driver's route and found no conflict with the work-rest cycle he described. The driver's schedule did not include the required 8 hours off-duty time, and the truck driver obtained 5.5 to 6.5 hours of sleep per night. He successfully steered the truck onto the exit ramp and applied the brakes in an attempt to slow the truck before the accident. Had the driver not applied the brakes, the truck would have been traveling much faster due to the downgrades on the interstate and ramp. While investigators could not determine whether the driver was fatigued, his actions just prior to the collision do not suggest that fatigue was a factor in this accident. There was no evidence of drug or alcohol use by the drivers and that the weather, mechanical condition of the school bus, design and signing of the highways, emergency response, and truck driver fatigue did not contribute to the accident.

Passengers

Our Client Seat 5A
Other Passengers

1A Alice Bates	9C Charles Barley
2A Amy Francs	10A Dan Thomas
2C Clarisa Howard	10E David Thompson
2E Doris Isaacs	11A Thomas Aaron
9A Harry Allen	

Other Drivers and Parties

School Bus Driver:	Robert Howard
Tractor-Trailer Driver:	Stephen Blanca
Truck Owner:	Ace Trucking Company, Inc.

School Bus

■ FACTUAL INFORMATION

Accident Narrative

On May 31, 2001, about 3:28 P.M. central daylight time, a southbound Ace Trucking, Inc. (Stuart Trucking) truck-tractor semitrailer exited Interstate 540 (I-540) at State Highway 282 (SH-282) near Mountainburg, Arkansas. The driver was unable to stop the tractor semitrailer at the stop sign at the bottom of the ramp. The 79,040-pound tractor semitrailer was traveling approximately 48 mph when it entered the intersection and collided with the right side of a westbound, 65-passenger, 1990 Blue Bird Corporation school bus, traveling about 50 mph, and operated by the Mountainburg, Arkansas, Public Schools. The school bus rotated approximately 300 degrees clockwise, overturned, and came to rest on its right side on the eastbound shoulder of SH-282. The tractor semitrailer continued across SH-282, rotated about 60 degrees clockwise, overturned, and came to rest on its left side.

Collision

The tractor semitrailer hit the bus on the right side in the area of the rear axle. The truck continued south across SH-282, traveled 73 feet from the point of impact, rolled on its left side, and traveled an additional 78 feet, rotating about 60 degrees clockwise (see Figures 2 and 3). The school bus traveled 96 feet southwest from the area of impact, rotating about 300 degrees clockwise. The body, which partially separated from the chassis, rolled onto its right side, while the chassis remained partially upright.

Medical and Pathological Information

The passengers who sustained minor injuries were seated in seats 1A, 2A, 2C, and 2E (see Figure 5). The passenger in seat 1A sustained a contusion on the left side of his scalp. The passenger in seat 2A sustained a contusion on the left side of her scalp and a possible contusion or laceration of the spleen. The passenger in 2C sustained lacerations and contusions on the right elbow, and the passenger in seat 2E had lacerations and contusions on her right elbow and on the back of both knees. Two seriously injured passengers were seated in the rear of the bus. One was seated in the area of impact (seat 10E) and sustained lacerations to his head and elbow and a closed head injury. The other, seated across from the area of impact (seat 10A), sustained multiple spinal fractures and a fractured right arm and leg. The three fatally injured passengers were seated across from the area of impact. The passenger in seat 9A sustained a fractured skull, fractured left clavicle, three fractured ribs, and a compound fracture of the left leg; the passenger in 9C sustained multiple lacerations and contusions, a right pelvic fracture, a liver laceration, a right renal laceration, ruptured right hemidiaphragm, and vena cava injury; the passenger in 11A, who was partially ejected, had a skull fracture, multiple spinal fractures, and a fractured left tibia.

Emergency Response

The Crawford County Communications Center and the Mountainburg Police Department received notification of the accident at 3:29 P.M. The Mountainburg police chief arrived on scene at 3:31 P.M. and two rescue vehicles arrived at 3:35 P.M. The rescue vehicles were manned by eight firefighters, five of whom were qualified first responders and emergency medical technicians (EMTs). A triage area, where the injured were evaluated and treated, was established on the left side of the school bus. After the triage site was set up, a Lifeflight Air Ambulance (helicopter) was dispatched from Branson, Missouri, about 45 minutes flying time from the accident site. Four additional fire departments and one ambulance service, comprising 25 firefighters and EMTs, three rescue vehicles, a pumper truck, and seven ambulances, responded to the accident. By 3:45 P.M., the ambulances had transported eight of the injured passengers, the bus driver, and the truck driver from the scene (the helicopter was not needed). One partially ejected passenger (seat 11A) was under the bus. He was extricated by 3:52 P.M. and pronounced dead at the scene.

Survivability

EMTs and passersby removed two fatally injured passengers (seats 9A and 9C), one seriously injured passenger (seat 10A), and two passengers with minor injuries (seats 2A and 2D) from the bus. EMTs extricated the third fatally injured passenger (seat 11A) from underneath the bus; this passenger had been partially ejected through the right side window at row 11. The passenger in the front of the bus said that at the end of the impact sequence, he was lying on the "floor," which, post-collision, was the right side of the bus.

The passenger in seat 10E said he was lying on the right side of the bus when it came to rest and that the passenger in seat 9A was lying across his legs. Evidence indicates the passengers in the back of the bus struck the ceiling, right-side windows, and sidewall during the impact sequence.

Damage

Both the school bus and truck tractor were completely destroyed. The semitrailer received minor damage and the load was unusable.

Highway Information

Highway Design

The accident occurred at the intersection of SH-282 and the exit ramp from southbound I-540 (see Figure 10). Construction on this part of I-540 began in January 1987, and it opened to traffic in January 1999. The exit ramp from southbound I-540 to SH-282 was completed summer 1999. Arkansas State Highway and Transportation Department (ASHTD) records show that no accidents were reported in the intersection since it had been open.

The exit ramp from I-540 is a 15-foot-wide paved concrete lane, with tined surface texture, bordered by 6-foot paved asphalt shoulders to the west and 4-foot paved asphalt shoulders to the east, each delineated with thermoplastic edge lines. The exit ramp, as measured from the gore area to the intersection curb line of SH-282, is approximately 1,342 feet long, with a difference in elevation of about 85 feet. The only ramp curvature is a horizontal curve as the ramp transitions from the interstate. The average grade of the ramp is about 6 percent; the steepest grade is 9.42 percent, encompassing a distance of about 293 feet and ending about 413 feet from the end of the ramp, after which the ramp transitions to a 0.03 percent grade 69 feet before the intersection, as measured on scene.

A 36-inch stop sign was in place on the traffic island north of the intersection. An advance traffic control sign indicating "stop ahead" was about 581 feet north of the stop sign in the grassy right-of-way on the right side of the exit ramp. A recreational area guide sign was approximately 191 feet north of the "stop ahead" sign. Following the accident the state installed additional signing. The 36-inch stop sign was replaced with a 48-inch stop sign and erected another 48-inch stop sign on the left side of the ramp. It placed an additional 48-inch "stop ahead" sign on the left side of the ramp across from the original one, which is approximately 581 feet north of the stop sign. The state added a third 48-inch "stop ahead" sign on the right side of the ramp, approximately 881 feet north of the stop sign, and moved the recreation guide sign to the left side of the ramp.

The speed limit on I-540 is 70 mph for cars and 65 mph for trucks. No advisory speed signs are present on the exit ramp.

A review of the I-540 construction plans indicates that the truck descended four hills (and ascended three) between the Bunyard tunnel and the accident location. While traveling southbound from the tunnel, the truck descended an average grade of 2.7 percent (steepest grade was 4.9 percent) over 3.84 miles; an average grade of 2.3 percent (steepest grade, 4.1 percent) over 3.40 miles; and an average grade of 1.8 percent (steepest grade, 2.5 percent) over 0.47 mile. On its approach to the ramp, the truck was descending an average grade of 3.3 percent (steepest grade, 4.4 percent) over 0.66 mile.

The annual average daily traffic for I-540 was 14,600 vehicles, of which about 21 percent were trucks. A 24-hour traffic count showed that 36.7 percent of the 312 vehicles exiting onto the southbound ramp from I-540 were trucks. The June 13 ASHTD traffic count showed that trucks accounted for 32.3 percent of the 460 eastbound and 13.2 percent of the 988 westbound vehicles on SH-282. In the vicinity of the accident, SH-282 is a two-way, two-lane paved asphalt roadway running east-west. At the time of the accident, a combination of painted markings and raised, mountable concrete islands (2 inches high at the edges and 6 inches high overall) channelized the traffic lanes on both sides of the intersection. A left turn lane, about 12 feet wide, was available for westbound traffic turning onto the entrance ramp to southbound I-540. The east- and westbound traffic lanes were about 11 feet wide and bordered by paved shoulders about 8 feet wide and delineated by painted edge lines. Standard pavement markings (a yellow painted, double centerline) divided opposing lanes of traffic. The speed limit for SH-282, as posted on a sign approximately 1 mile east of the accident site, was 55 mph.

Tire Marks

The truck-tractor semitrailer produced multiple tire marks beginning on the east shoulder of the exit ramp, about 30 feet north of the area of impact, and continuing southwest across the intersection. The left front tire created a scuff mark, and a series of chips in the asphalt surface were in line with the scuff mark. From the area of impact, the longest tire mark, about 89 feet, traversed the south traffic island and continued toward the area where the truck tractor came to rest. The truck-tractor semitrailer produced multiple north-south scrape marks after the unit had rolled onto its left side. Scuff marks result when a tire slides while the wheel is still rotating. Scrape marks are produced when any part of a vehicle, other than the tires, contacts the ground while the vehicle is still in motion. Investigators observed no tire marks on SH-282 leading to the area of impact. The school bus produced multiple tire marks beginning at the area of impact and continuing southeast intermittently over a distance of about 110 feet. The longest tire marks terminated in the area where the school bus came to rest. The school bus produced a single deep scrape mark that ran west to east at the area of impact; investigators found no other scrape marks related to the collision.

Meteorological Information

At the Fort Smith, Arkansas, Regional Airport, approximately 23 miles from the accident site, the weather was partly cloudy with winds from the west at about 13 mph at 3:53 P.M.

The temperature was 69°F and the dew point was 60°.

Tests and Research

Sight Distance

At a driver eye height of 74 inches above the pavement, a motorist could see the stop sign from the transition area to the end of the ramp, a distance greater than that prescribed by the American Association of State Highway and Transportation Officials (AASHTO). The "state park" sign then in place north of the "stop ahead" sign could impede a motorist's view of the "stop ahead" sign from a distance of 684 feet until the driver was about 569 feet from the "stop ahead" sign (see Figure 13). Since the accident, Arkansas has moved the "state park" sign to the other side of the ramp, where it does not impede a driver's view of the "stop ahead" sign, and has added "stop ahead" signs. When the ramp was constructed, it was cut into existing terrain, and a grass berm runs parallel to and east of the ramp. A stop sign for traffic exiting I-540 onto SH-282 is in place at the intersection. Visibility test results showed that, when stopped at the intersection, a driver has a clear line of sight to the east exceeding 582 feet. A driver on westbound SH-282 is not able to see traffic on the exit ramp until the driver is 51 feet east of the intersection.

■ SUMMARY OF STATEMENT

School Bus Driver

The 76-year-old school bus driver possessed a current Arkansas class B CDL, with a passenger endorsement and a school bus restriction that was issued on April 7, 1999, and scheduled to expire on March 18, 2003. A review of the bus driver's record revealed no traffic convictions. He had been involved in a traffic accident on February 15, 2001; while exiting school property, the bus struck the right side of a passenger car as he entered the roadway. No one was injured and the bus driver was not cited for the accident. The bus driver had passed his most recent annual physical examination on August 1, 200X, as required by the Mountainburg Public Schools. He had been driving school buses for 14 years and had been driving this route for 3 years.

The school bus picked up students at Mountainburg Elementary School about 2:50 P.M., drove to Mountainburg High School to pick up more students, and departed the high school between 3:00 and 3:05 P.M. for the afternoon route home. The bus had made three stops on the route to unload students before dropping off a student at a truck stop on SH-282 and proceeding westbound on SH-282 at a driver-estimated speed of 45 mph. The driver stated that as he was nearing the ramp, he heard a passenger shout that a truck was not going to stop at the stop sign on the ramp. The driver said he briefly looked to his right, glimpsed the truck, and heard the loud sound of the collision.

The school bus driver stated that he was wearing his lap belt (the bus was only equipped with a lap belt), which was found tied in a knot during post-accident examination but still useable; no striations were found on the belt webbing. The driver reported that he was unable to get out of the lap belt after the bus came to rest because the weight of his body against the belt jammed the buckle and prevented him from unlatching it. One of the passengers unlatched the driver's belt. The driver reported that he struck his head, elbows, and chest on the interior of the bus as it rolled over. The bus driver's minor injuries included contusions on the left side of his face, left shoulder, and left hip. Because of a coronary condition, he was hospitalized after the accident as a precaution.

The bus driver and two passengers (seats 1A and 2B) were able to exit from the bus on their own via the rear emergency door. The bus driver helped the seriously injured passenger in seat 10E exit the bus.

Post-accident toxicological tests conducted by the Arkansas State Police for the school bus driver were negative for alcohol and other drugs.

■ SUMMARY OF STATEMENT

Truck Driver

Truck

The truck driver departed his home in Vandalia, Missouri, on May 28, 200X, for a 4-day trip through Iowa, Missouri, and Arkansas. On May 31, the day of the accident, the driver stated that he awoke about 8:00 P.M., conducted a 30-minute pretrip inspection, and departed Kingdom City, Missouri, where he had slept in his sleeper berth the previous night. He had picked up a load of bean meal in Mexico, Missouri, earlier that morning (approximately 1:44 P.M., according to the bill of lading) and was en route to Atkins, Arkansas (see Figure 1). The driver stopped near Joplin, Missouri, about 1:30 P.M. for a sandwich.

The driver said that in the vicinity of Fayetteville, Arkansas, he determined that he would need fuel near Mountainburg, where he knew of a truck stop on SH-282. The driver stated that he had stopped at the truck stop on several occasions while traveling northbound on I-540, but had not exited there before while traveling southbound. About 3:28 P.M., as the driver was southbound on I-540, he exited the ramp to SH-282; he estimated his speed to be approximately

20 to 25 mph, and he indicated that his truck was in sixth gear. He said that he attempted to downshift and brake at the top of the ramp, but the brakes did not operate. He stated that he continued to apply the brakes but was unsuccessful in slowing the vehicle, and it continued to accelerate down the ramp. The driver indicated that as he approached the intersection, he did not see any traffic ahead and was unable to see any traffic on westbound SH-282 due to a berm to the left (east) of the ramp. The driver said that he planned to try to stop the vehicle by proceeding directly across SH-282 and onto the upgrade of the I-540 southbound entrance ramp. As he entered the intersection, the driver stated that he saw the westbound school bus and was unable to avoid the collision.

The truck driver's minor injuries included contusions on the right side of his head, upper right arm, and left shoulder.

The 25-year-old truck driver possessed a current Missouri class A commercial driver's license (CDL), with no restrictions or endorsements, issued on March 15, 1999, and scheduled to expire on March 15, 2002. A review of the driver's record revealed a speeding conviction while driving a personal vehicle on November 19, 2000, and a failure-to-keep-right conviction while driving a commercial vehicle on July 30, 1999.

The driver had a valid medical certificate. Interviews with the truck driver and an examination of his employment records showed that he started driving commercial vehicles professionally in March 1999.

Ace Trucking was his first employer. He subsequently worked for McDowell Farms of Perry, Missouri; Target Aluminum of Vandalia, Missouri; and Jennings Implement of Curryville, Missouri. He returned to Ace Trucking in April before the accident.

The truck driver acknowledged that the logs he kept between May 28 and 31 were not accurate because he had reconstructed his activities and completed the logs at the end of each day.

Table 2, which follows, shows the driver's stated rest time, the times on the receipts, and the driver's likely hours of sleep during the days prior to the accident.

The driver stated that he was in good general health, but occasionally suffered from a chronic back problem stemming from a childhood injury. He said he was not experiencing back pain on the day of the accident. He also suffered from a dust allergy and occasionally took Zyrtec for relief of symptoms. He said he last used the medication 2 weeks before the accident, and toxicological tests did not reveal any Zyrtec in the driver's blood. The driver's medical records did not indicate any other medical conditions. The post-accident toxicological tests on the truck driver, conducted by Arkansas State Police and Crawford Memorial Hospital, were negative for alcohol and other drugs.

The truck driver said he was wearing his lap belt only; the truck was equipped with a separate shoulder belt. He said that during the accident sequence, his leg became wedged under the dashboard due to the deformation of the cab. After the truck came to rest, he was able to slide the seat back to free his leg and climb out through the broken windshield.

The driver said that the brakes on the tractor were adjusted weekly, even though doing so might not be necessary, and he described to investigators the correct procedure for adjusting brakes. He also stated a preference for adjusting the trailer axle brakes "loose" to prevent the trailer from slipping in wet and other conditions. He said that he had not personally adjusted the brakes on the trailer but was present when the mechanic at Ace Trucking did so 2 to 3 weeks before the accident.

■ VEHICLE AND WRECKAGE INFORMATION

Truck-Tractor Semitrailer

The accident vehicle, a 1989 Kenworth Truck Company (Kenworth) model T600A conventional-cab, three-axle tractor, was equipped with a nine-speed transmission and had a sleeper berth; it was towing a two-axle, 43-foot hopper semitrailer, model DWH-400, built by Wilson Trailer Company in 1996. The tractor was powered by a six-cylinder Caterpillar diesel engine without an engine brake; it was originally equipped with an electronic control module that had been removed in 1999.

Both the odometer, which read 2,967.2 miles at the time of the accident, and speedometer had been replaced. The tractor had a wheelbase of 222 inches and a curb weight of 16,805 pounds. According to Ace Trucking records, the tractor had received its mandatory annual inspection, performed by an employee of Ace Trucking, on April 17, 2001; the inspection form listed all brake components as "OK." Prior to that inspection, the tractor had been idle for about 2 years.

The hopper, owned by Ace Trucking and used to haul grain and animal feed, weighed about 10,100 pounds empty. It had received its annual inspection, performed by an employee of Ace Trucking, on July 3, 201X; the inspection form listed all brake components as "OK." The hopper had been used as a spare at least once a month for about 18 months prior to the accident.

Damage

The tractor sustained damage to the front part of the frame, which was bent to the right about 10 degrees; the entire cab was shifted rearward, the windshield and right door window were broken, and both doors were damaged. The engine was dislodged from its mount, and parts within the engine compartment, as well as the front engine support, were broken; the left fuel tank was dislodged and the right fuel tank was punctured; and the muffler stack was broken off. Due to accident damage, the tractor lights could not be tested to determine whether they were operational. The hopper trailer's front-left upper clearance lights were damaged, the left side of the trailer was scraped, both outside left trailer wheels were bent, and the tires were flat.

Post-Accident Examination

All three tractor axles had air brakes (see Figure 6) with standard S-cam/drum foundation (service) brakes (see Figure 7) fitted with manual slack adjusters. The semitrailer (hopper) had air brakes with standard S-cam/drum foundation brakes; its two axles had automatic slack adjusters. The third axle of the tractor and both trailer axles had emergency-parking spring brakes.

State Police investigators conducted tests 4 weeks after the accident, to determine whether the trailer brakes were operational. The trailer was connected to a truck tractor and driven at 20 mph and 40 mph. When the service brakes were applied at both speeds, only the 4L (fourth axle, left side) and 5R (fifth axle, right side) trailer brakes locked, and the tires slid on the roadway; wheels 4R (fourth axle, right side) and 5L (fifth axle, left side) were free rolling with the brakes fully applied.

Investigators tested the semitrailer's emergency-parking brakes, using an auxiliary tractor to pull the trailer on the cement pavement, on June 6, 2001. When the emergency-parking brake was applied, only the 5R wheel locked. When pulled on gravel on a slight downhill slope, both the 4L and 5R wheels locked. In all tests, the 4R and 5L wheels rolled freely.

Investigators also measured brake shoe lining thickness. On brake 5R, the lining was 3/16 inch, or 1/16 inch less than the required minimum of 4/16 inch; all other brake shoes were in compliance with minimum requirements. The brake drums were examined and the inside diameters measured. While none of the drums exceeded the manufacturers' maximum service diameter, they did approach it, making them more susceptible to brake heat than new drums because less drum mass was available to absorb the heat. The drums on brakes 1R, 4R, and 5L exhibited rust.

Background

About 95 percent of large (26,000 pounds or greater) commercial vehicles are equipped with air brakes with S-cam/drum foundation brakes. The purpose of the service brake components is to convert air pressure into mechanical forces used to decelerate the vehicle. Once air has been directed through lines and valves, it reaches a brake chamber (see Figure 6).

■ VEHICLE AND WRECKAGE INFORMATION

School Bus

The 65-passenger, 1990 Blue Bird Corporation school bus had a Chevrolet model 60 chassis with a V-8, 366-cubic-inch engine reconfigured to operate with propane. The school bus was equipped with a four-speed General Motors Corporation manual transmission with a two-speed differential, power-assisted steering, hydraulic brakes with a dual master cylinder, and a motorized booster pump. The tire tread depths exceeded FMCSR's and CVSA requirements. After the accident, the front brakes were tested and operated properly. The rear brakes could not be tested because of a severed hydraulic line caused by collision damage. The lights that were not damaged in the accident operated during post-accident testing.

The bus had 10 rows of three-passenger bench seats on both sides of the bus. The eleventh row had a three-passenger bench seat on the right side and a two-passenger bench seat on the left side to accommodate the vehicle's one emergency exit door at the rear.

The school bus had been retrofitted with a 66.5-gallon propane tank located 34 inches forward of the rear axle on the right side, about 4 inches behind the caged gasoline tank, which had been drained (see Figure 8). The propane tank was mounted outside the frame and was secured by two steel straps. The cylindrical propane tank, manufactured by Brunner Engineering and Manufacturing, was 64 inches long and 18 inches in diameter. The tank shell was 0.187 inch thick and the heads (ends of the tank) were 0.173 inch thick. The tank was equipped with an overfill protection device valve, designed to vent in case of overfill or fire. Part of the valve was inside the propane tank and part outside; if the outer part of the valve was damaged or destroyed, gas flow to the engine was supposed to shut off automatically.

Background

Buses manufactured before September 1, 1994, were only required to have one emergency exit door.

Post-Accident Examination

The tire tread depths exceeded FMCSR's and CVSA requirements. After the accident, the front brakes were tested and operated properly. The rear brakes could not be tested because of a severed hydraulic line caused by collision damage. The lights that were not damaged in the accident operated during post-accident testing.

CASE B

Multi-vehicle Collision
Interstate 90
Hampshire–Marengo Toll Plaza
Near Hampshire, Illinois
October 1, 2003

Abstract

On October 1, 2003, a multi-vehicle accident occurred on the approach to an Interstate 90 toll plaza near Hampshire, Illinois. About 2:57 P.M., a 1995 Freightliner tractor-trailer chassis and cargo container combination unit was traveling eastbound on the interstate, approaching the Hampshire–Marengo toll plaza at milepost (MP) 41.6, when it struck the rear of a 1999 Goshen GC2 25-passenger specialty bus. As both vehicles moved forward, the specialty bus struck the rear of a 2000 Chevrolet Silverado 1500 pickup truck, which was pushed into the rear of a 1998 Ford conventional tractor-box-trailer. As its cargo container and chassis began to overturn, the Freightliner also struck the upper portion of the pickup truck's in-bed camper and the rear left side of the Ford trailer. The Freightliner and the specialty bus continued forward and came to rest in the median. The pickup truck was then struck by another eastbound vehicle, a 2000 Kenworth tractor with Polar tank trailer. Eight specialty bus passengers were fatally injured, and 12 passengers sustained minor-to-serious injuries. The bus driver, the pickup truck driver, and the Freightliner driver received minor injuries. The Ford driver and co-driver and the Kenworth driver were not injured.

Interview Notes

Our Client

Jonathan Leonard,
152 Timber Ridge Road
Piedmont, Your State and Zip
Phone 555 432-1098
Social Security Number 111-22-3333

NOTE TO FILE: I agreed to a contingent fee for the personal injury case. Usual rates unless he brings in other passengers as clients, then reduced to 20%.

NOTE: Someone needs to check if that reduction is allowed under our state law and ethics rules.

O.M.

Passengers

Refer to seat numbers on National Transportation Safety Board (NTSB) seating chart

1A Alice Bates	2A Amy Francs
1B Betty Charles	2B Allan Gordon
1C Clara Donald	2C Clarisa Howard
1D Donna Edwards	2D Doris Issacs

3A Agnes Jones
3B Beth Kaye
3C Callie Leonard
3D Delia Masons

4A Ariel Nathan
4B Barbara Osgood
4C vacant
4D vacant

5A Ashley Peters
5B Bently Quist
5C Colleen Roberts
5D vacant

6A vacant
6B Beula Victors
6C vacant
6D Davia Thompson
6E Elisabeth Stein

■ OTHER DRIVERS AND PARTIES

Note: Names are fictional and not actual passenger names.

Chevrolet Silverado
    Robert Howard
Freightliner Tractor-Trailer
    Stephen Blanca

Kenworth Tractor-Trailer
    Glen Davids
Ford Tractor-Box-Trailer
    Sigmund Curtis

■ DETAILS

Freightliner Tractor-Trailer

The Freightliner driver reported that on the morning of the accident, about 6:00 A.M., he picked up his tractor at a rental space in Chicago, Illinois, and completed a 10- to 15-minute pretrip inspection, verifying that the lights, tires, brakes, and other equipment were in safe operating condition. Before picking up the accident chassis, he picked up another chassis trailer and cargo container and delivered both to a rail yard. He then drove to the Hamilton rail yard, where he picked up the accident chassis and empty cargo container. He reported conducting a 14-minute inspection of the chassis trailer and container—including the brakes, tires, and lights—and also said that he inspected the cargo container for cleanliness and damage. From the Hamilton yard, he drove to Midwest Recycling in Rockford, Illinois, where the cargo container was loaded with bundled recycling paper. He then departed for the return trip to Chicago.

The Freightliner driver reported that he was traveling at a speed of 40 to 45 mph in the right lane of I-90 East, following a specialty bus by about two car lengths. He stated that he routinely maintained this vehicle separation distance to prevent other vehicles from changing lanes into his path. He reported that he remained in the right lane from the time he departed Rockford until he reached the accident location and that he experienced difficulty pulling the loaded container because of the small engine in his truck. The driver said that traffic was moving normally into the toll plaza and that the sun was high and to his rear, without glare or reflection. He stated that he maintained a constant view ahead and was startled when he saw the specialty bus stopped just in front of his vehicle. According to the Freightliner driver, the bus was not displaying brake lights. The driver stated that he braked hard and turned the steering wheel to the left in an unsuccessful attempt to avoid a collision. He said that he felt the truck brakes "grab," but the braking action was insufficient to stop the truck, and the trailer shifted to his left and went out of control; the trailer overturned and the truck came to a stop in the median. The driver remained in his truck until the police arrived and asked him to exit the vehicle.

Goshen Specialty Bus

On October 1, 2003, about 9:25 A.M., the 25-passenger specialty bus left Chicago, with 20 passengers on board, for a round-trip sightseeing charter to Rockford. About 2:15 P.M., the bus departed Rockford for the return trip to Chicago. The bus driver stated that he was in the left lane while on I-90 East and switched to the right lane 1 to 1.5 miles prior to the accident location. He reported that he was traveling at a speed of approximately 45 mph about 1 mile west of the Hampshire–Marengo toll plaza when he observed a line of vehicles approaching the plaza and gradually began to reduce speed to ensure passenger comfort. The driver stated that the line of traffic was a little longer than usual and that only one manual toll booth appeared to be in operation. According to the driver, this toll plaza does not operate an automatic toll lane for commercial vehicles.

The bus driver reported that the sun was above and behind him at the time of the accident and that he did not experience adverse sun glare or reflection. He said that he was driving 10 mph about 0.5 mile from the toll plaza, when he observed in his left side mirror a red tractor-trailer approaching in his lane at a high rate of speed. The driver reported feeling the impact of the tractor-trailer and feeling his vehicle hit a vehicle ahead of him in the right lane. The driver's air bag deployed, the bus was pushed into the median, and the driver reported steering to the right to avoid entering the westbound traffic lanes. The driver said that he unbuckled his seat belt and stepped out of the bus to call for emergency assistance.

Chevrolet Pickup, Ford Tractor-Box-Trailer, and Kenworth Tractor-Tank-Trailer

When the specialty bus was struck by the Freightliner, it was pushed forward and struck a 2000 Chevrolet Silverado pickup truck equipped with a bed-mounted camper. The pickup truck driver stated that he had been traveling eastbound in the right lane at a constant speed of 50 mph when he suddenly heard a loud crash and was simultaneously forced back into his seat by the impact of something striking his vehicle from behind. The driver reported that he had been looking forward and did not observe the traffic behind him and had no recollection of the vehicles ahead of him. He stated that he heard no other sounds prior to the collision and had not braked, changed lanes, or made any other maneuver before the accident. He remembered that his vehicle came to rest beneath a large truck and that he was trapped in the driver's seat. He had been wearing his three-point seat belt, and his air bag deployed.

When the pickup truck was struck from behind by the specialty bus, the truck was pushed forward into the rear of a 1998 Ford tractor pulling a box trailer. The driver of the Ford combination unit stated to Safety Board investigators that he had been traveling in the right lane at a speed of 30 to 35 mph while approaching the toll plaza. He recalled following another tractor-semi-trailer that was about two truck-lengths ahead of him and said that he had not noticed the traffic to his rear. He reported hearing a loud "explosion" and feeling a simultaneous impact involving the rear of his vehicle, followed by two other impacts, and immediately brought his truck to a stop. After departing his vehicle, he said that he talked to the driver trapped in the cab of the pickup truck until emergency personnel arrived.

The fifth vehicle involved in this accident was a 2000 Kenworth tractor-tank-trailer. The driver reported that he drove the same route weekly and, on the day of the accident, was traveling eastbound in the right lane after reducing his speed from 62 mph in the posted 45-mph work area speed zone, anticipating slower traffic on the approach to the toll plaza. He stated that he was following a pickup truck, which was 50 to 100 feet ahead of his vehicle, and the pickup truck was closely following a Ford tractor-box-trailer, when the specialty bus and the Freightliner tractor-trailer passed him in the left lane and then merged back into the right lane in front of him. He reported that, as he approached the toll plaza, he did not notice whether a line of vehicles was waiting to go through the manual toll booth. The Kenworth driver said that he observed the Freightliner in the left lane, braking hard with brake lights illuminated, and then watched it collide with the Ford tractor-box-trailer and overturn. According to the Kenworth driver, he saw the pickup truck collide with the Ford and then lost sight of it as his vehicle skidded forward. During this sequence, he reported that he braked hard in an attempt to avoid becoming involved in the accident and later realized that the front of his vehicle had collided with the pickup truck.

■ DRIVER INFORMATION

Freightliner Driver

Certification and Experience. The 49-year-old Freightliner driver held a valid Illinois Class A commercial driver's license (CDL), with a corrective lenses restriction and an expiration date of January 5, 2006. He possessed a valid medical certificate issued August 6, 2003, approximately 2 months prior to the accident, with an expiration date of August 6, 2005. The driver had 13 years of truck driving experience and had been employed full time by Frontline Transportation Company for 6 weeks at the time of the accident.

Medical. According to the Freightliner driver, he did not take any prescription medications, was wearing his prescription eyeglasses at the time of the accident, and was not fatigued.

Duty Status. The Freightliner driver reported that he picked up his tractor about 6:00 A.M.; picked up and delivered a chassis trailer and cargo container; and then picked up the accident chassis and cargo container and traveled to Midwest Recycling in Rockford, Illinois, where the container was loaded. He said that he had driven the Chicago–Rockford route on four or five previous occasions.

Class-A license classification includes any combination of vehicles with a gross combination weight rating (GCWR) of 26,001 pounds or more, provided that the gross vehicle weight rating (GVWR) of the vehicle(s) being towed exceeds 10,000 pounds. (Holders of a Class A license may, with appropriate endorsements, operate all vehicles within classes B, C, and D.)

Bus Driver

Certification and Experience. At the time of the accident, the 57-year-old bus driver held an Illinois Class B9 CDL, with a passenger endorsement and an expiration date of September 27, 2007. The bus driver did not possess a valid medical certificate in accordance with 49 CFR 391.41. His medical certificate had been issued in 1999 and had expired in 2001. While working for Leisure, the bus driver had accumulated 6.5 years of experience driving buses similar to the accident bus. He said that he was very familiar with the I-90 route, having traveled it many times. He had previously worked as a professional firefighter with the Great Lakes Naval Training Center, where he operated heavy fire department vehicles and served as a driving instructor.

Medical. During an interview with Safety Board investigators, the bus driver stated that he was a Type II diabetic and used prescribed medications to control the condition. The driver reported that he was taking the prescription medications Lotensin, Actose, Amaryl, and Metformin daily; monitored his blood sugar and diet; and had undergone cataract surgery on his right eye during the year prior to the accident. On October 10, 2003, following the accident, the bus driver passed a complete physical examination for commercial driver fitness and was issued a valid medical certificate. The medical examination report indicated that the driver's Type II diabetes was well controlled through the use of prescribed oral medication.

Duty Status. The bus driver reported for duty at 7:00 A.M. on October 1, 2003. He then drove the accident bus 35 miles from the company headquarters in Lake Bluff, Illinois, to downtown Chicago, where he arrived at 9:15 A.M. He loaded his passengers and departed on a round-trip route from Chicago to Rockford at 9:25 A.M. At 2:15 P.M., he departed Rockford for the return trip to Chicago.

The bus driver was not required to keep driver logs due to the local nature of his operations.

Class B license classification includes any single vehicle with a GVWR of 26,001 pounds or more, or any such vehicle towing a vehicle not exceeding 10,000 pounds GVWR. (Holders of a Class B license may, with appropriate endorsements, operate all vehicles within class C, which includes any vehicle weighing 26,000 pounds [GVWR] or less designed to transport 16 or more people.)

The bus driver's operations fell within the 100-air-mile exemption. See <www.fmcsa.dot.gov/rulesregulations/administration/fmcsr/395.1.htm#e>, January 31, 2006.

■ OTHER DRIVERS

Chevrolet Pickup Truck

The 67-year-old pickup truck driver was traveling eastbound on I-90 from Beaver Dam, Wisconsin, to Bartlett, Illinois. The evening prior to the accident day he had been camping in Horicon, Wisconsin, and reported that he slept from 11:00 P.M. until 8:00 A.M. in his camper, which was mounted in the bed of his truck.

Ford Tractor-Box-Trailer

The 56-year-old Ford driver had 27 years of truck driving experience as an employee of Penner International, Inc. At the time of the accident, he was driving eastbound on I-90 en route to Durham, North Carolina, from Steinbach, Manitoba, Canada, transporting a box trailer containing 25 pallets of prescription medication. His co-driver was asleep in the sleeper berth.

Kenworth Tractor-Tank-Trailer

The 59-year-old Kenworth driver was an employee of Carl Klemm, Inc., and had 36 years of truck driving experience. At the time of the accident, he was transporting a tanker load of ink dye capsule liquid and was traveling eastbound on I-90, en route to West Carrollton, Ohio, from Portage, Wisconsin. The driver said that he had been on vacation for several days before returning to work on the day of the accident.

HIGHWAY INFORMATION

General

The accident occurred on I-90 east at MP 41.6, approximately 2,600 feet west of the Hampshire–Marengo toll plaza. I-90—a divided, straight, and level four-lane asphalt roadway—is classified as an urban principal arterial road. As part of the Illinois State Toll Highway, this section of roadway is referred to as the "Northwest Tollway," 76.5 miles stretching from I-294 in Chicago northwest to the Wisconsin state line. At the accident location, the 41-foot-wide paved portion of roadway comprised two main travel lanes (25 feet total width), an 11-foot-wide right shoulder, and a 5-foot-wide left shoulder. A 50-foot-wide depressed grassy median separated the eastbound and westbound lanes. Because of a construction work zone that extended from MPs 25.5 to 62.5, the posted speed limit for I-90 at the accident site was 45 mph. The signage for the reduced speed limit began 5.3 miles prior to the accident site, and toll information signage began 0.5 mile prior to the accident site (at MP 42.1).

Hampshire–Marengo Toll Booth Configuration

Figures 14 and 15 show the Hampshire–Marengo approach view and toll booth and toll lane configuration at the time of the accident. Lanes 1–3 (from right to left) were manual cash lanes with toll collectors for all vehicles, and lanes 4–6 (from right to left) were automatic coin lanes for cars only. At the time of the accident, the only manual lane available for commercial traffic was lane 3. Lane 1 was open weekdays during peak commercial hours, from 6:00 A.M. to 2:00 P.M., and closed the rest of the day. At the time of the accident, the toll collector for lane 2 was on break, and this lane was closed. The lane 3 toll collector stated that he observed no unusual queuing of traffic in lane 3 before the accident; he said that four or five tractor-semi-trailers were in line to pass through the toll plaza.

METEOROLOGICAL INFORMATION

The National Weather Service at DeKalb-Taylor Municipal Airport, 21 miles south of the accident site, reported the weather at 3:00 P.M. on October 1, 2003, as mostly sunny and clear, with a temperature of 50 degrees Fahrenheit, 23 percent humidity, and winds northwest at 15 mph.

TOXICOLOGICAL INFORMATION

Toxicological specimens were collected from the Freightliner driver at a local hospital following the accident. The ISP laboratory tested the specimens and found the driver's blood and urine to be negative for alcohol and other drugs of abuse. The Safety Board also had the specimens tested and determined that no carbon monoxide, cyanide, ethanol, or other drugs were present.

Toxicological specimens were collected from the bus driver 2 days after the accident, on October 3, 2003. The specimens were evaluated locally and were found to be negative for drugs of abuse. No alcohol testing was conducted. According to 49 CFR 382.303, the employer of a driver of a commercial motor vehicle operating on a public road in commerce is required to conduct alcohol and controlled substance testing on that driver if the vehicle is involved in a fatal accident. Safety Board investigators found no evidence that Leisure completed any post-accident alcohol testing on the bus driver, as required.

Figure 1 Regional map of accident location

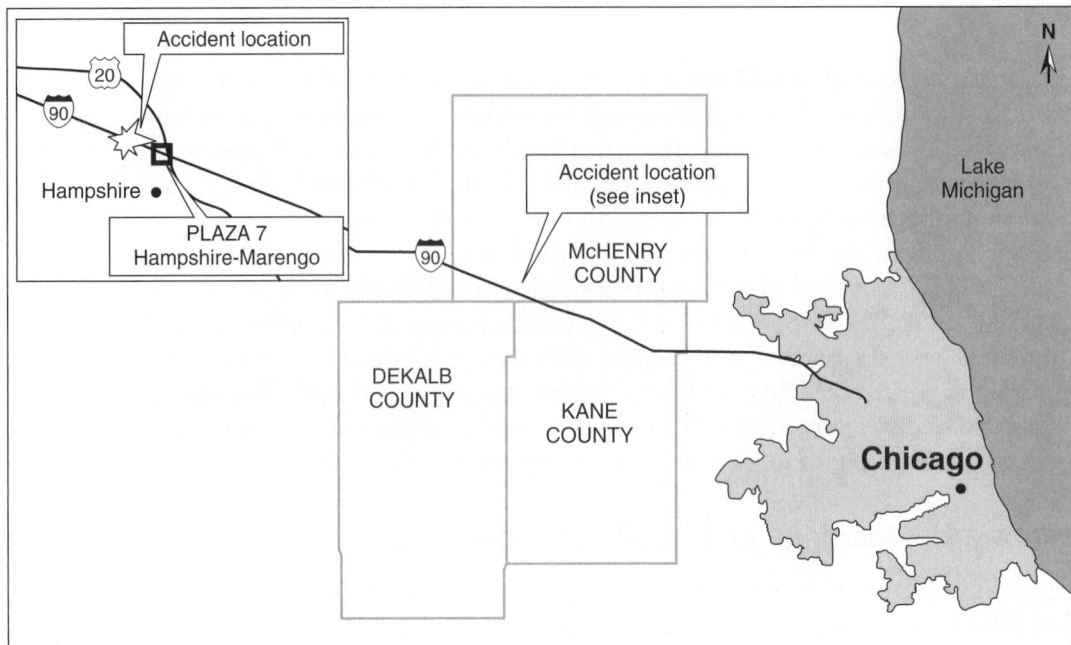

Figure 2 View of accident location, I-90 eastbound

Figure 3 Damaged Freightliner tractor-trailer

Courtesy of Illinois State Police

Figure 4 Damaged Goshen specialty bus

Figure 5 Damaged pickup truck

Courtesy of Illinois State Police

Figure 6 Damaged Ford tractor-box trailer

Figure 7 Damaged Kenworth tractor-tank trailer

Figure 8 Accident scene diagram

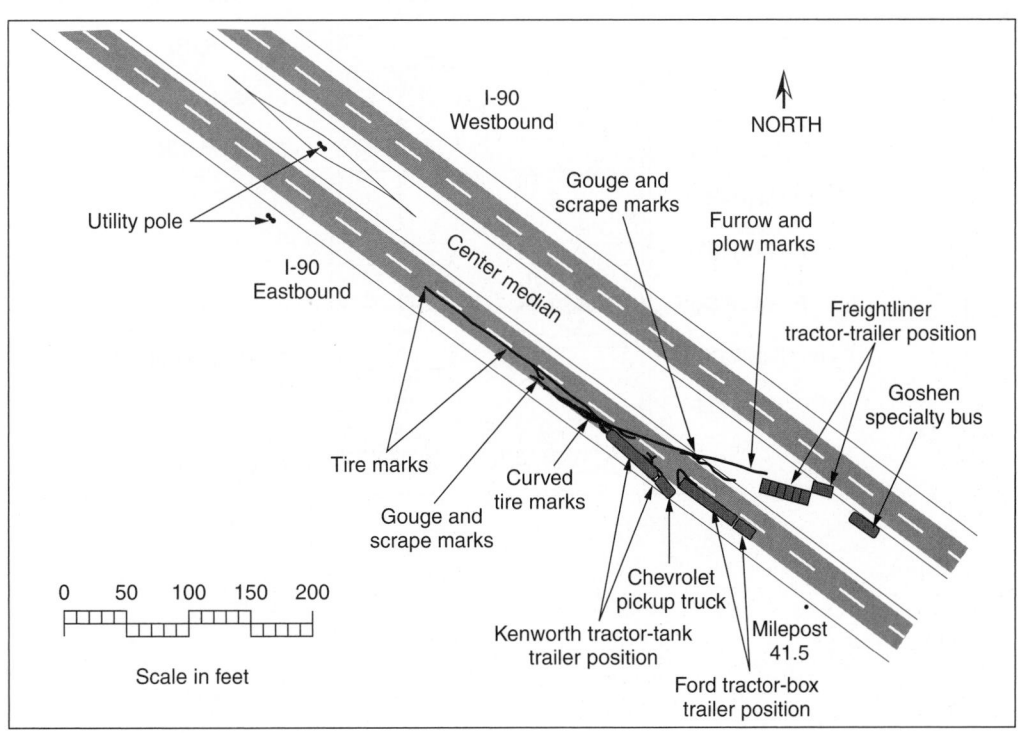

Figure 9 Specialty bus seating diagram

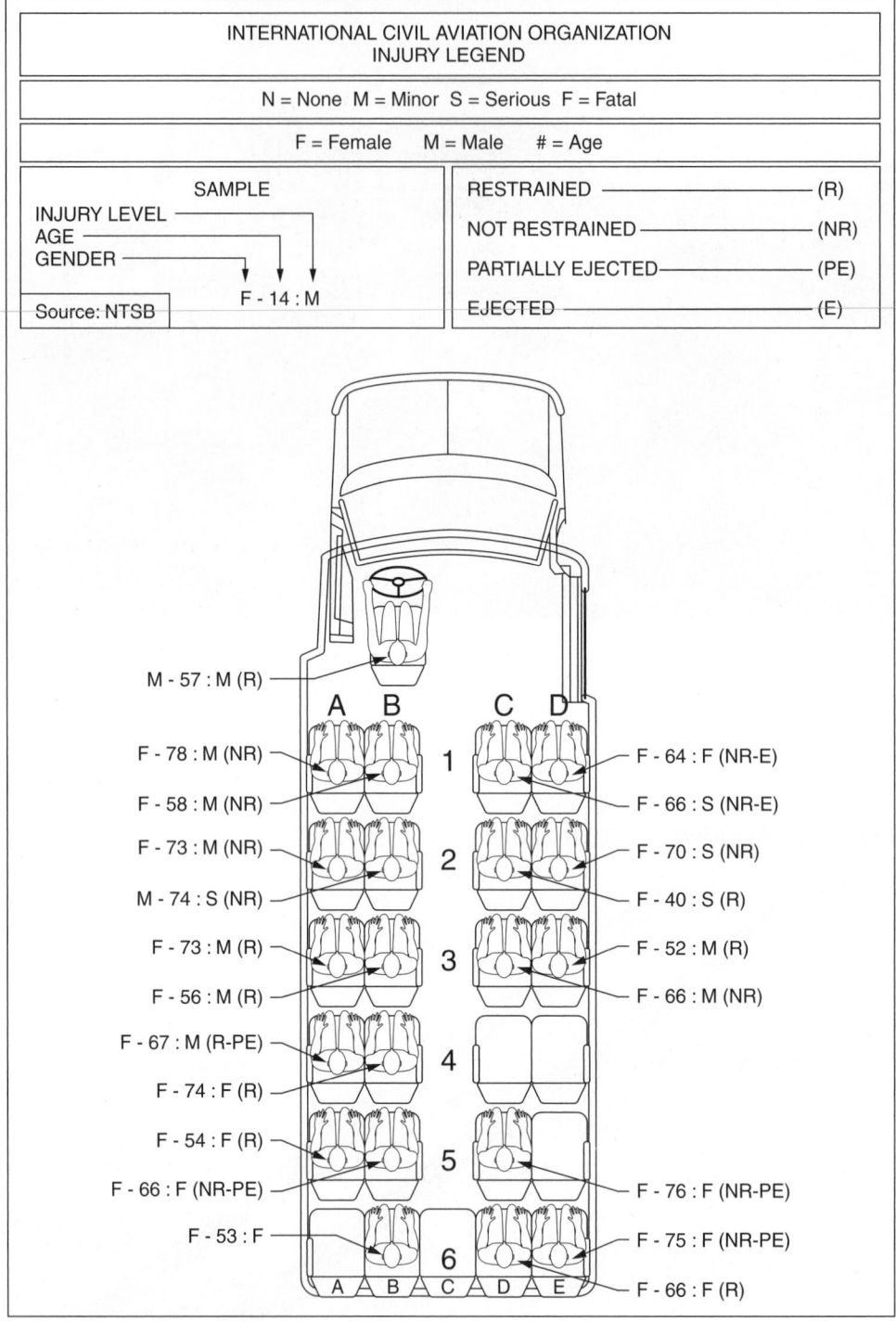

Figure 10 Specialty bus rear-impact damage

Note: Figures 11, 12, and 13 have been omitted from the orginal report.

Figure 14 Approach view of accident toll plaza

Figure 15 Accident scene toll plaza lanes

Figure 16 Graphic depiction of open road toll system

Courtesy of Illinois State Toll Highway Authority

Acronyms and Abbreviations

AAMVA	American Association of Motor Vehicle Administrators
ABS	antilock brake system
ADT	average daily traffic
ASA	automatic slack adjuster
ASE	National Institute for Automotive Service Excellence
ATA	American Trucking Associations, Inc.
Blossom Valley	Blossom Valley Farms, Inc.
CCMTA	Canadian Council of Motor Transport Administrators
CDL	commercial driver's license
CFR	*Code of Federal Regulations*
CVSA	Commercial Vehicle Safety Alliance
EDSMAC4	Engineering Dynamics Simulation Model of Automobile Collisions, 4th revision
FHWA	Federal Highway Administration
FMCSA	Federal Motor Carrier Safety Administration
FMCSRs	*Federal Motor Carrier Safety Regulations*
GVWR	gross vehicle weight rating
HVE	Human, Vehicle, Environment
ISS-2	Inspection Selection System
MCMIS	Federal Motor Carrier Management Information System
NHTSA	National Highway Traffic Safety Administration
NPRM	notice of proposed rulemaking
OOIDA	Owner-Operator Independent Drivers Association
PennDOT	Pennsylvania Department of Transportation
psi	pounds per square inch
SafeStat	Safety Status Measurement System
SIMON	Simulation Model Non-linear
SRPD	Southern Regional Police Department
THC	tetrahydrocannabinol
UMTRI	University of Michigan Transportation Research Institute
USDOT	U.S. Department of Transportation

CASE C

Collision Between a Ford Dump Truck and Four Passenger Cars
Glen Rock, Pennsylvania
April 11, 2003
Highway Accident Report
NTSB/HAR-06/01. Washington, D.C.

Abstract

About 3:36 P.M. on April 11, 2003, in the Borough of Glen Rock, Pennsylvania, a 1995 Ford dump truck owned and operated by Blossom Valley Farms, Inc., was traveling southbound on Church Street, a two-lane, two-way residential street with a steep downgrade, when the driver found that he was unable to stop the truck (Figure 1). The truck struck four passenger cars, which were stopped at the intersection of Church and Main Streets, and pushed them into the intersection. One of the vehicles struck three pedestrians (a 9-year-old boy, a 7-year-old boy, and a 7-year-old girl), who were on the sidewalk on the west side of Church Street. The

Figure 1 Accident truck

Source: Southern Regional Police Department

truck continued across the intersection, through a gas station parking lot, and over a set of railroad tracks before coming to rest about 300 feet south of the intersection. As a result of the collision, the driver and an 11-year-old occupant of one of the passenger cars received fatal injuries, and the three pedestrians who were struck received minor-to-serious injuries. The six remaining passenger car occupants and the truck driver were not injured.

Narrative

The 21-year-old accident truck driver worked for Blossom Valley Farms, Inc., (Blossom Valley) an agricultural nursery, making deliveries of landscaping materials, including mulch, dirt, and stone. He had been working for Blossom Valley for 10 days when the accident occurred. According to the accident driver, on the day of the accident, he started work about 8:00 A.M., and his first delivery in the 1995 Ford dump truck consisted of 8 yards of mulch to an address in Parkton, Maryland. (See Figure 2.) He also made his second and third deliveries, of 4 yards of mulch and 2 yards of Red Mountain Stone, respectively, to Parkton. On the way back from the third delivery, he stopped at a fast-food restaurant in Shrewsbury, Pennsylvania, where he picked up food and then returned to Blossom Valley. He ate lunch in the truck while topsoil was loaded into the truck. The fourth delivery of the day was a load of 14 yards of unscreened topsoil, which was being delivered a day late. The driver indicated that he knew it should take three trips to complete the topsoil delivery because the truck's capacity was limited to 5 scoops of wet topsoil (it was raining at the time). The employee who loaded the truck told the driver he had loaded 7 scoops and that the driver should go on with the delivery.

The driver indicated that he followed the directions printed on the delivery invoice given to him by his employer. He traveled north on the Susquehanna Trail and turned left on Church Street toward Glen Rock. He said he saw the "3/4 ton limit, Except Local Deliveries" signs at the beginning of Church Street but continued

Figure 2 Map of the general region of the accident site

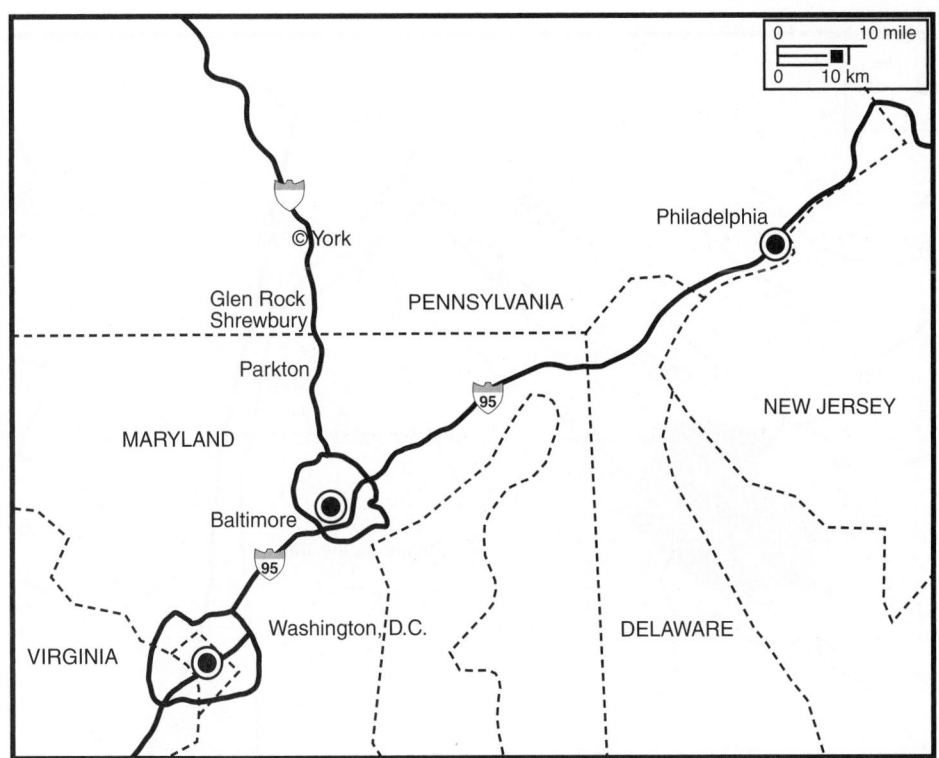

anyway because the directions given him by Blossom Valley told him to use that street and he thought he was making a local delivery. (See Figures 3 and 4.) He said that he was traveling 25 to 35 mph on Church Street and stopped at the top of the hill near a water tower and electrical substation. (A witness following the truck indicated in a police interview that the accident truck did not stop.)

The accident driver stated that as he started down the hill (see Figure 5), he did not select a lower gear. He said that at some point during the descent, he pumped his brakes and the truck began to speed up. He also stated that about a quarter of the way down the hill, he lost his brakes and the brake warning light in the truck began to flash. He said he knew then that he had brake problems because his boss and a coworker had told him that if the brake light flashed, he did not have enough pressure [air pressure]. He said he could not stop the truck, and he saw children and cars at the bottom of the hill. He indicated that he leaned out the window and yelled, "No brakes, get out of the way" as the truck neared Center Street (about 3 blocks from the accident site). He said he struck the back of a black car and thought he "went airborne." He said that he did not sound the horn and that he was not wearing a seat belt. He stated that his recollection of the events after the initial impact was "vague."

Witnesses reported that just before the accident, a school bus had unloaded students on Main Street. After exiting the bus, the students crossed Church Street and, as the bus began to leave, they walked up the sidewalk on the west side of Church Street. Witnesses also reported that four passenger cars were stopped at the "STOP" sign for southbound traffic on Church Street, where it intersects with Main Street. The first car in the queue was a 1997 Pontiac Grand Prix, occupied by a driver and three passengers; the second was a 1996 Mazda Protégé, occupied by a driver; the third was a 1987 Chevrolet Nova, occupied by a driver and a front seat passenger; and the fourth was a 1993 Chevrolet Camaro, occupied by a driver.

Figure 3 Map of the accident area, showing the Borough of Glen Rock (shaded area), the location of Blossom Valley Farms, and the intended delivery destination. The large arrows show the direction of the accident truck's travel

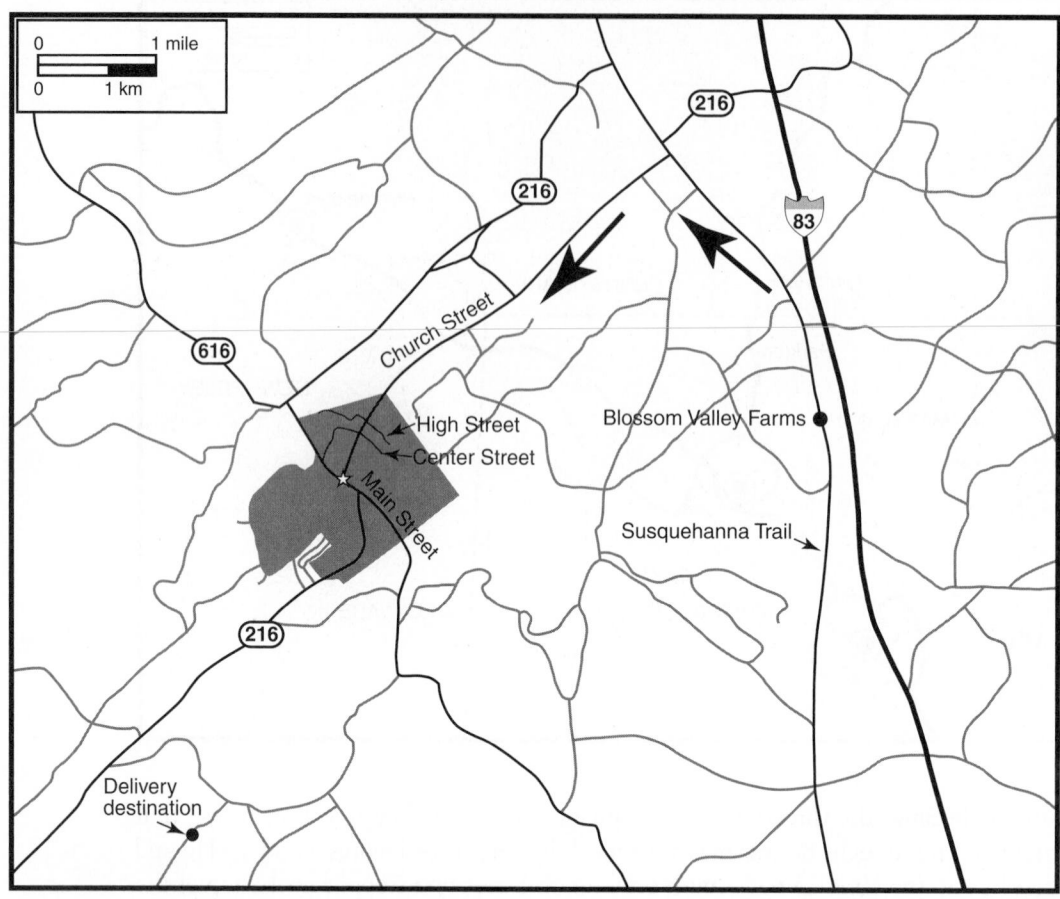

Figure 4 Weight prohibition signs at the beginning of Church Street

Source: Pennsylvania Department of Transportation

Figure 5 Descending grade on southbound Church Street

Source: Pennsylvania Department of Transportation

About 107 feet north of the intersection, the accident truck struck the rear of the Camaro, causing it to rotate clockwise and pushing it into the Nova. The Nova rotated counterclockwise; the rear of the vehicle climbed the 6-inch-high curb and struck three children on the sidewalk and a metal post on a fence on the west side of the sidewalk. The Nova continued to rotate counterclockwise and struck the Mazda, pushing it forward into the rear of the Pontiac. The truck pushed the passenger cars into the intersection.

The Camaro came to rest near the northwest corner of the intersection of Church and Main Streets, facing south. The Nova came to rest with its front wheels on the southern sidewalk in front of the gas station, facing south. The Mazda and Pontiac came to rest in the parking area of the gas station, west of the Nova by about 25 feet and facing southeast. The accident truck proceeded across Main Street, through the western portion of the gas station parking lot, onto Water Street, across the railroad tracks, and then west into an alley, coming to rest about 130 feet west of the intersection of the alley and Water Street. The truck traveled about 407 feet from its initial point of impact with the Camaro to its point of rest. (See Figures 6 and 7.)

Emergency Response

SRPD, Glen Rock Fire and Ambulance, and Loganville Fire Company responders were dispatched at 3:36 P.M. Glen Rock Ambulance responders were on scene within a minute, Glen Rock Fire Department personnel were on scene by 3:39 P.M., and SRPD officers arrived on scene about 3:44 P.M. In addition, the Shrewsbury and New Freedom, Pennsylvania, fire companies responded to the accident. Glen Rock, Rose Fire Company, and Jacobus ambulance services transported patients to Penn State Hershey Medical Center and York Hospital.

Figure 6 Intersection of Church Street and Main Street looking southbound on Church Street

Source: Southern Regional Police Department

Figure 7 At-rest positions of the vehicles at the accident scene

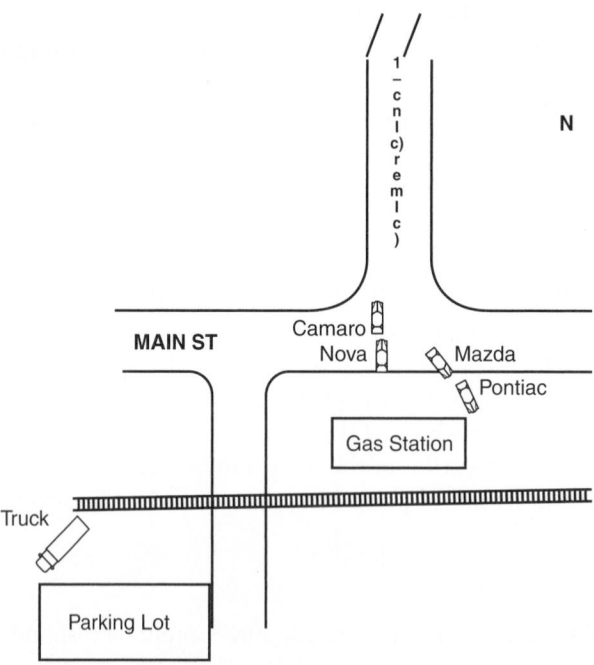

Driver Information

The 21-year-old truck driver lived in White Hall, Maryland, and had been working for Blossom Valley as a truck driver since April 1, 2003. He possessed a Maryland Class "C" noncommercial driver's license. This license permitted the driver to operate an automobile, station wagon, light truck, or any motor vehicle, except a motorcycle, with a gross vehicle weight of 26,000 pounds or less. A commercial driver's license (CDL) is required to drive a single vehicle weighing 26,001 pounds or more.

On the day of the accident, the driver was operating a commercial truck with a gross vehicle weight rating (GVWR) of 26,000 pounds that was equipped with an air brake system, which does not operate in the same way that hydraulic brake systems for automobiles do. (This report will discuss operation of air brake systems in a subsequent section.) According to the accident driver, he had no experience driving an air-braked truck before Blossom Valley hired him, and the largest vehicle he had previously driven was a pickup truck. According to the driver and his employer, he received no air brake training. He said that he had been shown how to operate the lift on the accident truck. At the time of the accident, he had been driving the accident truck for less than a week. Postaccident, he told investigators that he did not know that pumping an air brake-equipped truck's brakes depleted the brakes' air pressure.

Three days before the accident, on April 8, 2003, the driver had a minor accident in the same truck, which he stated was due to loss of braking. (The driver's truck rolled into the back of a stopped passenger car. Neither vehicle suffered substantial damage.)

Truck Information

The accident truck was a 1995 Ford Motor Company, F-800 Series, 2-axle truck with a dump body. It was equipped with a Ford FD-1060 6-cylinder diesel engine that produced 175 horsepower at 2,500 rpm, an Allison model AT-545 4-speed automatic transmission, air brakes, and a hydraulic dump bed. It did not have an antilock brake system (ABS). The truck had an odometer reading of 145,095 miles. According to the manufacturer, the truck's GVWR was 26,000 pounds. The SRPD weighed the truck during the postaccident investigation and found the total weight to be 26,600 pounds. In July 2003, the Pennsylvania Department of Transportation (PennDOT) weighed the truck on portable scales with the load removed, and the empty weight was 15,540 pounds. The wheelbase was 207 inches, and the overall truck length was 25 feet, 5.5 inches.

The truck was equipped on the front and rear axles with standard S-cam drum foundation air brakes with automatic slack adjusters (ASAs). A Bendix model 2150 single-cylinder, gear-driven compressor supplied air to the system. The air governor was a Bendix model D-2, permanently set at 110 pounds per square inch (psi).

As part of the Safety Board's normal protocol, investigators tested the brakes postaccident. The diesel engine was operable, and all air testing was done with air supplied by the engine-mounted Bendix compressor, using the vehicle foot valve (brake pedal) for brake testing. The diesel engine was started and full brake applications were made at about 90 psi of air pressure. No air leaks were discovered in the air brake system.

The brake testing results, summarized in Table 2, indicated that the pushrod stroke for both rear brakes exceeded the adjustment limit by 1/2 inch, resulting in little or no brake force for the rear wheels.

The truck was equipped with Gunite ASAs on all four brakes. After the accident, Safety Board investigators removed the automatic adjusters from the rear brakes, along with the quick-connect devises and clevis pins, and took them to the Gunite facility for testing. The quick-connect devises had wear in the clevis holes,

Table 2 Accident truck brake test results summary

Axle	Air chamber size	Slack arm length"	Pushrod stroke	Adjustment limit[B]	Rated stroke
Left front	T-16	5 1/2 in.	1 1/2 in.	1 3/4 in.	2 1/4 in.
Right front	1-16	5 1/2 in.	1 1/2 in.	1 3/4 in.	2 1/4 in.
Left rear	1-30	5 1/2 in.	2 1/2 in.	2 in.	2 1/2 in.
Right rear	1-30	5 1/2 in.	2 1/2 in.	2 in.	2 1/2 in.

"The distance from the center of the splined camshaft to the center of the clevis pin, which secures the pushrod to the slack adjuster; also known as the "lever arm length."

[B]The maximum pushrod stroke permitted. The values utilized for the "brake adjustment limit" are those stated in the *Commercial Vehicle Safety Alliance (CVSA) North American Standard Out-of-Service Criteria.* (Revised edition, April 2003.)

"The total length the pushrod can travel inside the air chamber." (When the "pushrod stroke" is equivalent to the "rated stroke," generally no braking forces are obtained when the brakes are applied.)

where they attached to the slack adjusters, and some flexing was observed where the two parts met. The combination of wear in the clevis pin holes and flexing of the joints rendered the automatic feature of the ASAs inoperative. When tested with the devises and clevis pins from the accident truck, the pushrod stroke would not go below 2 1/2 inches, at which point it produced little or no brake force. When the two rear adjusters were tested at the Gunite facility with new devises and clevis pins, the adjusters worked correctly and kept the adjustment well under 2 inches.

All four brake drums were removed, examined, photographed, and measured. The front axle had 15-inch drums and the rear axle had 16.5-inch drums. Heat cracks were present in all the drums, and some discoloration (bluing) was found on the front drums, which were smooth. The drum diameters were measured with a calibrated Central Tool digital brake drum gauge, and all were within manufacturer's tolerances. The brake shoe widths were 4 inches for the front wheels and 7 inches for the rear wheels. The brake shoes had no observable cracks and exhibited no anomalies All the shoes were measured and found to be within CVSA-established tolerances.

The truck was equipped with a dash-mounted red brake warning light, which illuminated when the air pressure went below 70 psi. An audible alarm accompanied this illumination. The spring brakes (parking brakes) were automatically fully applied on the rear axle when the system air reached about 40 psi. Investigators installed air gauges in all the air chambers, or in the service air line just outside the chamber, to check the amount of air going into the chamber during a service brake (foot pedal) application. When a forceful application was made at 90 psi, the chamber gauge pressure read about 75 psi on all four wheel positions (about 15 pounds less than the applied pressure).

The parking brake test was conducted by pulling the parking brake valve that applied the spring brakes. The engine was started and the transmission was moved into "DRIVE" in an attempt to move the vehicle forward on a concrete floor. The truck moved forward with only a slight increase in engine rpm. The truck was then placed in "REVERSE" and, with minimal engine acceleration, it went backward, even with the parking brake applied.

Highway Information

Church Street (State Route 3008) is a two-lane, two-way rural road 27 miles long between the Susquehanna Trail (State Route 3001) to the north and Main Street (State Route 216) to the south. The Susquehanna Trail is a two-lane, north/south roadway, which parallels Interstate Highway 83 on the west between

Harrisburg and the Pennsylvania/Maryland State Line. The topography of the surrounding area is rolling hills.

As Church Street enters the Borough of Glen Rock, the downgrade becomes increasingly steep, from 3.4 percent near the top of the hill to 13 percent at the base of the hill (intersection with Main Street). According to PennDOT, the roadway width varies from 20 feet before entering the borough to 26 feet inside the borough. There is an 8-foot-wide parking lane on the west side of Church Street in the borough, next to housing, and the travel lanes are 9 feet wide. Solid, double, yellow lines separate the north/south lanes.

Main Street is a two-lane, two-way, east/west roadway traversing the Borough of Glen Rock. Immediately to the east of the intersection between Main Street and Church Street, a painted pedestrian crosswalk traverses Main Street. A gas station is located on the south side of the T-intersection of Church Street and Main Street.

The speed limit on Church Street traveling south from the Susquehanna Trail is 55 mph. The speed limit changes 1.2 miles south of the intersection to 40 mph and again 1.8 miles south of the intersection, as Church Street enters the Borough of Glen Rock, to 25 mph. The speed limit at the accident site (intersection of Church Street and Main Street) is 25 mph.

According to PennDOT, the average daily traffic (ADT) on Church Street in 1998 was 3,213, of which 8 percent was trucks and buses. In 2001, the ADT was 3,915, of which 9 percent was trucks and buses.

PennDOT data indicated that from January 1999 to December 2002, 11 traffic accidents occurred on Church Street within the Borough of Glen Rock. Of the 11 accidents, 1 involved a fatality, 1 a major injury, 4 moderate injuries, and 5 minor injuries. Two of the 11 accidents involved trucks.

According to PennDOT, in 1965, after a fatal accident involving a truck at or near the April 11, 2003, accident intersection, the Borough of Glen Rock requested and obtained a weight restriction of 1,500 pounds (load capacity) on Church Street, and the street was so posted. At the intersection of the Susquehanna Trail and Church Street are R5-2 signs conforming to the *Manual on Uniform Traffic Control Devices* indicating that Church Street is a weight-restricted street. The signs indicate that the load weights are limited to 3/4 ton (1,500 pounds), except for local deliveries. The weight restriction applies only in the Borough of Glen Rock. (Refer to Figures 3 and 4.) For traffic traveling northbound on the Susquehanna Trail, an additional sign reads, "Trucks over 1 ton use [Pennsylvania State Route] 216 to Glen Rock." (See Figure 8.)

Additional signs and updated signs have periodically been erected in an effort to keep vehicles with weights in excess of the restriction from using Church Street. The borough ordinance, reads (in part)

> It shall be unlawful for any person to operate a motor vehicle, trailer, or semi-trailer, as defined in The Vehicle Code, having a load capacity in excess of fifteen hundred (1,500) pounds, on Church Street.... [except] (a) Delivering goods or supplying services to any location on said street or accessible only by the use of said street; and (b) Moving any such vehicle to the residence of the owner of such vehicle or to the customary place of parking such vehicle at any location on said Street or accessible only by the use of said Street.

PennDOT officials indicated that the restriction applies to vehicles "having a load capacity" in excess of 1,500 pounds; many of today's vehicles, including many pickup trucks, have a load-carrying capacity in excess of 1,500 pounds. According to PennDOT and the SRPD, enforcement of the weight restriction on Church Street is sporadic and complicated due to the wording of the ordinance

Figure 8 Intersection of Susquehanna Trail and Church Street. (Note the weight restriction sign directing trucks over 1 ton to use Pennsylvania State Route 216)

Source: Pennsylvania Department of Transportation

and a local magistrate's interpretation of the ordinance to allow use of this street for local deliveries to addresses that are not on or intersecting the street.

Motor Carrier Information

General

At the time of the accident, Blossom Valley was a private interstate carrier located in New Freedom, Pennsylvania. It was registered as a motor carrier with the U.S. Department of Transportation (USDOT). The carrier began operations in 1987; it transported building and construction materials, agricultural and farm supplies, and nursery stock. Blossom Valley trucks covered about 16,000 miles a year, including about 2,500 interstate miles. The majority of the interstate miles involved delivery of mulch, topsoil, stone, and nursery items. According to Blossom Valley's owner, before the accident, he was unaware of many of the Federal regulations and requirements concerning motor carrier operations.

The Blossom Valley fleet consisted of five trucks—two straight trucks, a 1994 Chevrolet dump truck, a 1995 Ford utility dump truck (the accident truck), and a 1990 International truck tractor with a 1997 Reit flatbed semitrailer. The tractor-semitrailer combination truck was the only vehicle in the fleet that required a driver with a CDL. It had a combined GVWR of 80,000 pounds and, like the accident truck, was air brake-equipped. The Chevrolet dump truck was equipped with hydraulic brakes. The carrier employed two drivers, one with a CDL and one without (the accident driver). The driver with a CDL drove the two straight trucks and the tractor-semitrailer.

According to statements made during Safety Board interviews with the accident driver, the motor carrier owner, and the other driver, Blossom Valley did not give the accident driver a road test. Title 49 CFR 391.31-33, "Road test," specifies that "a person shall not drive a commercial motor vehicle unless he/she has first successfully completed a road test and has been issued a certificate of driver's road test...." Title 49 CFR 390.5 defines a commercial motor vehicle as "any self-propelled motor vehicle...used on a highway in interstate commerce... [with] a gross vehicle weight rating of...10,001 pounds or more..." The road test certificate or a copy of a valid CDL is to be retained in the driver's qualification files.

The accident driver operated within a 100-mile radius of the home terminal and returned to that location every night, so, according to 49 CFR 395.1(e), he was not required to keep a record of duty status. However, as a motor carrier, Blossom Valley was required to maintain driver time records. After the accident, Blossom Valley was unable to provide investigators with the required time records. The accident driver's actual hours of service are unknown.

On March 10, 2004, another Blossom Valley truck, driven by a different driver, was ticketed for traveling down Church Street, because the vehicle was in violation of the weight restriction.

Accident Truck Maintenance History

At the time of the accident, Blossom Valley did not have a regular, scheduled vehicle maintenance program in place as required by 49 CFR 396.3. Safety Board investigators obtained maintenance records from four facilities that serviced Blossom Valley's vehicles: RG Group and Beasley Ford, both in York, Pennsylvania; Truck Specialties, Inc., in Shrewsbury, Pennsylvania; and C & T Transport in Parkton, Maryland. The service facilities did not have preventative maintenance agreements with Blossom Valley. Rather, they serviced the carrier's vehicles when Blossom Valley brought them in for repairs.

Truck Specialties completed Pennsylvania State inspections of the accident truck in 2001 and 2002. The facility had last serviced the truck in May 2002 for non-brake-related repairs.

On April 10, 2002, about 1 year before the accident, the accident truck was stopped in Maryland and subjected to a CVSA level 1 inspection, which included checking the brakes for adjustment. At that time, the pushrod stroke for the left rear brake was 2 1/4 inches and the pushrod stroke for the right rear brake was 2 1/2 inches. The adjustment limit is 2 inches, so the brake condition resulted in the truck being placed out of service. Safety Board investigators interviewed the driver who was operating the truck at the time of this inspection. (Blossom Valley no longer employs this driver.) He stated that he [manually] adjusted the brakes before departing the inspection site. He also indicated he had adjusted the accident truck's brakes three or four times during his seasonal employment with Blossom Valley during 2002. He further stated that he had worked full-time as a mechanic for a construction company, was a Pennsylvania State-certified truck inspection mechanic, and had been a truck mechanic for more than 20 years.

On January 20, 2003, the accident truck underwent a Pennsylvania State annual inspection performed by the Beasley Ford dealership in York, Pennsylvania. According to the service manager, the truck mechanics at Beasley are certified by the National Institute for Automotive Service Excellence (ASE). (For more information, see the section in this report on "Inspector and Mechanic Certification Requirements" under "Other Information.") The dealership pays

Table 3   Glen Rock accident vehicle inspection history

Date	Type of inspection	Comments
August 2, 2001	Pennsylvania State annual	Inspection and subsequent repairs performed by Truck Specialties mechanics; no brake problems noted
March 27, 2002	Pennsylvania State annual	Inspection and subsequent repairs performed by Truck Specialties mechanics; no brake problems noted
April 10, 2002	Roadside, CVSA level 1	Placed out of service for out-of-adjustment brakes; driver adjusted brakes and left inspection site
January 20, 2003	Pennsylvania State annual	Inspection and subsequent repairs performed by Beasley Ford; rear brakes out of adjustment
April 15–18, 2003	Postaccident inspection (CVSA level 1)	Placed out of service for out-of-adjustment brakes, a loose brake component, and an inoperative turn signal

the expenses of acquiring and maintaining certification. The mechanic who performed the annual inspection was a Pennsylvania State-certified truck inspector. He told Safety Board investigators that the rear brakes were out of adjustment and that he had [manually] adjusted them.

According to the dealer's service manager, ASAs, which work "pretty well," still require inspection and manual adjustment, particularly if the vehicle operates in hilly or mountainous areas, or in dirt, gravel, or mud. The Ford owner's manual for a year 2003 model F650/750 (a vehicle similar to the accident truck) states

> Inspect standard air brakes equipped with automatic slack adjusters for proper brake adjustment every 4 months or 20,000 miles, and more frequently if operated in hilly or mountainous regions or in mud.

At the time of the January 2003 inspection, the recorded mileage on the truck was 142,810. The accident occurred less than 3 months later, at which time the odometer read 145,095 miles No manual adjustments are known to have been made to the brakes between the January 20 inspection and the April 11 accident. The truck had traveled a total of 2,285 miles during that period. Table 3 summarizes the inspection history of the accident truck, indicating the date of each inspection, the type of inspection performed, and whether the brakes were adjusted.

Motor Carrier Oversight

General

At the time of the accident, Blossom Valley had not undergone a Federal Motor Carrier Safety Administration (FMCSA) compliance review or been assigned a safety rating, so it was considered an unrated carrier. Because the carrier had been involved in this multiple-fatality accident, the FMCSA conducted a compliance review of Blossom Valley's safety management controls on May 2, 2003. The compliance review revealed discrepancies in the areas of drug/alcohol testing, driver qualification files, records of duty status, vehicle inspection record-keeping, and driver/vehicle inspection reports. The compliance review resulted in a safety rating of "Conditional" for Blossom Valley. As of October 13, 2005, the FMCSA safety rating had not changed.

FMCSA standards require a motor carrier to have adequate management controls in place to comply with applicable safety requirements. The FMCSA uses a rating formula to determine a motor carrier's safety fitness. The safety fitness rating methodology begins with an FMCSA-conducted compliance review, applying the six factors shown in Table 4 that rate the carrier's compliance with the *Federal Motor Carrier Safety Regulations* (FMCSRs).

Table 4 Factors for FMCSA safety compliance and the results of Blossom Valley's compliance review

Factors	Applicable FMCSRs and other criteria	Results of May 2, 2003, Blossom Valley compliance review
1—General	Parts 387 and 390	Satisfactory
2—Driver	Parts 382, 383, and 391	Satisfactory
3—Operational	Parts 392 and 395	Satisfactory
4—Vehicle	Parts 393 and 396 and out-of-service rate	Unsatisfactory
5—Hazardous materials	Parts 107, 171, 172, 173, 177, 180, and 397	Not applicable
6—Accident	Recordable accident rate	Satisfactory

Table 5 Other Blossom Valley vehicle inspections

Date	Type of inspection	Comments
June 3, 2003	Roadside	Chevrolet pickup with a trailer: trailer brakes inoperative (no actuator switch); breakaway brake device not connected; vehicle placed out of service
June 27, 2003	Roadside	International tractor with Reit trailer: 4 of 10 brakes out of adjustment; vehicle placed out of service

Factors 1—General, 2—Driver, 3—Operational, 4—Vehicle, and 5—Hazardous Materials are rated "Satisfactory," "Conditional," or "Unsatisfactory." Factor 6—Accident is rated either "Satisfactory" or "Unsatisfactory"; a "Conditional" rating is not given. The ratings are defined as follows:

- "Satisfactory"—Carrier has not violated any acute regulations or shown a pattern of noncompliance with critical regulations for that factor.
- "Conditional"—Carrier has violated an acute regulation or had a pattern of noncompliance with critical regulations.
- "Unsatisfactory"—Carrier has violated two or more acute regulations or has patterns of noncompliance with two or more critical regulations.

After the FMCSA May 2003 compliance review, two other vehicles in Blossom Valley's fleet underwent roadside inspections and were placed out of service. (See Table 5.)

Toxicological Information

The accident truck driver told police that he began using illicit drugs in October 2002 (about 6 months before the accident). He acknowledged use of cocaine, marijuana, heroin, rock cocaine, and hydrocodone. (The driver did not have a prescription for the prescription medication hydrocodone.) He admitted using marijuana 2 days before the accident and estimated that he had last used cocaine about 2 weeks before the accident. He denied use of any controlled substance on the day of the accident.

Blood and urine specimens were collected from the driver at 6:33 P.M. and 6:55 P.M., respectively (about 3 and 3 1/4 hours postaccident). At the request of the York County, Pennsylvania, District Attorney, National Medical Services of Willow Grove, Pennsylvania, conducted postaccident toxicological testing of the truck driver's blood and urine. Postaccident urinalysis showed the presence of methylecgonine and benzoylecgonine (both metabolites of cocaine), morphine, and Δ^9-carboxy-tetrahydrocannabinol, an inactive metabolite of Δ^9-tetrahydrocannabinol (THC, the active hallucinogenic compound in marijuana). Blood was tested only for THC and metabolites; test results were negative. Urinalysis testing results for ethyl alcohol and cocaethylene were also negative.

Tests and Research

To evaluate the effectiveness of the truck's brakes, the Safety Board conducted computer simulations of the truck's descent on Church Street to the accident site and its impact with the four passenger cars. Investigators used a Human, Vehicle, Environment (HVE) system that employed two physics modules, the Simulation Model Non-linear (SIMON) for the truck descent and EDSMAC4 for the impact. The driver estimated his speed at the time of impact at 40 to 45 mph but stated that when he last looked at the speedometer, the truck was going 25 mph. The speed at impact was needed to determine a target speed for the truck at the bottom of the hill.

SIMON uses Brake Designer to assess the effects of temperature on the brake drums and linings. The HVE system has a Ford F-800 truck in its vehicle library. The size and adjustment of the brakes, the engine power curve, the transmission ratios, the differential ratio, and the load of the vehicle were set to replicate the accident truck in the simulation. Using the simulation tools, the brakes could be applied and released at different intervals as the vehicle descended the hill. SIMON does not model the compressor output and determine the available air pressure, but the force applied to the brake pedal can be varied. SIMON does model aerodynamic drag and rolling resistance. For the simulation, the down-grade was modeled as one grade that was 3,350 feet long at an average grade of 7.7 percent. This is equivalent to the grade at the accident site hill, which varied continuously. Based on the physical evidence (including tire marks and final vehicle positions) and HVE default vehicles for the 1993 Chevrolet Camaro, 1996 Mazda Protégé, 1987 Chevrolet Nova, and 1997 Pontiac Grand Prix, the EDSMAC4 simulations of the vehicle collisions near the intersection indicated that the speed of the truck at impact with the Camaro was about 35 mph.

The impact speed of 35 mph was used as a target for the SIMON downhill final speed. Witness statements concerning the speed of the truck on the hill varied. The driver stated that he stopped near the water tower and electrical substation at the top of the hill. He indicated that he pumped the brakes and that a quarter of the way down the hill, he lost the brakes. He said that as he was traveling about 25 mph, the brake warning light on the dashboard began to flash. A witness following the truck, however, stated that the truck did not stop and was traveling 25 to 30 mph at the top of the hill and then increased speed as it went down the hill. Numerous scenarios were simulated, including having the accident truck stop at the top of the hill and having it crest the hill at 25, 35, 45, and 55 mph. Simulations were made with and without sufficient brake pressure, for a total of 35 simulation runs. The simulations showed that the front brake drums could have heated from 615°F to 1,441°F. (At temperatures in excess of 900°F, brakes fade rapidly.) See appendix B (pages 550–51) for information on the simulations.

The simulations showed that if the driver had pumped the brakes rapidly and depleted the truck's air pressure to below 50 psi, the truck would not have been able to stop. If the driver had applied the brakes too late on the descent, the front brakes would have overheated, and the driver would not have been able to stop. If the driver had allowed the speed of the truck to exceed 38 mph on the descent, the front brakes would have overheated and faded. The simulations showed that the lowest brake drum temperatures occurred when the brakes were continually snubbed on and off as the truck went down the hill. The simulations indicated that the front brakes would have slowed the truck somewhat, keeping the truck to about 35 mph at the time of impact.

Other Information

Commercial Driver's License

The majority of States (32) have a classified license system, which is one in which the State issues different licenses for specific classes of vehicles. Before the CDL program was instituted (see below), in States that did not have a classified license system, any person licensed to drive an automobile could drive a commercial motor vehicle.

The CDL requirement was established under the Commercial Vehicle Safety Act of 1986 and became effective nationwide in 1992. It established testing and license requirements for drivers of commercial motor vehicles. The main purpose of the act was to reduce or prevent truck and bus accidents and fatalities by disqualifying unsafe commercial motor vehicle drivers. The classifications of CDL, by vehicle group descriptions, are

- Combination Vehicle (Group A)—Any combination of vehicles with a gross combination weight rating of 11,794 kilograms or more (26,001 pounds or more) provided the GVWR of the vehicle(s) being towed is in excess of 4,536 kilograms (10,000 pounds).
- Heavy Straight Vehicle (Group B)—Any single vehicle with a GVWR of 11,794 kilograms or more (26,001 pounds or more), or any such vehicle towing a vehicle not in excess of 4,536 kilograms (10,000 pounds) GVWR.
- Small Vehicle (Group C)—Any single vehicle, or combination of vehicles, that meets neither the definition of Group A nor that of Group B as contained in this section, but that either is designed to transport 16 or more passengers including the driver, or is used in the transportation of materials found to be hazardous for the purposes of the Hazardous Materials Transportation Act and which require the motor vehicle to be placarded under the Hazardous Materials Regulations.

Any CDL driver operating a commercial motor vehicle equipped with air brakes must pass an air brake test indicating that the driver has specific knowledge about air brake systems, inspection of the brakes, and "implications of low air pressure warning." If a CDL driver has not passed the air brake test, the CDL will display an "L" restriction, meaning the driver is prohibited from driving air brake-equipped vehicles. A CDL driver may have this restriction removed by passing a State air brake test at a later date.

Canadian Air Brake Endorsement

Since 2001, Transport Canada has required all drivers to have an air brake endorsement to drive any vehicle equipped with air brakes. According to the Canadian National Safety Code #4, "Classified Driver's Licence Program," a driver must possess a valid driver's license of an appropriate class to operate the assigned vehicle, including an air brake endorsement when the vehicle is equipped with air brakes. Transport Canada reports that Canada has experienced a reduction in brake-related accidents since the adoption of this requirement. Also, between September 1999 and September 2004, Canada experienced a 25-percent reduction in brakes found to be out of adjustment to the point of being out of service.

Brake Systems

Passenger cars are usually equipped with hydraulic brake systems. Trucks are equipped with either hydraulic brakes or air brakes. The two brake systems operate differently. A hydraulic brake system is filled with hydraulic fluid. When the brake pedal is depressed, a proportional force is applied to the fluid, which in turn forces the brake shoes against the drums, creating friction, which stops the vehicle. When the brake is released, the pressure is released, and the brakes release. Hydraulic brake systems are closed systems, so there is no depletion of the brake fluid. Also, hydraulic systems have little discernible lag time between pedal depression and brake application.

An air brake system converts compressed air into a linear force that acts upon a number of components, including the pushrod, slack adjuster, and camshaft, to apply the brake shoes against the brake drum, creating friction, which stops the vehicle. The compressor provides a supply of air to the holding tanks (also known as air supply reservoirs). When the brakes are applied, the stored air is distributed in the system through relay valves to the brake chambers, which convert the air pressure to a linear force. Using this force, the pushrod moves a slack adjuster that is attached to a camshaft, which rotates and causes the brake shoes to expand and contact the brake drum. When the brakes are released, the air used to activate the brakes is exhausted to the atmosphere.

The air brake system is an open system, in that the air used to apply the brakes is lost, and the air supply must be replenished before the brakes can operate. Repeated brake applications in succession (pumping the brakes) may prevent an air brake system from resupplying the air expended during braking quickly enough to maintain a supply of air sufficient to stop the vehicle.

Another distinct characteristic of an air brake system is the mechanical lag time, that is, the interval between the depression of the brake pedal and the application of the brakes. The lag time varies from about 0.20 to 0.55 second and may be longer in poorly maintained systems. The mechanical lag time adds to the overall stopping distance. For instance, at 50 mph, a vehicle travels at 73.30 feet per second. In a typical air brake system for which the lag time is 0.50 second, the vehicle will travel an additional 36 feet from the moment of brake pedal depression until the brakes are fully applied.

Vehicles that are typically equipped with air brakes include dump trucks, large transport trucks, and many types of buses. Some motor homes also have air brakes. Air brakes are optional on many trucks in the 19,501- to 33,000-pound weight classes. Hydraulic brakes typically wear out faster. In addition, air brake replacement parts are generally cheaper and more readily available than hydraulic brake system parts.

Figure 9 Brake schematic

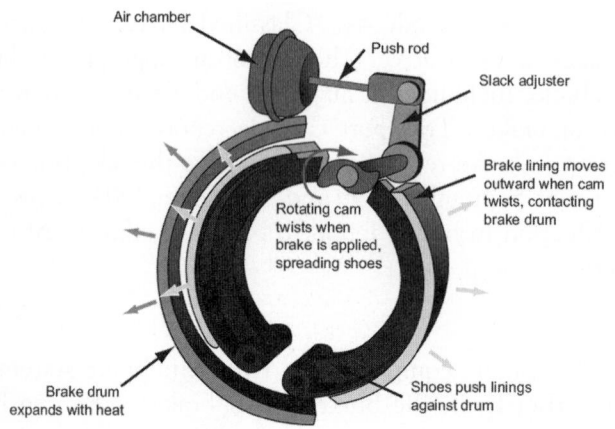

Automatic Slack Adjusters

ASAs, which are components of air brakes and are also known as automatic brake adjusters, have been offered as optional equipment on some commercial vehicles since the late 1960s. In 1992, the Safety Board noted, "The majority of truck tractors and about half the trailers currently being manufactured are equipped with automatic adjusters." When the rule requiring automatic adjusters on all air brake-equipped vehicles built on or after October 20, 1994, was enacted, most heavy vehicles were already in compliance. The primary purpose of ASAs is to maintain brake adjustment levels without a mechanic or driver having to adjust the brakes manually. (See Figure 10.)

The accident truck was equipped with Gunite ASAs. The Gunite service manual states (bold print in original), **"An automatic slack adjuster should not have to be manually adjusted except for initial installation and at the time of brake reline."** This manual also explains how to troubleshoot to find the cause of excessive pushrod stroke. It does not suggest that manual adjustment is a way to correct excessive pushrod stroke.

Inspector and Mechanic Certification Requirements

The ASAs on the accident truck were manually adjusted at different times by at least two individuals—a former Blossom Valley driver, who was a truck mechanic with 20 years' experience, and the mechanic from the Beasley Ford dealership in York, Pennsylvania. Both individuals were Pennsylvania State-certified truck inspection mechanics; the Ford dealership mechanic was also ASE certified.

Knowledge and Skills Needed to Drive Air Brake-Equipped Vehicles

Although the Glen Rock accident driver said that he slowed the truck before starting down the hill, he did not select a lower gear, which would have provided

Figure 10 Schematic of a Gunite automatic slack adjuster

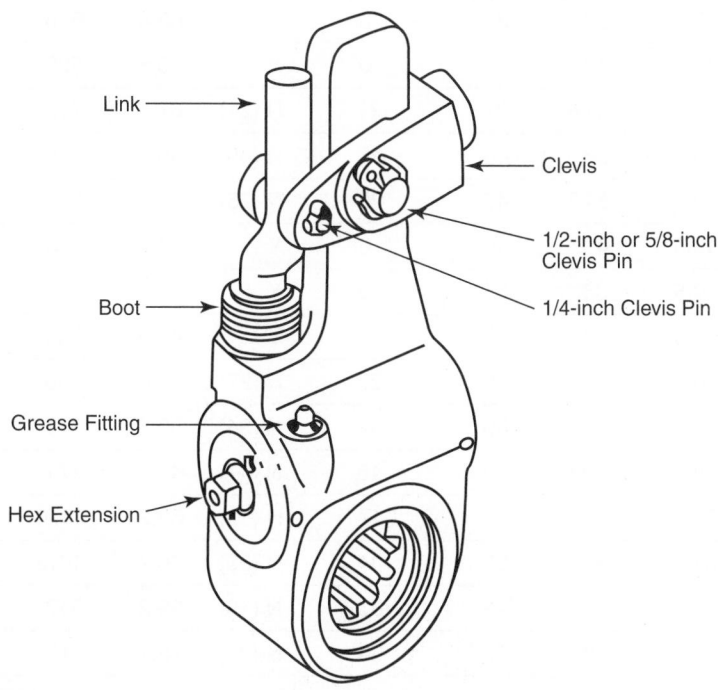

Source: Adapted from a figure that appears in the *Gunite Corporation Automatic Slack Adjuster Service Manual,* June 1994 edition.

engine braking, an action recommended by the AAMVA model *Commercial Driver License Manual* and experienced truck drivers. Had he used a lower gear, the vehicle would have slowed due to normal engine compression. In addition, he pumped the brakes, reducing the capability of the front brakes and exacerbating the loss of braking capability in the out-of-adjustment rear brakes. Until recent widespread use of ABS brakes, drivers of hydraulically braked vehicles (passenger cars, sport utility vehicles, and pickups and other light-duty trucks) were taught to pump their brakes in emergencies. But in an air-braked vehicle, pumping the brakes depletes the air pressure, thereby drastically reducing the brakes' capability.

Appendix B

Results of Safety Board computer simulations of accident events

Sim. no.	Initial speed (mph)	In gear (Y/N)	Brake forces (drag or pulse)	Time 10 to 15 (psi)	Time 30 (psi)	Time 50 (psi)	Highest speed (mph)	Lowest speed (mph)	Able to stop (speed end)	Length sim. (sec.)	Brake drum temp. (°F)	Brake lining temp. (°F)
1	1	Y	Drag	12	75.2	77.7	27	0	Y	92.7	737	485
2	1	Y	Drag	12	65.2	67.7	26	0	Y	82.4	676	438
3	1	Y	Drag	12	65.2	67.7	26	0	Y	81.7	669	430
4	1	Y	Drag	22	85.2	—	26	1	N (30)	86.2	588	399
5	1	Y	Drag	32	80.5	—	27	1	N (33)	81.8	546	358
6	1	Y	Drag	32	—	—	37	1	N (37)	73	540	323
7	1	Y	Drag	32	—	72	37	1	N (36)	73	516	320
8	25	Y	Drag	3	79.3	81.8	27	16	N (16)	87.7	761	500
9	25	Y	Drag	3	69.3	71.8	26	0	Y	85.1	763	506
10	25	Y	Drag	3	59.3	61.8	27	0	Y	75.2	707	458
11	25	Y	Drag	3	50.5	53	27	0	Y	66.6	656	417
12	25	Y	Drag	3	40.5	43	27	0	Y	56.6	595	370
13	25	Y	Drag	21	55.3	57.8	37	21	N (21)	67.4	768	408
14	25	Y	Drag	39.5	50.5	53	48	25	N (40)	58.2	550	259
15	25	Y	Drag	38	49	51.5	47	25	N (35)	59.1	638	289
16	35	Y	Drag	3	40.5	43	40	0	Y	54.7	918	552
17	35	Y	Drag	3	30.5	33	38	0	Y	53.9	838	489
18	35	Y	Drag	3	20.5	23	38	0	Y	42.9	733	415
19	35	Y	Drag	3	50.5	53	39	27	N (27)	60.6	850	474
20	35	Y	Drag	3	53.5	56	39	34	N (34)	59.8	746	446
21	45	Y	Drag	3	38	40.5	53	45	N (47)	45.4	771	401
22	45	Y	Drag	3	28	30.5	51	17	N (17)	53.2	1170	642
23	45	Y	Drag	3	34.5	37	52	34	N (36)	46.7	1012	489
24	55	Y	Drag	3	34.5	37	59	53	N (53)	39.2	817	402
25	55	Y	Drag	3	25.5	28	58	34	N (34)	42.1	1177	549

(continued)

Sim. no.	Initial speed (mph)	In gear (Y/N)	Brake forces (drag or pulse)	Time 10 to 15 (psi)	Time 30 (psi)	Time 50 (psi)	Highest speed (mph)	Lowest speed (mph)	Able to stop (speed end)	Length sim. (sec.)	Brake drum temp. (°F)	Brake lining temp. (°F)
26	55	Y	Drag	3	26	28.5	58	35	N (35)	41.8	1158	536
27	25	N	None	—	—	—	70	25	N (70)	46.6	150	150
28	1	N	None	—	—	—	67	1	N (67)	63.9	150	150
29	1	Y/N	None	Neutral at 11.6 sec			67	1	N (67)	61.9	150	150
30	1	Y	Pulse	12	32	—	28	0	Y	80.1	570	416
31	1	Y	Pulse	12	32 (pump down)		31	1	N (31)	119.6	573	504
32	1	Y	Pulse	12	32 (pump down)		30	1	N (30)	118	543	480
33	1	Y	Pulse	12	32 (pump down)		36	1	N (36)	111.4	488	431
34	25	Y	Pulse	3	Pumped down to 0		36	25	N (36)	75.6	466	356
35	25	Y	Pulse	3	Pumped down to 0		35	25	N (35)	75.6	456	349

APPENDIX III

SUPPLEMENTAL CASE STUDIES

Additional case studies are provided for use in completing independent case analysis, using the Comprehensive Case Study: School Bus–Truck Accident Case as an example.

Two of the additional case studies, New York School Bus Accident and Virginia School Bus Accident, are similar in nature to the Comprehensive Case Study: School Bus–Truck Accident Case. Additional cases are provided for a property damage case, a simple personal injury case, a tort action based on a civil assault, a commercial breach of contract, and an airplane crash.

List of Additional Cases:

- **Case 1: Simple motor vehicle accident with property damage claim**
- **Case 2: Student injured on school bus with a delay in treatment**
- **Case 3: Civil assault on a school bus and failure to protect**
- **Case 4: Breach of commercial contract**
- **Case 5: New York school bus accident**
- **Case 6: Virginia school bus accident**
- **Case 7: Aircraft fatality**

Several of the scenarios and parties in the non-NTSB cases are semi-fictional and loosely based on facts and situations from a number of sources woven together to provide a variety of case types. Some liberty has been taken with the identity of the parties, and no names used represent or are actual parties involved in the tragic accidents reported in the NTSB-based case studies.

■ CASE 1: SIMPLE MOTOR VEHICLE ACCIDENT WITH PROPERTY DAMAGE CLAIM

Joel Wilkenson is a regular client of the law firm. He recently had a fender bender for which there is no insurance coverage. He was stopped at the traffic light at Fourteenth and Market Streets waiting to make a left-hand turn when an SUV driven by a woman talking on her cell phone ran the red light from the other direction. He is seeking to sue the woman who hit him to recover the costs of the repair to his automobile.

Parties

Joel Wilkenson

Mary Smith
Mike Pope of Acme Garage—to testify for damage and repair to car
Tom Horton—a fact witness who observed the accident

■ CASE 2: STUDENT INJURED ON A SCHOOL BUS WITH A DELAY IN TREATMENT

Mandy Stein was returning from a class trip. She was seated in the rear of the school bus. Located directly behind her at the back of the bus were some boxes containing supplies and beverages. The bus stopped suddenly and a box fell on Mandy's head, injuring her. Mandy was taken to the emergency room, where treatment was provided until her mother arrived at the hospital. Mrs. Stein's religious beliefs do not allow submission to traditional medical treatment, but rather rely on higher powers for healing and recovery. She insisted that any treatment be stopped and took Mandy home. Mandy's father does not hold the same religious beliefs, and he sought court permission to have Mandy's injuries treated. Mandy suffered a head/scalp laceration, which was stitched in the emergency room, but there was no follow-up treatment or care until her father received court permission to have her treated by Dr. Lee. Because of the delay in treatment, the stitches became infected and surgery was required to remove the dead and infected skin, facial muscle, and nerves. She has permanent scarring and some loss of the use of her facial muscles.

Parties

Mandy Stein, a minor

Larry Stein, her father
Samantha Stein, her mother
Dr. Lee, plastic surgeon
Ron Clemmons, bus driver
Yourtown School District

■ CASE 3: CIVIL ASSAULT ON A SCHOOL BUS AND FAILURE TO PROTECT

Davis Hilary was riding home from school when Bobby Jones confronted him and prevented him from exiting the bus at his regular stop. Bobby held Davis down and threatened to harm him. A girl shouted that Bobby had a knife and the bus driver stopped the bus to investigate the matter. Bobby was restrained and taken back to school, where an investigation began.

Parties

Bobby Jones, a minor

Robert Jones, Sr., Bobby's father
Davis Hilary, a minor
Katy Hilary, Davis's mother
Lower Council School District
Ron Clemmons, bus driver

■ CASE 4: BREACH OF COMMERCIAL CONTRACT

The comprehensive case study is based on actual facts as reported in public documents. Content has been edited and reproduced in the words of the original documents to provide as much authenticity as possible. The use of an actual case is to allow you to perform basic legal and factual research that will present actual information that would be found in a real case on which you may in the future work.

Breach of Commercial Contract
Abstract

Melford Olson Honey, Inc. (Mel-O), a Minnesota honey wholesaler, sued Richard Adee (Richard) doing business as Adee Honey Farms (Adee Honey), a South Dakota honey farmer, in a Minnesota state court for breach of contract and specific performance, alleging Adee Honey failed to provide the requisite quantity of honey set forth in a June 2002 contract. Adee Honey removed the case to federal court on diversity jurisdiction and counterclaimed for money owed under the same contract. The district court denied both parties' motions for partial summary judgment, and the case proceeded to a jury trial.

Parties

Richard Adee, doing business as Adee Honey Farms

Bruce, SD
with regional offices in Bakersfield, CA, Cedar Rapids, NE, Roscoe, SD, and Woodville, MS, USA

Melford Olson Honey, Inc

Cannon Falls, MN

■ EXECUTIVE SUMMARY

Adee Honey, formed by Richard in 1957, operates honey farms in California, Nebraska, Mississippi, and South Dakota. Adee Honey's principal place of business is in South Dakota. Mel-O is owned by William Sill, and Curt and Darcy Riess. They bought the company in 1997 and were referred to Richard by Mel-O's prior owners.

In March 2002, Adee Honey and Mel-O entered into an oral agreement for the sale of honey. At the time, Adee Honey possessed a sufficient inventory of honey and agreed to sell approximately thirty loads, or 1.5 million pounds, to Mel-O for 82¢ per pound. Shortly thereafter, Mel-O sent a purchase order to Adee Honey memorializing the sale of 1.5 million pounds of honey for 82¢ per pound. The purchase order noted it was a contract with a "Good Thru" date of April 11, 2002. It was sent to Adee Honey's South Dakota office although Mel-O allegedly knew Richard was working at the Mississippi facility until mid-June.

At approximately the same time, Adee Honey called Mel-O to discuss the possibility of selling up to twelve loads of its inventoried honey to a competitor.

According to Adee Honey, Mel-O agreed, thereby altering the quantity term of the March 2002 contract. According to Mel-O, it permitted Adee Honey to sell twelve loads of inventoried honey to another distributor, provided the terms of the March 2002 contract were fulfilled with other honey. Between the months of May and September 2002, Adee Honey sent Mel-O eighteen loads of honey at 82¢ per pound.

In May 2002, honey prices began to rise due to a contamination in major Chinese honey supplies. In June 2002, Mel-O contacted Adee Honey about purchasing an additional 3.2 million pounds, and the parties agreed on a $1.00 per pound purchase price for the additional quantity. Mel-O sent a contract to Adee

Honey detailing the new arrangement, and Richard added a handwritten *force majeure* clause, specifically excusing performance in the event of "an act of God such as a drought or flood."

Later in the summer of 2002, South Dakota was experiencing drought-like conditions, and Adee Honey unilaterally stopped performing its obligations under the June contract. According to Mel-O, Richard contacted it to discuss the possibility of increasing the price of honey by 10¢ per pound to cover losses Adee Honey would suffer due to the production shortage. By the time Mel-O grudgingly decided to accept the terms, Adee Honey instead stated that the new price would be $1.55 per pound instead of $1.00 to $1.10 per pound.

In the early fall of 2002, Adee Honey began delivering honey to Mel-O at an invoice price of $1.55 per pound. Mel-O, however, refused to pay for this honey. By November 2002, its account was roughly $1.7 million in arrears. In November and December, Mel-O paid Adee Honey 82¢ per pound for approximately 575,000 pounds received, claiming this honey fulfilled the terms of the March 2002 contract. Mel-O did not pay anything for an additional 602,206 pounds received. Mel-O admits owing $1.00 per pound on this quantity, subject to some adjustments.

Adee Honey admits it contracted with Mel-O for eighteen loads of honey.

Miscellaneous Information

The Minnesota statute of frauds provides that oral contracts for the sale of goods for $500.00 or more are unenforceable "unless there is some writing sufficient to indicate that a contract for sale has been made between the parties and signed by the party against whom enforcement is sought." Minn. Stat. § 336.2-201(1).

The statute is applicable because the March 2002 contract for the sale of honey, goods priced over $500.00, was not reduced to writing and signed by Adee Honey, the party against whom enforcement was sought.

Under the merchant exception, Minnesota law provides:

(2) Between merchants if within a reasonable time a writing in confirmation of the contract and sufficient against the sender is received and the party receiving it has reason to know its contents, it satisfies the requirements of subsection (1) [regarding the general applicability of the statute of frauds] against such party unless written notice of objection to its contents is given within ten days after it is received.

The June 2002 contract contains a handwritten *force majeure* clause. Next to the 3.2 million-pound quantity, Richard added: "provided production of said pounds is NOT impeded by an Act of God such as by drought or flood."

Minnesota law provides:

Except so far as a seller may have assumed a greater obligation and subject to the preceding section on substituted performance:

(a) Delay in delivery or nondelivery in whole or in part by a seller who complies with paragraphs (b) and (c) is not a breach of duty under a contract for sale if performance as agreed has been made impracticable by the occurrence of a contingency the nonoccurrence of which was a basic assumption on which the contract was made or by compliance in good faith with any applicable foreign or domestic governmental regulation or order whether or not it later proves to be invalid.

(b) Where the causes mentioned in paragraph (a) affect only a part of the seller's capacity to perform, the seller must allocate production and deliveries among the seller's customers but may include regular customers not then under contract as well as the seller's own requirements for further manufacture. The seller may so allocate in any manner which is fair and reasonable.

(c) The seller must notify the buyer seasonably that there will be delay or non-delivery and, when allocation is required under paragraph (b), of the estimated quota thus made available for the buyer.

■ CASE 5: NEW YORK SCHOOL BUS ACCIDENT

The comprehensive case study is based on actual facts as reported in a National Transportation Safety Board (NTSB) report. Content has been edited and reproduced in the words of the report to provide as much authenticity as possible. Figures are reproduced from the same report. Some liberty has been taken with the identity of the parties, and no names used represent or are actual parties involved in the tragic accident reported. We use an actual incident to allow you to perform basic legal and factual research that will present actual information that would be found in a real case on which you might in the future work.

School Bus and Dump Truck Collision
Central Bridge, New York
October 21, 1999

Abstract

On October 21, 1999, about 10:30 a.m. near Central Bridge, New York, a school bus was transporting 44 students and 8 adults on a field trip. The bus was traveling north on State Route 30A as it approached the intersection with State Route 7. Concurrently, a dump truck, towing a utility trailer, was traveling west on State Route 7. As the bus approached the intersection, it failed to stop as required and was struck by the dump truck. Seven bus passengers sustained serious injuries; 28 bus passengers and the truck driver received minor injuries. Thirteen bus passengers, the bus driver, and the truck passenger were uninjured.

Passengers

Refer to seat numbers on the National Transportation Safety Board (NTSB) seating chart (NTSB report Figure 4) on page 553.

Other Drivers and Parties

School Bus Driver:	Sam Carole
School Bus Company:	*Kinnicutt Bus Company*
Tractor-Trailer Driver:	Dave Smith
Trucking Company	*MVF Construction Company*

■ EXECUTIVE SUMMARY

About 10:30 a.m. on October 21, 1999, in Schoharie County, New York, a Kinnicutt Bus Company school bus was transporting 44 students, 5 to 9 years old, and 8 adults on an Albany City School No. 18 field trip. The bus was traveling north on State Route 30A as it approached the intersection with State Route 7, which is about 1.5 miles east of Central Bridge, New York. Concurrently, an MVF Construction Company dump truck, towing a utility trailer, was traveling west on

Figure 4 School bus seating and injury diagram.

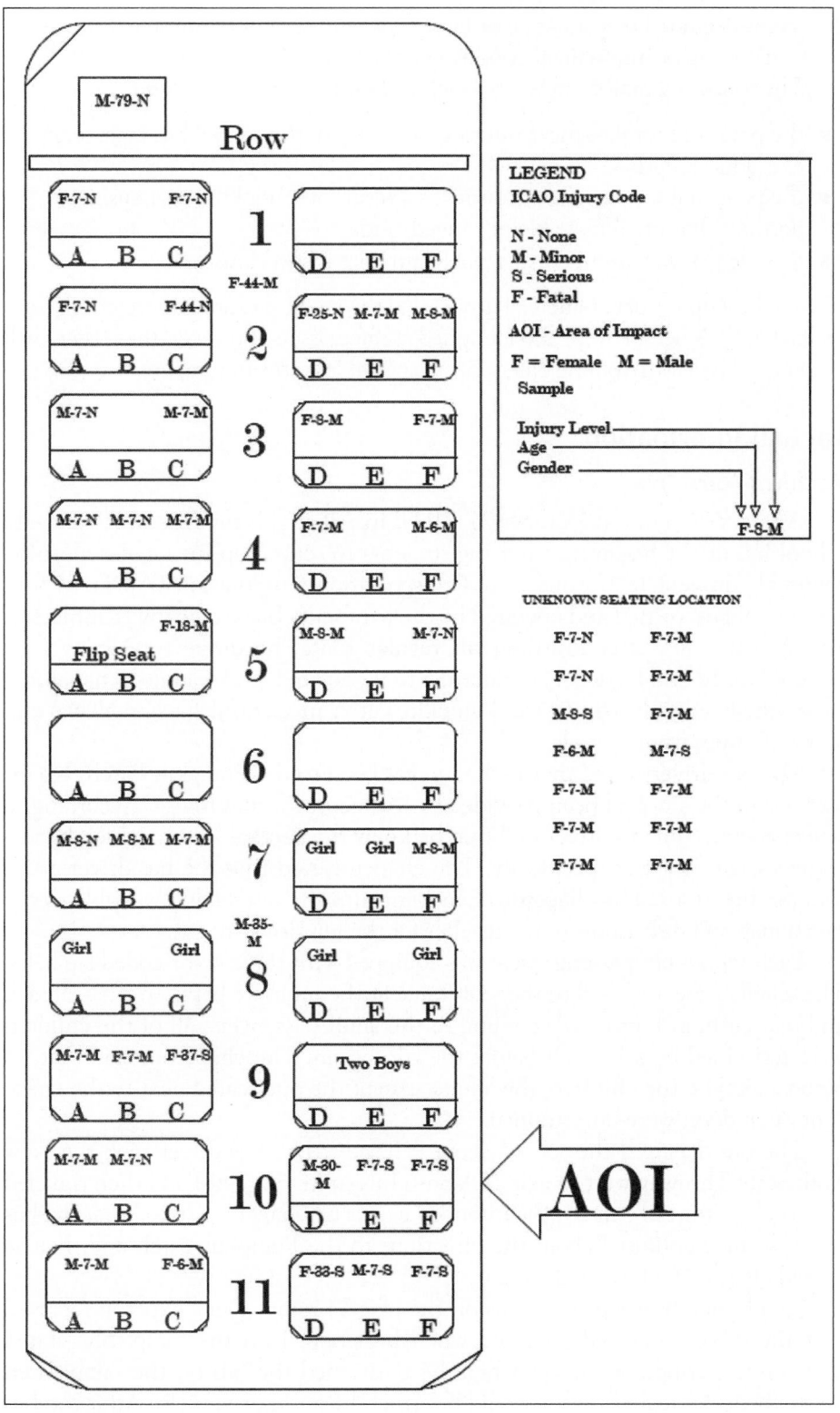

State Route 7. The dump truck was occupied by the driver and a passenger. As the bus approached the intersection, it failed to stop as required and was struck by the dump truck. Seven bus passengers sustained serious injuries; 28 bus passengers and the truck driver received minor injuries. Thirteen bus passengers, the bus driver, and the truck passenger were uninjured.

The National Transportation Safety Board determines that the probable cause of this accident was the school bus driver's failure to stop for the stop sign due to his degraded performance or lapse of attention as a result of factors associated with aging or his medical condition or both.

The following major safety issues were identified in this accident:

- the potential for passenger injuries as a result of the school bus emergency exit door design,
- the potential for passenger injuries as a result of school bus seat cushion bottoms that are removable or hinged, and
- the adequacy of commercial vehicle airbrake inspections.

The medical fitness of commercial drivers and the medical examination for the commercial driver's license were also identified as safety issues; however, these issues will be analyzed in a forthcoming Safety Board special investigation report.

Factual Information

Accident Narrative

About 7:20 a.m. on October 21, 1999, in Albany, New York, a 79-year-old school bus driver began transporting students to school on his regular morning route. He drove a 1997 American Transportation Corporation (AmTran) full-size school bus, owned and operated by the Kinnicutt Bus Company (Kinnicutt). About 8:50 a.m., after finishing his regular route, he drove to Albany City School No. 18 and loaded 44 children, 5 to 9 years old, and 8 adults (chaperons) for a scheduled field trip to the Pumpkin Patch in Central Bridge, New York, about 40 miles from the school.

The bus driver stated that he had never been to the Pumpkin Patch. No directions to the site had been provided by Kinnicutt for him to use. According to one chaperon, the bus driver said that he knew the general area to which he was going vaguely but not specifically. The chaperon said that the bus driver asked him for directions. The chaperon then went into the school and was able to obtain a map and directions from a teacher for the bus driver to use.

Each school bus passenger seat was equipped with three color-coded lap belts. These belts were attached to the seat frame at the juncture between the seatback and seat cushion bottom. According to the adult passengers, all of the children were restrained by a lap belt before the trip began. The chaperons said that, to better supervise the children, the adults, except the one seated next to the emergency exit door, were unrestrained.

The bus departed the school about 9:20 a.m. The bus driver took the New York State Thruway west to exit 25A onto Interstate-88 (I-88) and then traveled west on I-88 toward exit 23, the intended exit. The chaperons stated that the bus driver seemed confused about the directions to the Pumpkin Patch and that he turned off at exit 24, the wrong exit.

He ultimately stopped the bus on the exit 24 ramp. One chaperon reported that the driver appeared confused when he stopped on the ramp. She stated that she was concerned about where he positioned the bus on the ramp when he stopped; she feared that it would be struck by another vehicle. After the bus driver received directions from a chaperon, the driver returned to I-88 and continued traveling to exit 23, the correct exit.

The bus driver stated that at the top of the exit 23 ramp, he turned right onto State Route 30A (SR-30A) and started looking for State Route 7 (SR-7). About 10:30 a.m., the bus was traveling north on SR-30A between 15 and 25 mph as it approached the intersection with SR-7. The intersection was about 1.5 miles east of Central Bridge. The north- and southbound traffic on SR-30A were controlled by an advance warning sign that indicated a stop ahead, a stop sign, flashing red intersection control beacons, and pavement markings that included the word "stop" and a stop bar.

At the same time, an MVF Construction Company (MVF) dump truck, towing a utility trailer, was traveling about 45 mph west on SR-7. East- and westbound traffic on SR-7 at the intersection were controlled by flashing yellow intersection control beacons. The dump truck was occupied by its 52-year-old driver and a passenger. As the school bus approached the intersection, according to the chaperons, several children on board saw the sign for the Pumpkin Patch that was beyond the intersection and yelled. These children may also have released their belt buckles. One child reportedly stood up in the seating compartment. The bus driver, who was looking for SR-7, told investigating police that he saw the posted stop sign, slowed, but did not stop the bus, which then entered the intersection where the dump truck struck it on the right side behind the rear axle. (See Figure 1.)

The school bus, after rotating about 145 degrees clockwise, slid approximately 100 feet and came to rest facing south. The dump truck, after rotating about 150 degrees clockwise, struck three highway guide signs and a utility pole; it then came to rest facing northeast. (See Figure 3.)

The complete National Transportation Safety Board report is available and may be downloaded from the Technology Resources Website, www.pearsonhighered .com/goldman, together with selected exhibits.

SOURCE: http://www.ntsb.gov/publictn/2000/HAR0002.pdf

Figure 1 Exterior crush damage of school bus

Figure 3 Final rest position

■ CASE 6: VIRGINIA SCHOOL BUS ACCIDENT

The comprehensive case study is based on actual facts as reported in a National Transportation Safety Board (NTSB) report. Content has been edited and reproduced in the words of the report to provide as much authenticity as possible. Figures are reproduced from the same report. Some liberty has been taken with the identity of the parties, and no names used represent or are actual parties involved in the tragic accident reported. We use an actual incident to allow you to perform basic legal and factual research that will present actual information that would be found in a real case on which you might in the future work.

Multi-Vehicle Collision between Trash Truck and School Bus
Arlington, Virginia
April 18, 2005

Abstract

A 52-passenger school bus was traveling westbound on Columbia Pike (State Route 244) in Arlington County, Virginia, transporting 15 elementary school children, grades pre-K through 5, to the nearby Hoffman-Boston Elementary School. On approaching the signaled intersection with Courthouse Road, the school bus driver began moving the bus into the left turn lane and slowed it nearly to a stop. As the driver turned the vehicle, its left front encroached slightly into the left lane of the eastbound side of Columbia Pike. A 2003 Mack trash truck was traveling with the flow of traffic in the left eastbound lane on Columbia Pike. The truck reached the intersection with Courthouse Road, continued through it on a green signal, and deviated slightly leftward from its lane toward the yellow centerline. The truck collided with the school bus; the impact involved the front-left corners of both vehicles and a sideswipe.

Drivers and Parties

School Bus Driver:	Kathryn Salvatore
School Bus Operator:	Arlington County School District
Truck Driver:	John Gonzales
Trucking Company:	AAA Recycling and Trash Removal Services

■ EXECUTIVE SUMMARY

Accident Description

Shortly before 8:40 a.m., on Monday, April 18, 2005, a 52-passenger school bus was traveling westbound on Columbia Pike (State Route 244) in Arlington County, Virginia, transporting 15 elementary school children, grades pre-K through 5, to the nearby Hoffman-Boston Elementary School. On approaching the signaled intersection with Courthouse Road, the school bus driver began moving the bus into the left turn lane (from which it would turn south onto Courthouse Road) and slowed it nearly to a stop. As the driver turned the vehicle, its left front encroached slightly into the left lane of the eastbound side of Columbia Pike. The driver later stated that distractions inside the bus might have affected her driving at this time. She said her attention was drawn to a student standing on a seat and to a clipboard that fell to the floor at her driving station.

About 8:40 a.m., a 2003 Mack trash truck was traveling with the flow of traffic in the left eastbound lane on Columbia Pike, at a speed one witness who

Passengers

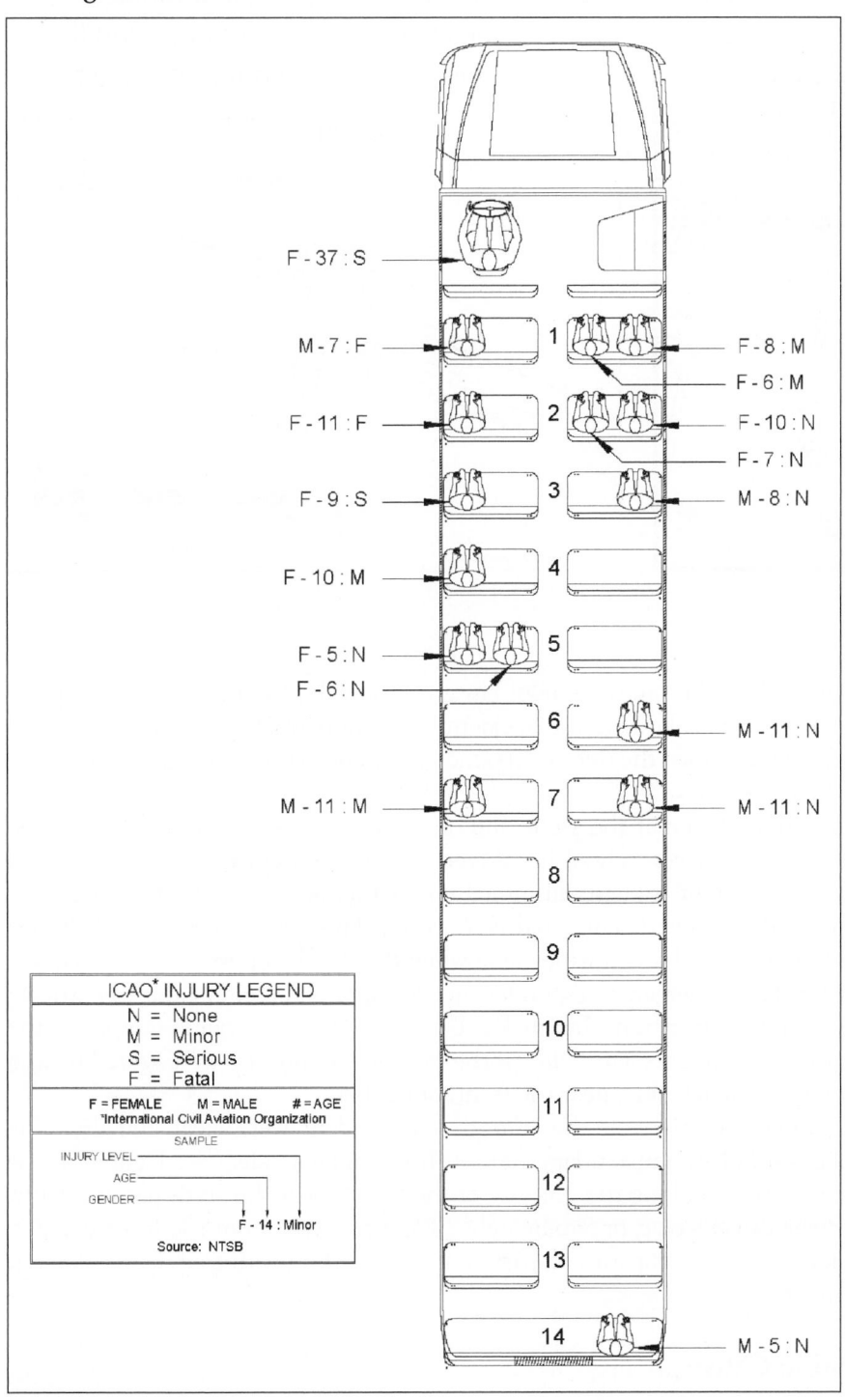

was traveling on the road in the same direction estimated to be approximately 30 mph. The truck reached the intersection with Courthouse Road, continued through it on a green signal and, according to several witnesses, deviated slightly leftward from its lane toward the yellow centerline. The truck collided with the school bus; the impact involved the front-left corners of both vehicles and a sideswipe. (See Figures 1 and 2 for a map of the accident location area and a diagram representing the vehicles at the point of impact.)

Figure 1 Map showing the area of Arlington, Virginia, where the accident occurred

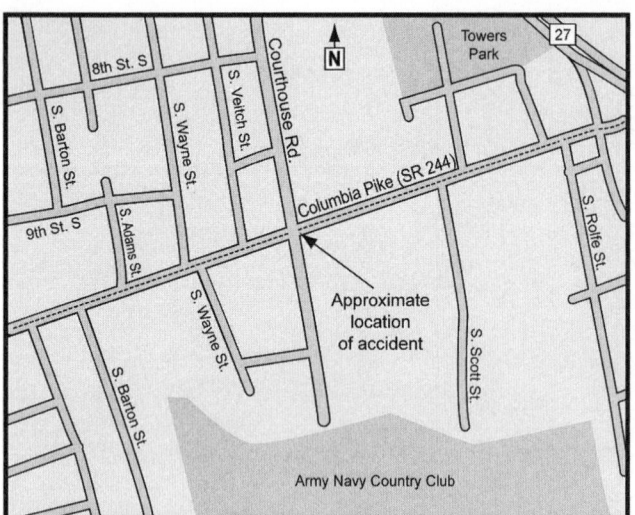

Figure 2 Diagram showing the estimated positions of the school bus and the trash truck at the point of impact

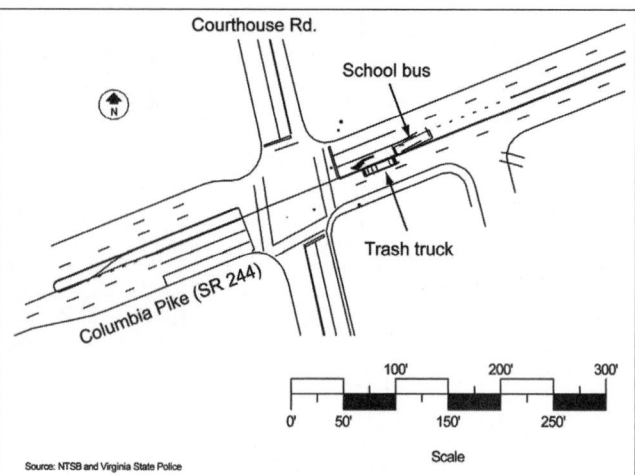

During the collision, the school bus was pushed backward, but it remained in the left turn lane following the accident. The trash truck continued eastbound about 200 feet, crossed the right eastbound lane, jumped the right curb of Columbia Pike, and came to rest.

One student died at the scene and one student died 3 days later in the hospital. The truck driver, school bus driver, and one student on the bus sustained serious injuries; four students sustained minor injuries; and the remaining eight students were uninjured. The bus driver, who had been wearing her seat belt, was ejected through the broken windshield when the shoulder portion of the belt was sheared in half. Emergency responders needed approximately 1 hour to extricate the trash truck driver from the truck cab because of his legs being trapped in the wreckage. The students who suffered the most severe injuries were seated behind the driver on the left side, near the front, of the bus.

Weather conditions at the time of the accident were clear and dry. The school bus sustained impact damage to its front and left side. (See Figure 5.) The damage continued along the left side of the bus to near the sixth passenger row behind the driver's seat, approximately 20 feet rearward from the front bumper. Intrusion into the occupant compartment extended inboard to a depth of about 6 1/2 inches.

Probable Cause

The National Transportation Safety Board determines that the probable cause of this accident was the school bus driver's encroachment into the trash truck's lane and the trash truck driver's failure to maintain proper lane position, for undetermined reasons, causing the front-left sides of the two vehicles to collide and the vehicles to sideswipe each other.

The complete National Transportation Safety Board report is available and may be downloaded from the Technology Resources Website, www.pearson highered.com/goldman, together with selected exhibits.

SOURCE: http://www.ntsb.gov/publictn/2008/HAB0801.pdf

Figure 5 Damage to the school bus

■ CASE 7: NEW YORK AIRPLANE CRASH

The comprehensive case study is based on actual facts as reported in a National Transportation Safety Board (NTSB) report. Content has been edited and reproduced in the words of the report to provide as much authenticity as possible. Figures are reproduced from the same report. Some liberty has been taken with the identity of the parties, and no names used represent or are actual parties involved in the tragic accident reported. We use an actual incident to allow you to perform basic legal and factual research that will present actual information that would be found in a real case on which you might in the future work.

Aircraft Accident
Clarence Center, New York
February 12, 2009

Abstract

On February 12, 2009, about 2217 (10:17 p.m.) eastern standard time, a Colgan Air, Inc., Bombardier DHC-8-400, N200WQ, operating as Continental Connection flight 3407, was on an instrument approach to Buffalo-Niagara International Airport, Buffalo, New York, when it crashed into a residence in Clarence Center, New York, about 5 nautical miles northeast of the airport. The 2 pilots, 2 flight attendants, and 45 passengers aboard the airplane were killed, one person on the ground was killed, and the airplane was destroyed by impact forces and a post crash fire.

■ EXECUTIVE SUMMARY

On February 12, 2009, about 2217 eastern standard time, a Colgan Air, Inc., Bombardier DHC-8-400, N200WQ, operating as Continental Connection flight 3407, was on an instrument approach to Buffalo-Niagara International Airport,

Buffalo, New York, when it crashed into a residence in Clarence Center, New York, about 5 nautical miles northeast of the airport. The 2 pilots, 2 flight attendants, and 45 passengers aboard the airplane were killed, one person on the ground was killed, and the airplane was destroyed by impact forces and a post-crash fire. The flight was operating under the provisions of *14 Code of Federal Regulations* Part 121. Night visual meteorological conditions prevailed at the time of the accident.

The home base of operations for both the captain and the first officer was Liberty International Airport (EWR), Newark, New Jersey. On February 11, 2009, the captain had completed a 2-day trip sequence, with the final flight of the trip arriving at EWR at 1544. Also that day, the first officer began her commute from her home near Seattle, Washington, to EWR at 1951 Pacific standard time (PST), arriving at EWR (via Memphis International Airport [MEM], Memphis, Tennessee) on the day of the accident at 0623. The captain and the first officer were both observed in Colgan's crew room on February 12 before their scheduled report time of 1330. The flight crew's first two scheduled flights of the day, from EWR to Greater Rochester International Airport (ROC), Rochester, New York, and back, had been canceled because of high winds at EWR and the resulting ground delays at the airport.

The company dispatch release for flight 3407 was issued at 1800 and showed an estimated departure time of 1910 and an estimated en route time of 53 minutes. The airplane to be used for flight 3407, N200WQ, arrived at EWR at 1854. A first officer whose flight arrived at EWR at 1853 saw, as he exited his airplane, the flight 3407 captain and first officer walking toward the accident airplane. The airplane's aircraft communications addressing and reporting system (ACARS) showed a departure clearance request at 1930 and pushback from the gate at 1945. According to the cockpit voice recorder (CVR) recording, the EWR ground controller provided taxi instructions for the flight at 2030:28, which the first officer acknowledged.

About 2041:35, the first officer stated, "I'm ready to be in the hotel room," to which the captain replied, "I feel bad for you." She continued, "this is one of those times that if I felt like this when I was at home there's no way I would have come all the way out here." She then stated, "if I call in sick now I've got to put myself in a hotel until I feel better…we'll see how…it feels flying. If the pressure's just too much… I could always call in tomorrow at least I'm in a hotel on the company's buck but we'll see. I'm pretty tough." The captain responded by stating that the first officer could try an over-the-counter herbal supplement, drink orange juice, or take vitamin C.

The CVR recorded the tower controller clearing the airplane for takeoff about 2118:23. The first officer acknowledged the clearance, and the captain stated, "alright cleared for takeoff it's mine." According to the dispatch release, the intended cruise altitude for the flight was 16,000 feet mean sea level (msl) The flight data recorder (FDR) showed that, during the climb to altitude, the propeller deice and airframe deice equipment were turned on (the pitot static deicing equipment had been turned on before takeoff) and the autopilot was engaged.

The airplane reached its cruising altitude of 16,000 feet about 2134:44. The cruise portion of flight was routine and uneventful. The CVR recorded the captain and the first officer engaged in an almost continuous conversation throughout that portion of the flight, but these conversations did not conflict with the sterile cockpit rule, which prohibits nonessential conversations within the cockpit during critical phases of flight. About 2149:18, the CVR recorded the captain making a sound similar to a yawn. About 1 minute later, the captain interrupted his own conversation to point out, to the first officer, traffic that was crossing left to right. About 2150:42, the first officer reported the winds to be from 250° at 15 knots gusting to 23 knots; afterward, the captain stated that runway 23 would be used for the landing.

About 2153:40, the first officer briefed the airspeeds for landing with the flaps at 15° (flaps 15) as 118 knots (reference landing speed [Vref]) and 114 knots (go-around speed [Vga]), and the captain acknowledged this information. About 2156:26, the first officer stated, "might be easier on my ears if we start going down sooner." About 2156:36, the captain instructed the first officer to "get discretion to twelve [thousand feet]." Less than 1 minute later, a controller from Cleveland Center cleared the flight to descend to 11,000 feet, and the first officer acknowledged the clearance.

About 2203:38, the Cleveland Center controller instructed the flight crew to contact BUF approach control, and the first officer acknowledged this instruction. The first officer made initial contact with BUF approach control about 2203:53, stating that the flight was descending from 12,000 to 11,000 feet with automatic terminal information service (ATIS) information "romeo," and the approach controller provided the airport altimeter setting and told the crew to plan an instrument landing system (ILS) approach to runway 23.

About 2204:16, the captain began the approach briefing. About 2205:01, the approach controller cleared the flight crew to descend and maintain 6,000 feet, and the first officer acknowledged the clearance. About 30 seconds later, the captain continued the approach briefing, during which he repeated the airspeeds for a flaps 15 landing. FDR data showed that the airplane descended through 10,000 feet about 2206:37. From that point on, the flight crew was required to observe the sterile cockpit rule.

About 2207:14, the CVR recorded the first officer making a sound similar to a yawn. About 2208:41 and 2209:12, the approach controller cleared the flight crew to descend and maintain 5,000 and 4,000 feet, respectively, and the first officer acknowledged the clearances. Afterward, the captain asked the first officer about her ears, and she indicated that they were stuffy and popping.

About 2210:23, the first officer asked whether ice had been accumulating on the windshield, and the captain replied that ice was present on his side of the windshield and asked whether ice was present on her windshield side. The first officer responded, "lots of ice." The captain then stated, "that's the most I've seen—most ice I've seen on the leading edges in a long time. In a while anyway I should say." About 10 seconds later, the captain and the first officer began a conversation that was unrelated to their flying duties. During that conversation, the first officer indicated that she had accumulated more actual flight time in icing conditions on her first day of initial operating experience (IOE) with Colgan than she had before her employment with the company. She also stated that, when other company first officers were "complaining" about not yet having upgraded to captain, she was thinking that she "wouldn't mind going through a winter in the northeast before [upgrading] to captain." The first officer explained that, before IOE, she had "never seen icing conditions...never deiced...never experienced any of that."

About 2212:18, the approach controller cleared the flight crew to descend and maintain 2,300 feet, and the first officer acknowledged the clearance. Afterward, the captain and the first officer performed flight-related duties but also continued the conversation that was unrelated to their flying duties. About 2212:44, the approach controller cleared the flight crew to turn left onto a heading of 330°. About 2213:25 and 2213:36, the captain called for the descent and approach checklists, respectively, which the first officer performed. About 2214:09, the approach controller cleared the flight crew to turn left onto a heading of 310°, and the autopilot's altitude hold mode became active about 1 second later as the airplane was approaching the preselected altitude of 2,300 feet. The airplane reached this altitude about 2214:30; the airspeed was about 180 knots at the time.

About 2215:06, the captain called for the flaps to be moved to the 5° position, and the CVR recorded a sound similar to flap handle movement. Afterward, the approach controller cleared the flight crew to turn left onto a heading of 260° and maintain 2,300 feet until established on the localizer for the ILS approach to runway 23. The first officer acknowledged the clearance.

The captain began to slow the airplane less than 3 miles from the outer marker to establish the appropriate airspeed before landing. According to FDR data, the engine power levers were reduced to about 42° (flight idle was 35°) about 2216:00, and both engines' torque values were at minimum thrust about 2216:02. The approach controller then instructed the flight crew to contact the BUF air traffic control tower (ATCT) controller. The first officer acknowledged this instruction, which was the last communication between the flight crew and air traffic control (ATC). Afterward, the CVR recorded sounds similar to landing gear handle deployment and landing gear movement, and the FDR showed that the propeller condition levers had been moved forward to their maximum RPM position and that pitch trim in the airplane- nose-up direction had been applied by the autopilot.

About 2216:21, the first officer told the captain that the gear was down; at that time, the airspeed was about 145 knots. Afterward, FDR data showed that additional pitch trim in the airplane-nose-up direction had been applied by the autopilot and that an "ice detected" message appeared on the engine display in the cockpit. About the same time, the captain called for the flaps to be set to 15° and for the before landing checklist. The CVR then recorded a sound similar to flap handle movement, and FDR data showed that the flaps had been selected to 10°. FDR data also showed that the airspeed at the time was about 135 knots.

At 2216:27.4, the CVR recorded a sound similar to the stick shaker. (The stick shaker warns a pilot of an impending wing aerodynamic stall through vibrations on the control column, providing tactile and aural cues.) The CVR also recorded a sound similar to the autopilot disconnect horn, which repeated until the end of the recording. FDR data showed that, when the autopilot disengaged, the airplane was at an airspeed of 131 knots. FDR data showed that the control columns moved aft at 2216:27.8 and that the engine power levers were advanced to about 70° (rating detent was 80°) 1 second later. The CVR then recorded a sound similar to increased engine power, and FDR data showed that engine power had increased to about 75 percent torque.

FDR data also showed that, while engine power was increasing, the airplane pitched up; rolled to the left, reaching a roll angle of 45° left wing down; and then rolled to the right. As the airplane rolled to the right through wings level, the stick pusher activated (about 2216:34), and flaps 0 was selected. (The Q400 stick pusher applies an airplane-nose-down control column input to decrease the wing angle-of-attack [AOA] after an aerodynamic stall.) About 2216:37, the first officer told the captain that she had put the flaps up. FDR data confirmed that the flaps had begun to retract by 2216:38; at that time, the airplane's airspeed was about 100 knots. FDR data also showed that the roll angle reached 105° right wing down before the airplane began to roll back to the left and the stick pusher activated a second time (about 2216:40). At the time, the airplane's pitch angle was −1°.

About 2216:42, the CVR recorded the captain making a grunting sound. FDR data showed that the roll angle had reached about 35° left wing down before the airplane began to roll again to the right. Afterward, the first officer asked whether she should put the landing gear up, and the captain stated, "gear up" and an expletive. The airplane's pitch and roll angles had reached about 25° airplane nose down and 100° right wing down, respectively, when the airplane entered a steep descent. The stick pusher activated a third time (about 2216:50). FDR data showed that the flaps were fully retracted about 2216:52. About the same time, the CVR recorded the captain stating, "we're down," and a sound of a thump. The airplane impacted a single-family home (where the ground fatality occurred), and a postcrash fire ensued. The CVR recording ended about 2216:54.

ABBREVIATIONS

AC	advisory circular
ACARS	aircraft communications addressing and reporting system
AFM	airplane flight manual
agl	above ground level
AOA	angle-of-attack
ATC	air traffic control
ATCT	air traffic control tower
ATIS	automatic terminal information service
ATOS	air transportation oversight system
BTV	Burlington International Airport
BUF	Buffalo-Niagara International Airport
CVR	cockpit voice recorder
CWA	Center Weather Advisory
eice	en route ice accumulation
FDR	flight data recorder
IFR	instrument flight rules
ILS	instrument landing system
msl	mean sea level
nm	nautical mile
PIC	pilot-in-command
SIC	second-in-command

The complete National Transportation Safety Board report is available and may be downloaded from the Technology Resources Website, www.pearsonhighered .com/goldman, together with selected exhibits and simulation, or in PDF format.

SOURCE: http://www.ntsb.gov/publictn/2010/AAR1001.pdf

APPENDIX IV

SELECTED PORTIONS OF THE FEDERAL RULES OF CIVIL PROCEDURE AND FEDERAL RULES OF EVIDENCE

■ RULE 16. PRETRIAL CONFERENCES; SCHEDULING; MANAGEMENT

(a) **Purposes of a Pretrial Conference.**

In any action, the court may order the attorneys and any unrepresented parties to appear for one or more pretrial conferences for such purposes as:

(1) expediting disposition of the action;

(2) establishing early and continuing control so that the case will not be protracted because of lack of management;

(3) discouraging wasteful pretrial activities;

(4) improving the quality of the trial through more thorough preparation, and;

(5) facilitating settlement.

(b) **Scheduling.**

(1) **Scheduling Order.**

Except in categories of actions exempted by local rule, the district judge—or a magistrate judge when authorized by local rule—must issue a scheduling order:

(A) after receiving the parties' report under Rule 26(f); or

(B) after consulting with the parties' attorneys and any unrepresented parties at a scheduling conference or by telephone, mail, or other means.

(2) **Time to Issue.**

The judge must issue the scheduling order as soon as practicable, but in any event within the earlier of 120 days after any defendant has been served with the complaint or 90 days after any defendant has appeared.

(3) **Contents of the Order.**

(A) *Required Contents*. The scheduling order must limit the time to join other parties, amend the pleadings, complete discovery, and file motions.

(B) *Permitted Contents*. The scheduling order may:

   (i) modify the timing of disclosures under Rules 26(a) and 26(e)(1);

   (ii) modify the extent of discovery;

   (iii) provide for disclosure or discovery of electronically stored information;

   (iv) include any agreements the parties reach for asserting claims of privilege or of protection as trial-preparation material after information is produced;

   (v) set dates for pretrial conferences and for trial; and

   (vi) include other appropriate matters.

(4) **Modifying a Schedule.**

A schedule may be modified only for good cause and with the judge's consent.

(c) Attendance and Matters for Consideration at a Pretrial Conference.

(1) Attendance.

A represented party must authorize at least one of its attorneys to make stipulations and admissions about all matters that can reasonably be anticipated for discussion at a pretrial conference. If appropriate, the court may require that a party or its representative be present or reasonably available by other means to consider possible settlement.

(2) Matters for Consideration.

At any pretrial conference, the court may consider and take appropriate action on the following matters:

(A) formulating and simplifying the issues, and eliminating frivolous claims or defenses;

(B) amending the pleadings if necessary or desirable;

(C) obtaining admissions and stipulations about facts and documents to avoid unnecessary proof, and ruling in advance on the admissibility of evidence;

(D) avoiding unnecessary proof and cumulative evidence, and limiting the use of testimony under Federal Rule of Evidence 702;

(E) determining the appropriateness and timing of summary adjudication under Rule 56;

(F) controlling and scheduling discovery, including orders affecting disclosures and discovery under Rule 26 and Rules 29 through 37;

(G) identifying witnesses and documents, scheduling the filing and exchange of any pretrial briefs, and setting dates for further conferences and for trial;

(H) referring matters to a magistrate judge or a master;

(I) settling the case and using special procedures to assist in resolving the dispute when authorized by statute or local rule;

(J) determining the form and content of the pretrial order;

(K) disposing of pending motions;

(L) adopting special procedures for managing potentially difficult or protracted actions that may involve complex issues, multiple parties, difficult legal questions, or unusual proof problems;

(M) ordering a separate trial under Rule 42(b) of a claim, counterclaim, crossclaim, thirdparty claim, or particular issue;

(N) ordering the presentation of evidence early in the trial on a manageable issue that might, on the evidence, be the basis for a judgment as a matter of law under Rule 50(a) or a judgment on partial findings under Rule 52(c);

(O) establishing a reasonable limit on the time allowed to present evidence; and

(P) facilitating in other ways the just, speedy, and inexpensive disposition of the action.

(d) Pretrial Orders.

After any conference under this rule, the court should issue an order reciting the action taken. This order controls the course of the action unless the court modifies it.

(e) Final Pretrial Conference and Orders.

The court may hold a final pretrial conference to formulate a trial plan, including a plan to facilitate the admission of evidence. The conference must be held as close to the start of trial as is reasonable, and must be attended by at least one attorney who will conduct the trial for each party and by any unrepresented party. The court may modify the order issued after a final pretrial conference only to prevent manifest injustice.

(f) Sanctions.

(1) In General.

On motion or on its own, the court may issue any just orders, including those authorized by Rule 37(b)(2)(A)(ii)-(vii), if a party or its attorney:

(A) fails to appear at a scheduling or other pretrial conference;

(B) is substantially unprepared to participate—or does not participate in good faith—in the conference; or

(C) fails to obey a scheduling or other pretrial order.

(2) Imposing Fees and Costs.
Instead of or in addition to any other sanction, the court must order the party, its attorney, or both to pay the reasonable expenses—including attorney's fees—incurred because of any noncompliance with this rule, unless the noncompliance was substantially justified or other circumstances make an award of expenses unjust.

■ RULE 26. DUTY TO DISCLOSE; GENERAL PROVISIONS GOVERNING DISCOVERY

(a) Required Disclosures.
   (1) Initial Disclosures.
      (A) In General. Except as exempted by Rule 26(a)(1)(B) or as otherwise stipulated or ordered by the court, a party must, without awaiting a discovery request, provide to the other parties:
         (i) the name and, if known, the address and telephone number of each individual likely to have discoverable information—along with the subjects of that information—that the disclosing party may use to support its claims or defenses, unless the use would be solely for impeachment;
         (ii) a copy—or a description by category and location—of all documents, electronically stored information, and tangible things that the disclosing party has in its possession, custody, or control and may use to support its claims or defenses, unless the use would be solely for impeachment;
         (iii) a computation of each category of damages claimed by the disclosing party—who must also make available for inspection and copying as under Rule 34 the documents or other evidentiary material, unless privileged or protected from disclosure, on which each computation is based, including materials bearing on the nature and extent of injuries suffered; and
         (iv) for inspection and copying as under Rule 34, any insurance agreement under which an insurance business may be liable to satisfy all or part of a possible judgment in the action or to indemnify or reimburse for payments made to satisfy the judgment.
      (B) Proceedings Exempt from Initial Disclosure. The following proceedings are exempt from initial disclosure:
         (i) an action for review on an administrative record;
         (ii) a forfeiture action in rem arising from a federal statute;
         (iii) a petition for habeas corpus or any other proceeding to challenge a criminal conviction or sentence;
         (iv) an action brought without an attorney by a person in the custody of the United States, a state, or a state subdivision;
         (v) an action to enforce or quash an administrative summons or subpoena;
         (vi) an action by the United States to recover benefit payments;
         (vii) an action by the United States to collect on a student loan guaranteed by the United States;
        (viii) a proceeding ancillary to a proceeding in another court; and
         (ix) an action to enforce an arbitration award.
      (C) Time for Initial Disclosures—In General. A party must make the initial disclosures at or within 14 days after the parties' Rule 26(f) conference unless a different time is set by stipulation or court order, or unless a party objects during the conference that initial disclosures are not appropriate in this action and states the objection in the proposed discovery plan. In ruling on the objection, the court must determine what disclosures, if any, are to be made and must set the time for disclosure.
      (D) Time for Initial Disclosures—For Parties Served or Joined Later. A party that is first served or otherwise joined after the Rule 26(f) conference must make the initial disclosures within 30 days after being served or joined, unless a different time is set by stipulation or court order.
      (E) Basis for Initial Disclosure; Unacceptable Excuses. A party must make its initial disclosures based on the information then reasonably available to it. A party is not excused from making its disclosures

because it has not fully investigated the case or because it challenges the sufficiency of another party's disclosures or because another party has not made its disclosures.

(2) Disclosure of Expert Testimony.

(A) In General. In addition to the disclosures required by Rule 26(a)(1), a party must disclose to the other parties the identity of any witness it may use at trial to present evidence under Federal Rule of Evidence 702, 703, or 705.

(B) Written Report. Unless otherwise stipulated or ordered by the court, this disclosure must be accompanied by a written report—prepared and signed by the witness—if the witness is one retained or specially employed to provide expert testimony in the case or one whose duties as the party's employee regularly involve giving expert testimony. The report must contain:

(i) a complete statement of all opinions the witness will express and the basis and reasons for them;

(ii) the facts or data considered by the witness in forming them;

(iii) any exhibits that will be used to summarize or support them;

(iv) the witness's qualifications, including a list of all publications authored in the previous 10 years;

(v) a list of all other cases in which, during the previous 4 years, the witness testified as an expert at trial or by deposition; and

(vi) a statement of the compensation to be paid for the study and testimony in the case.

(C) Time to Disclose Expert Testimony. A party must make these disclosures at the times and in the sequence that the court orders. Absent a stipulation or a court order, the disclosures must be made:

(i) at least 90 days before the date set for trial or for the case to be ready for trial; or

(ii) if the evidence is intended solely to contradict or rebut evidence on the same subject matter identified by another party under Rule 26(a)(2)(B), within 30 days after the other party's disclosure.

(D) Supplementing the Disclosure. The parties must supplement these disclosures when required under Rule 26(e).

(3) Pretrial Disclosures.

(A) In General. In addition to the disclosures required by Rule 26(a)(1) and (2), a party must provide to the other parties and promptly file the following information about the evidence that it may present at trial other than solely for impeachment:

(i) the name and, if not previously provided, the address and telephone number of each witness— separately identifying those the party expects to present and those it may call if the need arises;

(ii) the designation of those witnesses whose testimony the party expects to present by deposition and, if not taken stenographically, a transcript of the pertinent parts of the deposition; and

(iii) an identification of each document or other exhibit, including summaries of other evidence— separately identifying those items the party expects to offer and those it may offer if the need arises.

(B) Time for Pretrial Disclosures; Objections. Unless the court orders otherwise, these disclosures must be made at least 30 days before trial. Within 14 days after they are made, unless the court sets a different time, a party may serve and promptly file a list of the following objections: any objections to the use under Rule 32(a) of a deposition designated by another party under Rule 26(a)(3)(A)(ii); and any objection, together with the grounds for it, that may be made to the admissibility of materials identified under Rule 26(a)(3)(A)(iii). An objection not so made—except for one under Federal Rule of Evidence 402 or 403—is waived unless excused by the court for good cause.

(4) Form of Disclosures.

Unless the court orders otherwise, all disclosures under Rule 26(a) must be in writing, signed, and served.

(b) Discovery Scope and Limits.

(1) Scope in General.

Unless otherwise limited by court order, the scope of discovery is as follows: Parties may obtain discovery regarding any nonprivileged matter that is relevant to any party's claim or defense—including the existence, description, nature, custody, condition, and location of any documents or other tangible things and the identity and location of persons who know of any discoverable matter. For good cause, the court may order discovery of any matter relevant to the subject matter involved in the action. Relevant information need not be admissible at the trial if the discovery appears reasonably calculated to lead to the discovery of admissible evidence. All discovery is subject to the limitations imposed by Rule 26(b)(2)(C).

(2) **Limitations on Frequency and Extent.**

(A) When Permitted. By order, the court may alter the limits in these rules on the number of depositions and interrogatories or on the length of depositions under Rule 30. By order or local rule, the court may also limit the number of requests under Rule 36.

(B) Specific Limitations on Electronically Stored Information. A party need not provide discovery of electronically stored information from sources that the party identifies as not reasonably accessible because of undue burden or cost. On motion to compel discovery or for a protective order, the party from whom discovery is sought must show that the information is not reasonably accessible because of undue burden or cost. If that showing is made, the court may nonetheless order discovery from such sources if the requesting party shows good cause, considering the limitations of Rule 26(b)(2)(C). The court may specify conditions for the discovery.

(C) When Required. On motion or on its own, the court must limit the frequency or extent of discovery otherwise allowed by these rules or by local rule if it determines that:

(i) the discovery sought is unreasonably cumulative or duplicative, or can be obtained from some other source that is more convenient, less burdensome, or less expensive;

(ii) the party seeking discovery has had ample opportunity to obtain the information by discovery in the action; or

(iii) the burden or expense of the proposed discovery outweighs its likely benefit, considering the needs of the case, the amount in controversy, the parties' resources, the importance of the issues at stake in the action, and the importance of the discovery in resolving the issues.

(3) **Trial Preparation: Materials.**

(A) Documents and Tangible Things. Ordinarily, a party may not discover documents and tangible things that are prepared in anticipation of litigation or for trial by or for another party or its representative (including the other party's attorney, consultant, surety, indemnitor, insurer, or agent). But, subject to Rule 26(b)(4), those materials may be discovered if:

(i) they are otherwise discoverable under Rule 26(b)(1); and

(ii) the party shows that it has substantial need for the materials to prepare its case and cannot, without undue hardship, obtain their substantial equivalent by other means.

(B) Protection Against Disclosure. If the court orders discovery of those materials, it must protect against disclosure of the mental impressions, conclusions, opinions, or legal theories of a party's attorney or other representative concerning the litigation.

(C) Previous Statement. Any party or other person may, on request and without the required showing, obtain the person's own previous statement about the action or its subject matter. If the request is refused, the person may move for a court order, and Rule 37(a)(5) applies to the award of expenses. A previous statement is either:

(i) a written statement that the person has signed or otherwise adopted or approved; or

(ii) a contemporaneous stenographic, mechanical, electrical, or other recording—or a transcription of it—that recites substantially verbatim the person's oral statement.

(4) **Trial Preparation: Experts.**

(A) **Expert Who May Testify.** A party may depose any person who has been identified as an expert whose opinions may be presented at trial. If Rule 26(a)(2)(B) requires a report from the expert, the deposition may be conducted only after the report is provided.

(B) **Expert Employed Only for Trial Preparation.** Ordinarily, a party may not, by interrogatories or deposition, discover facts known or opinions held by an expert who has been retained or specially employed by another party in anticipation of litigation or to prepare for trial and who is not expected to be called as a witness at trial. But a party may do so only:

(i) as provided in Rule 35(b); or

(ii) on showing exceptional circumstances under which it is impracticable for the party to obtain facts or opinions on the same subject by other means.

(C) **Payment.** Unless manifest injustice would result, the court must require that the party seeking discovery:

    (i) pay the expert a reasonable fee for time spent in responding to discovery under Rule 26(b)(4)(A) or (B); and

    (ii) for discovery under (B), also pay the other party a fair portion of the fees and expenses it reasonably incurred in obtaining the expert's facts and opinions.

(5) Claiming Privilege or Protecting Trial- Preparation Materials.

  (A) Information Withheld. When a party withholds information otherwise discoverable by claiming that the information is privileged or subject to protection as trial-preparation material, the party must:

    (i) expressly make the claim; and

    (ii) describe the nature of the documents, communications, or tangible things not produced or disclosed—and do so in a manner that, without revealing information itself privileged or protected, will enable other parties to assess the claim.

  (B) Information Produced. If information produced in discovery is subject to a claim of privilege or of protection as trial preparation material, the party making the claim may notify any party that received the information of the claim and the basis for it. After being notified, a party must promptly return, sequester, or destroy the specified information and any copies it has; must not use or disclose the information until the claim is resolved; must take reasonable steps to retrieve the information if the party disclosed it before being notified; and may promptly present the information to the court under seal for a determination of the claim. The producing party must preserve the information until the claim is resolved.

(c) Protective Orders.

(1) In General.

A party or any person from whom discovery is sought may move for a protective order in the court where the action is pending—or as an alternative on matters relating to a deposition, in the court for the district where the deposition will be taken. The motion must include a certification that the movant has in good faith conferred or attempted to confer with other affected parties in an effort to resolve the dispute without court action. The court may, for good cause, issue an order to protect a party or person from annoyance, embarrassment, oppression, or undue burden or expense, including one or more of the following:

(A) forbidding the disclosure or discovery;

(B) specifying terms, including time and place, for the disclosure or discovery;

(C) prescribing a discovery method other than the one selected by the party seeking discovery;

(D) forbidding inquiry into certain matters, or limiting the scope of disclosure or discovery to certain matters;

(E) designating the persons who may be present while the discovery is conducted;

(F) requiring that a deposition be sealed and opened only on court order;

(G) requiring that a trade secret or other confidential research, development, or commercial information not be revealed or be revealed only in a specified way; and

(H) requiring that the parties simultaneously file specified documents or information in sealed envelopes, to be opened as the court directs.

(2) Ordering Discovery.

If a motion for a protective order is wholly or partly denied, the court may, on just terms, order that any party or person provide or permit discovery.

(3) Awarding Expenses.

Rule 37(a)(5) applies to the award of expenses.

(d) Timing and Sequence of Discovery.

(1) Timing.

A party may not seek discovery from any source before the parties have conferred as required by Rule 26(f), except in a proceeding exempted from initial disclosure under Rule 26(a)(1)(B), or when authorized by these rules, by stipulation, or by court order.

(2) Sequence.

Unless, on motion, the court orders otherwise for the parties' and witnesses' convenience and in the interests of justice:

(A) methods of discovery may be used in any sequence; and

(B) discovery by one party does not require any other party to delay its discovery.

(e) Supplementation of Disclosures and Responses.

(1) In General.

A party who has made a disclosure under Rule 26(a)—or who has responded to an interrogatory, request for production, or request for admission—must supplement or correct its disclosure or response:

(A) in a timely manner if the party learns that in some material respect the disclosure or response is incomplete or incorrect, and if the additional or corrective information has not otherwise been made known to the other parties during the discovery process or in writing; or

(B) as ordered by the court.

(2) Expert Witness.

For an expert whose report must be disclosed under Rule 26(a)(2)(B), the party's duty to supplement extends both to information included in the report and to information given during the expert's deposition. Any additions or changes to this information must be disclosed by the time the party's pretrial disclosures under Rule 26(a)(3) are due.

(f) Conference of the Parties; Planning for Discovery

(1) Conference Timing.

Except in a proceeding exempted from initial disclosure under Rule 26(a)(1)(B) or when the court orders otherwise, the parties must confer as soon as practicable—and in any event at least 21 days before a scheduling conference is to be held or a scheduling order is due under Rule 16(b).

(2) Conference Content; Parties' Responsibilities.

In conferring, the parties must consider the nature and basis of their claims and defenses and the possibilities for promptly settling or resolving the case; make or arrange for the disclosures required by Rule 26(a)(1); discuss any issues about preserving discoverable information; and develop a proposed discovery plan. The attorneys of record and all unrepresented parties that have appeared in the case are jointly responsible for arranging the conference, for attempting in good faith to agree on the proposed discovery plan, and for submitting to the court within 14 days after the conference a written report outlining the plan. The court may order the parties or attorneys to attend the conference in person.

(3) Discovery Plan.

A discovery plan must state the parties' views and proposals on:

(A) what changes should be made in the timing, form, or requirement for disclosures under Rule 26(a), including a statement of when initial disclosures were made or will be made;

(B) the subjects on which discovery may be needed, when discovery should be completed, and whether discovery should be conducted in phases or be limited to or focused on particular issues;

(C) any issues about disclosure or discovery of electronically stored information, including the form or forms in which it should be produced;

(D) any issues about claims of privilege or of protection as trial-preparation materials, including—if the parties agree on a procedure to assert these claims after production—whether to ask the court to include their agreement in an order;

(E) what changes should be made in the limitations on discovery imposed under these rules or by local rule, and what other limitations should be imposed; and

(F) any other orders that the court should issue under Rule 26(c) or under Rule 16(b) and (c).

(4) Expedited Schedule.

If necessary to comply with its expedited schedule for Rule 16(b) conferences, a court may by local rule:

(A) require the parties' conference to occur less than 21 days before the scheduling conference is held or a scheduling order is due under Rule 16(b); and

(B) require the written report outlining the discovery plan to be filed less than 14 days after the parties' conference, or excuse the parties from submitting a written report and permit them to report orally on their discovery plan at the Rule 16(b) conference.

(g) Signing Disclosures and Discovery Requests, Responses, and Objections.
  (1) Signature Required; Effect of Signature.
  Every disclosure under Rule 26(a)(1) or (a)(3) and every discovery request, response, or objection must be signed by at least one attorney of record in the attorney's own name—or by the party personally, if unrepresented—and must state the signer's address, e-mail address, and telephone number. By signing, an attorney or party certifies that to the best of the person's knowledge, information, and belief formed after a reasonable inquiry:
  (A) with respect to a disclosure, it is complete and correct as of the time it is made; and
  (B) with respect to a discovery request, response, or objection, it is:
      (i) consistent with these rules and warranted by existing law or by a nonfrivolous argument for extending, modifying, or reversing existing law, or for establishing new law;
      (ii) not interposed for any improper purpose, such as to harass, cause unnecessary delay, or needlessly increase the cost of litigation; and
      (iii) neither unreasonable nor unduly burdensome or expensive, considering the needs of the case, prior discovery in the case, the amount in controversy, and the importance of the issues at stake in the action.
  (2) Failure to Sign.
  Other parties have no duty to act on an unsigned disclosure, request, response, or objection until it is signed, and the court must strike it unless a signature is promptly supplied after the omission is called to the attorney's or party's attention.
  (3) Sanction for Improper Certification.
  If a certification violates this rule without substantial justification, the court, on motion or on its own, must impose an appropriate sanction on the signer, the party on whose behalf the signer was acting, or both. The sanction may include an order to pay the reasonable expenses, including attorney's fees, caused by the violation.

■ RULE 33. INTERROGATORIES TO PARTIES

(a) In General.
  (1) Number.
  Unless otherwise stipulated or ordered by the court, a party may serve on any other party no more than 25 written interrogatories, including all discrete subparts. Leave to serve additional interrogatories may be granted to the extent consistent with Rule 26(b)(2).
  (2) Scope.
  An interrogatory may relate to any matter that may be inquired into under Rule 26(b). An interrogatory is not objectionable merely because it asks for an opinion or contention that relates to fact or the application of law to fact, but the court may order that the interrogatory need not be answered until designated discovery is complete, or until a pretrial conference or some other time.
(b) Answers and Objections.
  (1) Responding Party.
  The interrogatories must be answered:
  (A) by the party to whom they are directed; or
  (B) if that party is a public or private corporation, a partnership, an association, or a governmental agency, by any officer or agent, who must furnish the information available to the party.
  (2) Time to Respond.
  The responding party must serve its answers and any objections within 30 days after being served with the interrogatories. A shorter or longer time may be stipulated to under Rule 29 or be ordered by the court.
  (3) Answering Each Interrogatory.
  Each interrogatory must, to the extent it is not objected to, be answered separately and fully in writing under oath.

(4) Objections.

The grounds for objecting to an interrogatory must be stated with specificity. Any ground not stated in a timely objection is waived unless the court, for good cause, excuses the failure.

(5) Signature.

The person who makes the answers must sign them, and the attorney who objects must sign any objections.

(c) Use.

An answer to an interrogatory may be used to the extent allowed by the Federal Rules of Evidence.

(d) Option to Produce Business Records.

If the answer to an interrogatory may be determined by examining, auditing, compiling, abstracting, or summarizing a party's business records (including electronically stored information), and if the burden of deriving or ascertaining the answer will be substantially the same for either party, the responding party may answer by:

(1) specifying the records that must be reviewed, in sufficient detail to enable the interrogating party to locate and identify them as readily as the responding party could; and

(2) giving the interrogating party a reasonable opportunity to examine and audit the records and to make copies, compilations, abstracts, or summaries.

■ RULE 34. PRODUCING DOCUMENTS, ELECTRONICALLY STORED INFORMATION, AND TANGIBLE THINGS, OR ENTERING ONTO LAND, FOR INSPECTION AND OTHER PURPOSES

(a) In General.

A party may serve on any other party a request within the scope of Rule 26(b):

(1) to produce and permit the requesting party or its representative to inspect, copy, test, or sample the following items in the responding party's possession, custody, or control:

(A) any designated documents or electronically stored information—including writings, drawings, graphs, charts, photographs, sound recordings, images, and other data or data compilations—stored in any medium from which information can be obtained either directly or, if necessary, after translation by the responding party into a reasonably usable form; or

(B) any designated tangible things; or

(2) to permit entry onto designated land or other property possessed or controlled by the responding party, so that the requesting party may inspect, measure, survey, photograph, test, or sample the property or any designated object or operation on it.

(b) Procedure.

(1) Contents of the Request.

The request:

(A) must describe with reasonable particularity each item or category of items to be inspected;

(B) must specify a reasonable time, place, and manner for the inspection and for performing the related acts; and

(C) may specify the form or forms in which electronically stored information is to be produced.

(2) Responses and Objections.

(A) *Time to Respond.* The party to whom the request is directed must respond in writing within 30 days after being served. A shorter or longer time may be stipulated to under Rule 29 or be ordered by the court.

(B) *Responding to Each Item.* For each item or category, the response must either state that inspection and related activities will be permitted as requested or state an objection to the request, including the reasons.

(C) *Objections.* An objection to part of a request must specify the part and permit inspection of the rest.

(D) *Responding to a Request for Production of Electronically Stored Information.* The response may state an objection to a requested form for producing electronically stored information. If the responding party objects to a requested form—or if no form was specified in the request—the party must state the form or forms it intends to use.

(E) *Producing the Documents or Electronically Stored Information.* Unless otherwise stipulated or ordered by the court, these procedures apply to producing documents or electronically stored information:

(i) A party must produce documents as they are kept in the usual course of business or must organize and label them to correspond to the categories in the request;

(ii) If a request does not specify a form for producing electronically stored information, a party must produce it in a form or forms in which it is ordinarily maintained or in a reasonably usable form or forms; and

(iii) A party need not produce the same electronically stored information in more than one form.

(c) Nonparties.

As provided in Rule 45, a nonparty may be compelled to produce documents and tangible things or to permit an inspection.

■ RULE 37. FAILURE TO MAKE DISCLOSURES OR TO COOPERATE IN DISCOVERY; SANCTIONS

(a) Motion for an Order Compelling Disclosure or Discovery.

(1) In General.

On notice to other parties and all affected persons, a party may move for an order compelling disclosure or discovery. The motion must include a certification that the movant has in good faith conferred or attempted to confer with the person or party failing to make disclosure or discovery in an effort to obtain it without court action.

(2) Appropriate Court.

A motion for an order to a party must be made in the court where the action is pending. A motion for an order to a nonparty must be made in the court where the discovery is or will be taken.

(3) Specific Motions.

(A) To Compel Disclosure. If a party fails to make a disclosure required by Rule 26(a), any other party may move to compel disclosure and for appropriate sanctions.

(B) To Compel a Discovery Response. A party seeking discovery may move for an order compelling an answer, designation, production, or inspection. This motion may be made if:

(i) a deponent fails to answer a question asked under Rules 30 or 31;

(ii) a corporation or other entity fails to make a designation under Rule 30(b)(6) or 31(a)(4);

(iii) a party fails to answer an interrogatory submitted under Rule 33, or

(iv) a party fails to respond that inspection will be permitted—or fails to permit inspection—as requested under Rule 34.

(C) Related to a Deposition. When taking an oral deposition, the party asking a question may complete or adjourn the examination before moving for an order.

(4) Evasive or Incomplete Disclosure, Answer, or Response.

For purposes of this subdivision (a), an evasive or incomplete disclosure, answer, or response must be treated as a failure to disclose, answer, or respond.

(5) Payment of Expenses; Protective Orders.

(A) If the Motion Is Granted (or Disclosure or Discovery Is Provided After Filing). If the motion is granted—or if the disclosure or requested discovery is provided after the motion was filed—the court must, after giving an opportunity to be heard, require the party or deponent whose conduct necessitated the motion, the party or attorney advising that conduct, or both to pay the movant's reasonable expenses incurred in making the motion, including attorney's fees. But the court must not order this payment if:

(i) the movant filed the motion before attempting in good faith to obtain the disclosure or discovery without court action;

(ii) the opposing party's nondisclosure, response, or objection was substantially justified; or

(iii) other circumstances make an award of expenses unjust.

(B) If the Motion Is Denied. If the motion is denied, the court may issue any protective order authorized under Rule 26(c) and must, after giving an opportunity to be heard, require the movant, the attorney filing the motion, or both to pay the party or deponent who opposed the motion its reasonable expenses incurred in opposing the motion, including attorney's fees. But the court must not order this payment if the motion was substantially justified or other circumstances make an award of expenses unjust.

(C) If the Motion Is Granted in Part and Denied in Part. If the motion is granted in part and denied in part, the court may issue any protective order authorized under Rule 26(c) and may, after giving an opportunity to be heard, apportion the reasonable expenses for the motion.

(b) Failure to Comply with a Court Order.

(1) Sanctions in the District Where the Deposition Is Taken.

If the court where the discovery is taken orders a deponent to be sworn or to answer a question and the deponent fails to obey, the failure may be treated as contempt of court.

(2) Sanctions in the District Where the Action Is Pending.

(A) For Not Obeying a Discovery Order. If a party or a party's officer, director, or managing agent—or a witness designated under Rule 30(b)(6) or 31(a)(4)—fails to obey an order to provide or permit discovery, including an order under Rule 26(f), 35, or 37(a), the court where the action is pending may issue further just orders. They may include the following:

  (i) directing that the matters embraced in the order or other designated facts be taken as established for purposes of the action, as the prevailing party claims;

  (ii) prohibiting the disobedient party from supporting or opposing designated claims or defenses, or from introducing designated matters in evidence;

  (iii) striking pleadings in whole or in part;

  (iv) staying further proceedings until the order is obeyed;

  (v) dismissing the action or proceeding in whole or in part;

  (vi) rendering a default judgment against the disobedient party; or

  (vii) treating as contempt of court the failure to obey any order except an order to submit to a physical or mental examination.

(B) For Not Producing a Person for Examination. If a party fails to comply with an order under Rule 35(a) requiring it to produce another person for examination, the court may issue any of the orders listed in Rule 37(b)(2)(A)(i)-(vi), unless the disobedient party shows that it cannot produce the other person.

(C) Payment of Expenses. Instead of or in addition to the orders above, the court must order the disobedient party, the attorney advising that party, or both to pay the reasonable expenses, including attorney's fees, caused by the failure, unless the failure was substantially justified or other circumstances make an award of expenses unjust.

(c) Failure to Disclose; to Supplement an Earlier Response, or to Admit.

(1) Failure to Disclose or Supplement.

If a party fails to provide information or identify a witness as required by Rule 26(a) or 26(e), the party is not allowed to use that information or witness to supply evidence on a motion, at a hearing, or at a trial, unless the failure was substantially justified or is harmless. In addition to or instead of this sanction, the court, on motion and after giving an opportunity to be heard:

(A) may order payment of the reasonable expenses, including attorney's fees, caused by the failure;

(B) may inform the jury of the party's failure; and

(C) may impose other appropriate sanctions, including any of the orders listed in Rule 37(b)(2)(A)(i)-(vi).

(2) Failure to Admit.

If a party fails to admit what is requested under Rule 36 and if the requesting party later proves a document to be genuine or the matter true, the requesting party may move that the party who failed to admit pay the reasonable expenses, including attorney's fees, incurred in making that proof. The court must so order unless:

(A) the request was held objectionable under Rule 36(a);

(B) the admission sought was of no substantial importance;

(C) the party failing to admit had a reasonable ground to believe that it might prevail on the matter; or

(D) there was other good reason for the failure to admit.

(d) Party's Failure to Attend Its Own Deposition, Serve Answers to Interrogatories, or Respond to a Request for Inspection.

(1) In General.

(A) Motion; Grounds for Sanctions. The court where the action is pending may, on motion, order sanctions if:

(i) a party or a party's officer, director, or managing agent—or a person designated under Rule 30(b)(6) or 31(a)(4)—fails, after being served with proper notice, to appear for that person's deposition; or

(ii) a party, after being properly served with interrogatories under Rule 33 or a request for inspection under Rule 34, fails to serve its answers, objections, or written response.

(B) Certification. A motion for sanctions for failing to answer or respond must include a certification that the movant has in good faith conferred or attempted to confer with the party failing to act in an effort to obtain the answer or response without court action.

(2) Unacceptable Excuse for Failing to Act.

A failure described in Rule 37(d)(1)(A) is not excused on the ground that the discovery sought was objectionable, unless the party failing to act has a pending motion for a protective order under Rule 26(c).

(3) Types of Sanctions.

Sanctions may include any of the orders listed in Rule 37(b)(2)(A) (i)-(vi). Instead of or in addition to these sanctions, the court must require the party failing to act, the attorney advising that party, or both to pay the reasonable expenses, including attorney's fees, caused by the failure, unless the failure was substantially justified or other circumstances make an award of expenses unjust.

(e) Failure to Provide Electronically Stored Information.

Absent exceptional circumstances, a court may not impose sanctions under these rules on a party for failing to provide electronically stored information lost as a result of the routine, good-faith operation of an electronic information system.

(f) Failure to Participate in Framing a Discovery Plan.

If a party or its attorney fails to participate in good faith in developing and submitting a proposed discovery plan as required by Rule 26(f), the court may, after giving an opportunity to be heard, require that party or attorney to pay to any other party the reasonable expenses, including attorney's fees, caused by the failure.

■ RULE 45. SUBPOENA

(a) In General.

(1) Form and Contents.

(A) *Requirements—In General.* Every subpoena must:

(i) state the court from which it issued;

(ii) state the title of the action, the court in which it is pending, and its civil-action number;

(iii) command each person to whom it is directed to do the following at a specified time and place: attend and testify; produce designated documents, electronically stored information, or tangible things in that person's possession, custody, or control; or permit the inspection of premises; and

(iv) set out the text of Rule 45(c) and (d).

(B) *Command to Attend a Deposition—Notice of the Recording Method.* A subpoena commanding attendance at a deposition must state the method for recording the testimony.

(C) *Combining or Separating a Command to Produce or to Permit Inspection; Specifying the Form for Electronically Stored Information.* A command to produce documents, electronically stored information, or tangible things or to permit the inspection of premises may be included in a subpoena commanding attendance at a deposition, hearing, or trial, or may be set out in a separate subpoena. A subpoena may specify the form or forms in which electronically stored information is to be produced.

(D) *Command to Produce; Included Obligations.* A command in a subpoena to produce documents, electronically stored information, or tangible things requires the responding party to permit inspection, copying, testing, or sampling of the materials.

(2) Issued from Which Court.

A subpoena must issue as follows:

(A) for attendance at a hearing or trial, from the court for the district where the hearing or trial is to be held;

(B) for attendance at a deposition, from the court for the district where the deposition is to be taken; and

(C) for production or inspection, if separate from a subpoena commanding a person's attendance, from the court for the district where the production or inspection is to be made.

(3) Issued by Whom.

The clerk must issue a subpoena, signed but otherwise in blank, to a party who requests it. That party must complete it before service. An attorney also may issue and sign a subpoena as an officer of:

(A) a court in which the attorney is authorized to practice; or

(B) a court for a district where a deposition is to be taken or production is to be made, if the attorney is authorized to practice in the court where the action is pending.

(b) Service.

(1) By Whom; Tendering Fees; Serving a Copy of Certain Subpoenas.

Any person who is at least 18 years old and not a party may serve a subpoena. Serving a subpoena requires delivering a copy to the named person and, if the subpoena requires that person's attendance, tendering the fees for 1 day's attendance and the mileage allowed by law. Fees and mileage need not be tendered when the subpoena issues on behalf of the United States or any of its officers or agencies. If the subpoena commands the production of documents, electronically stored information, or tangible things or the inspection of premises before trial, then before it is served, a notice must be served on each party.

(2) Service in the United States.

Subject to Rule 45(c)(3)(A)(ii), a subpoena may be served at any place:

(A) within the district of the issuing court;

(B) outside that district but within 100 miles of the place specified for the deposition, hearing, trial, production, or inspection;

(C) within the state of the issuing court if a state statute or court rule allows service at that place of a subpoena issued by a state court of general jurisdiction sitting in the place specified for the deposition, hearing, trial, production, or inspection; or

(D) that the court authorizes on motion and for good cause, if a federal statute so provides.

(3) Service in a Foreign Country.

28 U.S.C. § 1783 governs issuing and serving a subpoena directed to a United States national or resident who is in a foreign country.

(4) Proof of Service.

Proving service, when necessary, requires filing with the issuing court a statement showing the date and manner of service and the names of the persons served. The statement must be certified by the server.

(c) Protecting a Person Subject to a Subpoena.

(1) Avoiding Undue Burden or Expense; Sanctions.

A party or attorney responsible for issuing and serving a subpoena must take reasonable steps to avoid imposing undue burden or expense on a person subject to the subpoena. The issuing court must enforce this duty and impose an appropriate sanction—which may include lost earnings and reasonable attorney's fees—on a party or attorney who fails to comply.

(2) Command to Produce Materials or Permit Inspection.

(A) *Appearance Not Required.* A person commanded to produce documents, electronically stored information, or tangible things, or to permit the inspection of premises, need not appear in person at the place of production or inspection unless also commanded to appear for a deposition, hearing, or trial.

(B) *Objections.* A person commanded to produce documents or tangible things or to permit inspection may serve on the party or attorney designated in the subpoena a written objection to inspecting, copying, testing or sampling any or all of the materials or to inspecting the premises—or to producing electronically stored information in the form or forms requested. The objection must be served before the earlier of the time specified for compliance or 14 days after the subpoena is served. If an objection is made, the following rules apply:

　(i) At any time, on notice to the commanded person, the serving party may move the issuing court for an order compelling production or inspection.

　(ii) These acts may be required only as directed in the order, and the order must protect a person who is neither a party nor a party's officer from significant expense resulting from compliance.

(3) Quashing or Modifying a Subpoena.

(A) When Required. On timely motion, the issuing court must quash or modify a subpoena that:

　(i) fails to allow a reasonable time to comply;

　(ii) requires a person who is neither a party nor a party's officer to travel more than 100 miles from where that person resides, is employed, or regularly transacts business in person—except that, subject to Rule 45(c)(3)(B)(iii), the person may be commanded to attend a trial by traveling from any such place within the state where the trial is held;

　(iii) requires disclosure of privileged or other protected matter, if no exception or waiver applies; or

　(iv) subjects a person to undue burden.

(B) When Permitted. To protect a person subject to or affected by a subpoena, the issuing court may, on motion, quash or modify the subpoena if it requires:

　(i) disclosing a trade secret or other confidential research, development, or commercial information;

　(ii) disclosing an unretained expert's opinion or information that does not describe specific occurrences in dispute and results from the expert's study that was not requested by a party; or

　(iii) a person who is neither a party nor a party's officer to incur substantial expense to travel more than 100 miles to attend trial.

(C) Specifying Conditions as an Alternative. In the circumstances described in Rule 45(c)(3)(B), the court may, instead of quashing or modifying a subpoena, order appearance or production under specified conditions if the serving party:

　(i) shows a substantial need for the testimony or material that cannot be otherwise met without undue hardship; and

　(ii) ensures that the subpoenaed person will be reasonably compensated.

(d) Duties in Responding to Subpoena.

(1) Producing Documents or Electronically Stored Information.

These procedures apply to producing documents or electronically stored information:

(A) *Documents.* A person responding to a subpoena to produce documents must produce them as they are kept in the ordinary course of business or must organize and label them to correspond to the categories in the demand.

(B) *Form for Producing Electronically Stored Information Not Specified.* If a subpoena does not specify a form for producing electronically stored information, the person responding must produce it in a form or forms in which it is ordinarily maintained or in a reasonably usable form or forms.

(C) *Electronically Stored Information Produced in Only One Form.* The person responding need not produce the same electronically stored information in more than one form.

(D) *Inaccessible Electronically Stored Information.* The person responding need not provide discovery of electronically stored information from sources that the person identifies as not reasonably accessible because of undue burden or cost. On motion to compel discovery or for a protective order, the person responding must show that the information is not reasonably accessible because of undue burden or cost. If that showing is made, the court may nonetheless order discovery from such sources if the requesting party shows good cause, considering the limitations of Rule 26(b)(2)(C). The court may specify conditions for the discovery.

(2) Claiming Privilege or Protection.

    (A) *Information Withheld.* A person withholding subpoenaed information under a claim that it is privileged or subject to protection as trial-preparation material must:

        (i) expressly make the claim; and

        (ii) describe the nature of the withheld documents, communications, or tangible things in a manner that, without revealing information itself privileged or protected, will enable the parties to assess the claim.

    (B) *Information Produced.* If information produced in response to a subpoena is subject to a claim of privilege or of protection as trial-preparation material, the person making the claim may notify any party that received the information of the claim and the basis for it. After being notified, a party must promptly return, sequester, or destroy the specified information and any copies it has; must not use or disclose the information until the claim is resolved; must take reasonable steps to retrieve the information if the party disclosed it before being notified; and may promptly present the information to the court under seal for a determination of the claim. The person who produced the information must preserve the information until the claim is resolved.

(e) Contempt.

The issuing court may hold in contempt a person who, having been served, fails without adequate excuse to obey the subpoena. A nonparty's failure to obey must be excused if the subpoena purports to require the nonparty to attend or produce at a place outside the limits of Rule 45(c)(3)(A)(ii).

▪ ARTICLE V. PRIVILEGES

Rule 501. General Rule

Except as otherwise required by the Constitution of the United States or provided by Act of Congress or in rules prescribed by the Supreme Court pursuant to statutory authority, the privilege of a witness, person, government, State, or political subdivision thereof shall be governed by the principles of the common law as they may be interpreted by the courts of the United States in the light of reason and experience. However, in civil actions and proceedings, with respect to an element of a claim or defense as to which State law supplies the rule of decision, the privilege of a witness, person, government, State, or political subdivision thereof shall be determined in accordance with State law.

Notes

Rule 502. Attorney-Client Privilege and Work Product; Limitations on Waiver

(a) Scope of waiver.

In federal proceedings, the waiver by disclosure of an attorney-client privilege or work product protection extends to an undisclosed communication or information concerning the same subject matter only if that undisclosed communication or information ought in fairness to be considered with the disclosed communication or information.

(b) Inadvertent disclosure.

A disclosure of a communication or information covered by the attorney-client privilege or work product protection does not operate as a waiver in a state or federal proceeding if the disclosure is inadvertent and is made in connection with federal litigation or federal administrative proceedings—and if the holder of the privilege or work product protection took reasonable precautions to prevent disclosure and took reasonably prompt

UNITED STATES DISTRICT COURT
for the

<_____> DISTRICT OF <_____>

<Name(s) of plaintiff(s)>,   )
)
Plaintiff(s)   )
)   Civil Action No. <Number>
v.   )
)
<Name(s) of defendant(s)>,   )
)
Defendant(s)   )

REPORT OF THE PARTIES' PLANNING MEETING

(1) The following persons participated in a Rule 26(f) conference on <Date> by <State the method of conferring>:
<Name>, representing the <plaintiff>
<Name>, representing the <defendant>

(2) Initial Disclosures. The parties [have completed] [will complete by <Date>] the initial disclosures required by Rule 26(a)(1).

(3) Discovery Plan. The parties propose this discovery plan:
<Use separate paragraphs or subparagraphs if the parties disagree.>
  (a) Discovery will be needed on these subjects: <Describe>.
  (b) <Dates for commencing and completing discovery, including discovery to be commenced or completed before other discovery.>
  (c) <Maximum number of interrogatories by each party to another party, along with the dates the answers are due.>
  (d) <Maximum number of requests for admission, along with the dates responses are due.>
  (e) <Maximum number of depositions by each party.>
  (f) <Limits on the length of depositions, in hours.>
  (g) <Dates for exchanging reports of expert witnesses.>
  (h) <Dates for supplementations under Rule 26(e).>

(4) Other Items:
  (a) <A date if the parties ask to meet with the court before a scheduling order.>
  (b) <Requested dates for pretrial conferences.>
  (c) <Final dates for the plaintiff to amend pleadings or to join parties.>
  (d) <Final dates for the defendant to amend pleadings or to join parties.>
  (e) <Final dates to file dispositive motions.>
  (f) <State the prospects for settlement.>
  (g) <Identify any alternative dispute resolution procedure that may enhance settlement prospects.>
  (h) <Final dates for submitting Rule 26(a)(3) witness lists, designations of witnesses whose testimony will be presented by deposition, and exhibit lists.>
  (i) <Final dates to file objections under Rule 26(a)(3).>
  (j) <Suggested trial date and estimate of trial length.>
  (k) <Other matters.>

Date: <Date>   <Signature of the attorney or unrepresented party>
                                   _____
                    <Printed name>
                    <Address>
                    <E-mail address>
                    <Telephone number>

Date: <Date>   <Signature of the attorney or unrepresented party>
                                   _____
                    <Printed name>
                    <Address>
                    <E-mail address>
                    <Telephone number>

Source: http://www.uscourts.gov/uscourts/RulesAndPolicies/Rules/Usable_Rules_Forms_Civil/ CIV52-Report_of_the_Parties-_Planning_Meeting.wpd

measures, once the holder knew or should have known of the disclosure, to rectify the error, including (if applicable) following the procedures in Fed. R. Civ. P. 26(b)(5)(B).

(c) Selective waiver.

In a federal or state proceeding, a disclosure of a communication or information covered by the attorney-client privilege or work product protection—when made to a federal public office or agency in the exercise of its regulatory, investigative, or enforcement authority—does not operate as a waiver of the privilege or protection in favor of non-governmental persons or entities. The effect of disclosure to a state or local government agency, with respect to non-governmental persons or entities, is governed by applicable state law. Nothing in this rule limits or expands the authority of a government agency to disclose communications or information to other government agencies or as otherwise authorized or required by law.

(d) Controlling effect of court orders.

A federal court order that the attorney-client privilege or work product protection is not waived as a result of disclosure in connection with the litigation pending before the court governs all persons or entities in all state or federal proceedings, whether or not they were parties to the matter before the court, if the order incorporates the agreement of the parties before the court.

(e) Controlling effect of party agreements.

An agreement on the effect of disclosure of a communication or information covered by the attorney-client privilege or work product protection is binding on the parties to the agreement, but not on other parties unless the agreement is incorporated into a court order.

(f) Included privilege and protection.

As used in this rule:

(1) "attorney-client privilege" means the protection provided for confidential attorney-client communications, under applicable law; and

(2) "work product protection" means the protection for materials prepared in anticipation of litigation or for trial, under applicable law.

■ ARTICLE IX. AUTHENTICATION AND IDENTIFICATION

Rule 901. Requirement of Authentication or Identification

(a) General provision.

The requirement of authentication or identification as a condition precedent to admissibility is satisfied by evidence sufficient to support a finding that the matter in question is what its proponent claims.

(b) Illustrations.

By way of illustration only, and not by way of limitation, the following are examples of authentication or identification conforming with the requirements of this rule:

(1) *Testimony of witness with knowledge.* Testimony that a matter is what it is claimed to be.

(2) *Nonexpert opinion on handwriting.* Nonexpert opinion as to the genuineness of handwriting, based upon familiarity not acquired for purposes of the litigation.

(3) *Comparison by trier or expert witness.* Comparison by the trier of fact or by expert witnesses with specimens which have been authenticated.

(4) *Distinctive characteristics and the like.* Appearance, contents, substance, internal patterns, or other distinctive characteristics, taken in conjunction with circumstances.

(5) *Voice identification.* Identification of a voice, whether heard firsthand or through mechanical or electronic transmission or recording, by opinion based upon hearing the voice at any time under circumstances connecting it with the alleged speaker.

(6) *Telephone conversations.* Telephone conversations, by evidence that a call was made to the number assigned at the time by the telephone company to a particular person or business, if (A) in the case of a person, circumstances, including self-identification, show the person answering to be the one called, or (B) in the case of a business, the call was made to a place of business and the conversation related to business reasonably transacted over the telephone.

(7) *Public records or reports.* Evidence that a writing authorized by law to be recorded or filed and in fact recorded or filed in a public office, or a purported public record, report, statement, or data compilation, in any form, is from the public office where items of this nature are kept.

(8) *Ancient documents or data compilation.* Evidence that a document or data compilation, in any form, (A) is in such condition as to create no suspicion concerning its authenticity, (B) was in a place where it, if authentic, would likely be, and (C) has been in existence 20 years or more at the time it is offered.

(9) *Process or system.* Evidence describing a process or system used to produce a result and showing that the process or system produces an accurate result.

(10) *Methods provided by statute or rule.* Any method of authentication or identification provided by Act of Congress or by other rules prescribed by the Supreme Court pursuant to statutory authority.

Notes

Rule 902. Self-authentication

Extrinsic evidence of authenticity as a condition precedent to admissibility is not required with respect to the following:

(1) Domestic public documents under seal. A document bearing a seal purporting to be that of the United States, or of any State, district, Commonwealth, territory, or insular possession thereof, or the Panama Canal Zone, or the Trust Territory of the Pacific Islands, or of a political subdivision, department, officer, or agency thereof, and a signature purporting to be an attestation or execution.

(2) Domestic public documents not under seal. A document purporting to bear the signature in the official capacity of an officer or employee of any entity included in paragraph (1) hereof, having no seal, if a public officer having a seal and having official duties in the district or political subdivision of the officer or employee certifies under seal that the signer has the official capacity and that the signature is genuine.

(3) Foreign public documents. A document purporting to be executed or attested in an official capacity by a person authorized by the laws of a foreign country to make the execution or attestation, and accompanied by a final certification as to the genuineness of the signature and official position (A) of the executing or attesting person, or (B) of any foreign official whose certificate of genuineness of signature and official position relates to the execution or attestation or is in a chain of certificates of genuineness of signature and official position relating to the execution or attestation. A final certification may be made by a secretary of an embassy or legation, consul general, consul, vice consul, or consular agent of the United States, or a diplomatic or consular official of the foreign country assigned or accredited to the United States. If reasonable opportunity has been given to all parties to investigate the authenticity and accuracy of official documents, the court may, for good cause shown, order that they be treated as presumptively authentic without final certification or permit them to be evidenced by an attested summary with or without final certification.

(4) Certified copies of public records. A copy of an official record or report or entry therein, or of a document authorized by law to be recorded or filed and actually recorded or filed in a public office, including data compilations in any form, certified as correct by the custodian or other person authorized to make the certification, by certificate complying with paragraph (1), (2), or (3) of this rule or complying with any Act of Congress or rule prescribed by the Supreme Court pursuant to statutory authority.

(5) Official publications. Books, pamphlets, or other publications purporting to be issued by public authority.

(6) Newspapers and periodicals. Printed materials purporting to be newspapers or periodicals.

(7) Trade inscriptions and the like. Inscriptions, signs, tags, or labels purporting to have been affixed in the course of business and indicating ownership, control, or origin.

(8) **Acknowledged documents**. Documents accompanied by a certificate of acknowledgment executed in the manner provided by law by a notary public or other officer authorized by law to take acknowledgments.

(9) **Commercial paper and related documents**. Commercial paper, signatures thereon, and documents relating thereto to the extent provided by general commercial law.

(10) **Presumptions under Acts of Congress**. Any signature, document, or other matter declared by Act of Congress to be presumptively or prima facie genuine or authentic.

(11) **Certified domestic records of regularly conducted activity.** The original or a duplicate of a domestic record of regularly conducted activity that would be admissible under Rule 803(6) if accompanied by a written declaration of its custodian or other qualified person, in a manner complying with any Act of Congress or rule prescribed by the Supreme Court pursuant to statutory authority, certifying that the record:
   (A) was made at or near the time of the occurrence of the matters set forth by, or from information transmitted by, a person with knowledge of those matters;
   (B) was kept in the course of the regularly conducted activity; and
   (C) was made by the regularly conducted activity as a regular practice.
   A party intending to offer a record into evidence under this paragraph must provide written notice of that intention to all adverse parties, and must make the record and declaration available for inspection sufficiently in advance of their offer into evidence to provide an adverse party with a fair opportunity to challenge them.

(12) **Certified foreign records of regularly conducted activity.** In a civil case, the original or a duplicate of a foreign record of regularly conducted activity that would be admissible under Rule 803(6) if accompanied by a written declaration by its custodian or other qualified person certifying that the record:
   (A) was made at or near the time of the occurrence of the matters set forth by, or from information transmitted by, a person with knowledge of those matters;
   (B) was kept in the course of the regularly conducted activity; and
   (C) was made by the regularly conducted activity as a regular practice.
   The declaration must be signed in a manner that, if falsely made, would subject the maker to criminal penalty under the laws of the country where the declaration is signed. A party intending to offer a record into evidence under this paragraph must provide written notice of that intention to all adverse parties, and must make the record and declaration available for inspection sufficiently in advance of their offer into evidence to provide an adverse party with a fair opportunity to challenge them.

Notes

Rule 903. Subscribing Witness' Testimony Unnecessary

The testimony of a subscribing witness is not necessary to authenticate a writing unless required by the laws of the jurisdiction whose laws govern the validity of the writing.

Notes

Adapters   Devices for changing the connection on a connector to a different configuration.

Agent   A person authorized to act on behalf of another.

Annotation monitor   Monitor that allows a witness to easily make on-screen annotations with the touch of a finger.

Antivirus software   Programs that scour the computer for the presence of viruses; the better programs eliminate the virus.

Applications software   A collection of one or more related software programs that enables a user to enter, store, view, modify, or extract information from files or databases. The term is commonly used in place of "program" or "software." Applications may include word processors, Internet browsing tools, and spreadsheets.

Assets   Things that have value.

Attachment   An attachment is a record or file associated with another record for the purpose of storage or transfer.

Attachments   A popular method of transmitting text files and graphic images by attaching the file to an email.

Attorney–client privilege   A rule of evidence permitting an attorney to refuse to testify as to confidential client information, and specifically protecting the communication between the attorney and client for the purpose of obtaining legal advice.

Authentication of documents   The process of determining that the proposed evidence is what it is purported to be and is genuine.

Auto coding   The electronic scanning and coding of documents by selected key terms and dates.

Backup   A copy of data created as a precaution against the loss of or damage to the original data.

Bates production numbering   A Bates production number is a tracking number assigned to each page of each document in the production set.

Boilerplate   Standard language used in other documents.

Boolean   A computer search using words and phrases and logical operators such as AND, OR, and NOT.

Browser   A software program that allows a person to use a computer to access the Internet.

Cable   Operates over cable TV lines.

Candor   The ethical obligation to not mislead the court or opposing counsel with false statements of law or of facts that the lawyer knows to be false.

Capacity   Technical specifications such as CPU speed and computer memory.

Case management system   Software for organizing the parts of a case in a central repository that can be shared by all members of the legal team.

Case Management/Electronic Case Files (CM/ECF)   The federal court's electronic access an filing system.

Case   Issues that a client has presented to a legal team to handle and resolve.

Cell   In a spreadsheet, the box at the intersection of a row and a column for text or numerical data.

Central Processing Unit (CPU) The computer chip and memory module that perform the basic computer functions.

Chain of custody A written record showing the identity of everyone accessing evidence and showing that the evidence was not altered while in possession of the law firm.

Chart of accounts A listing of all the names of the accounts used in a particular financial entity.

Check register A chronological record of disbursements of checks and deposits.

Claim of privilege Prevents the disclosure of confidential communications as evidence based on a recognized privilege.

Claim of privilege The person claiming the privilege—usually the client—has the burden to establish its existence.

Claw-back provision A provision contained in the report of counsels' meet and confer and included in the court's scheduling order that describes what to do with privileged materials that are disclosed inadvertently through e-discovery. The provision should address return of the materials and waiver of the privilege.

Coding The process of capturing case-relevant information (i.e., author, date authored, date sent, recipient, date opened, etc.) from a document.

Column A vertical set of cells in a spreadsheet.

Compatibility In software usage, means software is designed to work on a particular type of computer or operating system.

Competent Having or providing the requisite knowledge, skill, thoroughness, and preparation necessary for representation of a client.

Computer hardware A tangible or physical part of a computer system.

Computer system A combination of an input device, a processor, and an output device.

Computer virus A program that attacks and destroys computer programs, internal computer operating systems, and occasionally computer hard drives.

Concept search Using a list of terms statistically related to the words in a query.

Confidentiality In the law field, any information with regard to a client, learned from whatever sources, that is to be kept in confidence by the legal team.

Conflict of interest Representation of one client that will be directly adverse to the interest of another client, the attorney, or another third party that is not a client.

Conflict report generator A program for sorting names of parties and clients to identify similar names or cases.

Connections The way in which workstations, file servers, and other peripheral devices are joined to the network.

Content (application) metadata Information about the contents of a document.

Content metadata Information about the contents of a document.

Database A collection of similar records.

De-duplication/de-duping The process of comparing electronic records based on their characteristics and removing duplicate records from the data set.

Deposition A form of discovery available to ask questions and obtain oral answers under oath from a witness or party to a lawsuit. Questions and answers are recorded stenographically.

Dial-up access Uses a modem connected to a PC to connect to the Internet by dialing a phone number.

Digital format A computerized format that allows information to be transmitted electronically.

Digital Subscriber Line (DSL) A line that is always connected using existing telephone lines.

Discovery   A step in the litigation process where the plaintiff and defendant share information relevant to their dispute.

Document camera   A portable evidence presentation system equipped with a high-resolution camera.

Documents   In Abacus, documents are any previously saved word processing files, scanned images, pleadings, correspondence, or Internet web pages.

Domain nomenclature   Part of the URL naming protocol.

Drivers   A program that allows the computer to communicate with a peripheral and tell it what to do.

Due process   An established course of judicial proceedings or other activity designed to ensure the legal rights of an individual.

E-discovery   Discovery of documents created, disseminated, and stored via electronic means.

E-repositories   Web or cloud based services that store electronic information.

Electronic courtroom   Courtroom equipped with electronic equipment for use in trial presentations.

Electronic database   An electronic repository of information of all types that can be sorted by a computer program and presented in a meaningful manner.

Electronic Discovery Reference Model   A suggested model for the procedures in electronic discovery.

Electronic repository   An off-site computer used to store records that may be accessed over secure Internet connections.

Electronically Stored Information (ESI)   Any type of information that can be stored electronically.

Email archiving   The continuous saving of email data.

Encryption   Scrambling documents using algorithms (mathematical formulas).

End User License Agreement (EULA)   The contract between the software company and the user authorizing the use of the program and setting the limitations of that use.

Entry of appearance   An attorney for one of the litigants files papers officially identifying himself or herself as representing the client before the court.

Equity   The value of the assets of an entity reduced by the claims of outsiders.

Ethical wall   Restricting access to information or files from those with a potential conflict of interest or who do not have a need to know the client information.

Ethics   Minimally acceptable standards of conduct in a profession.

Events   Any appointments, tasks, reminders, or things to do that are scheduled for specific dates.

Expenses   The decreases in the owner's equity caused by an outflow of assets from the entity in the delivery of goods and services.

Expert witness   A person qualified by education, training, or experience to render an opinion based on a set of facts that are outside the scope of knowledge of the fact finder.

Federal rules of evidence   The rules governing the admissibility of evidence in federal court.

Fiduciary relationship   A relationship where one is under a duty to act for the benefit of another under the scope of the relationship.

Field   Information located in vertical columns.

File extension   A tag of three or four letters, preceded by a period, that identifies a data file's format or the application used to create the file.

File format   The internal structure of a file, which defines the way it is stored and used.

File server   A computer in a network that controls the flow of information in the network.

Filtering The process used to scan or search documents for relevant terms in an attempt to narrow the focus, such as by filtering to eliminate documents created before or after a certain date.

Firewalls Programs designed to limit access to the authorized users of an application.

Footer Items at the bottom of each page of the document.

Form views An alternative way of viewing and presenting the information in a database.

Formula bar In Excel, the area at the top of the spreadsheet for entering formulas and data into spreadsheet cells.

Freeware Software distributed, generally over the Internet, at no charge to the user.

Graphic User Interface (GUI) A set of screen presentations and metaphors that utilize graphic elements such as icons in an attempt to make an operating system easier to use.

Hard copy The paper copy of a document.

Header Items at the top of each page of the document.

Host Every computerized device, like a computer, printer, or fax machine, that is connected to a network.

Hotspot A wireless access point, usually in a public area.

Hub A device used for sharing a signal among multiple computer devices.

Inadvertent disclosure An unintended disclosure of privileged, confidential, or work product information to the opposing side.

Information Management Reference Model (IMRM) A proposed model for e-discovery that balances business and litigation needs.

Information technologist A member of the legal team who has legal and technology skills and primarily supports electronic discovery activities.

Infrared headphones An assisted listening device for the hearing impaired.

Intake form A form for obtaining information to enter into a computerized office or case management system.

Integrated functions The sharing of data among different functions in a software program.

Integration Direct input from one program into another program.

Internet backbone The Internet connection between countries that carries information around the world.

Internet Browser A program that allows the user to access the Internet.

Internet Service Provider (ISP) A company that provides users with local access to the Internet.

Internet The interconnecting global public network made by connecting smaller shared public networks. The most well-known is the Internet, the worldwide network of networks, which uses the TCP/IP protocol to facilitate information exchange.

Interpreter box Routes language translations from an interpreter to the witness/defendant's headphones or the courtroom's public address system.

Interrogatories A form of discovery in which written questions are addressed to a party to a lawsuit and require written answers made under oath.

Interrogatories Interrogatories request written answers to questions, which in some cases may be substituted with the production of documents.

IOLTA Trust accounts used for holding small amounts of client funds or that will be held for too short a period of time to generate income sufficient to allocate to the client. Interest is paid to state designated agencies to aid nonprofit legal aid providers. www.IOLTA.org

IP Internet protocol address. A string of four numbers separated by periods used to represent a computer on the Internet.

ISDN   Integrated services digital network, uses digital telephone lines.

IT   Information technology, or the technology support staff within organizations.

Journals   Chronological listings of financial transactions of a business.

Laptop port   A connection into which a laptop may be plugged.

Laptop   Small, portable computer.

Large-screen monitor   A video monitor conveniently located in the courtroom that is large enough for all to see the graphics displayed.

Ledger   The individual records for each account.

Legal specialty software   Programs that combine functions found in software suites for performing law office management functions.

Liabilities   Claims of outsiders to the assets of the entity.

List serves   An automatic mailing list, usually for specific topics.

Litigation hold   A process whereby a company or individual determines that an unresolved dispute may result in litigation and, as a result, that documents should not be destroyed or altered.

Local Area Network (LAN)   Usually refers to a network of computers in a single building or other discrete location.

Logical address   Addresses for delivering messages.

Macro   A set of instructions or keystrokes (a program within a program).

Macros   Small programs that execute software functions when activated.

Mail Merge   A macro that combines a document with a list of recipients.

Mailbox   An electronic storage location for email messages.

Mainframe   A large computer system used primarily for bulk processing of data and financial information.

Matters   Any item, case, file, or project that you need to track.

Media Access Control (MAC) address   A physical address that is unique and that is stored in a special memory location in a computerized device.

Metadata   Information about a particular data set that may describe, for example, how, when, and by whom it was received, created, accessed, and/or modified and how it is formatted.

Metadata   Information about a particular data set, which may describe, for example, how, when, and by whom it was received, created, accessed, and/or modified, and how it is formatted.

Minimum requirements   The minimum computer requirements in terms of memory, speed, and other characteristics necessary for software to run properly.

Mobile operating system   The software that controls the functions of mobile operating devices.

Model rules of professional conduct   The American Bar Association's set of proposed ethical standards for the legal profession.

Modem   A piece of hardware that lets a computer talk to another computer over a phone line.

Motherboard   A printed circuit board that holds electronic components of the computer.

Multi-user license   Authorizes the installation of software on multiple computers.

Municipal Area Network (MAN)   A network in a specific geographic municipality; usually wireless.

Native file format   An associated file structure defined by the original creating application of electronic documents.

Native format   A file structure defined by the original creating application.

Network administrator   The person with the highest level of access to or authority over the network.

Network file server   A computer that controls the flow of information over the network.

Network license   Authorizes the use of software on a computer network with a specified number of simultaneous users on the network.

Network rights and privileges   Rights to access the different information on the network.

Network   A group of computers or devices that is connected together for the exchange of data and the sharing of resources.

Networked computer   Any combination of workstations (stand-alone computers) electronically connected, usually to a central computer that acts as a server on which files and data are stored for access by all other computers and shared software programs.

Networked   A group of computers or devices that is connected together for the exchange of data and sharing of resources.

Non-waiver agreement   In discovery, an agreement that any privilege is not waived if a privileged document is accidently submitted to opposing counsel.

Objective coding   Also referred to as a bibliographic indexing. This includes the author, type of document, recipient, and date.

Office suites   Software consisting of commonly used office software programs that manage data and database programs; manipulate financial or numeric information and spreadsheet programs; and include displayed images and presentation graphics programs.

Online collaboration   Using the Internet to conduct meetings and share documents.

Operating system   The software that the rest of the software depends on to make the computer functional. On most PCs this is Windows or the Macintosh OS. Unix and Linux are other operating systems often found in scientific and technical environments.

Optical Character Recognition (OCR)   A technology that takes data from a paper document and turns it into editable text data. The document is first scanned, and then OCR software searches the document for letters, numbers, and other characters.

Outsourcing   The use of persons or services outside of the office staff.

Passwords   Combinations of letters, numbers, and symbols used to restrict access to files and computers.

PC   Personal computer.

Physical address   The media access control, or MAC, address.

Portable Document Format or PDF   An open standard format for document exchange that enables a document to be processed and printed on any computer.

Principal   One who authorizes another to act on his or her behalf.

Private cloud   An Internet-based service that allows restricted access to information stored on servers of a third-party host company.

Privilege log   A list of documents claimed by the submitting party to contain material subject to privilege or work product exclusion.

Privilege review   A review of documents for privileged or confidential content or attorney work product.

Privilege   A rule of evidence that protects certain forms of communication from disclosure at trial.

Program shell   A software program containing a platform for using different software programs. See integrated functions.

Property bar   In Quattro Pro, the area at the top of the spreadsheet for entering formulas and data into spreadsheet cells.

Proportionality   Weighing the cost against the benefits of preserving and obtaining evidence.

Random Access Memory (RAM) Temporary computer memory that stores work-in-process.

Read Only Memory (ROM) A type of nonvolatile memory that does not require power to retain its contents.

Recommended requirements Computer system configurations of memory, speed, and other characteristics for the maximum utilization of the software.

Record retention Keeping documents and electronically stored information for a period of time.

Record In a database, the information in a horizontal row.

Redaction The removal of confidential information (or at least that which is claimed to be confidential) or material prepared for trial under the work product doctrine.

Relevant That which tends to prove the existence of facts important to the resolution of a case or may lead to such evidence that is admissible.

Remote access Accessing a file server or computer from a remote location using the Internet.

Remote collaboration Two or more parties working on a common document through remote access.

Requests for production Requests for production seek the identification and physical location of relevant documents, or request copies.

Resource (system) metadata Data such as file names, size, and location.

Retention policy A formal process for retaining and destroying files and electronically stored information.

Revenue The increases in the owner's equity from the delivery of goods or services.

Review Checking documents for confidential, privileged, or work product content.

Ribbon A term used to describe the new user interface in the Microsoft Office 2007 suite of products.

Router A piece of hardware that routes data from a local area network (LAN) to a phone line.

Row A horizontal set of cells in a spreadsheet.

Rules of court Rules governing the practice or procedure in a specific court.

Rules-based calendaring Custom dates or reminders created for a set period before or after a selected event.

Safe haven Procedures and circumstances under which a party will not be penalized.

Sampling The testing of a search query by running it against a limited set of documents to measure the accuracy of the response to the search query.

Save As A command that allows the user to selected the location and file name before writing (saving) the file, allowing user to change the original file name and location from which it was originally opened.

Save A command that writes (saves) the document using the original file name and location from which it was opened.

Search queries Specific words used in a computerized search.

Security protocols Software programs that limit access to the file server and peripherals such as printers or other workstations.

Self-defense exception The right of an attorney to reveal a client confidence when necessary to defend himself or herself against a claim of wrongful conduct.

Server Any computer on a network that contains data or applications accessed by users of the network on their client PCs.

Shareware Software that the author has chosen to make available free to the using public on the honor system.

Single-user license   Authorizes the installation of software on one computer.

Smartphone   Generally a wireless telephone with features such as a camera and an Internet connection.

Smoking gun   A document hidden among old files that would conclusively impeach or destroy the credibility of a witness or be evidence that conclusively determines an issue.

Software   Coded instructions (programs) that make a computer do useful work.

Specialized search engines   Search engines that use highly developed algorithms to search for relevant information and return a listing in order of relevancy with amazing accuracy.

Specialty applications   Specialty programs combine many of the basic functions found in software suites: word processing, database management, spreadsheets, and graphic presentations.

Spoliation   Destruction of records that may be relevant to ongoing or anticipated litigation, government investigation, or audit. Courts differ in their interpretation of the level of intent required before sanctions may be warranted.

Spreadsheet   A computer software program with rows and columns in which primarily numeric data may be manipulated using formulas. Also sometimes called electronic accounting worksheets.

Stand-alone computer   A computer on which all of the software used is installed and on which all of the data or files are electronically stored.

Satic files   A file that contains only data.

Subjective coding   Identifies keywords within a document or other criteria not related to bibliographic information.

Supervising attorney   The attorney managing or supervising the members of the legal team.

Switch   A high-performance alternative to a hub.

System metadata   The data such as file names, size, and location.

Table of authorities   A list of the references in a document and the numbers of the pages where they are located.

Table   Data that is organized in a format of horizontal rows and vertical columns.

Tablet PC   Laptop that allows input from a pen device instead of a mouse or keyboard.

teleworkers   People who work from remote locations, typically from home.

template   A form or standard document.

thin client   A computer system where programs and files are maintained on a centralized server.

TIFF   Tagged Image File Format, one of the most widely used formats for storing images. TIFF graphics can be black and white, gray-scaled, or color.

Time line   Chronological listings of the facts of a case.

Timekeeping   The recording of all time spent performing activities during the work day.

Trial notebook   Summary of the case usually contained in a tabbed, three-ring binder with sections such as pleadings, motions, law, pretrial memo, and witnesses.

Trial presentation programs   Computer program that organizes and controls documents, depositions, photographs, and other data as exhibits for trial, and displays them.

Type-ahead feature   This feature completes the address after a few letters of the address are typed.

Uninterruptible Power Supply (UPS)   A battery system that can supply power to a computer or computer peripheral for a short period of time.

URL (uniform resource locator)   The Internet address for a website.

Utility software   Programs that perform functions in the background that are related to the operation of the computer.

Videoconferencing   Conferencing from multiple locations using high-speed Internet connections to transmit sound and images.

Visual presentation cart   Media center located in the courtroom.

Voice recognition   Computer programs for converting speech into text or commands without the use of other input devices such as keyboards.

VoIP   An Internet replacement for traditional telephone connections.

Webex viewer   A plug-in software program that allows the use of webinars.

Webinar   A program presented over the Internet for viewing at the user's computer.

Wide Area Network (WAN)   A network generally covering a large geographic area and made up of other networks; a network of networks.

Wireless computer networks   Networks using wireless technology instead of wires and cables for connecting people and equipment.

Wireless network   A network in which computers communicate over the airwaves wirelessly instead of through wired connections.

Word processor   A computer software program for creating, editing, and producing word documents in various formats.

Work product doctrine   The rule of evidence that allows the attorney to treat work product as confidential, and protects it from disclosure to the opposing side.

Work product   In the law field, material prepared for trial that is protected from disclosure.

Workbook   A collection of worksheets.

Workstation   Consists of a computer, monitor, and input device and is connected to a network that is used for access.

World Wide Web   The WWW is made up of all of the computers on the Internet that use HTML-capable software (Netscape, Explorer, etc.) to exchange data. Data exchange on the WWW is characterized by easy-to-use graphical interfaces, hypertext links, images, and sound. Today the WWW has become synonymous with the Internet, although technically it is really just one component of it.

ZIP file   An open standard for compression and decompression used widely for PC download archives. ZIP is used on Windows-based programs such as WinZip and Drag and Zip. The file extension given to ZIP files is .zip.

INDEX